Illustrator® CS2
Bible

Illustrator® CS2 Bible

Ted Alspach and Brian Underdahl

Wiley Publishing, Inc.

Illustrator® CS2 Bible

Published by
Wiley Publishing, Inc.
111 River Street
Hoboken, NJ 07030
www.wiley.com

Copyright © 2005 by Wiley Publishing, Inc., Indianapolis, Indiana

Published simultaneously in Canada

ISBN: 0-7645-9581-4

Manufactured in the United States of America

10 9 8 7 6 5 4 3 2 1

1B/RZ/QX/QV/IN

For general information on our other products and services or to obtain technical support, please contact our Customer Care Department within the U.S. at (800) 762-2974, outside the U.S. at (317) 572-3993 or fax (317) 572-4002.

Wiley also publishes its books in a variety of electronic formats. Some content that appears in print may not be available in electronic books.

Library of Congress Control Number: 2005924598

About the Authors

Ted Alspach is the author of many books on desktop publishing and graphics, as well as hundreds of articles on related topics, including *Illustrator 7 Studio Secrets, Illustrator 7 Bible, Photoshop Complete, Kai's Power Tools Studio Secrets,* and *Illustrator Filter Finesse.* He is a contributing editor to *Adobe Magazine.*

Brian Underdahl is the author of 70 books on many different, mostly computer-related topics. His books have won several awards including the *Referenceware Excellence Award 2003,* which was awarded at the Waterside Berkeley Publishing Conference for the best book in the Graphic Design and Multimedia category.

Credits

Acquisitions Editor
Tom Heine

Project Editor
Martin V. Minner

Technical Editor
Dennis R. Cohen

Copy Editor
Gwennette Gaddis Goshert

Editorial Manager
Robyn Siesky

Vice President & Executive Group Publisher
Richard Swadley

Vice President and Publisher
Barry Pruett

Project Coordinator
Erin Smith

Graphics and Production Specialists
Sean Decker
Lauren Goddard
Joyce Haughey
Jennifer Heleine
Heather Ryan
Amanda Spagnuolo

Quality Control Technicians
David Faust
Leeann Harney
Jessica Kramer
Brian H. Walls

Proofreading and Indexing
TECHBOOKS Production Services

Cover Image
Daniela Richardson

Special Help
Adrienne D. Porter

Preface

You are holding in your hands the biggest, most thorough, and most helpful guide to Adobe Illustrator you'll find anywhere.

Gives you a bit of a rush, doesn't it?

The *Illustrator CS2 Bible* is the book we wrote because we couldn't find the book we wanted about Adobe Illustrator. Now we have it, and believe it or not, we're constantly using our own book as a reference. We'd love to tell the world, "sure, we know that," without putting them on hold while we search the index for the "Reset Tracking to 0" Mac key command (⌘+Shift+X, by the way). There's just too much about Illustrator for any one person to keep in his or her head at one time; now, this latest edition of the book gathers all the Illustrator information you can't remember and makes it more available and easier to follow than the plot twists on your favorite soap opera.

If you're at your local bookstore looking at the different Illustrator books to choose from, don't just pick this one because it weighs the most (sorry about that . . . we get more thank-you letters from chiropractors who've stayed in business because of this monstrosity . . .) or because it works great as a booster seat for your two-year-old nephew. Instead, take a look-see through these pages, which are stuffed to overflowing with in-depth Illustrator information that you just won't find anywhere else.

What's New in This Edition

Illustrator CS2 has added many very cool new features as well as revamping some of the old standby tools. In this edition, you find complete coverage of the new functions and features and extensive explanations on how these new features work. For a complete listing of new features, see Chapter 1.

Is This the Illustrator Book for You?

We've been to bookstores. We've seen the other Illustrator books out there. Some of them are quite good. Some of them are fairly awful. But none of them can match the *Illustrator CS2 Bible* for thoroughness, usefulness, or completeness. We've left no vector-based stone unturned.

Here are more reasons why the *Illustrator CS2 Bible* is the best overall book on Illustrator:

✦ **The most complete coverage of Illustrator:** This book isn't big because we wanted to hog all the retail book space to ourselves (of course, that's not a bad idea), but because we've tried to include every possible thing you'd ever want to know about Illustrator. From learning the basics of drawing to creating outstanding special effects with vectors and rasters, it's all here.

✦ **Fun, original, different artwork to illustrate the techniques and capabilities of Illustrator:** When we say different, we're not talking about "performance art." Instead, we mean that each technique is created with a different piece of artwork. Some of it is simple, and some of it is complex — with each piece showing not only a particular feature, but other Illustrator capabilities as well.

✦ **Clean artwork without those annoying "jaggies":** This is vector software. When you think of vectors, you probably think of smooth, flowing paths that don't look like someone filled in a bunch of squares on a sheet of graph paper. So instead of using screen shots for paths shown in this book, each path was painstakingly drawn in Illustrator. We think you'll appreciate the difference.

✦ **Top-notch technical prowess:** Again, the *Illustrator CS2 Bible* has gotten the best possible people to do a technical review of the book. Previous editions were technically reviewed by Eric Gibson, the lead technical support engineer for Illustrator; Andrei Herasimchuk, who designed and implemented the Illustrator 7 interface; and Sandra Alves, a UI designer for Adobe Photoshop. This edition was tech edited by Dennis R. Cohen, author, consultant, and technical reviewer.

✦ **Perfect for teaching:** If you know Illustrator inside and out, you'll find the *Illustrator CS2 Bible* the best teaching tool available for Illustrator, with examples and explanations that complement a teaching environment perfectly. Many computer training companies teaching Illustrator use this book, as do schools and universities.

✦ **Real-world examples and advice:** Illustrator doesn't exist in a vacuum. Instead, it is often used in conjunction with other programs, in a variety of different environments and situations. Some people use Illustrator to create logos, others create full-page advertisements, and still others create entire billboards with Illustrator. Throughout this book, we present various real-world situations and examples that add to your understanding of each topic.

You don't need to be an artist or a computer geek to learn Illustrator with this book. No matter what your level of Illustrator experience is, you undoubtedly can find new things to try, and learn more about Illustrator along the way.

How to Get the Most Out of This Book

You may want to be aware of a few matters before you dive too deeply into the mysteries of vector-based graphics, Adobe-style:

✦ **Versions:** When you see the word *Illustrator,* it refers to all versions of Illustrator. When we stick a number after the word Illustrator, it's relevant to that version only. When Adobe releases the next major upgrade, look for a new version of this book to help you through it.

✦ **Menu and keyboard commands:** To indicate that you need to choose a command from a menu, we write something like MenuName ➪ Command — for example, File ➪ Save. If a command is nested in a submenu, it is presented as MenuName ➪ Submenu ➪ Command, as in Filter ➪ Distort ➪ Roughen. If a command has a keyboard command, we mention that as well for both Macintosh and Windows versions. For example, Save uses "Command+S" on the Mac, which we'll present as ⌘+S. ⌘ corresponds to the ⌘ symbol on your keyboard. The other Mac keys are spelled out — Option, Shift, Tab, and so forth. Save uses "Ctrl+S" in Windows (Ctrl corresponds to the Ctrl key on the Windows keyboard). So, both platforms are specified by saying, "to save a document, press Ctrl+S (⌘+S)." Notice that the Windows convention is stated first and the Mac convention follows it in parentheses. There are some other minor differences in things like menus, drop-down lists (pop-up menus), and so on between the Windows and Macintosh versions, but you won't have any problem identifying these elements, no matter what you call them.

✦ **This is not a novel:** As much as we'd like you to discover plot intricacies, subtle characterizations, and moral fabric woven into the story, none of those things exists in this book. You can use this book in two ways:

- Look up what interests you in the Contents or the Index, and refer to that section. Rinse and repeat as necessary.

- Slowly, calmly work your way through the entire book, trying out examples (the funky Steps that are almost everywhere) and techniques as you run across them. The book is designed to be read this way, each chapter building on the previous chapter.

What's a Computer Book without Icons?

Nonexistent, for the most part. We've included several icons throughout this edition that may make reading this book a little more enjoyable and helpful.

These icons indicate some sort of power-user secret that you absolutely need to know to be able to illustrate with the big kids.

This icon notes Interesting tidbits. It's sort of like having Cliff from *Cheers* rambling on about something every few pages — interesting, but not essential. Just something we thought you might want to know.

Danger Will Robinson!!! Caution icons let you know about all the nasty things that can happen and how to avoid them.

These icons indicate what's brand new in version CS2 of Illustrator. Kind of like finding a prize in your cereal box.

These icons point you to other places in the book where you can find more information on a given topic.

What's Inside the Book

Here's a brief rundown on what to expect in the *Illustrator CS2 Bible:*

✦ **Part I: Illustrator Basics:** This section introduces the new features you'll find in Illustrator CS2. It also has us pointing out all the funky elements of the cool Illustrator interface (can you say palettes a-plenty?) and how to work with documents (you know, the open, close, and save stuff). It also covers the basics of drawing, painting, and working with objects. You learn how to color things, how to uncolor things, and how to delete those things when you don't like their color.

✦ **Part II: Putting Illustrator to Work:** This section puts you to work learning about type and how to fine-tune those paths and objects you drew in Part I. It also gives you a chance to bend and distort paths. Part II also contains a healthy dose of the hard stuff — such as compound paths, masks, blends, patterns, and type.

✦ **Part III: Mastering Illustrator:** This is the section that contains the nitty-gritty — and we don't mean the dirt band. Hot topics such as using Illustrator styles, effects, filters, and techniques for creating fantastic graphics are presented. This section includes several newer features such as transparency and working with raster images. We even show you how to customize Illustrator to work better and faster.

✦ **Part IV: Getting Art Out of Illustrator:** This section describes the ways to get stuff out of Illustrator. Artwork can leave to go to the print world, or go on an all-expenses-paid trip to the Web.

✦ **Appendixes:** The two appendixes contain information on Illustrator CS2 shortcuts and Illustrator resources.

Acknowledgments

Whew. As we write these acknowledgments, we're just about finished with the total revamping of this gigantic book. And while we're just plain exhausted, we know we'd be much more tired if it were not for the help and support of several key people. This list is by no means exhaustive, but the individuals named here are the ones most responsible for getting this book out the door.

Tom Heine at Wiley Publishing is always a great support to have on our side. Thanks to Marty Minner, who led the project to its completion.

We also acknowledge all the great artists who contributed images for the color insert section: Joe Barsin, Cory Gray, Joe Jones, Todd Macadangdang, Jason McQuitty, Martin Mendelsberg, Chris Spollen, and Brian Warchesik.

Contents at a Glance

Preface vii
Acknowledgments xiii

Part I: Illustrator Basics 1

Chapter 1: What's New in Illustrator CS2? 3
Chapter 2: Understanding Illustrator's Desktop 13
Chapter 3: Working with Illustrator Documents 45
Chapter 4: Understanding Drawing and Painting Techniques 73
Chapter 5: Creating Objects, Graphs, and Symbols 115
Chapter 6: Learning How to Select and Edit 157
Chapter 7: Understanding Color, Gradients, and Mesh 205

Part II: Putting Illustrator to Work 243

Chapter 8: Using Illustrator to Organize Objects 245
Chapter 9: Working with Type 283
Chapter 10: Using Creative Strokes and Fills with Patterns 339
Chapter 11: Applying Transformations and Distortions 363
Chapter 12: Using Path Blends, Compound Paths, and Masks 401
Chapter 13: Using Live Trace 445
Chapter 14: Using Live Paint 461

Part III: Mastering Illustrator. 469

Chapter 15: Working with Graphic Styles, Filters, and Effects 471
Chapter 16: Creating 3D in Illustrator 513
Chapter 17: Customizing and Automating Illustrator 543

Part IV: Getting Art Out of Illustrator 573

Chapter 18: Understanding PostScript and Printing 575
Chapter 19: Creating Web Graphics 601
Appendix A: Shortcuts in Illustrator CS2 649
Appendix B: People and Resources 679

Index 687

Contents

Preface vii

Acknowledgments xiii

Part I: Illustrator Basics   1

Chapter 1: What's New in Illustrator CS2? 3

Improving Your Drawings with Live Trace 3
Painting Pretty Pictures with Live Paint 5
Using the Control Palette 7
Finding Your Images Easily with Adobe Bridge 8
Enhancing Illustrator with Photoshop Import Enhancements 9
Improving Your Workspace 10
Saving Color Information with Spot Color Rasters 11
Welcoming SVG 1.1 Support 11
Using Offset Paths 11
Handling Text with Underline and Strikethrough 12
Summary 12

Chapter 2: Understanding Illustrator's Desktop 13

Picasso Meets Illustrator: Getting Started 13
Getting started with Illustrator 14
Quitting Illustrator 15
Working with Illustrator's Interface 15
Working in the document window 16
Working with the toolbox 20
Viewing Tool Tips 22
Using the palettes 22
Using Illustrator's menus 26
Using the status bar 27
Navigating Around Your Document 29
Understanding the Zoom tool 29
Using the Zoom tool 30
Other zooming techniques 31
Zooming with the Navigator palette 33
Using the scroll bars to view your document 34
Scrolling with the Hand tool 35
Scrolling with the Navigator palette 36
Opening a new window 36

Working in Outline Mode versus Preview Mode 36
Using custom views 40
Using screen modes 40
Using the Edit Commands 40
Using the Clear command 41
Cutting, copying, and pasting 42
Undoing and redoing 43
Summary 43

Chapter 3: Working with Illustrator Documents 45
Setting Up a New Document 45
Modifying the Setup of a Document 47
Understanding the Artboard options 48
Changing Type options 50
Working with Transparency options 51
Opening and Closing Illustrator Files 52
Saving Files 53
Using the Save As command 54
Understanding the Save a Copy command 55
Reverting to the last saved version 55
Saving for Web option 56
Understanding file types and options 57
Using Illustrator's compatibility options 57
Saving as Illustrator EPS 58
Saving files in Adobe PDF format 60
Saving files in SVG 62
Using the Export Command 63
Placing Art 65
Placing Photoshop Art in Illustrator: Understanding Vectors and Pixels . . 67
Placing raster images 68
Using the Clipboard 68
Dragging and dropping 69
Working with Document and File Information 69
Looking at document information 69
Saving document information 70
Finding file information 71
Summary 71

Chapter 4: Understanding Drawing and Painting Techniques 73
Working with Paths 73
Understanding types of paths 74
Understanding anchor points 74
Understanding control handles and control handle lines 76
Understanding how fills and strokes relate to paths 78

Drawing Paths with Illustrator Tools 82
   Using the Pencil tool 83
   Working with the Smooth tool 88
   Erasing with the Erase tool 88
   Drawing with the Pen tool 89
   Using the various line tools 97
   Understanding Paintbrush types 103
   Using brushes 104
   Using the Calligraphic brush 105
   Creating with the Scatter brush 106
   Working with the Art brush 108
   Creating tiles using the Pattern brush 109
   Making a custom brush 111
   Understanding colorization tips 112
   Checking out the Brush Libraries 112
Summary 114

Chapter 5: Creating Objects, Graphs, and Symbols **115**
Making Basic Shapes 115
   Drawing shapes from their centers 118
   Drawing symmetric shapes (circles and squares) 118
   Drawing shapes at an angle 120
   Drawing rectangles using the Rectangle tool 120
   Defining properties with the Rectangle dialog box 122
   Drawing rounded rectangles and squares 122
   Using the round corners filter to round straight corners 126
   Rounding corners backward 126
   Drawing ellipses 127
   Creating polygons 128
   Seeing stars 130
Working with the Flare Tool 134
   Understanding Flare options 134
   Using a flare to add highlight 135
   Editing a flare 135
Filling and Stroking Shapes 136
   Using fills 136
   Using strokes 137
   Combining strokes with fills 139
   Applying fills and strokes 140
Creating and Embellishing Graphs and Charts 142
   Importing Microsoft Excel graph data 143
   Making and editing graphs 144
   Customizing graphs 145
   Choosing a graph type 147
Creating Flowcharts, Diagrams, and Site Maps 150

Using Symbols 151
    Spraying with the Symbol Sprayer tool 151
    Making a new symbol 154
    Using the Symbol tool 155
Summary 156

Chapter 6: Learning How to Select and Edit 157

Selecting a Path for Editing 157
    Understanding the selection methods 157
    Deciding which selection tool to use 162
    Selecting, moving, and deleting entire paths 166
    Using different selection options 167
    Keeping and labeling a selection 173
    Custom paint style selections 173
Editing Paths in Illustrator 174
    Editing with anchor points 175
    The Add Anchor Points function 176
    Removing anchor points 177
    Simplifying paths by removing anchor points 178
    Splitting paths 180
    Sectioning and repeating paths 181
    Reshaping paths 182
    Cleaning up a path 183
    Offsetting a path 184
    Outlining a path 185
    Averaging and joining 186
Converting Anchor Points 190
Converting Smooth Points 190
    Converting straight-corner points 191
    Converting combination-corner points 192
    Converting curved-corner points 193
Using Illustrator's Pathfinder Functions 193
    Setting the Pathfinder options 194
    Adding to a shape 195
    Subtracting from a shape 196
    Intersecting and excluding shapes 197
    Using the Expand button 198
    Dividing paths 198
    Trimming paths 199
    Merging 199
    Cropping paths 200
    Outlining paths 200
    Using Minus Back 201
    Trapping 201
Summary 202

Chapter 7: Understanding Color, Gradients, and Mesh 205

Working with the Swatches Palette 205
   Using the color swatches 206
   Using the Swatches pop-up menu 208
   Using other swatch libraries 210
   Using color space options in the Color palette 211
   Using the Color Ramp 214
   Working with gamut 215
   Spot colors 215
   Applying colors with the Color palette 216
   Transferring color from one object to another 216
Using Transparency 218
Creating Gradients 231
   Using preset gradients 231
   Using the Gradient palette 231
   Working with Gradient tool 233
   Creating shadows, highlights, ghosting, and embossing. 235
   Expanding gradient objects 237
   Printing gradients 237
Adding Realism with Mesh 238
   Enhancing with highlights and color 239
   Adding multiple highlights 240
Summary 241

Part II: Putting Illustrator to Work   243

Chapter 8: Using Illustrator to Organize Objects 245

Locking and Hiding Objects 245
   Locking objects 246
   Hiding objects 247
   Setting object attributes 247
Understanding Object Stacking Order 248
   Controlling the stacking order for objects 249
   Understanding stacking order for text 250
   Stacking order for strokes and fills 250
   Pasting objects in front of and behind selected objects 250
Creating and Deconstructing Groups 251
   Grouping objects 251
   Ungrouping 252
Layering Your Artwork 253
   Getting started with layers 254
   Using the Layers palette 256
   Moving and layers 259
   Using the Layers palette pop-up menu 259

Working with Templates in Illustrator 261
    Placing a template on a layer 262
    Using a template to trace an image 263
Using Align and Distribute 264
Measuring an Image 265
    Changing the measurement units 266
    Using the Measure tool 267
    Sizing objects with the Transform palette 269
    Using rulers 270
    Measuring with objects 270
    Using Offset Path (for equidistant measuring) 271
Working with Grids 271
    Creating grid color, style, and spacing 273
    Spinning grids 274
Using Guides 274
    Creating guides 275
    Locking, unlocking, and moving guides 275
    Releasing guides 275
    Deleting guides 276
    Changing guide preferences 276
    Understanding Smart Guides 277
    Using angles as guides 278
Measuring for Printing 278
    Tiling 279
    Creating crop marks 280
Summary 281

Chapter 9: Working with Type **283**

Understanding Fonts 283
    Understanding Bitmap fonts 283
    Understanding PostScript fonts 284
    Understanding TrueType fonts 284
    Understanding OpenType fonts 284
    Adding type with Multiple Master fonts 285
Understanding Basic Type Menu Commands 285
    Using the Font submenu 286
    Understanding the Recent Fonts submenu 287
    Selecting the font size 288
    Using alternate glyphs 288
Using the Type Tools 289
    Using the Type tool 290
    Using the Area Type tool 290
    Using the Type on a Path tool 290
    Using the Vertical Type tool 292
Creating Individual Type 292
Placing Area Type in a Rectangle 293

Working with Type Areas 294
Creating Area Type 295
    Using area type functions 295
    Choosing good shapes for area type 296
    Outlining areas of area type 297
    Selecting carefully with area type 297
    Changing the area, not the type 298
    Flowing area type into shapes 298
Placing Type on a Path 300
    Adding effects to type on a path 301
    Using vertical type 302
Selecting Type 305
Editing Type 306
Using the Type Palettes 306
    Working with the Character palette 307
    Changing font and style 308
    Using text underlining and strikethrough 308
    Measuring type 308
    Changing type size 309
    Adjusting the leading 310
    Kerning and tracking 311
    Using vertical scale and horizontal scale 313
    Using character rotation 313
    Understanding the language barrier 314
    More multinational options 314
    Adding paragraph options 315
    Aligning type 316
    Indenting paragraphs 316
    Spacing before or after paragraphs 317
    Spacing through justification 317
    Hyphenating text 318
    Using every-line and single-line composer 319
    Controlling punctuation 319
    Working with OpenType 320
    Using the Tabs palette 321
Using Advanced Type Functions 322
    Threading text 322
    Unthreading text 323
    Fitting a headline 324
    Finding and replacing text 324
    Finding fonts 326
    Checking spelling 327
    Changing case 328
    Using Smart Punctuation 328
    Adding rows and columns 329
    Showing hidden characters 331

Changing type orientation 331
Updating legacy text 331
Exporting and placing 331
Creating Outlines 332
Distorting characters for special effects 334
Masking and other effects 334
Avoiding font conflicts by creating outlines 335
Understanding hinting 336
Understanding Other Type Considerations 336
Summary 337

Chapter 10: Using Creative Strokes and Fills with Patterns 339

Using Creative Strokes 339
Stroke essentials 340
Using the stroke charts 341
Creating parallel strokes 344
Creating map elements 346
Creating Perfect Patterns 352
Using the default patterns 353
Creating custom patterns 354
Understanding pattern backgrounds and boundaries 355
Making seamless patterns 355
Creating symmetrical patterns 356
Creating line patterns and grids 356
Using diagonal-line and grid patterns 358
Using transparency and patterns together 359
Transforming patterns 360
Summary 361

Chapter 11: Applying Transformations and Distortions 363

Adding a Transformation with Tools 363
Rotating with the Rotate tool 366
Reflecting with the Reflect tool 367
Scaling with the Scale tool 368
Shearing with the Shear tool 369
Reshaping with the Reshape tool 370
Moving objects 372
Using the Free Transform tool 373
Working with the Transform Palette 374
Using Transform Each 376
Using Transformations 378
Creating shadows 378
Rotating into a path 379
Making tiles using the Reflect tool 380

Using transformation tools on portions of paths 381
Transforming patterns 382
Using Liquify Tools on Objects 383
Warping objects 384
Twirling objects 384
Puckering 385
Bloating 386
Scalloping 386
Crystallizing 386
Wrinkling 387
Distorting with Commands 388
Using free distortions 389
Using Pucker & Bloat 389
Roughening objects 391
Transforming objects 393
Tweaking transforms 394
Using the Twist command 395
Working with the Zig Zag filter 396
Using Warp Effects 397
Understanding Warp types 398
Summary 400

Chapter 12: Using Path Blends, Compound Paths, and Masks . . . 401

Understanding the Difference between Blends and Gradients 401
Creating Path Blends 403
Defining Linear Blends 404
Working with Blend Options 406
Using the Blend option 406
Blending multiple objects 407
Editing a blended object 407
Releasing a blend 408
Expanding blends 408
Replacing the spine 409
Reversing the spine 410
Reversing front to back 410
Using nonlinear blends 412
Finding end paths for linear blends 413
Calculating the number of steps 414
Creating radial blends 415
Making a Color Blend 416
Using multiple colors with linear blends 416
Using guidelines for creating color linear blends 418
Creating Shape Blends 419
Complex-shape blending 419
Creating realism with shape blends 420

Blending symbols 423
Blending envelopes 423
Blending 3D objects 125
Airbrushing shadows 425
Creating glows 427
Softening edges 428
Designing neon effects 429
Using Compound Paths 430
Creating compound paths 431
Releasing compound paths 432
Understanding holes 433
Overlapping holes 433
Creating compound paths from separate sets of paths 434
Working with type and compound paths 435
Finding Path Directions 436
Figuring out which way to go 437
Reversing path directions 438
Faking a compound path 439
Using Clipping Masks 439
Creating masks 440
Masking raster images 441
Using a mask with other masks 442
Releasing masks 442
Masking and printing 442
Masking and compound paths 443
Summary 444

Chapter 13: Using Live Trace **445**

Understanding Live Trace 445
Learning Live Trace Modes 446
Getting to know outline mode 447
Using tracing result mode 448
Combining outline and tracing result modes 448
Setting Live Trace Options 449
Understanding the Live Trace presets 449
Choosing custom Live Trace options 456
Tracing Raster Images with Live Trace 457
Summary 458

Chapter 14: Using Live Paint **461**

Understanding Live Paint 461
Setting the Live Paint Options 463
Using Live Paint 465
Summary 468

Part III: Mastering Illustrator   **469**

Chapter 15: Working with Graphic Styles, Filters, and Effects 471

Understanding how Graphic Styles Work 471
    Using the Appearance palette 472
    Working with the Graphic Styles palette 477
Using Filters in Illustrator 481
    Finding the Plug-Ins folder 482
    Understanding the color filters 482
    Manipulating colors with the color filters 486
    Understanding the create filters options 488
    Understanding the Distort filters 493
    Using the Stylize filters 494
    Reapplying the last filter used 497
Using Photoshop-Compatible Filters in Illustrator 497
    Working with rasterized Illustrator artwork 497
    Using Illustrator's Photoshop plug-ins 499
Using Effects 500
    Understanding 3D effects 500
    Converting to Shape effects 501
    Distorting and transforming effects 502
    Creating Path effects 502
    Understanding the Rasterize effect 502
    Stylizing effects 503
    Using SVG Filters effects 509
    Warp effects 510
    Creating Photoshop filter effects 510
Summary 510

Chapter 16: Creating 3D in Illustrator 513

Using 3D Inside Illustrator 513
Understanding the Three-Dimensional World 514
    Changing from two dimensions to three dimensions 514
    Three-dimensional positioning 515
Extruding and Revolving 2D Objects 516
    Extruding flat art 516
    Extruding a stroke 518
    Understanding bevels 519
    Revolving objects 521
Rotating Objects 523
Changing the Appearance of Three-Dimensional Objects 523
    The Surface characteristics 524
    Understanding lighting 525
    Lighting options 525

Using the Appearance palette with 3D 527
Mapping 2D art to 3D surfaces 527
Using Other 3D Techniques 531
Using gradients to make bumps and dents 531
Perspective drawing 531
Guest Artist How-To: Using Illustrator to Create 3D Texture Maps
(by Joe Jones) 532
Conceptualization 533
Modeling 534
Texture mapping 535
Summary 542

Chapter 17: Customizing and Automating Illustrator **543**

Who's Responsible for Illustrator? 543
Customization Options 544
Modifying the Startup File 545
Changing Preferences 547
Altering the Keyboard Increment option 547
Using the Constrain Angle option 548
Changing the Corner Radius option 549
Adjusting the General options 550
Changing Preferences for Type 554
The Size/Leading option 555
The Baseline Shift option 555
The Tracking option 555
The Greeking option 556
The Type Object Selection by Path Only option 556
The Show Asian Options option 556
The Show Font Names in English option 556
Setting the Number of Recent Fonts option 556
Choosing a font preview size 556
Using Units & Display Performance 557
Changing Units settings 557
Changing Display Performance 558
Changing Guides and Grid Preferences 558
Adjusting Smart Guides & Slices 559
Changing Display options 560
Altering Angles 560
Changing Snapping Tolerance 560
Adjusting Slices 560
Changing Hyphenation 561
Adjusting the Plug-ins and Scratch Disks 561
Customizing the File Handling and Clipboard 562
Setting the Appearance of Black Options 563
Altering Placement and Toolbox Value Preferences 564
Adding Keyboard Customization 564
Knowing What You Can't Customize 565

Using Actions 565
    Using a Default Action 565
    Creating a new action 566
    Creating a new set 567
    What is recordable? 567
    Duplicating and deleting an action 567
    Starting and stopping recording 568
    Inserting a menu item 568
    Inserting a stop 568
    Action options 569
    Playback options 569
    Inserting a selected path 570
    Selecting an object 570
    Clearing, resetting, loading, replacing, and saving actions 570
Summary 571

Part IV: Getting Art Out of Illustrator   573

Chapter 18: Understanding PostScript and Printing 575

Understanding the Benefits of PostScript 576
Using PostScript 577
Knowing What to Do Prior to Printing 578
    Understanding document setup 578
    Printing composites 579
    Working with gray colors 582
Using the Separation Setup 583
    Understanding the printer's marks and bleeds 583
    Changing printer information 584
    Changing page size 584
    Changing the orientation 585
    Understanding emulsion 585
    Changing from positive to negative to positive 587
    Working with different colors 587
Outputting a Color-Separated File 588
    Using spot color separations 588
    Printing process color separation 590
    Choosing numerous colors 590
    Combining spot and process color separations 593
Using Other Applications to Print 594
Understanding Trapping 594
    Understanding misaligned color separations 596
    Knowing how much you need to trap 597
    Trapping Illustrator files 598
    Using complex trapping techniques in Illustrator 599
Summary 600

Chapter 19: Creating Web Graphics **601**

Designing for the Web versus Designing for Print 601
Illustrator and the Web — the Basics 602
Understanding pixel preview 603
Using Web-safe colors 605
Understanding hexadecimal colors 608
Optimizing and Saving Web Graphics 609
Introducing the Save for Web dialog box 610
Previewing Web graphics 610
Learning the Web-graphic formats 615
Choosing output options 617
Creating Vector Graphics for the Web 620
Using Flash graphics 620
Creating SVG files 623
Understanding Web Slicing 628
Object-based Web Slicing 629
Working with slices 630
Understanding CSS Layers 632
Getting Interactive 633
Specifying an image map 633
Creating animations 634
Adding rollovers with Adobe ImageReady 638
Using Data-Driven Graphics to Streamline Design Work 639
Understanding variables 640
Using the Variables palette 641
Understanding scripting 641
Scripting versus Actions 642
Setting up a data-driven graphics template 643
Taking advantage of data-driven graphics with Adobe GoLive 645
Summary 647

Appendix A: Shortcuts in Illustrator CS2 . . . . **649**

Appendix B: People and Resources **679**

Index 687

Illustrator Basics

In This Part

Chapter 1
What's New In
Illustrator CS2?

Chapter 2
Understanding
Illustrator's Desktop

Chapter 3
Working with
Illustrator Documents

Chapter 4
Understanding
Drawing and
Painting Techniques

Chapter 5
Creating Objects,
Graphs, and Symbols

Chapter 6
Learning How to
Select and Edit

Chapter 7
Understanding Color,
Gradients, and Mesh

What's New in Illustrator CS2?

✦ ✦ ✦ ✦

In This Chapter

Using Live Trace

Adding color with
Live Paint

Controlling Illustrator
with the Control
palette

Browsing file types
with Adobe Bridge

Working with
Photoshop import
improvements

Enhancing your
workspace

Colorizing images
with spot-color rasters
and other fun stuff

Being efficient with
SVG 1.1

Offsetting paths for
more control

Improving text
handling

✦ ✦ ✦ ✦

It's always exciting to see what's new in new versions of your favorite software. Long-time Adobe Illustrator fans certainly have a great interest in learning about the new features in Illustrator CS2, but those changes aren't of interest only to people who've used Illustrator extensively in the past. New users and people who currently use competing products also want to know if this new version adds must-have features.

In this chapter, I introduce several features that have been added to Illustrator CS2 as well as some changes that make existing features easier to use or simply more powerful. Fortunately, Illustrator CS2 maintains a strong connection with the past so that you don't have to relearn the entire application. Still, the changes that have been made are important ones that you'll find useful and fun. Let's dig in!

Improving Your Drawings with Live Trace

There's probably little doubt that the two most exciting new features in Illustrator CS2 are *Live Trace* and *Live Paint*. In this section, I introduce Live Trace — a very powerful tool that replaces the old and quite limited Auto Trace tool. In the next section, you learn more about Live Paint — the much appreciated replacement for the Paint Bucket tool.

Cross-Reference This chapter merely introduces Live Trace. For a complete discussion of the Live Trace tool, see Chapter 13.

The Live Trace tool converts imported bitmap (raster) images into vector images. This makes it possible to manipulate those images in Illustrator using the same tools and techniques that you use for artwork created entirely within Illustrator. This capability opens up a whole new world of possibilities because you can now take an existing digital photo and quickly convert that photo into a native Illustrator object. As a result, you can create complex artwork in Illustrator in minutes using an existing digital image rather than spending hours drawing the art manually.

Cross-Reference See Chapter 3 to learn more about the important differences between vector and raster images.

Previous versions of Illustrator had a tool called the Auto Trace tool that was used to trace bitmap images. Although the Auto Trace tool did trace bitmap images and convert them into vector-based objects, the whole process was quite tedious and the end results typically weren't very good. Oh sure, you could spend lots of time carefully tracing an image, but you had to keep manually selecting colors, adding new areas to the trace, and hoping you didn't make any mistakes along the way. As a result, many Illustrator users made heavy use of layers as they manually traced bitmap images using the Pencil tool.

The Live Trace tool turns the whole process of tracing bitmap images into vector objects upside down. Instead of hours of painstaking manual labor, using the Live Trace tool is a breeze. You make a few selections in a dialog box and bingo — Live Trace automatically does the work for you. But don't think that just because the process is automated, the results won't be as good as (or better than) the old manual process. You can tweak every Live Trace setting to get exactly the results you want.

Figure 1-1 shows an example of how the Live Trace tool compares to the old Auto Trace tool. In this example, I began by placing a bitmap image into an Illustrator document. Below the original bitmap is an example of how the old Auto Trace tool worked. In this case, I clicked the image in several different places to convert areas of the image into vectors. Because I didn't change the default fill color, the traced areas were filled with white. The lower image shows how the new Live Trace tool quickly converted the bitmap into vectors using one of the tool's preset tracing options. With just a few clicks, the image became a fully editable Illustrator object that looks far more realistic than what hours with the Auto Trace tool could produce.

The Live Trace tool offers many different preset tracing options so that you can begin using the tool immediately. In addition, you have the option of saving your own presets so that you can apply the same processing to a series of imported bitmap images. If your projects involve using bitmap images in conjunction with Illustrator artwork, the Live Trace tool can save you many hours of tedious work. But even if you only occasionally want to start with a bitmap image, you'll find the new Live Trace tool invaluable.

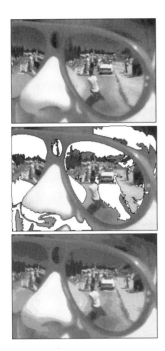

Figure 1-1: The top image is the raw imported bitmap, the middle image was traced using the old Auto Trace tool, and the bottom was traced using the new Live Trace tool.

Painting Pretty Pictures with Live Paint

Anyone who has ever used a paint program on a computer has probably used a paint bucket-style tool. This staple of bitmap paint programs fills a closed area with a selected color — one click, and you've poured the paint into the area.

Illustrator has long had a Paint Bucket tool that worked very much like the similar tool in a bitmap-based paint program. But fundamental differences between bitmap graphics and vector graphics have a major effect on how these types of tools function in the different types of programs. The new Live Paint tool in Illustrator CS2 provides you with much of the intuitive functionality found in bitmap-based graphics while giving you the power of vector-based graphics.

When you use the Live Paint tool, the paint you add remains live — meaning that you can modify a path, and the paint effect automatically updates to reflect the new shape or position of the path. The Live Paint tool works with both fills and strokes (depending on the settings you choose for the tool).

Figure 1-2 shows an example of applying the Live Paint tool to an image that was converted from a bitmap to vectors using the Live Trace tool.

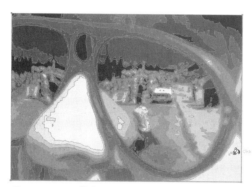

Figure 1-2: Click an image with the Live Paint tool to create a Live Paint group that remains live as you continue to modify the drawing.

Figure 1-3 shows an example of one type of effect that you can create using the Live Paint tool. In this case, the color of the sunglass frame was changed from a dull brown to a glowing fluorescent green.

Figure 1-3: This image was modified with the Live Paint tool to create a very different look from the original bitmap image.

In most cases, you use both the Live Trace and Live Paint tools to process images, but the Live Paint tool also works with objects you create completely within Illustrator.

Cross-Reference For a complete discussion of the Live Paint tool, see Chapter 14.

If you have used paint bucket tools in a bitmap-based graphics program, you can certainly appreciate one powerful feature of the Illustrator CS2 Live Paint tool. Unlike the paint buckets in bitmap graphics programs, the Live Paint tool can automatically close small gaps to prevent the paint from flowing outside of the desired object. The gap detection feature is fully controllable too, so you can set the size of gaps that you want to ignore.

Using the Control Palette

Illustrator makes extensive use of *palettes* — objects similar to non-modal dialog boxes that enable you to choose various settings for selected objects. Illustrator CS2 adds a convenient new palette called the Control palette that provides quick access to a number of the most common properties for an object. (If you have used Adobe InDesign, the Illustrator CS2 Control palette will seem quite familiar because it appeared first in InDesign.)

Figure 1-4 shows how the Control palette might appear when a drawn object such as a rectangle is selected. Notice that the Control palette provides quick access to settings such as the fill and stroke colors, the width of the stroke, the style of the brush, and so on. The Control palette actually can take on many different appearances because the controls in the palette reflect options suitable for the selected object.

Figure 1-4: The new Control palette provides quick access to the properties of the currently selected object.

Illustrator's palettes are discussed throughout the chapters as appropriate. As you work with the various palettes, remember that the Control palette often may provide the settings you need without the necessity of hunting down the specific palette where that setting normally resides.

Finding Your Images Easily with Adobe Bridge

Adobe Bridge is a new standalone program that is included with Illustrator CS2. Bridge is designed to make it easier for you to browse all the various file types that are supported by the Adobe Creative Suite applications. Using Bridge, you can view the contents of a file before opening it. Figure 1-5 shows an example of using Bridge to view various files.

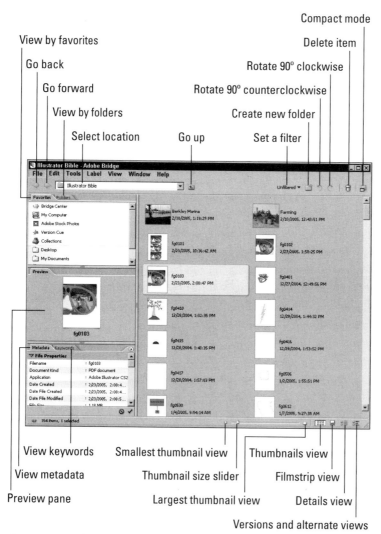

Figure 1-5: Adobe Bridge makes it easy to choose the file you want to open.

Bridge also allows you to apply *metadata* — various types of information about your files, such as who created them, your copyright notice, and so on. To apply metadata, you click an item in the Metadata pane of the Bridge window. You can modify only certain metadata properties. The properties you can modify have a pencil icon to the right of the data.

One of the handier features in the Bridge window is the thumbnail size slider along the bottom edge of the window. You can drag the slider to the right to make the thumbnails larger or to the left to make them smaller. This feature allows you to easily locate specific files, especially if you have saved several versions of a file containing slight differences.

If you have additional Adobe Creative Suite applications beyond Illustrator, Bridge also supports automating tasks between applications and setting global color settings for all the applications.

Enhancing Illustrator with Photoshop Import Enhancements

Illustrator CS2 also adds support for Photoshop layer comps when you place a Photoshop file into an Illustrator document. *Layer comps* are multiple compositions of a page layout that you create in order to have multiple versions of a layout within a single Photoshop file. Using layer comps allows you to show a client several versions of the layout from a single file.

Figure 1-6 shows the Photoshop Import Options dialog box displaying a Photoshop file containing multiple layer comps. You use the Layer Comp drop-down list (pop-up menu) at the top of the dialog box to choose which of the comps you want to import into your Illustrator document.

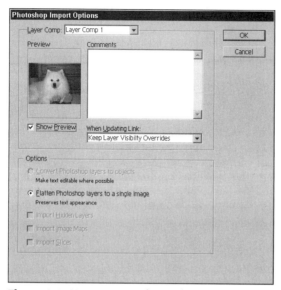

Figure 1-6: You can now choose between various layer comps when you import a Photoshop file containing multiple layer comps.

Improving Your Workspace

If you are a typical Illustrator user, you probably have your own preferred desktop layout (or maybe even several for different tasks). That is, you want this palette to sit right here and that palette to sit over there. Setting up your preferred layout is likely the first thing you do when you open Illustrator.

The people at Adobe have finally listened to users and added several commands to help you manage your workspace so that it is now easier to get just the screen layout you want in Illustrator CS2. The Window ⇨ Workspace submenu includes commands that enable you to restore the default layout, choose a minimal layout for maximum workspace, save your favorite layout, or load a saved layout. Figure 1-7 shows the Save Workspace dialog box that you use to save and name your workspace layouts.

Figure 1-7: Illustrator CS2 enables you to save and restore your favorite workspace layouts.

Tip

The workspace layout feature also supports dual monitors, if you happen to be lucky enough to have two displays.

Saving Color Information with Spot Color Rasters

Spot colors are special colors you use to ensure an exact match with a specific color. Illustrator CS2 now includes support for spot color rasters so that you can create a drop shadow in a specific color and have Illustrator generate the correct color separations for printing. You can also colorize an embedded grayscale image with one spot or process color, and any spot color rasters are preserved when you save the file.

Cross-Reference

See Chapter 18 for more information about spot colors.

Welcoming SVG 1.1 Support

Previous versions of Illustrator have included support for SVG (*Scalable Vector Graphics*) version 1.0. Illustrator CS2 adds support for SVG 1.1 — a more capable version that produces better output.

Most image formats used on the Web are bitmap formats. Although bitmap formats are vital for photographs, the resulting file sizes make bitmap formats less efficient than vector-based formats for many types of graphics. SVG is an XML-based vector image format that can be programmed to respond to user interaction.

Cross-Reference

See Chapters 3 and 19 for more information about SVG.

Using Offset Paths

Objects that you draw in Illustrator can have both a stroke and a fill. In previous versions, the stroke was always centered on the path, which limited your ability somewhat in creating precisely the effect you may want. Illustrator CS2 now offers you the option to offset stroke alignment around a path. It is now possible to offset the stroke to be completely inside or outside a path as needed. You use the Stroke palette to control the offset.

Cross-Reference

See Chapter 5 for more information about strokes and paths.

Handling Text with Underline and Strikethrough

Although this final new feature isn't likely to be a determining factor for anyone contemplating an upgrade from a previous version of Illustrator, the ability to underline or strikethrough text is a needed improvement. Illustrator CS2 is generally a bit faster at text handling than previous versions, but underlining and strikethrough are the only visible text-related changes new to this version.

See Chapter 9 for more information about working with text and type in Illustrator CS2.

Summary

Illustrator CS2 has some major changes and several minor ones compared to earlier versions of the application. This chapter introduced several of the new features in order to give you a bit of the flavor of the new version. You learned that:

✦ Live Trace takes the place of the Auto Trace tool and provides far more power to help you use raster images in your Illustrator documents.

✦ Live Paint is a worthwhile upgrade to the old Paint Bucket tool that enables paint effects to remain live while you work.

✦ The Control palette provides a convenient place to find the most common settings for selected objects so that you don't always have to hunt down some obscure palette to adjust a property.

✦ Adobe Bridge is a standalone application that allows you to browse files in all Adobe-supported formats and to change some of the metadata associated with those files.

✦ You can now work with Photoshop layer comps directly inside Illustrator CS2.

✦ The workspace enhancements enable you to save and recall custom desktop layouts for increased efficiency.

✦ Spot color rasters are saved with your files for more accurate printing of spot color separations.

✦ SVG 1.1 support increases the accuracy of vector graphics you create in Illustrator CS2 for use on the Web.

✦ Offset paths allow you to place a stroke inside or outside a path in addition to directly centered over the path.

✦ Improved text handling features now include support for underlining and strikethrough.

✦   ✦   ✦

Understanding Illustrator's Desktop

✦ ✦ ✦ ✦

In This Chapter

Getting Illustrator started

Using shortcut keys

Working with Illustrator's interface

Moving around in Illustrator

Outline versus Preview mode

Understanding the Edit functions

✦ ✦ ✦ ✦

Not too long ago, commercial artists and illustrators worked by hand, not on computers. You might find it hard to believe, but they spent hours and hours with T-squares, rulers, French curves, and type galleys from their local typesetters.

Now, of course, most artists and artist wannabes spend hours and hours with their computers, mice, digitizing tablets, monitors, and onscreen type that they set themselves. A few traditional artists are still out there, but more and more make the transition to the digital world every day.

After that transition, computer artists usually come face-to-face with Illustrator, the industry-standard, graphics-creation software for both print and the Web. The following is a typical example of how people get to know Illustrator.

Picasso Meets Illustrator: Getting Started

Illustrator arrives and the enthusiastic artist-to-be — we'll call him Picasso — opens the box, pops in the CD-ROM, and installs the product. A few minutes later Picasso launches Illustrator and is faced with a clean, brand-new, empty document. A world of possibilities awaits, only a few mouse clicks away. But Picasso is a little intimidated by all that white space, just as many budding young writers wince at a new word-processing document with the lone insertion point blinking away.

So, Picasso decides he'll "play" with the software before designing anything "for real." He chooses the rectangle tool first, clicks, drags, and voilà! A rectangle appears on the screen! His confidence soars. He may try the other shape tools next, but sooner or later Picasso starts playing with some of the software's other features. Eventually, he eyes the dreaded Pen tool. And thus starts his downward spiral into terror.

Confusion ensues. Hours of staring at an Illustrator document and wondering "Why?" take up the majority of his time. Picasso doesn't really understand fills and strokes, he doesn't understand stacking order and layers, and he certainly doesn't understand Bézier curves.

Picasso goes through the tutorial three times, but whenever he strays one iota from the set-in-stone printed steps, nothing works. Picasso becomes convinced that the Pen tool is Satan's pitchfork in disguise. Patterns make about as much sense as differential equations. Then he encounters things such as effects that can be edited later (huh?), miter limits for strokes (yeah, right), and the difference between targeting a group or all the objects in that group (huh? again). All are subjects that seem quite foreign and impossible to understand.

Picasso had never used or seen software as *different* as Illustrator.

Ah, but you have an advantage over Picasso. You have this book. The following sections in this chapter take you through the interface and common editing commands that help you construct better illustrations. The other areas focused on are the basic Illustrator functions, from setting up a new document to understanding exactly what paths are and how Illustrator uses them.

Control palet

Don't worry if you don't already know what the Pen tool is — you'll learn lots more about each of the drawing tools in Chapter 4.

Getting started with Illustrator

The first step in getting started is to install the software, which is slightly different depending on whether you're using a Macintosh or a Windows computer. After the software is installed, you can launch Illustrator in one of the following ways:

✦ Double-click Illustrator's application icon.

✦ Double-click an Illustrator document, which automatically launches Illustrator.

✦ In Windows, choose Start ➪ Programs ➪ Adobe Illustrator.

Quitting Illustrator

Now that you know how to open the program, it's time to learn how to close it. You can end your Illustrator session at any time by choosing File ➪ Exit (or Illustrator ➪ Quit). This action closes the current document and exits the application. If you have not previously saved your document, Illustrator prompts you to do so before exiting the application. You can also close Illustrator in one of these ways:

✦ **Mac OSX:** Click and hold the Illustrator icon in the Dock and then click Quit, or Ctrl-click the Dock icon and then click Quit. You can also choose Illustrator ➪ Quit. You also have the option of pressing Ctrl, clicking the Illustrator icon in the dock, and choosing Quit, or pressing ⌘+Q.

✦ **Windows:** Right-click Illustrator's taskbar icon and click Close, or press Alt+F4 and click Close from the pop-up menu. You can also close Illustrator by right-clicking the taskbar icon and picking Close, or by pressing Ctrl+Q.

Working with Illustrator's Interface

Understanding the interface is the first step in learning Illustrator. Adobe has kept its products looking consistent so that using all its programs together is easy. The tools, palettes, and menus are pretty similar when using Illustrator, Photoshop, and InDesign.

Illustrator's interface holds many elements that let you work in optimum productivity. After you understand the interface, the creation process is much easier. When looking at Illustrator, you'll find the following:

✦ **Document window:** The document window appears when you open an existing document or start a new document.

✦ **Toolbox:** The toolbox houses the tools you need to create amazing artwork. The tools are set as icons that represent what the tool looks like.

✦ **Palettes:** The palettes enable you to choose options such as colors, line width, styles, and so on. You can move the palettes around (floating) to any location. You can also close or open palettes, as needed.

✦ **Control palette:** The control palette is a special palette that normally appears just below the menu bar. This palette enables you to quickly select settings that apply to the currently selected tool.

✦ **Menu:** The main menu is across the top of the window and allows you to access many of Illustrator's powerful commands. Illustrator also makes use of pop-up context menus that appear when you right-click (Ctrl-click) many objects.

✦ **Zoom control:** The zoom control provides a quick method of zooming in or out in the document window so that you can see fine details or the entire drawing.

✦ **Status bar:** The status bar typically shows you what tool is currently being used. You can also choose from several different status bar options if you prefer to see other information such as the current date and time, the number of undo levels that are available, the color profile that is being used, or the status of shared documents.

✦ **Artboard:** The Artboard is the part of the document window that contains the art you want to print. It is typically shown as a thin black rectangle.

Working in the document window

The document window, shown in Figure 2-1, is where you perform all your work. It contains two main elements: the Artboard and the page, or pasteboard.

Tip   You can move the printable area represented by the dashed lines using the Page tool (one of the two optional modes of the Hand tool). More detail on the Page tool is covered later in this chapter.

Illustrator windows act like windows in most other programs. You use the title bar at the top of the window to move the window around your screen. On the title bar is the name of the document. If you have not yet saved your document, the name of the document is Untitled-1, with the number changing for each new document you create. (Hint: Save it as soon as you create it!) Next to the title of the document is the current viewing percentage relative to actual size.

Note   If you have not maximized the document window, the document's name appears in the document window's title bar rather than in Illustrator's title bar on Windows PCs. This extra document window title bar reduces the size of your workspace, so you may want to maximize the document window in order to gain a little more room to work on your document.

Tip   If you're using a Mac, once you've saved a document, you can ⌘+click the document name in the title bar to see a full path to its location on disk.

The scroll bars let you see what is above and below or right and left of the current viewing area.

Cross-Reference   See "Using the scroll bars to view your document" later in this chapter for more on scroll bars.

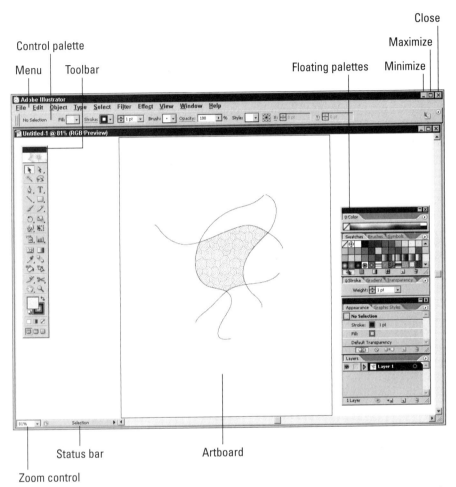

Figure 2-1: The document window contains the page, surrounded by the Artboard.

Three vital buttons help you close, minimize, and maximize the various windows you open in Illustrator. You find these buttons on the upper-left corner in OS X, and on the upper-right corner in Windows. In Windows you'll find a second set of these buttons — the upper set controls the entire Illustrator window while the lower set controls the document window.

In addition to these buttons, the Windows version of Illustrator offers four options that help you quickly access your files. The Cascade, Tile, and Arrange Icons commands are all accessible via the Window menu:

✦ **Cascade:** When you have multiple files open, this command lines up all the title bars in a staggered (stairstep) arrangement going down and to the right.

✦ **Tile:** With multiple files open, this command tiles the windows next to one another to fill the application window. Figure 2-2 shows two document windows tiled next to each other.

✦ **Arrange Icons:** This command arranges your open files into neat rows.

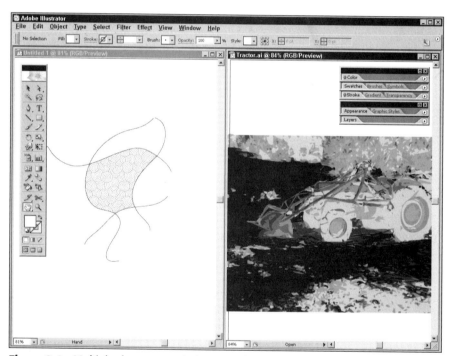

Figure 2-2: Multiple document windows can be tiled next to each other.

Understanding the Artboard

The Artboard is the area of your document that will print. The area of the Artboard doesn't have to be the same as the printed document. The Artboard is designated by black lines that form a rectangle in the document window and shows the largest area in which you can print. To set the size, orientation, and units for the Artboard, use the Document Setup dialog box. Open the Document Setup box by choosing File ➪ Document Setup. If you don't want to see the Artboard (perhaps because you're working on a large document that won't entirely fit on the Artboard), choose View ➪ Hide Artboard. To show the Artboard again, choose View ➪ Show Artboard.

Tip   To change the overall page size, use the Media options in the Print dialog box. To access the Print dialog box, choose File ➪ Print.

If you are taking your Illustrator artwork into another application, such as Photoshop or InDesign, the size of the Artboard is irrelevant; your entire illustration appears in most other software applications even if that artwork is larger than the Artboard.

Getting to know the work area

When using Illustrator, the worst thing that can happen is for you to lose an illustration on which you are working. "Where'd it all go?" you cry. This can happen very easily in Illustrator. Just click a few times on the gray parts of the scroll bars at the bottom of the document window. Each time you click, you move about half the width (or height) of your window, and three clicks later, your page and everything on it is no longer in front of you. Instead, you see the work area's scratch area, usually a vast expanse of white nothingness.

The work area measures 227.5×227.5 inches, which works out to about 360 square feet of drawing space. At actual size, you see only a very small section of the Artboard. A little letter-size document looks extremely tiny on a work area this big. If you get lost in the work area, a quick way back is to choose View ➪ Actual Size. Doing this puts your page in the center of the window at 100 percent view, at which time you can see at least part of your drawing. To see the whole page quickly, choose View ➪ Fit in Window, which resizes the view down to where you can see the entire page.

Note   Although the View ➪ Actual Size and View ➪ Fit in Window commands may seem to do the same thing, look closely and you'll see a subtle difference between the two. The View ➪ Fit in Window command always shows the entire Artboard — which, depending on your monitor's resolution setting, may not be the same as the 100 percent view produced by the View ➪ Actual Size command.

This discussion assumes, of course, that you have actually drawn artwork on the Artboard. If you have drawn your artwork way off to the side of the work area away from the Artboard, you may have more difficulty finding your drawing.

Using the Page tool

The Page tool, which you access via the Hand tool, shown in Figure 2-3, changes how much of your document prints; it does this by moving the printable area of the document without moving any of the printable objects in the document. Clicking and dragging the lower-left corner of the page relocates the printable area of the page to the place where you release the mouse button.

Cross-Reference The Hand tool is located in Illustrator's toolbox. For more on the toolbox, see the next section.

Figure 2-3: You access the Page tool by clicking the Hand tool and then selecting the tool from the flyout menu that appears.

Tip Double-clicking the Page tool slot resets the printable-area dotted line to its original position on the page.

The Page tool is useful when your document is larger than the biggest image area that your printer can print. The tool enables you to tile several pages to create one large page out of several sheets of paper. *Tiling* is the process by which an image is assembled by using several pieces of paper arranged in a grid formation. A portion of the image prints on each page, and when you fit the pages together, you can view the image in its entirety. Tiling is good only for rough prints, because you typically need to manually trim about a quarter inch around the edge of each sheet of paper; most printers don't print to the edge of the paper.

Cross-Reference To learn more about how to print and all that the process entails, see Chapter 18.

Working with the toolbox

The Illustrator toolbox contains all the tools that you use to draw objects in your documents. The toolbox normally appears on top of your document window, covering up part of your document window in the upper-left corner. The toolbox, shown in Figure 2-4, has no close box. To close it, you must choose Window ➪ Tools. You make the toolbox visible by placing a check mark next to the Window menu's Tools menu item. You hide the toolbox by clicking the check-marked item, so that no check mark appears next to the Tools menu item. The tools are discussed through-out the book in the chapters that use those tools.

Tip To toggle the display of *all* palettes, not just the toolbox, press the Tab key. Each time you press Tab, the palettes either hide or are redisplayed — depending on their current state. This won't work if you are using the Type tool with an active insertion point, of course.

Figure 2-4: The toolbox holds all the tools you need to draw in Illustrator.

Tip You can show and hide all the palettes *except* the toolbox by pressing Shift+Tab (again, don't try this when you are using the Type tool with an active insertion point).

To choose a tool, click the tool you want to use in its slot within the toolbox and release the mouse button. Doing this highlights it on the toolbox. You can also choose tools by pressing a key on the keyboard. For example, pressing P selects the Pen tool. You can inactivate a tool only by selecting another one.

Cross-Reference Appendix A lists all the shortcut keys for selecting each of the tools.

Many tools have additional pop-up tools called *flyouts*, which are tools that appear only when you click and hold down the mouse on the default tool. Illustrator denotes the default tools that have pop-up tools with a little triangle in the lower-right corner of the tool. To select a pop-up tool, click and hold a tool with a triangle until the pop-up tools appear; then drag to the pop-up tool you want. The new pop-up tool replaces the default tool in that tool slot.

Tip You can browse through the tools on any flyouts by pressing Alt (Option) while clicking a toolslot. Each click displays the next tool.

Tip You can customize the tool shortcuts under the Keyboard Shortcuts dialog box found under the Edit menu. In this dialog box, simply select the tool you want to change and enter the new shortcut letter, number, or symbol. You can also do this in Adobe Photoshop and Adobe InDesign.

Any tool with a pop-up option also has a tearoff tab on the right side of the flyout. You can make the flyout a free-floating palette by clicking this tearout tab. Use this feature if you find that you are constantly switching between tools in that tearoff. Then you won't have to click+hold and drag to the next tool.

Viewing Tool Tips

What if you forget the function of a specific tool or you can't tell the difference between the various tools in Illustrator? No problem! Illustrator comes equipped with a handy Tool Tips feature that identifies tools quickly and easily. When you have Tool Tips activated, you simply move your cursor over the element you want to identify, and a yellow text box pops up and tells you its name. For example, when you place your cursor over the Type tool, a box appears with the words Type Tool (T). The letter within the parentheses indicates the keyboard shortcut for the tool. In this example, if you press T, you activate the Type tool without clicking it. Illustrator provides Tool Tips for every tool in the toolbox as well as for the palette controls.

Illustrator provides Tool Tips by default. However, if you find them annoying, or if you know the tips well enough not to need the Tool Tips, you can disable them in the General screen of the Preferences dialog box. To open the Preferences dialog box, simply choose Edit (Illustrator) ➪ Preferences ➪ General and deselect the Show Tool Tips option.

Using the palettes

Palettes are small windows that are similar to dialog boxes. The palettes enable you to control virtually every aspect of the Illustrator drawing environment. Illustrator has more than two dozen palettes, all of which can remain open while you work on your document (provided that you can still see your document through all those palettes). Technically speaking, a palette is a *modeless* window. The big difference between a modeless window and a dialog box is that you don't have to close the modeless window to perform other tasks. Therefore, you can work with the features on one palette without having to close another palette.

Unlike windows, palettes are never really active. Instead, the one you are working in is in the front. If the palette has editable text fields, Illustrator highlights the active one or makes the text cursor blink. To bring a palette to the forefront — that is, bring it into focus — simply click it anywhere.

Palettes are like regular windows in many ways. Each palette has a title bar that you can click and drag to move it. The title bar also has buttons for minimizing (Windows) or zooming (Macintosh OS) and closing the palette. Each palette also has a tab with the name of the palette within it.

Note   You can use the title tab to toggle between the minimized state (showing only the title tab and the maximized state (showing the entire palette) by double-clicking the title tab.

Occasionally, a palette has a handle on the lower-right corner that looks like a triangle with two lines, as seen in Figure 2-5. You can use this handle for changing the palette's size by clicking and dragging the corner containing the handle.

Figures 2-5: You can resize a palette that has a triangle on its lower-right corner.

Tip   For some palettes (such as the Color palette), a double arrow icon appears to the left of the title name. Clicking this icon toggles the palette size among several different sizes.

Linking together and tearing apart palettes

You can place palettes together in different combinations by *tabbing* and *docking* them. Tabbing stacks the tabs for several palettes into a single palette. Docking aligns the palettes without stacking them into the same space.

Each palette (except for the toolbox) has a tab on it. Clicking the tab of a palette brings it to the front. Dragging a tab from one palette to another moves that palette into another palette. Dragging a tab out of a palette makes the palette separate from the previous palette. Figure 2-6 includes a set of palettes that have been tabbed together.

Note   By default, Illustrator tabs certain palettes together. You can drag them apart and tab others together to suit your method of working.

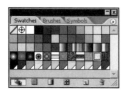

Figure 2-6: A palette contains a number of tabs.

You can dock palettes together by dragging the tab of one palette to the bottom of another palette. When the bottom of the other palette darkens, releasing the mouse button "docks" the moved palette to the bottom of the other one. Then, when you move the other palette, the docked palette moves with it. To separate a palette from the others, click and drag the tab away from the original palette.

Tip To restore the default palette layout, use the Window ➪ Workspace ➪ Default command.

Working with palettes

Palettes are even more useful when you can reveal and hide them to suit your needs. Under the Window menu, you can choose which palettes show and which ones hide. Simply check next to a palette to show it, and uncheck next to the palette to hide it. Some palettes use a keyboard shortcut to access them, and others are accessed through the Window menu. To see the shortcuts, look to the right of the palette name. Under the Window menu, you can see what palettes are visible by the checkmark next to them.

The palettes are discussed throughout the books in various chapters. The palettes are listed as they appear under the Windows menu. These are the palettes available:

✦ **Actions:** Use this palette to record a sequence of events to play at any time.

✦ **Align:** This palette lets you align objects (Shift+F7).

✦ **Appearance:** Use this palette to check the attributes of a selected object (Shift+F6).

✦ **Attributes:** Use this palette to view the overprinting and any URLs associated with the selected object (Ctrl+F11/⌘+F11).

✦ **Brushes:** Use this palette to select a brush type (F5).

✦ **Color:** This palette lets you apply color to your illustrations (F6).

✦ **Document Info:** This palette shows information on the document such as color mode, Artboard dimensions, and other options.

✦ **Flattener Preview:** Use this to see certain areas of flattened artwork. You can also adjust the flattener options here.

✦ **Gradient:** This palette is used for changing and applying gradients (Ctrl+F9/⌘+F9).

✦ **Graphic Styles:** This palette lists the default graphic styles and lets you save graphic styles (Shift+F5).

✦ **Info:** This palette displays information on the selected object that is used for measuring objects or distance (F8), among other things.

✦ **Layers:** This palette lets you put objects on different layers for easier organization (F7).

✦ **Links:** This lists the placed objects that are linked to the document.

✦ **Magic Wand:** Use this to adjust the settings for the Magic Wand tool.

✦ **Navigator:** Use this to quickly move around a large document.

✦ **Pathfinder:** Use this to combine, split, divide, and do more to multiple paths (Shift+Ctrl+F9/Shift+⌘+F9).

✦ **Stroke:** This palette lets you adjust the width and style of the stroke (Ctrl+F10/⌘+F10).

✦ **SVG Interactivity:** Use this palette to set options for Scalable Vector Graphics.

✦ **Swatches:** This palette houses preset colors, gradients, and patterns.

✦ **Symbols:** This palette houses preset symbols and lets you define new symbols (Shift+Ctrl+F11/Shift+⌘+F11).

✦ **Tools:** This palette contains all of Illustrator's tools.

✦ **Transform:** This palette lets you move, scale, and apply other transformations (Shift+F8).

✦ **Transparency:** Use this palette to adjust the opacity of objects (Shift+Ctrl+F10/Shift+⌘+F10).

✦ **Type:** Use this palette to adjust a variety of type options such as Character (Ctrl+T/⌘+T), Character Styles, Glyphs, OpenType (Alt+Shift+Ctrl+T/Option+Shift+⌘+T), Paragraph (Alt+Ctrl+T/Option+⌘+T), Paragraph Styles, and Tabs (Shift+Ctrl+T/Shift+⌘+T).

✦ **Variables:** This palette is used for data-driven graphics to set the options.

Using Illustrator's menus

Although Adobe places more emphasis on Illustrator's palettes and other elements, such as its toolbox, you will still find many important and useful features in Illustrator's menus.

Some general rules apply to Illustrator menus:

✦ To select a menu item, pull down the menu, highlight the menu item you want, and release or click the mouse button. If the cursor is not on that item but is still highlighted, the command will not take effect.

✦ Whenever an ellipsis appears (three little dots that look like this...), choosing that menu item brings up a dialog box where you must verify the current information by clicking an OK button or by entering more information and then clicking OK. If the option has no ellipsis, the action you select takes place right away.

✦ When you see a key command listed on the right side of the menu, you can type that key command instead of using the mouse to pull down this menu. Using key commands for menu items works just like clicking the menu bar and pulling down to that item.

✦ If you see a little triangle next to a menu item, it means the menu possesses a submenu. You can choose items in the submenu by pulling over to the menu and then pulling up or down to select the menu item needed. Submenus usually appear on the right side of the menu, but due to space limitations on your monitor, submenus may appear on the left side for certain menus.

Palette menus

Not only does the main document window have menus; so do palettes. You can find a variety of features and options to meet your creative needs. To open these menus, simply find and click the round button with the arrow in the middle, located on the top-right corner of most palettes. Figure 2-7 gives an example of the options you have available when you access the Character palette's menu. These options and features change with each palette.

Figure 2-7: You can find a multitude of options by accessing the palette menu.

Context-sensitive menus

Illustrator provides context-sensitive menus that appear right under your cursor as you're working. To access them, right-click (Ctrl+click) anywhere in the document window, and a context-sensitive menu appears. These menus contain commands that relate to the type of work you're doing and the specific tool you have. Figure 2-8 shows a context-sensitive menu that appears in a document when a rectangle shape is created and selected. This menu looks different if another object is selected.

Figure 2-8: When you right-click the document window, Illustrator reveals a context-sensitive menu.

Typing keyboard commands

Keyboard commands are shortcuts for common activities that you perform in Illustrator. These shortcuts typically use the Ctrl (⌘) key in combination with other keys. Some menu items do not have keyboard commands; usually, you have to choose those items from the menu.

Keyboard commands are as important to an Illustrator artist as the mouse is; with a little practice, you can learn them quickly. Besides, many of the default keyboard commands are the same from program to program, which makes you an instant expert in software that you haven't used yet! Good examples of this are the Cut/Copy/Paste, Select All; and Save commands:

✦ **Cut/Copy/Paste:** You activate these by pressing Ctrl+X, Ctrl+C, and Ctrl+V (⌘+X, ⌘ +C, and ⌘+V).

✦ **Select All:** You can select everything in a document by pressing Ctrl+A (⌘+A).

✦ **Save:** You can quickly save your work by pressing Ctrl+S (⌘+S).

Using the status bar

The status bar, located on the lower left of your document window, has a Zoom pop-up list and a button that displays useful and otherwise difficult to find information. To change the item shown in the status bar, click the triangle to the right of

Show and select a different item. Although the default for this button displays the tool that you are currently using, you can change the information to display one of the following instead:

✦ **Version Cue Status:** Select this to see the Version Cue information for shared files. This option is available only if you have Adobe Creative Suite installed.

✦ **Current Tool:** Select this to show the selected tool's name.

✦ **Date and Time:** Use this to show the current date and time.

✦ **Number of Undos:** This is a handy option that shows the number of queued undos and redos.

✦ **Document Color Profile:** This shows the current Color Profile.

Mousing Around in Illustrator

Illustrator requires the use of a mouse for selecting items, pulling down menus, moving objects, and clicking buttons. Learning to use the mouse efficiently requires patience, practice, and persistence.

You use the mouse to perform five basic functions in Illustrator:

✦ **Pointing:** Move the cursor around the screen by moving the mouse around your mousepad.

✦ **Clicking:** Press and release the left mouse button (or the only button on some Macs) in one step. You click to select points, paths, and objects, and to make windows active.

✦ **Dragging:** Press the mouse button and keep pressing it while you move the mouse. You drag the cursor to choose items from menus, select contiguous characters of text, move objects, and create marquees (dotted rectangles used for zooming the view).

✦ **Double-clicking:** Quickly press and release the mouse button twice in the same location. You double-click to select a word of text, select a text field with a value in it, access a dialog box for a tool, and run Illustrator (by double-clicking its icon).

✦ **Right-clicking (Ctrl+clicking):** This displays a context-sensitive menu when you press the right mouse button (or Ctrl+click on the Mac).

The cursor is the little icon (usually an arrow) that moves in the same direction as the mouse. In Illustrator, the cursor often takes the form of a tool that you are using. When the computer is busy, an ugly little watch or a spiraling circle (Macintosh) or hourglass (Windows) takes its place.

Navigating Around Your Document

Being able to move through a document easily is a key skill in Illustrator. Rarely can you fit an entire illustration in the document window at a sufficient magnification to see much of the image's detail. Usually, you are zooming in, zooming out, or moving off to the side, above, or below to focus on certain areas of the document.

Understanding the Zoom tool

The most basic navigational concept in Illustrator is the ability to zoom to different magnification levels. Illustrator's magnification levels work like a magnifying glass. In the real world, you use a magnifying glass to see details that aren't readily visible without it. In the Illustrator world, you use the different magnification levels to see details that aren't readily visible at the 100 percent view.

Changing the magnification levels of Illustrator does not affect the illustration. If you zoom in to 200 percent and print, the illustration still prints at the size it would if the view were 100 percent. It does *not* print twice as large. Figure 2-9 shows the same Illustrator document at 100 and 200 percent magnification.

Figure 2-9: An Illustrator document at 100 percent (left) and 200 percent (right) magnifications

In Illustrator, 100 percent magnification means that the artwork you see on the screen has the same physical dimensions when it prints. If you place a printout next to the onscreen image at 100 percent magnification, it appears at exactly the same size, depending on your monitor resolution (the higher the resolution, the smaller the document looks onscreen).

Tip   For those of you who plan to use Illustrator with Photoshop, remember that in Photoshop, 100 percent view is different. In Photoshop, each pixel onscreen is equal to one pixel in the image. Unless the pixels per inch (ppi) of the image match those of the screen (and they would if Web graphics were being designed), the 100 percent view tends to be larger than the printed dimensions of the image.

Using the Zoom tool

Perhaps the easiest way to control the magnification of your artwork is with the Zoom tool. This tool (which looks like a magnifying glass and is located in the right column of the toolbox) can magnify a certain area of artwork and then return to the standard view.

To use the Zoom tool to magnify an area, select it in the toolbox by clicking it once. The Zoom cursor takes the place of the Arrow cursor (or whatever tool was previously selected). It looks like a magnifying glass with a plus sign in it. Clicking any spot in the illustration enlarges the illustration to the next magnification level, with the place you clicked centered on your screen. The highest magnification level is 6,400 percent — which, as all you math aficionados know, is 64 times (not 6,400 times!) bigger than the original. Where you click with the Zoom tool is very important:

✦ **Clicking the center of the window** enlarges the illustration to the next magnification level.

✦ **Clicking the edges (top, bottom, left, and right) of the window** makes the edges that you did not click (and possibly some or all of your artwork) disappear as the magnification increases.

✦ **Clicking the upper-right corner** hides mostly the lower-left edges and so forth.

If you are interested in seeing a particular part of the document close up, click that part at each magnification level to ensure that it remains in the window.

If you zoom in too far, you can use the Zoom tool to zoom out again. To zoom out, press the Alt (Option) key when you have the Zoom tool active (releasing the Alt [Option] key restores the Zoom In tool). Clicking with the Zoom Out tool reduces the magnification level to the next lowest level. You can zoom out to 3.13 percent (1/32 actual size). To access the Zoom out, hold the Alt (Option) key to see the minus sign indicating that you are zooming out.

When you use the Zoom tool, you magnify everything in the document, not just the illustration. You magnify all paths, objects, the Artboard, and the Page Setup boundaries equally. However, the way certain objects appear (the thickness of path selections, points, handles, gridlines, guides, and Illustrator user interface [UI] components such as palettes and windows) does not change when you zoom in.

If you need to zoom in to see a specific area in the document window, use the Zoom tool to draw a marquee by clicking and dragging diagonally around the objects that you want to magnify. The area thus magnifies as much as possible so that everything inside the box just fits in the window that you have open. If you drag a box as you press and hold the Alt (Option) key to zoom out, you do the same thing as if you had just clicked to zoom out.

Tip

To move a zoom marquee around while you're drawing it, press and hold the spacebar after you've begun drawing the marquee but before you release the mouse button. When you release the spacebar, you can continue to change the size of the marquee by dragging.

Other zooming techniques

You also can zoom in and out by using commands in the View menu. Choose View ➪ Zoom In to zoom in one level at a time until the magnification level is 6,400 percent. The Zoom In menu item zooms from the center out. Choose View ➪ Zoom Out to zoom out one level at a time until the magnification level is 3.13 percent.

Although Illustrator can zoom to any level, it uses 23 default zoom levels when you click the Zoom tool or when you access the Zoom In and Zoom Out menu items (or their respective keyboard commands). Table 2-1 lists each of the default Zoom In and Zoom Out default levels.

Table 2-1
Zoom In and Zoom Out Default Levels

Zoom Out	Ratio	Zoom In	Ratio
100%	1:1	100%	1:1
66.67%	2:3	150%	3:2
50%	1:2	200%	2:1
33.33%	1:3	300%	3:1
25%	1:4	400%	4:1
16.67%	1:6	600%	6:1

Continued

Table 2-1 *(continued)*

Zoom Out	Ratio	Zoom In	Ratio
12.5%	1:8	800%	8:1
8.33%	1:12	1,200%	12:1
6.25%	1:16	1,600%	16:1
4.17%	1:24	2,400%	24:1
3.13%	1:32	3,200%	32:1
		4,800%	48:1
		6,400%	64:1

Tip   You can quickly zoom in or out using the scroll wheel on your mouse. Rotate the wheel away from you to zoom out (move your view away from the document), or rotate the wheel toward you to zoom in (move your view closer to the document).

Zooming to Actual Size

You can use different methods to automatically zoom to 100 percent view. The first method is to double-click the Zoom tool slot in the toolbox. This action changes the view to 100 percent instantly. Your other choices are as follows:

✦ **Using the Zoom feature in the status bar:** To do this, simply click the drop-down arrow in the left corner of the status bar and select 100%.

✦ **Using the View menu:** This is the best way to zoom to 100 percent magnification because it not only changes the image size to 100 percent, but also centers the page in the document window. Simply choose View ➪ Actual Size.

Zooming to Fit in Window size

Fit in Window instantly changes the magnification level of the document so that the entire Artboard (not necessarily the artwork, if it isn't located on the page) fits in the window and is centered in it. You can choose from two different methods to change the document view to the Fit in Window size:

✦ **Use the View menu:** One way to automatically change to the Fit in Window view is to choose View ➪ Fit in Window.

✦ **Use the Hand tool slot:** Simply double-click the Hand tool slot.

Tip   You can quickly go to 3.13 percent by Ctrl (⌘)+double-clicking the Zoom tool slot in the toolbox.

Zooming to a specific magnification

If you'd like to view a document at a specific zoom level, double-click the view area at the bottom-left corner of the active document window; then type the magnification you want to zoom to, and press Enter or Return.

Note When you specify a magnification, you do not change the document. Rather, you change how you view the document. For this reason, you can never undo any type of magnification-level change. Choosing Edit ⇨ Undo after zooming undoes the last change you made to the document before you changed the magnification level, *not* the magnification-level change.

Zooming with the Navigator palette

Of course, being able to zoom in very closely to your artwork does have a pitfall. The more you zoom in on an illustration, the less of that illustration you see at one time. The Navigator palette (shown in Figure 2-10), which you access by choosing Window ⇨ Navigator, helps you out by letting you see the entire illustration as well as the portion into which you're zoomed (indicated by a red viewing rectangle). You have several options within the Navigator palette for changing your view:

Figure 2-10: The Navigator palette shows a snapshot of the document.

✦ **The red rectangle:** You can stay zoomed in and move easily to another section by dragging the red rectangle (which actually scrolls), in the center of the Navigator palette, to another area.

✦ **The pop-up menu:** You access this menu by clicking the circular icon with a left-pointing arrow located on the upper-right corner of the palette. The Navigator palette's pop-up menu includes a View Artboard Only option. This option sets the thumbnail in the Navigator palette to show only the extent of the Artboard. If this option isn't set, the thumbnail shows all objects included in the document.

✦ **The magnification level box:** You can type an exact magnification level in the box in the lower-left corner of the Navigator palette.

✦ **The slider:** Located at the bottom of the Navigator palette is a slider giving you yet another way to zoom in and out by dragging the slider to the left or right.

✦ **The Zoom In and Zoom Out tools:** The Zoom In and Zoom Out tools look like little triangles and big triangles on either side of the slider triangle. You can zoom in and out a preset amount (using the same amounts used by the Zoom In and Zoom Out tools and menu items) by pressing the Zoom In or Zoom Out icons. These buttons are located on either side of the triangle slider.

Caution

The Navigator palette can slow down Illustrator if your artwork contains many patterns, gradients, and gradient mesh objects. To avoid this slowdown, you can close the Navigator palette by choosing Window ➪ Navigator.

Using the scroll bars to view your document

Sometimes, after you zoom in to a high magnification, part of the drawing that you want to see is outside the window area. Instead of zooming in and out repeatedly, you can use the scroll bars on the right side and bottom edges of the document window to move around inside the document. The right scroll bar controls where you are vertically in the document. The bottom scroll bar controls where you are horizontally in the document window.

The scroll bars contain three elements: up and down arrows, a gray area (or bar), and a *thumb*, also called the *elevator box*, which is the blue oval (on a Mac) or gray square (in Windows) that rides along the scroll bar. The gray area of the right scroll bar is proportionate to the vertical size of the work area (the space around the Artboard). If the little elevator box is at the top of the scroll bar, you are viewing the top edge of the work area. If it is centered, you are viewing the vertical center of the work area. The techniques are as follows:

✦ **Using the up and down arrows:** When you click the up arrow, you display what is above the window's boundaries by pushing everything in the window down in little increments. Clicking the down arrow displays what is below the window's boundaries by pushing the document up in little increments.

✦ **Using the thumbs:** Dragging the thumb up displays what is above the window's boundaries proportionately by whatever distance you drag it. Dragging the thumb down displays what is below the window's boundaries proportionately by whatever distance you drag it.

✦ **Using the gray bar:** Clicking the gray bar above the thumb and between the arrows displays what is above the window's boundaries in big chunks. Clicking the gray bar below the thumb, between the arrows, displays what is below the window's boundaries in big chunks.

Caution Be careful not to drag too far, or you will be previewing beyond the top of the Artboard.

Note In OS X, if you want to specify how far Illustrator scrolls when you click the gray bar, you can set this in the System Preferences. Also, on a Mac, the default is for the up and down arrows to be together. You can change this in your system's preferences for General to place the scroll bars together or at the top and bottom.

Scrolling with the Hand tool

The Hand tool improves on the scroll bars. The Hand tool—which looks like a hand—is located at the bottom of the first column of tools just above the color options.

Instead of being limited to horizontal and vertical movement only, you can use the Hand tool to scroll in any direction, including diagonally. The Hand tool is especially useful for finding your way around a document when you're viewing it at a high magnification level. The higher the magnification level, the more you're likely to use the Hand tool.

To use the Hand tool, select it from the Hand tool slot in the toolbox.

Tip To quickly access the Hand tool, press H, or press and hold the spacebar. Clicking and dragging the page moves the document around inside the document window while the spacebar is held down. If you release the spacebar, you return to the previous tool. This works for all tools, but the Type tool works a little differently. If you're currently using the Type tool in a text area, press Ctrl+spacebar (⌘+spacebar) to access the Zoom tool, and release Ctrl (⌘) while keeping the spacebar pressed to gain access to the Hand tool.

When you click in the document, be sure to click the side that you want to see. Clicking at the top of the document and dragging down enables you to scroll down through almost an entire document at a height of one window. Clicking in the center and dragging enables you to scroll through only half a window's size at a time.

The best thing about the Hand tool is that it works live. As you drag, the document moves under "your Hand." If you don't like where it is going, you can drag it back, still live. The second best thing is that accessing it requires only one keystroke, a press of the spacebar.

Note You cannot use Undo to reverse scrolling that you have done with the scroll bars and the Hand tool.

Scrolling with the Navigator palette

Use the red viewing rectangle in the Navigator palette to scroll quickly to another location within a document. Clicking and dragging within the red rectangle moves the viewing area around "live," whereas clicking outside the rectangle "snaps" the view to a new location.

Tip   You can change the red rectangle to another color by choosing Palette Options in the Navigator palette pop-up menu.

Cross-Reference   For more on the features of the Navigator palette, see the section "Zooming with the Navigator palette" earlier in this chapter.

Opening a new window

So now you've learned how to zoom and pan around the document window, and you probably have many different sections of your artwork that you want to focus on. Illustrator lets you create a number of windows for the current artwork using the Window ⇨ New Window option.

This option creates a new window that is the same size as the current window. You can then zoom and pan within this new window while maintaining the previous window. You can then place these windows side by side to see the artwork from two unique perspectives. Illustrator gives each new window a different reference number, which appears in the title bar.

Working in Outline Mode versus Preview Mode

In the old days, everyone worked in Outline mode (previously called Artwork mode). In Outline mode, you see only the "guts" of the artwork—the paths without the fills and strokes applied. To see what the illustration looked like with the fills and strokes applied, you had to switch to Preview mode. Usually, the preview was not quite what you had in mind, but to make changes, you had to switch back to Outline, and then to Preview again to check, and so forth. Many users of Illustrator from that time refer to it as the golden age, with not a little trace of sarcasm.

Today, Illustrator enables you to edit your work in both Outline and Preview modes, both shown in Figure 2-11. You can print a document from either mode. Saving the document while you are in Outline mode does not affect anything in the document, but the next time you open it, it displays in Outline mode. The same thing applies to Preview mode: Whatever mode you are in is saved with the artwork.

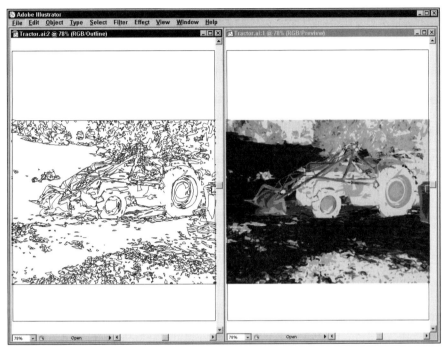

Figure 2-11: Artwork shown in both Outline mode (left) and Preview mode (right)

You cannot undo a Preview or Outline mode change (going from Preview to Outline, for example). If you make a Preview or Outline mode change and then close your document, Illustrator asks you if you want to save changes, which in this case refers only to the view change.

The current view mode is always displayed in the title bar next to the document name.

Understanding Outline mode

You may find working with a drawing in Outline mode significantly faster than working with it in Preview mode (discussed in the next section). In more complex drawings, the difference between Outline mode and Preview mode is significant, especially if you are working on a very slow computer. The speed that you gain is even greater when the artwork contains gradients, patterns, placed artwork, and blends. Outline mode is much closer to what the printer sees — as paths. *Paths* define the edges of the objects with which you are working.

Cross-Reference

For more on paths, see Chapter 4. To learn how to edit and select paths, see Chapter 6.

Getting used to Outline mode can take some time. Eventually, your brain can learn to know what the drawing looks like from seeing just the outlines, which show all of the paths. The one big advantage of Outline mode is that you can see every *path* (a single entity in your drawing made up of one or more straight or curved lines) that isn't directly overlapping another path. In Preview mode, many paths can be hidden. In Outline mode, invisible masks are normally visible as paths, and you can select paths that were hidden by the fills of other objects. To select paths in Outline mode, you must click the paths directly or draw a marquee across them.

To change the current document to Outline mode, choose View ➪ Outline. In Outline mode, the illustration disappears and is replaced onscreen by outlines of all the paths. Text that has yet to be converted into outlines looks fine, although it is always black.

Note   You can change how a placed image displays in Outline mode by selecting or deselecting the Show Images in Outline Mode option in the Document Setup dialog box. To display the Document Setup dialog box, choose File ➪ Document Setup. A placed image displays as a box if you check the Show Placed Images option. If you leave this option unchecked, the image displays only in black and white surrounded by a box.

Understanding Preview mode

In Preview mode, you can see which objects overlap, which objects are in front and in back, where gradations begin and end, and how patterns are set up. In other words, the document looks just the way it will look when you print it.

Note   In Preview mode, the color you see onscreen only marginally represents the actual output because of the differences between the way computer monitors work (red, green, and blue colors — the more of each color, the brighter each pixel appears) and the way printing works (cyan, magenta, yellow, and black colors — the more of each color, the darker each area appears). Monitor manufacturers make a number of calibration tools that decrease the difference between what you see on the monitor and the actual output. You can also use software solutions. One software solution, CIE calibration, is built in to Adobe Illustrator (choose Edit ➪ Color Settings). OS X users also can use ColorSync.

Choosing View ➪ Preview changes the view to Preview mode.

The biggest disadvantage of Preview mode is that Illustrator begins to draw and fill in the various parts of your image, which can take some time, especially if your computer is slow. When you change the image, the screen redraws. You can stop screen redraw by pressing Ctrl+Y (⌘+Y) at any time.

Another disadvantage of Preview mode is being unable to select the path you want to change in the image. Sometimes, so much stuff appears on your screen that you don't know what to click! This problem can become more complicated when you include fills in the mix, because the strokes on those paths are also visible. Instead of selecting a path by clicking it, you can select entire paths by clicking the insides of those paths in a filled area.

Understanding Overprint Preview mode

Drawing in Illustrator often results in one or more objects overlapping each other, meaning that the colors of these objects overlap as well. When you print these objects, the top color blocks, or *knocks out,* anything below it. The advantage of using this feature is that your illustration becomes cheaper and easier for a printer to generate. To see how your overprint will look after you've set the Overprint feature, you can view it in Overprint Preview mode by choosing View ➪ Overprint Preview.

For more on color and overprinting, see Chapters 7 and 18.

Understanding Pixel Preview mode

Because most Web page graphics are pixel-based, the Pixel Preview mode is specifically intended for graphics that designers want to place on Web pages. This mode lets you view images before converting them to a Web graphics format. Choose View ➪ Pixel Preview, and Illustrator places a check mark next to the Pixel Preview option and then shows a raster form of your image. Figure 2-12 shows what you would see in these two previews. In the figure, both windows are zoomed to 800 percent to more clearly show the effect of the Pixel Preview mode.

For more on creating Web graphics, see Chapter 19.

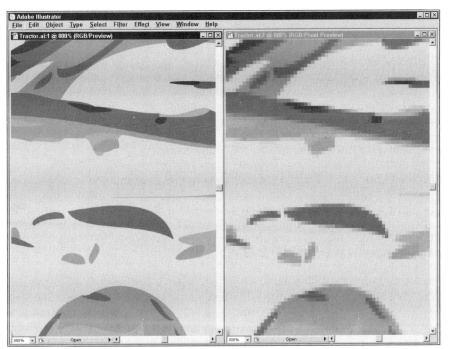

Figure 2-12: With Illustrator's Pixel Preview option, you can view an image in Preview mode (left) and in Pixel Preview mode (right).

Using custom views

Illustrator has a special feature called custom views that enables you to save special views of an illustration. Custom views contain view information, including magnification, location, and whether the illustration is in Outline or Preview mode. If you have various layers or layer sets in Preview mode and others in Outline mode, custom views can also save that information. Custom views, however, do not record whether templates, rulers, page tiling, edges, or guides are shown or hidden.

If you find yourself continually going to a certain part of a document, zooming in or out, and changing back and forth between Preview and Outline mode, that document is a prime candidate for creating custom views. Custom views are helpful for showing clients artwork that you created in Illustrator. Instead of fumbling around in the client's presence, you can, for example, show the detail in a logo instantly if you have preset the zoom factor and position and have saved the image in a custom view.

To create a new view, set up the document in the way that you would like to save the view. Then choose View ➪ New View, and name the view in the New View dialog box. Each new view name appears at the bottom of the View menu. No default keyboard shortcuts exist for these views, but you can create your own shortcuts by using the Keyboard Shortcuts dialog box, available under the Edit menu. You can create up to 25 custom views. Custom views are saved with a document as long as you save it using the Illustrator format.

Using screen modes

So you've been working on an illustration for an important client (actually, they all are important), and the client scheduled an appointment to see your progress, but the best part of the work is hidden behind the palettes and the toolbox. You can turn off the palettes and the toolbox, or you can switch between the different screen modes.

Illustrator uses three different screen modes represented by the three icon buttons at the bottom of the toolbox. They are Standard Screen Mode, Full Screen Mode with Menu Bar, and Full Screen Mode. In addition to clicking the screen mode buttons in the toolbox, you can also press F to switch between the three modes.

Using the Edit Commands

In most software, including Illustrator, many basic functions of the Edit menu work the same way. If you've used the Edit menu in Photoshop or Microsoft Word, for example, you should have no trouble using the same functions in Illustrator, because the menu options are located in the same place in each program, as you can see in Figure 2-13.

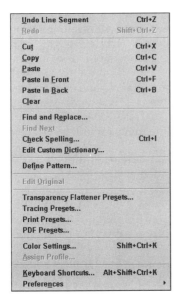

Figure 2-13: The various commands under the Edit menu help you to quickly cut, copy, and paste objects from place to place, as well as help you undo and redo previously applied commands.

Using the Clear command

The most simplistic Edit command is Clear. In Illustrator, it works almost exactly like the Backspace (Delete) key on the keyboard. When something is selected, choosing Clear deletes or gets rid of what is selected.

You're probably asking yourself, "If the Backspace (Delete) key does the same thing, why do we need Clear?" or "Why didn't they just call the Clear command Backspace (Delete)?" Ah, the makers of Illustrator are a step ahead of you in this respect. Note that we said "almost" the same way; there is a subtle yet important difference in what the Clear command does and what the Backspace (Delete) key does, due to Illustrator's abundant use of palettes.

If you are working on a palette and have just typed a value in an editable text field, the Backspace (Delete) key deletes the last character typed. If you tabbed down or up to an editable text field and highlighted text, or if you dragged across text in an editable text field and highlighted text, then the Backspace (Delete) key deletes the highlighted characters. In all three situations, the Clear command deletes anything that is selected in the document.

Cutting, copying, and pasting

The Cut, Copy, and Paste commands in Illustrator are very handy. Copying and cutting selected objects places them on the clipboard, which is a temporary holding place for objects that have been cut or copied. After you place an object on the clipboard, you can paste it in the center of the same document, the same location as the cut or copied object, or another document in Illustrator, InDesign, or Photoshop.

Choosing Cut from the Edit menu deletes the selected objects and copies them to the clipboard, where they are stored until you cut or copy another object or until you shut down or restart your computer. Quitting Illustrator does not remove objects from the clipboard. Cut is not available when no object is selected.

Choosing Copy from the Edit menu works like Cut, but it doesn't delete the selected objects. Instead, it just copies them to the Clipboard, at which time you can choose Paste and slap another copy onto your document.

Choosing Paste from the Edit menu places any objects on the Clipboard into the center of the document window. Paste is not available if nothing is in the clipboard.

Tip   Alternatively, you can use the Paste in Front and Paste in Back options to position the object you are pasting relative to other objects.

Now, here's the really cool part: Just because you've pasted the object somewhere doesn't mean it isn't in the clipboard anymore. It is! You can paste again and again, and keep on pasting until you get bored or until your page is an indecipherable mess, whichever comes first. The most important rule to remember about Cut, Copy, and Paste is that whatever is currently in the clipboard is replaced by anything that subsequently gets cut or copied to the Clipboard.

Cut, Copy, and Paste also work with text that you type in a document. Using the Type tools, you can select type, cut or copy it, and then paste it. When you're pasting type, it will go wherever your blinking text cursor is located. If you have type selected (highlighted) and you choose Paste, the type that was selected is replaced by whatever you had on the Clipboard.

You can cut or copy as much or as little of an illustration as you choose; you are limited only by your hard disk space (which is used only if you run out of RAM).

Tip   If you ever get a message saying you can't cut or copy because you are out of hard disk space, it's time to start deleting stuff from your hard drive. Or simply get a bigger hard drive.

Thanks to the Adobe PostScript capability on the clipboard, Illustrator can copy paths to other Adobe software, including InDesign and Photoshop. Paths created in those packages (with the exception of InDesign) can be pasted into Illustrator. With Photoshop, you have the option of pasting your clipboard contents as rasterized pixels instead of as paths.

You have the ability to drag Illustrator artwork from an Illustrator document right into a Photoshop document. In addition, because Adobe lets you move things in both directions, you can drag a Photoshop selection from any Photoshop document right into an Illustrator document.

Undoing and redoing

You can keep undoing in Illustrator until you run out of either computer memory or patience. After you undo, you can redo by choosing Redo, which is found right below Undo in the Edit menu. And, guess what? You can redo everything you've undone.

Choosing Undo from the Edit menu undoes the last activity that was performed on the document. Successive undos undo more and more activities, until the document is at the point where it was opened or created or you have run out of memory.

Choosing Redo from the Edit menu redoes the last undo. You can continue to redo undos until you are back to the point where you started undoing or you perform another activity, at which time you can no longer redo any previous undos.

If you undo a couple of times and then do something, you won't be able to redo. You have to undo the last thing you did and then actually do everything again. In other words, all the steps that you undid are gone. It's fine to use the Undo feature to go back and check out what you did, but after you have used multiple undos, don't do anything if you want to redo back to where you started undoing from. Got that?

Summary

In this chapter, you learned the following:

✦ Illustrator may seem difficult to learn at first, but with this book and a bit of dedication, you can master it.

✦ Illustrator has many keyboard shortcuts that increase productivity.

✦ Adobe has kept the interface similar through its products.

✦ The document window, toolbox, palettes, menu, and status bar look the same in many Adobe applications.

✦ You can view Illustrator documents at virtually any magnification level without actually changing them.

✦ Use the Hand tool to scroll around your document.

✦ Illustrator's Outline mode lets you see paths without their strokes and fills.

✦ Cut, Copy, and Paste are under the Edit menu with Undo and Redo.

✦ Illustrator provides virtually unlimited undos and redos.

✦   ✦   ✦

Working with Illustrator Documents

✦ ✦ ✦ ✦

In This Chapter

Creating new
documents

Changing the
document setup

Opening and closing
Illustrator files

Saving files

Using the Export
command

Placing art

Understanding vector-
based and
pixel-based images

Placing raster images

Working with
rasterized Illustrator
artwork

Using raster images

Working with
document and file
information

✦ ✦ ✦ ✦

When you create an illustration in Illustrator, you are actually creating a document, which you can place on the Web, send to a printer, or simply save on your computer. This chapter covers how to set up and change a document, how to open and save files, and how to export and place files. You also find out the difference between pixel-based documents and vector-based documents.

Setting Up a New Document

When you first load Illustrator, you see a window, shown in Figure 3-1, that enables you to choose to create a new document from scratch or from an existing Illustrator template. Alternatively, you can choose to open an existing document so that you can do some additional work with that document.

If you have Illustrator already up and running, you can create a new document by choosing File ⇨ New or by pressing Ctrl+N (⌘+N). This new document now becomes the active document. An *active document* means that the document is in front of any other documents.

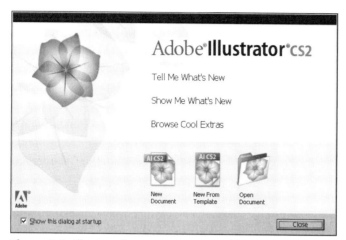

Figure 3-1: Illustrator's startup screen enables you to create a new document or open an existing one.

The New Document dialog box lets you enter the name, size, units, Artboard in width and height, orientation, and color mode. Figure 3-2 shows the New Document dialog box. Although the default dimensions in the New Document dialog box are for Letter size, you can set the new document to any size you want:

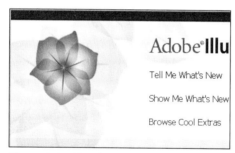

Figure 3-2: Use the New Document dialog box to choose the basic settings for a new document.

✦ **Name:** You can give your new document a name.

✦ **Size:** This allows you to choose standard preset dimensions, such as Letter or Legal, for your document.

✦ **Units:** You can also select the units you prefer to work in. Most artists choose points, but some prefer working in picas, inches, millimeters, centimeters, or pixels.

✦ **Width and Height:** Instead of selecting a preset size, you can specify exact dimensions in Width and Height boxes.

✦ **Orientation:** You can also choose the orientation of the page. The orientation options are portrait (meant to be viewed vertically) and landscape (meant to be viewed horizontally).

✦ **Color Mode:** Finally, you can choose from CMYK and RGB color modes.

Chapter 7 covers CMYK and RGB color modes in greater detail.

The document window initially shows up at Fit in Window size. In the title bar at the top of the window, you see Untitled-1 and the percentage zoom the document is displayed at. As soon as you save the document, the title bar contains the name of the document.

You cannot change the way that some of the palettes or presets appear when you first start Illustrator. For example, the Selection tool is always selected in the toolbox. Another unchangeable item is the initial paint style with which you begin drawing: a fill of white and a stroke of 1-point black. The character attributes are always the same: 12-point Myriad Roman, auto leading, flush-left alignment.

See Chapter 18 for more on changing the startup file.

Modifying the Setup of a Document

To change almost anything about the document structure and how you work with that document, you need to go to the Document Setup dialog box, seen in Figure 3-3, by choosing File ⇨ Document Setup. As with the New Document dialog box, you can change the size of the Artboard, the page orientation, the ruler units, and whether you want to view the file in Outline mode.

At the top of this dialog box is a list box (a pop-up menu on the Mac) that includes options for Artboard, Type, and Transparency. When you choose an option, the Document Setup dialog box displays a group of settings that apply to the selected option. Each of these options is discussed in the following sections.

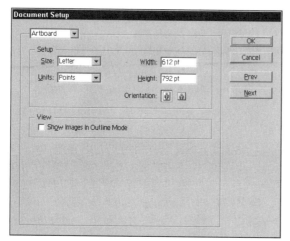

Figure 3-3: The Document Setup dialog box provides options for controlling your document's settings.

Understanding the Artboard options

In Illustrator, the Artboard defines the maximum drawing area that you can print. The Artboard is useful as a guide to where objects on a page belong. In older versions of Illustrator, the maximum printable size was 11 x 17 inches; with version 6, it increased to 227 x 227 inches or 358 square feet (provided that you can find a printer to print that big).

Cross-Reference   See Chapter 2 for more on the Artboard and pasteboard.

Commercial printers print colored artwork using separate plates for each of the different primary colors (typically they use four different plates). An application such as Illustrator can break down color images into the *separations* that are used to create these plates. *Crop marks* are lines that are printed as an aid to determining where to trim (or "crop") the printed page when the document is printed on over-sized paper.

Illustrator's separation setup ignores the Artboard and places crop marks around the entire imageable area. The *imageable area* is only the area where artwork exists. It may be within the Artboard, but it also may extend onto the pasteboard. When you export an illustration to another program, such as QuarkXPress or InDesign, the Artboard is ignored entirely.

Choosing the Artboard measurement units

You can view a document in points, picas, inches, centimeters, millimeters, or pixels. The measurement units affect the numbers on the rulers and the locations of the hash marks on those same rulers. The measurement system also changes the way measurements display in the Info palette and in all dialog boxes where you enter a measurement other than a percentage.

You change the measurement system in one of two ways:

✦ **Using the Preferences dialog box:** Use this method if you want to change all documents. To do so, choose Edit (Illustrator) ➪ Preferences ➪ Units & Display Performance.

✦ **Using the Document Setup dialog box:** Use this method for the currently active document. You open this box by choosing File ➪ Document Setup.

Choosing the Artboard size

Choose the size of the Artboard by selecting one of the following preset sizes in the Size drop-down list (pop-up menu on the Mac):

✦ **Custom:** Any size you type into the Width and Height fields of the Document Setup dialog box automatically changes the Size drop-down (pop-up) to Custom.

✦ **640 x 480:** Makes your Artboard 640 x 480 pixels.

✦ **800 x 600:** Makes your Artboard 800 by 600 pixels.

✦ **468 x 60:** Makes your Artboard 468 x 60 pixels.

✦ **Letter:** 8.5×11 inches.

✦ **Legal:** 8.5×14 inches.

✦ **Tabloid:** 11×17 inches.

✦ **A4:** 8.268×11.693 inches (21×29.7 centimeters).

✦ **A3:** 11.693×16.535 inches (29.7×42 centimeters).

✦ **B5:** 7.165×10 inches (18.2×25.4 centimeters).

✦ **B4:** 10.118×14.331 inches (55.7×36.4 centimeters).

Note   A4, A3, B5, and B4 are non-U.S. paper sizes.

Setting the Artboard orientation

You define the orientation of your Artboard by choosing one of the two Orientation pages. On the left is Portrait orientation, and on the right is Landscape orientation:

✦ **Portrait orientation:** You use this when the document is taller than it is wide. You can also think of portrait orientation as the vertical view.

✦ **Landscape orientation:** You use this when the document is wider than it is tall. You can also think of landscape orientation as the horizontal view.

Understanding the Show Images In Outline option

The last option in the Document Setup dialog box is the Show Images In Outline Mode option. Checking this box displays all placed EPS images in Outline mode. The placed image shows up in the file as a grayscale image. Fear not, the color is still there. You can see the color image by looking at the Navigator palette. Using this option allows for quicker redraw time when working with large placed image files.

Cross-Reference   For more on the Outline option, see Chapter 2.

Changing Type options

In the Document Setup dialog box, you can also change the Type options, as shown in Figure 3-4. Choose Type from the list box as the top of the dialog box to set these options. The following options are available under the Type options:

✦ **Highlight:** The options here are to check the Substituted Fonts or Substituted Glyphs in the document. This shows the fonts and glyphs (different forms of the same character) that have used a substitute because the current system does not have the actual font or glyph for that particular document.

✦ **Language:** Choose a desired language from the menu. You can choose from a variety of languages including English, French, Finnish, and so on, but you must have the language set up on your system to be able to use that language. All computers are set up, and you choose the language you are using.

✦ **Double Quotes:** Choose the style from the drop-down list (pop-up menu). You have a variety of quotes to choose from. Some users like the "curly" quotes rather than the straight ones.

✦ **Single Quotes:** Choose the style from the drop-down list (pop-up menu). The choices of single quotes are the same as the double quotes.

✦ **Use Typographer's Quotes:** Select this option to use the fancy quotes rather than the straight ones.

✦ **Options:** Choose the Size and Position for Superscripts, Subscripts, and Small Caps as a percentage of the original size.

✦ **Export:** In this list box (pop-up menu), choose from Preserve Text Editability and Preserve Text Appearance. In this case, you can either choose to be able to edit the text (but it may not look like you intended), or let the text look like it should (but make it so you can't edit it).

Type, the Type options, and the Type panel of the Document Setup dialog box are covered in more detail in Chapter 9.

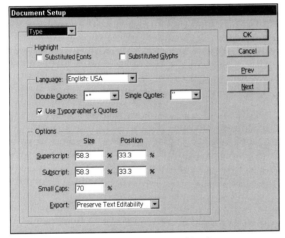

Figure 3-4: The Type options found in the Document Setup dialog box enable you to control the appearance of text in your Illustrator documents.

Working with Transparency options

Transparency options refer to making a transparent background screen. Many users like to use a transparent grid to see the opacity of their objects. On a white background, the opacity isn't easy to see. Just as in Photoshop, you can see a checkered grid that shows the opacity of the objects in front. The Flattener settings let you pick a resolution for the object when you change it to a rasterized (pixel) object when it is flattened — converted into a single layer with all overlapping objects combined. The Transparency options are also found in the Document Setup dialog box as shown in Figure 3-5. Choose Transparency from the list box at the top of the dialog box to display the following options:

✦ **View:** In this area, you can change your grid size to small, medium, or large. You can customize your own grid color. The Simulate Colored Paper check box makes the Artboard color match the grid color you have chosen.

✦ **Export and Clipboard Transparency Flattener Settings:** Select a preset (high, medium, or low resolution) from the Preset list box (pop-up menu), or choose a Custom setting.

Cross-Reference The Transparency options are covered in Chapters 7 and 15.

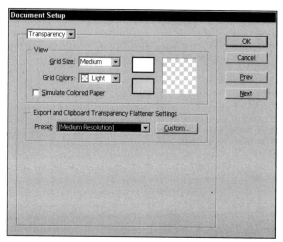

Figure 3-5: Use these options in the Document Setup dialog box to set the Transparency options.

Opening and Closing Illustrator Files

You can open many different types of files in Illustrator CS2. To open a file, choose File ➪ Open or press Ctrl+O (⌘+O) to display the Open dialog box. Find the file you want to open, and double-click it to open it into a document window on the screen.

To close the active Illustrator file, choose File ➪ Close or press Ctrl+W (⌘+W). The active document is the one that is in front of all other documents. Closing an Illustrator document does not close Illustrator; it continues running until you choose File ➪ Exit (Illustrator ➪ Quit Illustrator).

If you saved the file prior to closing it, the file just disappears. If you have modified the file since the last time you saved it, a message box appears, asking whether you want to save changes before closing. If you have not saved the file at all, the Save As dialog box appears so that you can name the file and choose a location for it. If you click the Don't Save button (or press the D key while the message box is showing), then any changes that you made to the document since you last saved it (or if you have never saved it, all the changes you made since you created it) are lost. Clicking Cancel or pressing Esc, takes you back to the drawing, where you can continue to work on it.

Saving Files

Saving and backing up Illustrator documents are some of the most important Illustrator activities you can do.

To save a file, choose File ➪ Save or press Ctrl+S (⌘+S). If you have previously saved the file, updating the existing file with the changes that you have made takes just a fraction of a second. If you have not yet saved the file, the Save As dialog box similar to the one shown in Figure 3-6 appears (in this case the Adobe version of the dialog box was selected by clicking the Use Adobe dialog button). Illustrator files are best saved as .AI files because this is the native Illustrator format, which preserves all Illustrator-specific information.

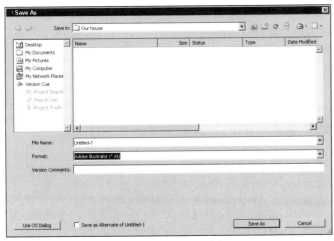

Figure 3-6: The Save As dialog box enables you to save your document in several different formats.

When saving files, remember the following tips and tricks:

✦ **Decide where to save the file.** Make sure that the name of the folder where you want to save the file is displayed above the file-list window. Saving your working files in a location other than the Illustrator folder is a good habit. Otherwise, you can have trouble figuring out which files are yours, which files are tutorial files, and so on.

✦ **Name the file something distinctive.** If you look for a file six months from now, you may not recognize it. Avoid using Untitled-1, Untitled-2, and so on. Such names are non-descriptive, and you can too easily replace the file at a later date with a file of the same name. For the same reasons, do not use Document 1, Document 2, and so on.

These are your formatting choices for saving an Illustrator file:

✦ **Adobe Illustrator Document:** For use when passing between users who have Adobe Illustrator.

✦ **Adobe PDF (pdf):** For use in sending the file to anyone who has or can download Adobe Reader or Acrobat Standard or Professional.

✦ **Illustrator EPS (eps):** For use when sending or passing files between users who may not have Illustrator, but can place or open the files in another program such as InDesign or Photoshop.

✦ **Illustrator Template (ait):** For use in creating templates that you can use as guides for future drawings.

✦ **SVG (svg):** For use when creating a Web page. SVG stands for Scalable Vector Graphics, and is an XML-based format that can produce much smaller file sizes than the typical bitmap formats such as JPEG and TIF.

✦ **SVG Compressed (svgz):** For use when creating a Web page. This option generally produces smaller files than the uncompressed SVG format.

Using the Save As command

You activate the Save As command by selecting File ➪ Save As or by pressing Shift+Ctrl+S (⌘+Shift+S). By using this command, you can save multiple versions of the document at different stages of progress. If you choose Save As and do not rename the file or change the save location, Illustrator prompts you to replace the existing file. If you choose Replace, Illustrator erases the file that you saved before and replaces it with the new file that you are saving.

When Should I Save?

You really can't save too often. Whenever I put off saving for "just a few minutes," that's when the application aborts or unexpectedly quits. Depending on your work habits, you may need to save more frequently than other people do. Here are some golden rules about when to save:

✦ **Save as soon as you create a new file.** Get it out of the way. The toughest part of saving is deciding how and where you are going to save the file and naming it. If you get those things out of the way in the beginning, pressing Ctrl+S (⌘+S) later is fairly painless.

✦ **Save before you print.** It is just a good idea in case your program quits when you print.

✦ **Save before you switch to another application.** This is another good idea in case you forget that you still have the application running or another application forces you to restart, such as when you're loading new programs.

✦ **Save right after you do something that you never want to have to do again.** For example, you want to save after getting the kerning "just right" on a logo or matching all the colors in your gradients so that they meet seamlessly.

✦ **Save after you use a filter that takes more than a few seconds to complete.**

✦ **Save before you create a new document or go to another document.**

✦ **Save at least every 15 minutes.** This is just a good, basic rule; that way, you are sure to have the latest version in case of a power outage that can shut your system down immediately.

Understanding the Save a Copy command

The Save a Copy command that you activate by selecting File ⇨ Save a Copy or by pressing Ctrl+Alt+S (⌘+Option+S), saves a copy of your document at its current state (with "copy" appended to the filename) without affecting your document or its name. The next time you press Ctrl+S (⌘+S), Illustrator saves your changes to the original and the copy isn't affected by any of your changes.

Reverting to the last saved version

Choosing File ⇨ Revert is an option that automatically closes the document and opens the last saved version of it. This option is grayed out if you have not yet saved the file. When you select it, a dialog box appears, asking you to confirm that you actually do want to revert to the last saved version of the document.

Caution You cannot undo a Revert action, and you cannot redo anything you've done up to that point with the document.

Saving for Web option

Saving an Illustrator file for the Web is an easy step that ensures Illustrator properly saves your file for Web usage. This option enables you to choose various settings such as the amount of compression that is applied to your document in order to reduce the file size so that your Web pages load faster. Choose File ➪ Save for Web, or press Alt+Shift+Ctrl+S (⌘+Shift+Option+S) to access the Save for Web dialog box shown in Figure 3-7.

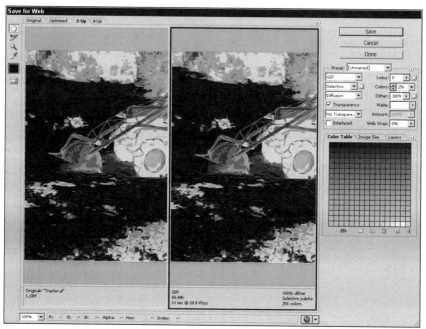

Figure 3-7: The Save for Web dialog box enables you to save your document in a format suited for use on the Web.

The tabs you see in the Save for Web dialog box are Original, Optimized, 2-Up, and 4-Up. The first tab, Original, shows the file in its original state. The second tab, Optimized, shows the file in the optimized settings you chose at the right of the Save for Web dialog box. The third and fourth tabs, 2-Up and 4-Up, respectively, show the figure in the original state along with 1 or 3 of the other default options so you can decide which option best suits your needs.

More on the Save for Web dialog box is presented in Chapter 19.

Understanding file types and options

You can save and export Illustrator files in several ways. Actually, you can save in and export them to many different formats using the File ⇨ Save As and File ⇨ Export commands.

Saving an Illustrator file with the wrong options can dramatically affect whether you can place or open that file in other software, as well as what features Illustrator includes with the file when Illustrator reopens it. Saving a document as an older version of Illustrator may alter the document if the older version is missing features you used in your document.

As a rule, unless you're going to take your Illustrator document into another program, you can save it as an Adobe Illustrator (.ai) file without any problems. Doing this keeps the file size down and makes saving and opening the file much quicker.

Using Illustrator's compatibility options

Most software packages are forward compatible for one major version, but Illustrator is novel in that you can open an Illustrator 1.1 file in the CS2 version of the software, even though many years have passed between those product versions.

If necessary, you can also export an Illustrator document to certain older Illustrator formats using the Illustrator Legacy Options dialog box shown in Figure 3-8. To open this dialog box, select File ⇨ Export and then choose Illustrator Legacy from the Save as type list box. (To save in a Legacy format on the Mac, select Save As, choose Illustrator document from the Format pop-up, and in the Illustrator Options dialog box, choose the legacy format you desire.)

The only real reason to save illustrations in older versions of Illustrator is to exchange files with clients who haven't upgraded from an old version. The following list provides information about saving files in each version:

- ✦ **Illustrator CS:** Saves the file with all Illustrator CS-compatible features intact.
- ✦ **Illustrator 10:** Saves the file with transparency, color profiles, and embedded fonts.
- ✦ **Illustrator 9:** Saves the file with transparency and color profiles.
- ✦ **Illustrator 8:** Saves the file in a cross-platform (Mac and Windows) Illustrator 8 format. Illustrator 8 added support for EMF file format, and drag-and-drop to Microsoft Office products (Windows), Japanese format FreeHand files, and DXF file formats.

✦ **Illustrator 3:** Saves the file in the Illustrator 3 format. In fact, you can use the Illustrator 3 format for lots of cheating—doing things that Illustrator normally doesn't enable you to do. For example, technically, you can't place gradients or masks into patterns. But if you save a gradient as an Illustrator 3 file and reopen it in Illustrator 7, the gradient becomes a blend, which you can use in a pattern (although Illustrator's Expand feature is quicker for this sort of thing).

✦ **Japanese Illustrator 3:** Saves the file in the Japanese Illustrator 3 format, which preserves the Japanese type options.

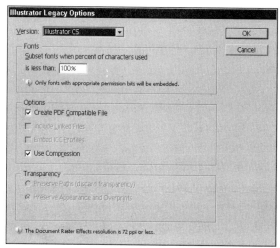

Figure 3-8: The Illustrator Legacy Options dialog box enables you to save your document in older Illustrator formats.

Saving as Illustrator EPS

If you do have to place your Illustrator document in another program, such as QuarkXPress, you may want to save the file as Illustrator EPS (Encapsulated PostScript). First choose File ➪ Save As to display the Save As dialog box. Then select the Illustrator EPS option in the Save as type list box (Format pop-up menu), name the file, and click the Save button to open the EPS Options dialog box, shown in Figure 3-9.

The following Preview options affect the way that other software programs see Illustrator files when you save them as Illustrator EPS files:

✦ **None:** This option lets most software programs recognize the Illustrator document as an EPS file, but instead of viewing it in their software, you see a box with an X in it. Usually, this box is the same size as the illustration and includes any stray anchor points or control handles. The file prints fine from other software.

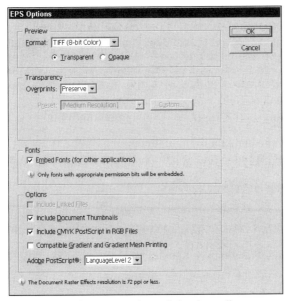

Figure 3-9: The EPS Options dialog box allows you to specify how EPS files are saved.

✦ **TIFF (Black & White):** This option saves the file with a preview for IBM systems. Page-layout or other software programs for PCs that can import EPS files can preview illustrations that you save with this option.

✦ **TIFF (8-bit Color):** This option saves the file with a color preview for IBM systems. Page-layout and other software programs display this file in 8-bit color (256 colors) when you place it in a document. An Illustrator file that you save with a color preview takes up more file space than a file saved with any other option.

Note Two additional preview options are available in Mac. Macintosh (8-bit color) maps to a selected 256-color palette. In Macintosh (Black & White), anything at 50 percent or higher intensity maps to black, and everything else maps to white.

In addition to the preview options, you can choose from several other options that affect how the EPS file is saved:

✦ **Transparency:** You can Preserve or Discard Overprints. Overprinting allows underlying colors to appear through transparent areas of the drawing.

✦ **Fonts:** Choose to embed the fonts with the file (although this makes the file larger) so you don't have to worry about font substitution if someone else doesn't have your font.

✦ **Options:** These let you include linked files to ensure that any necessary files are included; include document thumbnails so someone can determine the file contents without opening the file; include CMYK PostScript in RGB for more accurate color printing; use compatible gradient and gradient mesh printing so that older printers can do a better job of printing gradients; and choose your level of PostScript for compatibility with applications that don't support newer PostScript versions.

Note   The Mac version also provides a Use Printer's Default Screen checkbox. It instructs Illustrator to use any default screen defined in the printer's PPD file.

Saving files in Adobe PDF format

Another choice for saving a file in Illustrator is PDF (Portable Document Format) because anyone can load Adobe Reader for free and view the file. To save your document in PDF, first choose File ⇨ Save As and select Adobe PDF in the Save as type list box (Format pop-up menu). Click the Save button to display the Save Adobe PDF dialog box, as shown in Figure 3-10.

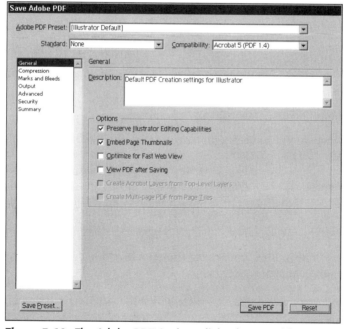

Figure 3-10: The Adobe PDF Options dialog box provides many options for controlling how PDF files are saved.

This dialog box includes seven different areas that you can use to set options. You select the settings by choosing from the list along the left side of the dialog box. The following lists the areas and their options:

✦ **General:** Under this category, you can set the Compatibility ranging from Acrobat 7 (PDF 1.6) to Acrobat 4 (PDF 1.3). If a user has an older version of Acrobat, you may need to save with backward compatibility so the user can read the file. Depending on the PDF version you select, the following options may also be available:

- **Preserve Illustrator Editing Capabilities:** Saves all Illustrator data in the PDF file so that you can reopen and edit the PDF file in Illustrator.

- **Embed Page Thumbnails:** Includes a thumbnail image that appears in the Open or Place dialog boxes.

- **Optimize for Fast Web View:** Creates a file that can be viewed more quickly in a Web browser.

- **View PDF after Saving:** Opens the document in your PDF viewing application after it is saved.

- **Create Acrobat Layers from Top-Level Layers:** Creates layers in the PDF file (useful for multi-language versions of your file, for example).

- **Create Multi-page PDF from Page Tiles:** Combines all pages of your document into a multi-page PDF file.

✦ **Compression:** In this area, you can change compression settings for Color Bitmap Images, Grayscale Bitmap Images, and Monochrome Bitmap Images. You also have a check box that determines whether to compress text and line art. This makes for a smaller file for emailing or uploading files to other users. These image types offer similar options, but you can choose different compression settings for each of them. These options are available:

- **Downsampling:** Reduces the file size by reducing the number of pixels in the image.

- **Compression type:** Enables you to choose from no compression, JPEG, JPEG2000, and ZIP compression. You may need to experiment with the various options so see which type of compression produces optimal results for your particular document.

- **Image Quality:** Allows you to choose the level of quality for JPEG and JPEG2000 image files. Lower-quality files are smaller, but may not result in quite the appearance you want.

✦ **Marks & Bleeds:** In this area, you set the Printer's Marks — lines printed outside the image area that show how to trim the drawings once you get them back from the printer or how to register the multiple color pages, Printer Mark Type, Trim Mark Weight, and how far to offset it from the artwork. The Bleeds for the top, bottom, left, and right of the page are set here. Bleeds are used to print images slightly oversize so that white edges won't appear once the images are trimmed.

✦ **Output:** You use this category to specify how colors are converted between the RGB and CMYK color profiles when the file is saved. RGB is typically used for onscreen display and CMYK is generally considered a more accurate profile for printed documents.

✦ **Advanced:** The Advanced PDF settings are Fonts and Overprint and Transparency Flattener Options. Use these options to Embed Fonts for use in other applications and to set your Transparency and Overprinting abilities in other applications (if you are saving the file in PDF version 1.3). The Transparency and Overprinting options control the way underlying colors appear through transparent areas of the drawing.

✦ **Security:** Under the Security area, you set whether the document requires a password for a user to open it and whether the password restricts editing. You also set the Security Permissions and the Acrobat Permissions (printing allowed, changes allowed, copying of text, images, or other content, and enabling text access of screen reader devices for the visually impaired).

✦ **Summary:** In the Summary area, you can see all the other options that Illustrator saves with the file.

Tip   You can save all the options under the Adobe PDF dialog box as presets by clicking the Save Preset button. This makes it easier for you to reuse the same settings in the future.

Saving files in SVG

Scalable Vector Graphics, or SVG, is a *vector-based* image format based on XML (eXtensible Markup Language), and it is one of the formats supported by Illustrator. Vector-based formats often have smaller file sizes than do bitmap image formats, so utilizing vector-based images for the Web can offer some important advantages in keeping Web page load times to a minimum. Figure 3-11 shows the SVG Options dialog box with its options.

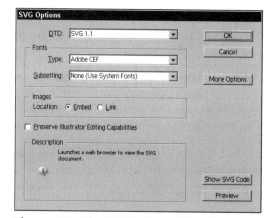

Figure 3-11: The SVG Options dialog box enables you to create vector-based images for the Web.

To save Illustrator documents in SVG format, choose File ➪ Save As to display the Save As dialog box. In the Save As dialog box, choose SVG from the Save as type list box (Format pop-up menu). You can also choose the compressed SVG option to create an even smaller file.

These are the SVG Options:

✦ **DTD:** This option enables you to specify the *Document Type Definition* level for your XML file. Older browsers may not support all features of newer DTD levels, but you'll generally want to choose SVG 1.1 for maximum flexibility.

✦ **Fonts Type and Subsetting:** This option enables you to specify the type of fonts to embed and to choose which characters are included — such as the characters that are actually used, rather than the entire font set. You can choose None, Only Glyphs used, Common English, Common English and Glyphs used, Common Roman, Common Roman and Glyphs used, and All Glyphs.

✦ **Images Location (Embed or Link):** If you choose to Embed, the file size is larger because it includes the placed image as part of the file. If you choose Link, it looks for the file on the system and accesses it that way (smaller file size).

✦ **Preserve Illustrator Editing Capabilities:** This option lets you choose to keep the editing capabilities in Illustrator. That way, you can use Illustrator to do any edits on the file.

Cross-Reference

The more advanced options are the CSS Properties, Decimal Places, Encoding, Optimize for Adobe SVG Viewer, Include Extended Syntax for Variable Data, and Include Slicing Data. These options are covered in depth in Chapter 19.

Using the Export command

Adobe Illustrator allows you to export to several different file formats. Most of the export formats are bitmap formats, such as TIFF and JPEG. You can also export in PDF format so that you can read Illustrator documents with Adobe Acrobat Reader. When you choose the Export option, these formats are available (the file extensions are shown in parentheses):

✦ **AutoCAD Drawing (dwg):** This is the standard format for vector drawings created in AutoCAD.

✦ **AutoCAD Interchange File (dxf):** This is the tagged data of the information in an AutoCAD file.

✦ **BMP (bmp):** This is the standard Windows format. In BMP format, you choose the color model, Resolution, Anti-alias (jaggy edges), File format, Depth (number of colors or gray), and Compression.

✦ **Enhanced Metafile (emf):** Windows users use this format for exporting vector data.

✦ **Illustrator Legacy (ai):** Using this saves the file as an older version of native Illustrator format.

✦ **Illustrator Legacy EPS (eps):** This is like Illustrator Legacy (ai), except that you can place the files in other programs such as InDesign.

✦ **JPEG (jpg):** You use this format mainly to show photographs on the Web.

✦ **Macintosh PICT (pct):** You use this format with Macintosh graphics and page-layout programs for transferring files.

✦ **Macromedia Flash (swf):** Macromedia Flash Player uses this format for animated Web graphics.

For more information on the various options in the Macromedia Flash (SWF) Formation Options dialog box, see Chapter 19.

✦ **PCX (pcx):** This is an older bitmap format that is not used very often because better options, such as JPEG, exist.

✦ **Photoshop (psd):** You use this format for taking the file into Photoshop by saving it as a raster image in the Photoshop format.

✦ **Pixar (pxr):** This is a Macintosh-only format.

✦ **PNG (png):** This is the alternative to GIF and JPEG. Use this for lossless compression. However, not all Web browsers support PNG.

✦ **Targa (tga):** You use this format for systems that use the Truevision video board.

✦ **Text Format (txt):** Use this format to export text into a plain text format.

✦ **TIFF (tif):** You use this format to move files between different programs and different computer platforms.

✦ **Window Metafile (wmf):** You mainly use this on Windows applications for 16-bit color. WMF is supported by most Windows layout and drawing applications.

When you choose a format type, a specific dialog box that relates to that particular format appears. For example, Figure 3-12 shows the Macromedia® Flash™ (SWF) Format Options dialog box that appears when you export an Illustrator document as a Flash file.

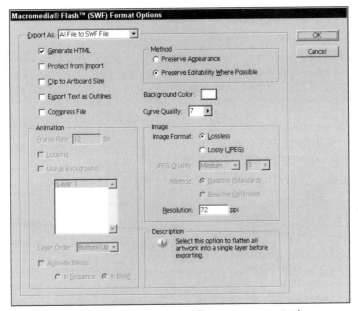

Figure 3-12: The Macromedia® Flash™ (SWF) Format Options dialog box enables you to specify options for saving in Flash format.

Placing Art

It is not necessary to create your entire Illustrator document from scratch if you already have some existing artwork that you would like to use. You can use most types of image files in an Illustrator document, including both bitmap and vector-based images.

To place files into an Illustrator document, follow these steps:

1. **Choose File ➪ Place** to display the Place dialog box. Figure 3-13 shows the Place dialog box.

Note Figure 3-13 shows the Windows dialog box. The Adobe dialog box gives you the choice of viewing the files as a list, icons, thumbnails, or tiles. List is the default. The other three options show the preview. The Mac dialog box looks and acts like a Mac Finder window. It includes a sidebar and offers a choice of list or column presentation.

Figure 3-13: The Place dialog box allows you to choose image files to add to your Illustrator document.

2. **Navigate to the folder containing the file.** You can click the drop-down arrows on the Look in list box to navigate to your file.

3. **Select the files that you want to place.** Only files that you can place appear in the file window. Because you can also place text files, be sure that the file you've chosen is indeed an image document.

4. **Choose how you want to place the art.** You have three options:

   • **Link:** Normally, the option is unselected. Illustrator places the art within the Illustrator file. You generally do not want to select this option, because it prevents the two files from being separated; if you have one but not the other, you are out of luck. However, there are several good reasons to link the file. First, placed art can be huge and may make your Illustrator file too large. Second, if you need to make changes to a placed art file included in an Illustrator file that you have saved with a preview, you must replace the placed art in the preview file with the new version. Preview shows the actual placed image and Outline shows a box with an X through it. If you link the placed art instead of including it, the art is automatically updated when you make changes. And finally, you can share placed art that you've linked across multiple files. For example, you can place a business letterhead or logo in all your company files.

- **Template:** The template option makes your placed file a template. When you make a placed file a template, it automatically locks in on a template layer in the Layers palette and dims the image so that you can use it to trace over.

- **Replace:** You may want to replace placed art with new versions or completely different artwork. Illustrator has made this process painless. If you select placed artwork, a dialog box appears asking if you want to replace current artwork or place new artwork, not changing the selected artwork. Use this to keep a certain size or transformation that you used in another placed image. Simply choose Replace, and the selected image replaces the existing one, transformation and all.

5. **Click the Place button at the bottom of the Place dialog box.** After you place art into Illustrator, you can transform it (move, scale, rotate, reflect, and shear it) in any way.

Tip

The really cool part about changing placed art this way is that if you have placed transformed artwork, the artwork you exchange with it via the Place Art command has the exact same transformation attributes! For example, if you scale down placed artwork to 50 percent and rotate it 45 degrees, artwork that you exchange also scales down 50 percent and rotates 45 degrees.

Caution

Be careful when importing artwork other than EPS images into Illustrator, because TIFF and most other bitmap formats increase the size of your document dramatically.

Placing Photoshop Art in Illustrator: Understanding Vectors and Pixels

The main use of the Place command is to import raster-based images into Illustrator. These can be photographic images used within your design or images that you can trace, but this raises a critical question, the answer to which will help you understand how images created with a paint program like Photoshop differ from Illustrator: What is the difference between raster and vector images?

In its original version, Illustrator was a pure vector piece of software. But since Version 8, the border has been crossed, and Illustrator is just this side of the pixel border. What does this mean? It means that you can do things to pixels in Illustrator that you can't do in Photoshop. (Ah, now I've got your attention!) For example, you can use Photoshop filters in Illustrator, but you cannot apply these filters to vector images. Because Photoshop filters work only on pixel-based images, you can rasterize—that is, convert your paths into a pixel-based image—or simply use the Effects menu to get some amazing effects.

Cross-Reference — For more on the Effects menu and Filters, see Chapter 15.

You can move between Photoshop and Illustrator in one of three ways:

✦ Place the raster image using the File ➪ Place menu.

✦ Use the clipboard to transfer images.

✦ Drag and drop your art between the two programs.

But before you get into the ins and outs of moving Photoshop art to Illustrator, and vice versa, you first need to understand the difference between vectors and pixels.

The essence of Illustrator is the ability to manipulate outlines. When you think vectors, think Illustrator's paths. Illustrator's paths consist of *outlines*, which you can resize and transform into any imaginable shape and fill with various colors and gradients. You can stretch vector-based images, and they won't look any worse — unless you scale blends and gradients too large. This means that when you create a curve in Illustrator, it's really a curve — not a jagged mass of pixels.

When you think pixels, think Photoshop's little teeny-tiny squares of color — squares that don't ever change position and that you don't add to or subtract from. The only characteristic you change about pixels is their color. Pixels can only be square, and they take up space. Pixels exist on an immobile grid. Enlarging a pixel-based image results in giant, ugly squares of color.

Placing raster images

Even with its pixel capabilities, Illustrator is no Photoshop. There are tools and features in Photoshop that are invaluable for adjusting pixel-based artwork. Adobe recognizes this, so it has provided several methods for moving pixels to Photoshop from Illustrator and from Photoshop to Illustrator.

The most rudimentary way, which has existed for several versions of both software packages, is to save art in a format the other program can read and then to open or place the art in the other program. To place Illustrator art into Photoshop, save the art in Illustrator format and then open the art in Photoshop. To place Photoshop art into Illustrator, save in Photoshop as a format that Illustrator can read, such as TIFF, and then in Illustrator, choose File ➪ Place and select the file.

Using the Clipboard

The next way is through Adobe's wonderful PostScript on the Clipboard process, which allows for transferring artwork between Adobe software programs by simply copying in one program and pasting in another. To place Illustrator art in Photoshop, copy the art in Illustrator, switch to Photoshop, and paste the art into any open document. To place Photoshop art in Illustrator, copy the art in Photoshop, switch to Illustrator, and paste the art into an open document. This process works best for smaller files.

Dragging and dropping

The easiest way to move art between these programs is to drag it from one program to the other. To drag art from Illustrator to Photoshop, select the art in Illustrator and drag it out of the Illustrator window onto a Photoshop window. To drag art from Photoshop to Illustrator, select the art in Photoshop and drag it out of the Photoshop window onto an Illustrator window.

Tip

You must have a window from the "to" application open when you start dragging for drag-and-drop to work between programs. If the window is hidden behind other windows, drag to the destination application's taskbar button, pause while the window is displayed, and then drop into the destination window.

Running Mac OS X 10.3 (Panther) or later, press F9 to invoke Exposé and tile all the windows of all running applications. Select the one containing the item you want to drag, select the item in that window and start the drag. While keeping the mouse button down, press F9 again and continue the drag to the window where you want to drop your selection.

To place paths from Photoshop into Illustrator, select the paths in Photoshop with the Path Selection tool, copy the paths, and then paste them in Illustrator.

Working with Document and File Information

All files have information that is recorded when you save a file. You can see most of the information about a file by looking at the Document Info palette. You can use this information to see the graphic styles, patterns, gradients, custom colors, fonts, and placed art. Knowing what the file consists of when saving it or choosing an option to save or export is helpful. Another option is to save the document information as its own file.

Document Info and File Info are two different things. Document Info is a palette found under the Window menu. File Info is found under the File menu, and you can make additions to the information.

Looking at document information

You find general file information in the Document Info palette. You can use the Document Info feature in any document by choosing Window ➪ Document Info. The Document Info palette offers a number of different types of information that you can access through the palette's menu:

✦ **Document:** Lists the Color Mode, Color Profile, Ruler Units, Artboard Dimensions, Show Images in Outline mode (off or on), Highlight substituted fonts (off or on), Highlight Substituted Glyphs (off or on), Preserve Text Editability, and Simulate Colored Paper (off or on).

✦ **Objects:** Lists the Paths, Compound Paths, Gradient Meshes, Symbol Instances, All Type Objects, Individual Type Objects, Area Type Objects, Type on Path Objects, Clipping Masks, Opacity Masks, Transparent Groups, Transparent Objects, RGB Objects, CMYK Objects, Grayscale Objects, Spot Color Objects, Pattern Objects, Gradient Objects, Brushed Objects, Styled Objects, Fonts, Linked Images, Embedded Images, and Non-Native Art Objects.

✦ **Graphic Styles:** Lists the Graphic styles used by name.

✦ **Brushes:** Lists the Brushes used by name.

✦ **Spot Color Objects:** Lists any objects that have a Spot color applied by name.

✦ **Pattern Objects:** Lists any objects with a pattern by name.

✦ **Gradient Objects:** Lists any objects with a Gradient by name.

✦ **Fonts:** Lists all fonts used.

✦ **Linked Images:** Lists any images that are linked by Location, Name, Type, Bits per channel, Channels, Size, Dimensions, and Resolution.

✦ **Embedded Images:** Lists any images that are embedded by Type, Bits per channel, Channels, Size, Dimensions, and Resolution.

✦ **Font Details:** Lists more information such as PostScript name, Language, and Font type.

Tip If you check the Selection Only option in the Document Info palette menu, the palette contains only information about the document's selected objects.

Saving document information

The last option in the Document Info palette's menu is the Save option. You select this option to save the information in a text file that you can view in any text editor. This method of viewing the document information offers the advantage of being able to see all the various pieces of information at once without needing to select different menu options.

Finding file information

In addition to the document information, you can also view (and modify) the information about the file. To access File Info, choose File ➪ File Info. The file info dialog box (which is unnamed except for the name you used to save the Illustrator document) has several areas of information (although they are not all relevant for every file). You can use this dialog box to enter the information you want to be saved with the file, such as the name of the author and a copyright notice.

Summary

Understanding Illustrator's documents is one of the basic yet most important areas of Illustrator. The main thing to keep in mind is to save and save often. This chapter covered the following topics:

✦ Use File ➪ New to set up a New document with Artboard dimensions and units.

✦ You can change the document setup at anytime by accessing the Document Setup dialog box. Access this box quickly by choosing File ➪ Document Setup.

✦ You can add a variety of files to an Illustrator document with the Place command.

✦ Illustrator files are best saved as .ai files.

✦ You can also export Illustrator files into a variety of formats. Keep in mind that if you want to retain editing capabilities, save a version as an Illustrator file as well.

✦ Document Info and File Info are two different things. The Document Info is a palette found under the Window menu. The File Info is found under the File menu, and you can make additions to the information.

✦　✦　✦

Understanding Drawing and Painting Techniques

✦ ✦ ✦ ✦

In This Chapter

Working with paths

Understanding anchor points and control handles

Drawing paths with Illustrator Pencil and Pen tools

Using the miscellaneous line tools

Using the Paintbrush tool

✦ ✦ ✦ ✦

In this chapter, you learn about *paths*, which are the underlying lines that make up the various objects. This chapter also covers using Illustrator's drawing tools, including the Pen, Pencil, and Paintbrush tools to create these paths. And we talk about the techniques behind many cool effects that you can create using these tools.

Working with Paths

The most basic element in Illustrator is a path. A *path* is what Illustrator calls the black line segment that appears when you draw a line. When you select a path, its anchor points appear. A path must have at least two *anchor points*, which appear as small squares along the path; these anchor points control which way the path goes. Paths look different in Preview and Outline modes. In Preview mode, you actually see the line weight, dashed style, color, and any effects applied to that line. In Outline mode, you simply see a thin line. Without two anchor points, you cannot draw a path like the one shown in Figure 4-1. Conceptually, there is no limit to the number of anchor points or segments that you can have in any one path. Depending on the type of anchor points that are on either end of a line segment, you can make a segment straight or curved. A single anchor point will never print anything.

Cross-Reference For more on viewing modes, see Chapter 2. For more on selecting paths, see Chapter 6.

Figure 4-1: This whole illustration was created with paths consisting of two anchor points with a line segment between them.

Understanding types of paths

Now that you know what a path is, you should understand the three major types of paths:

✦ **Open paths:** Two distinct end points, with any number of anchor points in between. An example of this is a simple line that you draw with the Pencil tool.

✦ **Closed paths:** Continuous paths, with no end points and no start or end — a closed path just continues around and around. An example of this is a shape that you create with one of Illustrator's shape tools, such as a rectangle or circle.

✦ **Compound paths:** Two or more open or closed paths.

Cross-Reference For more on creating shapes in Illustrator, see Chapter 5. For a detailed look at compound paths, see Chapter 12.

Understanding anchor points

As stated earlier, paths consist of a series of points and the line segments between these points. These points are commonly called anchor points because they anchor the path; paths always pass through or end at anchor points.

Anchor points consist of control handles and control handle lines. *Control handles*, which appears as small squares along the path, determine how tightly or loosely the curve bends at each anchor point. Control handle lines run on a tangent along the path and are attached to the path by the control handle. They determine the direction of the curved path. The next section discusses control handles and control handle lines in more detail. Anchor points, control handles, and control handle lines do not appear on the printed output of your artwork. In fact, they appear only in Illustrator and Photoshop, never on artwork imported into other applications.

There are two classes of anchor points:

✦ **Smooth points:** These anchor points have a curved path flowing smoothly through them. Most of the time, you don't know where a smooth point is unless you select the path. Smooth points keep the path from changing direction abruptly. Every smooth point has two linked control handles.

✦ **Corner points:** In this class of anchor points, the path changes direction noticeably at those specific points. There are three different corner points:

• **Straight corner points:** These are anchor points where two straight line segments meet at a distinct angle. There are no control handles on this type of anchor point.

• **Curved corner points:** These are points where two curved line segments meet and abruptly change direction. Each curved corner point has two independent control handles. Each handle controls a curve, and you can change only one side if you'd like.

• **Combination corner points:** These are the meeting places for straight and curved line segments. A combination corner point has one independent control handle. The one control handle controls the curve.

Figure 4-2 shows the different types of anchor points in Illustrator.

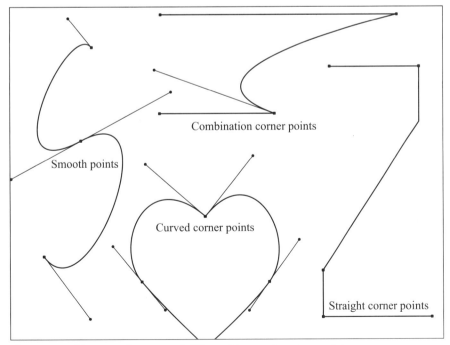

Combination corner points

Smooth points

Curved corner points

Straight corner points

Figure 4-2: Illustrator has several different types of anchor points.

Understanding control handles and control handle lines

If an anchor point has a control handle coming out of it, the next segment is curved. No control handle, no curve. Couldn't be simpler.

As stated before, control handles are connected to anchor points with control handle lines. Figure 4-3 shows what happens when an anchor point with no control handle and an anchor point with a control handle are connected to another anchor point. Figure 4-4 shows the anchor points, control handles, and the control handle lines on a path.

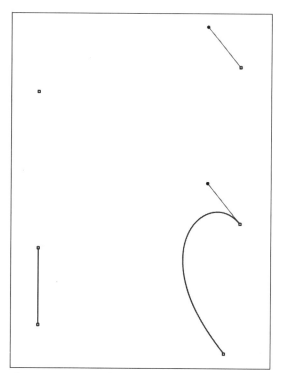

Figure 4-3: An anchor point without a control handle (top left) and an anchor point with a control handle (bottom left) are connected to new anchor points, resulting in a straight line segment (top right) and a curved line segment (bottom right).

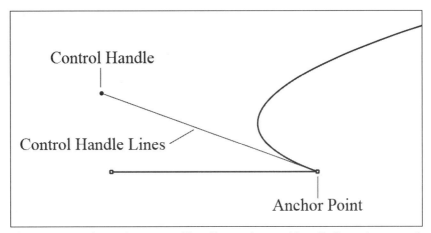

Figure 4-4: Anchor points, control handles, and control handle lines along a path

The basic concept to remember about control handles is that they act as magnets by pulling the curve toward them. This presents an interesting problem because each curved line segment usually has two control handles. Just as you might suspect, the control handle exerts the greatest amount of force on the half of the curved segment nearest to it. If there is only one control handle, the segment curves more on the side of the segment with the control handle than on the side with no control handle.

The greater the distance between a control handle and its corresponding anchor point, the farther the curve (on that end of the curve segment) pulls away from an imaginary straight segment between the two points, as shown in Figure 4-5. If the control handles on either end of the segment are on different sides of the curved segment, the curved segment takes on an S shape, as the bottom path in Figure 4-6 shows. If the control handles on the ends of the curved segment are on the same side, the curve takes on a U shape.

Regardless of whether the anchor point is a smooth point, a curved corner point, or a combination corner point, control handle lines coming out of an anchor point are always tangent to the curved segment where it touches the anchor point. Tangent refers to the touching of the control handle line to the curved segment as it crosses the anchor point, as shown in Figure 4-6.

Tip To adjust the curves without moving the control handles, click the curve and drag it. Keep in mind that you're changing both control handles at once, which can make adjusting the curve hard to control.

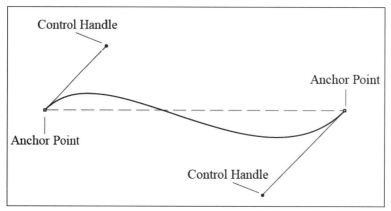

Figure 4-5: Control handles pull the line segment away from the straight line that would normally exist between them. The bottom path is an S shape because the control handles are pulling in opposite directions.

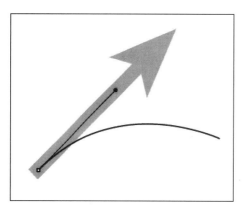

Figure 4-6: Control handle lines run tangent to the path where the path meets the anchor point.

Understanding how fills and strokes relate to paths

If paths are the basic concept behind Illustrator, you may be wondering where the colors and patterns fit in. You apply all colors and patterns to Illustrator paths using fills and strokes. Basically, a fill is a color or pattern that appears within a path, and a stroke is a special style that you apply along a path.

Cross-Reference For more on applying fills and strokes to shapes, see Chapter 5. To create fills and strokes, see Chapter 10.

A Little History on Bézier Curves

If you don't know much about geometry (or maybe don't remember much — it was back in high school, after all), you may find the very concept of creating curves by using math frightening. But most of the curve creation in Illustrator takes place behind the scenes when you use a tool such as the Pen tool.

PostScript curves are based on Bézier curves (pronounced bez-ee-ay), which were created by Pierre Bézier in the early 1970s as a way of controlling mechanical cutting devices, commonly known as Numerical Control. Bézier worked for Renault (the car manufacturer) in France, and his mission was to streamline the process by which machines were controlled.

A mathematician and engineer, Bézier developed a method for creating curves using four points for every curved segment. He placed two points at either end of the segment — in Illustrator, these correspond to the anchor points — and made two points float around the curve segment to control the curve's shape — these are control handles in Illustrator. Using these four points, you can create any curve; using multiple sets of these curves, you can create any possible shape. John Warnock and Chuck Geschke, of Adobe, decided that Bézier curves were the best method for creating curves in a page description language (PostScript), and suddenly those curves became a fundamental part of high-end graphic design.

Bézier curves are anything but intuitive, and in fact, they represent the most significant stumbling block for beginners learning Illustrator. After you've mastered the concept and use of these curves, everything about Illustrator suddenly becomes easier and friendlier. Don't try to ignore them, because they won't go away. You'll find it easier in the long run to try to understand how they work.

You should remember from Chapter 2 that when you work in Illustrator in Outline mode (View ➪ Outline), only paths are visible. In Preview mode (View ➪ Preview), fills and strokes applied to paths are visible. Unless a path is selected in Preview mode, that path (anchor points and line segments) isn't visible. You can toggle between Outline mode and Preview mode by pressing Ctrl+Y (⌘+Y). Figure 4-7 shows closed paths with different fills in both Outline mode and Preview mode.

You can also fill open paths. The fill goes straight across the two end points of the path to enclose the object. Figure 4-8 displays different types of filled open paths. Filling an open path is usually not desirable, although in some circumstances doing so may be necessary. Because the fill goes from the endpoints of the path, if you have an irregular shaped path, the fill can look strange. If you are looking to get a cool pair of sunglasses, use a filled path for an unusual look.

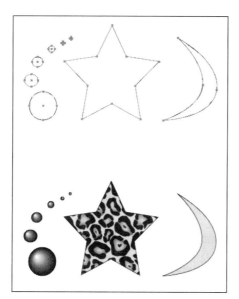

Figure 4-7: Closed paths with different fills: The top row shows how they appear in Outline mode, while the bottom row shows what they look like in Preview mode.

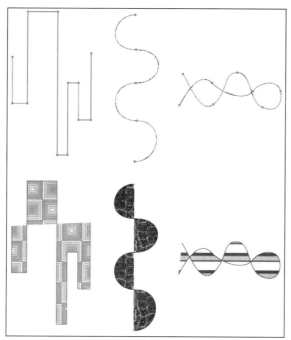

Figure 4-8: Open paths with different fills: The top row shows how they appear in Outline mode, while the bottom row shows how they appear in Preview mode.

Caution

A straight line with a fill can cause problems when you go to print. In PostScript, when you specify a fill, but only have two dimensions to an object (a straight line), it prints (rasterizes) at one "device pixel." At 100 percent onscreen, the filled line looks exactly like a 1-point stroked line (72 dpi = 1 device pixel = $\frac{1}{72}$ inch and 1 point = $\frac{1}{72}$ inch). When you zoom in to 200 percent, the stroked line scales by 200 percent, but the filled line stays the same (1 device pixel or $\frac{1}{72}$ inch). When you print this line to a typical laser printer, one device pixel is as tiny as $\frac{1}{300}$ or $\frac{1}{600}$ inch. By the time you print to a typical Imagesetter printer, one device pixel becomes $\frac{1}{2570}$ inch, making it too small to be visible in most situations. The key to fixing it is to ensure, for any paths you don't want filled, that they have no fill before sending the document to print.

Cross-Reference

For more about printing, see Chapter 18.

Besides filling paths, you can also stroke paths with a tint of any color or a pattern. These strokes can be any weight (thickness), and the width of the stroke is equally distributed over each side of the path. Open paths have ends on the strokes; these ends can be cropped, rounded, or extended past the end of the stroke by half the width of the stroke. Several different paths with strokes are shown in Figure 4-9.

Figure 4-9: Various paths with different strokes applied to them

For more on Stroke weight, color, and attributes, see Chapter 5.

A single point is also considered a path; however, single points in Illustrator have no printable qualities. This isn't readily noticeable, because you can assign a fill or stroke color to a single point, although you can't see it in Preview mode or when you print it. When the document is color separated, it causes a separation of the color to print, even if nothing else on that page uses that same color, and the separation appears blank.

If you think that you may have individual anchor points floating around your illustration, you can select all of them at once by choosing Select ➪ Object ➪ Stray Points and then deleting them.

Fills and strokes in Illustrator can be colors or an opaque white, which knocks out any color underneath. Fills and strokes may also be transparent. Transparency in Illustrator is commonly referred to as a fill, stroke, or none.

For more on Transparency, see Chapter 15.

Drawing Paths with Illustrator Tools

The most effective (and challenging) way to create paths is to draw them with one of the drawing tools. The Pen, Paintbrush, and Pencil tools are the most common drawing instruments, but Illustrator has a Brushes palette as well with three key brushes — the Art Brush, the Scatter Brush, and the Pattern Brush. If you are looking for the Calligraphic option, you find it as a brush option that you can choose in the Brushes palette. The Smooth tool and the Erase tool are two more helpful tools. They are located in the Pencil tool's pop-up menu. These two tools cut editing time drastically by letting you clean up lines and fix errors with the stroke of a brush.

Of the three main tools used to draw paths in Illustrator (the Pen, Pencil, and Paintbrush), the Pen is the most difficult to use, but it often yields the best results. The Pencil by far is the easiest but requires some editing to smooth the bumpy lines. The Paintbrush tool combined with a tablet can create some amazing hand-drawn looks in your art.

Each tool has its place, and you use all three to achieve the most productivity. So practice using all the tools, and find which one works best for whatever you may be working on. Figure 4-10 shows an illustration created using several different tools.

Figure 4-10: In this illustration, the various objects were created using several tools.

Using the Pencil tool

When you want to draw rough edges or realistic illustrations that don't look "computery," for example map drawing with beautiful bumpy edges, the Pencil tool is the tool to use. The Pencil tool is housed in the Illustrator toolbox with the tools that edit it — the Smooth and Eraser tools — and draws a freeform stroked path wherever you drag the cursor. However, instead of creating a closed path that is a certain width, the result is a single path that approximately follows the route you've taken with the cursor. The Pencil tool has the unique capability to make the lines you draw look . . . well . . . good.

Actually, part of the Pencil tool's charm is also its biggest drawback. Unlike the Pen tool — which creates precise, super-straight lines, but which is difficult to control — the Pencil tool is much easier to use, but it draws lines that are far from perfect. This is because the Pencil tool creates only smooth points and corner anchor points. When you select it, the Pencil tool's anchor point has two control handles. If you remember the earlier discussion on anchor points, you'll know this means that you can neither draw a smooth anchor point — although at first glance, you may think you can—nor a straight corner point with the Pencil tool. This makes the construction of precise objects nearly impossible.

Before you use the Pencil tool for the first time, you should change the Paint Style attributes to a fill of None and a stroke of Black, 1 point. Having a fill other than None while drawing with the Pencil tool often results in bizarre-looking shapes. To select these settings, begin in the color section near the bottom of the Illustrator toolbox. Click the Fill square; then click the None (red slash) box to make sure the fill is None. Select the stroke (outlined rectangle), and click the black to make sure the stroke has a black stroke. Then use the Window ⇨ Stroke command to display the Stroke palette, and choose 1 point from the weight list box.

To use the Pencil tool, follow these steps:

1. **Double-click the Pencil tool.** The Pencil tool is the fifth tool down in the second column of the toolbox and is housed with the Smooth tool and the Erase tool, which help smooth and edit Pencil tool paths. The Pencil tool, obviously, has a pencil for its icon. Double-clicking this icon opens the Pencil Tool Preferences dialog box. Figure 4-11 shows the Pencil Tool Preferences dialog box.

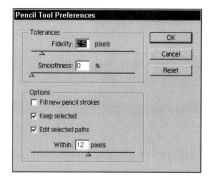

Figure 4-11: In the Pencil Tool Preferences dialog box, you can change the fidelity and smoothness for the Pencil tool.

Cross-Reference   For more on the Erase and Smooth tools, see the sections "Working with the Smooth tool" and "Erasing with the Erase tool," covered later in this chapter.

2. **Adjust the options in the Pencil Tool Preferences dialog box.** The options are as follows:

   • **Fidelity:** The Fidelity setting controls how far (measured in pixels) curves may stray from the original dotted line that you draw with the mouse. A low fidelity value results in sharper angles; a high fidelity value results in smoother curves. The lowest Fidelity number is .5 pixels, the highest is 20 pixels, and the default is 2.5 pixels.

Note As stated previously, although you think you can create them at first glance, you cannot create smooth anchor points. You may find this especially deceiving when you set the Fidelity option to a high number so that all the anchor points look like they are smooth points. This is **not** the case. In fact, most anchor points created with the Pencil tool — with the exception of end points — are curved corner points, which are anchor points with two independent control handles shooting out.

- **Smoothness:** Measured as a percentage, the Smoothness value determines how well the Pencil controls the bumpiness or irregularity of the line. A low Smoothness value results in a course, angular path, while a high Smoothness value results in a much smoother path with fewer anchor points.

- **Fill new pencil strokes:** Applies a fill to new pencil strokes when checked and applies no fill when unchecked.

- **Keep selected:** The Keep selected option keeps the last path you drew selected in case you want to edit or do any changes right after drawing the path.

- **Edit selected paths:** If you check this option, you can edit the path with the Pencil tool. If you don't check this option, you can still edit, but you have to use the Selection tools.

- **Within pixels:** The Within pixels option sets how close your drawing has to match the existing path to be editable; this works only when Edit selected paths is checked.

3. **Click OK.** Illustrator applies your preferences.

4. **Begin dragging the mouse.** The Pencil tool resembles a little pencil when you are drawing. As you drag, a series of dots follows the cursor. These dots show the approximate location of the path you have drawn. The location of a path drawn with the Pencil tool is directly relevant to the speed and the direction in which the cursor is moving.

Tip Pressing the Caps Lock key (engaging it) changes the cursor from the Pencil shape to crosshairs, which looks suspiciously like the crosshairs from the Paintbrush tool. The line of points comes from the dot in the center of the crosshairs. Use the crosshairs if you want to see exactly the point from which the drawing starts. You can set your cursors to always be crosshairs style just by opening the Preferences dialog box (by pressing Ctrl+K [⌘+K]) and checking the Use Precise Cursors check box. When this option is checked, the Caps Lock key changes the cursor back to the regular tool.

5. **Release the mouse button.** The path of dots is transformed into a path with anchor points, all having control handle lines and control handles shooting off from them. The faster you draw with the Pencil tool, the fewer points that are created; the slower you draw, the more points that are used to define the path.

Tip   You can repeat the item you just drew quickly and easily. Using a Selection tool, click the objects you drew and press Alt (Option). Next, drag the items side by side to make more of those objects. (See Chapter 6 for more on the Selection tools.)

Tip   You can instantly transform a swooping, uneven, jagged line that looks terrible as you draw into a beautifully curved piece of artwork reminiscent of lines drawn traditionally with a French curve using the Smooth tool.

Drawing open paths and closed paths

You can draw both open and closed paths with the Pen and Pencil tools. Paths in Illustrator may cross themselves. When these paths cross, the fills may look a little unusual. Strokes look normal; they just overlap where paths cross.

Cross-Reference   For more on paths, see the section "Understanding types of paths" earlier in this chapter.

To create an open path, draw a path with the Pencil or Pen tool, but make sure that the beginning and end of the path are two separate points at different locations. Open paths with fills may look a little bizarre because Illustrator automatically fills in between the end points on the path, even if the imaginary line between the end points crosses the path. Figure 4-12 shows both open and closed paths drawn with the Pencil tool.

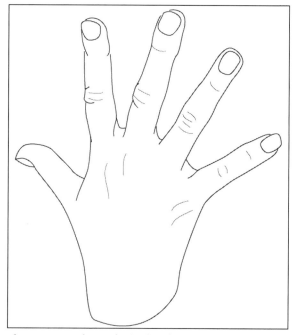

Figure 4-12: The paths in this drawing were created by the Pencil tool.

How the Fidelity and Smoothness Options Affect a Line

Because drawing nice-looking paths with the Pencil tool and a mouse is just a tad difficult and frustrating, Illustrator provides a way to determine how rough or smooth your path will be before you draw it.

Normally, paths that appear from the dotted lines created with the Pencil tool are fairly similar to those dotted lines in direction and curves and such. When lines are being drawn, though, human error can cause all sorts of little bumps to appear, making the path look lumpy. In some cases, as in map creation, lumpy is good. More often than not, though, lumpy is an undesirable state for your illustrations.

The smoothness—or jaggedness—of the resulting paths drawn with the Pencil tool depends on the Fidelity and Smoothness options in the Pencil Tool Preferences dialog box, which determines how jagged or smooth each section appears from the dotted line to the path. As stated before, a low Fidelity value results in sharper angles, and a high Fidelity value results in smoother curves, while a low Smoothness value results in a course, angular path, and a high Smoothness value results in a much smoother path with fewer anchor points.

At a Fidelity setting of .5, paths appear jagged and rough. Also, many more anchor points are present, although there are still no straight corner points. A setting of .5 is great for creating some photorealistic illustrations of complex, detailed objects, such as tree leaves and textures. When the setting is this low, the resulting path follows the dotted line as closely as possible.

When the Fidelity option is set to 20, paths created with the Pencil tool appear extremely smooth. Illustrator uses the smallest number of anchor points, and the curve of the line appears to be very graceful. Because so few anchor points are used, much detail is lost, and the path wavers from the original dotted line of the Pencil tool by a significant amount. Even though it appears that all the anchor points are smooth points, they are actually curved corner points with two independent control handles.

To create a closed path, end your path at the same place that you started the path. While drawing, press the Alt (Option) key. When the pencil cursor is directly over the location where the line begins, a little circle appears to the lower right of the pencil. This change means that the path is a closed path if you release the mouse button when that particular cursor is showing.

Connecting Pencil paths

You can quickly connect the Pencil drawn paths you draw in Illustrator. While drawing with the Pencil tool, press the Alt (Option) key and when you release the mouse button, a line automatically connects the beginning anchor point to the ending anchor point resulting in a closed path. You can try to draw back to the beginning line, but they probably won't connect. You can also draw the paths close to one another; select the two endpoints, and press Ctrl+J (⌘+J) to join the paths.

Adding to an existing open path

To continue drawing on an existing path (which could have been drawn with the Pen tool or the Pencil tool), the existing path must first be an open path with two distinct end points. Pass your drawing tool over one end of the path with the Pencil tool, and watch for the pencil cursor to change — the little x beside the pencil disappears. This action means that if you click and drag, you can extend the path with the Pencil tool. If the Caps Lock key is engaged, the cursor changes from an X (crosshairs) to a +.

You can add on only to end points on an existing path. Anchor points that are within paths cannot be connected to new (or existing, for that matter) segments. If you attempt to draw from an anchor point that is not an end point, you create an end point for the path you are drawing that is overlapping but not connected to the anchor point you clicked above.

Working with the Smooth tool

The Smooth tool came into being in version 8. This extremely cool editing tool makes changing any path a breeze. The Smooth tool works on any path regardless of what tool created it. You can apply the Smooth tool in one of two ways:

✦ **Using the toolbox:** Select the path you want to edit, click the Smooth tool found in the Pencil tool's pop-up tools, and drag your mouse over a selected path to smooth out the line.

✦ **While using other tools:** You can also access the Smooth tool while using the Pencil tool by pressing the Alt (Option) key. The tool changes to the Smooth tool while you keep the key pressed.

Figure 4-13 shows a path before and after using the Smooth tool. As you can see, the top path has more anchor points than the smoothed bottom path.

Double-clicking on the Smooth tool opens a dialog box where, just as with the Pencil tool, you can set Fidelity and Smoothness values.

Cross-Reference For more on the Fidelity and Smoothness values, see the section "Using the Pencil tool" earlier in this chapter.

Erasing with the Erase tool

You find the Erase tool with the Pencil tool in the toolbox. Like the Smooth tool, the Erase tool works on any path, no matter how you created it. The Erase tool does what you'd think; it erases a path at the point where you have dragged the Erase tool over the path. You can use the Erase tool to cut a path by first selecting the path and then dragging across a section. Illustrator removes the section you drag over. You can use the Erase tool to cut a line, just as you would use the Scissor tool. If you just click one time on the path, Illustrator cuts the path exactly in that spot. Unlike Photoshop's clunky eraser-looking tool, this is much more refined and easier to use.

Figure 4-13: The top illustration is pretty bumpy. The same illustration below had the Smooth tool applied to it. Notice the smoothness especially in the eye area.

Drawing with the Pen tool

The Pen tool is the most powerful tool in Illustrator's arsenal because you are dealing more directly with Bézier curves than with any other tool. Drawing objects with any other tool is one thing, but using the Pen tool to create paths out of nothing is dumbfounding.

During the first several months of using Illustrator, you may find yourself avoiding the Pen tool like the plague. Then you slowly work up to where you can draw straight lines comfortably and finally curved segments. Even after you draw curved segments for a while, you still may not understand how the tool works, and you may miss out on many of its capabilities because of that lack of knowledge. While practicing with the Pen tool, you begin to understand the four types of anchor points—smooth points, straight corner points, curved corner points, and combination corner points—and you discover that understanding how anchor points work is the key to using the Pen tool. The first click of the Pen tool produces one anchor point. The second click (usually in a different location) creates a second anchor point that is joined to the first anchor point by a line segment. Clicking without dragging produces a straight corner point.

Although the Pen tool is a little frustrating and confusing to use at first, it is the most important tool to learn. It saves you so much time and effort because, with it, you can draw the most accurately and smoothly with fewer edits. After you master this tool, you will use it for most of your drawing and tracing needs.

Unfortunately, the Pen tool does not do all the work; you do have to perform some of the labor involved in creating curves and straight lines. Drawing with the Pen tool isn't just placing anchor points.

Here are some things to consider when you're drawing with the Pen tool:

✦ **The first obstacle is to figure out where the heck those anchor points are going to go.** Two drawings with the same number of anchor points can look totally different, depending on anchor point placement. You have to think ahead to determine what the path will look like before you draw it. You should always locate points where you want a change in the path. That change can be a different curve or a corner. Look for these three changes:

  • A corner of any type

  • The point where a curve changes from clockwise to counterclockwise or vice versa

  • The point where a curve changes *intensity:* from tight to loose or loose to tight (by far, the hardest change to judge)

✦ **The second obstacle is to decide what type of anchor point you want to use.** Remember that you have four different anchor points to choose from when drawing with the Pen tool—smooth, straight corner, curved corner, and combination corner. If the path is smoothly curving, you use a smooth point. If it has a corner, use one of the corner points.

✦ **The third obstacle arises when you decide that the anchor point should be anything but a straight corner point because all the other anchor points have control handles.** The obstacle is figuring out how to drag the control handles, how far to drag them, and in which direction to drag them.

Drawing straight lines with the Pen tool

The easiest way to start learning to use the Pen tool is by drawing straight lines. The lightning bolt in Figure 4-14 was created entirely with straight lines. The great thing about straight lines drawn with the Pen tool is that you don't have to worry about or fuss over control handles.

Figure 4-14: Straight lines drawn with the Pen tool are all you need to create something like this lightning bolt.

The simplest straight line is a line drawn with only two anchor points. To draw straight lines:

1. **Select the Pen tool.** This tool is located on the third row of the first column in the toolbox and looks like an old-fashioned ink pen tip.

2. **Click and release where you want the first end point to appear.** This becomes the beginning of your line.

3. **Click and release where you want the second end point (the end of the line) to appear.** A line appears between the two points. Too easy, isn't it?

Tip

Hold down the Shift key to keep the line constrained to a 45-degree angle (0, 45, 90, and so on).

4. **To draw another separate line, first click the Pen tool in the toolbox or hold down the Ctrl (⌘) key and click.** Either action tells Illustrator that you are finished drawing the first line.

5. **Clicking and releasing again in one spot and then another draws a second line with two end points.** Be careful not to drag when clicking the Pen tool to form straight lines. If you drag the mouse, you create a smooth point and the path curves.

Paths drawn with the Pen tool, like the Pencil tool, may cross themselves. The only strange result you may see involves the fills for objects whose paths cross. In open paths created with the Pen tool, fills may look unusual because of the imaginary line between the two end points and any paths that the imaginary line crosses.

Closing paths with the Pen tool

If you want to create a closed path (one with no end points), return to the first anchor point in that segment and click. As the Pen tool crosses over the beginning anchor point, the cursor changes to a pen with a circle in the lower-right corner. After you have created a closed path, you don't need to click the Pen tool again. Instead, the next click of the Pen tool in the document automatically begins a new path.

Tip   You must have at least three anchor points to create a closed path with straight lines.

Drawing curves with the Pen tool

Initially, you may find the whole process of drawing curves with the Pen tool rather disorienting. You actually have to think differently to grasp what the Pen tool is doing. To draw a curve, you need to drag with the Pen tool, rather than click and release when you draw straight lines. This section gives two sets of instructions for creating two basic curve shapes: the bump and the S shape.

The most basic curve is the bump (a curved segment between just two points). Follow these steps to create the bump that is illustrated in Figure 4-15.

Figure 4-15: You can create a basic bump curve like this in four simple steps.

1. **Click with the Pen tool, and drag up about ½ inch.** You'll see an anchor point and a control handle line extending from it as you drag.

2. **Release the mouse button.** When you do so, you see the anchor point and a line extending to where you dragged with a control handle at its end.

3. **Position the cursor about 1 inch to the right of the place you first clicked.**

4. **Click with the mouse, and drag down about ½ inch.** As you drag, you see a curve forming that resembles a bump.

5. **Release the mouse.** The curve fills with the current Fill color. You also see the control handle you just dragged.

Before you try to draw another curve, remember that the Pen tool is still in a mode that continues the current path; it does not start a new one. To start a new path, choose Select ⇨ Deselect, or press Shift+Ctrl+A (⌘+Shift+A). Alternatively, you can hold down Ctrl (⌘) and click an empty area on-screen. The next time you use the Pen tool, you can draw a separate path.

To create an S shape, one more set of steps is needed. With these steps, you can create the S shape, as illustrated in Figure 4-16.

1. **Click and drag with the Pen tool about ½ inch to the left.**

2. **Release the mouse button.** You should see the anchor point and the control handle that you just drew with a control handle line between them.

3. **Position the cursor about 1 inch below where you first clicked.**

4. **Click and drag to the right about ½ inch.**

5. **Release the mouse button.**

6. **Position the cursor about 1 inch below the last point you clicked.**

7. **Click and drag to the left, about ½ inch.** Now you have an S shape.

Cross-Reference

For more on changing strokes and fills, see Chapter 7.

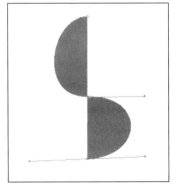

Figure 4-16: It is also very easy to create a basic S curve like this one.

All the anchor points created in these two examples are smooth points. You drag the control handles in the direction of the next curve that you want to draw. The lengths of the control handle lines on either side of the anchor point are equal. However, you do not have to make the lengths of the control handle lines on either side of the smooth point the same. Instead, you can make a smooth point have both long and short control handle lines coming out of it. The length of the control handle line affects the curve, as shown on the S curve in Figure 4-17.

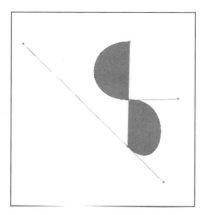

Figure 4-17: The length of the control handle lines controls the shape of the curve.

Follow these steps to create a smooth point with two control handle lines of different lengths:

1. **Create a smooth point along a path.** See the last set of steps to learn how to do so.

2. **Select the newly created smooth point with the Direct Selection tool.** For more on using these tools, see Chapter 5.

3. **Click and drag the control handle again.**

4. **Adjust the angle for both control handle lines and the length for the new control handle line that you are dragging.** Note that as you drag out this control handle line, the other control handle line wobbles to the angle that you are dragging. This happens because on any smooth point the control handle lines must be at the same angle, and as you drag out the new control handle line, you are changing the angle for both control handle lines simultaneously.

Closing curved paths with the Pen tool

The majority of the paths you draw with the Pen tool will be closed paths, not the open ones we've drawn so far. Like open curved paths, any closed curved path must have at least two anchor points, just as paths with straight corner points need three distinct points to create a closed path.

When the Pen tool is placed over the starting point of the path you've drawn, a little circle appears to the right of the pen shape. This indicates that the path will become a closed path if you click this anchor point.

Of course, to ensure that the initial anchor point remains a smooth point, you need to click and drag on the initial anchor point. Simply clicking produces a combination corner point, which has only one control handle associated with it.

Working with curved corner points

Curved corner points are points where two different, usually distinct, curved segments meet at an anchor point. Because the two curves meet this way, a smooth point does not provide the means for their joining correctly. Instead, a smooth point would make the two different curves blend into each other smoothly.

The main difference between a curved corner point and a smooth point is that a smooth point has two linked control handles on their ends; a curved corner point has two *independent* control handles. As the name indicates, control handles and their associated control handle lines move independently of each other, enabling two different, distinct types of curves to come from the same anchor point.

To create a curved corner point, create a smooth point in a path and then press Alt (Option) and drag the control handle you just drew. As you do this, you are creating the control handles independently. The next segment will curve as controlled by the newly split control handle, not by the original combined one.

Tip   When creating curved corner points, you can press the Alt (Option) key to create independent points all the time, not just when starting a new segment.

Combination corner points

A combination corner point is a point where a curved segment and a straight segment meet each other. At this corner point, there is one control handle coming from the anchor point from the side where the curved segment is located and, on the other side, there is no control handle, indicating a straight segment.

To create a combination corner point with the Pen tool, draw a few curved segments and then go back to the last anchor point. You should see two linked control handles displayed at this point. Simply click once on the anchor point, and one of the two control handles disappears. The next segment then starts out straight.

Tip   You can change existing smooth and curved corner points into combination corner points simply by dragging one of the control handles into the anchor points.

Using basic Pen tool drawing techniques

Now that you've gained some experience with the Pen tool, you'll benefit by living by the Pen Rules. The Pen Rules are laws to live by — or at least to draw by.

Follow these rules:

✦ **Remember not to drag where you want to place the next point; instead, go just one-third of that distance.** You must determine where you want to locate the next anchor point before you can determine the length of the control handle line you are dragging. Dragging by one-third is always a good approximation to make. You may run into trouble when the control handle line is more than half or less than one-quarter of the next segment. If your control handle line is too long or too short, chances are good that the line will curve erratically.

✦ **Don't get the outside of the curve and the outside of the shape you are drawing confused — they may well be two different things.** Remember that control handle lines are always tangent to the curved segment they are guiding. Tangent? Well, here's a simpler way of putting this rule: It's a line that touches the curve but does not cross or intersect the curve. If your control handle lies inside the curve you are drawing, it becomes too short and overpowered by the next anchor point. Control handles *pull* the curve toward themselves; this makes them naturally curve out toward the control handle lines. If you fight this natural pull, your illustrations can look loopy and silly.

✦ **Drag the control handle in the direction that you want the curve to travel at that anchor point.** The control handle pulls the curve toward itself by its very nature. If you drag backward toward the preceding segment, you create little curved spikes that stick out from the anchor points. This commandment applies *only* to Smooth Points. If the anchor point is a curved corner point, you must make the initial drag in the direction the curve was traveling and the next drag (an Alt (Option)+ drag) in the direction that you want the curve to travel. If the anchor point is a combination curve point and the next segment is straight, make the dragging motion in the direction that the curve was traveling. Next, click and release the anchor point. If the combination curve point's next segment is curved, click and release the first click, and the second click should be dragged in the direction of the next curve.

✦ **Use as few anchor points as possible.** If your illustration calls for smooth, flowing curves, use very few anchor points. If, on the other hand, you want your illustration rough and gritty, use more anchor points. The fewer anchor points you use, the smoother the final result. When only a few anchor points are on a path, changing its shape is easier and faster. More anchor points mean a bigger file and longer printing times as well. If you're not sure whether you need more anchor points, don't add them. You can always add them later with the Add anchor point tool.

For more on the Add anchor point tool, see Chapter 6.

✦ **Place anchor points at the beginning of each "different" curve.** You should use anchor points as *transitional* points, where the curve either changes direction or increases or decreases in size dramatically. If it looks as though the curve changes from one type of curve to another, the location to place an anchor point is in the middle of that transitional section.

✦ **Do not overcompensate for a previously misdrawn curve.** If you really messed up on the last anchor point you've drawn, don't panic and try to undo the mistake by dragging in the wrong direction or by dragging the control handle out to some ridiculous length. Doing either of these two things may temporarily fix the preceding curve but usually wrecks the next curve, causing you to have to overcompensate yet again.

Using the various line tools

In addition to the Pencil and Pen tools, Illustrator includes several unique tools that you can use to create specialized types of lines. From straight lines with the Line Segment tool to spiral lines using the Spiral tool, these line tools fall into the convenience category. Housed with the Line Segment tool, these tools include the Line Segment, Arc, Spiral, Rectangular Grid, and Polar Grid tools.

Using the Line Segment tool

Now that you've learned how to create straight lines the hard way with the Pen tool, here's an easy way — use the Line Segment tool. After you learn to use the Line Segment tool, you'll think that using the Pencil or Pen tool to draw straight lines is just plain ridiculous. Any amount of caffeine in your system results in a jittery line with either tool. Using this tool is a breeze. Simply click and drag the line where you want it to go, as indicated in Figure 4-18. Holding the Shift key while drawing a line constrains the line to 45-degree increments. If you press the Alt (Option) key while drawing a line, your starting point begins in the middle of the line.

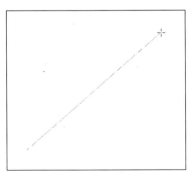

Figure 4-18: A line segment being drawn with the Line Segment tool

Double-clicking the Line Segment tool, or clicking one time on the Artboard, brings up the Line Segment Tool Options dialog box, as shown in Figure 4-19. In this dialog box, you can set the length and angle and whether to fill the line with the defaulted Fill color. You can use the Pen tool to draw straight lines, but when you have a tool specifically made for lines, use it.

Figure 4-19: The Line Segment Tool Options dialog box lets you draw exactly the line you want without dragging the mouse.

Tip

The Pen tool versus the Line Segment tool: The Pen tool can also draw straight lines and constrained lines, so why use the Line Segment tool at all? Well, one small slip of the Pen tool, and you have a curved line. In addition, you can get the precise length and angle using the Line Segment tool because you actually see the line rubberbanding from the original point.

Working with the Arc Segment tool

Arcs are now easily drawn using the Arc tool. The old-fashioned way used to be to draw an oval and remove the sections you didn't need via the Direct Selection tool or Scissor tool. Figure 4-20 shows an Arc drawn with the Arc tool.

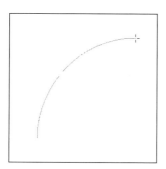

Figure 4-20: An arc being drawn with the Arc tool

The Arc tool is housed with the Line Segment tool. You can have an arc that sweeps inward or outward depending on your settings. Double-clicking the Arc tool accesses the Arc Segment Tool Options dialog box, shown in Figure 4-21. These are the Arc Segment Tool Options:

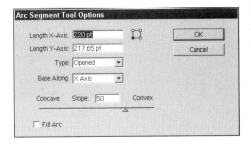

Figure 4-21: The Arc Segment Tool Options dialog box includes several options for the properties of the arc.

✦ **Length X-Axis:** Enter the value for the length of the slope along the X-Axis.

✦ **Length Y-Axis:** Enter the value for the length of the slope along the Y-Axis.

✦ **Type:** Choose whether you want the arc to be an open or closed path.

✦ **Base Along:** This is where you choose the direction of the slope, either along an X-axis or Y-axis.

✦ **Slope:** Dragging the slider to the left results in a concave slope. Dragging the slider to the right results in a convex slope.

✦ **Fill Arc:** Checking this option fills the inside of the arc with the default color.

Tip

When dragging out an arc, pressing the F key or the X key toggles the arc between convex and concave. Press the spacebar while you draw to move the whole arc. These keyboard shortcuts are true with all shapes that you draw in Illustrator.

Creating spirals with the Spiral tool

The Spiral tool (located with the Line Segment tool) makes spirals — all sorts of spirals. What can you use a spiral for? Well, you can use the Spiral tool to create a simulated record. Of course, the path was exceedingly long and refused to print on most Imagesetters. Other than that, you can use them to simulate nature patterns, such as snails, shells, an eddy, or a whirlpool. Figure 4-22 shows several spirals manufactured with the Spiral tool.

Tip

Spirals beg to be stroked, not filled. Putting just a fill on a spiral makes it look lumpy and not quite round.

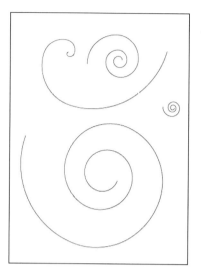

Figure 4-22: These spirals were created with the Spiral tool.

If you click in your document with the Spiral tool, the Spiral dialog box, as shown in Figure 4-23, appears, and you can enter specific values for a spiral. This is handy for those times your client or boss wants that 82.5 percent decay spiral.

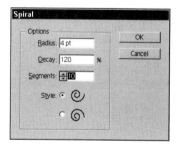

Figure 4-23: The Spiral dialog box enables you to modify how the Spiral tool works.

Making grid lines using the Rectangular Grid tool

You can easily create a grid using the Grid tool, which is housed with the Line Segment tool. For example, you could use a grid to create a perspective drawing. Use the Skew tool to give an angled view. You can create a unique Rubik's cube. You can also create nice grid paper or use the Grid tool to create a data chart. Figure 4-24 shows a grid being drawn.

Pressing these keys while creating grids makes life easier:

✦ **Up or Down arrow:** Increases or decreases the number of horizontal lines

✦ **Left or Right arrow:** Increases or decreases the number of vertical lines

✦ **Shift key:** Creates a perfect square grid

✦ **Alt (Option) key:** Creates a grid from a central point

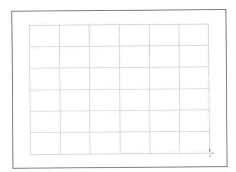

Figure 4-24: This grid was created using the Grid tool.

Double-clicking the Grid tool accesses the Rectangular Grid Tool Options dialog box, shown in Figure 4-25. Under the Grid Options, you can choose to skew the Grid. That is, you can make the lines closer to the top or bottom and left or right. You can change the following options:

✦ **Default Size:** Enter the width and height in points.

✦ **Horizontal Dividers:** Enter how many dividers and how much they will be skewed.

✦ **Vertical Dividers:** Enter the number of dividers and how much they will be skewed.

✦ **Use Outside Rectangle As A Frame:** This option causes a rectangle to frame the grid.

✦ **Fill Grid:** Checking this box fills the grid with the set default fill color.

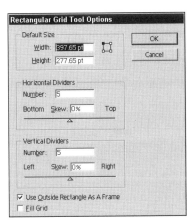

Figure 4-25: The Rectangular Grid Tool Options dialog box lets you specify dividers.

Understanding the Polar Grid tool

The Polar Grid tool is found with the Line Segment tool. A Polar Grid is also referred to as a radar grid. You would recognize it as a dartboard, or a bull's-eye, as shown in Figure 4-26.

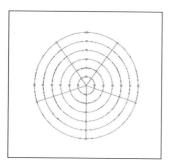

Figure 4-26: A polar grid looks like a bull's-eye.

The Polar Grid Tool Options dialog box, seen in Figure 4-27, lets you set the same options as those found in the Rectangular Grid options, except that the dividers are radial and concentric instead of horizontal and vertical:

✦ **Default Size:** Enter the width and height in points.

✦ **Concentric Dividers:** Enter how many dividers and how much they will be skewed (distributed) away from the center.

✦ **Radial Dividers:** Enter the number of dividers and how much they will be skewed top to bottom.

✦ **Create Compound Path From Ellipses:** This option causes ellipses to create a compound path.

✦ **Fill Grid:** Checking this box fills the polar grid with the set default fill color.

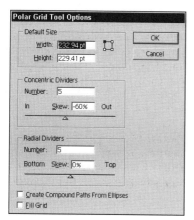

Figure 4-27: Use the Polar Grid Tool Options dialog box to adjust the settings for your polar grid object.

Pressing these keys while creating grids makes life easier:

✦ **Up or Down arrow:** Increases or decreases the number of concentric circles

✦ **Left or Right arrow:** Increases or decreases the number of radial lines

✦ **Shift key:** Creates a perfect round polar grid

✦ **Alt (Option) key:** Creates a polar grid from a central point

Understanding Paintbrush types

The Paintbrush tool draws a stroked path—that is, a path that is also a brush stroke. This makes life so much easier when it comes to editing. The Paintbrush tool is similar to paintbrush-type tools in painting programs. The Paintbrush has a certain width, and you can paint with this Paintbrush at this width anywhere in your document. The big difference between paint programs' paintbrushes and Illustrator's Paintbrush tool is that when you finish drawing with Illustrator's Paintbrush tool, you create a stroked path.

To use the Paintbrush tool, choose the tool, then choose the brush from the Brush palette, and start drawing. A freeform path appears wherever you drag. That's all there is to it, kinda. Figure 4-28 shows a drawing that was created with the Paintbrush tool set to a variable width with a pressure-sensitive stylus.

Drawing with the Paintbrush tool is a bit more complicated than I just explained. The most important consideration is the width of the paintbrush stroke. The paintbrush stroke can be as narrow as 0 points and as wide as 1,296 points (that's 18 inches to you and me).

Although 0 is the smallest width, a paintbrush stroke drawn with a width of 0 points actually has a width bigger than 0 points. To change the paintbrush stroke width (the default is 9 points), open the Stroke palette (*not* the toolbox) and enter a number in the Weight field. Remember that you are actually changing that default brush.

A mouse is *not* an intuitive drawing tool, and not being able to draw in the first place makes it even more difficult to draw with the Paintbrush tool. So, if artists have trouble with the mouse, what's the point of having the Paintbrush tool at all? Well, instead of a mouse, you can use several types of alternative drawing devices. The best of these is a pressure-sensitive tablet (for more information about pressure-sensitive drawing tablets visit the Wacom Web site as www.wacom.com). Trackballs with locking buttons are also good for drawing with the Paintbrush tool; this allows more control over the direction and speed of the Paintbrush.

Tip   When you're drawing with any of the tools in Illustrator, dragging off the edge of the window causes the window to scroll, which creates a frightening effect for the uninitiated. If you don't want the window to remain where it scrolled to, don't let go of the mouse button; instead, drag in the opposite direction until the window returns to the original position.

Figure 4-28: This drawing of a horse was created with the Paintbrush tool using a pressure-sensitive tablet and a stylus.

To help you draw more precisely, you have the option of changing the cursor shape from the cute little brush into crosshairs. Press the Caps Lock key (to engage it), and the cursor changes into crosshairs with a dot in the center. Press the Caps Lock key again (to release it), and the cursor returns to the brush shape. The dot at the center of the crosshairs is the center of any paintbrush stroke drawn with the Paintbrush tool. Normally, when the cursor is in the shape of a paintbrush, the tip is the center of the paintbrush stroke. Some people find it easier to draw when the paintbrush cursor is replaced with the precise crosshairs.

Using brushes

If you want to create a totally new brush, choose New Brush from the Brushes palette pop-up menu to display the New Brush dialog box, shown in Figure 4-29. You then select the type of new brush you want to create. You can choose from Calligraphic, Scatter, Art, and Pattern brushes. The Brushes palette includes samples of each of these brush types. Calligraphic brushes make strokes similar to a calligraphic pen. Scatter brushes scatter an object along the brushed path. The Art brush takes an object and stretches it along the brush path length. The Pattern brush uses repeated tiles along the brush path.

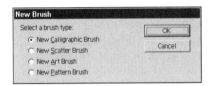

Figure 4-29: The New Brush dialog box lets you choose to create one of four different brush types.

Using the Calligraphic brush

A Calligraphic brush was made to simulate the actual calligraphic pen tip. You set the angle and size and draw to your heart's content. You can also create a perfectly round brush in the Calligraphic Brush Options dialog box by not entering an angle and by keeping the Roundness at 100%.

The Calligraphic Brush Options, shown in Figure 4-30, are as follows:

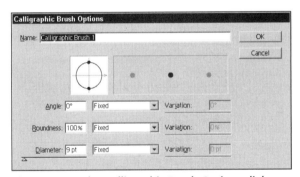

Figure 4-30: The Calligraphic Brush Options dialog box enables you to customize a brush.

✦ **Name:** This option lets you give your new brush a name or rename an existing brush (maximum of 30 characters).

✦ **Angle:** You can set the angle of the Calligraphic paintbrush. The angle you should choose depends on what is going to be drawn. To mimic hand-drawn lettering in a calligraphic style, the angle should be set to 45° (or if you're left-handed, it should be set to –45°).

✦ **Roundness:** This does what you'd think it does. It sets the roundness of the brush. The higher you make the value, the rounder the brush.

✦ **Diameter:** The diameter option sets the maximum diameter of the brush.

✦ **Variation:** If you choose the Random option from the Angle or Roundness list boxes, you then enter a value for Variation. The Variation for the Angle value is in a degree that you want to vary from the original setting. The Variation for the Roundness is set in percentages. A slider sets the Variation for the Diameter, or you can enter a number. The Diameter Variation goes from your original value up to the Variation value. This is a great way to simulate a hand-drawn look if you don't have a pressure-sensitive tablet.

Creating a Calligraphic brush

You can use a Calligraphic brush many ways. You can choose an existing brush and get started. If you load additional brush libraries, you'll find quite a variety of brushes to choose from. You can also create your own brush from an existing one or from scratch. To create a new brush, use an existing style that you like, but that you want to alter. To create a brush like this, select the brush that you want to duplicate and choose Duplicate Brush from the Brush palette pop-up menu. To edit that duplicated brush, double-click the duplicate brush or select Brush Options from the pop-up menu. In the Brush Options dialog box, change the brush to your specifications.

Variable widths and pressure-sensitive tablets

If you have a pressure-sensitive tablet — some call them Wacom (pronounced "walk 'em") tablets because a large majority are made by Wacom — you can select the Pressure option beside the Diameter field in the Brush Options dialog box (accessed by double-clicking on a brush in the Brushes palette). If you don't have a pressure-sensitive tablet, the Pressure option is grayed out (unselectable).

Note

A pressure-sensitive tablet is a flat, rectangular device over which you pass a special stylus. The more pressure exerted by the stylus on the tablet, the wider a paintbrush stroke becomes, provided that you select the Pressure option in the Calligraphic dialog box. When using the Pressure option, try to set the Variation different from the original specified diameter to see the difference when you press harder or softer.

Creating with the Scatter brush

The Scatter brush copies and scatters a predefined object along a path. Illustrator has a number of brush libraries containing artwork that you can use for a Scatter brush, or you can select a piece of artwork that you create to use as a Scatter brush. Use the Window ➪ Brush Libraries command to view the available brush libraries. Figure 4-31 shows an example of a path drawn with one of the available Scatter brushes.

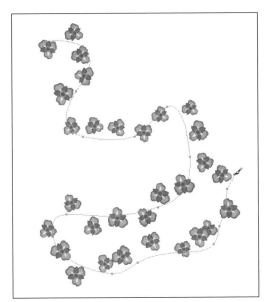

Figure 4-31: The Scatter brush enables you to draw some very interesting paths.

These are your choices in the Scatter Brush Options dialog box, as seen in Figure 4-32:

✦ **Name:** You can name your brush with up to 30 characters.

✦ **Size:** In the size area, you have several options that enable you to set the size. If you want really big images and small images that vary in size, then drag the sliders in opposite directions.

✦ **Spacing:** This option adjusts the space between each object.

✦ **Scatter:** This option adjusts how the objects follow the original path on each side of the path. If you set a high value, the objects are farther away from the original path.

✦ **Rotation:** This option adjusts how much the object rotates from its original position.

✦ **Rotation relative to:** This option gives you two choices from a pop-up menu. The Page option rotates objects according to the page setup. The Path option rotates objects tangent to the path.

✦ **Colorization:** You have four Colorization choices: None, Tints, Tints and Shades, and Hue Shift. For more on colorization and colorization tips, see "Understanding colorization tips," later in this chapter.

Tip

The Scatter Brush Options dialog box shows the brush preview only when you are creating a new brush.

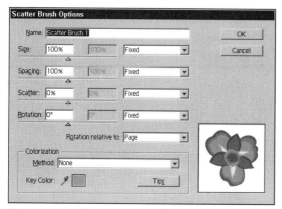

Figure 4-32: The Scatter Brush Options dialog box

Working with the Art brush

The Art brush, like the Scatter brush, uses an object along a path. The difference is that the Art brush stretches the object to the length of the path rather than repeating and scattering the object. Illustrator centers the object evenly over the path and then stretches it. Figure 4-33 shows several different Art brush examples.

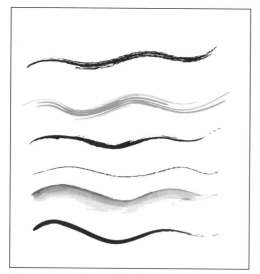

Figure 4-33: The Art brush creates artistic-looking paths.

These are your choices in the Art Brush Options dialog box, shown in Figure 4-34:

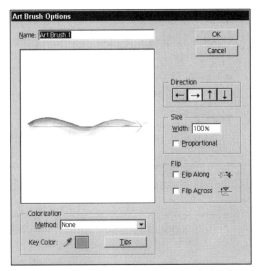

Figure 4-34: The Art Brush Options dialog box enables you to create your own Art brush.

✦ **Name:** You can name your new Art brush or rename an existing Art brush with up to 30 characters.

✦ **Direction:** This option lets you choose from four directions. The directions are relative to how you drag the paintbrush.

✦ **Size:** This option scales the art when it is stretched. You can choose Proportional to keep the object in proportion.

✦ **Flip:** This option lets you flip your object along or across the path.

✦ **Colorization:** You have four Colorization choices: None, Tints, Tints and Shades, and Hue Shift. For more on colorization and colorization tips, see "Understanding colorization tips" later in this chapter.

Creating tiles using the Pattern brush

The Pattern brush repeats a tiled object along a path. The Pattern brush can have tiles to display the sides, inner corner, outer corner, beginning, and end. If you think of a Pattern brush as you would a regular Pattern tile, but keep in mind the corners, you'll have no problem creating your own interesting Pattern brushes. Figure 4-35 shows an example of one of the Pattern brushes.

Figure 4-35: The Pattern brush draws a stroke using a repeating pattern.

These are your choices in the Pattern Brush Options dialog box, shown in Figure 4-36:

✦ **Name:** Enter a new name, or change an existing name (up to 30 characters).

✦ **Tile buttons:** This is where you choose which of the five tiles you want to create.

✦ **Size:** This option lets you enter the size in proportion and the space between the tiles.

✦ **Flip:** This option lets you flip the pattern along or across the path.

✦ **Fit:** In this option, you can choose Stretch to Fit, Add Space to Fit, or Approximate Path. Stretch lengthens or shortens a tile to fit your object. Add Space adds a blank space between the tiles to fit the path proportionately. Approximate Path makes the tile fit as close to the original path without altering the tiles.

✦ **Colorization:** You have four Colorization choices: None, Tints, Tints and Shades, and Hue Shift.

The list box in the Pattern Brush Options dialog box allows you to choose an existing pattern instead of the selected artwork.

Cross-Reference For more on colorization and colorization tips, see "Using colorization tips" later in this chapter.

Figure 4-36: The Pattern Brush Options dialog box enables you to create some very interesting brushes.

Making a custom brush

You can create a brush several ways. If you like a brush, but not all aspects of it, you can duplicate that brush (by choosing Duplicate Brush from the Brushes palette menu) and edit its options to make it as you like. To edit a brush, double-click the brush, choose Brush Options from the pop-up menu, or click the Brush Options icon at the bottom of the Brushes palette. You can also create a brush by choosing New Brush from the pop-up menu or clicking the New Brush icon at the bottom of the Brushes palette. Doing this brings up a dialog box asking you to choose the type of brush you want to create.

Note You can create a Calligraphic Brush by filling in the text fields of the Calligraphic Brush dialog box. To create any of the other brushes, you must have your art drawn first and then choose New Brush.

To create your own brush design, first create the object that you want to use. Next, select all the parts of the object that you want as a brush and choose New Brush from the Brushes palette pop-up menu. Then choose the type of brush you want to create. The Brush Options dialog box appears, and you see your new design there. Now all you have to do is set the rest of the options, and you are ready to use your new brush.

Understanding colorization tips

The Tips button in the Art, Scatter, and Pattern Brush dialog boxes displays a dialog box explaining the different colorization options. Figure 4-37 shows the Colorization Tips dialog box, which has four areas of colorization: None, Tints, Tints and Shades, and Hue Shift.

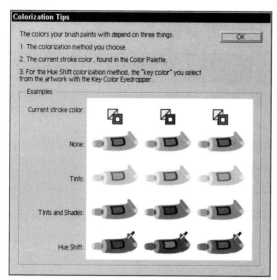

Figure 4-37: The Colorization Tips dialog box provides visual examples of the various colorization options.

To see how the Colorization options work, first create four copies of a brush. For the first copy, use the default of None. For the next three copies, change the Stroke color (you won't see anything happen yet). Double-click the second copy, and select Tint. Apply to stroke when asked to do so in the dialog box. The color should change at this point. Double-click the third copy, and select Tints and Shades. Double-click the last copy, and select Hue Shift. All the copies should look different.

Checking out the Brush Libraries

The Brush Library that displays when you choose the Brush palette is the default Library. You have additional Libraries from which to choose. Adobe has really come up with some cool brushes for our creative pleasure. The Brush Libraries are found under the Window menu, as shown in Figure 4-38.

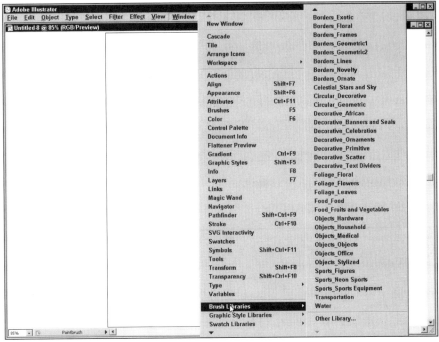

Figure 4-38: The Brush Libraries submenu under the Window menu contains many different libraries.

To use a brush from one Brush Library, choose the brush you want from the scrolling list. Figure 4-39 shows just one of the many Brush Libraries that are included with Illustrator.

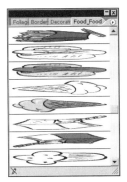

Figure 4-39: The Brush Libraries include a variety of interesting brushes you can use.

Summary

Illustrator's drawing tools provide you with many powerful methods of quickly creating artwork. In this chapter, you learned the following important points about using these tools:

✦ Illustrator includes four anchor point types: straight corner points, combination corner points, smooth points, and curved corner points.

✦ Edit curves with the control handles.

✦ Curves are based on the Bézier principle.

✦ Use the Pencil tool to create paths quickly.

✦ Use the Smooth and Erase tools to edit your paths.

✦ Although the Pen tool is the most difficult to learn, it yields the smoothest results.

✦ The Paintbrush tool creates a free-formed stroked path.

✦ A pressure-sensitive tablet can mimic hand drawing.

✦ The Line Segment tool can create straight lines. Other tools with the Line Segment tool let you create arcs, grids, polar grids, and spirals.

✦ The Scatter Brush repeats objects along a path rotated and sized differently.

✦ The Art Brush stretches an object to the length of the path.

✦ The Pattern Brush repeats a pattern on a path.

✦ You can create a new brush in the Brushes palette.

✦   ✦   ✦

Creating Objects, Graphs, and Symbols

✦ ✦ ✦ ✦

In This Chapter

Creating rectangles, ellipses, polygons, and stars

Using the Flare tool

Understanding Fills and Strokes

Designing graphs, charts, flowcharts, and diagrams

Creating with the Symbol Sprayer tools

Editing and altering symbols

✦ ✦ ✦ ✦

I n this chapter, you learn how to create objects such as rectangles, ellipses, stars, and polygons. In addition, you find out how to create and enhance graphs, add touches of light with the Flare tool, and create really cool repeating effects with the Symbolism tools.

This is actually a very important chapter because it introduces the objects, graphs, and symbols that you will use often in later chapters. Be sure to take the time to understand the concepts that are presented in this chapter so that you'll have an easier time later.

Making Basic Shapes

Drawing the most basic shapes — rectangles, ellipses, polygons, and stars — is precisely what a computer is for. Try drawing a perfect ellipse by hand. Troublesome, isn't it? How about a square that doesn't have ink bubbles or splotches at the corners? A nine-pointed star? Drawing these objects and then coloring them in Illustrator is so easy and so basic that after a few weeks of using Illustrator, you'll never be able to draw a shape by hand again without wincing, maybe even shuddering.

Illustrator exemplifies the true power of object-oriented drawing programming. No matter what you draw, you can adjust and move each piece of the drawing independently until it's just right. Don't like the sun so high in your background? Pull it down and tuck it in just a bit behind those mountains. Is the tree too small for the house in your illustration? Scale it up a bit. This feature is great not only for artists, but also for your pesky client (or boss) who demands that everything be moved except that darned tree.

And after you create the shape, you can move, rotate, scale, and manipulate it in any way you like. Figure 5-1 shows an illustration drawn one way and then modified in a matter of seconds by moving existing elements and adding a few anchor points.

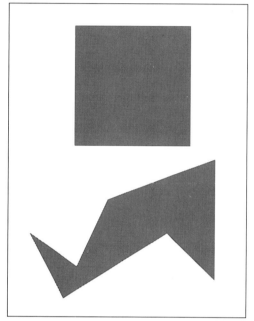

Figure 5-1: A basic square becomes a more interesting shape with a few simple modifications.

Remember these general things when you're drawing basic shapes:

✦ **Creating common shapes:** You can draw common objects (or shapes) in Illustrator including squares and rectangles, rectangles with rounded corners, circles and ellipses, polygons, and stars. Tools for creating these objects are found as pop-up tools in the toolbox under the Rectangle tool. You basically use all these tools in the same manner. So after you learn how to use the Rectangle tool later in this chapter, you'll know how to use the other tools.

Cross-Reference

To learn the basic way to use a shape tool, see the section "Drawing rectangles using the Rectangle tool." For more on paths, see Chapter 4, and for more on selecting objects, see Chapter 6.

✦ **Lines and points that appear when you select an object:** After you draw a shape, an outlined closed path appears with blue points indicating the anchor points. The edge of the path has thin blue lines surrounding it. These blue lines indicate that the object is currently selected.

Tip   Note that the closed path appears in black unless you've changed the default line and fill color. For more on changing the fill or line color, see "Filling and Stroking Shapes" later in this chapter. Also, the anchor points appear as blue points only if you are in Preview mode, the default viewing mode. To learn more about the various view modes in Illustrator, see Chapter 2.

✦ **Changing an object's shape:** The initial click you make with any of the shape tools is called the origin point. While you drag a shape, the origin point never moves, but the rest of the shape is fluid, changing shape as you drag in different directions and to different distances with your mouse. Dragging horizontally with almost no vertical movement results in a long, flat shape. Dragging vertically with very little horizontal movement creates a shape that is tall and thin. Dragging at a 45-degree angle (diagonally) results in a regular shape.

✦ **Entering exact dimensions in a shape's dialog box:** If you click a tool without dragging it, the shape's dialog box appears. The center of the shape is now where you clicked (normally, the corner of the shape is where you click). Unlike manually drawing (dragging) centered shapes, the dimensions you enter are the actual dimensions of the shape. The dimension is *not* doubled as it is when you drag a centered shape.

**Cross-
Reference**   For the exact steps on entering dimensions in the shape's dialog box, see the section "Defining properties with the Rectangle dialog box" later in this chapter.

✦ **Changing units of measure:** When you first run Illustrator, all measurements are set to points. Therefore, the values inside the various shape dialog boxes appear in so many points (12 points in a pica). To change the units of measure to something else (for example, millimeters or inches), see Chapter 8.

✦ **Moving shapes while you draw them:** While drawing a shape, you may realize that you want to move it. In Illustrator, you can move any shape by holding down the spacebar while depressing your mouse button and dragging your shape to a new location. When you let up on the spacebar, you can continue to draw your object.

✦ **Deleting shapes:** Getting rid of the shape you've drawn is even easier than creating it — you simply delete it by pressing the Delete or Backspace key.

✦ **Tool information:** If you click a tool picture, Illustrator gives you some information about that particular tool.

> Traditional bitmap paint applications do not have the capability to move sections of a drawing (with the exception of the use of layers in software such as Photoshop and Painter). After you move a section of an image in a bitmap program, a *hole* appears in the place where the section used to be. And if the new location already has an object, you delete this section of the object, replacing it with the new image.

Drawing shapes from their centers

When you draw a shape, Illustrator starts from the corner, and you have to move your mouse to form your shape. However, if you often place shapes on top of or under other objects, you may need to have an even amount of space between your shape and the object it surrounds. Instead of drawing a shape from a corner, you can draw one from its center. Drawing from the corner forces you to eyeball the space around the object, while drawing from the center of the other object ensures that space surrounding the object is the same.

To draw a shape from its center, hold down the Alt (Option) key and then click and drag. The origin point is now the center of the shape. The farther you drag in one direction, the farther the edges of the shape go out in the opposite direction. Drawing from the center of a shape lets you draw something twice as big as the same shape drawn from a corner. As long as you press the Alt (Option) key, the shape continues drawing from its center. If you release the Alt (Option) key before you release the mouse button, the origin of the shape changes back to a corner. You can press and release the Alt (Option) key at any time while drawing, toggling back and forth between drawing from a corner and drawing from the center. You can switch back and forth when drawing rectangles and ellipses only.

Drawing symmetric shapes (circles and squares)

You can force Illustrator to create symmetric shapes by holding down the Shift key as you draw a shape. For example, when you press the Shift key while drawing a rectangle, the rectangle constrains to a square. Likewise, you can draw a perfect circle by holding down the Shift key as you draw an ellipse. You can do this for all the Shape tools as well as the Line and Pencil tools.

> For more on drawing rectangles, see the next section. For more on drawing ellipses, see the section "Drawing ellipses" later in this chapter. You can also create a square using the Polygon dialog box. To learn how to do so, see the section "Creating polygons."

Creating Drop Shadows for Shapes

A useful way to add depth to an object, such as a rectangle, is with a drop shadow. You can use this technique on any type of object or text. To create a drop shadow for a shape, follow these steps:

1. **Draw a shape.** Using the shape's tool, draw a shape to the size you want it. This example uses a rectangle.

2. **Change the Fill color of the shape to the shadow color you want.** You do this by clicking the Fill square in the toolbox and then choosing your color in the Color palette.

 Cross-Reference For more on palettes in general, see Chapter 2. For more on fills, see Chapter 10.

3. **Change the Stroke color of the shape to the shadow color you want.** You do this by clicking the Stroke icon in the toolbox and then choosing that color in the Color palette.

4. **Choose the Selection tool, and drag the rectangle object just a little while holding down the Alt (Option) key.** This creates a copy of the original shape. The farther you drag, the greater the depth of the drop shadow. After you release the mouse button, you should have two overlapping shapes.

5. **Change the Fill color of the top shape to a color other than the shadow color.** You do this by clicking the Fill square in the toolbox and then clicking the desired color in the Color palette. The following figure shows a drop shadow for a rectangle.

A basic drop shadow box

You can create drop shadows manually in this manner, but Illustrator also includes a Drop Shadow filter and effect in the Filter ➪ Stylize and Effect ➪ Stylize menus. These features offer many more options for creating drop shadows automatically. You can learn to use these features in Chapter 15.

You can also use the Rectangle (or Ellipse) dialog box to draw a perfect square (or circle) by entering equal values for the width and height. Simply click without dragging to get the dialog box to appear.

Tip   To draw shapes from their centers and to make them symmetric at the same time, draw the shape while holding down both the Alt (Option) and Shift keys. Make sure that both keys are still pressed when you release the mouse button.

Drawing shapes at an angle

Usually, when you draw a shape with a tool, the shape orients itself with the document and the document window. For example, the bottom of a rectangle aligns parallel to the bottom of the document window.

But what if you want to draw shapes that are all angled at 45 degrees on the page? Well, one possibility is to rotate them after you draw them by using the Transform Each command or the Rotate tool. Better yet, you can set up your document so that every new shape automatically appears at an angle.

The angle of a shape depends on the Constrain Angle value. Usually, the Constrain Angle is 0°, where all shapes appear to align evenly with the borders of the document. To change the Constrain Angle, choose Edit (Illustrator) ⇨ Preferences ⇨ General and enter a new value in the Constrain Angle text field in the Preferences dialog box.

When you finish drawing these angled shapes, make sure that you change the Constrain Angle setting back to 0°, or you create all new shapes at the altered Constrain Angle.

Tip   Constrain Angle affects shapes and other objects created in Illustrator, such as type. In addition, dragging objects while pressing the Shift key constrains them to the current Constrain Angle or to a 45-degree or 90-degree variation of it. The Constrain Angle is much easier to see if you turn on Grids by choosing View ⇨ Show Grid or pressing Ctrl+" (⌘+"). When the grid option is turned on, it is always aligned with the Constrain Angle.

Drawing rectangles using the Rectangle tool

The most basic shape you can draw is a rectangle. Although the following steps explain how to draw a simple rectangle, you essentially use these same steps for all the other shape tools in Illustrator.

1. **Select the Rectangle tool.** You can do this by clicking it in the toolbox or by pressing the letter M on the keyboard. You find the Rectangle tool in the second column of the Toolbox on the fourth row from the top.

2. **Click your mouse on the Artboard, and hold down the mouse button.** This sets the origin point of the rectangle.

3. **Drag your mouse diagonally to the size you desire.** You can draw rectangles from any corner by clicking and dragging in the direction opposite from where you want that corner to be. For example, to draw a rectangle from the lower-right corner, click and drag up and to the left. As long as you have the Rectangle tool selected, dragging with it in the document window produces a new rectangle.

4. **Release the mouse button.** Illustrator creates a rectangle as shown in Figure 5-2. The farther the distance from the initial click to the point where you release the mouse button, the larger the rectangle.

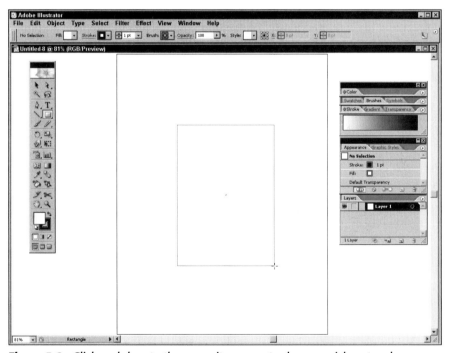

Figure 5-2: Click and drag to the opposite corner to draw a quick rectangle.

Defining properties with the Rectangle dialog box

If you want to create a rectangle with exact dimensions, all you have to do is open the Rectangle dialog box and enter the dimensions. The steps that follow also apply to the other basic shape tools in Illustrator. To draw a rectangle of an exact size, follow these steps:

1. **Click the Rectangle tool once, and release where you want to place the upper-left corner.** The Rectangle dialog box, shown in Figure 5-3, appears.

Figure 5-3: Use the Rectangle dialog box to specify the exact dimensions of a rectangle.

2. **Type in the width and height.** When the Rectangle dialog box appears, values are usually already inside the text fields. These numbers correspond to the size of the rectangle you last drew. To create another rectangle of the same size, just click OK (or press Return or Enter). To make the rectangle a different size, replace the values with your own measurements. If a text field is highlighted, typing replaces the text in the text field and deletes what had been highlighted.

Tip

To highlight the next field in a dialog box, press the Tab key. You can also highlight the preceding field in a dialog box by pressing Shift+Tab. If you'd like to highlight any text field instantly, double-click the value or click the label next to that value.

3. **Click OK.** Illustrator draws the rectangle using precisely the size that you specified. To get out of the Rectangle dialog box without drawing a rectangle, click the Cancel button, or just press Esc (⌘+Period). Anything you type in that dialog box is then forgotten. The next time the dialog box is opened, it still displays has the size of the previously drawn rectangle.

Rectangles whose sizes are specified in the Rectangle dialog box are always drawn from the upper-left corner. The largest rectangle you can draw is about 19 feet by 19 feet. It's a wonder you can get anything done at all with these limitations!

Drawing rounded rectangles and squares

Sometimes, straight corners just aren't good enough. That's when it's time to create a rectangle with rounded corners. Why? Maybe you want your rectangles to look less "computery." A tiny bit of corner rounding (2 or 3 points) may be just what you need.

Before we get into how to actually draw rounded rectangles, it helps to understand how Illustrator sets the roundness of your corners. It performs this feat in one of three ways:

✦ **Using most recently drawn rounded corner rectangle:** Illustrator sets the Corner Radius value using the dimensions of the most recently drawn rounded-corner rectangle and places this value in the General Preferences dialog box. In other words, after you draw a rectangle using the Rounded Rectangle tool, Illustrator saves those dimensions for the next time that you draw a rounded rectangle.

✦ **Using the General Preferences dialog box:** What if you don't want to use the radius of the last rounded rectangle? Why, you use the value in the General Preferences dialog box, of course! To do so, choose Edit (Illustrator) ⇨ Preferences ⇨ General or press Ctrl+K (⌘+K), and set the corner radius you desire. All rounded rectangles are now drawn with this new corner radius until you change this value.

✦ **Using the Rounded Rectangle dialog box:** Changing the value in the Corner Radius field in the Rounded Rectangle dialog box not only changes the current rounded rectangle's Corner Radius value but also changes the radius in the General Preferences box. Illustrator uses this corner radius for all subsequently drawn rounded rectangles until you change the radius value again. You learn how to access the Rounded Rectangle dialog box shortly.

Now that you understand how Illustrator works when you draw rounded rectangles, the next step is to learn how to draw one. You can create a rounded rectangle in one of two ways: You can accept the current radius and draw, or you can change the current radius and draw.

To draw a rounded rectangle with the current radius, use the Rounded Rectangle tool:

1. **Choose the Rounded Rectangle tool.** You do this by clicking the Rectangle tool in the toolbox until a pop-up tool appears. Next, drag your mouse to the right to select the Rounded Rectangle tool.

2. **Click and drag with the Rounded Rectangle tool as if you were drawing a standard rectangle.** The only difference is that this rectangle has rounded corners. The point at which you clicked is where the corner would be — if there were a corner. Of course, with rounded corners, there is no real corner, so the computer uses an imaginary point called the origin point, as its onscreen corner reference.

Alternatively, you can specify a Corner Radius value in the Rounded Rectangle dialog box by following these steps:

1. **Click the Rounded Rectangle tool as before.**

2. **Click the Artboard with the Rounded Rectangle tool.** The Rounded Rectangle box appears, shown in Figure 5-4.

Figure 5-4: The Rounded Rectangle dialog box includes a third field for defining the corner radius.

3. **Specify a value in the Corner Radius field.** The third text field is for the size of the corner radius. This option makes the corners of the rectangle curved, although leaving the setting at a value of 0 keeps the corners straight. The corner radius in Illustrator is the length from that imaginary corner (the origin point) to where the curve begins, as shown in Figure 5-5. The larger the value you enter in the Corner Radius field of the Rectangle dialog box, the farther the rectangle starts from the imaginary corner and the bigger the curve. For example, if you set the corner radius at 1 inch, the edge of the rectangle starts curving 1 inch from where a real corner would normally appear.

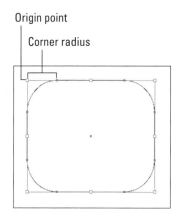

Figure 5-5: The corner radius defines the roundness of the corner.

4. **Click OK.** Illustrator applies your changes.

5. **Click and drag with this tool as if you were drawing a standard rectangle.** Your rounded rectangle appears.

How the Corner Radius Really Works

For all you geometry buffs, the whole corner radius business works this way: The width of the bounding box of any circle is called the *diameter* of that circle; half the diameter is the *radius* of the circle, as indicated in the figure that follows.

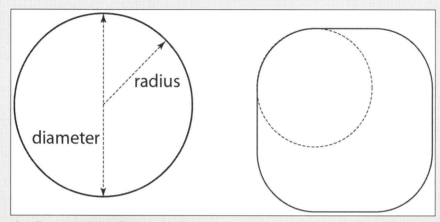

The diameter and radius of a circle

If you create a circle with a radius of 1 inch, the circle actually has a diameter of 2 inches. Put this 2-inch circle into the corner of the rectangle, as in the preceding figure, and the curve of the circle matches the curve of the rounded rectangle that has a corner radius of 1 inch.

To realistically determine the way a rounded corner will look, use the method that measures the distance from the imaginary corner to the place where the curve starts.

You are limited to a maximum of a 4,320-point corner radius, which works out to 5 feet. The largest rectangle you can create has a 10-foot length. So a 10-foot square with a 5-foot radius is another circle. (Those clever engineers . . .)

Tip   If the corner radius is more than half the magnitude of either the length or width of the rectangle, the rectangle may appear to have perfectly round ends on at least two sides. If the corner radius is more than half the magnitude of either the length or width of the rectangle, then the rectangle becomes an ellipse!

Cross-Reference   Need to draw a rounded rectangle from the center or create a rounded square? Use the Rounded Rectangle tool, and follow the instructions in the section "Drawing shapes from their centers," or "Drawing symmetric shapes (circles and squares)."

Using the round corners filter to round straight corners

If you have an existing rectangle with straight corners and you want to make the corners round, neither of the methods presented in the section "Drawing rounded rectangles and squares" are going to help you. Instead, you must choose Effect ➪ Stylize ➪ Round Corners and enter the value of the corner radius you want for the existing rectangle in the Round Corners dialog box. Using this command allows you to change straight-corner rectangles to rounded-corner rectangles. However this effect is not recommended for changing rounded-corner rectangles to straight-corner rectangles because it usually results in an unsightly distortion.

Furthermore, this command cannot change corners that you have rounded with either the Rounded Rectangle tool or through previous use of the Round Corners dialog box.

Rounding corners backward

What if you want your corners to round inward instead of out? Initially, it would seem that you are out of luck, because Illustrator doesn't provide any way for you to enter a negative value for a corner radius. However, you can manipulate the corners manually. The following steps explain how to create a reverse rounded-corner rectangle:

1. **Draw a rounded rectangle to the dimensions that you desire.** For more on drawing rounded rectangles, see the section "Drawing rounded rectangles and squares" earlier in this chapter.

2. **Select the leftmost point on the top of the rounded rectangle by dragging the Direct Selection tool (hollow arrow) over it.** One control handle appears, sticking out to the left.

3. **Click and drag the control handle down below the anchor point while pressing the Shift key, and then release the mouse button.** Holding the Shift key ensures that the control handle line is perfectly vertical.

4. **Select the topmost point on the left side by dragging the Direct Selection tool over it.** A control handle appears, sticking straight up out of this anchor point.

5. **Click and drag the control handle to the right while pressing the Shift key, and then release the mouse button.**

6. **Repeat these steps for each of the corners.** After you get the hang of it, the points start flying into position almost by themselves. Figure 5-6 shows an example of a rectangle with backward rounded corners on the left side.

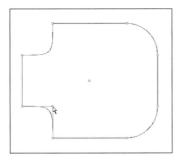

Figure 5-6: The final product of creating backward rounded corners on a rectangle

Drawing ellipses

Drawing an ellipse is harder than drawing a rectangle because the point of origin is outside the ellipse. With a rectangle, the point of origin corresponds to a corner of the rectangle, which also happens to be an anchor point. The ellipse is completely within the rectangle. Figure 5-7 shows that the top edge of the ellipse is at the midpoint of the dragged rectangle.

Origin point   Dragged area

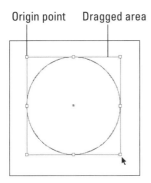

Figure 5-7: The curves of an ellipse extend to the boundaries of the dragged area.

Follow these steps (similar to those for drawing a rectangle) to create an ellipse:

1. **Click the Rectangle tool, and choose the Ellipse tool.** The Ellipse tool is housed with the Rectangle tool.

2. **Click and drag diagonally.** The outline of an ellipse forms.

3. **Release the mouse button.** The ellipse appears onscreen. Ellipses, like rectangles, have four anchor points, but the anchor points on an ellipse are at the top, bottom, left, and right of the ellipse.

Cross-Reference

Learn more about fills in the section "Filling and Stroking Shapes," later in this chapter. For the general steps of drawing a rectangle, see the section "Drawing a rectangle using the Rectangle tool." For the steps on entering exact values, see the section "Defining properties with the Rectangle dialog box." Both are covered earlier in this chapter.

Creating polygons

Although creating more and more ellipses, rectangles, and rounded rectangles is loads of fun, sooner or later you're going to get bored. I dare say that you can create more interesting shapes automatically by using some of the additional shape tools that come with Illustrator. Most of these tools are located in the Rectangle tool slot in the toolbox, as shown in Figure 5-8.

Figure 5-8: The Rectangle tool slot and the tools housed with it enable you to draw many shapes.

To create a polygon, you first want to specify the number of sides for your polygon and then you can draw it following these steps:

1. **Select the Polygon tool.** This tool is located to the right of the Ellipse tool in the Rectangle tool slot.

2. **Click the Artboard with the Polygon tool.** You want to do this before you draw the polygon. Clicking the Artboard displays the Polygon dialog box, shown in Figure 5-9.

Figure 5-9: Use the Polygon tool dialog box to create regular polygons.

3. **Specify values for the polygon.** The Polygon dialog box has the following options, both of which you must specify:

   • **Radius:** This is the distance from the center of the polygon to one of the vertices of the polygon. For even-sided shapes (4, 6, 8, 10, and so on sides), the radius is half the width of the object, from one corner to the opposite corner. For odd-sided shapes, the radius is the distance from the center of the polygon to any of the vertices. Its diameter is twice that value.

   • **Sides:** This is the number of sides that you want for the polygon.

4. **Click OK.**

While drawing a polygon, you can change the number of sides on the fly without re-opening the Polygon dialog box. To increase or decrease the number of sides, press the up arrow or the down arrow while you are dragging. Figure 5-10 shows different polygons drawn with the Polygon tool.

All polygons you create with the Polygon tool are equilateral polygons, meaning that they have sides of equal length. For this reason, every four-sided object that you create is a square and every six-sided object is a perfect hexagon. You may find the square capabilities of the Polygon tool useful; it can save you a step when you want to draw a square at an angle. You can't do this with the Rectangle tool unless you change the Constrain Angle in the General Preferences prior to drawing the square or use the Rotate tool on the square after you draw it.

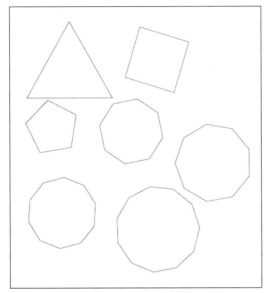

Figure 5-10: The number of sides on polygons drawn with the Polygon tool can easily be adjusted on the fly using the arrow keys.

If you press the Shift key while dragging your mouse, the polygon you're creating is upright. It aligns to the current Constrain Angle (usually 0°). Therefore, if you're creating a triangle and you press Shift, the triangle has one side that is perfectly horizontal (the bottom) unless you have a different Constrain Angle, in which case one edge of the triangle aligns to that angle.

Cross-Reference   For more on changing the Constrain Angle, see the section "Drawing shapes at an angle."

Note   Press the spacebar to move your polygon around when dragging with the Polygon tool. You can do this at any time during the creation of a Polygon. When you release the spacebar, the tool functions as before.

Possibly the more versatile function of the Polygon tool (and the Star and Spiral tools) is the wonderful function that comes from using the tilde (~) key. When you press the tilde key and draw, you see several shapes appear rapidly. As Figure 5-11 shows, this technique can create all sorts of interesting designs.

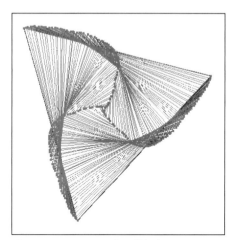

Figure 5-11: Press the tilde key to create fascinating designs.

Seeing stars

To create stars, choose the Star tool from its hiding place next to the Polygon tool in the Rectangle tool slot and drag in the document. As you drag, a star is created. Several stars are shown in Figure 5-12.

Figure 5-12: Use the Star tool when you want to draw stars.

Stars have several of the same controls as polygons when you're drawing them: Pressing the Shift key aligns the star to the Constrain Angle, the spacebar moves the star around, and the tilde (~) key makes lots more stars. The up and down arrows work a bit differently; instead of adding and removing edges, they add and remove entire points. So, in a way, they're actually adding two edges. Stars must have an even number of sides or they're not really stars; they're the pointy lumps you doodled during your Poly Sci classes as a sophomore.

The Star tool adds two additional keys for other functions. Pressing the Alt (Option) key positions the inner points relative to the outer points to produce a star with a corresponding side lying along the same line. Adobe refers to them as fixed stars. In case it's keeping you up at night, the Alt (Option) key has no effect on stars with three or four points.

Stars can come in all shapes, not just the fixed and standard shapes. You create these shapes by pressing the Ctrl (⌘) key when you drag the mouse. When you hold down the Ctrl (⌘) key, only the outer points are extended; the interior points remain fixed. Using this feature allows you build stars with long, thin points.

You can also specifically design a star by clicking with the Star tool to display the Star dialog box, shown in Figure 5-13, where you can enter the number of points and both the first and second radius of the points.

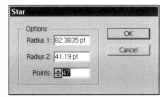

Figure 5-13: The Star dialog lets you specify both inner and outer radius values.

Turning Regular Stars into Something Spectacular

Of course, all the stars you create with the Star tool consist of regular-looking stars. However, using the steps that follow, you can turn an "ordinary" star into something spectacular. For example, you can use these stars to jazz up text for a more eye-catching look for an advertisement. Another good idea for using spectacular stars is for seals or official-looking approvals. For a more dramatic looking starburst, follow these steps.

1. **Create a star with about 30 points.** Make it look something like the one shown in Figure A.

Continued

Continued

Figure A: Start with a simple star.

2. Choose Effect ⇨ Distort & Transform ⇨ Roughen to display the Roughen dialog box, shown in Figure B.

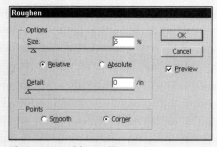

Figure B: Add an effect.

3. In the Roughen dialog box, change the Size to 5% and the Detail to 0. Keeping the Detail at 0 won't let Roughen add any anchor points. Applying the Roughen effect randomly makes some star points longer than others.

4. Choose the Corner radio button (so you don't have curves on your starburst) and click OK. You can also check the Preview check box; each time you check and uncheck it, a new random preview results; clicking OK uses the Roughen preview you see onscreen, as shown in Figure C.

Figure C: Apply your changes.

5. **Add any extras, like a drop shadow, text, and so on.** My end result is shown in Figure D.

Figure D: And there you have it! A work of art!

Working with the Flare Tool

The Flare tool came into being in Version 10 of Illustrator and is more than a welcome addition to Illustrator's amazing tools. Housed with the Rectangle tool, the Flare tool is used to create a flare. Seems simple, but what exactly is a flare? A *flare* is a highlight or reflection from a light source. Figure 5-14 shows a basic flare on a black background.

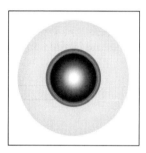

Figure 5-14: The Flare tool creates objects that appear to be reflections from a light source.

Understanding Flare options

With most tools, you have options. To access the Flare tool options, double-click the Flare tool to display the Flare Tool Options dialog box, as shown in Figure 5-15.

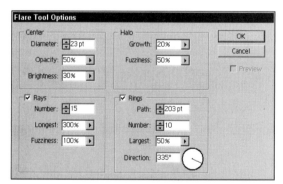

Figure 5-15: The Flare Tool Options dialog box enables you to select the settings for drawing flares.

In the Flare Tool Options dialog box, you can choose from many options, including these:

✦ **Center:** Sets the diameter, opacity, and brightness of the center of the flare.

✦ **Halo:** Sets the percentage of the halo's fade outward and fuzziness. A low fuzziness results in a clean, crisp halo.

✦ **Rays:** Sets the number of rays, longest ray length, and fuzziness of rays. If you don't want rays, enter 0 for the number of rays.

✦ **Rings:** Set the distance of the path between the halo's center and the center of the farthest ring, the number of rings, the size of the largest ring, and the ring direction.

After you create a flare, you can always edit it by selecting the flare first; then with the Flare tool, drag your mouse to change the direction or length. If you expand the object, the flare changes to a blended object (one with smooth transitions between the colors). That way, you can change the number of blend steps or colors if necessary.

The Flare tool is perfect for making a nighttime sky of stars. You can use any backdrop with your graphic illustration. For variation, drag small, medium, and large flares for depth to the stars. Dragging a small amount outward creates a small flare; a little larger drag creates a medium flare; a big drag outward creates a large flare.

Using a flare to add highlight

The best use of flares is to add a highlight to an object. For example, you can drag out a flare on the corner of an object to simulate the light reflecting off of it. You simply click and drag the mouse to place the center of the flare, and then click to set the size of the center and halo and rotate the ray angle.

You can use keyboard commands while drawing to modify the flare:

✦ **Shift key:** Constrains the rays of the flare to 45-degree increments.

✦ **Up arrow:** Adds rings. Each time you press the up arrow as you are drawing the flare, you add rings. Keep pressing for lots of rings.

✦ **Down arrow:** Deletes rings. Each time you press the down arrow as you are drawing the flare, it takes away rings.

✦ **Ctrl (⌘):** Press this key while dragging to hold the center of the flare constant.

Editing a flare

After you have drawn the flare, it is not set in stone. Maybe you don't like how far the flare is going out, or maybe you'd like to see additional rings. You can always go back and edit the flare to remove rings, change the distance, and so on. You have two ways to edit a flare:

✦ **Using the Flare tool:** Select the flare that you want to edit. Using the Flare tool, drag the end point to a new length or in a new direction. An example of this is shown in Figure 5-16.

✦ **Using the Flare Tool Options dialog box:** Select the flare that you want to edit. Double-click the Flare tool to open the Flare Tool Options dialog box. Change the values in the dialog box to edit the flare. Refer to Figure 5-15 to see the Flare Tool Options dialog box.

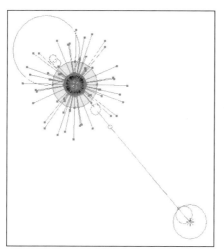

Figure 5-16: Editing a flare with the Flare tool produces a very different appearance.

Filling and Stroking Shapes

One of the most powerful features of Illustrator is its ability to color objects. In Adobe Illustrator, you can color both the fill and the stroke of the paths that you have created. The *fill* is the internal portion of a shape, while the *stroke* is the edge of a shape.

Using fills

The fill of an object is the color inside the shape. If a path is closed (a condition where there are no endpoints and the object's path is connected from end to end), the fill exists only on the inside of the path. If the path is open, or has two endpoints, the fill exists between an imaginary line drawn from endpoint to endpoint and the path itself. Fills in open paths can provide some very interesting results when the path crosses itself or the imaginary line crosses the path. Figure 5-17 shows examples of fills in open and closed paths. For text, the fill is the color of the text. Fills do not appear in Outline mode, only in Preview mode.

Figure 5-17: Open and closed paths result in very different use of fills.

Cross-Reference For more information on fills, see Chapter 10.

Besides white and black, the Fill color options include the following:

✦ **Process Colors:** A process color is made up of four inks: cyan, magenta, yellow, and black, also known as CMYK. Most commercial printers use these four colors to create your illustration.

✦ **Spot Colors:** Spot color is created using inks that have been premixed. A spot color uses its own printing plate rather than the standard CMYK plates.

✦ **Patterns:** A pattern consists of created artwork that is repeated or laid out like tiles to fill a space.

✦ **Gradients:** A gradient blends two or more colors together for a smooth transition between colors.

✦ **Gradient Meshes:** A gradient mesh changes the object by adding blended lines to accommodate the changes in colors.

✦ **None:** This is where the fill is transparent. This option lets you see behind a path to what is underneath it when the stroke of an object is the visible part.

Using strokes

A stroke is defined as the outline or the path of an object. Any object you draw can have a stroke applied to it, including shapes, lines, paths, and even text. The stroke of an object is made up of three parts: color, weight, and attributes. Strokes appear where there are paths or around the edges of type. Like fills, any one path or object may have only one type of stroke on it; the color, weight, and style of the stroke are consistent throughout the length of the path or the entire text object. Individual characters in a text object can have different strokes only if you select them with the Type tool after you apply the Stroke attributes.

Cross-Reference You can learn more about applying strokes to text in Chapter 9.

Setting stroke color

Besides white and black, the Stroke color options are the same as those for fills, except that you cannot apply gradients and gradient meshes to a stroke. To apply a Stroke color, simply select the Stroke color at the bottom of the toolbox, or press the X key and then select the color to use from the Color palette or from the Swatches palette.

Changing stroke weight

The weight of a stroke is how thick it is. On a path, Illustrator centers the stroke on that path, with half the thickness of the stroke on one side of the path and half the thickness on the other side of the path. So a 1-point stroke has ½ point on each side of the path.

You set Stroke weight in the Stroke palette's Weight menu or by typing a value in the Weight text field. Figure 5-18 shows the Stroke palette. You can also use the up and down arrows on the left of the text box to incrementally change the Stroke weight.

Figure 5-18: Choose from a preset Stroke weight in the pop-up menu, or enter your own value in the Weight text box.

Tip

Use mathematical operations in the Stroke weight palette! You can mathematically change the current Stroke weight by adding, subtracting, multiplying, or dividing by any value. Just place the appropriate symbol (+ for add, - for subtract, * for multiply, and / for divide) after the current value, and then the number by which you want to perform the operation. Use this when you are asked to increase the Stroke weight by, say, 2 times the current value.

Strokes have upper and lower limits. You can never create strokes wider than 1,000 points. A stroke with a weight of 0.001 can exist in Illustrator, although the recommendation is that you not choose such a value. Instead, set the stroke to None. Because a stroke of 0.001 changes to match the output device (it appears 1 pixel thick, or as a 1-point stroke onscreen), the potential changes in thickness can drastically change the way an image looks. Be very careful if you choose to venture into this area of Illustrator.

Modifying stroke attributes

The attributes of a stroke consist of several parts, including the cap style, join style, miter limit, and dash pattern. Figure 5-19 shows the Stroke palette where you choose these attributes.

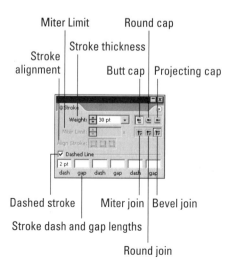

Figure 5-19: Use the options in the Stroke palette to set the stroke attributes.

The stroke attributes include the following options:

✦ **Cap style:** The way the ends of a stroke look. This style can be butt cap, rounded cap, or projected cap. Caps apply only to End Points on open paths. You can choose a Cap style for a closed path (with no End Points), but nothing happens; if the path is cut into an open path, that Cap style goes into effect.

  • **Butt Cap:** Chops the stroke off perpendicularly at the end of the path.

  • **Rounded Cap:** Results in smooth, rounded ends that resemble a half-circle. These caps protrude from the End Point ½ the Stroke weight.

  • **Projected Cap:** Projects from the endpoint ½ the Stroke weight and appear perpendicular to the direction of the path at its End Point.

✦ **Join style:** The join style is the manner in which the corner points on paths appear when you stroke them. You can apply one of three Join types to paths:

  • **Mitered Join:** Causes the outer edges of the stroke to meet at a point. This Join type is the only one affected by the Miter Limit.

  • **Rounded Join:** Rounds off the outside edge of corners.

  • **Beveled Join:** Is cropped off before the angle can reach a corner.

Joins affect only Corner points, including Straight Corner points, Curved Corner points, and Combination Corner points. In all cases, Join types affect only outside corners. Inside corners always appear mitered.

✦ **Miter Limit:** The Miter Limit option controls how far a corner can extend past the edge of the path. This is important for tight corners of paths with large Weights, because the place where the outside edges meet in a corner can be really far away from the original edges of the paths. The number in the Miter Limit controls how many times the width of the stroke the Miter can extend beyond the point. The default is 4, which is good for the majority of applications.

✦ **Align Stroke:** Use this option to control how the stroke aligns with the path. It can be centered over the path, inside the path, or outside the path. This option is new in Illustrator CS2.

✦ **Dash pattern:** Usually, the dash pattern for a stroke is solid, but you can create various dash patterns for different effects. The bottom of the Stroke palette controls if and how dashed strokes should appear. Checking the Dashed Line box allows you to enter different values for up to three dash and gap lengths.

Combining strokes with fills

Many times, paths in Illustrator require both fills and strokes. When you give both a fill and a stroke to a single path, the stroke knocks out the fill at the edges of the path by one-half the weight of the stroke. Figure 5-20 demonstrates this using a dashed stroke to make the point a little more obvious.

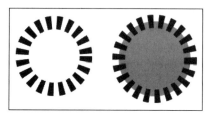

Figure 5-20: A stroke knocks out a fill by one-half the weight of the stroke, as shown on the right circle.

Tip   If knocking out the fill of a path hides part of the pattern that you want to be seen, you can correct this problem by copying the path and pasting it in front, removing the front-most path's stroke. Be warned, though, that the filled path, on top of the stroked path, knocks out the "inner" half of the stroke.

Applying fills and strokes

The toolbox contains two icons — one for fill and one for stroke, which are located in the Paint Style section of the toolbox and shown in Figure 5-21.

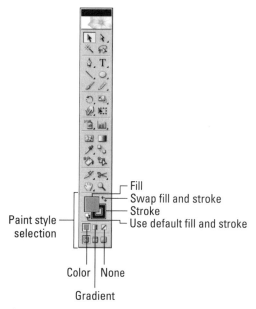

Figure 5-21: The Paint Style section of the toolbox

By default, the fill is set to white and the stroke is set to 1-point black. In fact, at any time you can reset to the default fill and stroke by clicking the Default Fill and Stroke icon in the lower-left corner of the Paint Style section.

You can quickly swap between the colors in the Fill and Stroke icons by clicking the Swap Fill and Stroke icon located in the upper-right of the Paint Style section.

When you first start Illustrator, the Fill icon is in front of the Stroke icon. This means that any changes made in the Color or Swatch palettes affect the fill. When the Fill icon is in front of the Stroke icon, the fill is said to be in *focus*. You can change the focus to the stroke by clicking the Stroke icon. When the focus is on the stroke, changes made in the Color or Swatch palettes affect the stroke, not the fill.

Tip   You can quickly reset the fill and stroke colors to their defaults by pressing the D key. You can quickly change the focus from the Stroke icon to the Fill icon by pressing Shift–X.

The Fill and Stroke icons change in appearance to match the current fill and stroke. For example, if you have a green fill and an orange stroke, the Fill icon is green and the Stroke icon is orange, and you obviously slept through the color-coordination lectures in your design classes. The Fill icon displays a gradient or pattern if that is the current fill.

You use the three icons at the bottom of the Paint Style section to determine the type of fill or stroke:

✦ **Color:** You use this icon when you want to have a solid color or pattern for the fill or stroke. Press the comma key (,) on the keyboard to quickly activate the color icon.

✦ **Gradient:** Use this icon when the fill contains a gradient. You cannot color a stroke with gradients; clicking this icon when the Stroke icon is in focus changes the fill to gradient and changes the focus to fill as well. Press the period key (.) to quickly activate the gradient icon.

✦ **None:** This creates an empty fill or no stroke. Fills of None are entirely transparent. Strokes of None are not colored and have no Stroke weight. Press the forward slash key (/) to quickly activate the None icon.

Oddly enough, you don't need to use the color and gradient icons to determine the type of fill when switching between color and gradient; you can simply click the appropriate swatch in the Swatches palette to change the fill type. No swatch for None is available; to change the fill or stroke to None, you must either click the icon or press the forward slash (/) key. Get used to the forward slash key; it saves you loads of time when you want to change colors for objects. You can quickly combine pressing the X and / keys to change focus and apply None to the stroke or fill.

Creating and Embellishing Graphs and Charts

Graphs are most useful when they show numerical information that normally takes several paragraphs to explain or that you can't easily express in words. You can easily overlook a significant difference between two numbers until you use a graph to represent them. The Graphs feature is one of the most underused features in Illustrator. Most people use programs such as Microsoft Excel to design their graphs. You just wouldn't think Illustrator can do graphs with accuracy, but it can and with more than just the boring graph visuals as well.

One of the most exciting things about graphs in Illustrator is their fluidity. Not only can you create graphs easily, but you can also change them easily. In addition, if the data that you used to create a graph changes, you can enter the new data and have it show up in the graph instantaneously.

Cross-Reference   For more on graph types, see the section "Choosing a Graph type" later in this chapter.

All the graph tools work in a manner similar to that of the shape creation tools. For example, when you select the Graph tool, you can click and drag to set the size of the graph, or you can display the tool's dialog box (in this case, the Graph Size dialog box) by clicking the Artboard without dragging to enter the size information.

The Graph Data box, shown in Figure 5-22, looks like a simple spreadsheet with rows and columns. Using this box, you can enter data to graph. After you enter the data, press the Apply button (which looks like a check mark) and Illustrator updates your graph.

Cross-Reference   For more on working with the shape tools, see "Making Basic Shapes," earlier in this chapter. For the basic steps of using a shape tool, see the section "Drawing rectangles using the Rectangle tool." For more on accessing a tool's dialog box, see the section "Defining properties with the Rectangle dialog box."

Caution   Make sure that the graph is never ungrouped (a graph always has all its elements grouped together, meaning that you can select them with the Selection tool as a whole rather than individual pieces), at least not until you finish making all graph data and graph style changes. If you ungroup the graph, you cannot use any of the graph options to change the ex-graph because Illustrator views it as just a set of paths and text.

Cross-Reference   For more on grouping and ungrouping, see Chapter 8.

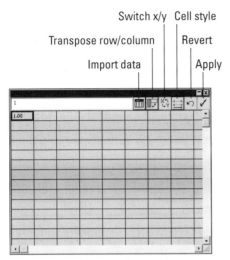

Figure 5-22: The Graph Data box resembles a simple spreadsheet.

Importing Microsoft Excel graph data

You can import graph data in tab-delimited text files such as those exported by Microsoft Excel. Tab-delimited files are text and numbers that are separated by tabs and newlines. To import data from another file, click the Import button, the leftmost icon at the top of the Graph Data box, and then choose the text file containing the information you want to graph.

Caution   The text file that you import cannot contain any punctuation except for decimal points. If you have formatted the text file with thousands separators, the numbers will not import correctly.

Because Illustrator is not really a graphing or spreadsheet program, many of the usual controls for arranging data in such programs are not available, including inserting rows and columns and creating formulas.

The Cut, Copy, and Paste functions work within the Graph Data box, so you can move and duplicate information on a very basic level.

One very useful feature in the Graph Data box is the Transpose row/column button. This function switches the x- and y-axes of the data, thus swapping the row and column layout of everything that you have entered.

Making and editing graphs

Follow the steps below to create a basic graph. The type of graph in this example is a grouped column graph, which you commonly use to compare quantities over time or between different categories.

1. **Select the Graph tool.** The tool is located midway down in the toolbox and looks like a bar graph.

2. **Click and drag to form a rectangular area.** You do this as you would when using the Rectangle tool. The size of the rectangle that you create becomes the size of the graph.

 For more on creating rectangles, see the section "Drawing rectangles using the Rectangle tool" earlier in this chapter.

3. **Release the mouse button.** As soon as you do so, an untitled floating window appears, containing a simple worksheet. This floating window is the Graph Data box; refer to Figure 5-22.

4. **Enter your data into the Graph Data box.** Information that you enter in the worksheet becomes formatted in graph form. The top row in the worksheet area should contain the labels for comparison within the same set. The items in the top row appear as legends outside the graph area. In the leftmost column, you can enter labels that appear at the bottom of the grouped column graph as categories. In the remaining cells, enter the pertinent information as shown in Figure 5-23.

 To get the labels on the legends to read numbers only, you must place quotation marks (" ") around the numbers. If you do not use quotation marks, Illustrator considers the numbers as data, not labels.

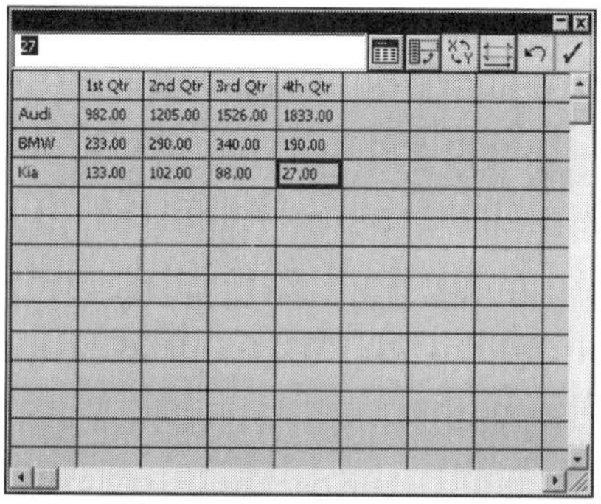

	1st Qtr	2nd Qtr	3rd Qtr	4th Qtr
Audi	982.00	1205.00	1526.00	1833.00
BMW	233.00	290.00	340.00	190.00
Kia	133.00	102.00	98.00	27.00

Figure 5-23: The graph data is now ready to be graphed.

5. **Close the window.** This signals Illustrator to use the data that you entered in the graph. The graph appears, and it should look something like the one in Figure 5-24.

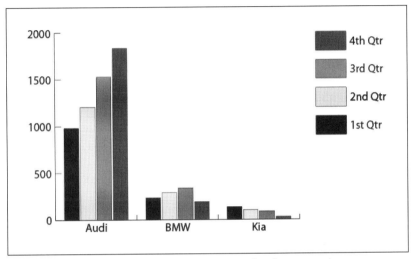

Figure 5-24: The final graph shown in Grouped Column Graph

6. **Change your Graph styles.** After you create the graph, you can change the Graph styles to see which graph shows my information the best.

You can change the numbers and the text in the Graph Data box at any time by selecting the graph and Object ➪ Graph ➪ Data. Illustrator recreates the graph to reflect the changes you make. If you have moved some of the graph objects around, they may revert to their original locations when Illustrator recreates the graph.

Customizing graphs

When a graph is selected, you can use the Object ➪ Graph ➪ Type menu to open the Graph Type dialog box, shown in Figure 5-25. Using this dialog box, you can quickly change between the different graph types while keeping the same data. Choosing a different graph type and clicking OK changes the tool to represent the type of graph you selected. You can choose from nine graph types; the column graph is the default.

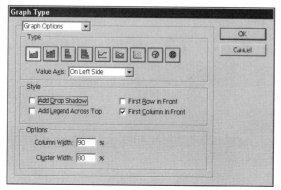

Figure 5-25: The Graph Type dialog box lets you choose the type of graph to use.

The Graph Type dialog box includes several options for controlling the look of the graph, including the following:

✦ **Type:** Separate icon buttons are available for each of the graph types, including Column, Stacked Column, Bar, Stacked Bar, Line, Area, Scatter, Pie, and Radar.

✦ **Value Axis:** The choices — On Left Side, On Right Side, On Both Sides — display the vertical values on the left side (the default), the right side, or both sides.

✦ **Style:** Under these options, you can add a drop shadow or add a legend across the top of the graph. You can also opt to place the first row in front or the first column in front (for when the columns or rows stack closely together).

✦ **Options:** These options are specific to the graph you select. The default graph (grouped column graph) has options to set the column and cluster width in percentage. Each type of graph has its own customization options.

Tip

To make visually striking graphs, use a combination of graph types. Simply use the Group Selection tool to select all the objects that are one legend type and then choose Object ⇨ Graph ⇨ Type, and enter the new graph type for that legend.

In the Graph options pop-up menu in the Graph Type dialog box, you can find other options such as Value Axis and Category Axis. These are the Value Axis and Category Axis options:

✦ **Tick Values:** This Value Axis option sets the minimum, maximum, and divisions and includes a check box to override calculated values.

✦ **Tick Marks:** This Value Axis option sets the length and how many ticks are drawn per division.

✦ **Add Labels:** This Value Axis option sets a prefix and/or a suffix for labels.

✦ **Tick Marks:** This Category Axis option sets the length and how many are drawn per division and includes a check box to draw tick marks between labels.

Choosing a graph type

You can choose from nine different types of graphs in Illustrator. Each type gives a specific kind of information to the reader. Certain graphs are better for comparisons, others for growth, and so on. The following sections describe the graphs, explain how to create them, and tell how you can use them.

Grouped-column graphs

You primarily use grouped-column graphs to show how something changes over time. Often, they are referred to as bar graphs because the columns that make up the graphs resemble bars.

The real strength of a grouped-column graph is that it provides for the direct comparison of different types of statistics in the same graph.

Column width and cluster width are two customizable options for grouped-column graphs and stacked-column graphs. Column width refers to the width of individual columns, with 100% being wide enough to abut other columns in the cluster. Cluster width refers to how much of the available cluster space is taken up by the columns in the cluster. At 80% (the default), 20 percent of the available space is empty, leaving room between clusters.

You can widen columns and clusters to 1000 percent of their size and condense them to 1 percent of the width of the original column or cluster.

Stacked-column graphs

Stacked-column graphs are good graphs for presenting the total of a category and the contributing portions of each category as shown in Figure 5-26.

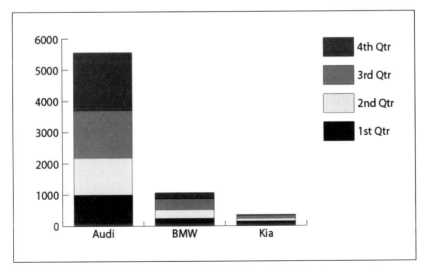

Figure 5-26: This shows the data displayed in a stacked-column graph.

This graph shows the same amount of information as the grouped-column graph, but the information is organized differently. The stacked-column graph is designed to display the total of all the legends, and the grouped-column graph is designed to aid comparison of all individual legends in each category.

Line graphs

Line graphs (also known as line charts) show trends over time. They are especially useful for determining progress and identifying radical changes as shown in Figure 5-27.

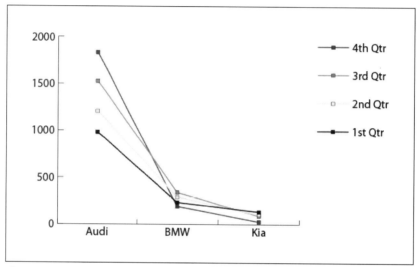

Figure 5-27: Here the graph type has been changed to a line graph.

The Line graph of the Graph Type dialog box (Object ⇨ Graph ⇨ Type) has several unique options:

✦ **Mark Data Points:** This forces data points to appear as squares. If this box is not checked, the data points are visible only as direction changes in lines between the data points.

✦ **Connect Data Points:** If you check this option, Illustrator draws lines between each pair of data points.

✦ **Draw Filled Lines (and the corresponding text box for line width):** This creates a line filled with the data point legend color and outlined with black.

✦ **Edge-to-Edge Lines:** This stretches the lines out to the left and right edges of the graph. Although the result is technically incorrect, you can achieve better visual impact by using this feature.

Area graphs

On first glance, area graphs may appear to be just like filled line graphs. Like line graphs, area graphs show data points that are connected, but area graphs, like the one shown in Figure 5-28, are stacked one on top of the other to show the total area of the legend subject in the graph. In the Area Graphs dialog box, you can add style to the graph by choosing from these options: Add Drop Shadow, Add Legend Across Top, First Row in Front, and First Column in Front.

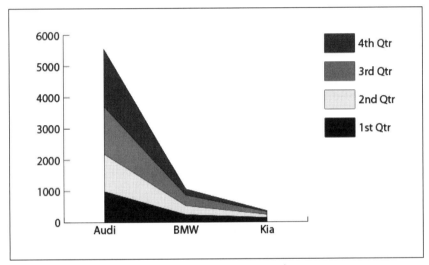

Figure 5-28: The data is shown here in an area graph.

Pie graphs

Pie graphs are great for comparing percentages of the portions of a whole, as shown in Figure 5-29. The higher the percentage for a certain activity, the larger its wedge. Some of the options for Pie Graphs are: Add Drop Shadow, Add Legend Across Top, First Row in Front, First Column in Front, Legend, Sort, and Position.

When you create pie graphs, you can remove the individual wedges from the central pie with the Group Selection tool to achieve an exploding pie effect.

The Legends in Wedges option is the only option in the Graph Type dialog box that is specifically for pie graphs. If you select this option, the name of each wedge centers within that wedge. Illustrator doesn't do a very good job of placing the legend names, many times overlapping neighboring names. In addition, the letters in the legend names are black, which can make reading some of the names difficult or impossible.

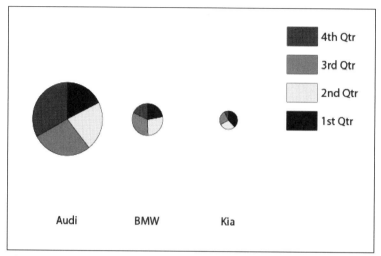

Figure 5-29: The pie graph displays proportionally sized pies and pie wedges.

Scatter graphs and radar graphs

Scatter graphs, which are primarily used for scientific charting purposes, are quite different from all the other types of graphs. Each data point is given a location according to its x-y coordinates instead of by category and label. The points are connected, as are the points in line graphs, but the line created by the data point locations can cross itself and does not go in any specific direction. Scatter graphs have the same customization options as line graphs.

A radar (or web) graph compares values set at a certain point. This type of graph is viewed as a circle graph. Categories are spread around the circle and the data with higher values extend further from the center.

Creating Flowcharts, Diagrams, and Site Maps

Illustrator can create a chart for a company's organization. Using the Rectangle tool and some effects, you can make a clean organization chart.

To create an organization chart, whether it is for a business or simply a family tree, follow these steps:

1. **Draw a rectangle.** See the section "Drawing rectangles with the Rectangle tool" for more on using this tool.

2. **Type a name inside the rectangle.** For more on entering text into graphics, see Chapter 9.

3. **Make copies of your rectangle.** Pressing the Alt (Option) key while dragging with the Selection tool allows you to make copies of the first rectangle. Create as many rectangles as you need; then, using the Type tool, edit the names appropriately.

Figure 5-30 shows an organization chart created using Illustrator.

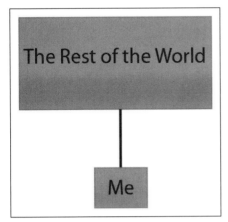

Figure 5-30: You can use Illustrator to create an organization chart that clearly defines your position.

You can use the same principle for the organizational chart to create a sitemap for a Web site. The main difference is that you'll organize the sitemap from left to right rather than top to bottom as in an organizational chart. The point is to show the smoothest way that information flows.

Using Symbols

Since the addition of the Symbol tools in Illustrator 10, the world has never been the same. Small children can now, with ease, make a sensible drawing using the Symbol Sprayer tool. Adults and professionals alike can create amazing designs with very little effort. Illustrator has included a bunch of symbols to use with the Symbol Sprayer tool. If you'd like to, create your own and add it to the Symbol palette.

Spraying with the Symbol Sprayer tool

To start using the Symbol Sprayer tool, follow these steps:

1. **Choose a Symbol from the Symbols palette.** Figure 5-31 shows the Symbols palette, which you access by choosing Window ➪ Symbols or Shift+Ctrl+F11 (Shift+⌘+F11).

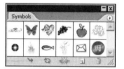

Figure 5-31: The Symbols palette contains various symbols that you can use in your drawings.

2. **Choose the Symbol Sprayer tool.** This tool is located midway down the left column of the toolbox next to the Graph tool. It has the icon that looks like a spray can.

3. **Start spraying away.** The longer you hold the mouse button down, the more symbols are sprayed in that area. Figure 5-32 shows a bunch of butterflies sprayed on a page.

Figure 5-32: The butterfly symbol was sprayed on the Artboard using the Symbol Sprayer tool.

To change the size of the sprayer or any other areas, double-click the Symbol Sprayer tool to access the Symbolism Tools Options dialog box, as shown in Figure 5-33.

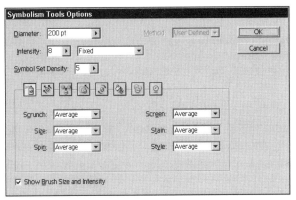

Figure 5-33: Use the Symbolism Tools Options dialog box to modify the way the Symbol Sprayer tool functions.

When you have a group of symbols, you can then alter them to look different. Editing the Symbol tools is done in the Symbolism Tools Options dialog box. These options are:

✦ **Diameter:** This sets the diameter of the sprayer in points.

✦ **Method:** This sets the method to User Defined, Average, or Random. The User Defined method lets you manually scrunch, size, spin, screen, stain, and style the symbols. The Average method scrunches, sizes, spins, screens, stains, and styles the symbols by averaging the spaces between symbols. The Random method randomly scrunches, sizes, spins, screens, stains, and styles the symbols.

✦ **Intensity:** This determines how many instances Illustrator sets when you use the mouse. *Instances* is the term for the number of symbols Illustrator sprays.

✦ **Pressure Pen:** Use this drop-down (pop-up) box if you are using a pressure-sensitive tablet to select the way that the Symbol Sprayer tool responds to different pen motions.

✦ **Symbol Set Density:** This sets the density of the symbol set for the tools. Density determines how close together the symbols are.

✦ **Scrunch, Size, Spin, Screen, Stain, and Style:** The Symbol Sprayer tool icon must be selected in order to access these options. Choose either User Defined or Average. The User Defined method lets you manually scrunch, size, spin, screen, stain, and style the symbols. The Average method scrunches, sizes, spins, screens, stains, and styles the symbols by averaging the spaces between symbols. The Random method randomly scrunches, sizes, spins, screens, stains, and styles the symbols.

✦ **Show Brush Size and Intensity:** Check this to see the actual size and intensity of the brush when using the Symbolism tools.

Making a new symbol

If you don't like the default images available in the Symbol palette, you can create your own. It's as simple as making your own symbol and adding it to the palette. You can either create a new symbol or use an existing symbol as a base.

To modify an existing symbol and add it to the palette, follow these steps:

1. **Select the existing symbol in the Symbol palette.** You can access the Symbol palette by choosing Window ➪ Symbols or Shift+Ctrl+F11 (Shift+⌘+F11).

2. **Choose Place Symbol Instance from the pop-up menu.** You find this option by clicking the right-pointing triangle in a circle on the upper-right side of the Symbol palette. Alternatively, you can simply drag the symbol from the palette to the page, as shown in Figure 5-34.

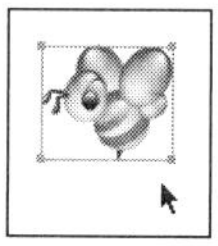

Figure 5-34: Place a symbol instance by dragging the symbol from the palette to the Artboard.

3. **With the symbol selected, choose Object ➪ Expand.** This displays the Expand dialog box so that you can choose the parts of the symbol you want to expand.

4. **Click OK to close the Expand dialog box.** This turns the object back into editable strokes and fills.

5. **Alter the object to your liking.** You may need to use the Object ➪ Ungroup command if you want to alter the existing design.

6. **Turn it back into a symbol by choosing New Symbol from the Symbols palette pop-up menu as shown in Figure 5-35.** Alternatively, you can drag the new symbol over the Symbols palette.

You can also totally create your own new symbol. Simply draw the object you want as a new symbol and drag it onto the Symbols palette (or choose New Symbol from the Symbols palette pop-up menu). After you have created a new symbol, you can use it the same way you use any of the built-in symbols.

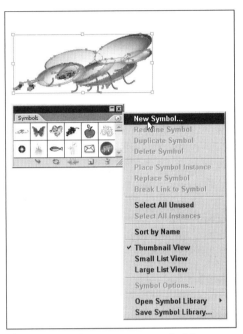

Figure 5-35: Create a new symbol from an existing one and either drag it to the Symbol palette or choose New Symbol from the pop-up menu.

Using the Symbol tool

Illustrator gives you lots of ways to edit your symbols after you've sprayed them on your Artboard. These Symbol tools change the spacing between the objects, their size, color, transparency, style, and direction. Located eight tools down on the left side of the toolbox, you access these tools by simply clicking and dragging to the tool you want.

To apply the effects of these tools, click the tool and then click the Artboard. Generally speaking, the longer you hold down the mouse, the more Illustrator applies the effect. For example, the longer you wait to release the mouse after clicking with the Symbol Scruncher tool, the more your image contracts. If you hold down the Alt (Option) key while clicking one of these tools, it reverses the effect of the tool. For example, pressing the Alt (Option) key while clicking the Symbol Scruncher tool pulls symbols apart. These tools are available:

✦ **Symbol Shifter tool:** Use the Symbol Shifter tool to totally move the symbols in the direction you drag. To change the stacking order with the Symbol Shifter tool, press the Shift key and click the symbol to bring it forward. To send a symbol backward, hold the Alt (Option) key while pressing the Shift key and clicking the symbol.

✦ **Symbol Scruncher tool:** This tool changes the location of your symbols by pulling them together and changing the density distribution of the sprayed symbols.

✦ **Symbol Sizer tool:** This tool increases the size of the symbols.

✦ **Symbol Spinner tool:** You use this tool to move symbols to a new location. Simply, choose the Symbol Spinner tool and drag the symbols in the direction you want them to go.

✦ **Symbol Stainer tool:** The Symbol Stainer tool could possibly be the coolest Symbol tool of all. Use this tool to change the color of the symbols based on the Fill Swatch in the toolbox. Keep changing the color to make the symbols look totally different. The longer you hold the mouse pointer over the symbol, the more color is infused. If you are between symbols, you'll get a mixture of the two colors.

✦ **Symbol Screener tool:** This tool changes the transparency of the symbols. The longer you apply this tool, the more the transparency.

✦ **Symbol Styler tool:** Use the Symbol Styler tool to apply a certain Style to a symbol. Choose the Style from the Styles palette, and apply it to the symbol.

Summary

In this chapter, you learned how to use some of the more advanced and interesting drawing tools that Illustrator offers. These topics were covered:

✦ Even the most basic shapes, such as the rectangle and ellipse, can create some pretty cool artwork.

✦ The Flare tool can quickly add a highlight or create art on its own.

✦ Illustrator has a variety of graph styles from which to choose.

✦ You can always edit a graph's data so long as you don't ungroup the graph.

✦ The Symbol Sprayer tool creates a bunch of objects quickly and efficiently.

✦ Use the other Symbolism tools to alter the objects for variety.

✦ Change any of the Symbol tool options to create just what you want.

✦ You can alter the transparency, size, color, and position of the symbols at any time.

✦   ✦   ✦

Learning How to Select and Edit

In This Chapter

Using the selection tools

Editing paths with the selection tools

Selecting with the Select menu

Editing with anchor points

Splitting paths

Averaging and joining paths

Erasing paths

Reshaping paths

Outlining paths

Using the Pathfinder palette

In Chapter 4, you learned how to create paths, and in Chapter 5, you learned how to create various objects; now you need to know how to change them. This chapter explains how to select what you want to change and how to change it.

After you've created, traced, or even legitimately borrowed someone else's artwork, there's always that period where you look at the artwork and realize that it's not quite right. That's where this chapter comes in. No, I won't do your finishing for you, but I'll show you how to take advantage of Illustrator's many tools to get the best end result, from slight control-handle manipulations to massive scalings and rotations, to dramatic effects created with the Pathfinder palette.

The focus of this chapter is modifying individual paths and the points on those paths by cutting them, combining them, and adjusting them.

Selecting a Path for Editing

The key to editing a path is learning how to select that path. Maybe you don't want the whole path, just a section, or maybe only a point. This section explains the selection tools and how to use them.

Understanding the selection methods

If there is one group of tools in Illustrator that you absolutely must have, it is the set of five selection tools (one of them is a pop-up tool). As in most applications, to alter something (move, scale, and so on), you must first select it. When you draw a new path or paste in Illustrator, the program automatically selects the object you're working on. However, as soon as you draw another path, Illustrator deselects the preceding object and automatically selects the new path. The selection tools let you select paths and perform additional manipulations on them. Illustrator's five selection tools are the Selection tool, the Direct Selection tool, the Group Selection tool, the Magic Wand tool, and the Lasso tool, as shown in Figure 6 1.

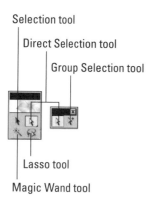

Selection tool

Direct Selection tool

Group Selection tool

Lasso tool

Magic Wand tool

Figure 6-1: The five selection tools are shown here with the tear off for the Direct Selection and Group Selection tools visible.

The following list details what these tools do. You can either click them in the Toolbox to select them (they're all housed together with the Selection tool), or you can press a keyboard shortcut to active them.

✦ **Selection tool:** This tool, which looks like an arrowhead pointing diagonally up, allows you to select an object, a path, or a bunch of paths at one time. You can press V to activate it.

✦ **Direct Selection tool:** You use this tool, which looks like a diagonally pointing white arrow, to select parts of an object or path. It's designed to select items on which you want to perform detailed work. You can press A to activate it.

✦ **Group Selection tool:** As its name suggests, this tool, which looks like a white arrow with a plus sign, allows you to select hierarchical groups of objects. Each click allows you to select a wider range of objects around the core object.

✦ **Magic Wand tool:** You use this tool, which looks like a magician's wand, to select groups of objects whose fills or strokes are similar in color. Because this tool detects drastic changes in color, you shouldn't use it for objects with subtle color differences. You can press Y to activate it.

✦ **Lasso tool:** This tool, which—you guessed—looks like a lasso, lets you draw around the objects that you want to choose. You generally use this tool for unevenly shaped objects. Because this tool detects large differences in contrast, you use this tool if your object contrasts sharply with surrounding objects. You can press Q to activate it.

The specific function of each tool is discussed in greater detail later in the chapter. Before this discussion, however, you need to know that there are different categories of selecting, depending on what you want to select. These categories are Intrapath, Path, Group, IntraGroup, and Selecting All.

Using intrapath selecting

Intrapath selecting means that you select at least one point or segment within a path — usually with the Direct Selection tool — to adjust individual points, segments, and series of points as shown in Figure 6-2. Note that the selected points appear as solid squares and that unselected points are hollow squares. Intrapath selecting also allows you to use most of the functions in the Object menu, such as hiding, locking, or grouping. But these options lock, hide, or group the entire path.

Figure 6-2: This figure shows an example of intrapath selection on paths using the Direct Selection tool.

Note   Although you may select just a portion of the path, many features affect the entire path, not just the selected points. For example, most of the attributes available in the Object menu (including Pathfinder, Masking, and Compound Paths) affect the entire path even when only a point or segment is selected.

Understanding path selecting

Path selecting means that all points and segments on a path are selected. When you click a path using the Group Selection tool or the Selection tool, Illustrator automatically selects the entire path. Drawing a marquee (a dotted rectangle indicating a selection) entirely around a path with the Direct Selection tool also selects the entire path. All the capabilities from Intrapath selecting are available, such as the entire Object menu and the Arrange menu and most of the functions in the Filter menu. After you select a path, the entire path is affected by moving, transforming, cutting, copying, pasting, and deleting. An example of Path selecting is shown in Figure 6-3.

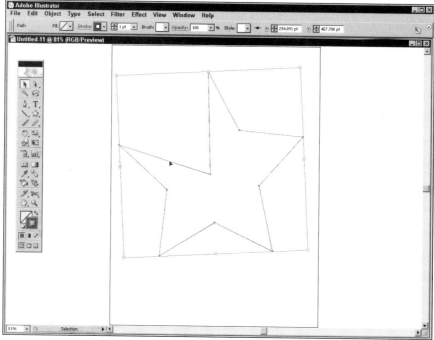

Figure 6-3: Path selection selects the whole path.

Selecting groups

You can select and affect a series of grouped paths as if it were a single object by using Group selecting. All paths in the group are affected in the same way as paths that you select with Path selecting. The Selection tool selects entire grouped paths at once. If you use the Group Selection tool instead, you need a series of clicks to select a group of paths. Figure 6-4 shows what you can accomplish with Group selecting.

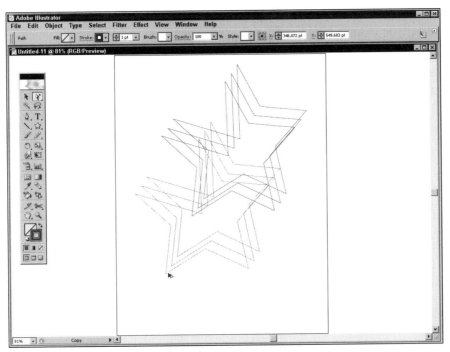

Figure 6-4: Group selection affects the entire group.

You can also select and affect groups of paths within other groups by using intra-group selecting. All paths in the group are affected in the same way as paths that you select with Path selection. Use the Group Selection tool to select a group of paths at once. Each successive click on the same path selects another set of grouped paths that the initial path is within.

Cross-Reference   See Chapter 8 for more information on groups.

Selecting All

To select everything in your document that hasn't been hidden or locked, choose Select ➪ Select All, or press Ctrl+A (⌘+A). This selects all the points and segments on every path that hasn't been locked in the document. You can also select everything in the document by drawing a marquee around all the paths with any selection tool.

Normally, after you select something new, everything that you have previously selected becomes deselected. To continue to select additional points, paths, or segments, you must hold down the Shift key while clicking.

The Shift key normally works as a toggle when used with a selection tool, selecting anything that is not selected and deselecting anything that is currently selected. Each selection tool works with the Shift key a little differently, as described in the following sections.

Tip

To deselect everything that is selected, click a part of the document that is empty (where you can see the Pasteboard or Artboard) without using the Shift key. You also can deselect everything by choosing Select ⇨ Deselect All, or by pressing Shift+Ctrl+A (Shift+⌘+A). Another choice under the Select menu is to Reselect. This option enables you to select the last thing selected.

You can use the selection tools for manually moving selected points, segments, and paths. You use automatic or computer-assisted manipulations when you type specific values in the Transform palette, for example. The next few sections cover the selection tools and their functions.

Deciding which selection tool to use

After the brief overview of the selection tools, you'll need to choose which one works best in which cases. For specific path editing, use the Selection, Direct Selection, or Group selection tools. For selecting areas or colored sections, use the Magic Wand or Lasso tools. The next sections describe the functions of the tools.

Using the Selection tool

The Selection tool selects entire paths or complete groups at one time. You can't select just one point or a few points on a path with the Selection tool. Instead, the entire path on which that point lies is selected (all the anchor points turn black). Drawing a marquee (clicking and dragging as a box forms behind the cursor) around parts of paths or entire paths also selects entire paths.

Illustrator has a bounding box that you can access when you use the Selection tool. This bounding box, shown in Figure 6-5, enables you to move or scale the selected objects by simply dragging the control handles. When you select an object, a bounding box appears around the whole object or around all the objects in a selected group. This bounding box has handles on the four corners as well as handles at the midpoint of each side of the box. These handles enable you to scale the object any way you like. By holding down the Shift key and dragging one of the corner handles, you can easily scale the selected object proportionately. You can also rotate the object using the bounding box. Look for the curved arrow to indicate rotation (move the cursor just outside one of the box corners to display the curved arrow). You can enable or disable the bounding box by choosing View ⇨ Show Bounding Box/Hide Bounding Box or by pressing Shift+Ctrl+B (Shift+⌘+B).

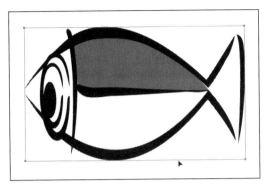

Figure 6-5: The bounding box is always rectangular, and it indicates that an object is selected.

Using the Direct Selection tool

To select individual points, line segments, or a series of specific points within a path, you need to use the Direct Selection tool. This tool is the only tool that enables you to select something less than an entire path. You can also draw a marquee over a portion of a path to select only those points and segments within the area of the marquee. If the marquee surrounds an entire path, the entire path is selected. You can also select Individual points or a series of points on different paths by drawing a marquee around just those points. You can switch to the Direct Selection tool by pressing A on the keyboard. Press A again to choose the Group Selection tool. Another press of the A key takes you back to the Direct Selection tool.

You use the Shift key with the Direct Selection tool to select additional points or segments or to deselect previously selected points. If you press the Shift key, the Selection tool works as a toggle between selecting and deselecting points or segments. You can use the Shift key in this way to add to or subtract from the current selection.

After you select a point, or series of points, you can manipulate those selected points by moving, transforming (via the transformation tools), and applying certain filters to them. You can select and modify individual segments and series of segments in the same way that you transform points.

Using the Group Selection tool

You can find the Group Selection tool as a pop-up tool under the Direct Selection tool. It first selects a path, then the group that the path is in, then the group that the other group with the path is in, and so on.

For the Group Selection tool to work properly, choose the first path or paths by either clicking them or drawing a marquee around them. To select the group that a particular path is in, however, requires you to click one of the initially selected paths. To select the next group also requires you to click; if you drag at any point, only the paths you drag over are selected. For example, suppose that you have a line of bicycles that belong to a group and each individual bicycle is also a group and each wheel on each bicycle is a group and each spoke is a separate path. Using the Group Selection tool, you can click once on a spoke to select it, and if you click it again, you select the wheel group; a third click selects the whole bicycle, and the fourth click the entire line of bicycles.

Caution   Still confused about how the Shift key selects and deselects paths? The Shift key is an odd duck when used with the Group Selection tool. What happens when you click an unselected path with this tool while holding down the Shift key? The path is selected. But what happens when you click a selected path? The process deselects just one path. What makes more sense is if you click again with the Shift key, and it then deselects the entire group. Nope. This isn't what happens. The Shift key works as a toggle on the one path you are clicking — selecting it, deselecting it, and so on.

Dragging a marquee around paths with the Group Selection tool works only for the first series of clicks; dragging another marquee, even over the already-selected paths, just reselects those paths.

Tip   You can use the keyboard to jump around each of the selection tools. No matter what tool you select in the toolbox, pressing Ctrl (⌘) toggles to and enables the Selection tool while you keep the Ctrl (⌘) key held down. You can toggle between the regular Selection tool and the Direct Selection tool by pressing V for the Selection and A for Direct Selection. When you have the Direct Selection tool, press Alt (Option) and you access the Group Selection tool!

If you have selected several paths at once, clicking a selected path selects only the group that the selected path is in. If other selected paths are in different groups, those groups are not selected until you click those paths with the Group Selection tool. However, clicking multiple times on any of the paths in the selected group continues to select "up" in the group that the selected path is part of.

The Group Selection tool is the most useful when dealing with graphs and blends, but it can be used in a number of other situations to greatly enhance your control of what is and is not selected. People who are always ungrouping and regrouping paths can greatly benefit from using the Group Selection tool. In fact, proper use of this tool frees you from ever having to ungroup and regroup objects for workflow reasons.

Tip   You can access the Group Selection tool when the Direct Selection tool is selected by holding down the Alt (Option) key. If the Direct Selection tool is not chosen, then select it by holding down the Ctrl (⌘) key (you may have to press V for the Selection and A for Direct Selection).

The Group Selection tool also selects compound paths. One click selects an individual path within the compound path, and the second click selects the entire compound path.

Using the Magic Wand tool

The Magic Wand tool lets you make a selection based on the same stroke weight, fill color, stroke color, opacity, and blending mode. Choose the Magic Wand tool from the toolbox (it looks like a magic wand), or press Y. Like Photoshop's Magic Wand, you make selections with a click of the tool. To select with the Magic Wand tool, click the object that you want to select. All the objects with the same attributes are selected.

You can set the options on the Magic Wand tool for selecting objects. Access the Magic Wand palette by double-clicking on the Magic Wand tool, or choose Window ➪ Magic Wand. The Magic Wand palette is shown in Figure 6-6.

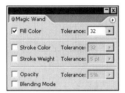

Figure 6-6: The Magic Wand palette enables you to fine-tune the operation of the Magic Wand tool.

You can set the following options in the Magic Wand palette:

✦ **Fill Color:** Check the Fill Color option to make your Magic Wand selection based on the object's fill color.

✦ **Stroke Color:** Use the Stroke Color option to make a Magic Wand selection based on the object's stroke color.

✦ **Stroke Weight:** Choose the Stroke Weight option to base your Magic Wand selection on the object's stroke weight.

✦ **Opacity:** Check the Opacity option to base your Magic Wand selection on the object's opacity.

✦ **Blending Mode:** Use the Blending Mode option to make a Magic Wand selection based on the object's blending mode.

✦ **Tolerance:** Set the tolerance for the Fill Color, Stroke Color, Stroke Weight, and Opacity. You can set the tolerance in pixels between 0 and 255 (for RGB objects) or between 0 and 100 (for CMYK objects). Setting the tolerance low results in a selection very close in the original selected object. A higher tolerance selects more objects.

Using the Lasso tool

The Lasso tool lets you make a free-form selection by dragging the mouse. Access the Lasso tool by choosing it from the toolbox (it looks like a rope) or by pressing Q. The Lasso tool selects paths and anchor points by dragging around the path or line segment.

With both the Magic Wand and Lasso tools, you can add to a selection by holding down the Shift key while clicking with either tool. Subtract from a selection by holding down the Alt (Option) key.

Selecting, moving, and deleting entire paths

Usually, the best way to select a path that is not currently selected is by clicking it with the regular Selection tool, which highlights all the points on the path and enables you to move, transform, or delete that entire path.

To select more than one path, you can use a number of different methods. The most basic method is to hold down the Shift key and click the successive paths with the Selection tool, selecting one more path with each Shift-click. Shift-clicking a selected path with the Selection tool deselects that particular path. Drawing a marquee with the Selection tool selects all paths that at least partially fall into the area drawn by the marquee. When drawing a marquee, be sure to place the cursor in an area where there is nothing. Finding an empty spot may be difficult to do in Preview mode because fills from various paths may cover any white space available. Drawing a marquee with the Selection tool while depressing the Shift key selects nonselected paths and deselects currently selected paths.

To select just a portion of a path, you must use the Direct Selection tool. To select an anchor point or a line segment, simply click it. To select several individual points or paths, click the points or paths that you want to select while holding down the Shift key. You can select a series of points and paths by dragging a marquee across the desired paths.

Individually selected points become solid squares. If these points are smooth, curved-corner, or combination-corner points, control handles appear from the selected anchor point.

The first time you click a straight-line segment, all the anchor points on the path appear as hollow squares, telling you that something on that path is selected. Selected points turn black, and curved line segments have one or more control handles and control-handle lines sticking out from the ending anchor points. Straight-line segments don't do anything when selected. The inventive side of you may think that you can get around this problem by dragging the selected segments to a new location or by copying and pasting them and then undoing. However, this solution doesn't work because of Illustrator's habit of selecting all points on paths when undoing operations on those paths.

If paths are part of either a compound path or a group, all other paths in that compound path or group are also selected.

To move a path, click the path and drag (in one motion) with the Selection tool. To move several paths, select the paths and then click an already-selected path with the regular Selection tool or the Direct Selection tool and drag.

Tip   If you have been selecting multiple paths by using the Shift key, be sure to release the Shift key before clicking and dragging on the selection. If the Shift key is still pressed, the clicked path becomes deselected and no paths move. If this does happen, just Shift-click the paths that were deselected and drag.

To delete an entire path, select it with the Selection tool and press the Backspace (Delete) key. To delete multiple paths, select them and press the Backspace (Delete) key. Remember that line segments exist only when one point is on either side of the segment. Even if the line segment is not selected, if one of its anchor points is deleted, the line segment is also deleted. A path is made up of points, and those points are connected via segments. If the points are gone, the paths disappear along with them. But if you delete all the segments, all the points can still remain.

You can duplicate portions of paths when pressing the Alt (Option) key while releasing the mouse button. Duplicating segments also duplicates the anchor points on either side of that segment.

Using different selection options

Illustrator has several special select functions (they are found under the Select menu). You use the Select functions for selecting paths with common or specific attributes. The Select functions make mundane, repetitive tasks easy to accomplish by doing all the nasty work for you.

To access the Select functions, choose them from the Select menu as shown in Figure 6-7.

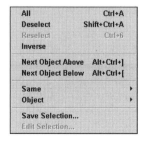

Figure 6-7: The Select functions found in the Select menu enable you to select objects.

Tip

You can redo the last selection type by choosing Reselect from the Select menu or by pressing Ctrl+6 (⌘+6).

You can find the following options under the Select menu:

✦ **All:** Choosing this selects everything in the document except locked objects.

✦ **Deselect:** Choosing this function deselects everything in the document.

✦ **Reselect:** This function reselects the last selection.

✦ **Inverse:** The Select Inverse function is perfect for selecting all paths that aren't selected. You can use this selection function to instantly select paths that are hidden, guides, and other unlocked objects that are hard to select.

✦ **Next Object Above:** Choosing this selects the next object above the selected object in stacking order (stacking order is the same as Layer order). See Chapter 8 for more on stacking order.

✦ **Next Object Below:** This function selects the next object below the selected object in stacking order.

✦ **Same:** Here, you can choose to select the same blending mode, fill and stroke, fill color, opacity, stroke color, stroke weight, style, symbol instance, or threaded block series. Figure 6-8 shows these options. For more on threaded blocks, see Chapter 9.

Figure 6-8: The Same options found under the Select menu

✦ **Object:** In this area, you can choose to select all objects on the same layer, the object's direction handles, brush strokes, clipping masks, stray points, or text objects. Figure 6-9 shows these options.

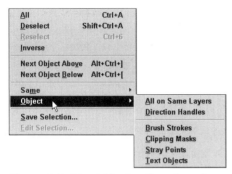

Figure 6-9: The Object options found under the Select menu

✦ **Save Selection:** Use this to save a particular selection.

✦ **Edit Selection:** Use this to edit a saved selection.

Select Inverse

Select Inverse (Select ➪ Inverse) quickly selects all unlocked and unhidden objects that are not currently selected while deselecting those objects that are currently selected. For example, if one object is selected and the document contains 15 other unlocked objects, the 15 objects become selected, and the one object that was selected originally becomes deselected.

Caution   Select Inverse does not cause locked or hidden objects to be selected and does not select guides unless guides are not locked. Objects on layers that are locked or hidden are not selected either.

Select Inverse is useful because selecting a few objects is usually quicker than selecting most objects. After you select the few objects, Select Inverse does all the work of selecting everything else.

When no objects are selected, Select Inverse selects all the objects, just as choosing Select ➪ Select All or pressing Ctrl+A (⌘+A) does. When all objects are selected, Select Inverse deselects all the objects, just as choosing Select ➪ Deselect or pressing Shift+Ctrl+A (Shift+⌘+A) does.

Select Same Blending Mode

Same Blending Mode (Select ➪ Same ➪ Blending Mode) selects objects that have the same Blending mode attributes of the currently selected object. The objects are selected regardless of their other attributes as long as the Blending Modes are the same.

Select Same Fill & Stroke

Same Fill & Stroke (Select ⇨ Same ⇨ Fill & Stroke) selects objects that have almost exactly the same paint style as the paint style of the selected object. The following information must be the same:

✦ The Fill color (as defined in the next section)

✦ The Stroke color

✦ The Stroke weight

Some items in the object's Paint Style that don't matter (that is, they don't prevent Same Paint Style from selecting an object) are any of the Stroke style attributes and the overprinting options.

Tip   If you select more than one object, don't select objects with different paint styles. The best thing to do with Same Paint Style, as with Same Fill Color, is to select only one object.

If you have a spot color selected, the Select functions select all other occurrences of that spot color, regardless of the tint. This can be troublesome when you want to select only a certain tint value of that spot color, not all the tint values.

Select Same Fill Color

Same Fill Color (Select ⇨ Same ⇨ Fill Color) selects objects that have the same Fill color as the currently selected object. This function selects objects regardless of their Stroke color, Stroke weight, or Stroke pattern. If you select objects with different fills, the Same Fill Color function won't work, but you may select two objects that have the same fill.

Same Fill Color considers different tints of spot colors to be the same color. This function works in two ways. First, if you select one object with any tint value of a spot color, Same Fill Color selects all other objects with the same spot color, regardless of the tint. Second, you can select more than one object, no matter what tint each object contains, provided that the selected objects have the same spot color.

Cross-Reference   For more on spot colors, see Chapter 7.

Tip   To be selected with Same Fill Color, process color fills must have the same values as the original. Even single colors, such as yellow, must be the same percentage. The Same Fill Color function considers 100% Yellow and 50% Yellow to be two separate colors.

Same Fill Color also selects objects that are filled with the same gradient, regardless of the angle or the starting or ending point of the gradient. This function does not, however, select objects that have the same pattern fill.

Select Same Opacity

Same Opacity (Select ⇨ Same ⇨ Opacity) selects objects that have the same Opacity value regardless of the other attributes of the object. Choosing Select ⇨ Same ⇨ Opacity selects all the objects with the same opacity value as the currently selected object.

Select Same Stroke Color

Same Stroke Color (Select ⇨ Same ⇨ Stroke Color) selects objects that have the same Stroke color, regardless of the Stroke weight or style and regardless of the type of fill.

The color limitations that are defined in the Select Same Fill Color section, earlier in the chapter, also apply to Same Stroke Color function.

Although you can choose a pattern for a Stroke that makes the Stroke look gray, the Same Stroke Color function does not select other objects that have the same Stroke pattern.

Select Same Stroke weight

Same Stroke Weight (Select ⇨ Same ⇨ Stroke Weight) selects objects that have the same Stroke weight, regardless of the stroke color, the style, or the fill color.

Even if the stroke is a pattern, Illustrator selects other paths that have the same Stroke weight as the patterned stroke when you apply this function.

Don't select more than one Stroke weight if you select more than one object. If you have selected different Stroke weights, Illustrator does not select any paths when you choose Select ⇨ Same ⇨ Stroke Weight. The best thing to do with the Same Stroke Weight function, as with Same Fill Color and Same Paint Style, is to select only one object.

Select Same Style

Same Style (Select ⇨ Same ⇨ Style) selects objects that have the same Style attributes. Choosing Select ⇨ Same ⇨ Style selects all the objects with the same style attributes as the currently selected object.

Select Same Symbol Instance

Same Symbol Instance (Select ⇨ Same ⇨ Symbol Instance) selects objects that have the same Symbol Instances. Choosing Select ⇨ Same ⇨ Symbol Instance selects all the objects with the same Symbol Instance as the currently selected object.

Select Same Link Block Series

Same Link Block Series (Select ⇨ Same ⇨ Link Block Series) selects all the threaded text link blocks with the initial selection. If you select only one block of text, choosing Select ⇨ Same ⇨ Link Block Series selects all the text that is linked with the currently selected text block.

All on Same Layers

Select Objects on the Same Layers (Select ➪ Object ➪ All on Same Layers) selects all objects on the currently selected objects' layers.

Direction Handles

Choosing Select ➪ Object ➪ Direction Handles selects all the direction handles on the currently selected object. This makes for easier editing of the object using its direction handles.

Brush Strokes

Select Object Brush Strokes (Select ➪ Object ➪ Brush Strokes) selects all brush strokes with the same attributes as the currently selected brush stroke.

Clipping Masks

You can select all clipping masks in your file by choosing Select ➪ Object ➪ Clipping Masks. Illustrator selects all unlocked and visible clipping masks, but the objects they mask are not selected. (A *clipping mask* is an object that hides other artwork that is outside the mask; see Chapter 12 for more information.)

Select Masks selects all the objects that are currently being used as masks. The only masks in the document that are not selected are the masks that are locked or hidden and the masks that are on layers that are locked or hidden.

Select Stray Points

Select Stray Points (Select ➪ Object ➪ Stray Points) selects all isolated anchor points in the document. Individual anchor points don't print or preview. You can see them in Preview mode only when they are selected. After you cut portions of line segments, stray points often appear. These individual points often interfere with connecting other segments. You can't use this selection function enough.

You can mistakenly create stray points in various ways:

✦ Clicking once with the Pen tool creates a single anchor point.

✦ Deleting a line segment on a path that has two points by selecting the line segment with the Direct Selection tool and pressing Backspace (Delete) leaves behind the two anchor points.

✦ Using the Scissors tool to cut a path, and while deleting one side or another of the path, not selecting the points turns these points into stray points.

Bringing an Illustrator 4 or older document that has still-grouped rectangles or ellipses into the CS2 version automatically deletes the center point and turns on the Show Center Point option in the Attributes palette (choose Window ➪ Attributes to display the Attributes palette).

Caution Center points of objects are not stray points, and you cannot select them without selecting the object to which they belong. Center points of objects are visible when you choose the Show Center Point option in the Attributes palette. Selecting the center point of an object selects the entire object, and deleting the center point deletes the entire object.

Text Objects

Choose Select ➪ Objects ➪ Text Objects to select all text objects in your document. Illustrator selects all unlocked and unhidden text objects.

Keeping and labeling a selection

After you have gone through any long process of selecting, you might want to save the selection, especially if you use a certain selection repeatedly. After you save a selection, you can make it reusable. To save a selection, create your selection first and then choose Select ➪ Save Selection to display the Save Selection dialog box, shown in Figure 6-10. By choosing Select ➪ Edit Selection, you can change the name of the selection. You access a saved selection by choosing Select ➪ name of selection.

Figure 6-10: The Save Selection dialog box enables you to name and save a selection.

Custom paint style selections

Unfortunately, you cannot do multiple-type selections with any of the special selection functions. You cannot, for example, select at one time all the objects that have the same Stroke color and Fill color, but have different Stroke weights.

The Lock Unselected command, which you activate by pressing Alt+Shift+Ctrl+2 (Option+Shift+⌘+2), is the key to specifying multiple selection criteria (this command does not appear on any of Illustrator's menus). The following steps describe how to perform multiple-type selections:

1. **Select a representative object that has Stroke and Fill colors that you want.**

2. **Choose Select ➪ Same ➪ Fill Color.** Illustrator selects all objects having the same Fill color as the original object, regardless of the objects' Stroke color.

3. **Press Alt+Shift+Ctrl+2 (Option+Shift+⌘+2).** This locks any objects that are not selected. This step is a key step. The only objects that you can modify or select now are the ones that have the same Fill color.

4. **Choose Select ⇨ Deselect, or press Shift+Ctrl+A (Shift+⌘+A), and select the original object.** The original object now has both the Fill color and the Stroke color that you want to select.

5. **Choose Select ⇨ Same ⇨ Stroke Color.** Only objects that have the same Stroke and Fill colors are selected.

6. **Choose Object ⇨ Unlock All, or press Alt+Ctrl+2 (Option+⌘+2), after you are finished** to make the other objects selectable.

Editing Paths in Illustrator

The path-editing tools are the Scissors tool; the Knife tool; and the Add Anchor Point, Delete Anchor Point, and Convert Anchor Point pop-up tools in the Pen tool slot. Clicking and holding down the Pen tool displays the Pen tool, Add Anchor Point, Delete Anchor Point, and Convert Anchor Point. (Although the Slice tool might seem similar to the path-editing tools mentioned in this section, it actually serves a very different purpose as discussed in Chapter 19.)

Dragging out to a path-editing tool replaces the default Pen tool with the newly selected pop-up tool. If you press the Caps Lock key at the same time that you choose a path-editing tool, the tool cursor resembles a cross hair. The cross-hair cursors enable precision positioning of cursors.

This list describes the purpose of each path-editing tool:

✦ **Add Anchor Point tool:** You use this tool to add anchor points to an existing path. If you add an anchor point to a straight segment (one that has no control handles on either end), the anchor point becomes a straight-corner point. If the segment is curved — meaning that you have at least one control handle for that segment — the new anchor point becomes a smooth point.

✦ **Delete Anchor Point tool:** This gets rid of the anchor point on which you click. Illustrator creates a new segment between the anchor points that were on either side of the anchor point you clicked. If the anchor point on which you clicked is an end point, no new segment is drawn; instead, the next or previous anchor point on the path becomes the new end point.

✦ **Scissors tool:** You use this tool to split paths. Clicking with the Scissors tool on a closed path makes that path an open path with the End Points directly overlapping each other where the click occurred. Using the Scissors tool on an open path splits that open path into two separate open paths, each with an end point that overlaps the other open path's end point.

✦ **Knife tool:** This tool slices through path areas. It is the only path-editing tool that doesn't require you to have paths selected; it works on all unlocked paths that fall under the blade. Use this to cut an object into two closed path objects.

✦ **Convert Direction Point tool:** This tool has two functions. The first is to simply change an anchor point from its current type to a straight-corner point by clicking and releasing it. You can also change the current type to Smooth by clicking and dragging on the anchor point. The second function is to move control handles individually by changing smooth points to curved-corner points and by changing combination-corner points and curved-corner points to smooth points. (Straight-corner points don't have any control handles, so using this method can't change them.)

You can add and remove anchor points in two different ways. I mentioned one method in Chapter 4, where I demonstrated how to add anchor points with the drawing tools and remove them simply by selecting them and pressing the Backspace (Delete) key.

The techniques that I cover in this chapter are unlike the methods discussed previously. Instead of adding new points that create an extension to an existing path, you learn how to add points in the middle of existing paths. Instead of deleting points and the line segments connected to them, you learn how to remove points between two anchor points and watch as a new line segment connects those two anchor points.

Editing with anchor points

To add an anchor point to an existing path, select the Add Anchor Point tool and click a line segment of a path. You may not place an anchor point directly on top of another anchor point, but you can get pretty close. Figure 6-11 shows a path before and after several anchor points are added to it.

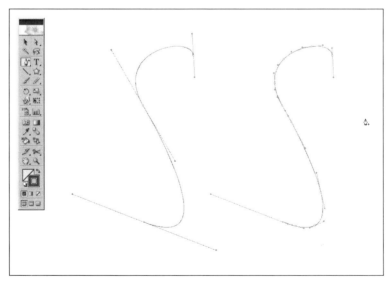

Figure 6-11: Adding anchor points to a path doesn't alter the shape of the path but allows the path to be modified more easily than if the points weren't added.

Tip   I like to select the paths to which I am adding anchor points before I start actually adding the points. This technique ensures that I don't accidentally get the annoying message "Can't Add Anchor Point. Please use the Add Anchor Point tool on a segment of a path." It seems that if there is just one point in the middle of a path, that's where I end up clicking to add the point. After I add one point, the path becomes selected automatically.

Tip   If that annoying message really bugs you, click the Don't show this message again box and instead you'll get a quiet noise alerting you that you can't add the anchor point.

Anchor points added to paths via the Add Anchor Point tool are either smooth points or straight-corner points, depending on the segment where the new anchor point is added. If the segment has two straight-corner points on either side of it, then the new anchor point is a straight-corner point. If one of the anchor points is any type of anchor point other than a straight-corner point, the new anchor point is a smooth point.

The Add Anchor Points function

The Object ➪ Path ➪ Add Anchor Points command adds new anchor points between every pair of existing anchor points it can find. New anchor points are always added halfway between existing anchor points.

Note   Add Anchor Points is related to the Add Anchor Point tool. This function adds anchor points the same way as the tool does, only more efficiently. Points that are added to a smooth segment are automatically smooth points; points added to a straight segment are automatically corner points.

For example, if you have one line segment with an anchor point on each end, Add Anchor Points adds one anchor point to the segment, exactly in the middle of the two anchor points. If you draw a rectangle and apply the Add Anchor Points function, Illustrator adds four new anchor points: one at the top, one at the bottom, one on the left side, and one on the right side.

Figure 6-12 shows an object that has had the Add Anchor Points function applied three times.

Tip   Want to know how many points Illustrator adds to your path when you apply the Add Anchor Points function? Each time you reapply the function, the number of anchor points doubles on a closed path and is one less than doubled on an open path.

Adding anchor points is useful before using the Pucker & Bloat filter and the Tweak filter, and before using any other filter that bases its results on the number and position of anchor points.

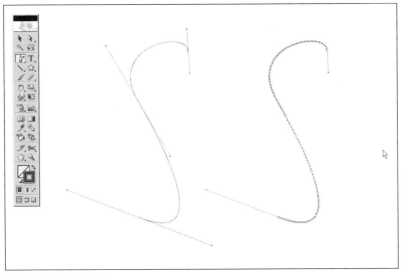

Figure 6-12: Using the Add Anchor points command doubles the number of anchor points, distributing new points evenly between existing points.

Cross-Reference

For more on filters and effects, see Chapter 15.

Tip

If you need to add a large number of anchor points quickly, use the Roughen filter (found under Filter ➪ Distort ➪ Roughen) with a size of 0% and the detail set to how many anchor points you want per inch. When you use Roughen, the anchor points are equally distributed, regardless of where the original anchor points were in the selected path (as opposed to Add Anchor Points, which places new points between existing ones, resulting in "clumping" in detailed areas).

Removing anchor points

Removing anchor points is a little trickier than adding them. Depending on where you remove the anchor point, you may adversely change the flow of the line between the two anchor points on either side of it, as shown in Figure 6-13. If the point removed had any control handles, the removal usually results in a more drastic change than if the anchor point was a straight-corner point. This situation occurs if control handles on the anchor point being removed are at least half the aspect of the curve. A straight-corner point affects only the location of the line, not the shape of its curve.

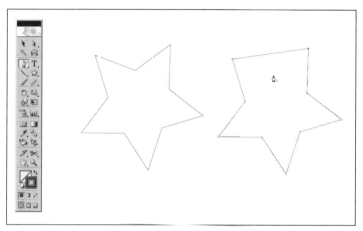

Figure 6-13: Removing an anchor point can drastically alter the shape of the original path.

To remove an anchor point, click an existing anchor point with the Delete Anchor Point tool. Like the Add Anchor Point tool, you can remove points without first selecting the path, but, of course, if the path is not selected, you can't see it or the points that you want to remove. If you miss and don't click an anchor point, you will get a message informing you that to remove an anchor point, you must click one.

After you remove anchor points, you cannot usually just add them back with the Add Anchor Point tool. Considering that the flow of the path changes when you remove a point, adding a point — even the correct type of point — does not give the same result as just undoing the point deletion.

If only two points are on an open path, the anchor point you click is deleted and so is the segment connecting it to the sole remaining anchor point. If there are only two points on a closed path, both line segments from the anchor point you click are deleted along with that point, leaving only one anchor point remaining.

Simplifying paths by removing anchor points

Some artwork can be unnecessarily complicated with many more anchor points than are actually needed. These additional anchor points most often occur with artwork that has been traced by Illustrator's Auto Trace tool or using Clip Art.

One solution to the problem of too many anchor points is to manually remove points via the Delete Anchor Point tool. This takes forever, but with patience you'll get good results. Unfortunately, the tool doesn't care what happens to the paths you're deleting from, and they'll change drastically in shape with each point removal.

An even better solution in most cases is to select the object and choose Object ➪ Path ➪ Simplify as discussed next. Doing this evenly removes anchor points.

Removing anchor points using Simplify

The Object ➪ Path ➪ Simplify command displays the Simplify dialog box that you use to remove excess anchor points. The Simplify dialog box shown in Figure 6-14 has four areas to adjust:

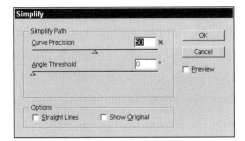

Figure 6-14: The Simplify dialog box helps you remove excess anchor points.

- ✦ **Curve Precision:** Adjust the Curve Precision by dragging the slider. Be sure to check the preview box first to see how much you want to keep the original curve.

- ✦ **Angle Threshold:** This option adjusts the smoothness of the corners.

- ✦ **Straight Lines:** Check this box to create straight lines between anchor points, even if they were curved in the original.

- ✦ **Show Original:** Check this to see the original path behind the path you are simplifying.

Figure 6-15 shows the results of applying Simplify to an illustration with way too many anchor points.

Figure 6-15: The original path (top) had twice as many points as the path after using Simplify (bottom).

Splitting paths

To change a single path into two separate paths that together make up a path equal in length to the original, you must use the Scissors tool. You can also split paths by selecting and deleting anchor points or line segments, although this method shortens the overall length of the two paths.

To split a path with the Scissors tool, click anywhere on a path. Initially, it doesn't seem like much happens. If you clicked in the middle of a line segment, a new anchor point appears. (Actually, two appear, but the second is directly on top of the first, so you see only one.) If you click directly on top of an existing anchor point, nothing at all seems to happen, but Illustrator actually creates another anchor point on top of the one that you clicked.

After clicking with the Scissors tool, you have separated the path into two separate sections, but it appears that there is still only one path because both sections are selected. To see the individual paths, deselect them by pressing Shift+Ctrl+A (Shift+⌘+A) and select one side with the Selection tool. After you split a path, you may move one half independently of the other half, as shown in Figure 6-16.

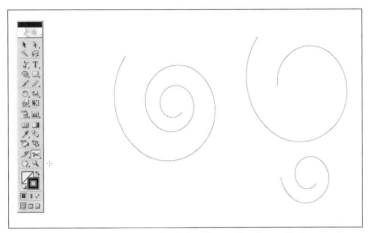

Figure 6-16: The original path (left); the path after splitting and moving the two pieces apart (right)

The anchor points created with the Scissors tool either become smooth points or straight-corner points, depending on the type of anchor point that is next along the path. If the line segment to the next anchor point has a control handle coming out of that anchor point that affects the line segment, the new end point becomes a smooth point. If there is no control handle for the line segment, the end point becomes a straight-corner point.

Caution   You cannot use the Scissors tool on a line's end point—only on segments and anchor points that are not end points.

Sectioning and repeating paths

Illustrator provides several capabilities that allow for multiple types of dividing and duplicating of paths, even paths that aren't selected. This section discusses those different features as well as the tool that makes this possible: the Knife tool.

The Knife tool

The Knife tool is located in the same area as the Scissors tool. The Knife tool divides paths into smaller sections as it slices through them as it goes through two sides of the closed path. Those sections are initially selected, but they're not grouped. Figure 6-17 shows a path before and after it crosses paths with the Knife.

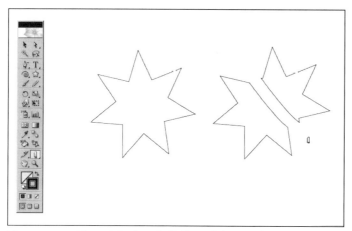

Figure 6-17: The original path (left) and the resulting paths (right) after being dragged apart

Tip   Pressing the Alt (Option) key when using the Knife tool cuts in a straight line rather than a curved one. The Shift key constrains the straight line to 45-degree angles when you also press the Alt (Option) key.

Caution   Remember that the Knife tool works on all paths that are under the existing path, selected or not.

The Slice tool

Another tool that looks like it cuts is the Slice tool. It does cut a path into sections. If you are creating artwork for the Web, this is one of the tools to use. The Slice tool slices the artwork into sections that are independent, each with its own specific information.

Cross-Reference   For more on slicing for the Web and the Slice tool, see Chapter 19.

Reshaping paths

You can reshape paths using the Reshape tool, which is housed with the Scale tool in the toolbox. Using the Reshape tool gets results, but maybe not exact editing. A great use for the Reshape tool is to edit multiple paths at the same time.

To use the Reshape tool, shown in Figure 6-18, on any path, just click where you want to bend the path and drag. To use the Reshape tool on several paths at once, first select the paths with the Direct Selection tool or Lasso tool, and then use the Reshape tool to drag-select the point(s) you want to move. You must select at least one point that is not a straight-corner point on each path. Then drag on a Reshape-selected point; Illustrator moves all the curved corner points as well.

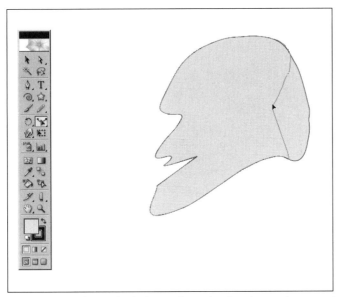

Figure 6-18: The paths being reshaped using the Reshape tool

Cleaning up a path

Clean Up removes three unwanted elements from Illustrator documents: stray points, unpainted objects, and empty text paths. Clean Up works on the entire document, regardless of what is selected. You apply this command by choosing Object ⇨ Path ⇨ Clean Up. The Clean Up dialog box is shown in Figure 6-19.

Figure 6-19: Use the Clean Up dialog box to specify what elements you want to clean up.

Clean Up doesn't work on locked or hidden paths, paths turned into guides, or paths on locked or hidden layers.

These are the Delete options in the Clean Up dialog box:

✦ **Stray Points:** Selects and deletes any little points flying around. These points can cause all sorts of trouble, as a point can have paint attributes but can't print. This option actually deletes the points.

Note Select All Stray Points under the Select menu selects the points, but you have to press the Backspace (Delete) key to delete them.

✦ **Unpainted Objects:** Gets rid of any paths that are Filled and Stroked with None, and that aren't masks (masks always have fills and strokes of None).

✦ **Empty Text Paths:** Finds any text paths with no characters and deletes them.

Note Empty Text Paths is not the same as the old Revert Text Paths from Illustrator 5/5.5, which changed empty text paths back into standard paths.

If you aren't sure whether your document contains these three items, run Clean Up. If none of these items is found, a message box, as shown in Figure 6-20, appears and tells you so.

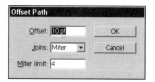

Figure 6-20: This message tells you that there was nothing to clean up in your document.

Offsetting a path

Offset Path, which you access by choosing Object ➪ Path ➪ Offset Path, draws a new path around the outside or inside of an existing path. The distance from the existing path is the distance that you specify in the Offset Path dialog box, which is shown in Figure 6-21. In a sense, you are creating a stroke, outlining it, and uniting it with the original all in one action. You can specify the distance the path is to be offset by entering a value in the Offset box.

Figure 6-21: Use the Offset Path dialog box to specify how to create the new offset path.

A positive number in the Offset Path dialog box creates the new path outside the existing path, and a negative number creates the new path inside the existing path. When the path is closed, figuring out where Illustrator will create the new path is easy. When working with an open path, for example, a vertical line, the outside is the left side and the inside is the right side of the path.

The Joins option enables you to select from different types of joins at the corners of the new path. The choices are Miter, Round, and Bevel, and the result is the same effect that you get if you choose those options as the stroke style for a stroke.

The Miter Limit affects the miter size only when you select the Miter option from the Joins drop-down list (pop-up menu). However, the option is available when you select round and bevel joins. Just ignore the Miter Limit when you are using round or bevel joins. (You cannot use a value that is less than 1.)

Often, when you are offsetting a path, the new, resulting path overlaps itself. This creates small, undesirable bumps in a path. If the bumps are within a closed-path area, select the new path and choose Unite from the Pathfinder palette. If the bumps are outside the closed-path area, choose Divide from the Pathfinder palette and then select and delete each of the bumps.

Tip

If you are thinking of using the Scale tool rather than Offset Path, you should know that the Scale tool does something totally different from Offset Path. Offset Path offsets lines around the original path equally. The Scale tool enlarges or reduces the path but does not add lines. Unless you are using a perfect square or circle, stick to Offset Path. That way, you get an even placement of the new path accurately around or inside the selected path.

Outlining a path

Outline Path creates a path around an existing path's stroke. The width of the new path is directly related to the width of the stroke.

I use Outline Path for two reasons. The first and most obvious reason is to fill a stroke with a gradient so you can view a pattern inside a stroke. The second reason is that when you transform an outlined stroke, the effect is often different from the effect that results from transforming a stroked path. Scaling an outlined stroke changes the width of the stroke in the direction of the scale. The same is true when using the Free Distort filter, which also changes the width of the stroke in the direction of the scale. This sometimes results in a nonuniform stroke. Figure 6-22 shows the difference between transforming/distorting a Stroked path and an Outlined Stroke. Both copies were scaled vertically to more clearly demonstrate the different behaviors. With the stroked path, the transformation resulted in the stroke expanding far beyond the fill, while with the outlined stroke the two remained in sync.

Consider these options for outlining a path:

✦ The End and Join attributes of the stroke's style determine how the ends and joins of the resulting stroke look.

✦ Outline Path creates problems for tight corners. It causes overlaps that are similar to those generated by Offset Path.

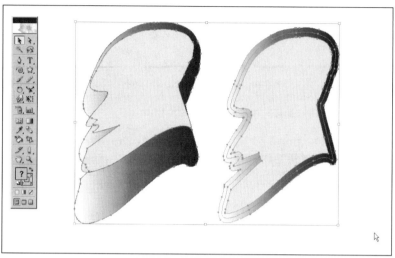

Figure 6-22: The original stroked path is on the left. The path on the right was outlined via Outline Path.

Note Using a Dash pattern on the stroke and using Outline Path changes the stroke back to a solid line and then outlines it.

Looking under the Effect menu, you'll find a Path effect with the following options: Offset Path, Outline Object, and Outline Stroke. These are the same as what is found under the Object ➪ Path menu. However, under Effect, you can always go back and edit the options. Choosing the Path functions from under the Object menu has a more permanent result.

Cross-Reference For more on the Effects menu, see Chapter 15.

Averaging and joining

Averaging points is the process in which Illustrator determines the location of the points and figures out where the center of all the points is on a mean basis. Joining is the process in which either a line segment is drawn between two end points, or two end points are merged into a single anchor point.

Averaging and joining are done together when two end points need to change location to be one on top of the other and then merged into one point. You can perform these steps one at a time, or you can have Illustrator do both steps automatically with the Object ➪ Path ➪ Average command or by pressing Alt+Ctrl+J (Option+⌘+J).

Averaging points

To line up a series of points either horizontally or vertically, use the Average command. The Average command also works to place selected points one on top of the other. Figure 6-23 shows the different types of averaging: horizontal and vertical.

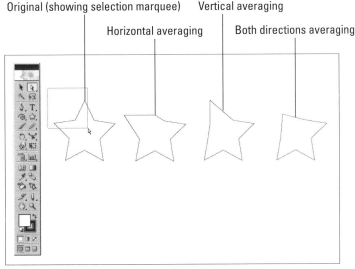

Figure 6-23: Different types of averaging produce quite different results.

To average points horizontally, select the points to be averaged with the Direct Selection tool and choose Object ➪ Path ➪ Average or press Alt+Ctrl+J (Option+⌘+J). The Average dialog box, shown in Figure 6-24, appears and asks which type of averaging you want to do. In this case, choose Horizontal, which moves selected points only up and down.

Caution   Be sure to select the points to be averaged with the Direct Selection tool. If you select a path with either the Group Selection tool or the regular Selection tool, every point in the path is averaged! This mistake can do quite a bit of damage when averaging both horizontally and vertically.

To average points vertically, choose the Vertical option in the Average dialog box. To average points both vertically and horizontally, choose Both. The Both option places all selected points on top of each other.

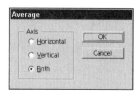

Figure 6-24: The Average dialog box lets you select Horizontal, Vertical, or Both.

When averaging points, Illustrator uses the mean method to determine the center. No, Illustrator isn't nasty to the points that it averages; rather, Illustrator adds together the coordinates of the points and then divides by the number of points. This provides the mean location of the center of the points.

If you want to average entire paths, see the section on Align and Distribution in Chapter 8.

Joining points

Joining is a tricky area to define. Illustrator's Join feature does two entirely different things. It joins two end points at different locations with a line segment, and it also combines two anchor points into one when they are placed one on top of the other.

To join two end points with a line segment, select just two end points in different locations (not on top of each other) with the Direct Selection tool and choose Object ➪ Path ➪ Join or press Ctrl+J (⌘+J). Illustrator forms a line segment between the two points, resulting in a closed path, as shown in Figure 6-25.

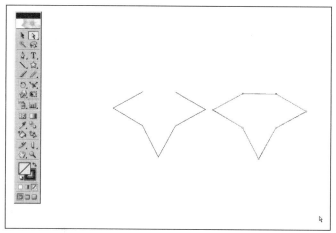

Figure 6-25: Joining two end points with a line segment using the Object ➪ Path ➪ Join command

To combine two end points into a single anchor point, select the two points that are directly one over the other and choose Object ⇨ Path ⇨ Join or press Ctrl+J (⌘+J). Not only can you join two separate paths, but you can also join together the end points on the same open path (overlapping end points) to create a closed path in the same way that two end points from different paths are joined.

To make sure that end points are overlapping, drag one end point to the other with a selection tool. When the two points are close enough, the arrowhead cursor (normally black) becomes hollow. Release the mouse button when the arrowhead is hollow, and Illustrator places the two points one directly above the other.

Another way to ensure that the end points are overlapping is to select them and choose Object ⇨ Path ⇨ Average or press Alt+Ctrl+J (Option+⌘+J). Next, select the Both option in the Average dialog box.

Caution When creating an anchor point out of two overlapping end points, make sure that the two points are precisely overlapping. If they are even the smallest distance apart, a line segment is drawn between the two points instead of transforming the two end points into a single anchor point.

Joining has these limitations:

✦ Joins may not take place when one path is part of a different group than the other path. If the two paths are in the same base group (that is, not in any other groups before being grouped to the other path, even grouped by themselves), the end points can be joined.

✦ If one path is grouped to another object and the other object has not been previously grouped to the path, the end points will not join.

✦ The end points on text paths cannot be joined.

✦ The end points of guides cannot be joined.

If all the points in an open path are selected (as if the path is selected with the regular Selection tool), then choosing Object ⇨ Path ⇨ Join or pressing Ctrl+J (⌘+J) automatically joins the end points. If the two end points are located one directly over the other, the Join dialog box appears, asking whether the new anchor point should be a smooth point or a corner point.

Joining is also useful for determining the location of end points when the end points are overlapping. Select the entire path, choose Object ⇨ Path ⇨ Join or press Ctrl+J (⌘+J), and choose smooth point. These steps usually alter one of the two segments on either side of the new anchor point. Undo the join, and you know the location of the overlapping end points.

Tip   If you are having trouble joining two open paths, make sure that they are not grouped. You cannot join grouped paths.

Converting Anchor Points

This section deals with the Convert Anchor Point tool. The Convert Anchor Point tool converts anchor points only by adjusting control handles. The Convert Anchor Point tool works differently with each type of anchor point.

Cross-Reference   See Chapter 4 for detailed definitions of the four different types of anchor points and how they're drawn with the Pen tool.

You can use the Convert Anchor Point tool either on extended control handles or on anchor points. When there are two control handles on an anchor point, clicking either control handle with the Convert Anchor Point tool does two things:

✦ It "breaks" the linked control handles so that when the angle of one is changed, the other is not changed as well. As a result, the two handles can be dragged to different angles.

✦ It makes them independent so that the control handle's length from the anchor point and the angle can be altered individually.

Converting Smooth Points

Smooth points can be changed into the other three types of anchor points by using both the Direct Selection tool and the Convert Anchor Point tool as follows:

✦ To convert smooth points into combination-corner points, use the Direct Selection tool or the Convert Anchor Point tool to drag one control handle into the anchor point.

✦ To convert smooth points into curved-corner points, use the Convert Anchor Point tool to drag one of the control handles. After being dragged with the Convert Anchor Point tool, the two control handles become independent of each other (the movement of one will not affect the other).

The following steps show you how you can use the Direct Selection tool and the Convert Anchor Point tool to change shapes — in this case, from a circle to a rhombus or diamond shape:

1. **Draw a circle with the Ellipse tool.** Remember to keep the Shift key pressed so you end up with a perfect circle.

2. **Select the Convert Anchor Point tool.**

3. **Click each of the anchor points and release.** Doing this converts the Smooth anchor points to Corner anchor points. The rhombus (diamond shape) should look like the illustration in Figure 6-26.

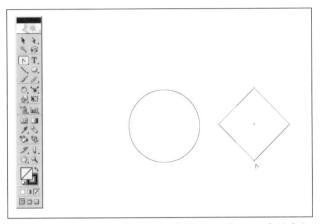

Figure 6-26: Convert the circle (left) to a diamond (right) by clicking on each anchor point with the Convert Anchor Point tool.

Converting straight-corner points

You can change straight-corner points into one of the other three types of anchor points by using both the Convert Anchor Point tool and the Direct Selection tool as follows:

✦ To convert straight-corner points into smooth points, use the Convert Anchor Point tool to click and drag on the anchor point. As you drag, linked control handles appear on both sides of the anchor point.

✦ To convert straight-corner points into combination-corner points, use the Convert Anchor Point tool to click and drag on the anchor point. As you drag, linked control handles appear on both sides of the anchor point. Select one of the control handles with the Convert Anchor Point tool or the Direct Selection tool and drag it toward the anchor point until it disappears.

✦ To convert straight-corner points into curved-corner points, use the Convert Anchor Point tool to click and drag on the anchor point. As you drag, linked control handles appear on both sides of the anchor point. Then use the Convert Anchor Point tool to drag one of the control handles. After being dragged with the Convert Anchor Point tool, the two control handles become independent of each other.

Converting combination-corner points

You can change combination-corner points into one of the other three types of anchor points by using both the Convert Direction Point tool and the Direct Selection tool as follows:

✦ To convert combination-corner points into smooth points, use the Convert Anchor Point tool to click and drag on the anchor point. As you drag, linked control handles appear on both sides of the anchor point.

✦ To convert combination-corner points into straight-corner points, use the Convert Anchor Point tool to click once on the anchor point. The control handle disappears.

✦ To convert combination-corner points into curved-corner points, use the Convert Anchor Point tool to click and drag the anchor point. As you drag, linked control handles appear on both sides of the anchor point. Then use the Convert Anchor Point tool to drag one of the control handles. After being dragged with the Convert Anchor Point tool, the two control handles become independent of each other.

The following steps are another example of how you can change shapes using the Direct Selection tool and the Convert Anchor Point tool — this time, changing a circle into a heart:

1. **Draw a circle with the Ellipse tool.** Remember to keep the Shift key pressed so that you end up with a perfect circle.

2. **Click the lowest point on the circle with the Direct Selection tool.**

3. **Click the right control handle of that anchor point, and drag it up using your eye to judge the heart shape.**

4. **With the Convert Anchor Point tool, click the left control handle of that point and drag it up.**

5. **Click the anchor point at the top of the circle, and drag it down a little using the Direct Selection tool.**

6. **With the Direct Selection tool, click the left control handle of the topmost point and drag it up.**

7. **Click the right control handle with the Convert Anchor Point tool, and drag it up.**

8. **Adjust the anchor points and control handles until the circle looks like a heart, as shown in Figure 6-27.**

Figure 6-27: Convert a circle into a heart using the Direct Selection tool and the Convert Anchor Point tool.

Converting curved-corner points

You can change curved-corner points into one of the other three types of anchor points by using both the Convert Anchor Point tool and the Direct Selection tool as follows:

✦ To convert curved-corner points into smooth points, use the Convert Anchor Point tool to click and drag on the anchor point. You can then use the Direct Selection tool to adjust the angle of both control handles at once.

✦ To convert curved-corner points into straight-corner points, use the convert anchor point tool to click once on the anchor point. The control handles disappear.

✦ To convert curved-corner points into combination-corner points, use the Direct Selection tool to drag one control handle into the anchor point.

Using Illustrator's Pathfinder Functions

The most powerful path functions in Illustrator are in the Pathfinder palette. They do things that would take hours to do using Illustrator's traditional tools and methods. The only drawback to the Pathfinder palette is that there are so many options that it's pretty hard to figure out which one to use for which job. Figure 6-28 shows the Pathfinder palette.

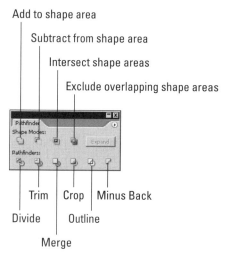

Add to shape area

Subtract from shape area

Intersect shape areas

Exclude overlapping shape areas

Trim | Crop | Minus Back

Divide | Outline

Merge

Figure 6-28: The Pathfinder palette enables you to quickly edit paths.

The Pathfinder options take over most of the mundane tasks of path editing that could otherwise take hours. Everything that the Pathfinder options do can be done manually with other Illustrator tools, but the Pathfinder options do them much more quickly. Common activities such as joining two paths together correctly and breaking a path into two pieces are done in a snap.

The Pathfinder options change the way that two or more paths interact. The cute little symbols on the Pathfinder options are supposed to clue you in to what each option can do, but the pictures are small and most don't accurately depict exactly how each option works.

If you have the Show Tool tips box checked, the name of each of the Pathfinder options pops up when you hold your cursor over its option symbol. However, these names can be a little confusing. The names were undoubtedly chosen to signify what each of the Pathfinder options can do, but most of them can't be defined easily with just one word.

Setting the Pathfinder options

To access the Pathfinder options, choose Pathfinder Options in the pop-up menu of the Pathfinder palette. This displays the Pathfinder Options dialog box, shown in Figure 6-29, which enables you to customize the way that the Pathfinders work.

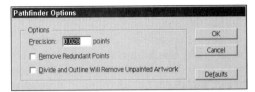

Figure 6-29: The Pathfinder Options dialog box enables you to configure the Pathfinders.

These are options in the Pathfinder Options dialog box:

✦ **Precision:** The value in the Precision text field tells Illustrator how precisely Pathfinders should operate. The more precisely they operate, the better and more accurate the results are, but the longer the processing time is. This speed differential is most apparent when you apply Pathfinders — especially Trap (found in the of Pathfinder palette's pop-up menu) — to very complex objects. The default value is 0.028 points, which seems to be accurate enough for most work.

✦ **Remove Redundant Points:** This option gets rid of overlapping points that are side by side on the same path. I can't think of why you would want over-lapping points, so keeping this option checked is a good idea.

✦ **Divide and Outline Will Remove Unpainted Artwork:** If you check this option, Illustrator automatically deletes unpainted artwork. This relieves you from having to remove all those paths that Divide always seems to produce that are filled and stroked with None.

Usually, the defaults in the Pathfinder Options dialog box are the best options for most situations, except for Remove Redundant Points, which is off by default. If you change the options, be aware that the Pathfinder Options dialog box resets to the defaults when you quit Illustrator.

Adding to a shape

The Add to shape area mode unites the selected objects if they are overlapping. A new path outlines all the previously selected objects. There are no paths where the original paths intersected. The new object takes the Paint Style attributes of the top-most object. If any objects are within other objects, those objects are assimilated. If there are "holes" in the object, the holes become reversed out of a compound path.

You'll find that Add to shape area is one Pathfinder option that you'll use often. Play with combining various paths for a while so you know what to expect, and you will develop a sense of when using Add to shape area is a better option than doing the same tasks manually.

Add to shape area combines two or more paths into one path, as described in these steps:

1. **Select the objects to which you want apply the Add to shape area mode.** In the example in Figure 6-30, the artwork is a rectangle with two ellipses resembling a can shape. Pathfinders work only with paths. You have to convert types into outlined paths, and you cannot use EPS or Encapsulated PostScript images.

2. **Choose Add to shape area from the Pathfinder palette.** Any overlapping artwork is united into one path. The color of the united path is always the color of the path that was the topmost selected path before you used Add to shape area.

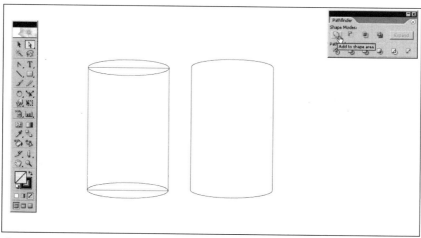

Figure 6-30: The objects on the left before using Add to shape area and on the right after using Add to shape area

When you use Add to shape area, paths that don't overlap but are outside of other paths become part of a group. Illustrator draws paths between end points of open paths before it unites those paths with other paths. Compound paths remain compound paths.

Subtracting from a shape

The Subtract from shape area mode does the opposite of Add to shape area. The topmost objects are subtracted from the bottom object. Figure 6-31 shows an object before (left) and after (right) using Subtract from shape area. The object retains the style (fill and stroke attributes) of the bottommost object.

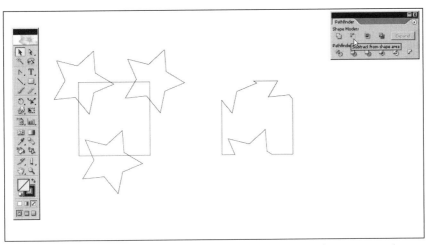

Figure 6-31: The objects on left before using Subtract from shape area and on the right after using Subtract from shape area

Intersecting and excluding shapes

Intersect and Exclude Shape Pathfinders are opposites. Using Intersect results in the opposite of what you get from using Exclude, and vice versa.

The Intersect shape areas mode creates only the intersection of the selected paths. Any part of a selected path that does not intersect is deleted. If two paths are intersecting and selected, only the area that is common to both paths remains. If three or more paths are selected, all must intersect in a common area for the function to produce results. If the paths selected do not intersect at all, they all get deleted. If one selected path is contained within all the other selected paths, the result is that contained path. The resulting path has the Paint Style attributes of the topmost path.

After you select two or more paths and click the Intersect button on the Pathfinder palette, only the overlapping portions of the paths remain. If you select three paths, the only area that remains is the area where all three selected paths overlap each other.

The Exclude overlapping shape areas mode is pretty much the opposite of Intersect. Choosing Exclude deletes the intersecting areas, grouping together the outside pieces. If you are having trouble making a compound path, use Exclude; any path within another path reverses, creating a compound path automatically.

If you use Exclude, only the areas that don't overlap remain. The color of the intersected or excluded path is always the color of the path that was the topmost selected path before you used Intersect or Exclude.

Tip

If you press and hold the Alt (Option) key when clicking any of the Pathfinder Shape Modes, the objects automatically expand.

Using the Expand button

The Expand button in the Pathfinder palette is used to ungroup the original objects to which you applied a Pathfinder function. The resulting paths form a new group.

Dividing paths

The Divide button in the Pathfinder palette checks to see where the selected paths overlap and then creates new paths at all intersections where the paths crossed, creating new paths if necessary. Fills and strokes are kept. In the process, the Divide command also groups the pieces of the fill together. Divide also keeps selections their original colors; the illustration appears to look the same even if it previously had strokes. To keep the strokes, copy before using Divide, and then choose Edit ➪ Paste In Back.

Simply put, Divide divides overlaying paths into individual closed paths, as described in the following steps and illustrated in Figure 6-32:

1. **Create the artwork that you want to divide into sections.**

2. **Create a path or paths where you want to divide the object.**

3. **Select all paths, both artwork and dividing paths, and choose the Divide option in the Pathfinder palette.** Use the Direct Selection tool to move them, because the Divide command groups them automatically.

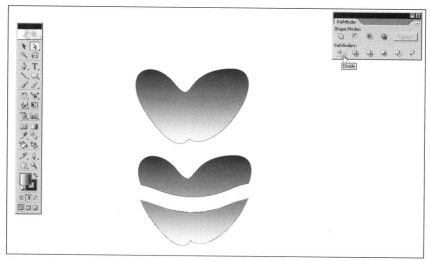

Figure 6-32: The object (above) before and (below) after separating the divided sections

Trimming paths

The Trim button removes sections of paths that are overlapped by other paths. Frontmost paths are the only ones that remain. This Pathfinder is very useful for cleaning up complex overlapping illustrations, although it can take a bit of time to complete. Figure 6-33 shows overlapping outlined type before (top) and after (bottom) applying Trim. You can best see the overlapping objects removed in Outline mode.

Figure 6-33: In Outline mode, you can best see how trim fixed the overlapping outlined text.

Tip   By trimming your blends, you can remove overlapping paths. This allows you to use Soft Mix and Hard Mix (found under Effects ➪ Pathfinder) with a blend. I trim blends to use them for shadowing or to apply highlights to objects.

Merging

The Merge button combines overlapping paths that have the identical fill applied to them. Even if the fill is different by as little as 1 percent, Merge creates two separate paths. This Pathfinder is much more efficient than Add to shape area for making areas of the same color into one object.

The following steps describe how to use Merge:

1. **Create the artwork for which you want to use Merge.**

2. **Select the artwork you want to merge.**

3. **Choose the Merge option in the Pathfinder palette.** Illustrator removes all overlapped paths, leaving only the paths that had nothing in front of them. All adjacent areas that contained identical colors are united.

Cropping paths

The Crop button works in much the same way as masks work, except that anything outside the cropped area is deleted, not just masked. Figure 6-34 shows the original objects on top and on the bottom, after using Crop. The topmost object acts as the mask on the object(s) underneath.

Follow these steps to use the Crop command:

1. **Bring the object that you want to use as a cropper to the front.**

2. **Select all the paths you want to crop with it and the cropper itself.**

3. **Choose the Crop option in the Pathfinder palette.** Illustrator deletes every-thing outside the cropper. The objects that were cropped are grouped together in the shape of the crop.

Figure 6-34: The object (top) before crop and after (below)

Unlike masks, there is no outside shape after a crop is made. The cropper used to crop the image is deleted when Crop is chosen.

 Cross-Reference   For more on masks, see Chapter 12.

Outlining paths

The Outline button creates small sections of paths wherever paths cross and color the strokes, using the fill of the path they were part of and giving the strokes a weight of 1 point. Outline is useful for spot trapping because it automatically creates the sections needed that have to be chosen for overprinting, although often the colors are incorrect. (*Trapping* is a process whereby colors are printed slightly beyond the edge of an object so that there won't be white gaps between adjacent colored areas when the document is printed on a commercial printing press.)

Outline creates smaller path pieces than Divide does; but, instead of making each section a closed path, each path maintains its individuality, becoming separate from adjoining paths. The result of outlining is several small stroke pieces. Instead of maintaining the Fill color of each piece, each piece is filled with None and stroked with the Fill color.

Using Minus Back

Each of the Pathfinders works on the principle that one path, either the frontmost or backmost path selected, will have all the other overlapping paths subtracted from it.

The Minus Back button subtracts all the selected paths behind the frontmost selected path from the frontmost selected path. With two objects, it is also quite simple. The object in the back is deleted, and the area where the object in back was placed is also deleted. Understanding Minus Back gets a little more confusing when you have more objects, but it does the same thing, all at once to all the selected paths. If the area to be subtracted is totally within the path it will subtract from, then a compound path results.

When you apply Minus Back, the color of the remaining path is the color of the frontmost path before you applied it.

Trapping

The Trap function in the Pathfinder palette is found under the pop-up menu. Trap takes some of the drudgery away from trapping. Traps solve alignment problems when color separations are produced. The most common problem that occurs from misalignment is the appearance of white space between different colors.

 The only limitation for Trap is that it doesn't work well on extremely complex illustrations because of time and memory constraints. The other concern with Trap is that it leaves your illustrations "pseudo-uneditable" because it creates extra paths around your original trap and makes it really difficult to edit. It doesn't affect the existing paths, but if you do much editing, you'll have to delete the trap paths and retrap.

Cross-Reference   For more on trapping, see Chapter 18.

Tip   Prior to trapping, I create a layer called Traps. Immediately after trapping, I move all the trap objects to the Traps layer. This keeps the traps together, in case I need to redo, adjust, or delete them.

Trap automatically creates a trap between abutting shapes of different colors. You set the amount (width) of trap in a dialog box that appears after choosing Trap.

To create a trap using the Trap option in the Pathfinder palette, follow these steps:

1. **Create and select the artwork that you want to trap.** If the artwork is overly complex, you may want to select only a small portion of the artwork before you continue.

2. **Choose the Trap option in the Pathfinder palette.**

3. **In the Trap dialog box, enter the width of the trap in the Thickness text field (the default is 0.25 points). Enter the amount that you want the height of the trap to differ from the width, which allows for different paper-stretching errors.** For example, entering the maximum, 400%, widens the horizontal thickness of the stroke to four times the amount set in the Thickness text field and leaves the vertical thickness the same.

4. **Enter a Tint reduction value that specifies how much the lighter of the two colors should be tinted on that area.** Check the Traps with Process Color check box to convert spot colors to process equivalents only in the resulting trap path that is generated from Trap.

5. **Check the Reverse Traps check box to convert any traps along the object that are filled with 100% Black but no other colors to be less black and more of the lighter abutting color.**

6. **Click OK.**

All traps generated by Trap result in filled paths, not strokes, and are automatically set to overprint in the Attributes palette.

Summary

Selecting the precise objects that you want to edit in an Illustrator document can be a little confusing until you learn the proper techniques. In this chapter, you learned how to select and edit. Specifically, this chapter covered the following topics:

✦ The first step in path editing is choosing the right tool.

✦ You can save selections and edit the names.

✦ Using Add Anchor Points doesn't change the shape.

✦ Using Delete Anchor Points changes the shape.

✦ Use Roughen from the Filter ⇨ Distort to add anchor points evenly.

✦ Use Clean Up to remove any hidden, unwanted, stray anchor points.

✦ Reshape paths with the Reshape tool.

✦ Change the object's anchor points with the Convert Anchor Point tool.

✦ Use the Pathfinder palette's Shape modes to add, subtract, intersect, and exclude shape areas.

✦ Use the Pathfinder palette's Pathfinder options to divide, trim, merge, crop, outline, or minus back.

✦ Under the Pathfinder palette's pop-up menu is a trap function.

✦   ✦   ✦

Understanding Color, Gradients, and Mesh

✦   ✦   ✦   ✦

In This Chapter

Using the Color, Swatches, and Stroke palettes

Defining paint styles

Using the Paint Bucket and Eyedropper tools

Working with transparency

Understanding and creating radial and linear gradients

Using the Gradient tool and Gradient palette

Changing gradients to blends or mesh

Using the Mesh tool

✦   ✦   ✦   ✦

This chapter covers color, gradients, and mesh. Gradients allow you to apply several different colors in a specific pattern across the surface of your image. You'll learn how to use and edit the preset gradients, as well as how to create gradients of your own.

Mesh changes your art into a grid of meshed lines, creating a 3D color look. You use the Mesh tool to add realistic shadows to your object through a delicate balance of color shifts.

You find color options in the Swatches palette, Color palette, or the Color Picker. You can also apply color to fills and strokes.

Working with the Swatches Palette

You can access the Swatches palette by choosing Window ⇨ Swatches. When you initially install Illustrator, the Swatches palette is housed with the Color palette, and you can switch between the palettes by clicking their respective tabs.

By default, the Swatches palette contains and displays several commonly used colors, patterns, and gradients. You change what displays by clicking the icons along the bottom of the palette. The following list describes the icons from left to right.

✦ **Show All Swatches:** This icon, which looks like three squares stacked, displays all color, gradient, and pattern swatches.

✦ **Show Color Swatches:** This icon, which looks like a solid block of color, displays only the color swatches.

✦ **Show Gradient Swatches:** This icon, which looks a block with a blend of colors on it, displays only the gradient swatches.

✦ **Show Pattern Swatches:** This icon, which looks like a block divided into fourths, displays only the pattern swatches.

✦ **New Swatch:** Clicking this icon, which looks like a little piece of paper with a bent corner, creates a new swatch. You can also create a new swatch by dragging it into the Swatches palette.

✦ **Delete Swatch:** When you select a swatch and click this trash can icon, Illustrator deletes it.

You can also view the swatches in either small or large thumbnail squares, or view all the swatches in a list, with names if they have them. You can change the view mode by selecting the appropriate option from the Swatches pop-up menu. Figure 7-1 shows the default view of the Swatches palette.

Show All Swatches

Show Gradient Swatches

New Swatch

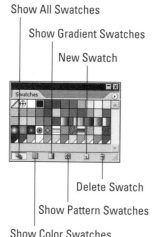

Figure 7-1: The Swatches palette enables you to select and apply various swatch patterns.

Delete Swatch

Show Pattern Swatches

Show Color Swatches

Using the color swatches

You can create a new swatch based on the current paint style, which appears in the Paint Style section of the toolbox, by clicking the New Swatch icon along the bottom of the Swatches palette. If you press Alt (Option) when creating a new swatch, the New Swatch dialog box appears, as shown in Figure 7-2. This dialog box enables you to initially name the swatch and set its color mode to either process color (CMYK) or spot color. *Process colors* are printed using a combination of the four standard printing inks — cyan, magenta, yellow, and black; *spot colors* are printed using a special premixed ink that is exactly the color you want to print.

Under the Color Mode in the New Swatch dialog box, you can set Grayscale, RGB, HSB, CMYK, Lab, or Web Safe RGB. Most default process color swatches are set up with RGB Color Mode. You can also create a new swatch by choosing New Swatch from the Swatches palette pop-up menu, which you access by clicking the right-pointing triangle in the circle on the upper-right corner of the palette.

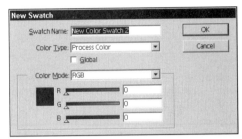

Figure 7-2: The New Swatch dialog box lets you name the new swatch.

Double-clicking a swatch displays the Swatch Options for that swatch. The Swatch Options dialog box is exactly like the New Swatch dialog box, except that it includes a Preview check box. The Swatch Options dialog box has the following options:

✦ **Swatch Name:** Lets you change the name of the swatch, which you can view only in List view mode.

✦ **Color Type:** Allows you to set the color type of the swatch to either process or spot.

✦ **Global:** Specifies that the changes should be applied throughout the document.

✦ **Color Mode:** Lets you change the mode to Grayscale, RGB, HSB, CMYK, Lab, or Web Safe RGB.

For more on Web Safe colors, see Chapter 19.

In addition, you can select one or more swatches to edit, duplicate, or remove from the Swatches palette. Click a swatch to select it; a frame appears on the selected swatch.

You can select more than one swatch by pressing the Ctrl (⌘) key and clicking additional swatches. If you press the Shift key and click additional swatches, a contiguous (connected) set of swatches is selected, from where you initially clicked to where you Shift-clicked. You can deselect individual swatches by pressing Ctrl (⌘) and clicking selected swatches. You deselect all the swatches by clicking an empty area of the Swatches palette. By selecting multiple swatches, you can duplicate and delete several swatches at once.

If you want to sort the swatches manually, you can do so by selecting any number of swatches and dragging them to a new location within the Swatches palette.

Using the Swatches pop-up menu

The Swatches pop-up menu, shown in Figure 7-3, has other functions as well, some of which we've already mentioned:

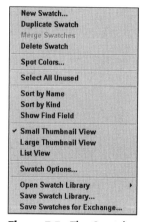

Figure 7-3: The Swatches pop-up menu provides additional options.

✦ **New Swatch:** This option works the same as the New Swatch icon at the bottom of the Color Swatch palette. A new swatch is created from whatever you select.

✦ **Duplicate Swatch:** This option duplicates the selected swatches. You can also drag a selected swatch to the New Swatch icon (the little piece of paper) to duplicate the swatch. If you press Alt (Option) while duplicating a swatch, the New Swatch dialog box appears.

✦ **Merge Swatches:** This option merges two or more selected swatches by using the first selected swatch's name and color. You must have two or more swatches selected to enable this option. It produces a new swatch that is a mixture of the selected swatches.

✦ **Delete Swatch:** To delete a swatch, select this option. You can also select the swatch and click the Trash icon. A warning dialog box, shown in Figure 7-4, appears and asks whether you want to delete the swatch selection. Click Yes to delete the swatch.

Figure 7-4: The Warning dialog box that appears when you try to delete a swatch

✦ **Spot Colors:** This option displays the Spot Color Options dialog box so that you can choose whether to use Lab values or CMYK values to describe any spot colors.

✦ **Select All Unused:** This option selects the swatches in the Swatches palette that you aren't using in the current document. You can then delete those swatches if desired.

✦ **Sort by Name:** This option organizes the swatches (regardless of which viewing mode the swatch palette is in) alphabetically.

✦ **Sort by Kind:** This option sorts the swatches to appear starting with color, then gradients, and then patterns.

✦ **Show Find Field:** This option opens a Find field so you can enter a specific swatch name to search for in the Swatches palette.

✦ **The View options:** You can also view the swatches in either small or large thumbnail squares, or view all the swatches in a list, with names if they have them.

✦ **Swatch Options:** Clicking this option displays the Swatch Options for the selected swatch. This dialog box was discussed in the preceding section.

✦ **Open Swatch Library:** This option displays a submenu so that you can choose to open a different swatch library.

✦ **Save Swatch Library:** Clicking this option presents the Save Palette as Swatch Library dialog box that enables you to save your custom swatches for future use.

✦ **Save Swatches for Exchange:** Clicking this option also displays the Save Palette as Swatch Library dialog box, except with the file type set to Swatch Exchange Files. Use this option if you are working with a group of people who all need to be using the same color swatches.

Using other swatch libraries

In addition to the standard Swatch Library palette, many other default Swatch Library palettes are accessible from the Swatch Libraries submenu of the Window menu, shown in Figure 7-5, or the Swatches palette pop-up menu. You can also create a new Swatch Library palette from any Illustrator document.

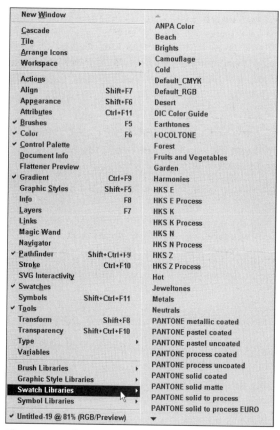

Figure 7-5: The Window menu's Swatch Libraries submenu enables you to choose different swatch libraries.

To view one of the other default Swatches palettes, choose it from the Swatch Libraries submenu. You cannot edit these Swatch libraries; you can only add swatches from these libraries to your main Swatches palette.

To add a swatch (or several selected swatches) to your main Swatches palette, do the following:

1. **Select the swatches you want to add.**

2. **Choose Add To Swatches from the library's pop-up menu.** You click the right-pointing triangle in a circle on the upper-right corner of the palette to access this pop-up menu.

3. **Drag the swatches to the main Swatches palette, or double-click the swatch.** Illustrator saves the main Swatches palette with your document. You can customize a palette for a specific document or edit the Adobe Illustrator Startup document's Swatches palette to use a certain set of colors in each new document you create.

See Chapter 17 for information on the Startup options.

Otherwise, these swatch libraries work the same way as your main Swatches palette; you can choose colors for fill and stroke, sort the swatches by Kind or Name, and view the swatches by List, Small Thumbnail View, or Large Thumbnail View. Figure 7-6 shows three swatch libraries.

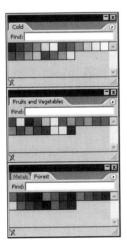

Figure 7-6: Three swatch libraries: Cold, Fruits and Vegetables, and Forest

Using color space options in the Color palette

The Color palette provides basic color selection via the Color Ramp along the bottom of the palette and more precise control via sliders and percentage entries in Grayscale, RGB, HSB, CMYK, and Web Safe RGB. Most users of Illustrator use either

RGB or CMYK color spaces. Heavy Web designers also use HSB and Web Safe RGB. If you are sure that you want to work only in black and white, choose Grayscale. Use the Color palette to add color to any object's stroke or fill. You can create any color to be used in an illustration by defining it in the Color palette, shown in Figure 7-7. Access the Color palette by choosing Window ➪ Color.

Figure 7-7: The Color palette enables you to define colors precisely.

The Color palette has a pop-up menu (and arrowheads next to the palette's name) that enables you to toggle the display of the options and and to choose from the available color spaces. The "options" are really the color mixing sliders; I've never found a reason to hide them. In fact, the sliders take up such a small amount of space that after they're in view, you'll probably never hide them either.

The color space options let you switch among the following:

✦ **Grayscale:** This option shows white to black with all shades of gray in between (see Figure 7-8).

Figure 7-8: The Color palette displaying the Grayscale color space

✦ **RGB:** The red, green, and blue color space is used by computer monitors, and it's perfect for multimedia and Web-page graphics. Refer to Figure 7-7 to see the RGB color space palette. You can enter RGB values as percentages or as values from 0 to 255. Double-click to the right of the text fields to change the RGB measurement system from percentages to the numeric 0 to 255 system and back.

✦ **HSB:** Hue, Saturation, and Brightness comprise this RGB-derived color space, which is best for adjusting RGB colors in brightness and saturation. Figure 7-9 shows the HSB color space palette.

Figure 7-9: The Color palette displaying the HSB color space

✦ **CMYK:** Cyan, magenta, yellow, and black are considered typical printing process colors, although Illustrator calls any colors process that aren't spot. Figure 7-10 shows the CMYK color space palette.

Figure 7-10: The Color palette displaying the CMYK color space

✦ **Web Safe RGB:** These colors are the 216 colors recognized by all graphic Web browsers on any platform. Figure 7-11 shows the Web Safe RGB color space palette.

Figure 7-11: The Color palette displaying the Web Safe RGB color space

As you drag a specific color's slider, the other sliders also change in color. Doing this gives you sort of a preview for what would happen if you were to drag along the sliders. The icon to the left of the sliders shows the current color and whether you're adjusting the fill (solid box) or stroke (box with a hole). Instead of dragging, you can also just simply click a different location along the slider to change its value.

Tip

Press the Shift key to adjust RGB and CMYK sliders proportionately. This is a great way to tint process colors. Shift-drag the slider with the largest value for the most control. When you release the mouse button, Illustrator makes the new color a tint of the original.

You can also change the slider values by typing values for each of the individual color channels (Cyan is a color channel in CMYK, for instance). Press the Tab key to highlight the next text field, or Shift-Tab to highlight the previous text field.

Tip Most of Illustrator's palettes' text fields are mathematically adept. You can add, subtract, multiply, and divide in them. This is useful when entering color percentages in the text fields of the Color palette. To add 5 percent to the current value, type +5 after the current value. To subtract 5 percent, type -5 after the current value. To divide the current value by 2, type /2 after the current value. To multiply the current value by 2, type *2 after the current value.

Using the Color Ramp

The Color Ramp is the bar along the bottom of the Color palette. It looks like a rainbow of colors. The Color Ramp enables you to quickly pick a color from the current color space. Resting your cursor above the Color Ramp area changes the cursor into an eyedropper.

When you change to a different color space, the Color Ramp along the bottom of the palette also changes to show the rainbow of colors in that particular color space.

Tip Shift-click the Color Ramp to cycle through the color spaces; this is much faster than choosing a color space from the pop-up menu.

Click any portion of the Color Ramp to select that color. Illustrator provides large rectangles of black and white to make choosing black or white easier. The Grayscale and Spot Color Ramps have large areas for both 0% and 100% to make selecting those percentages easier. You can also drag over the Color Ramp, watching the large square in the top of the Color palette (if Options are showing) to see the color you're dragging over. If Options aren't shown, look at the active Fill/Stroke icon in the toolbox to see the color you're currently positioned over. (This works only when the mouse button is pressed as you pass across the Color Ramp.)

Tip You can press the X key while dragging around the Color Ramp to switch between the fill and stroke focus. This way, you can quickly select colors for both fill and stroke with one mouse click! If the fill is in focus, click and drag through the Color Ramp to the appropriate color. Then, with the mouse button still pressed, press the X key; you'll now be picking a color for the stroke. Want to change the fill again? Just press X while holding down the mouse button.

Tip Press Alt (Option) and click anywhere on a Color Ramp to affect the opposite attribute. For example, if stroke is in focus on the toolbox, pressing Alt (Option) and clicking on a Color Ramp changes the fill color, not the stroke. Be aware, however, that Alt (Option)+clicking on a swatch in the Swatches palette does not affect the opposite attribute; this works only on a Color Ramp (and the color box in the Color palette).

Working with gamut

If you choose certain colors, a little icon appears in the center left of the Color palette, as shown in Figure 7-12. This icon indicates that the current color is out of gamut with the color space. Therefore, the particular color you chose isn't within the range of colors that can be displayed or printed for the selected color space. This issue is generally important only if you plan to print the document using CMYK process colors. If you plan to use the image onscreen, such as in Web or multimedia publishing, whether the color is in gamut does not really matter.

Figure 7-12: The Out of Gamut indicator appears when the current color cannot be accurately displayed or printed.

The best way to reset the current color is to click the Out of Gamut icon. The RGB or HSB values change so that the resulting color is well within CMYK color space. Another way to change the current color to CMYK color space is to choose CMYK from the Color palette pop-up menu.

If you want to change the color space of several objects — or perhaps your entire document — to CMYK, select the objects that you want to change and choose Filter ➪ Colors ➪ Convert to CMYK. To change the whole document to a different color space, choose File ➪ Document Color Mode ➪ CMYK Color or RGB Color.

Spot colors

Spot colors are colors in Illustrator that aren't separated into process colors (cyan, magenta, yellow, and black) when printed. Instead, they are printed on a different separation. A commercial printer uses special ink (commonly Pantone) for this spot color. Spot colors are indicated in the Swatches palette in Small Thumbnail and Large Thumbnail views by a white triangle containing a black dot in the lower right of the spot color swatch. List view shows a square with a circle inside of it (a "spot") on the right edge of the swatch listing. In List view mode, both the color space (grayscale, RGB, or CMYK) and Process/Spot status are indicated to the right of the color chip and name.

You can use as many spot colors in an illustration as you want, though it isn't usually practical or desirable to have more than four in one document. (Because CMYK printing can duplicate most colors, process colors are often a better choice than four spot colors.) Illustrator's default Swatch libraries, accessible by choosing Window ➪ Swatch Libraries, mostly contain spot colors that you can choose among, or you can create your own. Follow these steps to create your own spot color:

1. **Create a new swatch with the appearance you want.** Use the color sliders to do this.

2. **Double-click the newly created swatch.** Doing this opens the Swatch Options dialog box.

3. **Change the Swatch type from Process to Spot.** Now, when you use that swatch as a fill or stroke, Illustrator considers it a spot color when it comes time to print.

Tip   You can convert any spot color to a standard CMYK color (the color, not the swatch) by selecting the spot color and then changing the color space in the Color palette to CMYK. You can even change the color space to grayscale, RGB, or HSB in this way. This works only on the selected paths; the swatch is not affected.

Applying colors with the Color palette

Now you know how the palettes work, but how do you change the color of paths to what's in the palettes? The easiest thing to do is to select the path you want to change the fill or stroke (or both) of, change the focus (if necessary) of the Fill/Stroke icons, and select a color from either the Color or Swatches palette. Press X to change the color for the other (fill or stroke).

The key here is selecting. If you have selected paths, any changes you make affect those selected paths.

When you create a new path, Illustrator uses the fill and stroke that are currently displayed in the Paint Style section of the toolbox.

To apply colors to text, you can either select an entire text area with a Selection tool or select individual characters with a Type tool.

Tip   Selecting Type with a Selection tool can cause type paths and type areas, as well as the type, to be filled and stroked. You can use the Group Selection tool to deselect the associated paths, or better yet, just use the Type tool and drag across the characters you want to select.

Transferring color from one object to another

The Eyedropper and Paint Bucket tools are lifesavers for those of us who are constantly using self-stick notes to jot down the percentages of CMYK (cyan, magenta, yellow, and black) in one path so that we can apply those same amounts to another path. A good reason to use the Paint Bucket and Eyedropper tools is to ensure that your colors are consistent throughout an illustration. So, for example, if you used a custom color somewhere that you want to use again somewhere else, you don't try to duplicate it with a CMYK mix that may not be an exact match. With a couple of clicks or keystrokes, you can easily transfer the color properties of one object to another. The tools work with paths, objects, type, and placed images.

The Eyedropper and Paint Bucket tools work similarly to the other tools in Illustrator in that their properties stay the same until you change them—in this case, by clicking a new path or object with a different color. The Eyedropper tool "sucks" up color from where you click. Use this to see the breakdown of a color in the area you clicked. The Paint Bucket tool fills in an area with the active color in the Color Swatch. Just click the Paint Bucket tool on the shape you want to fill with color. To give you more control over what the tools can pick up and apply, Illustrator gives you an exhaustive list of properties to select in the Eyedropper Options dialog box. Double-clicking the Eyedropper tool brings up this dialog box, shown in Figure 7-13, where you can select or deselect options depending on what attributes you want to apply. So, for example, you can have the Eyedropper tool pick up the color and Stroke weight of a path without transferring the path's transparency properties.

 Cross-Reference For more on paths, objects, and type, see Chapters 4, 5, and 9, respectively. Most of the properties listed in the Eyedropper Options dialog box are also discussed in these chapters.

 Cross-Reference For more on placed images, see Chapter 3.

At the bottom of the Eyedropper Options dialog box is the Raster Sample Size menu. From this menu, you can choose whether you suck up a Point Sample (samples the color from the point where you click), 3×3 Average (averages the color in an area of 3 pixels by 3 pixels), or 5×5 Average (averages the color in an area of 5 pixels by 5 pixels).

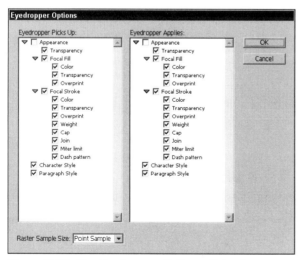

Figure 7-13: The Eyedropper Options dialog box enables you to fine-tune the operation of the Eyedropper tool.

The Eyedropper tool

The Eyedropper tool samples paint style information from a path and stores it in the Paint Style fill and stroke boxes (on the toolbox), without selecting that path. The information stays there until you change the information in the color palette, select another path with different paint style information, or click any other path or placed image with a different paint style.

Tip   If you have paths selected when you click with the Eyedropper tool, all selected objects in the document are changed to the paint style of the path that you clicked.

The Live Paint Bucket tool

You use the Live Paint Bucket tool to apply the current paint style to both paths and Live Trace images. You can apply any attribute that is active in the Appearance palette. Using the Live Paint Bucket tool is a quick and painless way to apply a set style or group of attributes you like to other objects.

Cross-Reference   See Chapter 14 for more information on the Live Paint Bucket tool and Chapter 13 for more on Live Trace.

Using Transparency

Transparency has changed the face of Illustrator. Being able to apply transparent live effects to any object in Illustrator is just plain amazing. It opens up many doors and lets in a kaleidoscope of colors to see through. Transparency is like looking through stained glass, a piece of plastic, anything you can see through. You can adjust the blending modes for a variety of effects. Blending modes are the interaction of the colors of an object with the objects underneath that object. Imagine that you are playing with Plexiglas blocks in three dimensions. You can see what is behind or in front of those blocks. You can even go as far as thinking that you are Superman looking through objects with X-ray vision. You can create stained glass effects, mixing color effects, and so much more. You can apply transparency to objects, groups of objects, or a whole layer.

In Illustrator, you apply Transparency in the Transparency palette as shown in Figure 7-14. If the Transparency palette isn't showing when you start up Illustrator, choose Window ⇨ Transparency. To see the options available with Transparency, click the upper-right triangle and choose Show Options. In the preview pane on the left side of the palette, you can see a thumbnail view of the current Opacity setting applied to the selected object.

These options are available in the Transparency palette:

✦ **Mode:** Use this option to choose the method used in the blend.

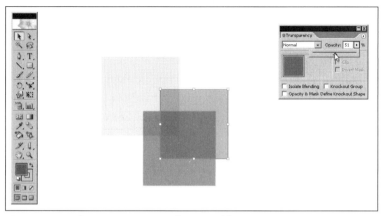

Figure 7-14: The Transparency palette enables you to create transparent objects.

✦ **Opacity:** Basically, you adjust an Opacity slider in the Transparency palette to determine how much you can see through that object.

✦ **Clip:** The Clip option gives the masks a black background.

✦ **Invert Mask:** This option reverses luminosity and opacity values of the masked objects.

✦ **Isolate Blending:** Check this option to affect only the group or layer opacity.

✦ **Knockout Group:** Selecting this option means that the opacity does not affect the group or layer, just the object.

✦ **Opacity & Mask Define Knockout Shape:** Selecting this option means that you can use a Mask to delineate where Illustrator applies the transparency settings.

Cross-Reference

The preceding options are discussed in greater detail later in this section.

Defining transparency between objects, groups, and layers

You can apply transparency to an object, group of objects, sublayer, or the entire layer. You can also apply transparency to symbols, patterns, type, 3D objects, graphic styles, strokes, and brush strokes. To define an object's transparency, select the object first and then drag the Opacity slider in the Transparency palette to the desired opacity. Figure 7-15 shows an example of changing the top object's opacity.

Figure 7-15: The top star object's opacity was changed to 60 percent so you can see the background through it.

Working with opacity

You adjust the transparency in the Transparency palette by dragging the Opacity slider. You access the slider by clicking the arrow on the side of the Opacity box. As mentioned previously, opacity is how see-through the object is. Applying no Opacity makes an object totally transparent. Applying any amount of opacity makes the object partially transparent. An opacity value of 100% makes the object totally opaque, which mean you can't see through it at all. If you check the Appearance palette, it shows you the amount of opacity applied to that particular object.

To apply opacity to a group of objects, or to a whole layer, start with the Layers palette and do the following:

1. **In the Layers palette, click the layer you want to adjust.**

2. **Adjust the Opacity slider or enter the Opacity value in the Transparency palette.**

Using blending modes

Within the Transparency palette, you find 16 blending modes similar to Photoshop's blending modes. Each mode creates a different effect when applied to the same object. Blending modes can totally change the look of the opacity applied to an object. Using blending modes lets you choose a variety of ways the colors of the objects blend when on top of another object. You create blending modes by combining a base color (the bottom object), the blend color (of the object on top), and the resulting color from the overlapping.

Illustrator supplies a variety of blending modes in the Transparency palette. Figure 7-16 shows the list of blending modes found in the Transparency palette in the pop-up menu. These blending modes are available:

✦ **Normal:** Use this for no interaction with the base color, only the blend color result.

✦ **Darken:** This mode uses the darker color (base or blend) as the resulting color.

✦ **Multiply:** This mode multiplies the base color by the blend color, creating a darker color.

✦ **Color Burn:** Use this to darken the base color.

✦ **Lighten:** This mode uses the lighter color (base or blend) as the resulting color.

✦ **Screen:** This multiplies the opposite color of the blend and base colors, creating a lighter color.

✦ **Color Dodge:** Use this to lighten and brighten the base color.

✦ **Overlay:** This mode either multiplies or screens, depending on the base color. The base color is mixed with the blend color, resulting in the lightness or darkness of the original color. With patterns or graphic styles, the highlights and shadows of the base color are kept and the blend color is mixed in to create lightness or darkness of the beginning color.

✦ **Soft Light:** This mode is like shining a softened light on the object. Blends less than 50 percent gray get lightened, and blends greater than 50 percent get darkened. If the blend is 50 percent, it is left alone.

✦ **Hard Light:** This mode is similar to soft light, but with a harsh light shining on the object. If the blend color is lighter than 50 percent gray, the object becomes lightened. If the blend color is darker than 50 percent gray, the object becomes darkened.

✦ **Difference:** This mode chooses the brighter color (either base or blend) and subtracts it from the other color.

✦ **Exclusion:** This mode is similar to Difference mode, but with lower contrast.

✦ **Hue:** This creates a result having the base color's saturation and the blend color's hue.

✦ **Saturation:** This creates a result having the base color's hue and the blend color's saturation.

✦ **Color:** This creates a result having the base color's luminance and the blend color's hue and saturation.

✦ **Luminosity:** This mode is the opposite of the Color mode. The result is the base color's hue and saturation and the blend color's luminance.

Figure 7-16: Under the pop-up in the Transparency palette, you see all the blending modes.

Isolating blending

Isolating blending is a necessary evil when too many objects are involved in a transparency illustration. When patterns are involved, you may lose the clarity of your artwork unless you limit how far the blending goes with the Opacity settings. In the Transparency palette, there is a check box for Isolate Blending. Use this to pick and choose how far you want the opacity to affect the underlying objects.

Follow these steps to apply a blending mode to an object:

1. **Click the drop-down list (pop-up menu) in the Transparency palette, and select a choice to apply that blending mode to the selected object.**

2. **Group together the objects that you want in the blend.** To learn more on how to group objects, see Chapter 7.

3. **In the Layers palette, click the radio button to the right of the layer that contains the selected group of objects to target the group of objects you want to isolate.**

4. **Check the Isolate Blending box in the Transparency palette.**

Figure 7-17 shows a group of objects without checking Isolate Blending (left) and the same objects with Isolate Blending checked (right). For the left image, the text, its text box, and the underlying bars are all blended together, making it difficult to read the text, but the right image isolates the blending so that only the text and its text box are blended.

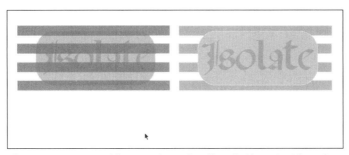

Figure 7-17: Text without Isolate Blending (left) and with Isolate Blending checked (right). The two text pieces are grouped.

Knocking out a group

Along with Isolate Blending is the Knockout Group check box in the Transparency palette. Knockout Group does the opposite of Isolate Blending. That is, you use the Knockout Group option to block the view of objects under the group.

Using opacity, clipping, and invert masks

A clipping mask crops the objects behind the mask to the edges of the mask. An opacity mask is similar to a clipping mask. Instead of clipping away other objects, it clips the objects to the defined area (mask) to show transparency. The opacity mask in Illustrator is like the layer mask concept in Photoshop. Use the opacity mask to clip objects to the top shape and apply the opacity mask's luminosity to the underlying objects. Where the top mask is white, you can see the artwork underneath, and where the mask is black, it is opaque. Figure 7-18 shows a group of 3D objects with a star shape on top. The star shape was then selected to be the opacity mask over the top of the other objects. Select Make Opacity Mask from the Transparency palette menu to apply an opacity mask.

After applying an opacity mask, the original shape disappears. If you don't believe me, check Outline mode. To get the shape back, simply release the opacity mask. You can release the opacity mask under the Transparency palette pop-up menu. Choose Release opacity masks, and the objects return to their original state.

Cross-Reference   For more on the different viewing modes in Illustrator, see Chapter 2.

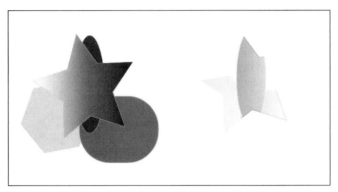

Figure 7-18: The objects before (left) and after (right) an opacity mask was applied to the star shape on top

Other choices under the Transparency menu are to unlink or relink an opacity mask. An opacity mask is automatically linked to the object that it is masking. To unlink the opacity mask, click the link symbol between the opacity mask and the object or choose Unlink opacity mask in the Transparency palette pop-up menu. When you unlink the object from the mask, you can move the object(s) around under the opacity mask and the mask stays put. To relink the two back together, click the link between the two thumbnails or choose Link Opacity mask from the Transparency palette pop-up menu.

You can disable an opacity mask, and Illustrator removes the Mask from its masking task, but does not delete the objects you used to make the mask from the file. To get the mask back, choose Enable opacity mask from the Transparency palette pop-up menu.

You can edit opacity masks if you click the thumbnail of the mask in the Transparency palette. Use Illustrator's editing tools to change the mask shape. Other options in the Transparency palette for the opacity mask are to make the opacity mask act as a Clipping mask with the Clip option. Check this to have the mask clip the area around the selected mask (like the clipping mask function). You can also use the Invert Mask option. Checking this inverts the dark and light, which reverses the original opacity.

Note   When using the Make Opacity Mask function, all the objects in the mask are automatically grouped together.

Viewing a transparency grid

Now that you are getting into this whole transparency thing, you may find it hard to see which objects have transparency applied to them. To see these transparent objects, you can enable a transparency grid. This grid shows up as a gray and white checkered pattern positioned behind all other objects.

To view the transparency grid, choose View ⇨ Show Transparency Grid or press Ctrl+Shift+D (⌘+Shift+D). If you want to change the look of the Transparency Grid, choose File ⇨ Document Setup and choose Transparency from the drop-down list (pop-up menu). You can also access the Document Setup by pressing Alt+Ctrl+P (⌘+Option+P). Figure 7-19 shows the Document Setup for Transparency options.

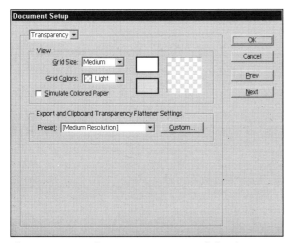

Figure 7-19: In the Document Setup dialog box, you can change the transparency grid.

Using these options, you can set the Grid Size and change the Grid Colors. A preview of the grid is also shown next to the color selection boxes. The Simulate Color Paper option shows you what your objects look like when printed on colored paper. At the bottom of the Document Setup dialog box are options for setting the Transparency Flattening settings.

Figure 7-20 shows an example of several objects as they appear above the transparency grid. Objects that are opaque completely block the view of the transparency grid, while those that that are partially transparent allow the grid to show through.

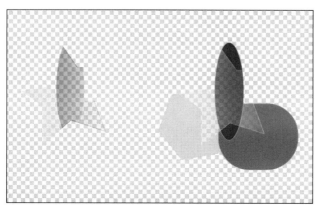

Figure 7-20: Opaque objects block the transparency grid, while transparent ones allow it to be seen.

Printing and flattening

Flattening is a process that removes transparency from objects and substitutes objects that have a similar appearance—only without any transparency. Flattening happens when transparency is not supported by other applications. Flattening actually creates more pieces of the objects. Flattening also changes your transparency. You lose transparency and instead a color is applied that reflects the opacity color. If you have two objects overlapping and you flatten the image, a third object is created where they overlap.

For more precise control over flattening, you can use the options that are available in the Flatten Transparency dialog box, shown in Figure 7-21. To use this option, select the object(s) you want to flatten and then choose Object ➪ Flatten Transparency. In the Flatten Transparency dialog box, choose your settings and then click OK. You also have the option to preview the settings by clicking the Preview box.

You can set these options in the Flatten Transparency dialog box:

✦ **Preset:** Choose from preset transparency flattening options of high, medium, or low resolution. Typically, you want to choose higher resolution for final printouts and lower resolution for draft output.

✦ **Raster/Vector Balance:** This option lets you choose the amount of rasterization. Set the balance high to retain as much vector information as possible. Set the balance lower, and more objects are rasterized into pixels.

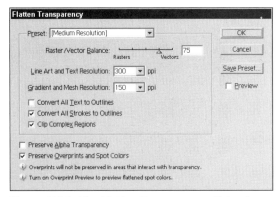

Figure 7-21: The Flatten Transparency dialog box provides more precise control over flattening.

✦ **Line Art and Text Resolution:** Set the resolution of the vector objects when they are rasterized.

✦ **Gradient and Mesh Resolution:** Set the resolution of the gradients and mesh objects when they are rasterized.

✦ **Convert All Text to Outlines:** This option changes all text to outlined paths.

✦ **Convert All Strokes to Outlines:** This option changes all the strokes to outlined paths.

✦ **Clip Complex Regions:** This option reduces the patching that happens to an object that is partially rasterized and partially vectored. This option also may result in very complex paths, making the image hard to print.

✦ **Preserve Alpha Transparency:** This option saves the opacity of flattened objects.

✦ **Preserve Overprints and Spot Colors:** This option saves the Overprinting and Spot color objects.

Transparency and type

Now that you have the basics, let's delve into using transparency on objects. You can create a plethora of different effects using transparency. The following sections cover just a few of the amazing things you can do with transparency.

Transparency is not limited to objects. It is fantastic to use on type as well. Take some text, and give it a three-dimensional feel using Effect ⇨ 3D ⇨ Extrude & Bevel (you must use the Selection tool to select the text before you can apply the effect). Then with color, highlights, and a background added, you can use the Transparency palette to really make the text sing. Figure 7-22 shows an illustration done with text and transparency.

Figure 7-22: Text and transparency create some fantastic effects.

Separating transparent objects

Transparency is useful with many different types of objects. Use it in a brush stroke, creating fills, styles, multiple fills, and more. If you choose to flatten the transparency, you'll see that Illustrator actually cuts it into sections. Figure 7-23 shows the objects from Figure 7-22 with transparency flattened and pulled apart so you can see the sections. To flatten a transparency, first select it and then choose Object ⇨ Flatten Transparency.

Figure 7-23: Objects with transparency flattened and pulled apart demonstrate how flattening creates many new objects.

3D, Symbols, and Transparency

Transparency is not limited to basic objects. You can use transparent effects on symbols, effects, patterns, brush strokes, and 3D objects. Figure 7-24 shows three-dimensional gears with different opacity settings. Anything you can do in Illustrator can have transparency applied. The Symbol tool has a Symbol Screener tool, which applies transparency in a brush-like fashion. You can also apply Opacity to the whole group of sprayed symbols using the Transparency palette.

The Symbol Screener tool is covered in Chapter 5.

Figure 7-24: Three-dimensional gears with different transparency effects applied

Using type with brush strokes and transparency can also result in some eye-catching effects. To create brush stroke type, follow these steps:

1. **Enter the type you want.** Don't worry about the typeface; just pick something plain.

2. **Convert the type to outlines.** You do this by selecting the type and then choosing Type ⇨ Create Outlines or by pressing Ctrl+Shift+O (⌘+Shift+O).

3. **Give the outlined type a stroke color, but no fill color.** For more on stroke and fill colors, see Chapter 10.

4. **With the type selected, click one of the Art Brush presets.** Access the Art Brush presets by clicking the Brushes tab or choosing Window ⇨ Brushes. Then choose a preset brush.

5. **Press Alt (Option) and drag to copy the type down and to the left a bit to create a drop shadow look.**

6. **Select the back type, and enter an Opacity value.** The example uses an Opacity value of 75%.

7. **Select the front type, and enter an Opacity value.** The example uses an Opacity value of 60%.

Doing this creates almost an embossed effect. Add a background, and the text lets the background shine through. Figure 7-25 shows an example of this embossed effect.

Figure 7-25: Brush strokes with transparency make for some interesting type effects.

Creating Gradients

The Gradient feature has no rivals. It is by far the most powerful gradient-creating mechanism available for PostScript drawing programs. Gradients in Adobe Illustrator can have 32 different colors, from end to end in a linear gradient, and from center to outside in a radial Gradient. Gradients can consist of custom colors, process colors, or just plain black and white. The midpoint of two adjacent colors can be adjusted smoothly and easily toward either color. You can make the Gradient palette available at all times because it is a floating palette. You can access it or view it by selecting Window ➪ Gradient or by pressing Ctrl+F9 (⌘+F9). And, for what they do, gradients are easier to use than blends.

Note You can apply gradients only to the fills of paths, not to strokes or text objects. Gradients also cannot be used in patterns.

Using preset gradients

To choose a preset gradient, select a path and make sure that the Fill box is active in the toolbox. In the Swatches palette, click the gradient swatch icon at the bottom of the palette. The four default gradient presets appear alone in the swatches. When you click a gradient swatch, Illustrator applies the gradient to the selected path.

Using the Gradient palette

The Gradient palette, if nothing else, is really neat looking, with all sorts of nifty little controls at your disposal for creating and modifying gradients; it's shown in Figure 7-26.

Figure 7-26: The Gradient palette enables you to create your own gradients.

The Type list box (pop-up menu) at the top of the Gradient palette lets you select from Radial or Linear gradient types. Radial gradients move from a center location of an object radial outward in all directions. Linear gradients move in one direction across the object.

The bottom of the Gradient palette is where you control what colors are in the gradient and where the colors are in relation to one another.

The default gradient is black and white and moves from white on the left to black on the right. To add a new color to the bar, click below the bar where you want the new color to appear. This causes a color marker (which appears as a small square). The new color becomes a step between the left color slider and the right color slider. The Location percentage value defines how close you click to either end with 0% on the left and 100% on the right. In other words, the closer you click to the left end, the closer that color is to the left slider.

If you then click the square marker, it becomes selected. You can tell when a gradient marker is selected because the small triangle above it turns dark. When selected, you can change its color by selecting a new color in the Color palette. You can enter up to 32 color stops between the two end colors. When a color stop is selected, entering a different percentage in the text field on the right changes the color stop's position.

The diamonds above the color bar show the midpoint between two color stops. By moving the midpoint left or right, you alter the halfway color between two color stops. When a diamond is selected, entering a different percentage in the text field on the right changes the diamond's position.

Tip   If you start with a black and white gradient and want to add color to the gradient, drag the color you want from the Color palette onto the marker to change the marker's color mode.

Working with Gradient tool

You use the Gradient tool to give a more 3D look to an object by changing the angle and the starting and ending points for a linear gradient, as well as the location of the center and edges of a radial gradient. The tool is also used to offset the highlight on a radial gradient.

Gradients are created with the Gradient palette and applied from the Gradient tool or palette:

1. **Double-clicking the Gradient tool displays the Gradient palette.** The Gradient tool in the toolbox looks like a blended rectangle.

2. **Select a Gradient type.** Select Radial or Linear.

3. **Select at least one path that is filled with a Gradient.**

4. **Drag with the Gradient tool on the object.** Dragging on linear gradients changes the angle and the length of the gradient, as well as the start and end points. Dragging with the Gradient tool on radial gradients determines the start position and end position of the gradient. Clicking with the Gradient tool resets the highlight to a new location.

Figure 7-27 shows a gradient original (left) and after changing the start position of the gradient (right).

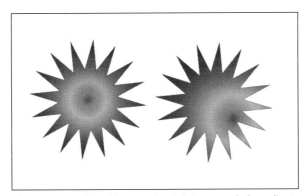

Figure 7-27: The object on the left has a radial gradient applied to it. The object on the right altered the highlight of the radial gradient.

Using Gradients to Create Bubbles

Gradients are a great tool to use when creating objects with a three-dimensional look. You can create great molecular pieces for a chemistry drawing, or bubbles for a fun illustration. Start out by drawing circles and using the Gradient tool to change the angle of the gradient. Use the Gradient tool to click where you want the highlight to be and drag where you want the darker area to be. You can create a set of random bubbles quite easily using gradients. To create bubbles, follow these steps:

1. Draw a circle using the Ellipse tool while holding down the Shift key.

2. Fill the circle with a radial gradient in a blue color. Figure A shows the Gradient palette with the settings I used for the bubbles.

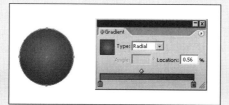

Figure A: The Gradient palette with the bubble settings

3. Using the Gradient tool, change the location of the highlight by clicking once where you want it to go, as shown in Figure B.

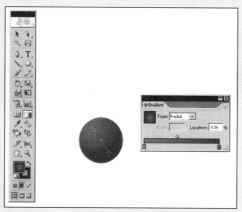

Figure B: Use the Gradient tool to change the highlight.

4. Drag the "bubble" to the Symbol palette creating a new bubble symbol.

5. Using the Symbol Sprayer tool, first select the bubble in the Symbol palette and then spray out a bunch of bubbles, as shown in Figure C.

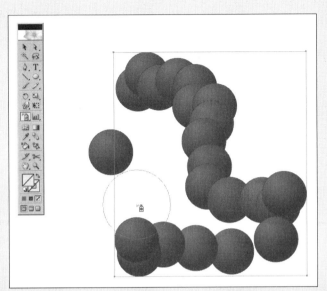

Figure C: Use the Symbol Sprayer tool to spray out a bunch of bubbles.

6. Using the other Symbolism tools, change the sizes, location, and transparency of the bubbles to give a more realistic look.

Creating shadows, highlights, ghosting, and embossing

You can use gradients to simulate special effects either by duplicating and altering a gradient or by using the Gradient tool on similar gradients.

Ghosting is a technique where an object such as text appears lightly against a background. You can simulate ghosting by using the Gradient tool to slightly alter the starting and ending locations of the gradient.

1. **Ghosting effects are easiest to see on text, so create a rectangle and then create a large section of text on top of the rectangle.**

2. **Convert the type into outlines by choosing Type ➪ Create Outlines.** Alternatively, you can press Ctrl+Shift+O (⌘+Shift+O).

3. **Position the type outline in the center of the rectangle.**

4. **Select both the type and the rectangle, and apply a Gradient Fill to them.**

5. **With both rectangle and type selected, drag from the bottom of the rectangle to the top with the Gradient tool.**

6. **Modify the opacity of both the type and the rectangle to get the effect you want.** Figure 7-28 shows an example of this effect.

Figure 7-28: Ghosting with gradients creates an interesting effect.

Another interesting technique you may want to experiment with involves offsetting two copies of the original graduated image to create an embossed gradient image. In one offset image, the gradient is lightened; in the other, the gradient is darkened. Typically, you place the lighter image above and to the left of the darker image to create a raised appearance. To make embossed images seem sunken rather than raised, make the lighter image below and to the right and the darker image above and to the left. To make the image seem further raised or recessed, increase the distance between the original path and the offset images. Figure 7-29 shows an example of this effect.

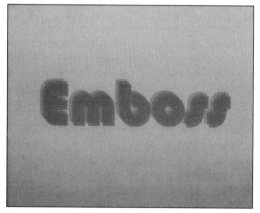

Figure 7-29: Offsetting copies of the image produces an embossed effect.

Expanding gradient objects

In Illustrator, you can automatically change gradients into blends by selecting the gradient you wish to change and then choosing Object ➪ Expand. You might want to expand a gradient into a blend to add special effects to the object with the paths rather than a gradient fill. Because you expand the object into paths, there are many more paths to change, twist, or mangle, creating lots of options for your object. Expanding the object changes the fill to a blend of paths. The Expand dialog box, shown in Figure 7-30, allows you to choose to Expand the Object, Fill, or Stroke. You also choose whether to Expand the Gradient to a Mesh, or the number of steps in the blend.

Cross-Reference

For more on blending, see Chapter 12.

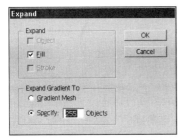

Figure 7-30: The Expand dialog box can convert a gradient into a blend.

Printing gradients

Checking the Compatible Gradient and Mesh Printing option check box in the Print dialog box prevents most gradient problems from occurring. Choose File ➪ Print, and then choose Graphics from the left side choices, as shown in Figure 7-31. When you're printing to PostScript Level 1 printers, checking this box speeds gradient printing dramatically. If your target printer is not a PostScript printer, then this check box is disabled. Compatible gradients bypass a high-level imaging system within Illustrator that older printers and printers without genuine Adobe PostScript may not be able to understand. Checking this box may cause documents to print slower on printers that would ordinarily be able to print those documents.

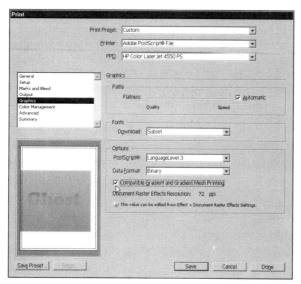

Figure 7-31: Use the Compatible Gradient and Mesh Printing option in the Graphics pane to resolve printing problems with certain printers.

Adding Realism with Mesh

The Mesh tool changes a normal filled path into a multicolored object with the click of a button. You use the Mesh tool to add highlights, shading, and three-dimensional effects. Figure 7-32 shows an object created with the Mesh tool. You click and create a new color at the clicked point. The new color blends smoothly into the object's original color. This section demonstrates how you enhance highlights and color, and add multiple highlights.

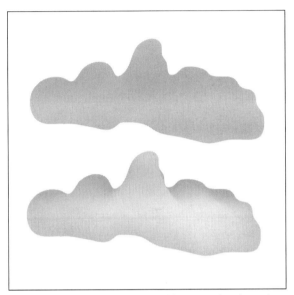

Figure 7-32: The Mesh tool adds more depth to the lower copy of the clouds.

Enhancing with highlights and color

The Mesh tool is found in the toolbox; it looks like a rectangle with squiggly lines inside. The Mesh tool adds highlights or shading with the click of a mouse. Follow these steps to apply a mesh:

1. **Deselect the object to which you want to add a point.**

2. **Pick the color of the highlight point in the Color palette.** If it isn't visible, choose Window ➪ Color.

3. **Select the Mesh tool from the toolbox.**

4. **Click to set the point.**

5. **To change the highlight color, with the Direct Selection tool, select a point on the mesh and change its color values in the Color palette.**

The Create Gradient Mesh dialog box, shown in Figure 7-33, is accessed by choosing Object ⇨ Create Gradient Mesh, and it allows you to create you own gradient meshes to use with the Mesh tool. To display this dialog box, you must have something selected; otherwise, Illustrator grays out the option. In the Create Gradient Mesh dialog box, you can set how many mesh lines form a row and a column; whether the appearance is flat, to center, or to the edge; and the highlight intensity from 0% to 100%.

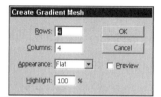

Figure 7-33: The Create Gradient Mesh dialog box enables you to customize the mesh settings.

Adding multiple highlights

Clicking more than once on an object with the Mesh tool adds more blends to the object. Each click creates a new horizontal and vertical axis. For this reason, the tool is called a "mesh." The more clicks that are created, the more individual lines appear until the base object appears as a complex mesh of lines. Each intersection of lines is a point of color that can be changed. However, when you change a color, adjacent intersecting points aren't updated. The following steps give you an example of what happens when you add multiple highlights to an object:

1. **Create a dark-colored rectangle, and deselect it.**

2. **Change the color in the Color palette to a bright color.**

3. **With the Mesh tool, click in the middle of the rectangle.** A point of light appears, creating a sort of radial gradient.

4. **Deselect the rectangle, change the fill color to another bright color, and click another point.** When you do this, two additional points that are somewhere between the dark background and the two bright highlights appear. Figure 7-34 shows an example of this.

Tip

If you never manually change the color of the two new points, they'll continue to update to match the color of the surrounding points. But, if you change the color of one of those points, they're no longer "smart" and remain that color regardless of the colors of the points around them.

You can create very complex Mesh objects with just a dozen or so clicks. These objects are editable, but you need to somehow keep track of which points were the originals, so that all the other ones update automatically.

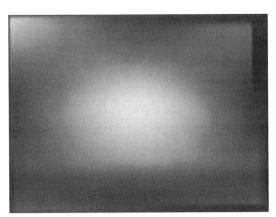

Figure 7-34: The rectangle with a highlight in the middle and additional highlights at each corner

Tip   You can change the background color of the object you're editing after several highlights have been added by selecting *all* the points on the perimeter of the original object with the Direct Selection tool. Every click with the Mesh tool adds four points to the perimeter of the object.

Summary

In this chapter, you learned some very important points about adding a bit of splash to your Illustrator documents using colors, gradients, and mesh. In particular, this chapter covered the following topics:

✦ You use the Swatches palette to store and apply commonly used colors.

✦ The Color palette enables you to choose colors from a Color Ramp and to mix colors using interactive sliders.

✦ You change the color space from grayscale to CMYK to RGB to HSB by selecting one from the Color pop-up menu.

✦ You can color paths and type quickly by using the Eyedropper tool to sample colors from paths or placed images.

✦ You can also create your own gradients and save them in the Swatches palette.

✦ You can quickly turn gradients into blends by selecting the gradient and applying the Expand option.

✦ The Mesh tool makes adding shadows and highlights a breeze.

✦   ✦   ✦

Putting Illustrator to Work

◆   ◆   ◆   ◆

In This Part

Chapter 8
Using Illustrator to
Organize Objects

Chapter 9
Working with Type

Chapter 10
Using Creative
Strokes and Fills
with Patterns

Chapter 11
Applying
Transformations
and Distortions

Chapter 12
Using Path Blends,
Compounds Paths,
and Masks

Chapter 13
Using Live Trace

Chapter 14
Using Live Paint

◆   ◆   ◆   ◆

Using Illustrator to Organize Objects

In This Chapter

Locking
and hiding objects

Understanding
stacking order

Using groups

Working with layers

Measuring with
the Measure tool

Using grids
and guides

As more and more objects are added to a document, the artwork can very quickly become unmanageable. To address this problem, Illustrator includes many features for organizing the various objects in the document. From locking or hiding objects that you don't want to accidentally move, to grouping a set of objects so they can all move together, these features are keys to success in Illustrator.

Another key way to organize objects covered in this chapter is by using the Layers palette. The Layers palette offers precise control over different objects by placing them on different layers and controlling what effects are applied to them.

This chapter shows you how to use Illustrator's features to organize the objects in your documents.

Locking and Hiding Objects

All objects in Illustrator can be locked or hidden — including guides. The process of locking and hiding work is about the same, and the results are only marginally different. In a way, hiding is an "invisible lock." Locking the artwork still leaves it visible and printable. When you hide an object, it is for all intents and purposes "gone" until you show it again. Locking is great to use when you still need to see the location of the object, but don't want to accidentally move or transform it. Hiding works nicely when you need the object out of the way but not gone.

You can quickly lock and hide layers using the Show/Hide and Lock/Unlock columns in the Layers palette. For more on the Layers palette, see the section "Using the Layers palette" later in this chapter.

Locking objects

Locking can be applied to more than just objects that you draw. Under the Object ⇨ Lock menu, you can choose to lock a selection, all artwork above, or other layers. To lock an object, select it and choose Object ⇨ Lock ⇨ Selection. You can also press Ctrl+2 (⌘+2). Illustrator not only locks the object, it also deselects it. In fact, you cannot select an object after you lock it. You cannot move or change locked objects, nor can you hide them. Because you cannot select a locked object, you can't change it — in Illustrator, as in most applications, you can modify objects only when you select them.

A locked object remains locked when you save and close the document. As a result, locked objects remain locked the next time you open the document. Because locked objects are always visible, they always print. You can't tell from the printed item whether or not it is locked.

To change a locked object, choose Object ⇨ Unlock All. You can also press Ctrl+Alt+2 (⌘+Option+2). This command unlocks (and selects) all objects. There is no way to unlock just a few objects locked with the Lock command. That's one reason why you may want to use the Layers palette to lock specific objects instead of using the Object ⇨ Lock command: Objects locked using the Layers palette can be individually unlocked.

A tricky way to invisibly "copyright" your illustration is to create a small text box in a far corner of the pasteboard with your copyright information in it, color the text white, and lock the text box. No one knows it is there, and it can't be easily selected. In fact, it'll even print if it is placed on top of a background in another program.

You should consider locking objects under the following circumstances:

✦ **When the document is full of complex artwork.** You can do a Select All and not have to wait forever for the selection tool to finish selecting all parts of the complex art before locking the artwork.

✦ **When you don't want to accidentally move or change certain artwork.**

✦ **When you can't easily select paths that are under other paths.** In this case, you lock the ones on top.

✦ **When you have to fit an illustration into a certain area.** In this situation, you create a box of that size and lock it so you have an instant boundary with which to work.

Hiding objects

Sometimes, you don't want to see certain objects on your document page — perhaps because they obstruct your view of other objects or they take a long time to redraw. In these cases, it's a good idea to hide the objects in question. To do so, select them and choose Object ➪ Hide ➪ Selection. Alternatively, you can press Ctrl+3 (⌘+3).

Hidden objects are invisible and unselectable; they still exist in the document, but they do not print. When a document is closed and reopened, hidden objects reappear.

To show (and select) all hidden objects, choose Object ➪ Show All. Alternatively, you can press Ctrl+Alt+3 (⌘+Option+3). Think of it as "unhide." There is no way to show just a few of the hidden objects when using the Show All command.

Setting object attributes

Choosing Window ➪ Attributes (Ctrl+F11/⌘+F11) displays the Attributes palette. In this palette, you have these options:

✦ The Overprint Fill and Overprint Stroke options control how Illustrator handles overlapping areas of different colors when printing the document.

✦ The Show or Hide Object's Center Point buttons let you choose whether to view the center point of a closed path.

✦ The Reverse Path Direction buttons are used when working with compound paths. Use these to reverse a path's direction when a multiple compound path isn't working.

✦ The Use Non-Zero Winding Fill Rule and Use Even-Odd Fill Rule buttons control how Illustrator fills areas defined by compound paths.

✦ The Image Map list box enables you to specify the shape of an area in an image map.

✦ The URL field allows you to specify a URL (Uniform Resource Locator) for a selected object or objects.

✦ Add notes about the document or specific objects in the text box at the bottom of the palette. You can use notes to tell different things about the document such as color space and special effects used.

Another useful way to "copyright" your artwork is to select all the objects and then go to the Attributes palette and enter your copyright information within the palette, as shown in Figure 8-1.

Don't Show Center

Show Center

Overprint Fill

Reverse Path Direction Off

Overprint Stroke

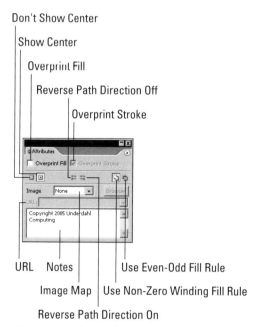

URL   Notes   Use Even-Odd Fill Rule

Image Map   Use Non-Zero Winding Fill Rule

Reverse Path Direction On

Figure 8-1: The Attributes palette allows you to add notes to your artwork.

Understanding Object Stacking Order

Stacking order is a crucial concept that you need to understand in the world of Adobe Illustrator. This concept is not the same as the layer concept; rather, it is the forward/backward relationship between objects within each layer.

After you create the first object, Illustrator places the next object you create in front of the first object, or on top of it. Likewise, Illustrator places the third created object in front of both the first and second objects. This cycle continues indefinitely, with objects being stacked one in front of another.

To make your life much more pleasant, Illustrator lets you move objects forward or backward through the stack of objects. In fact, Illustrator's method of moving objects forward and backward is so simple and basic that it is also quite limiting. You can also move objects via the Layers palette. The Layers palette offers a wide range of moving and organizing options.

Cross-Reference   For more on layers and moving objects, see "Moving and layers" later in this chapter.

Controlling the stacking order for objects

You can change the stacking order of objects in Illustrator from front to back, or you can move objects up or down through the stacking order. Figure 8-2 shows two versions of the same illustration after various objects were moved in the stacking order. Use these commands for moving objects in the stacking order:

Figure 8-2: The stacking order changed the look of the illustration.

✦ **Bring to Front:** To move an object to the front, choose Object ➪ Arrange ➪ Bring to Front, or press Ctrl+Shift+] (⌘+Shift+]). Illustrator moves the selected object forward so that it is in front of every other object (but only in that layer). Bring to Front is not available when no objects are selected. Multiple-selected paths and grouped paths still retain their front/back position relative to each other.

✦ **Bring Forward:** To move selected objects forward one object at a time, choose Object ➪ Arrange ➪ Bring Forward, or press Ctrl+] (⌘+]).

✦ **Send Backward:** To move selected objects backward one object at a time, choose Object ➪ Arrange ➪ Send Backward, or press Ctrl+[(⌘+[).

✦ **Send to Back:** To move an object to the back, choose Object ➪ Arrange ➪ Send to Back, or press Ctrl+Shift+[(⌘+Shift+[). Illustrator sends the selected object to the back so that it is behind every other object. Send to Back is not available when there are no objects selected. Multiple selected paths and grouped paths still retain their front/back position relative to each other.

✦ **Send to Current Layer:** Use the Object ➪ Arrange ➪ Send to Current Layer command to move the selected object to a different layer. You must first select the object and then select the destination layer in the Layers palette before choosing this command.

Understanding stacking order for text

Individual characters in a string of text work in a similar manner to their object cousins when it comes to front/back placement. The first character typed is placed at the back of the text block, and the last character typed is placed at the front, as shown in Figure 8-3. To move individual characters forward or backward, you must first choose Type ➪ Create Outlines, or press Ctrl+Shift+O (⌘+Shift+O), and then select the outline of the character that you want to arrange. The outlined text is now treated as an object. Use the same arranging commands from the Object ➪ Arrange submenu that you use for other types of objects to move the stacking order of the outlined type.

Figure 8-3: Text characters that overlap each other demonstrate stacking order.

 For more on text, see Chapter 9.

Stacking order for strokes and fills

Try as you might, you cannot change the front/back relationship of strokes and fills. Strokes are always in front of fills for the same path. To get the fill to cover or over-lap the stroke, you must copy the path, use the Paste in Front command by choosing Edit ➪ Paste in Front or pressing Ctrl+F (⌘+F), and then remove the stroke from the path that you pasted.

 For more on Strokes and Fills, see Chapter 10.

Pasting objects in front of and behind selected objects

Choosing Edit ➪ Paste in Front, or pressing Ctrl+F (⌘+F), pastes any objects you have on the Clipboard in front of any selected objects, or at the top of the current layer if no objects are selected.

Choosing Edit ➪ Paste in Back, or pressing Ctrl+B (⌘+B), pastes any objects on the Clipboard behind any selected objects, or at the bottom of the current layer if no objects are selected. When you paste an object in front of or behind, you also are pasting the attributes of that object (the stroke and fill).

In addition, both Paste in Front and Paste in Back paste objects in the same location as the copied object, even from document to document. If the documents are different sizes, Illustrator pastes them in the same location relative to the center of each document. If the Clipboard is empty, or if type selected with a Type tool is on the Clipboard, these options are not available.

Note Copied items in Illustrator retain their layer name and related layer information. When you copy an item that is on layer "X-Flies" and paste that item in another document that contains an X-Flies layer, the item appears on the X-Flies layer. If the document doesn't contain that layer, Illustrator creates a new layer with that name and the item appears on that layer. This works only if you select the Paste Remembers Layers option item in the Layers palette's pop-up menu.

Creating and Deconstructing Groups

Grouping is the process of putting together a series of objects that need to remain spatially constant in relationship to each other. You generally group objects if you intend to move them, flatten them, or perform one effect on all of them at once. Your group may contain as little as one path, to an unlimited number of objects. You generally ungroup a group of objects when you no longer need the grouping. For example, you may ungroup objects so that you can edit one of them. When you have objects that go together, such as the figure of a person you created, you may want to group all parts of that person to keep the figure neatly together. That way, when you want to move the person, all pieces move together as one unit. Often, you try to move a collection of objects, and you miss one or more pieces. When you group the pieces together, they all move together when one object is selected. Ungrouping is necessary when you want to separate the objects to make them a part of another group or you want them to stand individually. When applying transformations or special effects, you'll want to ungroup so the specific object can have the effect applied.

Grouping objects

In any illustration, objects are much easier to manipulate if they are grouped. Grouping similar areas is helpful for moving entire areas forward or backward, as well as for doing any type of horizontal or vertical movement or transformation upon a set of objects. Suppose that you drew a tree with a bunch of apples. You want to group the apples together so you can edit the apples all at one time, such as changing the color or the size.

To group objects together, follow these steps:

1. **Select the items you want to group with any of the Selection tools.** For a run down of the various Selection tools, see Chapter 6.

2. **Choose Object ➪ Group, or press Ctrl+G (⌘+G).** This command makes the separate objects stay together when you select them.

Now, when you select any object in a group with the regular Selection tool, Illustrator selects all the objects in that group and makes all the points in a path solid (selected).

Cross-Reference The Group Selection tool is covered in Chapter 6.

Not only can you group several objects together, but you can also group groups together to form a group of groups in which there is a hierarchical series of grouped groups. In addition, groups can be grouped to individual objects or to several other objects.

After a set of objects or groups is grouped together, grouping it again produces no effect. The computer does not beep at you, display a dialog box, or otherwise indicate that the objects or groups you are attempting to group together are already grouped. Of course, it never hurts to again choose Object ➪ Group if you are not sure whether they are grouped. If they weren't grouped before, they now are, and if they were grouped before, nothing unusual or unexpected happens.

Tip If you group several objects that are on different layers, all the objects move to the topmost layer that contains one of the grouped objects and form a group there. This means that the perceived stacking order may change, which can change the appearance of your Illustration.

Ungrouping

If you are looking to apply a specific effect to one object in the group, you'll have to ungroup the object so the whole group isn't affected. Suppose, in the apple tree, that you want to make one apple really big and rotten-looking. First, ungroup the apples, regroup the other apples (to keep them organized), and then apply the effect to the one apple. To ungroup groups (separate them into individual paths and objects), follow these steps:

1. **Select the group with either the Group Selection tool or the regular Selection tool.**

2. **Choose Object ➪ Ungroup, or press Ctrl+Shift+G (⌘+Shift+G).** Any selected groups become ungrouped.

Ungrouping, like grouping, works on one set of groups at a time. For example, if you have two groups that are grouped together, ungrouping that outer group results in the two original groups. If you again choose Ungroup, Illustrator also ungroups those two groups. Another way to understand grouping is to think of nesting. Each operation adds or subtracts only one level of nesting.

Tip   When you absolutely do not want anything in a group grouped with anything else —
and you suspect that there may be several mini-groups within the group you have
selected — simply press Ctrl+Shift+G (⌘+Shift+G) several times. You do not need to
select the subgroups individually to ungroup them. To get rid of all the groups in
your illustration, choose Select ➪ All, or press Ctrl+A (⌘+A) and then proceed to
ungroup by pressing Ctrl+Shift+G (⌘+Shift+G) several times. To remove certain
objects from a group or compound path, select just those objects, cut, and Paste in
Front (or Paste in Back).

Layering Your Artwork

Illustrator's layering feature provides an easy and powerful way to separate artwork
into individual sections. A layer is a separate section of the document that is on its
own level, above, under, or in between other layers, but never on the same level as
another layer. You can view these sections separately, locked, hidden, and rearranged
around each other. Figure 8-4 shows a logo illustration that has been layered; it also
shows the Layers palette representing the various layers. In this case, the layers have
been named to make it easier to keep track of what is on each layer.

As you can see from this illustration, having the various elements of your illustration on separate layers helps you organize them. Each area of the illustration has its
own layer. You use these layers to create the stacking order as well as to keep the
text on one layer for easier editing. You'll find that artists use layers to organize the
different grouped objects, shadows, borders, and backgrounds. You can also turn
layers off and on to give a client different options on a logo, Web site, or business
theme. Using the Layers palette, you can create, control, and manipulate layers to
suit your needs. Another use for layers is to trace placed images.

Cross-   For more on tracing placed images, see the section "Working with Templates in
Reference   Illustrator."

The biggest advantage for layers is that you can color-code them to further organize your work. By choosing Select ➪ All or pressing Ctrl+A (⌘+A), you can quickly
see which objects are on which layers, just by the color of the paths and points.
The selection boxes for each layer match the color shown in the right column of the
Layers palette (which is displayed when objects on that layer are selected). Using
the same colors for all layers makes you miss out on half the power of layers. Use
vivid, distinct colors for each layer.

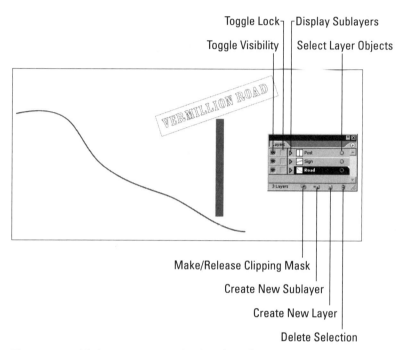

Figure 8-4: This logo was created using three layers to keep the illustration organized.

Of course, having too many layers can pose problems. Layers take up RAM (Random Access Memory) and computer power. Therefore, the more layers you have, the slower your system operates. For this reason, you should create layers only when they help you better organize an illustration. Even setting up one additional layer can dramatically ease selection and moving problems.

Tip   You can create as many layers as you want, up to the limitations of application memory. Suffice it to say, however, that the more layers you create after a certain point (several hundred), the slower Illustrator runs.

Getting started with layers

After you realize that you need to use layers, what do you do? The only way to manipulate, create, and delete layers is by using the Layers palette. If the Layers palette is not showing, choose Window ➪ Layers or press F7. When you open the Layers palette for the first time in a new document, you see only Layer 1 listed.

To create a new layer, do the following:

1. **Click the Create New Layer icon at the bottom of the palette.** The icon looks like a piece of paper with the corner folded over and is to the left of the Trash icon in Figure 8-4. You can also click the triangle in the upper right of the palette to display a pop-up menu. Clicking the first item, New Layer, displays the Layer Options dialog box shown in Figure 8-5. You can also display this dialog box by double-clicking the layer name.

Figure 8-5: The Layers Options dialog box lets you name the layer.

2. **Change the name of your layer.** In the Layer Options dialog box, the name of the new layer is highlighted. To change this name, type a new name, and it replaces the generic name.

3. **Select any of the options that you want for this layer.** The options below the name in the Layers Options dialog box affect how you view the layer and make it function. The options are as follows:

   - **Color:** The first option is the color of the paths and points when objects on that layer are selected. Choose one of the preset colors from the drop-down list (pop-up menu) or select the Other option to use a Custom Color. Each time you create a new layer, a different color (going in order from the list) is applied to that layer.

   - **Template:** Use this option when you want to trace something, but not have it print. If you check Template, Illustrator automatically unchecks the Print option and enables the Dim Images option. See more on the Dim Images option below.

   - **Show:** This option makes the objects in the layer visible.

   - **Preview:** This option lets you see a preview of objects on this layer.

   - **Lock:** This option prevents objects on this layer from being selected and prevents any objects from being put on this layer.

For more on the Lock feature, see the section "Locking and Hiding Objects."

- **Print:** This option enables you to print objects that are on this layer.
- **Dim Images to:** This option dims any placed images on the layer, making them 50 percent lighter as a default, or you can enter a value.

4. **Click OK.** The new layer appears above the existing layer in the Layers palette.

If you want the objects on the new layer to appear below the objects on the existing layer, click the name of the new layer and drag it below the existing layer. Be careful not to drop the new layer on top of the existing layer — doing so will make the new layer into a sublayer of the existing layer.

For more on sublayers, see the section "Moving and layers" later in this chapter.

To modify the existing layer, double-click it. You see the Layer Options dialog box again. Make the changes and choose the options that you want for this layer and then click OK.

Using the Layers palette

The Layers palette is the control center where all layer-related activities take place. Most activities take place on the main section of the Layers palette, which is always visible when the Layers palette is onscreen. Other activities take place in the pop-up menu that appears when you press the triangle in the upper right of the palette.

Illustrator has wonderful options in the Layers palette. First is the capability to thin the display of layers in the palette for those illustrations with tons of layers. Second is the capability to drag to a hidden layer. Third is that Illustrator displays in italic layers that you don't have set to print, so that you can see quickly what will and what will not print.

Clicking the Close button in the Layers palette closes the Layers palette. You can also close the Layers palette by choosing Window ⇨ Layers or by pressing F7. To bring the Layers palette back to the screen, choose Window ⇨ Layers or press F7 again.

Using Layers palette columns

Aside from the standard Minimize and Close (Zoom and Close) buttons at the top of the palette, the following gives an exhaustive list of the options in the Layers palette:

- ✦ **Show/Hide column:** The far-left column controls how you view each layer. If this column has a solid eye icon, the layer is in Preview mode. The hollow eye icon means that the layer is in Outline mode. No eye indicates a hidden layer.

Clicking a solid or hollow eye icon toggles it from showing to hidden. Clicking in the Show/Hide Column when no eye is present shows the layer. Pressing Ctrl (⌘) and clicking the eye toggles it from solid (Preview mode) to hollow (Outline mode) and back again. Pressing Alt (Option) and clicking an eye shows or hides all other layers. Layers that are set as template layers display a little icon with an overlaid square, triangle, and ellipse to indicate a template layer.

✦ **Lock/Unlock column:** The second column is the Lock/Unlock column. The lock icon indicates whether a layer is locked. An empty column means that the layer is not locked. A lock icon means that the layer is locked from use.

To manually activate the Lock and Hide commands and to learn about their various uses, see the section "Locking and Hiding Objects."

✦ **Layer Names:** The column in the center of the palette lists the names of all the layers in the document. When no documents are open, no layers are listed. If one layer is highlighted and has a triangle in the upper-right corner, that layer is active. All new objects are created on the active layer. You can select a range of layers by Shift-clicking each layer. Pressing Ctrl (⌘) allows you to select or deselect additional layers.

The layer at the top of the column is the layer that is on top of all the other layers. The layer at the bottom of the column is the layer that is at the bottom of all the other layers. To move a layer or layers, click and drag it up or down. As you drag, a dark horizontal line indicates where the layers are placed when you release the mouse button.

Ctrl+Alt+Click (⌘+Option+Click) on the eye icon to turn all layers into Outline mode except the selected layer.

You can undo all layer changes as they happen by choosing Edit ⇨ Undo or by pressing Ctrl+Z (⌘+Z) immediately afterward.

✦ **Target icon:** When an object is selected, the target icon displays as a double ring. It appears as a single ring when the object is not selected. You can also click the icon to select the object.

✦ **Object status:** To the right of the layer's name is the object status of the layer. If a square appears in that column, at least one object on that layer is selected.

Using the Layers palette icons

The four icons along the bottom of the Layers palette make layer manipulation very easy. This section explains what these icons do:

✦ **Make/Release Clipping Mask:** This icon, which looks like an overlapping rectangle and circle, lets you create a clipping mask in the layer. The topmost object in the layer acts as the masking shape. The difference between using

Make/Release Clipping Mask from the Layers palette rather than choosing
Object ➪ Clipping Mask ➪ Make is that the objects won't be grouped when
using the Layers palette.

Cross-Reference   For more on clipping masks, see Chapter 12.

✦ **Create New Sublayer:** You use this icon, which looks like an arrow pointing to
a piece of paper with a corner turned down, to add sublayers. To do so, select
the layer and choose the Create New Sublayer icon or choose Create New
Sublayer from the pop-up menu in the Layers palette. You can have as many
sublayers inside a layer as you want. To see the sublayers, click the triangle to
the left of the layer name. You can also change a layer into a sublayer by
dragging it under the layer you want it to go to. Figure 8-6 shows the sublayers
within a layer. You'll notice a sublayer is indicated by <> brackets and is
indented. Some sublayers have a triangle indicating that there are more sublayers within that sublayer. The sublayers also tell you what is in that layer,
for example <path>, <compound path>, and so on.

Figure 8-6: The sublayers of a layered illustration show
you the document layout.

✦ **Create New Layer:** Clicking this icon, which looks like a piece of paper with a
corner turned down, creates a new layer instantly, without the New Layer dialog
box appearing. If you press Alt (Option) and click the New Layer icon,
Illustrator creates a new layer by way of the Layer Options dialog box. Dragging
a layer to the New Layer icon duplicates that layer and everything on it.

✦ **Delete Selection:** Clicking this icon, which looks like a trash can, deletes the
selected layers. If there is art on a layer that is about to be deleted, a dialog
box appears to make sure that you really want to delete that layer; Figure 8-7
shows the warning you'll receive. Alt (Option)+clicking the Trash icon deletes
selected layers without a warning dialog box, whether or not art is on the
selected layers. You can also drag layers to the Trash icon; Illustrator deletes
the layers without a warning dialog box.

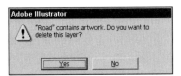

Figure 8-7: If you attempt to delete a layer that contains artwork, Illustrator warns you before actually deleting the layer.

Moving and layers

You can move selected objects to another layer. A selected object shows up on its layer with a square in the upper-right corner of that layer. Dragging that square to another layer moves the selected object to that layer. Figure 8-8 shows a selection marker being dragged to another layer. You can drag only to a layer that is not hidden or locked. Only one object at a time can be moved to another layer.

This box shows the items being dragged.

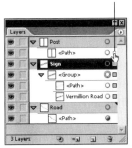

Figure 8-8: The selected object is being moved to another layer.

Using the Layers palette pop-up menu

Clicking the triangle in the upper right of the Layers palette displays a pop-up menu that shows the different options that are available relative to the selected layers; Figure 8-9 shows this pop-up menu. These options are available:

✦ **New Layer:** This option creates a new layer above the currently selected layer or, if no layer is selected, at the top of the list. When you select this option, the Layer Options dialog box appears. When you create a new layer, Illustrator automatically assigns the next color in the color list.

Figure 8-9: The Layers palette pop-up menu gives you more options for working with layers.

Tip   If you press the Alt (Option) key before you click the pop-up menu triangle, the first menu item reads New Layer Above First Layer, or New Layer Above whatever the name of the active layer is.

✦ **New Sublayer:** This option creates a new sublayer below the selected layer.

✦ **Duplicate Layer:** This option duplicates selected layers, along with any objects that are on those layers. You can also duplicate layers by dragging them to the New Layer icon at the bottom of the Layers palette.

✦ **Delete Layer:** This option deletes the layer and any artwork on the layer. If the layer you want to delete contains artwork, a dialog box warns you that you are about to delete it. If one or more objects are selected, the Layers palette menu says "Delete Selection." If you select several layers, the entry reads Delete Layers, and all selected layers are deleted. You can undo layer deletions using the Edit ➪ Undo command.

✦ **Options for Layer:** This option is called Options for whatever the name of the active layer is. The menu item reads Options for Selection if you select more than one layer. Clicking Options for Selection displays the Layer Options dialog box, in which you can choose a number of different options. If more than one layer is selected, the layer options affect all selected layers.

✦ **Make/Release Clipping Mask:** This option creates a clipping mask in the layer. The topmost object in the layer acts as the masking shape.

✦ **Locate Object:** Use this to find where an object is located in the Layers palette. Choose an object in the document, and then choose this option to see where it is in the Layers palette.

✦ **Merge Selected:** This option combines selected layers into one. Merging layers does two important things: First, it places art that you want on the same layer together in one step. Second, it eliminates all those empty layers automatically.

✦ **Flatten Artwork:** This option takes all your layers and combines them as one layer.

✦ **Collect in New Layer:** This option moves the selected objects to a new layer.

✦ **Release to Layers (Sequence):** Use this option to move the selected objects to new individual layers.

✦ **Release to Layers (Build):** Use this option to move the selected objects to layers in a cumulative sequence. You mainly use this option to create animation sequences where the first layer contains the first object, the second layer contains the first and second objects, the third layer contains the first three objects, and so on.

✦ **Reverse Order:** Use this to reverse the stacking order of the selected layers. The layers must be adjoining in the Layers palette.

✦ **Template:** You use this option to make your selection a template.

✦ **Hide Others:** This option hides all the layers except the selected ones.

✦ **Outline Others/Preview All Layers:** This option changes all unselected layers to Outline view or changes all unselected layers to Preview view.

✦ **Lock Others/Unlock All Layers:** This option locks all layers except the selected ones or unlocks all layers except the selected ones.

✦ **Paste Remembers Layers:** This option causes Illustrator to paste all objects on the layer from which you copied them, regardless of which layer is currently active. Unchecking this menu item causes objects on the Clipboard to be pasted on the current layer.

✦ **Palette Options:** Use this option to change the Row Size, Thumbnail views, and whether to Show Layers Only.

Tip Double-clicking a layer name displays the Layer options dialog box.

Working with Templates in Illustrator

It's often much easier to create artwork in Illustrator by starting with something to trace, whether it's a logo, a floor plan, or your cousin Fred's disproportionate profile. Even the best artists use some form of template when they draw to keep proportions consistent, to get angles just right, and for other reasons that help them to achieve the best possible result.

This section discusses methods and techniques for manually tracing different types of artwork within Illustrator. First, you place an image—the image that you eventually want to trace—on a layer, which is your template layer. Next, you use the template layer to trace your image.

Cross-Reference Illustrator CS2 offers a new feature called Live Trace that you can use to automatically trace raster images. For more information about Live Trace, see Chapter 13.

Placing a template on a layer

You can create a template in Illustrator by placing any image into a "template" layer. That image can then be used for tracing or as a guide for creating or adjusting artwork.

Follow these steps to create a template layer:

1. **Double-click the layer that you want to modify.** The Layer Options dialog box appears. For more about the various options in this dialog box, see the section "Getting started with layers."

2. **In the Layer Options dialog box, check the Template option.** By default, the Dim Images check box is checked, and all other options are grayed out.

3. **Enter a value in the Dim Images text field.** The lower the percent value, the lighter the image appears in Illustrator.

4. **Click OK to apply the change.** Illustrator creates a template layer from the image you selected.

Note Paths that you place on Template layers do not show when they're selected. Instead, an icon appears in the Layers palette's view column to indicate that the current layer is a template layer. Template layers do not print. For more on the columns in the Layers palette, see the section "Using Layers palette columns."

Tip You can make any vector artwork into a template by rasterizing it and then setting that layer into a template layer.

Figure 8-10 shows an image before and after dimming.

Placed images work well as templates because their resolution is independent of the Illustrator document. You can scale placed images up or down, changing their onscreen resolution as you change their size. For example, if you scale a 72-dpi (dots-per-inch) image down to one-fourth of its imported size (making the dpi of the placed image 4 x 72-dpi, or 288-dpi), you may zoom in on the image in Illustrator at 400 percent. At 400 percent, the placed image still has a 72-dpi resolution because one-fourth of 288-dpi is 72-dpi. The more you increase the placed image's dpi by scaling it down, the more you can zoom in to see the details of the image. Here's another plus: A placed image template is a full-color template that keeps all the shading and colors and enables you to see all the fine details easily. That way, you can trace all the tiny details that the color brings out.

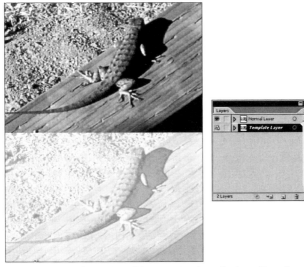

Figure 8-10: The original image (top) and after dimming (bottom)

Using a template to trace an image

Now that you've got your template (placed image) all set up, you're ready to trace it — or so you would think. You can go about tracing in lots of different ways, and I've included the "best of the best" techniques in this section to help you muddle through this mess.

You can trace templates in two ways: manually and automatically. Manually tracing consists of using the Pencil and Pen tools to tediously trace the edges of a template — often a very time-consuming task. You manually trace an image when you have lots of time on your hands, and when you want to retain every single detail of the traced image. As an alternative, you can use the Live Trace function, discussed in Chapter 13, to speed up the process.

Some designers prefer manually tracing templates. Using the Pen and Pencil tools allows illustrators to add detail, remove oddities, and change curves, angles, and the so on to their satisfaction. You'll also find that using a pressure-sensitive tablet makes for really nice, accurate tracing. The Pencil tool is great to use when creating more bumpy lines as in map drawing. The Pen tool is fantastic for creating smoother, more accurate lines.

Cross-Reference For more on using the Pen and Pencil tools, see Chapter 4.

Note   If you use a pressure-sensitive drawing tablet, you may find that manually tracing a printed copy of an image that you place under the clear plastic overlay on the surface of the tablet is easier than attempting to trace the image on the screen. You may need to experiment to see which method best suits your working style.

Using Align and Distribute

The Align palette, shown in Figure 8-11, contains several buttons for aligning and distributing objects with a simple click of a button. Align treats paths, type objects, and groups as single objects, allowing for quite a bit of flexibility when aligning and distributing. Aligning objects moves them to line up along a specified area (horizontal left, horizontal middle, horizontal right, vertical top, vertical center, and vertical bottom). Select the objects first; then choose an alignment. Distribute takes the selected objects and evenly move them a specified amount from each other (vertical distribute top, vertical distribute center, vertical distribute bottom, horizontal distribute left, horizontal distribute center, and horizontal distribute right).

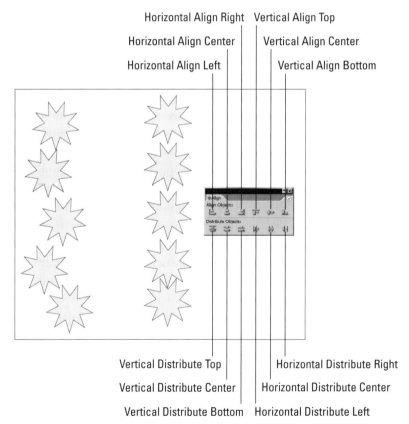

Figure 8-11: The Align palette and objects before alignment (left) and after aligning along the left (right)

To use the Align palette, follow these steps:

1. **Select the objects you want to align and/or distribute.** See Chapter 6 for more on selecting objects.

2. **Click the appropriate button in the palette.** The palette has two areas: Align Objects and Distribute Objects:

   - **The Align area:** In order from left to right, the icons in this area include: Horizontal Align Left, Horizontal Align Center, Horizontal Align Right, Vertical Align Top, Vertical Align Center, and Vertical Align Bottom.

   - **The Distribute areas:** In order from left to right, this area includes: Vertical Distribute Top, Vertical Distribute Center, Vertical Distribute Bottom, Horizontal Distribute Left, Horizontal Distribute Center, and Horizontal Distribute Right.

Tip
Each click in the palette counts as a change in Illustrator, which means that if you click 20 times, you'll need to undo 20 times to get back to where you started.

Measuring an Image

So you're drawing the blueprints for that new civic center downtown, and your boss wants everything to scale. Wouldn't it be great if Illustrator helped you with your gargantuan task? But, wait! It does! You can measure objects or distances between objects in Illustrator in several ways:

✦ Using the Measure tool

✦ Using the Transform palette

✦ Using the rulers along the side of the document window

✦ Placing objects whose dimensions are known against the edges

✦ Using Offset Paths

✦ Eyeballing it (popular since the first artist painted his recollections of the preceding day's battle with the saber-toothed animals of his time)

Different methods of measuring are appropriate for different needs. For example, you want to use the Measure tool to check the accuracy between objects or the size of the objects. When using the Transform palette, you can enter exact measurements of scaling, moving, rotating, shear, and reflecting. The rulers let you drag out guidelines for keeping your objects accurately sized and aligned. Offset path duplicates the selected path, offsetting it from the original by the specified distance. Eyeballing is fine as long as accuracy isn't a condition of your illustration.

The default unit of measure for all the measurement methods listed above is points. Before we discuss the various ways to measure, we start with a discussion of how to change units.

Changing the measurement units

The default of using points for measurement is great for type, but when was the last time your art director said, "I'd like you to design a 360 x 288-point ad and make the logo at least 144 points high." And your grandmother isn't likely to say to you, "Gosh, you must be at least 5,600 points tall, maybe taller. You've grown at least 100 points since I last saw you. Does your mother let you wear that to school?!"

Points don't work for everything, so Adobe lets us change the measurement units to picas, inches, centimeters, millimeters, or pixels. The way to choose from these measurements is to temporarily indicate a different unit of measurement each time you enter a value, by appending a character or two to the end of your numerical value.

In the metric system, there are 100 centimeters in a meter and 10 millimeters in a centimeter. The other system, which is much more significant to Illustrator users, is the pica/point system. When the pica measurement system is selected in the Units and Display Performance Preferences, measurements are displayed using the common (common to typesetters and designers, anyway) system of picas followed by points. So a distance of 3 picas and 6 points is displayed as 3p6. Such a measurement is displayed as 42 points using the point system.

You can change to a different unit of measure in one of three ways:

✦ **Using the Preferences dialog box:** Choose Edit (Illustrator) ➪ Preferences ➪ Units & Display Performance, and select the measurement system you want in the General list box. This permanently alters your measurement units. In other words, all dialog boxes in all new documents will express their measurements in the specified units, not points.

✦ **Using the Document Setup menu:** Choose File ➪ Document Setup, and choose the appropriate unit of measure in the Units list box. This changes the units to inches in that document only.

✦ **Using any dialog box:** Type the appropriate unit abbreviation, listed in Table 8-1, after the number in whatever dialog box you open, even if the text fields show points. Illustrator does conversions from points to inches and centimeters (and vice versa) on the fly, so after you enter a point value, the program converts the points into inches as soon as you press the Tab key. This little feature can be an excellent way for you to become more comfortable with points and picas. To get picas, enter "p0" after the number.

Table 8-1 Illustrator Unit Abbreviations		
Unit of Measure	**Abbreviation**	**Example**
Inches	inch, in or "	To enter 2 inches, type 2 inch, 2 in, or 2".
Millimeters	mm	To enter 2 millimeters, type 2 mm.
Centimeters	cm	To enter 2 centimeters, type 2 cm.
Points	pt	To enter 2 points, type 2 pt or p 2.
Picas	p	To enter 2 picas, type 2p.
Picas and points	p	To enter 2 picas 6 points, type 2p6.
Pixels	px	To enter 2 pixels, type 2px.

A quick refresher on measurement units and their relations:

$$1" = 6p = 72\ pt = 25.4\ mm = 2.54\ cm$$
$$.16667" = 1p = 12\ pt = 4.2\ mm = .42\ cm$$
$$.01389" = p1 = 1\ pt = .35\ mm = .035\ cm$$
$$.03931" = p2.83 = 2.83\ pt = 1\ mm = .1\ cm$$
$$.39305" = 2p4.35 = 28.35\ pt = 10\ mm = 1\ cm$$

Pixels cannot be directly related to the other measurement units because the size of each pixel varies according to screen resolution.

Using the Measure tool

The fastest way to obtain a precise, exact measurement in Illustrator is to use the Measure tool, shown in Figure 8-12. Follow these steps to use the tool:

1. **Click and hold the Eyedropper tool.** The Measure tool is a pop-up tool found with the Eyedropper and Paint Bucket tools.

2. **Click the Measure tool.** The icon looks like a ruler.

3. **Click an object where you want to begin measuring with the Measure tool.** The Info palette of the Measure tool appears.

4. **Click where you want to end your measurement.** The Info palette shows the distance between the location first clicked and the next location clicked or the distance between where the tool was first clicked and where the mouse was released after dragging.

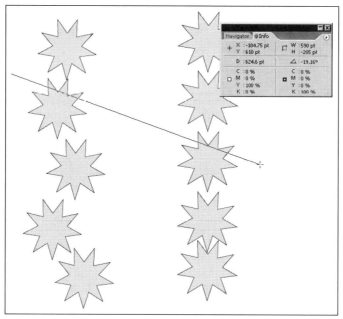

Figure 8-12: The Measure tool enables you to make very precise measurements.

Double-clicking the Measure Tool displays the Guides & Grid section of the Preferences dialog box where you can set the distance between grid lines if you use the grid to help in making more accurate drawings.

Cross-Reference To learn more about the Guides & Grid Preferences dialog box, see the sections "Working with Grids" and "Using Guides" later in this chapter.

You can use the measurements that you obtain with the Measure tool to move your object the distance you want. As soon as the Measure tool measures a distance, it routes that information to the Move dialog box, shown in Figure 8-13. The next time you open the Move dialog box, it holds the values sent by the Measure tool. You open the Move dialog box by choosing Object ⇨ Transform ⇨ Move or by double-clicking the Selection tool. If you hold down the Shift key, you can constrain the movement of the measuring line to 45 degrees or 90 degrees.

Figure 8-13: The Move dialog box allows you to move objects with great precision.

Sizing objects with the Transform palette

A great way to resize objects is using the Transform palette. When you have an object selected, you can enter a new height and width in the Transform palette and immediately the object changes to match the new measurements. The Transform palette also lets you know the placement of the object via the x and y units. The Transform palette, which you open by choosing Window ➪ Transform, shows the height, width, and location of any selected path or paths, as shown in Figure 8-14.

Figure 8-14: Use the Transform palette to set objects to specific sizes.

The options for the Transform palette are listed as follows:

✦ **X and Y:** These two options show the location of the object on the page, measured from the lower-left corner.

✦ **W:** This option shows the width of the selected object (or the total width of the selected objects when more than one is selected).

✦ **H:** This option shows the height or total height of the selected object or objects.

✦ **Rotate:** Located on the bottom left of the palette, you use this option to rotate an object by entering a value in degrees.

✦ **Shear:** Located on the bottom right, you can enter a value to slant the object along a horizontal or vertical axis.

To change the object's size, select the object first and then enter a new value for the height and width in the Transform palette. If you want the object to move, enter new X and Y values in the Transform palette.

Using rulers

You can toggle rulers on and off by choosing View ➪ Show/Hide Rulers or by pressing Ctrl+R (⌘+R). Normally, the rulers measure up and across from the artboard's lower-left corner; however, you can alter this orientation by dragging the ruler origin (where the zeros are) from its position in the upper-left corner, between where the two rulers meet. Because rulers take up valuable onscreen real estate, it's usually a good idea to leave them turned off unless you are constantly measuring things or you want to display your illustration at a higher magnification. Rulers are easy to show and hide—just press Ctrl+R (⌘+R) when you want to see them, and press Ctrl+R (⌘+R) again to hide them. To reset the rulers to their original location, double-click in the origin box of the rulers.

Tip If you change the ruler origin to the middle of the document page, move it back to a corner when you are finished. When you zoom in, rulers may be the only indicator of your location within the document.

One of the rulers' nicest features is the display of dotted lines on the rulers that correspond to the cursor's position. And yet, at times, measuring with rulers works no better than eyeballing; although the process requires precision, you are limited by the rulers' hash marks in pinpointing the cursor's exact position. The rulers are best suited for measuring when the document is at a very high zoom level.

Measuring with objects

Using objects to compare distances can be more effective than using either the Measure tool or the rulers, especially when you need to place objects precisely—for example, when you want several objects to be the same distance from one another.

If you place a circle adjacent to an object (so that the objects' edges touch), you know that the second object is placed correctly when it's aligned to the circle's other side. (A circle is the object most commonly used because the diameter is constant.)

You can use other objects for measuring, including these:

✦ **Squares:** When you need to measure horizontal and vertical distances

✦ **Rectangles:** When the horizontal and vertical distances are different

✦ **Lines:** When the distance applies to only one direction

To enable better precision, turn the measuring object into a guide using the View ➪ Guides ➪ Make Guides command.

Cross-Reference Guides are discussed in more detail in the section "Using Guides," later in this chapter.

Using Offset Path (for equidistant measuring)

Suppose that you want to place several objects the same distance from a central object. You may find that using any of the previously mentioned measuring techniques is time-consuming and even inaccurate, especially when you deal with complex images. However, Illustrator's Offset Path dialog box enables you to automatically align objects equidistantly from a central object.

To use an Offset Path to measure objects that are equally spaced apart, follow these steps:

1. **Select the central object.** See Chapter 5 for more on selecting objects.

2. **Choose Object ➪ Path ➪ Offset Path.** The Offset Path dialog box, shown in Figure 8-15, opens.

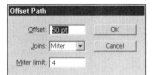

Figure 8-15: The Offset Path dialog box creates an offset path you can use for precise placement of objects.

3. **Enter the desired distance in the Offset text field.** You can enter a distance in points, millimeters, inches, or pixels. See the section "Changing the measurement" for more on entering the correct unit of measure.

For detailed coverage on the Offset Path dialog box and its settings, see Chapter 6.

4. **Click OK.** Illustrator creates the new Offset Path.

5. **Change the new path into a guide.** For more information, see the section "Creating guides" later in this chapter.

6. **Align your objects to this guide.**

Working with Grids

Nothing I've found is more useful on a day-to-day basis than the Grid feature. Grids act as a framework for your artwork, providing an easy method for aligning and positioning images. Figure 8-16 shows an Illustrator document that has grids turned on. One advantage of using grids is the Snap to Grid feature. With this feature, you can move objects near a gridline, and Illustrator automatically snaps the object directly on the grid line.

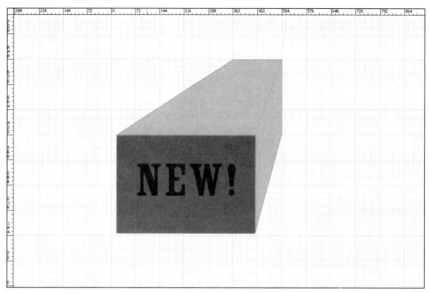

Figure 8-16: A document with Illustrator's Grid function turned on

Grids start from the origin of your artboard (usually the lower-left corner). If you want to change the position of the grid, you can do so by dragging the origin point (at the Origin Marker where the rulers meet) to the new starting position for the grid. You reset the grid position (and the ruler origin) by double-clicking the Origin Marker.

Instead of gridlines, you may want to use guides for layout purposes. For example, you may need a few lines in different locations to set a page for a flyer advertisement. Use guides by dragging them out from the rulers to the exact locations where you want to place art and enter type. Gridlines are great for using lines that are set a specific distance apart. Use gridlines to create a perspective drawing, or to place objects a specific distance apart.

This list shows the commands for displaying gridlines and the various Snap to Grid features, which are available only when gridlines are displayed:

   ✦ **Display grid lines:** Choose View ➪ Show Grid, or press Ctrl+" (⌘+").

   ✦ **Turn off grids:** Choose View ➪ Hide Grid, or press Ctrl+" (⌘+").

   ✦ **Snap to Grid:** Choose View ➪ Snap to Grid, or press Ctrl+Shift+" (⌘+Shift+"). This feature snaps the object to the nearest grid.

   ✦ **Snap to Point:** Choose View ➪ Snap to Point, or press Ctrl+Alt+" (⌘+Option+"). This feature snaps the dragged object to another object's point. More importantly, you can see this happen. As you drag, the cursor turns from black to white when you are directly over another point.

Tip

If you want to display grids in each new document, open your Illustrator startup file and turn on grids in that document. Then save the startup file. All new documents display grids when you first create them. See Chapter 17 for more information on modifying the startup file.

Creating grid color, style, and spacing

You can customize the way grids look by changing the Grid preferences. Choose Edit (Illustrator) ➪ Preferences ➪ Guides & Grid to display the Guides & Grid section of the Preferences dialog box, as seen in Figure 8-17. Here, you can change the grid color, style, and spacing.

These options are available in the Grid section of the Preferences dialog box:

✦ **Color:** In this area, you can pick a new color from the list of colors. If you choose Other, you can use the color picker to the right of the Color area to pick a new color for your grids.

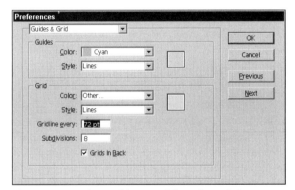

Figure 8-17: The Guides & Grid section of the Preferences dialog box enables you to set up the appearance options.

✦ **Style:** You can also choose between lines and dots as the grid style. I prefer to use lines for my grid, because dots can turn an already busy-looking page into one with all sorts of, well, dots all over the place.

✦ **Gridline every:** Enter the distance you want between gridlines. To change the space between the major (darker) gridlines, enter a value in the Gridline every text field.

✦ **Subdivisions:** To create subdivisions (minor) between the dark values, enter a number for how many sections should be created between the main lines. If you enter 1 as the value, no subdivisions are created. Because you're defining the number of divisions, not the number of lines, entering 2 creates one line between the two main lines. The standard 1-inch gridline with eight subdivisions creates ⅛-inch squares.

✦ **Grids In Back:** You can uncheck the Grids in Back check box in the Guides & Grid preferences to make your gridlines appear in front of your artwork. The box is checked by default so that the gridlines aren't running on top of your artwork.

Spinning grids

Your grid doesn't have to consist of just vertical and horizontal lines. You can rotate the grid to any angle you like by changing the Constrain Angle in the General section of the Preferences dialog box. Figure 8-18 shows a grid set at an angle of 6.275°. This is perfect for working with angled artwork; even if only a portion of the artwork is at an angle, the Constrain Angle can be set temporarily to the angle of the artwork.

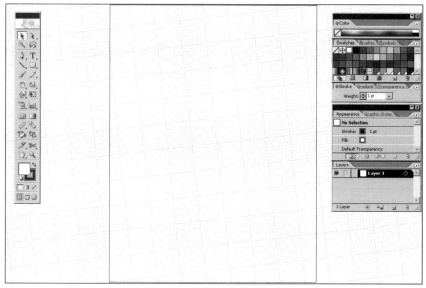

Figure 8-18: A grid rotated to 6.275° may help you create perspective drawings.

Using Guides

Guides are dotted or solid lines that help you align artwork. Guides do not print, and they are saved with documents. In Illustrator and most desktop-publishing software, guides are straight lines extending from one edge of a document to the other. But in Illustrator, you can also turn any path into a guide.

For the most part, guides behave exactly like their path counterparts. As long as you have them unlocked, you may select them, hide them, group them, and even paint them (although paint attributes are not be visible onscreen or on a printout until the guides are converted back into paths).

Creating guides

You can create guides in two ways: by pulling them out from the rulers and by transforming paths into guides.

To pull a guide from a ruler, first make the vertical and horizontal rulers visible by choosing View ➪ Show Rulers or by pressing Ctrl+R (⌘+R). To create guides that span the entire Pasteboard, click the vertical or horizontal ruler and drag out.

To transform an existing path into a guide, select the path and choose View ➪ Guides ➪ Make Guides or press Ctrl+5 (⌘+5).

Tip And now a word about the Magic Rotating Guide (possibly the coolest tip you'll ever learn): When you drag a guide out from the vertical ruler, press and hold Alt (Option) and the vertical guide becomes a horizontal guide. And vice versa.

Locking, unlocking, and moving guides

When you create a guide, you may want to make sure that it doesn't get moved when you are selecting and moving your objects. Locking your guide is a great way to ensure that the guide doesn't get picked up and moved. Moving a guide is necessary if you create a specific guide like the outline of a business card, and you want to move it to create a different business card. Moving an unlocked guide is simple — click it and drag. If guides are locked, unlock them by choosing View ➪ Guides ➪ Lock Guides or by pressing Ctrl+Alt+; (⌘+Option+;).

If you aren't sure whether the guides in your document are locked or unlocked, click and hold the View ➪ Guides menu. If you see a check mark next to Lock Guides, Illustrator locks the guides and also locks all new guides. To unlock all the document's guides, choose View ➪ Guides ➪ Lock Guides; to lock guides again, choose View ➪ Guides ➪ Lock Guides (yes, it's a toggle).

Releasing guides

Now that you are getting the hang of using the guides, you may want to delete them or release them to move. You can also release a guide if you have decided to make it into an object that you can stroke and fill. To release a guide or change it into a path, select the guide and choose View ➪ Guides ➪ Release Guides. Alternatively, you can press Ctrl+Alt+5 (⌘+Option+5).

To release multiple guides first, make sure that the guides are unlocked; in other words, make sure that no check mark appears next to Lock Guides in the View ⇨ Guides menu. Then select the guides, and choose View ⇨ Guides ⇨ Release Guides or press Ctrl+Alt+5 (⌘+Option+5).

Cross-Reference   You select multiple guides in the same way you select multiple paths: Drag a marquee around the guides, or press Shift and then click each guide. For more on selecting paths, see Chapter 6.

Tip   Selecting all guides — even those that are currently paths — by dragging a marquee or Shift-clicking can be a chore. Here's another way: First, make sure that the guides are not locked (see the previous section to unlock a guide). Next, choose Select ⇨ All, or press Ctrl+A (⌘+A). Select View ⇨ Guides ⇨ Release Guides, or press Ctrl+Alt+5 (⌘+Option+5). This releases all guides and, more importantly, selects all paths that were formerly guides (all other paths and objects are deselected). Finally, choose View ⇨ Guides ⇨ Make Guides, or press Ctrl+5 (⌘+5), and all selected paths become guides again and are selected.

Deleting guides

Suppose that you have just finished a fantastic drawing that you created with the help of many guides. Now that the image is complete, you want to delete those guides. Sure, you can unlock them and select them by holding down the Shift key. Or, if you were really thinking, you could put those guides on a layer and simply Select All and then Delete. Well, Illustrator has just made your life even easier. By choosing the Clear Guides option under the View menu's Guides submenu, all guides are miraculously deleted.

Changing guide preferences

In the Guides & Grid section of the Preferences dialog box (refer to Figure 8-17), you can change the style and the color of the guides. To open the Guides & Grid section of the Preferences dialog box, choose Edit (Illustrator) ⇨ Preferences ⇨ Guides & Grid.

In the Guides section of this dialog box, you have the following options:

✦ **Color:** Choose a color from the list box, or select Other to choose a color from the color picker. With guides, I like to use a darker, more vibrant color than a watered-down cyan. No matter which color you choose, keep it different from the Grid color and make sure it contrasts with the colors you're using in your document.

✦ **Style:** You can set the guide style to dots or lines; which you choose is a matter of preference. However, you may want to pick the opposite of what you've chosen for grids, to further differentiate the two.

Understanding Smart Guides

Smart Guides, which came into being in Version 8, pop up to help you create a shape with precision, align objects with accuracy, and move and transform objects with ease. Figure 8-19 shows an example of a Smart Guide. To activate Smart Guides, choose View ⇨ Smart Guides or press Ctrl+U (⌘+U).

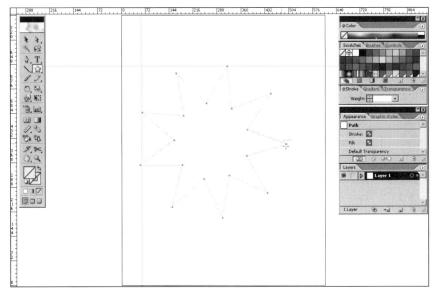

Figure 8-19: Smart Guides show you what is under the cursor in an illustration.

Check boxes enable you to turn these options on and off in the Smart Guides & Slices section of the Preferences dialog box, shown in Figure 8-20. These are some of the Smart Guide display options:

✦ **Text Label Hints:** These hints pop up when you drag over your object. They tell you what each area is. For example, if you drag over a line, the hint pops up with the word "path." If you drag over an anchor point, the hint reads "anchor point."

✦ **Transform Tools:** When you are rotating, scaling, or shearing an object with this option checked, Smart Guides show up to help you out.

✦ **Construction Guides:** These let you view guidelines (thin lines that pop up when moving or copying objects) when using Smart Guides.

✦ **Object Highlighting:** When you select this option, the object to which you point is highlighted.

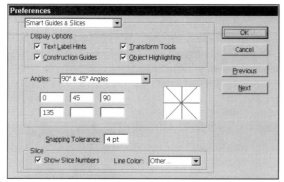

Figure 8-20: The Smart Guides & Slices section of the Preferences dialog box

Using angles as guides

The Smart Guides & Slices section of the Preferences dialog box, shown in Figure 8-20, lets you pick what angles display guides when you drag an object.

You have the following options in the Angles section of the dialog box:

✦ **Angles:** You can choose presets in this drop-down list (pop-up menu). The preset angles are 0, 45, 90, and 135. The angles are shown in the box to the right. When you add a custom angle, it shows up with the preset lines.

✦ **Custom Angles:** You can create a Custom Angle of your own in the boxes below the drop-down list (pop-up menu). To do so, simply enter the angle in one of the empty boxes.

✦ **Snapping Tolerance:** Snapping Tolerance lets you choose how close an object must be to another object before the first object automatically "snaps" to the second object. You set the Snapping Tolerance in points; the lower the number, the closer you have to move the objects to each other. If the number is pretty high, an object snaps to another object if it's merely passing by.

Measuring for Printing

Thinking ahead to the time when your job will print is always a good thing. Two of the most important areas of printing are the placement and the sizing of your artwork within the Illustrator document. This section deals with production-oriented issues you may face while using Illustrator to create printable pieces.

Tiling

Often, you'll create something that's quite small and you'll need to have several copies of the artwork on the page at once. Setting up your artwork for optimal spacing and printing is referred to as tiling.

Illustrator doesn't do tiling automatically, but it does provide the tools you need to tile your artwork.

1. **Select the finished artwork.** See Chapter 6 for more on selecting artwork.

2. **Open the Move dialog box.** You can do this by double-clicking the Selection tool or by choosing Object ➪ Transform ➪ Move.

3. **Enter the width of the art in the Horizontal field.** You may need to experiment to find the correct value to enter here.

4. **Enter 0 (zero) in the Vertical field.**

5. **Click the Copy button.**

6. **Choose Object ➪ Transform ➪ Transform Again.** You can also press Ctrl+D (⌘+D). This creates another duplicate of the artwork. Do this until you have the right number of pieces across the page.

7. **Select the entire row of artwork.**

8. **Open the Move dialog box again.**

9. **Enter 0 (zero) in the Horizontal field.**

10. **Enter the height of the art in the Vertical field.**

11. **Click the Copy button.**

12. **Choose Object ➪ Transform ➪ Transform Again.** Alternatively, you can press Ctrl+D (⌘+D). Again, this creates another duplicate of the row of artwork. Do this until you have the right number of pieces down the page, as shown in Figure 8-21.

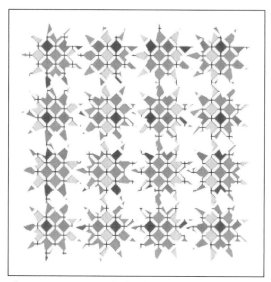

Figure 8-21: Artwork that has been tiled and repeated on a page

Creating crop marks

Crop marks are little lines that are designed to help you cut (or crop) along the edges of your illustration after the document has been printed. Crops (that's the slang term; if you're even half cool, you won't say "crop marks") don't intrude on the edges of the artwork, but instead are offset a bit from the corners of where the edges are.

You add crop marks using the Marks and Bleed pane of the Print dialog box, shown in Figure 8-22.

Instead of using standard crop marks, you can choose to use Japanese Crop Marks, which are different looking, yet seemingly no more functional than regular crop marks. You make this selection in the Printer Mark Type drop-down list (pop-up menu) of the Print dialog box.

Cross-Reference For more on printing, see Chapter 18.

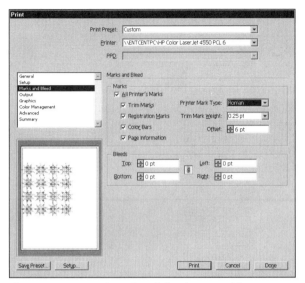

Figure 8-22: Use the Print dialog box to add crop marks.

Summary

Illustrator documents can quickly become very complex. You need to learn how to organize the objects in your documents in order to work efficiently. In this chapter, you learned valuable organization techniques, including the following:

✦ Locking and Hiding objects can help in creating illustrations.

✦ Grouping objects keeps artwork organized.

✦ You can use layers to effectively separate different sections of your artwork.

✦ Template layers are used in Illustrator to make your drawing easier and more precise, and it distinguishes them from Template documents.

✦ Manual tracing allows you to produce unique effects.

✦ The Measure tool provides a quick way to measure distances in Illustrator documents.

✦ Measurements generated by the Measure tool appear in the Move dialog box the next time you open it.

✦ Guides can be created from any object by selecting the object and pressing Ctrl+5 (⌘+5).

✦ You can quickly create document high/wide guides by dragging out from the rulers.

✦ Use the Copy button within the Move dialog box to tile and repeat artwork.

✦ Use the Smart Guides feature to make editing much easier.

✦   ✦   ✦

Working with Type

✦ ✦ ✦ ✦

In This Chapter

Understanding bitmap, PostScript, TrueType, OpenType, and Multiple Master fonts

Using the Character palette

Working with the Paragraph palette

Using area type

Working with type on a path

Adding type with the Type tool

Selecting and editing type

Threading and unthreading text blocks

Wrapping and creating headlines

Outlining type

Advanced type functions

Customizing fonts

✦ ✦ ✦ ✦

Fonts are a big deal to Illustrator users. For the seasoned graphic artist, the thousands of typefaces that are available provide a typesetting heaven on earth. For a newcomer to Illustrator and typesetting, fonts can be overwhelming. Illustrator ships with about 300 Adobe PostScript Type 1 fonts; other fonts are available for purchase at costs that range from about $2 per face to hundreds of dollars for a family. (A font face is a single variation, while a font family typically includes quite a few different variations.)

This chapter covers creating type with various Type tools, all the different formatting available, and cool things to do with type on a path and outlined type.

Understanding Fonts

Fonts come in various formats, each format having advantages and disadvantages over other formats. Fonts fall into the following categories: bitmap fonts, PostScript fonts (Type 1), TrueType fonts, OpenType fonts, and Multiple Master fonts.

Understanding Bitmap fonts

Bitmap fonts were the original fonts used for computers. They consist of a series of dots inside a grid pattern and worked well both onscreen and on the dot-matrix printers that were prevalent at the time of their introduction.

Each character in a bitmap font has a certain number of dots that define its shape. Some bitmap fonts include different point sizes, with the smaller point sizes having fewer dots than the larger point sizes. The larger the point size of the bitmap fonts, the more detail is available, and the better the letter looks.

Because bitmap fonts were originally designed for a computer screen, the dots in a bitmap font are set at 72 dpi (dots-per-inch). When you print a bitmap font on a laser printer, which has a resolution of at least 300 dpi, the letters tend to look blocky, even when their sizes are supported by the typeface.

Understanding PostScript fonts

Although PostScript fonts have in the past been the most popular font format in professional publishing circles, they also are the most confusing and frustrating fonts to use because they have two parts: the screen fonts (which are really bitmap fonts) and the printer fonts.

You need the printer fonts, as their name implies, for printing. Printer fonts consist of outlined shapes that get filled with as many dots as the printer can stuff into that particular shape. Because these printer fonts are mathematical outlines and not a certain number of dots, they make characters look good at any point size. In fact, PostScript printer fonts are device-independent, meaning that the quality of the type depends on the dpi of the printer (which is device-dependent). The higher the dpi, the smoother the curves and diagonal lines look. If printer fonts are missing, the printer either uses the corresponding bitmap font or substitutes another font whose printer font is available.

Adobe, just by coincidence, created the PostScript page description language based on outlines instead of dots, developed PostScript fonts, and also created typefaces in PostScript format called Type 1 format and Type 3 format. Since the rise of desktop publishing, the font standard has been PostScript.

Understanding TrueType fonts

The greatest advantage of TrueType fonts is that they have only one component — not separate screen fonts and printer fonts. Actually, many TrueType fonts do include screen fonts because hand-tuned screen fonts at small sizes tend to look better than filled outlines at screen resolution.

The quality of TrueType fonts is comparable to, if not better than, that of PostScript typefaces. Apple includes TrueType fonts with every new computer it sells. Microsoft includes a boatload of fonts with Windows, Office, and all the other applications it sells and licenses.

Understanding OpenType fonts

OpenType fonts take TrueType fonts a step further by including PostScript information. They also include a variety of features, such as ligatures (typographic replacement characters for certain letter pairs) and alternate glyphs that PostScript and TrueType don't offer. A glyph is the form of a character, such as a capital letter with a swash, making it a bit more exciting than the regular capital letter. Ligatures are replacement characters for paired letters such as ff, fi, and ffl. Illustrator offers an OpenType palette for you to specify alternate characters such as ligatures. You open the OpenType palette by choosing Window ➪ Type ➪ OpenType. The OpenType option lets you enhance the look of your OpenType fonts.

Cross-Reference

For more on glyphs, see the subsection "Using alternate glyphs" under the section "Understanding Basic Type Menu Commands" in this chapter.

Adding type with Multiple Master fonts

Multiple Master fonts, again from Adobe, provide a somewhat complex way to vary typestyles. Normally, a typeface may come in several weights, such as bold, regular, light, and black. But what if you want a weight that is between bold and black? Usually, you're out of luck.

The theory behind Multiple Master fonts was that a font has two extremes — black and light, for example. Multiple Master technology creates any number of in-betweens that range from one extreme to the other. Multiple Masters don't stop with weights, though. They also work to step between regular and oblique, wide and condensed, and serif and sans serif.

Although it seemed like a good idea when Adobe introduced the idea of Multiple Master fonts back in 1991, little interest was generated among users and Adobe is no longer developing this technology.

Understanding Basic Type Menu Commands

The Type menu, shown in Figure 9-1, contains all of Illustrator's type controls (with the exception of the Type tools).

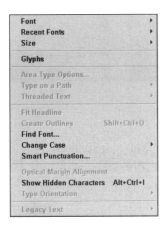

Figure 9-1: The Type menu enables you to select various type-related commands.

You can change most of the Type options in the Character palette, shown in Figure 9-2, by choosing Window ➪ Type ➪ Character or by pressing Ctrl+T (⌘+T). You can also change many text-related options using the Paragraph palette by choosing Window ➪ Type ➪ Paragraph or by pressing Alt+Ctrl+T (Option+⌘+T).

Figure 9-2: The Character palette provides access to many Type options.

Type is set in Illustrator in blocks of continuous, linked text. In most cases, text blocks in Illustrator are *threaded* — meaning that the text automatically reflows to fit the linked text boxes if they are resized.

Note   When the term *paragraph* is mentioned, it is usually referring to the characters that are between Returns. If there are no Returns in a story, then that story is said to have one paragraph. Returns end paragraphs and begin new ones. There is always exactly one more paragraph in a story than there are Returns.

The following sections describe each of the Type menu options. In the next four sections, we discuss the first four of these commands. The rest of the options are covered throughout this chapter.

Using the Font submenu

The Font submenu of the Type menu displays the typefaces in their actual form. The Font submenu displays all the fonts that are currently installed on the computer you are using. A check mark appears next to the font that is currently selected; an indicator as to whether it is a TrueType, Type 1, or OpenType font also appears. If no check mark appears next to any of the fonts, more than one font is currently selected. Figure 9-3 shows the Font submenu.

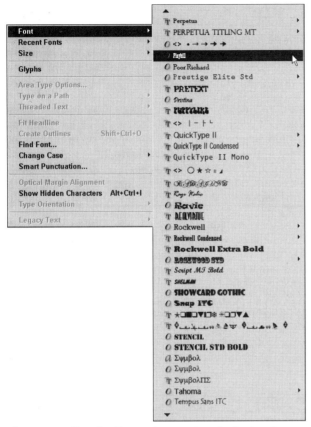

Figure 9-3: Use the Font submenu to select a typeface.

Understanding the Recent Fonts submenu

The Recent Fonts submenu of the Type menu displays the most recent fonts you have used in that document. The default setting for Recent Fonts is 5. You can change that number in the Type section of the Preferences dialog box. Access the type preferences by choosing Edit ➪ Preferences ➪ Type (Illustrator ➪ Preferences ➪ Type). In this dialog box, you can set the number of recent fonts using the Number of Recent Fonts list box (pop-up menu). The minimum for Recent Fonts is 1, and the maximum is 15.

Selecting the font size

Choosing Type ⇨ Size displays a submenu with Other and various point sizes listed. Choosing Other displays the Character palette with the font size field highlighted so that you can enter a specific font size. You can type any point size from 0.1 to 1296 in this field.

A check mark appears in the Size submenu next to the point size that is currently selected. If the point size currently selected does not correspond to a point size in the Size submenu, a check mark appears next to the Other menu item. Point size for type is measured from the top of the ascenders (like the top of a capital letter T) to the bottom of the descenders (like the bottom of a lowercase g). If no check mark appears next to any of the sizes, more than one size is currently selected (even if the different sizes are all Other sizes).

You can also increase and decrease the point size of type by using the keyboard shortcuts. Pressing Ctrl+Shift+> (⌘+Shift+>) increases the point size by the amount specified in the Size/Leading field of the Type section of the Preferences dialog box. Pressing Ctrl+Shift+< (⌘+Shift+<) decreases the point size.

Yet another way to change point size is to use the Scale tool. Using the Scale tool to change point size lets you change to any size; that size is displayed in the Character palette as soon as you are finished scaling. Again, remember that the limit in scaling type is 1296 points; you cannot exceed that limit even with the Scale tool unless the type has been converted to outlined paths.

Using alternate glyphs

A glyph is the form of a character of text. Some fonts have multiple forms for a letter, and the Glyphs palette is where you can choose those other options. Glyphs are also the ornamental forms, swashes, ligatures, and fractions that are part of OpenType fonts. Choosing Glyphs from the Type menu displays the Glyphs palette as shown in Figure 9-4. If no type is selected, the palette displays Entire Font in the Show list box (pop-up menu). The other choice in the Show list box (pop-up menu) is for Alternates for Current Selection. Use this palette to view some of the special character fonts such as Symbol or Zapf Dingbats.

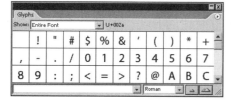

Figure 9-4: The Glyphs palette enables you to choose alternate glyphs for use in your documents.

Using the Type Tools

You use the Type tools to create and later edit type. The default tool is the standard Type tool, which creates both individual type and area type. Individual type is created when you click with the Type tool, creating a point for the type to begin. Area type is created by dragging a box that the type then fills. The pop-up tools on the tear-away Type palette, shown in Figure 9-5, are the Type tool, the Area Type tool, the Type on a Path tool, the Vertical Type tool, the Vertical Area Type tool, and the Vertical Type on a Path tool. Each of the type tools displays a different cursor.

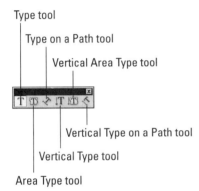

Type tool

Type on a Path tool

Vertical Area Type tool

Vertical Type on a Path tool

Vertical Type tool

Area Type tool

Figure 9-5: The Type tools provide many different ways to create interesting text.

Cross-Reference   All the tools shown in Figure 9-5 are explained in detail in the following sections.

You can select type in Illustrator with the Selection tool, in which case all the type in the text block is modified. You select type with a Type tool by dragging across either characters or lines — every character from the initial click until the release of the mouse button is selected. Double-clicking with a Type tool selects the entire word you clicked, including the space after it. Triple-clicking (clicking three times in the same place) selects an entire paragraph.

You can enter new type into an existing story by clicking with a Type tool where you want the new type to begin and then typing. If type is highlighted when you begin typing, the highlighted type is replaced with the new type.

The original reason for the inclusion of a vertical type capability in Illustrator was for Japanese type (commonly referred to as Kanji) compatibility. Vertical type can have a number of specialized uses as well. The following sections that discuss the different kinds of type blocks (Point, Rectangle, Area, and Path) address both normal (horizontal) type and vertical type capabilities.

Using the Type tool

With the Type tool, you can do everything you need to do with type. Clicking in any empty part of your document creates *individual type*, an anchor point to which the type aligns. Type created as individual type does not wrap automatically; instead, you must manually press the Enter (Return) key and start typing the next line. Individual type is usually used for creating smaller portions of type, like labels and headlines.

Clicking and dragging with the Type tool creates *area type* — type that is bordered by a box.

As the Type tool passes over a closed path, it changes automatically into the Area Type tool. Clicking a closed path results in type that fills the shape of the area you clicked. Holding down the Alt (Option) key as you pass over a closed path changes the tool into the Type on a Path tool. This intelligent switching of Type tools by Illustrator keeps you from having to choose different Type tools when you want a different kind of type.

If the Type tool crosses over an open path, it becomes the Type on a Path tool. Clicking an open path places type on the path, with the baseline of the type aligning along the curves and angles of the path. Holding down the Alt (Option) key when the Type tool is over an open path changes it into the Area Type tool.

You can toggle between the Type tool and the Vertical Type tool by pressing the Shift key. In fact, pressing the Shift key with the Area Type and Type on a Path tools automatically toggles those tools to their Vertical Type counterparts. This holds true even if you press Shift along with the Alt (Option) key (when toggling between Area Type and Type on a Path tools).

Using the Area Type tool

You use the Area Type tool for filling closed or open paths with type. You can even fill compound paths in Illustrator. Figure 9-6 shows an example of how the Area Type tool fills a path.

Using the Type on a Path tool

You use the Type on a Path tool for running type along any path in Illustrator. This is a great tool for placing type on the edges of a circle or wiggly lines. Figure 9-7 shows an example of type on a path.

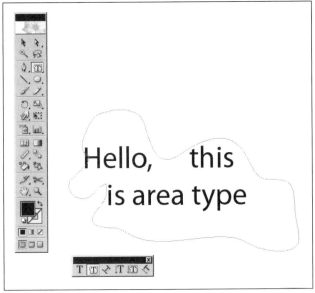

Figure 9-6: The Area Type tool creates text that fills a path.

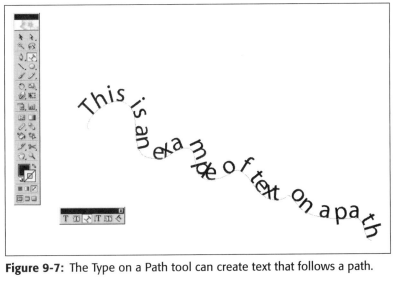

Figure 9-7: The Type on a Path tool can create text that follows a path.

Using the Vertical Type tool

Vertical type will probably remind you of the signs on the front of an old-time movie theater where the letters of the theater's name were stacked vertically rather than horizontally. The effect can be rather stunning when used properly. For the most part, the Vertical Type tool works like the regular Type tool, but instead of placing characters side by side, characters are placed from top to bottom as shown in Figure 9-8. Note that this is not the same as simply rotating the text 90 degrees.

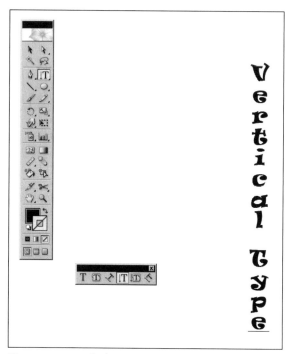

Figure 9-8: Vertical type can create an interesting effect.

Creating Individual Type

To create type with a single point defining its location, use the Type tool and click a single location within the document window where there are no paths. A blinking insertion point appears, signifying that type will appear where that point is located. When you type on the keyboard, text appears in the document at that insertion point.

Caution   When creating individual type, remember that only a hard return forces a new line of text to be created. If no returns are used, text eventually runs right off the document. When importing text used as individual type, be sure that the text contains hard returns, or the text will run into oblivion. Hard returns can be added after importing, but doing so may be difficult.

Placing Area Type in a Rectangle

You can create type in a rectangle in two ways. The easiest way is by clicking and dragging the Type tool diagonally, which creates a rectangle as you drag. The blinking insertion point appears in the top row of text, with its horizontal location dependent on the text alignment choice. Choosing flush right alignment forces the insertion point to appear in the upper-right corner; centered alignment puts the insertion point in the center of the top row; and flush left alignment, or one of the justification methods, makes the insertion point appear in the upper-left corner. Choose any alignment option in the Paragraph palette. Access this palette by choosing Window ➪ Type ➪ Paragraph or by pressing Alt+Ctrl+T (Option+⌘+T).

If you press the Shift key while drawing the rectangle, the rectangle is constrained to a perfect square. There is no need to drag from upper left to lower right — you can drag from any corner to its opposite — whichever way is most convenient.

To create type in a rectangle of specific proportions, click once in the document window with the Rectangle tool. The Rectangle Size dialog box appears, and you can enter the information needed. Then choose the Type tool and click the edge of the rectangle. The type fills the rectangle as you type.

Cross-Reference   For more on the using the Rectangle tool, see Chapter 5.

Note   If you use a rectangle as a type rectangle, it is always a type rectangle, even if you remove the text.

If you need to create a type container that is a precise size but don't want to draw a rectangle first, open the Info palette by choosing Window ➪ Info or by pressing F8. As you drag the type cursor, watch the information in the Info palette, which displays the dimensions of the type area. When the W field is the width you want and the H field is the height you want, release the mouse button.

Working with Type Areas

For type to exist in Illustrator, you must first define a type area. You can never have type outside these areas because type is treated very differently from any other object in Illustrator.

You can create different kinds of type areas:

✦ **Individual type:** Type that exists around a single point clicked with the standard Type tool.

✦ **Area type:** Type that flows within a specific open or closed path.

✦ **Type on a path:** Type whose baseline is attached to a specific open or closed path.

✦ **Vertical type:** Type that flows vertically rather than horizontally. As with normal horizontal type, vertical type can be individual type, area type, or type on a path.

Figure 9-9 shows examples of the variations of type you can create in Illustrator. In the figure, all the paths are selected to provide a clearer picture of how the type areas compare.

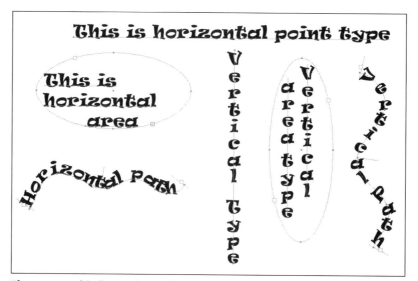

Figure 9-9: This figure shows the different kinds of type areas that you can create using the Type tools.

Creating Area Type

To create type within an area, first create a path that confines the area of your type. You can make the path closed or open, and any size. Remember that the area of the path should be close to the size needed for the amount of text (at the point size that it needs to fit). After you create the path, choose the Area Type tool and position the type cursor over the edge of the path and click.

The type in Figure 9-10 was flowed into the outline of a polygon that has been distorted.

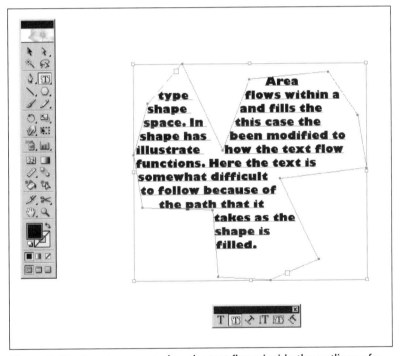

Figure 9-10: Area type created so the text flows inside the outlines of a modified polygon

Using area type functions

Within area types, you can choose several options. Double-click the Area Type tool or choose Type ➪ Area Type Options to access the Area Type Options dialog box, shown in Figure 9-11. You need to have some area type selected to access these options.

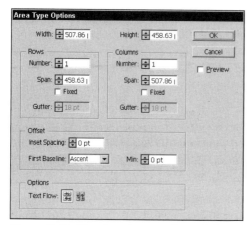

Figure 9-11: The Area Type Options dialog box enables you to set the parameters for area type.

You can set these options:

✦ **Width/Height:** Defines the area of the type

✦ **Rows/Columns:** Sets the number, size, and gutter of the horizontal rows and vertical columns

✦ **Offset:** Determines how far the text is offset from the edge of the path area

✦ **Text Flow:** Sets whether the text flows left to right and top to bottom, or top to bottom and left to right

Check the Preview box to see the settings you enter before hitting OK or Cancel.

Choosing good shapes for area type

What exactly constitutes a "good" shape to be used for area type? As a rule, gently curved shapes are better than harsh, jagged ones. Type tends to flow better into the larger lumps created by smoothly curving paths.

Try to avoid creating paths with wild or tight curves. Other designs that can cause problems are "hourglass" shapes or any closed path that has an area where the sides are almost touching. Type flows into a smoothly curved area, but it has trouble flowing into a sharp, spiky shape.

Try to make the top and bottom boundaries of the path have less "bumpiness" than the sides. This reduces the number of times that type jumps from one area to another.

Tip

For the best results with area type, make the type small and justify it by pressing Ctrl+Shift+J (⌘+Shift+J). This ensures that the type flows up against the edges of the path.

Outlining areas of area type

Placing a stroke on the path surrounding area type can be a great visual effect, but doing so and getting good results can be a bit tricky. If the stroke is thicker than 1 or 2 points, and you don't want the type to run into the edges of the stroke, there are a few things you can do. The best way to set the offset value is to use the Area Type Options dialog box and enter the value you want the text to offset away from the path. To do so, follow these steps:

1. **Create a path for your Area type with any drawing tool. For example, the Rectangle tool is a good tool to use.** For more on drawing tools, see Chapters 4 and 5.

2. **Click the shape with the Area Type tool.**

3. **Enter your text.**

4. **With the text selected, double-click the Area Type tool or choose Type ➪ Area Type Options.** Doing this opens the Area Type Options dialog box. For more on the options in this box, see the section "Using Area Type functions."

5. **Enter the value by which you want to offset the type away from the edge of the path.** You type this in the Inset Spacing area under the Offset section of the dialog box.

6. **Click the Preview button to see the result.**

7. **If you like what you see, click OK.**

Selecting carefully with area type

Probably the most overlooked rule when it comes to manipulating area type and the paths that create the type boundaries is the simple fact that Illustrator treats the path and the type equally, unless you choose the path with the Direct Selection (or Group Selection) tool. Area type is selected when you see an underline under all the characters in the area.

When using the transformation tools, be sure that if you don't want to change any of the characteristics of the type, you select just the path. Use the Group Selection tool to click once on the deselected path, and Illustrator selects only the path, not the type. If you transform the area text when you have both selected, the transformation applies to the text as well as the path.

Caution

If you have both the type and the path selected, the transformations affect both the type and the path.

Changing the area, not the type

Sometimes, you need to adjust the path that makes up the area of the area type—for example, when you scale a path up or down so that the text flows better. The trick here is to make sure that you select the entire path without selecting any of the characters. To do this, deselect the type and select the path with the Group Selection tool (the hollow arrow with the + sign).

Now any changes you make affect only the path, so you can scale it, rotate it, or change its Paint Style attributes without directly affecting the text within it. Figure 9-12 shows a transformed path, which allows the text inside to flow differently.

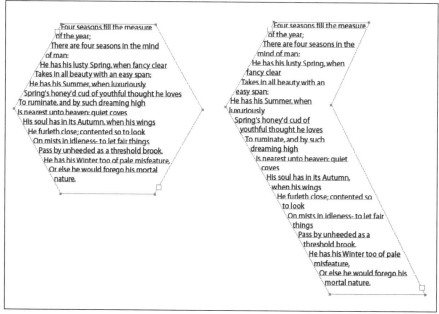

Figure 9-12: You can edit the original area type shape (left) to change only the text flow, not the type (right). (Poem by John Keats)

Flowing area type into shapes

You can do all sorts of nifty things with type that you flow into areas—from unusual column designs to fascinating shapes. Using nonrectangular columns can liven up a publication quite easily. Some magazines use curved columns that are easy to read and lend a futuristic, hip look to the publication. Angled and curved columns are simple to create in Illustrator by creating the shape of the column and flowing area type from one shape to the next.

Type Color and the Color of Type

Color of type and type color are two different things. You can paint type in Illustrator and make it any one of millions of different shades, which determines the color we normally think of.

The color of type, on the other hand, is the way the type appears in the document and is more indicative of the light or dark attributes of the text. The actual red-green-blue colors of the type do work into this appearance, but often the weight of the type and the tracking and kerning have a much more profound effect on the color of type.

To easily see the color of type, unfocus your eyes as you look at your document or turn the page upside down. Obviously, this works better on a printed area than onscreen (boy, those monitors get heavy when you hold them upside down). But you can still get the gist of the way the document appears when you view it on your monitor. Dark and light areas become much more apparent when you can't read the actual words on the path. This method of unfocusing your eyes to look at a page also works well when trying to see the "look" of a page and how it was designed. Often, unfocusing or turning the page upside down emphasizes the fact that you don't have enough white space or that all the copy seems to blend together.

Heavy type weights such as boldface, heavy, and black make type appear darker on a page. Type kerned and tracked very tightly also seems to give the type a darker feel.

The x-height of type (the height to which the lowercase letters, such as an x, rise) is another factor that determines the color of type. Certain italic versions of typefaces can make the text seem lighter, although a few typefaces make text look darker because of the additional area that the thin strokes of the italic type cover.

With red-green-blue colors, you can make type stand out by making it appear darker, or you can make it blend into the page when you make it lighter. When you add smartly placed images near the type, your page can come alive with color.

Traditionally, forcing type into an irregular (nonrectangular) area was quite a task. The typesetter had to set several individual lines of type, each specified by the art director or client to be a certain length so that when all the text was put together, the text formed the shape. This is probably the main reason the world has not seen much of this, except in overly zealous art students' portfolios.

For example, you can give a report on toxic waste more impact by shaping the text into the form of a hypodermic needle. Or you can make a seasonal ad in the shape of a Christmas tree. Look at some of the Absolut Vodka ads to see what they've done to flow text into that all-too-familiar bottle.

Placing Type on a Path

The unique thing about type on a path is that when the path is not visible, the type becomes the path, as shown in Figure 9-13. This can produce some really fascinating results, especially when combined with various fonts of different weights, styles, colors, and special characters.

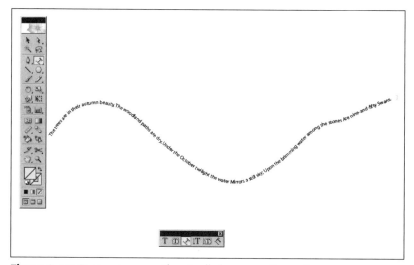

Figure 9-13: Type set on a path actually becomes the path.

Although using the Type on a Path tool can create some great effects, it has one glitch. You usually run into trouble when the path you're using has either corner anchor points or very sharp curves. Letters often crash (run into one another) when this occurs. Besides the most obvious way to avoid this problem, which is to not use paths with corner anchor points and sharp curves, you can sometimes kern (add or subtract space between specific pairs of characters) the areas where the letters crash until they aren't touching anymore.

When kerning type on a path, be sure to kern from the flush side first. For example, if the type is flush left, start your kerning from the left side and work to the right. If you start on the wrong end, the letters you kern apart move along the path until they aren't in an area that needs kerning, but other letters instead appear there.

Another method of fixing crashed letters is to tweak the path with the Direct Selection tool. Careful adjusting of both anchor points and control handles can often easily fix crashes and letters that have huge amounts of space between them.

Cross-Reference   For more on kerning, see the section "Kerning and tracking," later in this chapter.

To create type on a path:

1. **First, create a path in your document.** You should create a path that doesn't cross over itself.

2. **Click the path with the Type on a Path tool.** This creates an insertion point along the path. This works whether the path is a closed path or an open path.

3. **Start typing your text.** Type aligns to the insertion point; if the type is set to flush left, the left edge of the type aligns to the location where the Type on a Path tool was first clicked.

Tip Instead of typing your text in Illustrator, you can copy and paste it from another application using the Edit ➪ Paste command.

Note Although you can choose from different Type tools, you need to choose only one. If you have the standard Type tool selected, it changes into the Area Type tool when you pass over a closed path, and it changes into the Type on a Path tool when the cursor passes over an open path. You can access the Vertical Type versions of these tools by pressing Shift.

Adding effects to type on a path

Under the Type menu, you can warp type on a path by changing some of the settings. After you create type on a path, choose from the following effects: Rainbow, Skew, 3D Ribbon, Stair Step, or Gravity. To adjust the settings, choose Type ➪ Type on a Path ➪ Type on a Path Options to display the Type on a Path Options dialog box, shown in Figure 9-14, or double-click the Type on a Path tool.

Figure 9-14: The Type on a Path Options dialog box enables you to add some special effects to type.

In this dialog box, you can choose the following:

✦ **Effect:** Choose from Rainbow, Skew, 3D Ribbon, Stair Step, and Gravity, shown in Figure 9-15. The Rainbow effect places each letter's baseline along a path curved like a rainbow. Skew keeps all the letters' vertical edges strictly vertical. 3D Ribbon keeps all the letters' horizontal edges strictly horizontal. Stair Step does exactly what you'd expect; it raises (or lowers, depending on the settings) each letter as if the text were climbing (or descending) stairs. Gravity puts the center of each letter on the baseline of the path with increasing rotation.

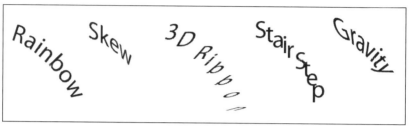

Figure 9-15: The Type on a Path effect options

✦ **Align to Path:** This option alters the path's alignment, with the choices being ascender, descender, center, or baseline, shown in Figure 9-16. Choosing ascender aligns the type higher on the path in line with the top of the highest part of the letter (an *h,* for example). The descender option aligns the type lower on the path in line with the hanging part of the letter (a *g,* for example). Choosing center aligns the type equally on the path with half being above the line and half being below the path. The baseline option aligns the base of the type (not the descender) to the path.

✦ **Spacing:** This allows you to space the path up or down from its original position.

✦ **Flip:** This option flips the type to the opposite side.

✦ **Preview:** This allows you to preview your changes before you click OK to commit to them.

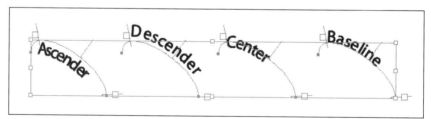

Figure 9-16: The Align to Path options

Using vertical type

Vertical type is a fascinating capability in Illustrator. If you use Kanji characters, you'll find it invaluable. But even if you don't, you may find some interesting uses for setting type vertically, instead of horizontally.

You can make your type appear vertical instead of horizontal in two ways. You can create type using any of the three Vertical Type tools, or you can convert horizontal type into vertical type with Type ➪ Type Orientation ➪ Vertical. Figure 9-17 shows area type both horizontally and vertically. Note that vertical type takes up a great deal more space than horizontal type and flows top to bottom, right to left.

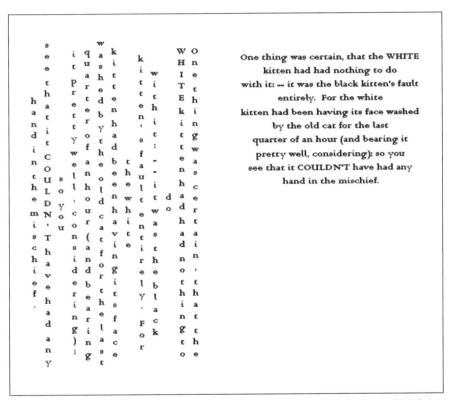

Figure 9-17: Vertical type (left) and the same type reoriented to horizontal (right)

Most of Illustrator's standard character and paragraph palette changes work with vertical type, but not always in ways you expect. For example, type is set on a centerline, not a baseline. The centerline runs vertically through the center of each character. Table 9-1 lists the differences in the way each major function works.

Table 9-1
Vertical Type Functions

Function	Difference
Font	Same as standard.
Size	Same as standard.
Leading	Changes the amount of space between the vertical "lines" of type, measured from centerline to centerline.
Kerning/Tracking	Changes the amount of vertical space between each pair of characters. Because very few Roman characters have both ascenders and descenders, tracking and kerning substantially can really help get rid of the excess white space between characters that makes vertical type so hard to read.
Vertical Scale	Changes the width (horizontal scale) of the characters.
Horizontal Scale	Changes the height (vertical scale) of the characters.
Baseline Shift	Moves the type left (negative values) and right (positive values) along the centerline.
Flush Left	Words are flush top.
Center	Words are vertically centered.
Flush Right	Words are flush bottom.
Justify Full Lines	Words on full (vertical) lines are justified from top to bottom.
Justify All Lines	All lines are vertically justified.
Left Indent	Top is indented. Positive numbers move the text down, and negative numbers move the text up.
Right Indent	Bottom is indented, with numbers working like Left Indent.
First Line Indent	The rightmost line is indented. Again, positive numbers move the text down, and negative numbers move the text up.
Space Before Paragraph	Paragraphs go from right to left, so this control increases the space to the right of the selected paragraph(s).
Auto Hyphenate	Hyphenates words the same way as horizontal type, but the hyphens appear at the bottom of each line.
Hang Punctuation	Punctuation hangs above and below the text area.
Tab Ruler	Appears to the right of text areas in vertical form.
Create Outlines	Same as standard.

Selecting Type

Before you can make changes to text, you must first select it. You can select text in two ways: You can select type areas with a Selection tool, which selects every character in the type area, or you can select characters individually or in groups with any of the Type tools.

To select the entire type area or multiple type areas, click the baseline of a line of type within the type area you want to select. Any changes made in the Type menu, Font menu, Character palette, or Paragraph palette affect every character in the selected type areas.

To select individual characters within a type area, you must use a Type tool. As you near text that has been typed in the document, the dotted lines surrounding the cursor disappear. The hot spot of the type cursor is the place where the short horizontal bar crosses the vertical bar.

To select an individual character, drag across the character you want to select. As you select a character, its colors reverse, so that black text appears white. To select more than one character, drag left or right across multiple characters; all characters from the location you originally clicked to the current location of the cursor are highlighted. If you drag up with the cursor over straight text, you select all the characters to the left and all the characters to the right of the cursor's current location. Dragging down does the reverse. The more lines you drag up or down, the more lines you select.

To select one word at a time (and the space that follows it), double-click the word you want to select. The word and the space after it reverse. The reason that Illustrator selects the space following the word has to do with the number of times you copy, cut, and paste words from within sentences. For example, to remove the word Lazy in the phrase "The Lazy Boy," you double-click the word Lazy and press Backspace (Delete). The phrase then becomes "The Boy," which only has one space where the word Lazy used to be. To select several words, double-click and drag the type cursor across the words you want to select. Illustrator selects each word you touch with the cursor, from the location you initially double-click to the current location. Dragging to the previous or next line selects additional lines, with at least a word on the first line double-clicked and one word on the dragged-to line.

For the nimble-fingered clickers, you may also click three times to select a paragraph. Triple-clicking anywhere inside the paragraph selects the entire paragraph, including the hard Return at the end of the paragraph (if there is one). Triple-clicking and dragging selects successive paragraphs, if you move the cursor up or down while pressing the mouse button during the third click.

To select all the text within a type area with a Type tool, click once in the type area and choose Select ➪ Select All or press Ctrl+A (⌘+A). As in most programs, you can select text only in contiguous blocks. You have no way to select two words in two different locations of the same type area without selecting all the text between them.

You can also select type through the use of the Shift key. Click one spot (we'll call it the beginning) and then Shift-click another spot. The characters between the beginning and the Shift-click are selected. Successive Shift-clicks select characters from the beginning to the current location of the most recent Shift-click.

Editing Type

Illustrator has limited text-editing features. By clicking once within a type area, a blinking insertion point appears. If you begin typing, characters appear where the blinking insertion point is. The Delete key removes the character to the right of the insertion point.

The arrow keys on your keyboard move the blinking insertion point around in the direction of the arrow. The right arrow moves the insertion point one character to the right, and the left arrow moves the insertion point one character to the left. The up arrow moves the insertion point to the previous line; the down arrow moves the insertion point to the next line.

Pressing the Ctrl (⌘) key speeds up the movement of the insertion point. Ctrl+right arrow (⌘+right arrow) or Ctrl+left arrow (⌘+left arrow) moves the insertion point to the next or preceding word, and Ctrl+down arrow (⌘+down arrow) or Ctrl+up arrow (⌘+up arrow) moves the insertion point to the next or preceding paragraph.

Tip   Pressing the Shift key while moving the insertion point around with the arrows selects all the characters that the insertion point passes over. This works for the Ctrl+arrow (⌘+arrow) movements as well.

When you select characters with a Type tool, typing anything deletes the selected characters and replaces them with what you are currently typing. Pressing Backspace (Delete) when characters are selected deletes all the selected characters. If you paste type by pressing Ctrl+V (⌘+V) when you have characters selected, the selected characters are replaced with the pasted characters.

Using the Type Palettes

Illustrator offers a variety of type palettes. The Character, Paragraph, and OpenType palettes are tabbed together. The Tabs palette is on its own. There is a Glyphs palette as well. You can also create character and paragraph styles and keep them in the Character Styles or Paragraph Styles palette. You can change typeface, style, alignment, kerning, and so much more with the palettes.

Working with the Character palette

The easiest way to change the attributes of characters is by using the Character palette, shown in Figure 9-18. Many of the changes in the Character palette are also available as options in the Type menu. As a rule, if you have more than one change to make, it is better to do it in the Character palette than the menu, if just so that everything you need is in one place.

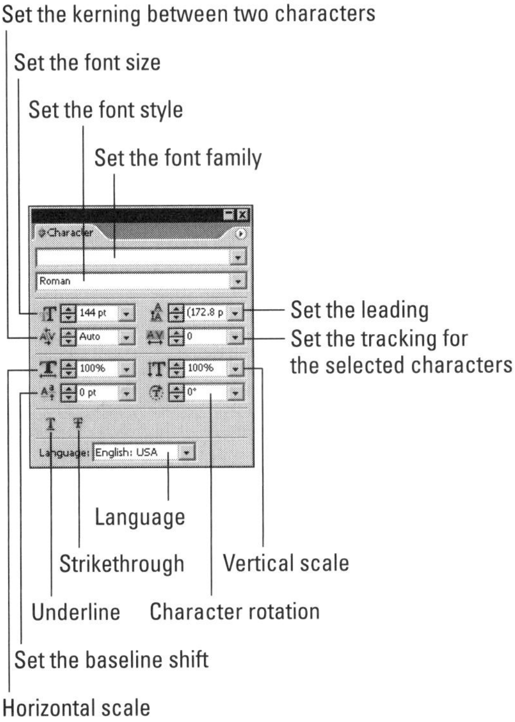
Set the kerning between two characters
Set the font size
Set the font style
Set the font family
Character
Roman
144 pt
(172.8 p
Auto
0
100%
100%
0 pt
0°
Language: English: USA
Set the leading
Set the tracking for the selected characters
Language
Strikethrough
Vertical scale
Underline
Character rotation
Set the baseline shift
Horizontal scale

Figure 9-18: The Character palette allows you to set a number of character properties in one place.

Character attribute changes affect only the letters that are selected, with the exception of leading (explained later), which should probably really be in the Paragraph palette.

Tip You can change several character attributes by increments. The increments are set in the General and Type sections of the Preferences dialog box. You can change increments for point size, leading, baseline shift, and tracking/kerning values. Where appropriate, the key commands for each attribute change are listed in the following sections.

You can use the Tab key to move across the different text fields in the Character palette. In addition to the Tab key tabbing forward through the text fields, pressing Shift+Tab tabs backward through the text fields.

Note

Choosing Edit ⇨ Undo, or pressing Ctrl+Z (⌘+Z), does not undo items typed in the Character palette while you are still in the text field. To undo something, you must first move along (tab) to the next field and then undo, and then Shift+Tab back. Canceling (Esc) does not cancel what you have typed but instead highlights the text (if you select a Type tool).

Tip

All the text fields in the Character palette have both a list box with common values in them for quick access and up and down arrows to the left of each field. These arrows increase (up) and decrease (down) the values of each of the currently selected text fields. Pressing the Shift key while clicking the little arrow buttons makes the change with each press even greater.

Tip

You can use the keyboard to press these buttons. When the field is highlighted, press the up arrow on your keyboard to press the up arrow button; press the down arrow on your keyboard to press the down arrow button. Press Shift at the same time to jump the value by a greater amount.

Changing font and style

The top field on the Character palette is called Set the font family. When you click the Set the font family field triangle, the list of fonts and how they look displays (that is, the fonts are displayed using actual characters from the font family). This also happens when you select Font under the Type menu.

Using text underlining and strikethrough

A new feature in Illustrator CS2 is the ability to use underlining or strikethrough with text you enter. To do so, you simply click the Underline or Strikethrough button near the bottom left of the Character palette.

Measuring type

Now that you understand points and picas, you're ready to move on and work with some type measurements.

At 72 points, the letter *I* is about 50 points tall. In inches, that is just under ¾ inch. To get better results for specially sized capital letters, a good rule is that every 100 points is about a 1-inch capital letter (because the height of a font includes the descenders). This works for most typefaces, and only for the first several inches, but it is a good start to getting capital letters that are sized pretty accurately.

Curves in capital letters are yet another wrench thrown into the equation. In many typefaces, the bottom and top of the letter *O* go beneath the baseline and above the ascender height of most squared letters. Serifs on certain typefaces may also cross these lines.

You measure type from the top of the ascenders (like the top of a capital *T*) to the bottom of the descenders (like the bottom of a lowercase *p*). So when people tell you they want a capital *I* that is 1-inch high, you can't just say, "Oh, there are 72 points in an inch, so I will create a 72-point *I* for them."

Under the Set the font family field in the Character palette, you find the Set the font style field. Clicking the arrow displays the styles available for the chosen font.

Tip   For every text field, you can apply the information you enter, either by tabbing to the next field (or Shift+Tabbing to the preceding text field) or by pressing Enter or Return.

Changing type size

The field below the Set the font style field on the left is the Set the font size field. You type the desired point size (from 0.1 point to 1296 points in increments of .001 point), and any selected characters increase or decrease to that particular point size. Next to the Set the font size field, you find a menu triangle, which lists the standard point sizes available. Point size for type is always measured from the top of the ascenders to the bottom of the descenders. You can increase or decrease type point size from the keyboard by typing Ctrl+Shift+> (⌘+Shift+>) to increase and Ctrl+Shift+< (⌘+Shift+<) to decrease the point size by the increment specified in the Preferences dialog box. Figure 9-19 shows the results of changing type size using the keyboard commands.

Figure 9-19: Original type on top, adjusted point size using the key commands on bottom

Tip   The keyboard commands for increasing and decreasing typographic attributes, such as point size, leading, baseline shift, and tracking, are more than just other ways to change those attributes. Instead, they are invaluable for making changes when the selected type has more than one different value of that attribute within it. For example, if some of the characters have a point size of 10 and some have a point size of 20, using the keyboard command (with an increment set to 2 points) changes the type to 12 and 22 points. This is tedious to do separately, especially if there are multiple sizes or just a few sizes scattered widely about.

Adjusting the leading

Next to the Set the font size field, you find the Set the leading field. Here, you enter the desired leading value between 0.1 point and 1296 points, in increments of .001 point. To the right of the Set the leading field is a pop-up menu triangle, from which you can choose common leading values. In Illustrator, leading is measured from the baseline of the current line up to the baseline of the preceding line, as shown in Figure 9-20. The distance between these two baselines is the amount of leading.

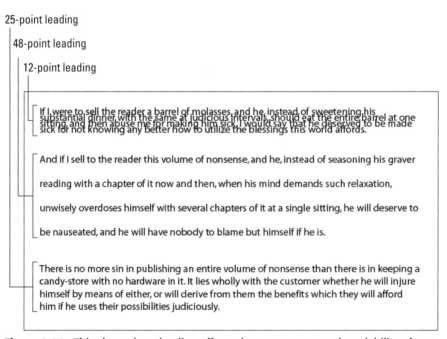

Figure 9-20: This shows how leading affects the appearance and readability of text.

If you change the field from the number that displays there by default, the Auto entry in the Set the leading list box becomes unchecked. The Auto option, when checked, makes the leading exactly 120 percent of the point size. This is just great when the type is 10 points because the leading is 12 points, a common point size-to-leading relationship. But as point size goes up, leading should become proportionately less, until, at around 72 points, it is less than the point size. Instead, when Auto Leading is checked, 72-point type has 86.5-point leading. That's lots of unsightly white space.

You can set Leading increments in the Type section of the Preferences dialog box.

Kerning and tracking

Kerning is the amount of space between any specific pair of letters. You can change kerning values only when there is a blinking insertion point between two characters.

Tracking is the amount of space between all the letters currently selected. If you select the type area with a Selection tool, it refers to all the space among all the characters in the entire type area. If you select characters with a Type tool, tracking affects only the space among the specific letters selected.

Although they are related and appear to do basically the same thing, tracking and kerning actually work quite independently of each other. They only look like they are affecting each other; altering one never actually changes the amount of the other. The Set the kerning between two characters field appears directly below the Set the font size field, while the Set the tracking for the selected characters field appears below the Set the leading field. Figure 9-21 shows examples of both leading and kerning.

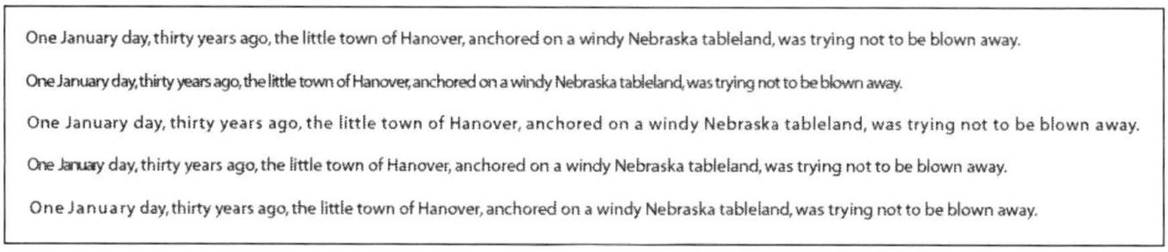

One January day, thirty years ago, the little town of Hanover, anchored on a windy Nebraska tableland, was trying not to be blown away.

One January day, thirty years ago, the little town of Hanover, anchored on a windy Nebraska tableland, was trying not to be blown away.

One January day, thirty years ago, the little town of Hanover, anchored on a windy Nebraska tableland, was trying not to be blown away.

One January day, thirty years ago, the little town of Hanover, anchored on a windy Nebraska tableland, was trying not to be blown away.

One January day, thirty years ago, the little town of Hanover, anchored on a windy Nebraska tableland, was trying not to be blown away.

Figure 9-21: The top line is the original, the second line has tracking set close, the third has tracking set apart, the fourth shows an example of kerning set close, and the last shows kerning set farther apart.

The Set the kerning field often reads Auto instead of a value when you select several letters. If Auto appears in that field, the kerning built into the font is used automatically. Choosing a different value overrides the Auto setting and uses the value you type. If you select several letters, you can choose only 0, but you can enter any number if a blinking insertion point appears between the letters. Auto kerning works by reading the kerning values of the typeface that were embedded by the type designer when the typeface was originally created. The typeface designer normally defines the space between letters; different typefaces look like they have different amounts of space between letters. There are usually a couple hundred preset kerning pairs for common Adobe typefaces, although the expert sets have quite a few more. When Auto kerning is in effect, you can see those preset kerning values by clicking between kerned letter pairs (capital *T* with most vowels is a good one to check) and reading the value in the Set the kerning field. If you use Auto kerning, Illustrator displays the value in parentheses. Different typefaces have different kerning pairs, and kerning pairs change from typeface to typeface, as well as from weight to weight and style to style.

For example, a kerning pair of the letters *AV* in Times New Roman Bold, when Auto kerning is on, is set to (–129). If you type a value of –250, that value overrides the Auto kerning, turning it off and using your new value of –250 (tracking and kerning are both measured in .001 em, a unit of measure that is relative to the current type size). Figure 9-22 shows the difference between a kerning value of –129 and –250.

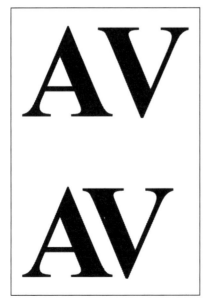

Figure 9-22: The top letters are using Auto kerning (–129). The bottom letters are using –250 kerning.

To decrease or increase the kerning or tracking by the increments specified in the Preferences dialog box, insert the Type tool between two letters and press Alt+left arrow (Option+left arrow) or Alt+right arrow (Option+right arrow). To increase or decrease the tracking or kerning by a factor of five times the amount in the Preferences dialog box, press Alt+Ctrl+right arrow (Option+⌘+right arrow) or Alt+Ctrl+left arrow (Option+⌘+left arrow).

Note An em space is the width of a capital M in a particular font at a particular point size.

The values entered for tracking and kerning must be between –1000 and 10,000. A value of –1000 results in stacked letters. A value of 10,000 makes enough space between letters for 10 em spaces. That's lots of space.

Note Different software works with kerning and tracking differently. In programs that do offer numerical tracking, it is usually represented in some form of a fraction of an em space, but the denominator varies from software to software.

The lower portion of the Character palette contains the Set the baseline shift field, which, unlike leading, moves individual characters up and down relative to their baseline (from leading). Positive numbers move the selected characters up, and negative numbers move the characters down by the amount specified. The maximum amount of baseline shift is 1296 points in either direction. Baseline shift is especially useful for type on a path. You can change baseline shift via the keyboard by selecting a letter with the Type tool and pressing Alt+Shift+up arrow (Option+Shift+up arrow) to increase. Pressing Alt+Shift+down arrow (Option+Shift+down arrow) decreases the baseline shift in the increment specified in the Preferences dialog box.

Using vertical scale and horizontal scale

Also in the Options section of the Character palette are the Horizontal Scale field and the Vertical Scale field. Horizontal scale controls the width of the type, causing it to become expanded or condensed horizontally. Vertical scale likewise controls the height of the type. You can enter values from 1% to 10,000% in these fields. Like most other fields in the Character palette, the values entered are absolute values, so whatever the horizontal scale is, changing it back to 100% returns the type to its original proportions.

Using character rotation

Along with the baseline and scale options, the Character palette also contains the Character Rotation field. This somewhat odd option tilts individual characters by rotating them relative to the baseline without changing the direction of the baseline. Figure 9-23 illustrates an example of how this works. In this case, the baseline is a line segment that slants downward at a 45-degree angle. The characters on the left use normal character rotation, while those on the right are rotated 45 degrees counterclockwise, producing a very interesting visual effect of letters falling down a hill.

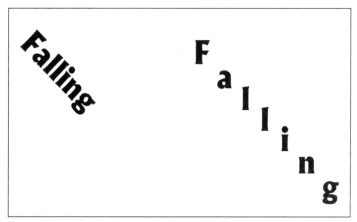

Figure 9-23: The characters on the right are rotated along the baseline to produce a greater visual impact.

Understanding the language barrier

If you're reading a translation of the Illustrator Bible in a language other than English, I'd like to welcome you by saying hello in your native language: "Hello." Okay, I'm probably not fooling you here; through the magic of translators who speak several languages much more fluently than I speak "westernized American English," my current language of choice, this book is translated into other languages without one iota of input from me.

If your language of choice is not English, you'll be interested in the Language option along the bottom of the Character palette. You can change to your language of choice, so that functions such as the spelling dictionary and hyphenation dictionary work for words that you'll be typing.

More multinational options

The other options along the bottom of the Character palette are specifically designed for Kanji character operations. To even see these options, you first have to choose Edit ➪ Preferences ➪ Type (Illustrator ➪ Preferences ➪ Type) and check the Show Asian Options box. This reconfigures the Character palette to show the Asian options for kerning and tracking.

Adding paragraph options

Some of the changes you make to text affect entire paragraphs at once. Paragraph attributes include things like alignment, indentation, hyphenation, spacing, and line breaking.

You can change paragraph attributes if you first select a type area using a Selection tool, in which case, the changes affect every paragraph within the entire type area. If you use the Type tool to select one or more characters, changes you make to paragraph attributes affect the entire paragraphs containing the selected characters.

To display the Paragraph palette, shown in Figure 9-24, using menu commands, choose Window ➪ Type ➪ Paragraph. To display the Paragraph palette with a key command, press Alt+Ctrl+T (Option+⌘+T).

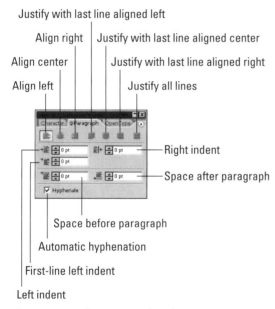

Figure 9-24: The Paragraph palette

Pressing Tab moves you forward through the text fields, and Shift+Tab moves you backward through the same text fields. Press Enter or Return to apply the changes that you made.

The bottom part of the Paragraph palette contains information that doesn't get changed often, so it almost doesn't need to be displayed. If you want to display it, choose Show Options from the Paragraph palette pop-up menu.

Aligning type

You can align paragraphs in different ways. Each way is represented by an icon in the Paragraph palette that shows a graphical representation of what multiple lines of type look like when that particular alignment is applied. The different types of alignment are Align left, Align center, Align right, Justify with last line aligned left, Justify with last line aligned center, Justify with last line aligned right, and Justify all lines. What these options do is listed here:

✦ **Align left:** Moves all your text so that it lines up with the left side of your page. The most common and the default setting, experienced typesetters often refer to this option as ragged right due to the uneven right side of the text. You can also apply this type of alignment by pressing Ctrl+Shift+L (⌘+Shift+L).

✦ **Align center:** All lines of type in the paragraph are centered relative to each other, to the point clicked, or to the location of the I-bar in type on a path. You can also apply this type of alignment by pressing Ctrl+Shift+C (⌘+Shift+C).

✦ **Align right:** Use this option to create a smooth, even right side and an uneven left side (no, ragged left isn't really a correct term). You can also apply this type of alignment by pressing Ctrl+Shift+R (⌘+Shift+R).

✦ **Justify with last line aligned left:** You apply this to make both the left and right sides appear smooth and even except the last line, which is aligned left.

✦ **Justify with last line aligned center:** Use this option to make both the left and right sides appear smooth and even except the last line, which is center aligned.

✦ **Justify with last line aligned right:** With this option, both the left and right sides appear smooth and even except the last line, which is aligned right.

✦ **Justify all lines:** Sometimes called Force Justify, this option is the same as Justify except that the last line of every paragraph is justified along with the other lines of the paragraph. This can create some really awful looking paragraphs, and it is done mainly for artistic emphasis, not as a proper way to justify type. The Justify all lines option is particularly useful for stretching a single line of type across a certain width. You can also apply this type of alignment by pressing Ctrl+Shift+F (⌘+Shift+F).

Note　Justification works only on area type. Illustrator does not allow you to select Justify or Justify all lines for type on a path or individual type.

Indenting paragraphs

Paragraphs can be indented within the Paragraph palette by choosing different amounts of indentation for the left edge, the right edge, and first line of each paragraph. The maximum indentation for all three fields is 1296 points and the minimum is –1296 points.

Using indents is a great way to offset type, such as quotes, that has smaller margins than the rest of the type surrounding the offset type. Changing the indentation values is also useful for creating hanging indents, such as numbered or bulleted text.

To create hanging indents easily, make the Left Indent as large as the width of a bullet or a number and a space, and then make the First Line value the negative value of that. If the left indent is 2 picas, the first line is –2 picas. This creates great hanging indents every time.

Spacing before or after paragraphs

Illustrator lets you place additional space between paragraphs by entering a number in the Space before paragraph field or the Space after paragraph field. You add this measurement to the leading to determine the distance from baseline to baseline before the selected paragraphs. You can also enter a negative number to decrease space between paragraphs, if necessary. You can make values for Space before paragraph between –1296 and 1296 points.

Spacing through justification

Illustrator enables you to control the spacing of letters, words, auto leading, and glyphs in text by changing the values you find in the Justification dialog box. You access this dialog box by choosing the Justification option in the Paragraph palette pop-up menu, shown in Figure 9-25. You can control these options in the Justification dialog box.

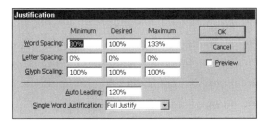

Figure 9-25: The Justification dialog box enables you to control how Illustrator applies paragraph justification.

✦ **Word spacing:** Word spacing is the space between the words that you create by clicking the spacebar. Set the Minimum, Desired, and Maximum values. The word space can range from 0% to 1000%; 100% is the default with no additional space being added. The minimum is the least amount of word spacing in percentage that you want to accept. Enter the exact percentage for the Desired setting. The maximum is the most amount of spacing you accept.

✦ **Letter spacing:** Letter spacing is the space between letters of words. The Letter spacing can be set from –100% to 500%. A value of 0% means that no space is added. Set the Minimum, Desired, and Maximum values.

✦ **Glyph scaling:** A glyph refers to any font character. Glyph scaling lets you change the width of the character as a percentage of the original. Set the Minimum, Desired, and Maximum scaling percentages. The range of glyph scaling is from 50% to 200%; 100% is the default where no scaling occurs.

✦ **Auto leading:** Set the Auto Leading as a percentage, which ranges from 0% to 500%, with 120% being the default.

✦ **Single word justification:** When there is a single word for the last line justification, choose one of these options from the pop-up: Full Justify, Align Left, Align Center, and Align Right.

Spacing affects the space between letters and words regardless of the alignment, although Justified text has even more spacing control than Flush Left, Flush Right, or Centered text.

When you choose Flush Left, Flush Right, or Centered alignment, the only text fields in the dialog box that you can change are the Desired fields for Letter Spacing and Word Spacing.

The Minimum and Maximum boxes in the Word Spacing, Letter Spacing, and Glyph Scaling areas are mainly used to control where the extra space goes and where it is removed from when stretching out and compressing the lines of text.

Hyphenating text

Hyphenation? In a drawing program? Unbelievably, but yes, and it's a nice addition to Illustrator's text-handling capabilities. Hyphenation works in the background, silently hyphenating when necessary.

To use Illustrator's hyphenation, you must select the Hyphenate check box in the lower left of the Paragraph palette.

Hyphenation in Illustrator works from a set of hyphenation rules that you define in the Hyphenation dialog box, shown in Figure 9-26. View the Hyphenation dialog box by choosing Hyphenation from the Paragraph palette pop-up menu. Here, you can specify how many letters must fall before the hyphen can appear and how many letters must fall after the hyphen. You can also limit the number of consecutive hyphens to avoid the "ladder look" of multiple hyphens.

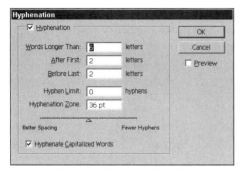

Figure 9-26: The Hyphenation dialog box allows you to fine-tune the way Illustrator hyphenates text.

Using every-line and single-line composer

In Illustrator, you can choose from two composition methods: Adobe every-line composer or Adobe single-line composer. These composer options are found in the Paragraph palette's pop-up menu. What this means is that in a paragraph, the composer checks and chooses the best breaks, hyphenation, and justification for the specific paragraph.

Every-line composer checks all the lines in the paragraph and makes its evaluation based on the paragraph as a whole. Single-line composer looks at each line of type rather than the whole paragraph to determine the best breaks, hyphenation, and justification. You can select both these options from the pop-up menu in the Paragraph palette.

Controlling punctuation

Roman Hanging Punctuation handles the alignment of punctuation marks for a specified paragraph. With the Roman Hanging Punctuation option turned on, apostrophes, quotes, commas, periods, and hyphens are 100 percent out of the margin. The characters — asterisks, tildes, ellipsis, en dashes, em dashes, colons, and semicolons — are 50 percent out of the margin.

If you check the Roman Hanging Punctuation option in the Paragraph palette's pop-up menu, punctuation at the left edge of a flush left, justified, or justified last line paragraph appears outside the type area. Punctuation on the right edge of a flush right, justified, or justified last line paragraph also appears outside the type area. Strangely enough, Illustrator is one of the few programs that support this very hip feature.

Another choice for punctuation is Optical Margin Alignment. Optical Margin Alignment handles the punctuation marks alignment for all paragraphs inside a type area. With this option turned on, all punctuation hangs outside of the margin so the type is aligned. You can find this feature under the Type menu.

Note   Additional options in the Paragraph palette's pop-up menu are Burasagari, Kinsoku Shori Type, Bunri-Kinshi, and Kurikaeshi Moji Shori. To see these options, you first must turn on Asian Options in the Type preferences. To do this, choose Edit ➪ Preferences ➪ Type (Illustrator ➪ Preferences ➪ Type), and then check the Show Asian Options box. Use these options for aligning double-byte punctuation marks, which aren't affected by choosing Roman Hanging Punctuation.

Working with OpenType

You can choose Window ➪ Type ➪ OpenType, or press Alt+Ctrl+Shift+T (Option+⌘+Shift+T), to access the OpenType palette. Use this palette to apply specific options to alternate characters with OpenType fonts. Figure 9-27 shows the OpenType palette.

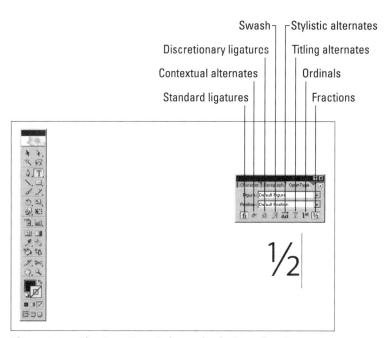

Figure 9-27: The OpenType Palette, displaying a fraction

Note Different OpenType fonts vary greatly in the features they offer. If you attempt to select one of the options in the OpenType palette that is not offered in the font you have selected, Illustrator changes the mouse pointer to a slashed circle to indicate that you cannot select that option.

Using the Tabs palette

You use the Tabs palette to set tabs the same way you would in your word-processing or page-layout program. To display the Tabs palette, shown in Figure 9-28, choose Window ➪ Type ➪ Tabs or Ctrl+Shift+T (⌘+Shift+T). The Tabs palette appears above the type you have selected and automatically assumes the width of the type area.

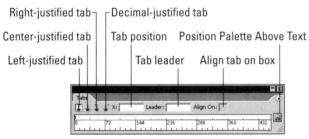

Figure 9-28: The Tabs palette allows you to set tabs in your text blocks.

To change the width of the Tabs palette, click and drag on the resize triangle in the lower-right corner of the palette. The Tabs palette can be made wider, but not taller. To reset the Tabs palette to the exact size of the type area, drag the resize box back.

Tip The Position Palette Above Text button moves the Tabs palette to make it flush left with the type and moves it up or down so that it is right above the selected text area.

Illustrator automatically sets tabs at every half inch. These are called Auto tab stops. After you set a tab, all the Auto tab stops to the left of the tab you have set disappear. The Auto tab stops work like left-justified tabs.

If you check the Snap to Unit option in the Tabs palette pop-up menu, tab stops correspond to ruler tick marks.

The measurement system shown on the ruler is the same system that the rest of the documents use. You can change the measurement system in the Units & Display Performance section of the Preferences dialog box. You can access this by choosing

Edit ➪ Preferences ➪ Units & Display Performance (Illustrator ➪ Preferences ➪ Units & Display Performance).

To set a tab, select a tab from the four Tab Style buttons on the upper left of the Tabs palette and click the ruler below to set exactly where you want the new tab. After the tab has been set, you can move it by dragging it along the ruler, or remove it by dragging it off the top or bottom edge of the ruler.

You can set four types of tabs:

✦ **Left-justified:** This option makes type align to the right side of the tab, with the leftmost character aligning with the tab stop.

✦ **Center-justified:** This option makes type align to the center of the tab, with half the characters aligning on either side of the tab stop.

✦ **Right-justified:** This option makes type align to the left side of the tab, with the rightmost character aligning with the tab stop.

✦ **Decimal-justified:** This option makes type align to the left side of the tab, with a decimal or the rightmost character aligning with the tab stop.

To change a tab from one style to another, select a tab stop and click the Tab style button to which you want to change. To deselect all tabs, click in the area to the right of the Tab position box. (If you don't click far enough away from the Tab position box, you end up changing the units.) It is a good idea to deselect tabs after setting them so that when you define a new tab style for the next tab stop, it does not change the tab stop that you just set.

Using Advanced Type Functions

Illustrator has built in some more advanced type functions that go beyond the basic user. In these functions, you find threading text, wrapping text, fitting headlines, find font, check spelling, and change case. You find each of these functions under the Edit and Type menus.

Threading text

The Threading Text option links text from one area to another, continuing a story from one area to another, as shown in Figure 9-29. Linked blocks act like groups, enabling you to use the regular Selection tool and click just one area to select all areas. (You can still select individual blocks with the Direct Selection tool.) Whenever you have more text than can fit into a text area, a tiny little red plus sign in a box appears, alerting you that there is more text in the box than you see.

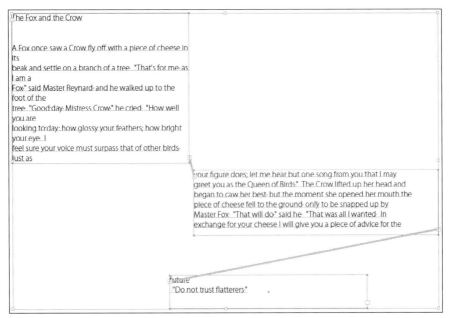

Figure 9-29: Text blocks are threaded together in the order of the arrows.

To use threaded text, select a text area or rectangle and any other shapes, even text rectangles and areas, and choose Type ➪ Threaded Text ➪ Create. The text areas then act as if they are grouped. Text flows from the backmost shape to the front-most in any group of linked blocks, so be careful to order your boxes correctly when setting up linked text. In fact, if you send a box to the back, Illustrator starts the thread from that location, then goes to the next box forward, and then the next, and so on. You cannot choose Type ➪ Threaded Text ➪ Create unless at least one text area and one other path or text area are selected.

Unthreading text

You can unthread text in various ways. To release the object from the text thread, choose Type ➪ Threaded Text ➪ Release Selection. This removes the text from the objects. To remove the thread, but leave the type in the objects, choose Type ➪ Threaded Text ➪ Remove Threading. You can also break the threads by double-clicking on an out port. The out port is the little box with the outward pointing arrow at the edge of the object that the type is flowing out of.

When you double-click the out port again, the text flows forward into the next object.

Fitting a headline

The Type menu's Fit Headline option is designed to automatically increase the width of type in order to fit type perfectly from the left side of a type area to the right side of that same type area, as shown in Figure 9-30. In this case, the Fit Headline option was used on the headline over the right-side text, while the left side uses normal text. Another option is to use Justify all lines in the Paragraph palette, but it doesn't do as nice of a job as Fit Headline.

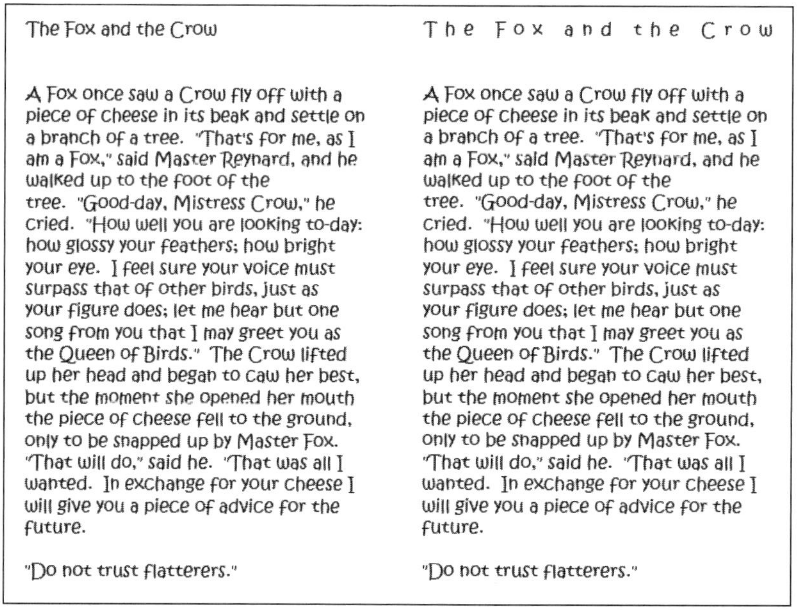

The Fox and the Crow | The Fox and the Crow

A Fox once saw a Crow fly off with a piece of cheese in its beak and settle on a branch of a tree. "That's for me, as I am a Fox," said Master Reynard, and he walked up to the foot of the tree. "Good-day, Mistress Crow," he cried. "How well you are looking to-day: how glossy your feathers; how bright your eye. I feel sure your voice must surpass that of other birds, just as your figure does; let me hear but one song from you that I may greet you as the Queen of Birds." The Crow lifted up her head and began to caw her best, but the moment she opened her mouth the piece of cheese fell to the ground, only to be snapped up by Master Fox. "That will do," said he. "That was all I wanted. In exchange for your cheese I will give you a piece of advice for the future.

"Do not trust flatterers."

Figure 9-30: The Fit Headline option makes headlines fit across the entire text block.

Finding and replacing text

Under the Edit menu are more choices for text editing. Illustrator lets you find certain text and replace with another text by choosing Edit ➪ Find and Replace to open the Find And Replace dialog box, shown in Figure 9-31. Use this to replace specific letters, words, or characters. In the Find And Replace dialog box, you have the following options:

Figure 9-31: Use the Find And Replace dialog box to edit your text.

✦ **Match Case:** Selects the characters only if they have the same uppercase and lowercase attributes as the characters you type in the Find text field.

✦ **Find Whole Word:** Tells Illustrator that the characters you type in the Find text field are an entire word and not part of a word.

✦ **Search Backwards:** Tells Illustrator to look before the current insertion point for the next instance of the characters, instead of using the default, which is to look after the current insertion point.

✦ **Check Hidden Layers:** Instructs Illustrator to look in the text in hidden layers.

✦ **Check Locked Layers:** Instructs Illustrator to look in the text in locked layers.

The following steps describe how to use these options to find and replace text:

1. **Choose Edit ➪ Find And Replace.** The Find And Replace dialog box appears.

2. **Type in the word, phrase, or characters that you want to find in the Find text field.**

3. **In the Replace with text field, type the word or characters that you want to use to replace the text.**

4. **Check the appropriate options described in the previous section.**

5. **Click the Find button to find the first occurrence of the word or characters.**

6. **Click the Replace button to replace the selected text.** Click the Replace & Find button to locate the next occurrence. If you want to change all occurrences, click the Replace All button.

Note   You do not need to select areas of type the Selection or Type tools — all that is necessary is that the document that you want to search is the open and active document.

Finding fonts

Find Font looks for certain fonts in a document and replaces them with fonts you specify. This can be especially handy if you have pasted in text from other applications and you want to make certain that your Illustrator document has a uniform appearance throughout.

To locate the fonts in your document, choose Type ➪ Find Font to display the Find Font dialog box, as shown in Figure 9-32.

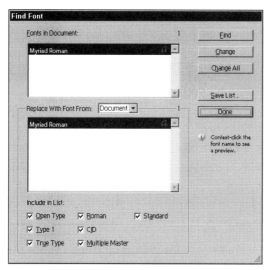

Figure 9-32: The Find Font dialog box helps you change the fonts that are in your document.

To change all occurrences of a certain font to another font, select the font you want to change in the top list box, titled Fonts in Document. Then select a font in the box in the lower section of the dialog box and click the Change All button. To change one particular instance, click the Change button. To find the next occurrence of that font, select Find Next. The Skip button skips over the currently selected text and finds the next occurrence of that font. Keep in mind that choosing System from the Replace With Font From list box can take a while for Illustrator to build and display the font list, especially if you have a ton of fonts on your system.

Clicking the Save List button enables you to save your font list as a text file.

Checking spelling

Spell checking checks all text in a document to see whether it is spelled (and capitalized) correctly. To use this feature, choose Edit ➪ Check Spelling to display the Check Spelling dialog box, shown in Figure 9-33.

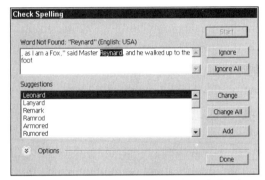

Figure 9-33: Use the Check Spelling dialog box to make certain your documents don't contain embarrassing spelling errors.

Note   Check Spelling uses a standard user dictionary as well as all foreign language and hyphenation dictionaries that are available.

If you have any misspelled words or words that are not in the spelling dictionaries, those words are listed at the top of the Check Spelling dialog box in the Misspelled Words list box. Selecting a word in this list displays similar words below in the Suggestions list box.

Some of the options you can change are to find repeated words or uncapitalized words at the start of a sentence. Other options are to ignore words that are all uppercase, Roman numerals, and words with numbers.

You use the Add button when you want to add the selected "misspelled" word to your custom dictionary.

As you're checking your spelling in the Check Spelling dialog box, clicking the Change button replaces the misspelled word with the highlighted word in the Suggested Corrections list. Clicking the Change All button replaces all misspelled occurrences of that word throughout the entire document with the correctly spelled word.

Clicking the Ignore button ignores that occurrence of the misspelled word. Clicking Ignore All skips all occurrences of that word in the document.

Clicking the Done button closes the Check Spelling dialog box.

Changing case

Change Case converts selected text to one of a variety of case options. To use this filter, select type with a Type tool and then choose Type ➪ Change Case. The four submenu choices are UPPERCASE, lowercase, Title Case, and Sentence case.

The four Change Case options affect only letters, not numbers, symbols, or punctuation. The options are as follows:

✦ **UPPERCASE:** Converts all selected letters into uppercase, regardless of whether any letters were uppercase or lowercase.

✦ **lowercase:** Converts all selected letters into lowercase, regardless of whether any letters were uppercase or lowercase. It also doesn't matter if the letters were originally uppercase because they were typed with the Caps Lock key engaged, or if the uppercase letters were uppercase because of a style format.

✦ **Title Case:** Capitalizes the first letter of each word.

✦ **Sentence case:** Uses periods, exclamation points, and question marks as the end of the sentence to capitalize the first letter of each sentence.

Tip

Be sure to check your text for proper capitalization after using any of these options. You're almost certain to find errors in things like proper names and acronyms.

Using Smart Punctuation

The Smart Punctuation filter looks for certain characters in a document and replaces them with characters you specify. To use this filter, select type with either a Selection tool or with a Type tool. Then choose Type ➪ Smart Punctuation. The Smart Punctuation dialog box, shown in Figure 9-34, appears.

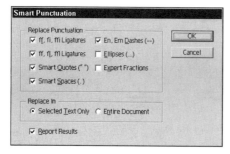

Figure 9-34: Use the Smart Punctuation dialog box to replace ordinary punctuation with typographer's punctuation.

The Smart Punctuation filter works after the fact, making changes to text already in the Illustrator document. There are no settings, for example, to convert quotes to curved quotes as you are typing them. The types of punctuation to be changed are determined by a set of check boxes in the Smart Punctuation dialog box. A checked box means that Illustrator looks for these certain instances and, if it finds them, corrects them with the proper punctuation.

The first two options are used for replacing ff, fi (or fl), and ffi (or ffl) with ligatures. Ligatures are characters that represent several characters with one character that is designed to let those characters appear better looking when placed next to each other. Most fonts have fi and fl ligatures, which look like fi and fl, respectively.

The remaining Smart Punctuation options work as follows:

✦ Smart Quotes replaces straight quotes (" " and ' ') with curly quotes, known as typesetter's quotes or printer's quotes (" " and ' ').

✦ Smart Spaces replaces multiple spaces after a period with one space. (In type-setting, there should only be one space following a period.)

✦ En, Em Dashes replaces hyphens (-) with en dashes (–) and double hyphens (--) with em dashes (—).

✦ Ellipses replaces three periods (. . .) with an ellipsis (...).

✦ Expert Fractions replaces fractions with expert fractions if you have the expert fractions for the font family you are using. Adobe sells "Expert Collection" fonts that contain these fractions. If you do not have expert fractions, your fractions remain unchanged.

Other options are to replace in Selected Text Only or in Entire Document. Checking the Report Results box displays a dialog box when the filter is finished, telling you how many of the punctuation changes were made.

Adding rows and columns

Area Type Options divides rectangular paths (text rectangles) into even sections. You can add rows, columns, or both to a text area using these options.

To add Rows and Columns, select a path and choose Type ➪ Area Type Options to display the Area Type Options dialog box, shown in Figure 9-35.

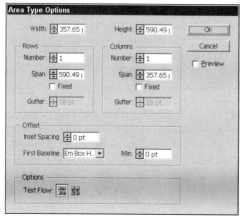

Figure 9-35: The Area Type Options dialog box enables you to create additional columns and rows in your text blocks.

You can select any text path, open or closed, and divide it into rows and columns, with one catch: The object becomes a rectangular shape, the size of the original path's bounding box (the smallest box that can completely contain the path). You cannot divide a nonrectangular path automatically. See the steps later in this section for a way to do this without Illustrator knowing about it. The Area Type Options dialog box has the following options:

✦ The left side at the top of the Area Type Options dialog box determines the width of the columns. The right side determines the height of the rows. At the bottom of the dialog box is a Preview check box; checking this displays changes as you make them in the Area Type Options dialog box.

Note   All measurements in the Area Type Options dialog box are displayed in the current measurement system.

✦ In the Rows section, the Number field specifies the number of rows into which the original path divides.

✦ The Span field is the height of each of the rows.

✦ The Gutter field specifies the space between rows.

✦ Check the Fixed check box to prevent the row height from changing if the text block is resized.

✦ In the Columns section, Number determines how many columns you get.

✦ The Span field determines the width of the columns.

✦ The Gutter field specifies the space between columns.

✦ Check the Fixed check box to prevent the column width from changing if the text block is resized.

Remember that using the Area Type Options feature actually divides the selected rectangle into several pieces.

✦ The Offset options are for Inset Spacing (from the edge of the object area) and First Baseline. Use the settings in this section to move text slightly away from the path for improved readability.

✦ The Text Flow options determine the direction of text as it flows from one section to the next. You may choose between text that starts along the top row and flows from left to right, and then goes to the next lowest row, flowing from left to right, and so on. The second option is to have text start in the left column, flowing from top to bottom, and then to the next column to the right, flowing from top to bottom.

Showing hidden characters

When you are typing, you typically add certain special characters — such as spaces, returns, and tabs. Typically, you don't see these characters. You can choose to view the hidden characters by choosing Show Hidden Characters from the Type menu. This option can be especially useful when you are working with imported text because it allows you to find any extra hidden characters that can interfere with proper text formatting.

Changing type orientation

You can easily change the orientation of your type by choosing Type Orientation from the Type menu. You then select either Horizontal or Vertical from the Type Orientation submenu. That way, if you wanted vertical type and did it as horizontal, you can change it easily without retyping it.

Updating legacy text

Legacy text is any text created in version 10 and earlier. Because Illustrator now uses a new Adobe Text Engine, the older text must be converted to take advantage of this new type engine. The changes are character positioning with tracking, leading, and kerning, shifts in the words resulting in different hyphenation, and changes in wordflow from threaded text. When you open an older file, a dialog box pops up, asking you if you want to update all legacy text. If you decline to do the update when opening the file, you can use the Legacy Text submenu entries to update all or selected legacy text while editing the file.

Exporting and placing

You can export text from your Illustrator documents for use in other applications. To export text, select the text you want to export and choose File ➪ Export to display the Export dialog box, shown in Figure 9-36. In the Export dialog box, select Text Format and enter a file name for the exported file. Click the Export button to save the file.

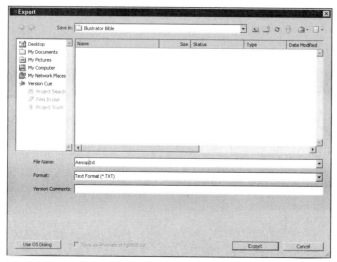

Figure 9-36: The Adobe Export dialog box is similar to the standard file dialog box that may appear.

You can import text back into Illustrator with the Place command (choose File ➪ Place when a text area is active with a Type tool). Word-processing software, page-layout software, or any other software that can read text files can open and use text that you saved in Illustrator.

Creating Outlines

After you create, edit, and spell check your text, you may want to create outlines from the characters so that you can modify the characters to produce some interesting visual effects. To do so, choose Type ➪ Create Outlines, or press Ctrl+Shift+O (⌘+Shift+O), and the selected type converts into editable paths, like those shown in Figure 9-37. To convert type to outlines, you need to select the type with a Selection tool, not a Type tool. Each letter is its own compound path, and you can edit each path with the Direct Selection tool.

Cross-Reference   For more on the Direct Selection tool, see Chapter 6.

OpenType and TrueType combine the screen and printer fonts into one file — if you can select any of these font types in Illustrator, you can create outlines from it. Illustrator locates the font file and uses that information to create the outlines.

Figure 9-37: Type converted into outlines can make for some cool effects.

After you convert type to outlines, you can apply gradients to its fill and you can apply patterns to its fill that you can preview onscreen. You can apply patterns to non-outline type.

Caution Although you can undo Create Outlines, be forewarned that you cannot convert back to type in case you made a spelling error or want to change the font or any other type attribute.

You can convert all forms of type, including individual type, type on a path, area type, and type containers to outlines.

Tip Creating outlines out of type is also very useful when you want to send the file to be outputted and the person doing the output does not have the font you are using. Simply use the Create Outlines option before you send the file, and it prints just fine. (This is not advised for 4-point type or smaller, as described in the "Understanding hinting" section later in this chapter.)

The process of creating editable type outlines has many uses, including distorting mild-mannered characters into grotesque letters. More practical uses for editable type outlines include making type-based logos unique, arcing type (where one side is flat and the other is curved), special effects and masking, and avoiding font compatibility problems. You can apply some of the basic effects by warping the text.

Cross-Reference

For more on warp effects, see Chapter 11.

Initially, when type is converted into outlines, individual characters are turned into compound paths. This ensures that holes in letters, such as in a lowercase a, b, or d, are see-through, and not just white-filled paths placed on top of the original objects.

Cross-Reference

See Chapter 12 for an in-depth discussion of compound paths.

Distorting characters for special effects

After letters have been turned into outlines, there is nothing to stop you from distorting them into shapes that resemble letters only in the most simplistic sense of the word.

The results of letter distortion usually aren't all that eye-pleasing, but they can be fun. Few things in life are as pleasing as taking a boring letter Q and twisting it into "the letter that time forgot." Or fiddling around with your boss's name until the letters look as evil as your boss does. Or adding pointed ears and whiskers to a random array of letters and numbers and printing out several sheets of them with the words "Mutant kittens for sale."

When modifying existing letters, use the Direct Selection tool. Select the points or segments you want to move, and drag them around to your heart's content. This can be great practice for adjusting paths, and you might accidentally stumble onto some really cool designs.

Type outlines provide you with the flexibility to manipulate letters to turn an ordinary, boring, letters-only logo into a distinct symbol embodying the company's image.

Outlines are flexible enough that there really are no limits to what can be done with something as simple as a word of type.

Masking and other effects

Standard type or type that has been converted into outlines can then be used as a mask or filled with a placed image or any objects, as shown in Figure 9-38.

For outlined words to work as a single mask, you must first change them into a compound path. Usually, individual letters of converted type are changed into individual compound paths, whether the letter has a hole in it or not. For masks to work properly, you must select the entire word or words you want to use as a mask and then choose Object ➪ Compound Path ➪ Make, or press Ctrl+8 (⌘+8). This changes all the selected letters into one compound path.

Figure 9-38: This shows type masking an image.

After the words are a compound path, place them in front of the objects to be masked, select both the words and the masked objects, and then choose Object ➪ Clipping Mask ➪ Make or press Ctrl+7 (⌘+7).

Tip   In some third-party (non-Adobe) and shareware typefaces, making a compound path out of a series of letters can produce results where the holes are not transparent. This issue is usually one of path direction, which can be corrected by selecting the inner shape (the hole) and changing the direction with the path direction buttons on the Attributes palette.

Avoiding font conflicts by creating outlines

If you ever give your files to a service bureau or to clients, you've probably already run into some font-compatibility problems. A font-compatibility problem usually means that the place you gave your file to doesn't have a typeface that you used in your Illustrator document or that they have a different version of the same typeface with different metrics.

This is a problem to which there is no great solution, and the trouble seems to be worsening as more font manufacturers spring up. And then there are shareware typefaces, some of which resemble Adobe originals to an uncanny degree of accuracy. All this leads to a great deal of confusion and frustration for the average Illustrator user.

But there is a way around this problem, at least most of the time. Convert your typefaces into outlines before you send them to other people with other systems — they don't need your typefaces for the letters to print correctly. In fact, converted letters aren't really considered type anymore, just outlines.

Tip   Save your file before converting the text to outlines, and then save it as a different file name after converting the text to outlines. This allows you to do text editing later on the original file, if necessary.

Understanding hinting

Most Type 1 fonts have *hinting* built into them. Hinting is a method for adjusting type at small point sizes, especially at low resolutions. Although hinting is built into the fonts, when those fonts are converted into paths via the Create Outlines command, the hinting functionality is gone. This is part of the reason that type converted to outlines can look heavier than it does otherwise.

Creating outlines shouldn't cause that much of a problem when the type is to be output to an imagesetter, because the high resolution of the imagesetter makes up for the loss of hinting. However, very small type — 4 points or less — could be adversely affected.

Note   Converting typefaces to outlines removes the hinting system that Adobe has implemented. This hinting system makes small letters on low-resolution (less than 600 dpi) devices print more accurately, controlling the placement and visibility of serifs and other small, thin strokes in characters. Type at small point sizes looks quite different on laser printers, although it retains its shape and consistency when it is output to an imagesetter or an output scanner system.

Understanding Other Type Considerations

When you're using type in Illustrator, remember these things if you want to get good results:

✦ Make sure that the person you are sending the Illustrator file to has the same fonts you have. It isn't enough just to have the same name of a font; you'll need the exact font that was created by the same manufacturer.

✦ Try not to mix TrueType fonts with PostScript fonts. This usually ends up confusing everyone involved.

✦ If the person you are sending Illustrator files to does not have your typeface, select the type in that font and choose Type ➪ Create Outlines or press Ctrl+Shift+O (⌘+Shift+O).

✦ If you are saving your illustration as an EPS file to be placed into another program and you are not going to open the file, you can select Include Document Fonts in the EPS Save dialog box. This forces any fonts used in the illustration to be saved with the illustration and allows the illustration to print as a placed image from within another program or to print from Illustrator as a placed EPS. The same goes for PDF files.

Summary

Text can be an important part of Illustrator documents. Understanding how Illustrator handles text-related issues is vital to getting the best results. In this chapter, you learned about the following important topics in this area:

✦ Individual type has one point as its "anchor," and the type is aligned to that point.

✦ There are four different ways to put type on a page: individual type, type containers, area type, and type on a path.

✦ Type containers exist within a rectangle drawn with the Type tool.

✦ Type can be selected all at once by clicking the path (or point) of the type with the Selection tool.

✦ Individual characters, words, and paragraphs can be selected by using any of the Type tools.

✦ Area type is type that exists within the confines of any path.

✦ Type on a path is type that runs along the edge of a path.

✦ The Character palette, accessed by pressing Ctrl+T (⌘+T), contains all the character-specific information about selected type and can be used to change that information.

✦ Tracking and kerning remove or add space between groups or pairs of letters, respectively.

✦ The Paragraph palette, accessed by pressing Alt+Ctrl+T (Option+⌘+T), contains all the paragraph-specific information about selected type and can be used to change that information.

✦ Most of the options used to control type can be found in the Type menu.

✦ Type can be set to wrap around selected paths by using the Text Wrapping feature.

✦ Type can be set to jump from text block to text block by threading text blocks together.

✦ The Tabs palette is used to set tabs for text areas.

✦ If you have both the screen font and the printer font of a Type 1 typeface, or if you have an OpenType or TrueType font installed, you can convert the font into outlines via the Create Outlines command.

✦ After type has been changed to outlines, you may use those outlines as a mask, or fill those outlines with gradients or patterns.

✦   ✦   ✦

Using Creative Strokes and Fills with Patterns

✦ ✦ ✦ ✦

In This Chapter

Using the default patterns

Creating your own patterns

Understanding how transparency works with patterns

Modifying existing patterns

Putting patterns and gradients into patterns

Transforming patterns

✦ ✦ ✦ ✦

No Illustrator book would be complete without discussing the how-to's of creating creative strokes, patterns, and textures with the Scribble effect. Sure, you can create these by simply drawing them, but Illustrator makes their creation a breeze. Illustrator enables you to create a pattern and save that pattern for future use.

We all have the desire to add some texture to make flat images pop up. The Scribble effect lets you add some sketchy or computery effects to a boring drawing. Scribble lets you add a loose, free quality look to your illustrations.

Using Creative Strokes

In Chapter 4, I discuss how to apply strokes to paths, and in Chapter 5, I discuss all the attributes of a stroke and how to apply them to objects. In this chapter, you find out how to use strokes to create something spectacular.

The ability to stroke a path in Illustrator is greatly underrated. Strokes can do more than just outline shapes and vary thickness and patterns. You can create illustrations with a combination of strokes. You can easily create a filmstrip or a railroad track with some Stroke attribute changes.

In the first part of this section, I explain some of the greatest mysteries and unlock some of the deepest secrets that surround strokes. If that sounds at all boring, take a look at the figures in this chapter. I created most of them by using strokes, not filled paths.

You create most effects with strokes by overlaying several strokes on top of one another. By using the Appearance palette's pop-up menu to Add New Stroke, you place an exact duplicate of the original path on top of itself.

Changing the weight and color of the top stroke gives the appearance of a path that is a designer, or custom, stroke. You can add strokes on top of or under the original stroke to make the pattern more complex or to add more colors or shapes.

Stroke essentials

Strokes act and work differently than fills. Remember these basic rules when using strokes:

✦ **Even distribution:** The most important thing to remember when using strokes is that you should evenly distribute stroke-weight width on both sides of a path. In other words, for a stroke with a 6-point weight, each side of the stroke's path should have 3 points of weight.

✦ **Using patterns in strokes:** You can place patterns into strokes, and you can see the pattern on the stroke.

✦ **No gradients allowed:** Due to PostScript limitations, you cannot use gradients to color strokes. The workaround for this is to use the Effect ⇨ Path ⇨ Outline Stroke command so you can edit later to fill with a gradient. Choosing Object ⇨ Path ⇨ Outline Stroke creates path outlines around the width of the stroke. When you convert a stroke into an outline, it is really an outlined path object and you can fill it with patterns and gradients (both of which appear when previewing and printing).

✦ **Consistent stroke weight:** Stroke weight never varies on the same path.

✦ **No stroke weight:** A stroke with a color of None has no Stroke weight.

✦ **Strokes and Pathfinder functions:** Strokes are, for the most part, ignored when combining, splitting, or modifying paths with the Pathfinder functions. Strokes are never considered when the Pathfinder functions search for the locations of the paths.

For more on applying patterns to strokes, see the section "Creating Perfect Patterns" later in this chapter. For more on Gradients, see Chapter 7. For more information on Stroke weights as they relate to paths and objects, see Chapters 4 and 5. For more on the Pathfinder functions, see Chapter 12.

Using the stroke charts

The stroke charts in Figures 10-1 through 10-3 show how some of the basic stroke-dash patterns look with various options checked, at different weights, and in different combinations. The great advantage of these charts is that you can find a style similar to the one you want and then modify it to suit your situation. The charts should help you determine when to use certain types of stroke patterns because, as you can see, some patterns work better than others with curves and corners. All the paths in the charts were taken from an original shape that included a straight segment, a corner, and a curve.

The first chart, shown in Figure 10-1, consists of 32 three-point stroke paths that have a variety of dash patterns and end and join attributes. The second chart, shown in Figure 10-2, shows 18 ten-point stroke paths with similar attributes. These two charts show stroke effects with only one path. The area in the middle of each path in the chart describes the path.

The third chart, shown in Figure 10-3, contains paths that have been copied on top of the original by using the Appearance palette. To copy the path this way, select the path and choose Add New Stroke from the Appearance palette pop-up menu. The paths are listed in the order that they were created. The first path is described at the bottom of the list. The first path is duplicated in the Appearance palette by choosing Add New Stroke from the pop-up menu, and given the Paint Style attributes of the item in the list. In the case of blended paths (the fourth one down in row 1 of Figure 10-3), you need to copy the original line and then choose Edit ➪ Paste In Front or press Ctrl+F (⌘+F) rather than use the Appearance palette to duplicate the path. You can't blend multiple paths in the Appearance palette because Illustrator reads the paths as one path. So in the case of blends, invoke the Paste in Front option before blending. Then you can just select all paths and choose Object ➪ Blend ➪ Make.

Tip To create some really great effects such as a pearl necklace, you need to blend the paths. You can blend paths from one to another. Simply select the paths and choose Object ➪ Blend ➪ Make. You can change the blend amount if necessary by choosing Object ➪ Blend ➪ Blend Options.

Cross-Reference For more on Blends, see Chapter 12.

When you create a stroke pattern, frequently the original path is selected in the Appearance palette and copied on top of the original by using the Appearance palette's pop-up menu (select the path and choose Add New Stroke) several times.

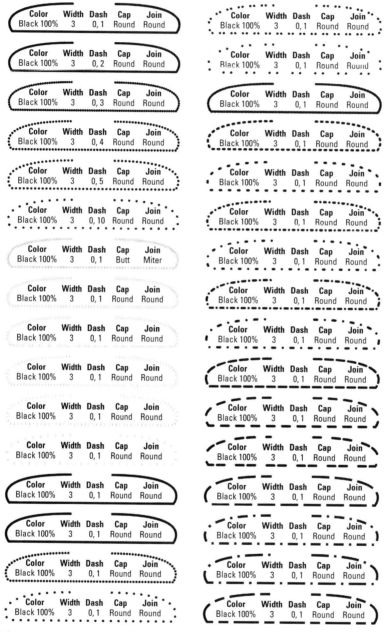

Figure 10-1: Thirty-two three-point stroke paths

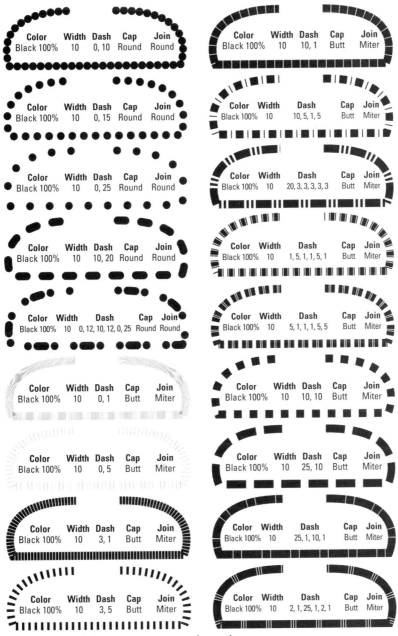

Figure 10-2: Eighteen ten-point stroke paths

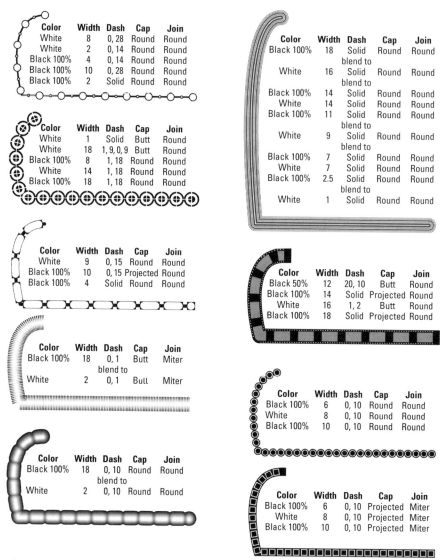

The following tables describe the stroke settings shown in the figure.

Color	Width	Dash	Cap	Join
White	8	0, 28	Round	Round
White	2	0, 14	Round	Round
Black 100%	4	0, 14	Round	Round
Black 100%	10	0, 28	Round	Round
Black 100%	2	Solid	Round	Round

Color	Width	Dash	Cap	Join
White	1	Solid	Butt	Round
White	18	1, 9, 0, 9	Butt	Round
Black 100%	8	1, 18	Round	Round
White	14	1, 18	Round	Round
Black 100%	18	1, 18	Round	Round

Color	Width	Dash	Cap	Join
White	9	0, 15	Round	Round
Black 100%	10	0, 15	Projected	Round
Black 100%	4	Solid	Round	Round

Color	Width	Dash	Cap	Join
Black 100%	18	0, 1	Butt	Miter
		blend to		
White	2	0, 1	Butt	Miter

Color	Width	Dash	Cap	Join
Black 100%	18	0, 10	Round	Round
		blend to		
White	2	0, 10	Round	Round

Color	Width	Dash	Cap	Join
Black 100%	18	Solid	Round	Round
		blend to		
White	16	Solid	Round	Round
		blend to		
Black 100%	14	Solid	Round	Round
White	14	Solid	Round	Round
Black 100%	11	Solid	Round	Round
		blend to		
White	9	Solid	Round	Round
		blend to		
Black 100%	7	Solid	Round	Round
White	7	Solid	Round	Round
Black 100%	2.5	Solid	Round	Round
		blend to		
White	1	Solid	Round	Round

Color	Width	Dash	Cap	Join
Black 50%	12	20, 10	Butt	Round
Black 100%	14	Solid	Projected	Round
White	16	1, 2	Butt	Round
Black 100%	18	Solid	Projected	Round

Color	Width	Dash	Cap	Join
Black 100%	6	0, 10	Round	Round
White	8	0, 10	Round	Round
Black 100%	10	0, 10	Round	Round

Color	Width	Dash	Cap	Join
Black 100%	6	0, 10	Projected	Miter
White	8	0, 10	Projected	Miter
Black 100%	10	0, 10	Projected	Miter

Figure 10-3: Paths that have been copied on top of the original paths

Creating parallel strokes

Do you need to create a railroad track or a racetrack quickly? Creating the curvy parallel lines to make your illustration realistic is easier than you think. The following steps describe how to create a specialty stroke that looks like parallel strokes.

Follow these steps to create the example:

1. **Use the Pen tool to draw a short curved line similar to the curves shown in Figure 10-4.** The example uses a fill of None and a stroke path weight that is 42-point and black (use the Stroke palette to set the size of the stroke).

2. **In the Appearance palette pop-up menu, choose Add New Stroke.** You access the pop-up menu by clicking the right-pointing arrow in the circle on the upper-right corner of the Appearance palette. The new stroke appears just above the existing stroke in the Appearance palette.

3. **Change the stroke weight of the new stroke to 30-point and the color to white.** Make certain that the new stroke is selected in the Appearance palette before making these changes. This overlays the new, narrower white stroke on top of the wider black stroke.

4. **Choose Add New Stroke from the Appearance palette pop-up menu.**

5. **Change the stroke weight of the new stroke to 18-point and the color to black.**

6. **Again, choose Add New Stroke from the Appearance palette pop-up menu.**

7. **Change the stroke weight of the new stroke to 6-point and the color to white.** In the final product, shown in Figure 10-4, the 30-point stroke is 12 points more than the 18 points of the black stroke, or 6 points on each side. The 42-point stroke is 12 points more than the white 30-point stroke.

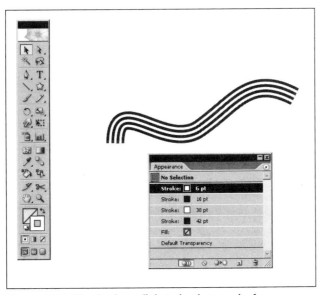

Figure 10-4: The final parallel stroke that results from overlaying new, smaller, contrasting strokes over existing ones

Caution   The order in which the overlapping strokes appear in the Appearance palette is very important. The widest stroke must be at the bottom of the list with the next widest just above it, and so on. If you don't have the strokes in the proper order, narrower strokes that are below wider strokes will not be visible. If necessary, you can drag the strokes in the Appearance palette to rearrange them into the correct order.

This example is just the tip of the iceberg in creating custom strokes. Not only can you have paths that overlap, but you also can give the stroke on each path different dash patterns, joins, and caps. You can even add fills to certain paths to make the stroke different on both sides of the path. And if all that isn't enough, you can use Outline Path to outline strokes.

Tip   When you are creating parallel strokes, determine how thick each of the visible strokes should be, multiply that number times the black and white visible strokes that you want for the base stroke, and work up from there. For example, if you want 10-point strokes, and there are four white strokes and five black strokes, make the first stroke 90-points thick and Black. Then make the next stroke 70-point White, and then 50-point Black, 30-point White, and 10-point Black.

Knowing the secrets doesn't let you in on the really good stuff, though. Read on to learn how to apply these to achieve truly amazing effects with strokes.

Creating map elements

Several effects that you can create with paths have a traveling theme, mainly because a path starts somewhere and finishes somewhere else. Railroad tracks, roads, highways, trails, and rivers all have a tendency to conform very nicely to stroke effects with paths.

Creating a railroad track with a gradient

One of the trickiest traveling paths to create is a railroad track. The practical point of creating this railroad track is to illustrate how to change a stroke into a gradient. As mentioned at the beginning of the chapter, you can do this only if you convert your stroke into an outline. Then you can fill it with the gradient of your choosing. To get the real railroad-track look, some innovative thinking is necessary, as described in the following steps.

1. **Draw a path to represent the railroad track with the Pen tool.** Set the fill to None.

2. **Give the path a desired Stroke weight.** This example uses a Stroke weight of 30 points as shown in Figure 10-5.

Creating a Film Strip Stroke

The stroke examples shown earlier in this chapter can help you find a specific style, which you can then modify for your situation. As an example, the stroke in the middle of the right column in the third stroke chart (refer to Figure 10-3) is a stroke that looks like a strip of film. The following steps describe how to create this film stroke, which is a basic stroke that produces a stunning effect.

1. **Draw a wavy path with the Pen tool.** For more on using the Pen tool, see Chapter 4.

2. **Change the stroke of the path to 18-point Black and the fill to None.**

3. **Choose Add New Stroke from the Appearance palette pop-up menu.** You access the pop-up menu by clicking the right-pointing arrow in a circle on the upper right of the Appearance palette. Change the new stroke to 16-point White, and use a Dash Pattern of Dash 1, Gap 2.

4. **Choose Add New Stroke from the Appearance palette pop-up menu again, and change the new stroke to 14-point Black, Solid.**

5. **Choose Add New Stroke from the Appearance palette pop-up menu once more, and change the new stroke to 50% Black, 12 points, with a Dash Pattern of Dash 20, Gap 10.**

The figure that follows shows the final filmstrip and the Appearance palette displaying the list of strokes. You can use this procedure to create any of the strokes in the third stroke chart (refer to Figure 10-3) by substituting the values that are listed in the chart for the stroke that you want.

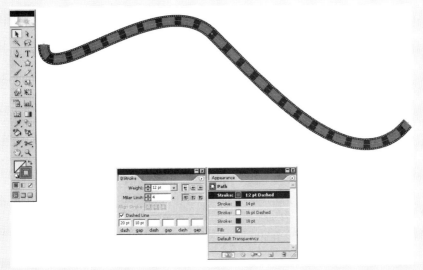

The film stroke created using a stroke pattern from Figure 10-3

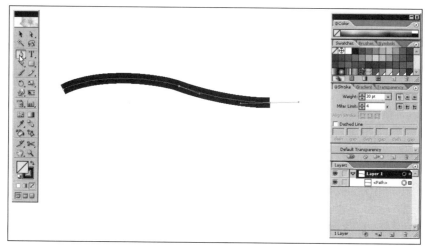

Figure 10-5: Begin by drawing a 30-point line with no fill.

3. **Copy the path by choosing Edit ➪ Copy.** Alternatively, you can press Ctrl+C (⌘+C).

4. **Choose Edit ➪ Paste in Front.** Alternatively, you can press Ctrl+F (⌘+F). You are still pasting the original copied path from the Clipboard. This creates a second path, which is the area between the two metal rails of the railroad.

5. **Give the inside path a desired Stroke weight.** The example uses a Stroke weight of 20 points, which is the inner track of the train track.

6. **Select both paths, and choose Object ➪ Path ➪ Outline Stroke.** This changes the paths into outlined paths because strokes cannot contain gradients.

7. **Fill the paths with a metallic gradient as shown in Figure 10-6.** For more on applying gradients, see Chapter 7.

8. **Select both paths, and click the Exclude overlapping shape areas button in the Pathfinder palette.** This command subtracts the inner section of the track from the two outer sections. Now you have two metal rails as shown in Figure 10-7.

9. **Choose Paste in Back.** This pastes the original copied path from the Clipboard. Alternatively, you can press Ctrl+B (⌘+B).

10. **Give the new path a Stroke weight that you want.** This example uses a Stroke weight of 40 points. This part becomes the wooden railroad ties that support the rails.

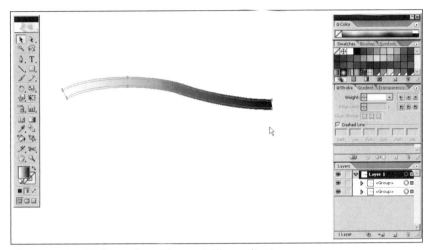

Figure 10-6: Fill the paths with a metallic gradient.

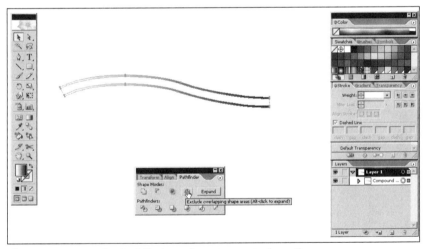

Figure 10-7: Use the Pathfinder palette to create the rails.

11. **Choose Object ➪ Path ➪ Outline Stroke.** This changes the strokes into out-lined paths. Fill this path with a gradient consisting of several wood-like browns as shown in Figure 10-8.

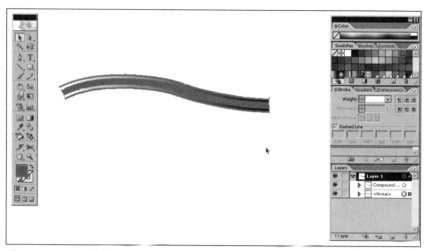

Figure 10-8: Add the stroke for the ties.

12. **Choose Edit ➪ Paste in Front.** You can also press Ctrl+F (⌘+F). This command pastes a path right on top of the wooden area.

13. **Give the stroke the same color as the background, give it a weight of 50, and give it a Dash Pattern of Dash 20, Gap 10.** The gaps are the see-through areas, showing the wood-filled path below them. Figure 10-9 shows the final result.

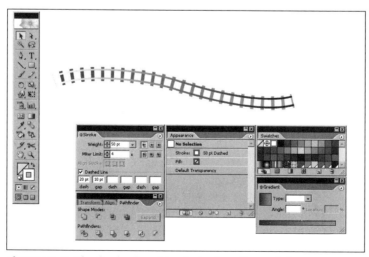

Figure 10-9: The final railroad tracks look pretty realistic.

Outline Path is often used on this type of stroke design because strokes can't have gradient fills. The reason that the railroad ties were not given a dash pattern before Outline Path was applied is that Outline Path doesn't work with dash patterns.

Creating a highway

Figure 10-10 shows a stroke design that I discovered a few years back while I was playing with Illustrator. It has the makings of a cute parlor magic trick that you can use to impress your friends. Back when you had to work in Artwork mode, that is, before Illustrator 5.0, creating designs with strokes was much more difficult. Artists couldn't see what they were drawing on-screen, so they had to envision it in their minds. Editing dashes and weights is almost a pleasure now that you can use the stroke palette and undo multiple changes.

Follow these steps to create a four-lane highway by drawing just one path:

1. **Use the Pen tool to draw a slightly wavy path from the left side of the Artboard to the right.**

2. **Change the Path to a fill of None, and create a 400-point stroke in green.** This path is the grass next to the highway.

3. **Choose Add New Stroke from the Appearance palette pop-up menu.** Change the paint style of the stroke to Cyan 25, Yellow 25, and Black 85, with a weight of 240 points. This path is the shoulder of the highway. Remember to double-click the stroke color picker to display the Color Picker dialog box and to use the Stroke palette to set the stroke width.

4. **Choose Add New Stroke from the Appearance palette pop-up menu.** Change the paint style to Cyan 5 and Black 10, with a weight of 165 points. This path is the white line at the edge of the highway.

5. **Choose Add New Stroke from the Appearance palette pop-up menu.** Change the paint style to Cyan 15, Yellow 10, and Black 50, with a weight of 160 points. This path is the highway's road surface.

6. **To create the dashed white lines for passing, choose Add New Stroke from the Appearance palette pop-up menu.** Change the paint style to Cyan 5 and Black 10, with a weight of 85 points, a dash of 20, and a gap of 20.

7. **Choose Add New Stroke from the Appearance palette pop-up menu.** Change the paint style to Cyan 15, Yellow 10, and Black 50, with a weight of 80 points. Uncheck the Dashed line box. This path is the inner part of the highway's road surface.

8. **To create the double yellow line, choose Add New Stroke from the Appearance palette pop-up menu.** Change the paint style to Cyan 15, Magenta 20, and Yellow 100, with a weight of 8 points.

9. **Choose Add New Stroke from the Appearance palette pop-up menu.** Change
the paint style to Cyan 15, Yellow 10, and Black 50, with a weight of 3 points.
This path is the piece of highway that divides the double yellow line.

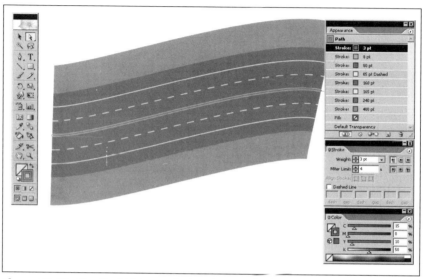

Figure 10-10: The final highway design that results from this exercise

Creating Perfect Patterns

"The Perfect Pattern is one in which you cannot determine the borders of its tiles,"
according to the Chinese Book of Patterns. If that is true, you can use Adobe
Illustrator to create perfect patterns.

The Pattern function in Illustrator is twofold. First, you can fill or stroke any path
with a pattern. Second, you can edit existing patterns or create new ones from
Illustrator objects. The real strength of Illustrator's pattern features is that you can
create patterns as well as apply them onscreen in almost any way imaginable.

A *pattern* in Illustrator is a series of objects within a rectangle that is commonly
referred to as a *pattern tile*. When you choose a pattern in the Swatches palette,
Illustrator repeats the selected pattern as necessary to fill the object, as shown in
Figure 10-11.

Illustrator places the pattern tiles together for you. After you apply a pattern to an
object, you can use any of the transformation tools to alter it.

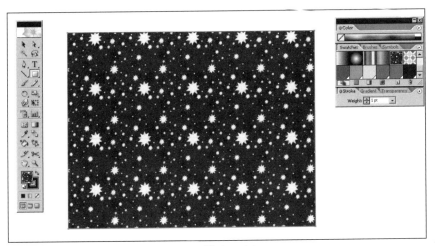

Figure 10-11: The pattern repeats to fill the object.

Note Tile patterns can either have a background color, or they can be transparent. Transparent patterns can overlay other objects, including objects filled with patterns.

Cross-Reference For more about creating objects with fills, see Chapter 5.

Using the default patterns

A few patterns are available at all times in Illustrator. You can open other libraries from the Swatch Libraries submenu of the Window menu. Under the Swatch Libraries submenu, you have a variety of libraries from which to choose. The last option is Other Library. Through Other Library, you can bring in saved libraries as well as the sample libraries that ship with Illustrator. Figure 10-12 shows one of the sample pattern libraries.

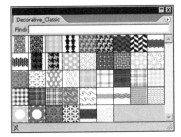

Figure 10-12: The Decorative_Classic pattern library is one of several sample libraries you can use in your Illustrator documents.

To fill a path with a pattern, select that path, make sure the Fill icon is active, and click the corresponding pattern swatch in the Swatches palette. Illustrator fills the path with the pattern you select.

Although there are a few different default Fill patterns, each one can take on a whole new perspective if you use the various transformation functions — move, rotate, scale, reflect, and skew — on them. The default patterns are stored in the Adobe Illustrator Startup file.

For more on the move, rotate, scale, reflect, and skew functions, see Chapter 11.

To learn how to modify the startup file to have a specific set of patterns available every time you use Illustrator, see Chapter 17.

Creating custom patterns

In addition to using the patterns provided with Illustrator, you can create custom patterns by following these steps:

1. **Create the artwork that you want to appear in the pattern tile.** This example uses a bunch of different stars created and arranged in a specific order.

2. **Select the artwork with the Selection tool.** For more on how to use the Selection tool, see Chapter 6.

3. **Drag your artwork into the Swatches palette.** A swatch with your new pattern appears on the palette.

4. **Select the object first, and then choose the new pattern you created in the Swatches palette.** This applies the new pattern to your object.

Figure 10-13 also shows the artwork applied as the fill of another shape.

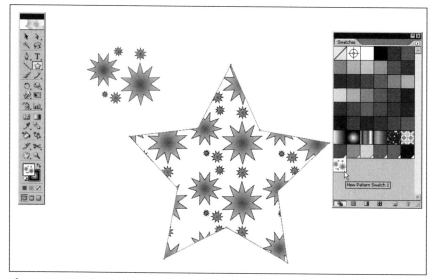

Figure 10-13: The final basic pattern tile is used here as a fill pattern in a star.

Understanding pattern backgrounds and boundaries

Any pattern tile you create can have the color background you specify, simply by making a rectangle the size of the tile and placing it behind the objects in the pattern. When you create the pattern on top of the background rectangle, just select the entire background along with the pattern objects to create the pattern.

If you don't create a background rectangle, Illustrator uses the bounding box, as shown in Figure 10-14, of the selected objects to determine the size of the pattern tile. The bounding box is the smallest rectangle that completely encloses all selected objects and paths.

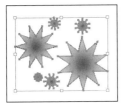

Figure 10-14: The bounding box is the smallest rectangle that completely encloses your selected objects and paths.

But what happens if you want the edge of the pattern tile to be somewhere inside the bounding box? Illustrator provides a way for you to define a bounding box to define pattern tiles that consist of objects that extend beyond the pattern edges. You create a bounding box by creating a Rectangle with the Rectangle tool, fill it with None, and make it the back-most object in the pattern tile.

Making seamless patterns

To make patterns seamless, you need to remember that objects that lie across the edge of the pattern border are cut into two sections, the outside section of which is invisible. You also need to make sure that lines that stretch from one edge of a pattern border to the other side connect to another line on the opposite edge of the boundary. The second problem is more difficult to deal with than the first one. To make a line match well from one side to the other, you usually have to move one or both of the ends up or down slightly.

For patterns to appear seamless, you cannot make the edges of the pattern noticeable. Avoiding this sounds rather easy: All you have to do is avoid placing any objects that touch the edges of a background rectangle. Well, that technique will do it, but when you use such a pattern, the lack of any objects along the borders of the tile can make the pattern look strange.

Creating symmetrical patterns

You can easily create symmetrical patterns in Illustrator. The key to creating them is to draw the bounding box after you create the rest of the objects, drawing outward from the center point of one of the objects.

When you create symmetrical patterns, the main difficulty is judging the space between the objects in the pattern. Objects can seem too close together or too far apart, especially in patterns that have different amounts of space between the objects horizontally and vertically. The solution is to use a square as the pattern tile boundary. This ensures that you have an equal amount of space from the center of one object to the center of the next object, both vertically and horizontally.

Creating line patterns and grids

Using lines and grids for patterns is ideal because they are so easy to create. The key in both types of patterns is the size of the bounding rectangle. You use a grid to draw accurate floor plans, or even for drawing perspective scenes. Line patterns are great for creating fences or any repeating linear paths.

Creating line patterns

Follow these steps to create a line pattern:

1. **Decide what point size you want for the lines and how far apart you want them.**

2. **Draw a rectangle making the height match the separation you want between the lines.** Make sure you draw the rectangle with a fill and stroke of None.

3. **Draw a horizontal line with a fill of None and a stroke of the point size you want from outside the left edge of the rectangle to outside the right edge of the rectangle.**

4. **Make a pattern out of the two objects.** You make a pattern by adding the image to the Swatches palette. In Figure 10-11, the upper selected object shows the pattern used in this example.

5. **Apply the pattern to the object of your choice.** You can apply a pattern by selecting the object and then clicking the pattern in the Swatches palette. The bottom image in Figure 10-15 shows the results.

You can use this technique with vertical lines as well. Just make the bounding rectangle's width the distance from line to line.

Illustrator made possible this suite of Aviation Nation 2004 art by Joe Jones. Joe developed at least two vector art files, usually a profile and cross-section file, for every object in each 3D model. Each B-17 Flying Fortress required more than 1,000 individual parts. Joe did the texture mapping for each object in Illustrator, often using gradients. He used Illustrator's scatter brushes to create the historically accurate rivet work. Joe developed "Lady Las Vegas" as an air-brush illustration from an original pencil sketch and created the layout and type in Illustrator.

ART BY JOE JONES

ART BY JOE JONES

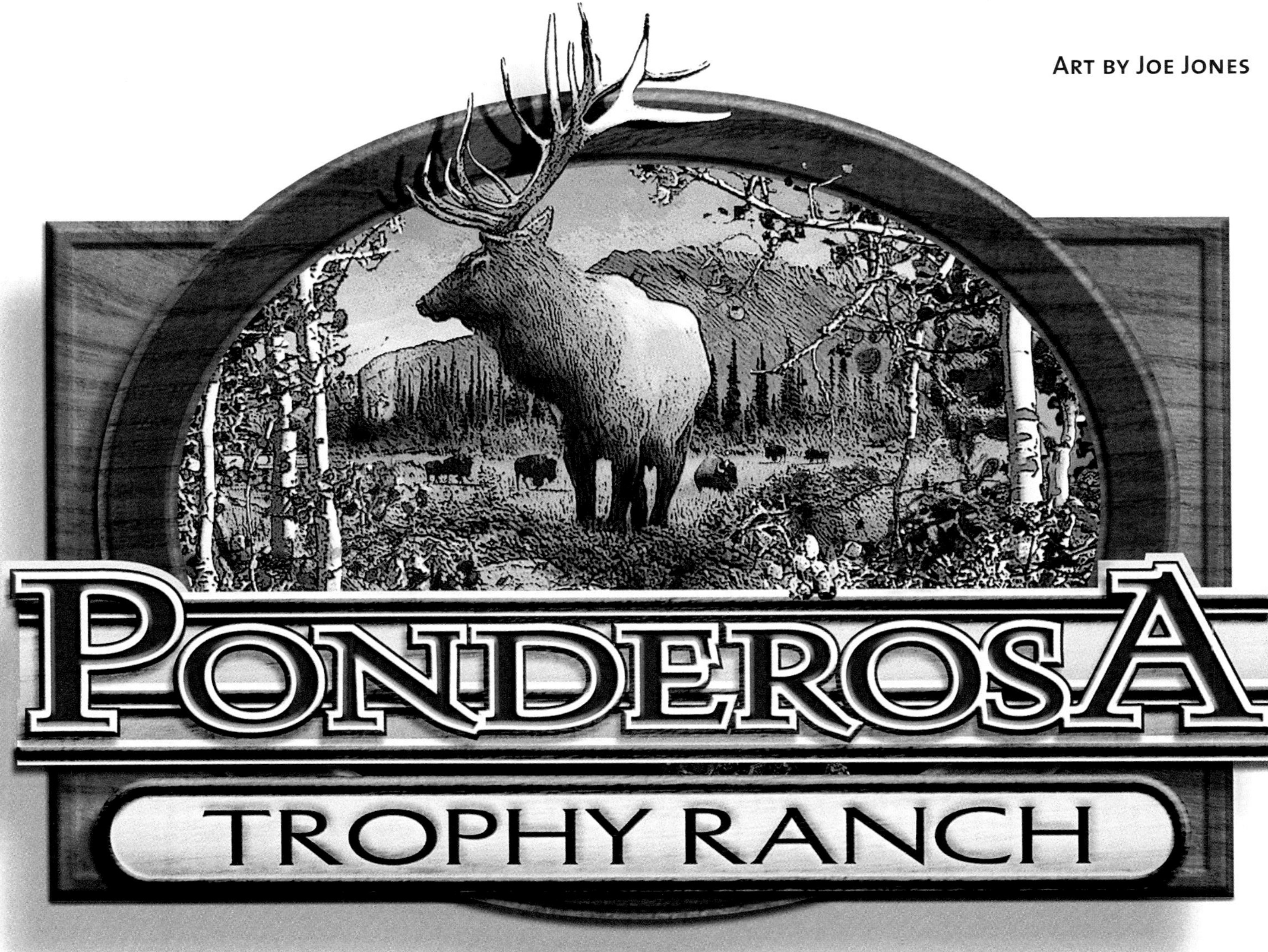

PONDEROSA
TROPHY RANCH

This logo by Joe Jones began in Illustrator, where he set up the art on separate layers. He then exported a layered Photoshop file and fully rendered the final logo in Photoshop.

ART BY JOE JONES

This is one of a series of graphics that Joe Jones created for a college's Web site. Joe developed the layout and built the Pantone chips in Illustrator. He copied and pasted the Illustrator path work into Photoshop before creating the masks and developing the graphic illustration.

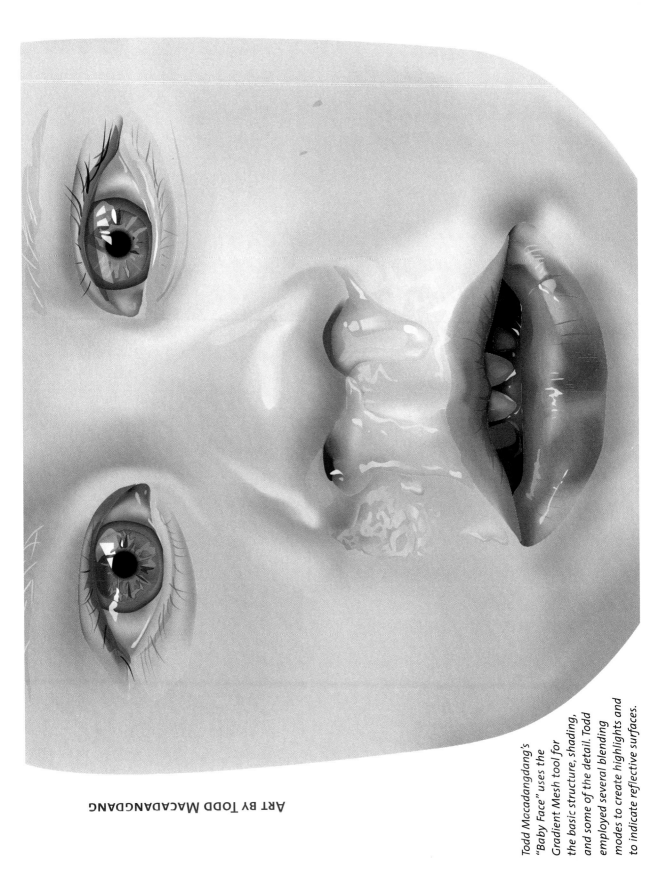

Todd Macadangdang's "Baby Face" uses the Gradient Mesh tool for the basic structure, shading, and some of the detail. Todd employed several blending modes to create highlights and to indicate reflective surfaces.

ART BY TODD MACADANGDANG

ART BY TODD MACADANGDANG

In "Kimberly," Todd Macadangdang began with a photo reference to obtain primary
values for skin and hair. He used the Gradient Mesh tool and a variety of blending modes.

Cory Gray used multiple layers and several color modes to produce "Gregory the Fish." Cory created the soft touches with Illustrator's Gradient Mesh tool and employed transparent blends with Gaussian Blur filters.

Four more pieces by Cory Gray show Illustrator's potential. Cory reports that bright colors and crisp, clean line work make Illustrator a perfect way to create children's art like "J.J.'s Dragon" (lower right).

ART BY CORY GRAY

Cory Gray used Illustrator's shape tools to create "Blue Moose Brew." Cory stamp-filtered the moose
in Photoshop, ran the image through Streamline, and vectorized it. He used Illustrator's art brush
to create the outer decoration and added some gradient for atmosphere. Cory designed the type in
Illustrator and used the Type on a Path tool for the circular elements.

THE BATTLE OF EVERMORE

Brian Warchesik

"The Battle of Evermore" is by Brian Warchesik. Brian usually begins with a hand-drawn sketch and refines his composition in Illustrator. In this stage, he separates the shapes within the composition and begins to define their separate values. He also defines the paths that he will export for painting. This approach prevents the need to clean and define edges later. Brian checks the pose and the anatomy of his main characters by taking reference photos or using Poser, and sometimes by doing both.

DREAM CATCHER

Brian W Warchesik

"Dream Catcher" is also by Brian Warchesik. After resolving his figures in Illustrator, Brian moves to Photoshop. He usually works with a grayscale image so that he can complete the composition without the encumbrances of adding color. He then switches to RGB and begins painting. Brian uses Photoshop and Painter for this stage, taking advantage of the strengths of each until the piece is complete.

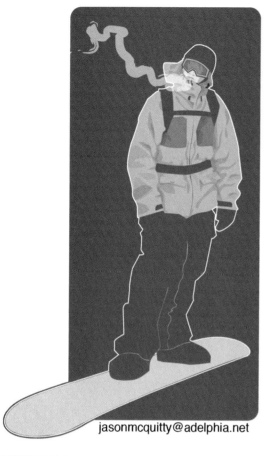

jasonmcquitty@adelphia.net

Jason McQuitty works with Illustrator to produce the hand-drawn effect visible in these images. Jason uses Illustrator's Pencil tool with a Wacom tablet. He creates a unique look by sketching, building up the color, and using transparencies for the shadows.

Joe Barsin used Illustrator's Gradient feature extensively in the license plate and the Chesapeake Bay Trust logo. He created the detailing in the heron's wing and the shading variations in the crab with the Gradient tool. The license plate required four Pantone colors, so keeping the colors separate for trapping was crucial. Joe's "Liberty" illustration employs straightforward Illustrator techniques. "Our World" is a complex illustration requiring the use of many layers.

JILL PATON WALSH &
DOROTHY L. SAYERS

A PRESUMPTION
OF DEATH

A NEW LORD PETER WIMSEY / HARRIET VANE MYSTERY

Chris Spollen used Illustrator to create this book cover. Chris reminds aspiring Illustrator artists of the importance of preliminary sketches.

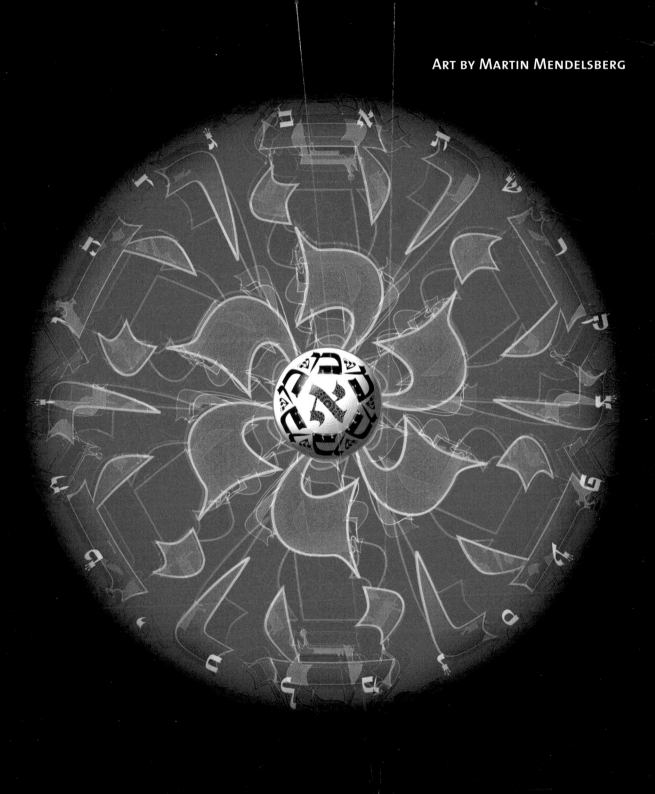

Martin Mendelsberg conceived his image "Tetra" through rough sketches and diagrams. He began with Hebrew letterforms based on ancient scribal models and produced as digital fonts using Illustrator and Macromedia Fontographer. He imported the finished composition into Photoshop for raster imaging, lighting, and refinements.

"Water" is also by Martin Mendelsberg. He based both of his images on research into the 10th-century Judaic text "Sefer Yetzirah," also known as the "Book of Creation."

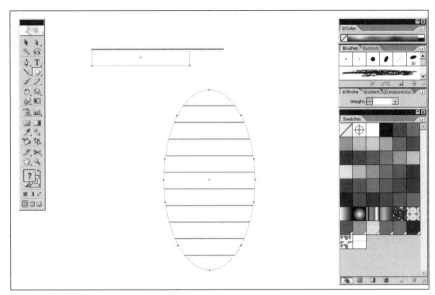

Figure 10-15: You can easily make a pattern from straight lines and apply it to any object.

Creating grid patterns

You can use a grid pattern to create graphing paper for a logo. Another good use of grid patterns is for grates or windows because you can use the transformation tools to add perspective. Creating grids is even easier than creating evenly spaced lines. Just follow these steps:

1. **Create a rectangle that is the size of the grid holes.** For example, for a ¼-inch grid, you make the rectangle ¼ inch×¼ inch. For more on creating rectangles, see Chapter 5.

2. **Apply a stroke to the object.** Make the stroke the weight that you want the gridlines to be.

Cross-Reference

For more on Stroke weights and applying strokes, see Chapter 5.

3. **Make that rectangle into a pattern.** You make a pattern by adding your object to the Swatches palette. That's it. You now have a pattern grid that is as precise as possible.

Tip

If you want the space between gridlines to be an exact measurement, make the rectangle bigger by the Stroke weight. A ¼-inch grid (18 points) with 1-point gridlines requires a rectangle that is 17 points×17 points.

Using diagonal-line and grid patterns

Shading effects, such as hatched lines, are easily created with a diagonal line and grid pattern. Figure 10-16 shows a close-up of a horse using a diagonal line pattern rotated and scaled to show a shaded effect. You may find creating diagonal-line and grid patterns difficult if you try to make a rectangle; draw a path at an angle, and then use the rectangle with the path in it as a pattern. Joining diagonal lines at the edges of the pattern is nearly impossible.

Using this technique is also a great way to avoid making several patterns when you need line patterns that are set at different angles. Just make one horizontal line pattern and rotate the patterns within the paths.

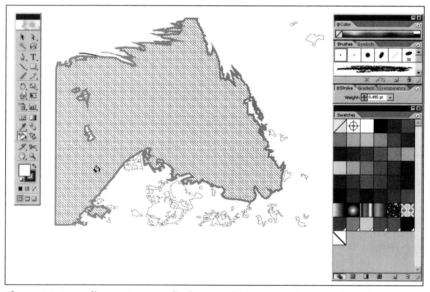

Figure 10-16: A line pattern applied to an object to create a shaded effect

Follow these steps for a better method of creating a shaded effect:

1. **Create a bounding box using the Rectangle tool.**

2. **Create lines (or grids) in horizontal or vertical alignment that extend beyond the bounding box.**

3. **Make the lines (or grids) into a pattern.** You can do this by dragging the lines (or grids) to the Swatches palette.

4. **Apply the pattern to an object.** You do this by selecting the object and clicking the pattern in the Swatches palette.

5. **Double-click the Rotate tool.** Doing this opens the Rotate dialog box.

6. **In the Rotate dialog box, enter the angle to change the lines and uncheck the Object check box.** Make certain that the Pattern check box is selected. The pattern rotates to the desired angle inside the path.

Using transparency and patterns together

Transparent patterns are great to use over the top of color, or gradients, or even other patterns. Instead of creating a bunch of specific patterns that use other patterns, use the transparent pattern option to layer over the top of other patterns. A great use of this option is to use a gradient and then use a line pattern to add a hatched shading look. To make the background of a pattern transparent, don't use a background rectangle. Only the objects in the pattern will be opaque.

You can use the simple line pattern with a transparent background alone or over another pattern. Figure 10-17 shows an object with a transparent pattern over a gradient.

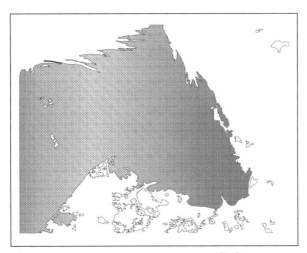

Figure 10-17: A transparent pattern applied over a gradient

One way to achieve interesting effects is by making a copy of the object behind the original:

1. **Select the object.**

2. **Choose Edit ➪ Copy.** Alternatively, you can press Ctrl+C (⌘+C). Doing this creates a copy of the object.

3. **Choose Edit ➪ Paste in Back.** You can also press Ctrl+B (⌘+B). Doing this pastes the object behind the original object.

4. **Change the fill in the copy of the object to a solid, a gradient, or another Pattern**.

5. **Use the Opacity slider to change the appearance as desired.**

Transforming patterns

After you create patterns and place them within paths, you may find that they are too big or at the wrong angle for the path. Likewise, they may start in an awkward location. You can use the transformation tools and the Move command to resolve these problems.

To transform a pattern inside a path:

1. **Select the path.**

2. **Double-click the transformation tool that corresponds to the change that you want to make to the pattern.** The transformation tool's dialog box appears, as shown in Figure 10-18.

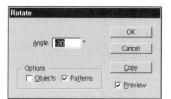

Figure 10-18: The Rotate dialog box (along with the other Transformation dialog boxes) lets you transform patterns independently of objects.

3. **In the Transformation dialog box, uncheck the Objects check box.** Doing this selects the Patterns check box. The Patterns and Objects check boxes are grayed out if the selected object does not contain a pattern.

Any changes that you make in the Transformation Tool's dialog box when only the Patterns check box is checked affect only the pattern, not the outside shape.

Cross-Reference For more on transforming objects, see Chapter 11.

To move a pattern within a path, choose Object ➪ Transform ➪ Move (or double-click the Selection tool). The Move dialog box also contains Patterns and Objects check boxes. If you uncheck the Objects check box, which selects the Patterns check box, only the pattern is moved.

Summary

Using patterns and strokes creatively makes drawing objects a far easier task. In this chapter, you learned about the following topics:

✦ The most attractive aspect of strokes is that you can use them together, on top of one another.

✦ The Stroke charts provided in this chapter show some of what you can do with strokes.

✦ Use Outline Path to create filled paths out of strokes.

✦ Use fills to create half-stroked paths.

✦ Patterns are a type of fill that provides texture to any path.

✦ Illustrator supplies several default patterns. You can transform these patterns in the same ways that you can transform other Illustrator objects.

✦ You can use almost anything you create in Illustrator as a pattern, with the exception of masks, gradients, placed images, and other patterns.

✦ You construct diagonal-line patterns by creating a horizontal-line pattern and rotating it with the Rotate tool when the pattern is filling a path.

✦　　✦　　✦

Applying Transformations and Distortions

✦   ✦   ✦   ✦

In This Chapter

Rotating, reflecting, shearing, scaling, and reshaping with tools

Using the Transform palette

Creating cool effects with the Liquify tools

Distorting objects

Creating distortion effects

Adding distortions with warps

✦   ✦   ✦   ✦

Illustrator has the capability to transform any object by scaling it, rotating it, reflecting it, shearing it, and reshaping it. In this chapter, you learn how to take advantage of this power using transformation functions with menus, palettes, and certain tools.

In addition to transformations, Illustrator really gets fun when you work with distortions. Distortions are accomplished with a number of different filters and effects, warps, and the amazing Liquify tools.

Adding a Transformation with Tools

Although there are many places to find the transformation functions, the first stop is the transformation tools. The transformation tools in the Illustrator toolbox address fundamental functions: rotating, reflecting, shearing, scaling, and reshaping. Before you can use any of these tools, however, you must select one or more objects (including paths, points, and segments). The selected paths are the paths that are transformed.

Using the various transformation tools, you can transform selected objects in five ways:

✦ Click with the transformation tool to set an origin point and then drag from a different location. This is called a manual transformation.

✦ Click and drag in one motion to transform the object from its center point or last origin point.

✦ Press Alt (Option) and click to set the origin, and then enter exact information in the tool's transformation dialog box. This method is more precise than manually transforming.

✦ Double-click a transformation tool to set the origin in the center of the selected object, and then enter information in the tool's transformation dialog box.

✦ Use the Transform palette (discussed later in this chapter).

All the transformations have additional options in their dialog boxes. The Copy button makes a copy of the original and transforms it to your settings. Selecting the Object check box applies the transformation only to the object (not the fill pattern inside). Selecting the Pattern check box applies the transformation to just the pattern (not the object). Selecting both check boxes applies any transformations to both the object and the pattern.

Cross-Reference   For more on copying and transforming patterns, see the "Transforming patterns" section later in this chapter.

All the transformation tools work on an accumulating basis. For example, if you scale an object 150 percent and then scale it again by 150 percent, the object becomes 225 percent of its original size ($150\% \times 150\% = 225\%$). If the object is initially scaled to 150 percent of its original size, and you want to return it to that original size, you must do the math and figure out what percentage you need to resize it — in this case, $100\% \div 150\% = 66.7\%$ — or you could just use the Undo feature. Entering 100% in the Scale dialog box leaves the selected objects unchanged.

Illustrator automatically creates a visible origin point, shown in Figure 11-1, when you use any of the transformation tools. Because the origin is in the center of the selection, if you just drag with the transformation tool, the origin point is visible as soon as you select the transformation tool. If you click without dragging to set the origin, it shows up at that location until the origin is reset. Having the origin point visible as a blue cross hair makes the transformation tools much more usable and functional.

When manually transforming objects, you can make a copy of the selected object — and thus leave the original untransformed — by holding down the Alt (Option) key before and after releasing the mouse button. In a transformation dialog box, you can make a copy by clicking the Copy button.

If the Patterns check box is available (you must have a pattern in one of the selected paths, or this option is grayed out) in any of the transformation dialog boxes, you can select its check box to transform your pattern along with the object. You can also transform the pattern only, leaving the object untransformed, by unchecking the Objects check box.

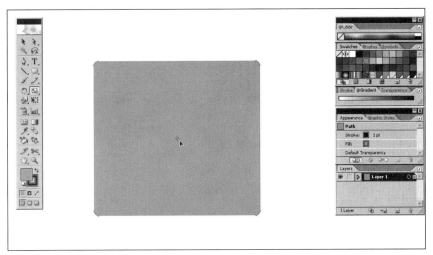

Figure 11-1: The origin point that appears when using any of the transformation tools

Cross-Reference You can learn more about patterns in Chapter 10.

Tip You can manually transform just patterns (and not the objects themselves) by pressing the grave (`) key while using any of the transformation tools, including the Selection tool for moving.

Manually transforming objects is fairly simple if you remember that the first place you click (the point of origin) and the second place should be a fair distance apart. The farther your second click is from the point of origin, the more control you have when dragging to transform.

All the transformation tools perform certain operations that rely on the Constrain Angle setting as a point of reference. Normally, this is set to 0 degrees, which makes your Illustrator world act normally. You can change the setting by choosing Edit (Illustrator) ➪ Preferences ➪ General, or by pressing Ctrl+K (⌘+K), and entering a new value.

You can access each of the transformation dialog boxes from the Object ➪ Transform submenu (see Figure 11-2).

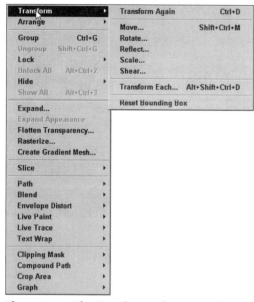

Figure 11-2: The Transform submenu under the Object menu

 Note   If the bounding box is visible (View⇨Show Bounding Box), you can use the Selection tool to rotate, scale, or move the object.

Rotating with the Rotate tool

The Rotate tool is found in the toolbox, and it rotates selected objects within a document. Double-clicking the Rotate tool displays the Rotate dialog box, shown in Figure 11-3, where you enter the precise angle of the selected item's rotation in the Angle text box. The object rotates around its origin, which by default is located at the center of the object's bounding box. A positive number between 0 and 180 rotates the object counterclockwise that many degrees. A negative number between 0 and –180 rotates the selected object clockwise. The Rotate tool works on a standard 360° circle of rotation,

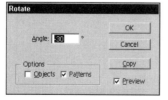

Figure 11-3: The Rotate dialog box allows you to rotate objects precisely.

Click once to set the origin point, which is the object's center of rotation, and then click fairly far from the origin and drag in a circle. The selected object spins along with the cursor. To constrain the angle to 45-degree increments as you are dragging, press and hold the Shift key. This angle is dependent on the Constrain Angle box and is in 45-degree increments plus the angle in this box. Figure 11-4 shows an illustration before and after rotation.

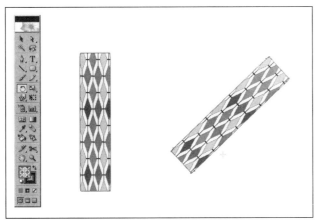

Figure 11-4: The object before (left) and after (right) rotation

Reflecting with the Reflect tool

The Reflect tool makes a mirror image of the selected objects, reflected across an axis of reflection. You can find the Reflect tool as a pop-up tool under the Rotate tool. Double-clicking the Reflect tool reflects selected objects across an axis of reflection that runs through the horizontal center or vertical center of the selected objects. In the Reflect dialog box, shown in Figure 11-5, you can enter the axis of reflection. If you want to reflect the object through either the horizontal or vertical axis, click the appropriate button.

Note
Pressing Alt (Option) and clicking in the document window also displays the Reflect dialog box; however, the axis of reflection is now not in the center of the selected object but in the location in the document where you Alt (Option)-clicked.

Figure 11-5: Use the Reflect dialog box to create mirror images of objects.

Manual reflecting is done by clicking once to set the origin point (the center of the axis of reflection) and again somewhere along the axis of reflection. If you click and drag after setting your origin point, you can rotate the axis of reflection and see what your objects look like reflected across various axes. The Shift key constrains the axis of reflection to 90° angles relative to the Constrain Angle. Pressing and holding the Alt (Option) key during the release of the click leaves a copy of the original object. Figure 11-6 shows an illustration before and after being reflected.

Figure 11-6: The object before (left) and after (right) being reflected across the vertical axis

Scaling with the Scale tool

The Scale tool resizes objects both uniformly and non-uniformly. You can also use the Scale tool to flip objects, but without the precision of the Reflect tool. It is impossible to keep both the size and proportions of an object constant while flipping and scaling.

Double-clicking the Scale tool displays the Scale dialog box, shown in Figure 11-7. All selected objects are scaled from their origin, which by default is located at the center of the object's bounding box. If the Uniform option is chosen, numbers typed into the text field result in proportionately scaled objects, where the width and height of the object remain proportional to each other. Numbers less than 100 percent shrink the object; numbers greater than 100 percent enlarge it.

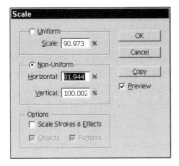

Figure 11-7: The Scale dialog box allows you to specify exactly how objects are scaled.

Non-uniform scaling resizes the horizontal and vertical dimensions of the selected objects separately, distorting the image. Non-uniform scaling is related to the constrain angle you set in the General Preferences dialog box; the angle set there is the horizontal scaling, and the vertical scaling is 90° from that angle.

Tip Pressing the Alt (Option) key and clicking in the document window also displays the Scale dialog box, but now the objects are scaled from the location in the document that was Alt (Option)-clicked.

You can achieve manual resizing by clicking your point of origin and then clicking away from that point and dragging to scale. If you cross the horizontal or vertical axis of the point of origin, the selected object flips over in that direction. Holding down the Shift key constrains the objects to equal proportions, if you drag the cursor at approximately 45-degree from the point of origin. Alternatively, holding down the Shift key constrains the scaling to either horizontal or vertical scaling only if you drag the cursor along at about a 90-degree angle from the point of origin relative to the constrain angle.

Shearing with the Shear tool

You find the Shear tool as a pop-up tool with the Scale tool. The Shear tool is somewhat tricky to use until you get the hang of it. Essentially, it pulls all points above the origin point to the side and pushes all points below the origin point in the opposite direction. The further the points are from the origin, the farther to the side they are moved. The effect gives a slanted, perspective-like look to your object. Use the Shear tool to add a shadow to an object or text. Another great use of shear is to make an object or text look like it is in perspective.

Double-clicking the Shear tool displays the Shear dialog box, shown in Figure 11-8, which is much more controllable. Double-clicking causes the origin to be in the center of the selected object. The Angle box is simple enough; in its text box, you enter the angle amount the object should shear. Any amount over 75° or less than –75° typically renders the object into an indecipherable mess, because at this angle or higher the art has been "flattened into a straight line." The Shear tool reverses the positive-numbers-are-counterclockwise rule: To shear an object clockwise, enter a positive number; to shear counterclockwise, enter a negative number. The Axis Angle box is for shearing an object along a specified axis.

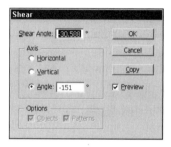

Figure 11-8: The Shear dialog box enables you to apply a shear transformation to an object.

Tip   Pressing Alt (Option) and clicking in the document window also displays the Shear dialog box, with the origin of the shear being the location of the preceding Alt (Option)-click.

Manual shearing is something else again because, while you click, hold, and drag with the Shear tool, you are doing two things at once. From the beginning of the second click until you release the mouse, you change the angle of shearing. Usually, it's best to start your second click fairly far away from the point of origin. Pressing and holding the Shift key constrains the axis of shearing to a 45-degree angle relative to the constraining angle. Figure 11-9 shows an illustration before and after being sheared.

Reshaping with the Reshape tool

You use the Reshape tool to select one or multiple anchor points in order to change an object's shape. You can also select parts of paths to change as well. Located as a pop-up tool under the Scale tool, you use the Reshape tool on any path by clicking where you want to bend the path and then dragging. To use the Reshape tool on several paths at once, use the Reshape tool to select the points you want to move first. You must select at least one point that isn't a straight corner point on each path. You then drag on a Reshape-selected point; all the curved points move as well. Figure 11-10 shows an example of what the Reshape tool does.

Figure 11-9: The horse before (left) and after (right) being sheared shows how the Shear tool affects objects.

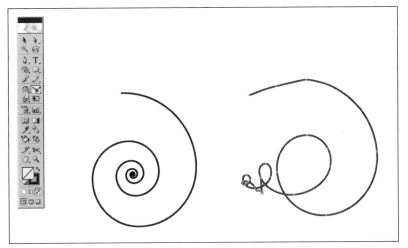

Figure 11-10: The spiral before (left) and after (right) using the Reshape tool

Tip   The Reshape tool works best on curved objects such as spirals, ovals, and so on.

Moving objects

The most common way to move an object is to use a Selection tool and drag the selected points, segments, and paths from one location to another.

The precise way to move an object is to use the Move dialog box, shown in Figure 11-11, or the Transform palette (see the next section). Select the object you want to move, and choose Object ➪ Transform ➪ Move. The Move dialog box appears, and you can enter the appropriate values in the horizontal or vertical text fields. If you want to move an object diagonally, enter a number in the Distance text field and then enter the angle of movement direction in the Angle text field.

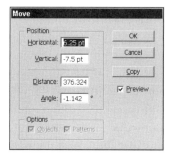

Figure 11-11: The Move dialog box enables you to specify an exact distance to move objects.

You can move any selected object (except for text selected with a Type tool) via the Move dialog box, including individual anchor points and line segments.

By default, the Move dialog box contains the distance and angle that you last moved an object, whether manually with a Selection tool or in the Move dialog box. If you use the Measure tool prior to using the Move dialog box, the numbers in the Move dialog box correspond to the numbers that appeared in the Info palette when you used the Measure tool.

Tip   Double-clicking the Selection tool in the toolbox displays the Move dialog box.

In the Move dialog box, positive numbers in the Horizontal text field move an object to its right, while negative numbers move an object to its left. Positive numbers in the Vertical text field move an object up, while negative numbers move an object down. Negative numbers in the Distance text field move an object in the opposite direction of the Angle text field. The Angle text field works a bit differently. Negative numbers in the Angle text field move the angle in the opposite direction from 0°, so entering –45° is the same as entering 315° and entering –180° is the same as entering 180°.

The measurement system in the Move dialog box uses the Units set in the General Preferences dialog box. To use units other than those of the current measurement system, use these indicators:

✦ For inches: 1", 1in, or 1 inch

✦ For picas: 1p, 1pica, or 1 pica

✦ For points: 1pt or 1 point

✦ For picas/points: 1p1, or 1 pica, 1 point

✦ For millimeters: 1mm or 1 millimeter

✦ For centimeters: 1cm or 1 centimeter

The Horizontal and Vertical text fields are linked to the Distance and Angle text fields; when you change one of the Horizontal or Vertical fields, Illustrator alters the Distance and Angle fields accordingly.

Pressing the Copy button duplicates selected objects in the direction and distance indicated, just as holding down Alt (Option) when dragging duplicates the selected objects.

Tip   The Move dialog box is a great place to enter everything via the keyboard. Press Tab to move from text field to text field, press Enter (Return) to push the OK button, and press Esc (⌘+Period) to push the Cancel button. Pressing Alt (Option)-Enter (Return) or pressing Alt (Option) while clicking OK is the same as clicking the Copy button. The same is true for all the transformation dialog boxes.

Using the Free Transform tool

Free Transform enables you to rotate, scale, reflect, and shear all with one tool. This way, you can create multiple transformations at one time. The Free Transform tool is located in the toolbox directly below the Scale tool.

What is unique about this tool is that you can select more than one object to change the size, shape, and placement in one step. The Free Transform tool does not replace the Free Distort filter. Using this cool tool to create distorted effects is different from using the Free Distort filter.

Cross-
Reference   The Free Distort effect is covered with the other effects in Chapter 15.

At first glance, they may seem the same, but they aren't. The Free Transform tool actually adds perspective, while the Free Distort effect mimics the shape, but keeps the spacing uniform. This sounds confusing, but the visual example in Figure 11-12 may help. The top row of objects shows the application of the Free Transform tool to the top and bottom of the row. This gives a tree-line effect with perspective. The bottom row of trees in the figure shows the application of the Frcc Distort effect to the top and bottom of the row again. Note the different results.

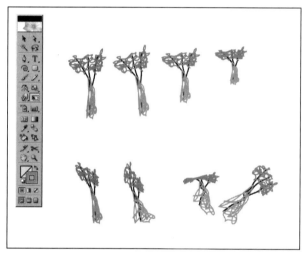

Figure 11-12: The top line of trees was created using the Free Transform tool. The bottom line of trees was created using the Free Distort effect.

Tip   To apply the Free Transform tool to the top and bottom at the same time, hold down the Alt (Option) key. For more control, hold down the Ctrl (⌘) key as you start to drag.

Working with the Transform Palette

Imagine a palette that combines four of Illustrator's five transformation capabilities into one place. Then take a look at Figure 11-13, which shows Illustrator's Transform palette in all its glory.

Y value   H value

X value   W value

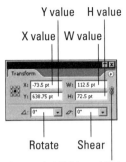

Rotate   Shear

Constrain Width and Height Proportions

Figure 11-13: The Transform palette enables you to apply several transforms in one place.

The Transform palette provides a way to move, scale, rotate, and shear selected artwork. You don't have a reflect option; you need to use the tool or the Transform submenu option to reflect artwork. Instead of manually setting an origin point or transforming from the center by default, the Transform palette gives you nine "fixed" origin points based on the bounding box of the selected objects; the bounding box is the blue box that surrounds any selected objects. You can select these fixed origin points using the square set of points in the left side of the palette. Choose an origin point before entering values in the palette, and the transformations will originate from the corner, center of a side, or the center of selected objects.

The text fields in the Transform palette are as follows:

✦ **X:** This is the horizontal location of the artwork, measured from the left edge of the document or horizontal ruler origin (if it has been moved from the left edge).

✦ **Y:** This is the vertical location of the artwork, measured from the bottom edge of the document or vertical ruler origin (if it has been moved from the bottom edge).

✦ **W:** This is the width of the artwork's bounding box.

✦ **H:** This is the height of the artwork's bounding box.

✦ **Rotate:** This field lets you apply a rotation to the selected artwork.

✦ **Shear:** This field lets you apply a shear to the selected artwork.

To use the palette, type the new value you'd like to use in any field and press Enter (Return). If you have another value to enter, press the Tab key to go to the next text field or Shift-Tab to go back a field. Pressing Alt (Option) when you press Enter (Return) or Tab creates a duplicate of the selected artwork with the transformations you specified.

For scaling, you can enter either absolute measurements (the size in inches, picas, and so on, that you want the artwork to be) or as a percentage by adding the % symbol after your value. You can also force Illustrator to scale uniformly, regardless of whether you're using absolute measurements or percentages, by clicking the Constrain Width and Height Proportions icon at the right side of the palette.

Using Transform Each

Transform Each provides a way to do several transformations in one shot, but that's only the beginning. The unique thing about Transform Each is that each selected object is transformed independently, as opposed to having all the selected objects transformed together. Figure 11-14 shows the difference between "normal" rotating and scaling, and the rotate and scale functions in Transform Each.

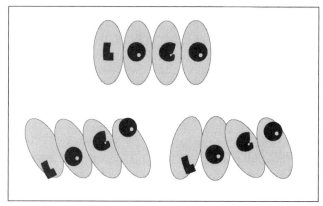

Figure 11-14: The logo original (top) with changes applied using the Transform Each dialog box (bottom, left) and with changes using the Random check box (bottom, right)

To access the Transform Each dialog box, shown in Figure 11-15, choose Object ➪ Transform ➪ Transform Each. In the dialog box, use the sliders/dial or type values for each of the transformations. The Random check box on the right side of the dialog box gives each object selected a random value that falls between the default (100% for Scale; 0 for Move and Rotate) and the value set by the slider/dial.

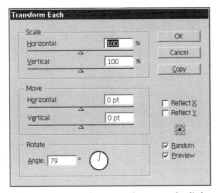

Figure 11-15: The Transform Each dialog box enables you to apply transforms to a number of objects at the same time.

In addition to controls for setting the Scale, Move, and Rotate values, the Transform Each dialog box includes check boxes to reflect the selected objects about the X or Y axes and an icon for selecting an origin point. But of all offerings, the Random function of Transform Each is its most powerful asset. Checking the Random check box can turn a grid into a distinct random texture, as shown in Figure 11-16.

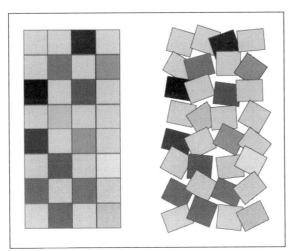

Figure 11-16: Transform Each's Random function applied to a pattern of columns of colored squares really mixes things up.

Using Transformations

The transformation tools open a world of possibilities within Illustrator. The following tips and ideas should give you a head start in exploring the amazing power of transformations.

Choosing Object ➪ Transform ➪ Transform Again or pressing Ctrl+D (⌘+D) redoes the last transformation that you performed on the selected object. Transformations include Move, Rotate, Scale, Reflect, Shear, and Transform Each. Transform Again also makes a transformed copy, if you made a copy either manually or by clicking the Copy button in the prior transformation dialog box.

Tip Transform Again remembers the last transformation no matter what else you do, and it can apply that same transformation to other objects or reapply it to the existing transformed objects.

Creating shadows

You can create all sorts of shadows by using the Scale, Reflect, and Shear tools. To create a shadow, follow these steps.

1. **Select the path where you want to apply the shadow.**

2. **Click the bottom of the path once with the Reflect tool.** This action sets the origin of reflection at the base of the image.

3. **Drag the mouse down while pressing the Shift key.** The image flips over, creating a mirror image under the original.

4. **Press the Alt (Option) key while keeping the Shift key pressed before and during the release of the mouse button.** Doing this makes a copy of the image.

5. **Using the Shear tool, click the base of the reflected copy to set the origin.**

6. **Click and drag left or right at the other side of the reflection.** Doing this sets the angle of the reflection.

7. **Using the Scale tool, click once again on the base of the reflected copy to set the origin.**

8. **Click and drag up or down at the other side of the reflection.** This step sets how far away from the original object, the shadow falls.

9. **Color the shadow darker than its background.** The resulting shadow is shown in the illustrations in Figure 11-17. You may have to experiment with these steps a bit to achieve the results you really want.

Figure 11-17: A shadow created with the transformation tools

Rotating into a path

Clever use of the Rotate tool can create a realistic, winding path by duplicating the same object at different rotational intervals, rotated from different origins. To create a path of objects using the Rotate tool, follow these steps.

1. **Start by creating an object of some sort.** The illustration in Figure 11-18 uses paw prints.

2. **Select the objects, and choose the Rotate tool.** You may find it helpful to group the objects together first. Group the objects by first selecting the objects and then choosing Object ➪ Group or Ctrl (⌘)+G.

Cross-Reference

For more on grouping objects, see Chapter 8.

3. **Click to set an origin to the side of the object.**

4. **Click the other side of the object and drag.** As you drag, you see the outline of the shape of the object that you are dragging.

5. **When the object is a good distance away, press the Alt (Option) key.** Doing this copies the object. Release the mouse button; then release the Alt (Option) key. A copy of the object appears.

6. **Press Ctrl+D (⌘+D) (Transform Again) to create another object the same distance away.** Repeat this step several times.

7. **Click with the Rotate tool on the other side of the object to set another origin.**

8. **Click and drag the outline of the object about the same distance; then press the Alt (Option) key and release the mouse button.**

9. **Use the Transform Again command several more times.**

The farther you click from the objects to set the origin, the smaller the curve of the path of objects. Clicking right next to the objects causes them to turn sharply.

If you want a quicker way to put paw prints on a path, create the paw print and then use the Scatter Brush to apply the paw prints to a path.

 For more on the Scatter Brush, see Chapter 4.

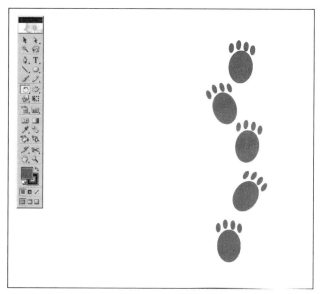

Figure 11-18: Using the Rotate tool and the Transform Again menu command, you can quickly make a path of objects.

Making tiles using the Reflect tool

You can make symmetrical tiles with the Reflect tool. You can use a set of four differently positioned, yet identical, objects to create artwork with a floor-tile look. To do this, follow these steps.

1. **Create the path (or paths) that you will make into the symmetrical tile.**

2. **Group the artwork together by selecting the artwork first, and then choosing Object ➪ Group or Ctrl (⌘)+G.**

3. **Select the Reflect tool, and click off to the right of it to set the origin.**

4. **Click and drag on the left edge of the object, and drag to the right while pressing the Shift and Alt (Option) keys.** Using the Shift key reflects the image at only 45-degree angles.

5. **When the object has been reflected to the right side, release the mouse button while still pressing the Alt (Option) key; then release the Alt (Option) key.** You now have two versions of the object.

6. **Select the original and reflected object, and reflect again across the bottom of the objects.** You now have four objects — each mirrored a little differently — that make up a tile. You can use this tile to create symmetrical patterns.

The resulting tile pattern is shown in Figure 11-19.

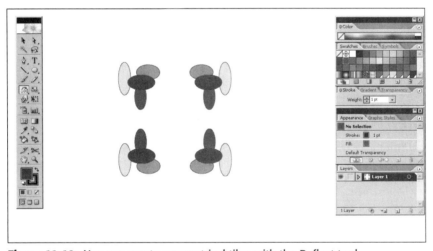

Figure 11-19: You can create symmetrical tiles with the Reflect tool.

Using transformation tools on portions of paths

When using the transformation tools, you don't need to select an entire path. Instead, try experimenting with other effects by selecting single anchor points, line segments, and combinations of selected anchor points and segments. Another idea is to select portions of paths on different objects.

Tip

When you're working with portions of paths, one of the most useful transformation tool procedures is to select a smooth point with the Direct Selection tool and then choose a transformation tool.

You can achieve precise control with the Rotate tool. Click the center of the anchor point, and drag around it. Both control handles move, but the distance from the control handles to the anchor point remains the same. This task is very difficult to perform with just the Direct Selection tool, which you can also use to accomplish the same task.

You can accomplish the exact lengthening of control handle lines by using the Scale tool. Click the anchor point to set the origin, and then drag out from one of the control handles. Both control handles grow from the anchor point in equal proportions.

When working on a smooth point, you can use the Reflect tool to switch lengths and angles between the two control handles.

Here are some more portion-of-path transformation ideas:

✦ Select all the points in an open path except for the end points, and use all the different transformation tools on the selected areas.

✦ Select the bottommost or topmost anchor point in text converted to outlines, and scale, rotate, and shear for interesting effects.

✦ Select two anchor points on a rectangle, and scale and skew copies into a cube to create a 3D appearance.

Transforming patterns

The option in all transformation dialog boxes and the Move dialog box to apply transformations to patterns can produce some very interesting results, as shown in Figure 11-20.

Figure 11-20: This shows a pattern that has been scaled up inside the text and rotated.

One of the most interesting effects results from using patterns that have transparent fills. Select an object that has a pattern fill, and double-click a transformation tool. Enter a value, check the Patterns check box, uncheck the Objects check box, and then click Copy. A new unchanged object overlaps the original object, but the pattern in the new object has changed. If desired, use the Transform Again command by pressing Ctrl+D (⌘+D) to create additional copies with patterns that have been transformed even more.

Tip   You can transform patterns "live" by pressing the grave (`) key while dragging with any transformation tool (including the Selection tool for moving).

Using Liquify tools on Objects

Illustrator has another group of tools called the Liquify tools, which includes the Warp tool, the Twirl tool, the Pucker tool, the Bloat tool, the Scallop tool, the Crystallize tool, and the Wrinkle tool. These tools are found housed with the Warp tool (a finger smushing a line) in the toolbox. The Liquify tools give you free-form morphing abilities unlike any other drawing tools.

All these tools work with a brush interface. You can alter the brush options and the individual tool options by double-clicking on the active tool. Figure 11-21 shows the Warp tool dialog box. In all the Liquify tools, you can always adjust the Global Brush Dimensions and even set it to use a pressure pen.

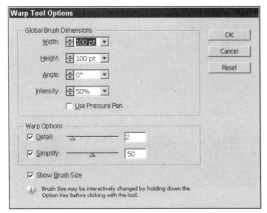

Figure 11-21: The Warp Tool Options dialog box gives you great latitude in warping objects.

The Global Brush Dimensions section includes settings for the Width, Height, and Angle of the brush. The Intensity setting controls how hard you need to move against the path before a change shows up. Using the Warp Option section, you can control the Detail and Simplify settings for each of the Liquify tools.

Tip Change the brush size while applying the tools by holding down the Alt (Option) key before clicking with the tool.

Warping objects

The Warp tool treats objects like modeling clay. You stretch, drag, or pull areas of an object. Figure 11-22 shows the original object on the left and the warped one on the right. You can push out the shape by dragging outward. Put dents in the object by dragging from the outside in.

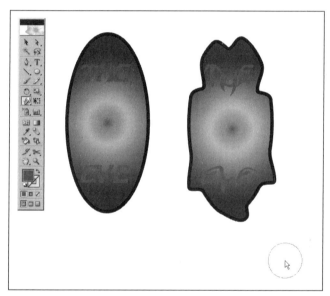

Figure 11-22: The object before (left) and after (right) using the Warp tool

Twirling objects

The Twirl tool applies a spiraled effect to the object. Use this to swirl and ripple distortions on your artwork. Figure 11-23 shows the original object on the left and the swirled object on the right.

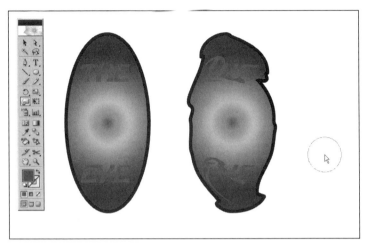

Figure 11-23: The object before (left) and after (right) using the Twirl tool

Puckering

The Pucker tool is similar to the Pucker effect. Using this tool in a brush fashion applies a pinched or pulled in look with spikes, as shown in Figure 11-24.

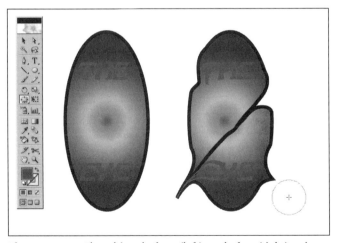

Figure 11-24: The object before (left) and after (right) using the Pucker tool

Bloating

The Bloat tool, like the Pucker tool, is similar to its effect counterpart. Use this to bulge out or puff out in a brushed controlled fashion. Figure 11-25 shows the original object on the left and the bloated object on the right.

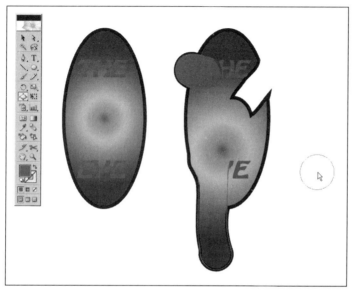

Figure 11-25: The object before (left) and after (right) using the Bloat tool

Scalloping

The Scallop tool is used to add arc shapes to your object. This tool randomly brushes the arc shapes along the area you brush over. Figure 11-26 shows the original object on the left and the scalloped object on the right.

Crystallizing

The Crystallize tool applies arcs and spikes by using a brush on the object. Click and drag outward to push the path out. Click and drag inward, and you push the path inward. The object does not have to be selected; simply drag the brush over the top of the object you want to crystallize. Figure 11-27 shows an example of this tool.

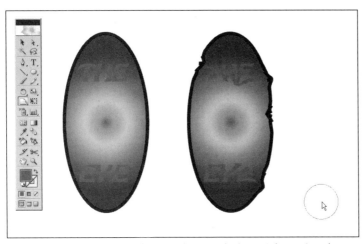

Figure 11-26: The object before (left) and after (right) using the Scallop tool

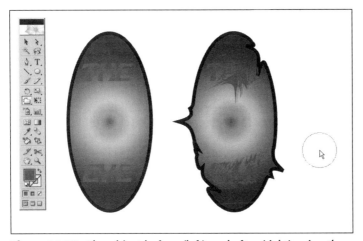

Figure 11-27: The object before (left) and after (right) using the Crystallize tool

Wrinkling

The Wrinkle tool applies a roughened edge to your artwork, similar to the Roughen effect but applied in a brush fashion. Figure 11-28 shows the Wrinkling tool.

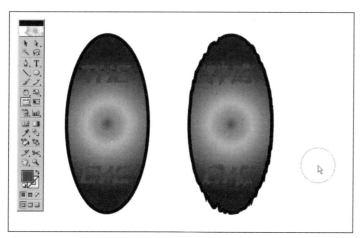

Figure 11-28: The object before (left) and after (right) using the Wrinkle tool

Distorting with Commands

I am calling this section "Distorting with Commands" because if you look under the Effect menu and the Filter menu, you find two different Distort submenus under each (although one of them in the Effect menu is actually Distort & Transform). You may wonder whether Adobe made an error in repeating itself, especially because both submenus include the same menu items. You can use either menu to apply the same commands. The difference is that effects are live and editable and filters are more permanent. Sure, you can undo, but that may change what you have done afterward. With effects, you can go back and edit or remove just the effect without losing any of your other applied options.

Cross-Reference   For more on filters and effects, see Chapter 15.

All effects produce the same look as filters but are fully editable via the Appearance palette. You'll find some filters and effects are exactly the same, except that using filters applies the effect permanently.

In the following examples, the commands used are those found in the Effect ⇨ Distort & Transform submenu.

Using free distortions

The first of the distortion effects is the Free Distort. This was discussed briefly with the Free transformation tool earlier in this chapter. The big difference between the Free transformation tool and the Free Distort command is that Free Distort keeps the spacing relevant and doesn't use the perspective as the Free transformation tool does.

The Free Distort command enables you to alter the shape of the selected object by dragging four corner points. Some may think of this as enveloping, but it is a much simpler effect. Figure 11-29 shows text that has the Free Distort command applied.

Figure 11-29: Free Distort effect applied on type

Using Pucker & Bloat

Although the Pucker & Bloat command undoubtedly has the coolest sounding name that Illustrator has to offer, this command also is one of the least practical. But Illustrator is a fun program, right? And these commands make it lots of fun.

Puckering makes objects appear to have pointy tips sticking out everywhere, and bloating creates lumps outside of objects. Puckering and bloating are inverses of each other; a negative pucker is a bloat, and a negative bloat is a pucker. If you are bewildered by these functions, stop reading right here. The following information spoils everything.

Selecting Pucker & Bloat opens the Pucker & Bloat dialog box, shown in Figure 11-30, where you may specify a percentage by which you want the selected paths to be puckered or bloated by either typing in the amount or dragging a slider.

Figure 11-30: The Pucker & Bloat dialog box

Bloating causes the segments between anchor points to expand outward. The higher the percentage, the more bloated the selection is. You can bloat from –200% to +200%. Using Bloat makes rounded, bubble-like extrusions appear on the surface of your object; using Pucker makes tall spikes appear on its path. When you drag toward Pucker, you can enter how much you want to pucker the drawing. Pucker amounts can range from –200% to +200%. The number of spikes is based on the number of anchor points in your drawing. Figure 11-31 shows text puckered (above) and the same text bloated (below).

Figure 11-31: Original type (above), with pucker applied (middle) and Bloat applied (below)

Note   Text is great to play with using these distortion commands because it is still fully editable. You don't have to create outlines first.

The Pucker & Bloat command moves anchor points in one direction and creates two independent direction points on either side of each anchor point. The direction points are moved in the opposite direction of the anchor points, and the direction of movement is always toward or away from the center of the object.

The distance moved is the only thing that you control when you use the Pucker & Bloat command. Entering a percentage moves the points that percentage.

Note Nothing about the Pucker & Bloat command is random. Everything about it is 100 percent controllable and, to some extent, predictable.

Roughening objects

Roughen adds anchor points and then moves them randomly by a percentage that you define. This gives objects a rough appearing outline.

Because the roughen commands work randomly, you get different results when you apply the same settings of the same command to two separate, identical objects. In fact, the results probably will never be duplicated. The Roughen command is a good reason for having the Undo command, so that you can apply the command, undo, and reapply until you achieve the desired effect. Figure 11-32 shows an example of using the Roughen command.

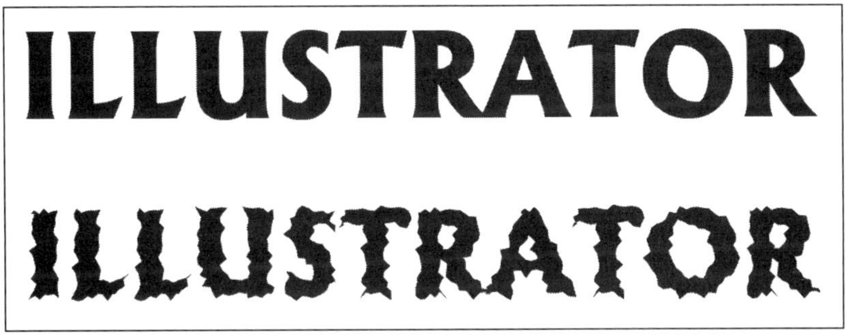

ILLUSTRATOR

ILLUSTRATOR

Figure 11-32: Original type (above) and Roughen applied to it (below)

Tip Using the keyboard, you can continually reapply any command that works randomly and get different results. Select the object, and apply the command by choosing the menu item and entering the values. If you don't like the result, press Ctrl+Z (⌘+Z) to undo it. Press Ctrl+E (⌘+E) to reapply the last filter and Ctrl+Shift+E (⌘+Shift+E) to reapply the last effect.

One important limitation of the Roughen command is that it works on entire paths, even if only part of the path is selected. The best way to get around this limitation is to use the Scissors tool to cut the path into separate sections.

The Roughen command does two things at once. First, it adds anchor points until the selection has the number of points per inch that you defined. Second, it randomly moves all the points around, changing them into straight corner points or smooth points, whichever you specified.

Selecting Roughen opens the Roughen dialog box, shown in Figure 11-33, where you can enter information to roughen the illustration — literally.

Figure 11-33: The Roughen dialog box

Three options are available:

✦ **Size:** How far points may move when roughened relative to the width or height (whichever is greater) of the selected path. Select higher values to increase the apparent roughness.

✦ **Detail:** How many points are created per inch. Select higher values to create more points.

✦ **Smooth or Corner Points:** If you select Smooth, all the anchor points added are smooth points. If you select Corner, all the points added are straight corner points. Use smooth to create soft edges and corner to create sharp edges.

Roughen never takes away points when roughening a path.

Tip

You can use the Roughen command as a very hip version of the Add Anchor Points command. If the Size box is set at 0%, the added points are added along the existing path all at once. Instead of going to Add Anchor Points again and again, just try entering a value of 25 in the Segments/Inch field of the Roughen command. You have instant multiple Add Anchor Points. This technique is great for Tweak or anything else where you need a bunch of anchor points quickly.

Transforming objects

You find the Transform command under the Distort & Transform submenu of the Effect menu. The transform effect is similar to the Transform palette, except that you can go back and edit as well as see the preview before applying.

Choosing Effect ⇨ Distort & Transform ⇨ Transform displays the Transform Effect dialog box, shown in Figure 11-34. One really cool feature of this dialog box is the Copies text box. Here, you can enter a multiple number of copies as shown in this re-creation of the paper doll in Figure 11-35.

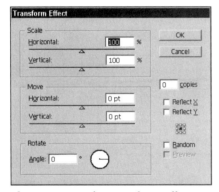

Figure 11-34: The Transform Effect dialog box

Figure 11-35: Paper dolls created using the Transform effect

Tip If the transform effect doesn't come out quite the way you'd like, double-click the name of the effect in the Appearance palette to reopen the Transform Effect dialog box. Make any further changes you want, and click OK to modify the effect.

Tweaking transforms

Selecting Tweak displays the Tweak dialog box, shown in Figure 11-36. In this dialog box, you define the amount of tweaking, including how much horizontal and vertical percentages and which points are moved (anchor points, in control points, or out control points). Choosing Relative applies the filter to the bounding box edges of the object. Choosing Absolute moves the points based on the absolute measurements that you enter.

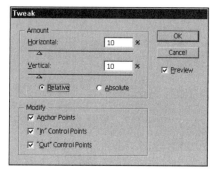

Figure 11-36: The Tweak dialog box

Note No anchor points are added with the Tweak dialog box.

If you enter 0% in either field, no movement occurs in that direction. Illustrator bases the percentage on the width or height of the shape — whichever is longer. If you check the Anchor Points option, all anchor points on the selected path move in a random distance corresponding to the amounts set in the Horizontal and Vertical text fields. If you check either In Control Points or Out Control Points, those points move the specified distance as well. The in control points are the points on one side of the anchor point that lead into the path. Out control points refers to the points on the other side of the anchor point that lead out of the path.

Tip Consider using the Tweak option when you are not sure of the size of the selected artwork or when you can determine only that you want points moved a certain portion of the whole, but cannot determine an absolute measurement.

Figure 11-37 shows an object that had the Tweak effect applied with the Relative option chosen (above) and the same values with the Absolute option chosen (below).

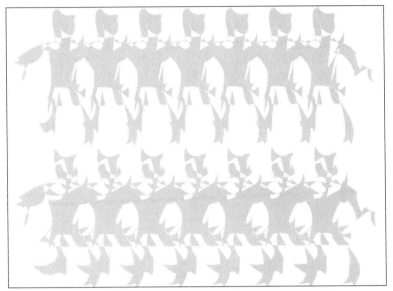

Figure 11-37: The top row was tweaked using the Relative option; the bottom row was tweaked using the Absolute option.

The percentages you enter pertain to the bounding box dimensions and move points up to those limits. The bounding box is an invisible box that surrounds each object. If the bounding box is 5 inches wide and 2 inches tall, and you enter a value of 10% for width and height, the points move randomly up to 0.5 inch horizontally and 0.2 inch vertically in either direction.

Using the Twist command

The Twist command is found under the Filter ➪ Distort ➪ Twist or Effect ➪ Distort &Transform ➪ Twist. This cool command rotates or twists the selected object, with more action being in the center of the object. Twist is the new name for Twirl in previous versions. In the Twist dialog box, shown in Figure 11-38, you set the amount of Twist.

Figure 11-38: The Twist dialog box

You can twist paths and text (without converting to outlines), to create some really great effects. One of my favorite looks is to take a starburst of lines and twist them into a flower or spirographic shapes using the Twist and Tweak effects, as shown in Figure 11-39. The top left has no Twist applied, and a 10-degree Twist is added to each consecutive one. A positive number twists the object clockwise; a negative number twists the object counterclockwise.

Figure 11-39: A range from 10 to 110 degree Twist was added to this object.

Working with the Zig Zag filter

The Zig Zag filter changes normally straight paths into zigzagged versions of those paths. When you first select Zig Zag, the Zig Zag dialog box appears, shown in Figure 11-40.

The dialog box enables you to specify various parameters of the Zig Zag effect, including the Amount, which is how large each zigzag is, and the number of Ridges, which is the number of zigzags. In addition, you can specify whether you want the zigzags to be curved (choose Smooth) or pointed (choose Corner). Like most of the other Illustrator filters, Zig Zag has a handy Preview check box. Figure 11-41 shows an example of zigzagged artwork.

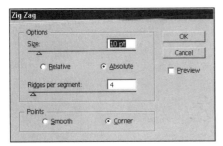

Figure 11-40: The Zig Zag dialog box

Figure 11-41: Art with Zig Zag applied to it

Using Warp Effects

Warp effects are also known as envelopes. Warp effects bend objects into a selected shape. Unlike Free Distort, you have many points to work with and a variety of pre-set options. You can choose from a variety of predefined Warp effects: Arc, Arc Lower, Arc Upper, Arch, Bulge, Shell Lower, Shell Upper, Flag, Wave, Fish, Rise, Fisheye, Inflate, Squeeze, and Twist.

You can find all these warp effects by choosing them from the Effect ➪ Warp submenu. Each of these predefined styles for Warp can also be altered into your own design in the Warp Options dialog box, shown in Figure 11-42.

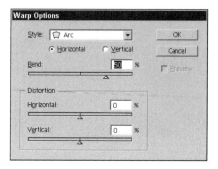

Figure 11-42: The Warp Options dialog box

In all the preset options, you have Warp Options to edit to your heart's desire. You can set these options:

✦ **Style:** Pick from 15 different predefined warps.

✦ **Horizontal or Vertical:** Edit this area to affect either the horizontal or vertical areas of the shape.

✦ **Bend:** Change how much of an effect is applied in percentage.

✦ **Distortion Horizontal:** This option enables you to increase or decrease the horizontal distortion in percentage.

✦ **Distortion Vertical:** This option enables you to increase or decrease the vertical distortion in percentage.

Understanding Warp types

This section provides more information on the 15 different Warp Style presets:

✦ **Arc:** Bends the shape top and bottom in an arc shape

✦ **Arc Lower:** Bends just the lower half of the shape in an arc

✦ **Arc Upper:** Bends just the upper half of the shape in an arc

✦ **Arch:** Bends the upper, middle, and lower areas into an arch shape

✦ **Bulge:** Pushes out the top and bottom of the shape

✦ **Shell Lower:** Squeezes in the middle and bulges out the lower area of the shape

✦ **Shell Upper:** Squeezes in the middle and bulges out the upper area of the shape

✦ **Flag:** Pushes the shape on the top and bottom into an upper and lower curve

✦ **Wave:** Pushes the shape on the top, middle, and bottom into an upper and lower curve

✦ **Fish:** Squeezes the shape into a fish shape

✦ **Rise:** Pushes the shape upward from lower left to upper right

✦ **Fisheye:** Bulges out just the center of the shape

✦ **Inflate:** Bulges out the whole shape instead of just the center

✦ **Squeeze:** Pushes in the left and right sides of the shape

✦ **Twist:** Twists the object around a center (like the twist effect)

Figure 11-43 shows all 15 presets applied to text.

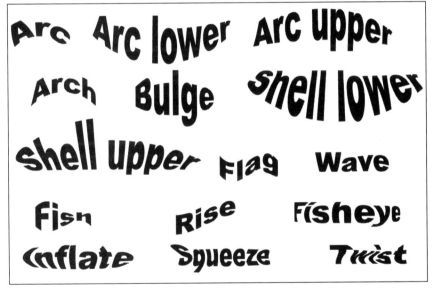

Figure 11-43: Each warp style is shown here in its own name.

Summary

Distortions and transformations are some of the most fun effects that are built into Illustrator. In this chapter, you learned the following:

✦ You can transform an object multiple ways. You can use the transformation tools, the transform menu, the Transform palette, transform filters, or transform effects.

✦ Add awesome effects by using the Liquify tools in a brush-like fashion.

✦ The Distort filters work by moving points around selected paths.

✦ The Pucker and Bloat features create spiked and bubbled effects, respectively.

✦ Roughen can be used to intelligently add anchor points.

✦ Use either the Twist filter alone or with the Twirl tool to twist artwork.

✦ Twirling adds anchor points as needed when twirling.

✦ Tweak is used to move existing points and control handles randomly.

✦ The Zig Zag filter creates even wavy or spiky paths.

✦ Warps push the object into a specific shape.

✦　　✦　　✦

Using Path Blends, Compound Paths, and Masks

✦ ✦ ✦ ✦

In This Chapter

Creating path blends

Using Blend options

Making a color blend

Creating shape blends

Using stroke blends

Creating compound paths

Figuring out path directions

Creating clipping masks

✦ ✦ ✦ ✦

Three of the more difficult areas of Illustrator to master are masks, path blends, and compound paths. Of course, these are also three of the more powerful functions in Illustrator. You use a *mask* to hide portions of an image, or mask them out. *Compound paths* consist of two or more separate paths that Illustrator treats as a single path. A *blend* is a bunch of paths created from two original paths. This chapter shows you how to get to know these three functions so that you can use them in your documents.

Understanding the Difference between Blends and Gradients

In Illustrator, a *blend* is a series of paths that Illustrator creates based on two other paths. The series of paths transforms from the first path into the second path, changing fill and stroke attributes as it moves. A *gradient* is a smooth blend of colors between two or more colors. The big difference is that the gradient shows up as a box rather than a series of paths as in a blend. With a gradient, you use a palette to signify where the colors start and stop.

At first glance, blends and gradients seem to do the same things but in different ways — so why have both? The Blend tool, moreover, seems to be much harder to use than the Gradient Vector tool. On the surface, it seems that you can do more with gradients than with blends. Blends take a long time to redraw; gradients take a fraction of the time.

After all, if gradients are so much easier to use and produce so much better results, is it really necessary to have a Blend tool or a Blend function? Students, clients, and the occasional passerby have asked me this question quite often, and they seem to have a good point at first. Upon further study, however, it becomes apparent that blends are quite different from gradients, both in form and function.

You use gradients only as fills for paths. You can make gradients either linear or radial, meaning that color can change from side to side, top to bottom, or from an interior point to the outside. Every gradient can have as many distinct colors in it as you can create, limited only by RAM. Gradients are simply an easier way to create blends that change only in color, not in shape or size.

Cross-Reference   You can read about gradients in Chapter 7.

Blends, on the other hand, are series of transformed paths between two end paths. The paths between the end paths mutate from one end path into the other. All the attributes of the end paths change throughout the transformed paths, including shape, size, and all Paint Style attributes. The major benefit is that you can blend multiple colors at one time.

Blends can be incredibly flexible when it comes to creating photorealistic changes in color, if you plan ahead. Changes to blends aren't really changes at all; instead, they are deletions of the transformed objects and changes in the attributes of the end paths. If you know what you want, blending colors can take on an incredibly realistic look by changing the shapes of the blend's end paths just slightly.

But even more useful than creating realistic changes in color is blending's capability to transform shapes from one shape to another (this is typically called *morphing*), as shown in the examples in Figure 12-1. With a bit of practice (and the information in this chapter), you can transform any illustration into another illustration. There is a limit to the complexity of the illustrations that you can transform, but the limit is due more to the time it takes to create the blends than to limitations inherent in Illustrator. Think of blends as morphing from one object into another.

Because blends work on both stroke and fill attributes of objects, you can create some really exciting effects that aren't possible by using any other technique, electronic or traditional.

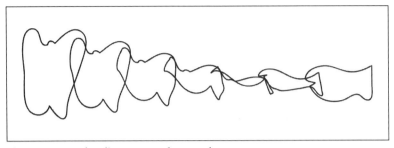

Figure 12-1: Blending to transform a shape

Creating Path Blends

Originally, Adobe marketed the Blend tool as a tool whose primary purpose was to transform shapes, not blend colors. Instead, designers used the tool for blending colors to create what were known as vignettes, or what traditional artists called gradients.

The Blend tool creates in-between steps in the area between two paths, where the paint style and shape of one path transform themselves into the paint style and shape of the second path.

Version 8 of Illustrator dramatically enhanced the Blending function. The big change is that blends became live, or editable. This huge change enables users to change the color, shape, and location of the blend shapes. The blend instantly reblends to the new changes. Another great change is the capability to blend along a path.

Although any blend takes into account both color and shape, I treat color and shape separately in this chapter because people using the Blend tool are often trying to obtain either a color effect or a shape effect, rather than both at once.

You use the Blend tool to create blends, which are a group of paths (commonly referred to as blend steps) that change in shape and color as each intermediate path comes closer to the opposite end path. Follow these steps to create a blend:

1. **Using a shape tool, create a small (1-inch) vertical shape.** For more on creating shapes, see Chapter 5. This example uses a rectangle.

2. **With the Selection tool, press Alt (Option) and drag a few inches to the right.** This copies the path a few inches to the side. Press Shift as you drag horizontally to constrain the movement of the path.

3. **On the left shape, change the fill and stroke to desired values.** This example uses a fill of black and a stroke of None. For more on changing the fill and strokes on shapes, see Chapter 4.

4. **For the right rectangle, change the fill and stroke to desired values.** This example uses a fill of white and a stroke of None.

5. **Select the Blend tool by pressing the W key.** Click the top-left point of the left path and then the top-left point of the right path. This step tells Illustrator to blend between these two paths, and it uses the top-left points as reference. The Blend tool cursor changes from x to + in the lower-right corner. Illustrator creates a spine between the two end paths, which are now transparent. Figure 12-2 shows the resulting blend.

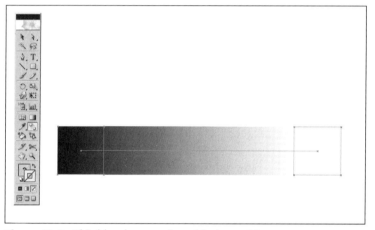

Figure 12-2: This blend moves from black to white.

6. **Press Ctrl+Shift+A (⌘+Shift+A).** This deselects all previously selected paths. The default Blend Option creates smooth color between the two shapes. The blend consists of 256 paths, including the two end paths. In the example, each path is a slightly different tint of black.

Defining Linear Blends

You create color blends by making two end paths, usually identical in shape and size, giving each path different Paint Style attributes, and generating a series of steps between them with the Blend tool. The more end paths you create, the more colors you can create.

Note The examples in this chapter are easier to understand when you are working in Preview mode.

Follow these steps to create a basic linear blend:

1. **Draw a curved path with the Pen tool, filling and stroking it as desired.** The example gives the path a fill of None and a stroke of two points black.

2. **Alt (Option)-copy the path to the right, filling and stroking the copied path as desired.** The example gives the new path a stroke of two points yellow.

3. **With the Blend tool, click the path on the left and then the path on the right.** Alternately, you can select both objects and choose Object ⇨ Blend ⇨ Make.

4. **Deselect all by pressing Ctrl+Shift+A (⌘+Shift+A) to see the result, as shown in Figure 12-3.**

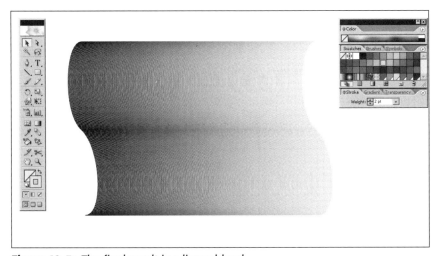

Figure 12-3: The final result is a linear blend.

Note The blend shown in Figure 12-3 demonstrates one of the hazards of creating blends — something often referred to as *banding*. See the sidebar "Avoiding Banding" later in this chapter to learn what to do to reduce or eliminate banding.

You have a variety of ways to blend objects. Keep in mind these suggestions when blending objects:

✦ You can edit blends by using the selection, rotate, or scale tools.

✦ You can perform blending with any number of objects, colors, opacities, and gradients.

✦ You cannot apply blending with mesh objects.

✦ You cannot edit the path (or *spine* as it is called) that the blend creates.

✦ The fill of the topmost object is used when blending patterns.

✦ When intermixing process and spot colors, the blend is colored with process colors.

✦ When blending with transparent objects, the topmost object's transparency is used.

✦ You can blend symbols.

✦ You can change the number of steps that Illustrator uses in the Blend Options dialog box.

✦ Blends create a knockout with transparency groups. (If you don't want this, change it in the Transparency palette by unchecking the Knockout Group.)

Working with Blend Options

Adobe has enhanced the Blending functions of Illustrator by making the Blend tool easier to use and faster, and by adding a Blend submenu under the Object menu. The Blend options are Make, Release, Blend Options, Expand, Replace Spine, Reverse Spine, and Reverse Front to Back. With Illustrator's Live Blend capability, you may not need to release a blend to change it. You can use the Direct Selection tool to select the path and edit or change the color, and the blend instantly updates. Live Blending is the capability to change the shape or color of a blend and update it automatically.

Using the Blend option

The Blend Options dialog box lets you change the Spacing and Orientation aspects. Select the blend that you want to adjust, and either double-click the Blend tool or choose Object ➪ Blend ➪ Blend Options to open the dialog box to change the settings.

Figure 12-4 shows the Blend Options dialog box. The three Spacing choices are Smooth Color, Specified Steps, and Specified Distance. The Orientation options are Align to Page and Align to Path.

Figure 12-4: The Blend Options dialog box enables you to set up blends the way you want.

These are the Blend options:

✦ **Smooth Color:** This option automatically determines the best number of steps needed to make this blend look very smooth.

✦ **Specified Steps:** This option lets you choose the number of intermediate steps you want in the blend.

✦ **Specified Distance:** This option enables you to type the distance between steps.

✦ **Align to Page:** This option runs the blend vertically or horizontally depending on your page orientation.

✦ **Align to Path:** This option runs the blend perpendicular to the path.

Blending multiple objects

Illustrator has the capability to blend multiple objects in one step. Long gone are the days of blending, hiding, blending, hiding, and so on. Select all the objects that you want to blend and choose Object ➪ Blend ➪ Make, or use the Blend tool to click all the objects that you want to blend. Figure 12-5 shows a blend that uses four different shaped rectangles. To create this effect I first drew four rectangles, each with a different fill. You need to use different fills in the objects to see a blend effect like this one.

Editing a blended object

The Live Blend option lets you change the colors of a blend without having to redo the whole blend. With the Direct Selection tool, select the path whose color you want to change in the blended shape. Select a new fill and/or stroke color. The blend updates instantly with the new color.

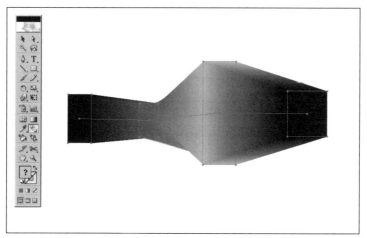

Figure 12-5: Blends can use multiple objects.

Another great aspect of Live Blend is the capability to edit the blend at any time and have it automatically update on the fly. As mentioned before, Illustrator creates a path, or spine, when you create a blend. With the Direct Selection tool, you can select an anchor point on the spine and move it. This changes the location of that point, and the blend updates accordingly.

Now you can edit lines by adding, deleting, or moving any part of your blend, and it updates automatically. You can delete and add points or change the shape of a path with the Direct Selection tool. Figure 12-6 shows a figure before and after editing the blend. In this case, the star that begins the blend was modified in the lower blend by dragging the upward pointing corner at the bottom of the figure downward.

Releasing a blend

If you want to redo a blend, you have to release it first using the Object ➪ Blend ➪ Release command. This command eliminates the intermediate objects and leaves you with just the original ones.

Expanding blends

If you want to retain the intermediate objects, choose Object ➪ Blend ➪ Expand. By choosing Object ➪ Blend ➪ Expand, you expand the blend into a series of individual shapes. You can then move or edit these shapes independently of the rest of the shapes.

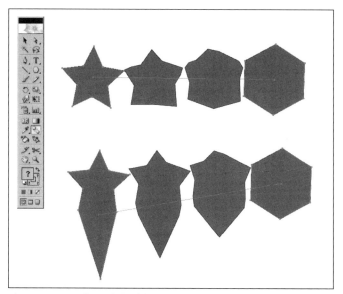

Figure 12-6: The original figure (top) and the edited blend (bottom) show how a simple modification can make quite a difference in the end result.

Replacing the spine

The Replace Spine option enables you to make a blend follow a selected path. Follow these steps to apply this effect:

1. **Create the blend as described earlier in this chapter.** For example, create a blend that blends a mostly vertical ellipse into a mostly horizontal ellipse.

2. **Draw a path in the shape that you want the spine of the blend to follow.** In this case, draw a large diameter circle to use as the path for the blend.

3. **Select the blend with the spine that you want to change and the path that you want to become the new spine.**

4. **Choose Object ➪ Blend ➪ Replace Spine.** The blend updates automatically. Figure 12-7 shows before and after a blend has been applied to a path. In this case, the path used in the lower instance is a circle.

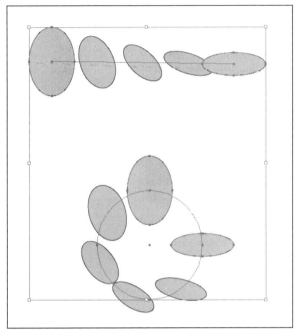

Figure 12-7: This demonstrates how the original blend (top) is changed after applying Replace Spine (bottom).

Reversing the spine

This menu option reverses the sequence of the objects that you are blending. If you have a rectangle on the right blended to a circle on the left, choosing Object ⇨ Blend ⇨ Reverse Spine places the circle on the right and the rectangle on the left. Reversing the spine flips the position of the shapes on the spine, as shown in Figure 12-8.

Reversing front to back

The Reverse Front to Back option reverses the order in which your paths were drawn when you created your blend. If you drew a small circle first and a large circle second, choosing Object ⇨ Blend ⇨ Reverse Front to Back places the small circle underneath and the large circle on top, as shown in Figure 12-9.

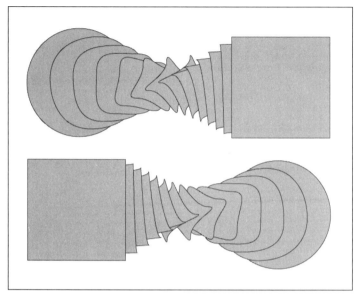

Figure 12-8: Reversing the spine changes the original (top) by swapping the position of the shapes (bottom).

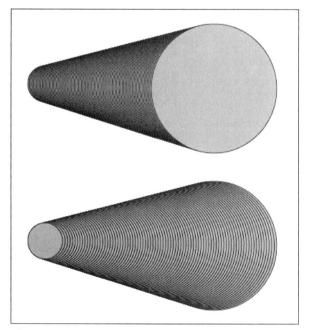

Figure 12-9: Reversing the spine front to back changes the stacking order of the original (top), creating the effect shown (bottom).

Using nonlinear blends

End paths with two endpoints (linear segments) used to make blends don't have to be just horizontal or vertical. And when you create multiple color blends, you don't have to align the intermediate end paths the same way as you align the end paths. Careful setup of intermediate blends can create many interesting effects, such as circular and wavy appearances, all created with straight paths.

Note   End paths that cross usually produce undesirable effects; if carefully constructed, however, the resulting blends can be quite intriguing. Blending crossed end paths creates the appearance of a three-dimensional blend, where one of the end paths blends "up" into the other.

To create nonlinear blends, set up the end paths and either rotate them or change their orientation by using the Direct Selection tool on one of the end points. Then blend from one end path to the intermediate end paths and then to the other end path. Figure 12-10 shows an example of a nonlinear blend.

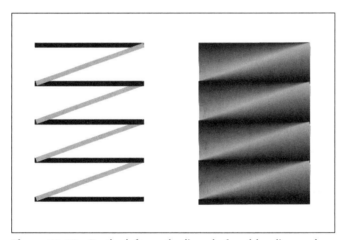

Figure 12-10: On the left are the lines before blending and on the right are the lines blended with the Blend tool (Smooth option).

Another good example of a nonlinear blend is to create a color wheel by aligning straight lines in a hexagon with differing colors and blending between them, as shown in Figure 12-11.

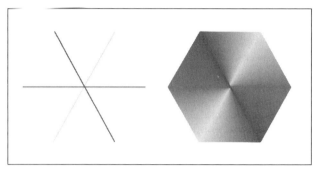

Figure 12-11: This is a linear blend applied in a perimeter fashion.

Finding end paths for linear blends

You can also use rectangles with fills and no strokes to achieve a linear blend effect. Figure 12-12 shows both lines and rectangles used for end paths.

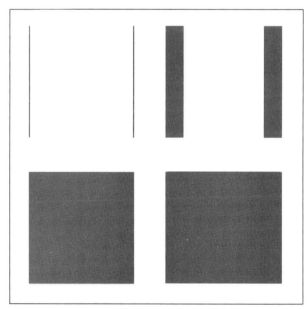

Figure 12-12: Lines and rectangles are both used for end paths in blends here.

Although you can use a rectangle as an end path, you should use a single line with two end points instead. In fact, lines are better than rectangles for three reasons. First, lines use half as much information as rectangles because lines have two anchor points, while rectangles have four anchor points. Second, it is much easier to change the width of a line (stroke weight) after you create the blend (just select the lines and enter a new weight in the Stroke palette) than it is to change the width of rectangles (you would have to use the Scale Each option). Third, creating a linear blend with lines (strokes) creates a thick mess of paths, but creating a linear blend with rectangles creates a thicker mess, so much so that it is difficult to select specific rectangles.

Tip   You can blend an open path with a closed path and vice versa with Illustrator. You can blend open or closed paths to any path by choosing Object ⇨ Blend ⇨ Make or using the Blend tool.

Calculating the number of steps

Whenever you create a blend, Illustrator provides a default value in the Specified Steps text field of the Blend Options dialog box that assumes that you want to print your illustration to an Imagesetter or other high-resolution device capable of printing all 256 levels of gray that PostScript allows.

The formula that Illustrator uses is quite simple. It takes the largest change that any one color goes through from end path to end path and multiplies that percentage by 256. The formula looks like this:

```
256 × largest color change % = the number of steps you want to
create
```

For example, using a linear blend example where the difference in tint values is 100 percent (100% – 0% = 100%), when you multiply 100 percent by 256, you get 256. Because the total number of grays must be 256 or fewer, Illustrator creates only 254. When you add this to the two ends, you have 256 tints.

But, of course, not everything you create outputs on an Imagesetter. Your laser printer, for example, cannot print 256 grays unless you set the line screen extremely low. To determine how many grays your laser printer can produce, you must know both the dpi (dots-per-inch) and the line screen. In some software packages, you can specify the line screen, but unless the printer is a high-end model, it is usually difficult to specify or change the dpi. Use the following formula to find out how many grays your printer can produce:

```
(dpi/line screen) × (dpi/line screen) = number of grays
```

For a 300-dpi printer with a typical line screen of 53, the formula looks like this:

```
(300/53) × (300/53) = 5.66 × 5.66 = 32
```

A 400-dpi printer at a line screen of 65 has the following formula:

```
(400/65) × (400/65) = 6.15 × 6.15 = 38
```

A 600-dpi printer at 75 lines per inch uses this formula:

```
(600/75) × (600/75) = 8 × 8 = 64
```

Sometimes, you may want to reduce the number of blend steps in a blend from the default because either your printer can't display that many grays or the distance from one end path to another is extremely small (see the sidebar "Airbrushing and the Magic of Stroke Blends" later in this chapter).

When reducing the number of blends, start by dividing the default by two and then continue dividing by two until you have a number of steps with which you are comfortable. If you aren't sure how many steps you need, do a quick test of just that blend with different numbers of steps specified and print it out. If you are going to an Imagesetter, don't divide by two more than twice, or banding can occur.

Creating radial blends

To create a radial blend, follow these steps:

1. **Make a shape about two inches in diameter.** See Chapter 4 for more on creating circles. Fill the circle. The example uses a fill of 100 percent black.

2. **Make a smaller shape inside the larger shape, and fill it as desired.** The example fills the smaller circle with white.

3. **Select both shapes, and choose Object ⇨ Blend ⇨ Make.**

4. **To change the number of steps, choose Object ⇨ Blend ⇨ Blend Options.** When blending black to white, Illustrator automatically uses 255 steps. When blending other colors, Illustrator automatically chooses the best amount.

You can create radial blends with almost any object. Figure 12-13 shows a radial blend using a star.

Caution   As with most other blends, when blending from two identically shaped end paths, always click the anchor point in the same position on each object. Figure 12-13 shows the difference between clicking the anchor points in the same position (left) and clicking those that are not in the same position (right).

Figure 12-13: Here are two examples of radial blends that differ because different anchor points were selected.

One of the nice things about creating radial blends manually (not using the gradient feature) is that by changing the location and the size of the inner object, you can make the gradient look vastly different. The larger you make the inner object, the smaller the blended area becomes.

The Gradient feature enables you to change the highlight point on a radial Gradient without changing the source, or angle, of the highlight.

Cross-Reference   The Gradient Mesh tool enables you to create easy highlights with the click of a mouse. See Chapter 7 for more information on this tool.

Making a Color Blend

Using colors in a blend is really no different from using black and white, except for the spectacular results. The only difficulty in using colors in blends is whether the colors look good together.

Using multiple colors with linear blends

To create linear blends that have multiple colors, you must create intermediate end paths, one for each additional color within the blend.

1. **Create two end paths at the edges of where you want the entire blend to begin and end.** Don't worry about colors at this time.

2. **Select the two paths, and choose Object ⇨ Blend ⇨ Make.** Alternatively, you can press Ctrl+Alt+B (⌘+Option+B).

3. **Choose Object ➪ Blend ➪ Blend Options.** This opens the Blend Options dialog box.

4. **Choose the values you want for the blend.** Change the Smooth Options to Specified Steps. Choose your orientation, and enter a number for the steps. (I entered 3 to create three evenly spaced paths between the two end paths.)

5. **Expand the newly created strokes by choosing Object ➪ Blend ➪ Expand.** Color each of the strokes of the paths differently, and then give them a desired weight. The example uses a weight of 2 points.

6. **Select all the paths, and choose Object ➪ Blend ➪ Make.** Alternatively, you can press Ctrl+Alt+B (⌘+Option+B). The result should look like the blend of colors in Figure 12-14.

Avoiding Banding

The graphic artist's worst nightmare: Smooth blends and gradations turn into large chunks of tints, and suddenly get darker or lighter instead of staying nice and smooth. *Banding*, as this nightmare is called, is an area of a blend where the difference from one tint to the next tint changes abruptly and displays a defining line showing the difference between the two tints. Individual tints appear as solid areas called bands.

Avoiding banding is easier when you know what causes it. Usually one of two factors in Illustrator is the cause: too few blend steps or too little variation in the colors of the end paths. Preventing banding due to any of these causes depends on the line screen setting and the capability of your printer to print it.

These causes pretty much make sense. Take the linear blend example earlier in this chapter. If you have only three intermediate steps between end paths, you have only five colors in the blend, thus creating five bands. If you place each of the end paths on one side of a 17-inch span, each created blend step takes up the five points of width of the stroke, making each shade of gray five points wide. If you make the color on the left 10 percent black instead of 100 percent black, Illustrator creates only 26 color steps between the two end paths. So, to avoid banding, use the recommended number of steps over a short area with a great variation of color.

If you find it hard to fix the banding problem and your blend consists of process colors, try adding a small amount of an unused color (black, for instance) to cover up the banding breaks. A 5 percent to 30 percent change over distances may provide just enough dots to hide those bands. Keeping this in mind, you have more of a chance for banding if you use the same tints for different process colors. Alter the tint values for one of the colors at one of the end paths just a little, and this alteration staggers the bands enough to remove them from sight.

See the "Calculating the number of steps" section earlier in this chapter for more information on banding.

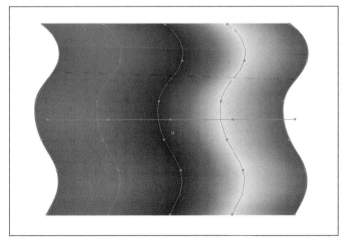

Figure 12-14: This is a multiple color linear blend with the paths and spine selected.

Using guidelines for creating color linear blends

Although the preceding procedure should have gone smoothly with no problems, follow these guidelines when creating blends to get good results each time you print:

✦ **For linear blends, use either rectangles with only four anchor points or a basic 2-point path.** If you use a shape with any more anchor points or if you use a curved shape with any paths that aren't perfectly straight, you get extra information that isn't needed to create the blend, and printing takes much longer than usual.

✦ **When creating linear blends, use one rectangle per end path and color the fills of the paths, not the strokes.** Coloring the strokes may appear to work, but it usually results in a moiré pattern when you print. Make sure that you set the stroke to None, regardless of what you have for the fill.

✦ **Don't change the number that appears in the Specified Steps text field in the Blend Options dialog box if you want smooth color.** Making the number higher creates additional paths that you can't print; making the number lower can result in banding when you print (see the "Avoiding Banding" sidebar earlier in this chapter).

Creating Shape Blends

The difference between color blends and shape blends is in their emphasis. Color blends emphasize a color change; shape blends emphasize blending between different shapes.

You have a number of details to remember when creating the end paths that form a shape blend. You must make both paths either open or closed. If open, you can only click end points to blend between the two paths. If the shapes also change color, be sure to follow the guidelines in the earlier section related to color blends.

For the best results, both paths should have the same number of anchor points selected before blending, and you should have the selected points in a relatively similar location. Illustrator pairs up points on end paths and the segments between them so that when it creates the blend steps, the lines are in about the same position.

Complex-shape blending

Whenever a shape is complex (that is, it isn't a perfectly symmetrical shape, such as a circle or a star), you may have to perform a number of functions to create realistic and eye-pleasing effects. Figure 12-15 shows a complex-shape blend.

Figure 12-15: It can be a little difficult to get the results you want with complex-shape blends.

One function that you can perform to improve the blend involves adding or removing anchor points from the end paths. Even if you select the same number of points and those points are in similar areas on each path, Illustrator may not give you an acceptable result. The Add Anchor Point and Delete Anchor Point tools become quite useful here. By adding points in strategic locations, you can often fool Illustrator into creating an accurate blend; otherwise, the blend steps can resemble a total disaster.

Tip   As a general rule, you disturb the composition of the graphic less if you add anchor points rather than remove them. On most paths, removing anchor points changes the shape of the path dramatically.

Another method of getting the paths to blend more accurately involves shortening them by splitting a long, complex path into one or two smaller sections that aren't nearly as complex. You must blend each path, which you can do in one step by choosing Object ➪ Blends ➪ Make.

Creating realism with shape blends

To create a realistic effect with shape blends, the paths you use to create the blends need to resemble objects you see in life, which are generally curved rather than straight. Take a look around you and try to find a solid-colored object. Doesn't the color appear to change from one part of the object to another? Shadows and reflections are everywhere. Colors change gradually from light to dark, not in straight lines but in smooth, rounded curves.

You can use blends to simulate reflections and shadows. You usually create reflections with shape blends and create shadows with stroke blends.

This section shows you how to simulate reflections with shape blends. This procedure is a little tricky for any artist because the environment determines a reflection. The artwork you create may be viewed in any number of environments, so the reflections have to compensate for these differences. Fortunately, unless you create a mirror angled directly at the viewer (impossible, even if you know who the viewer is in advance), you can get the person seeing the artwork to perceive reflection without really being aware of it.

The chrome-like type in the word *DON'T* in Figure 12-16 was created by masking shape blends designed to look like a reflective surface.

1. **Type the word or words you want to use for masking the reflective surface.** The typeface and the word itself have an impact on how an observer perceives the finished artwork. The example uses the word *DON'T* and the typeface Stencil. The example also required a great deal of tracking to make all the letters touch so that the word looks like one piece of material. In addition, the example uses baseline shift to move the apostrophe up several points.

2. **Select the text using the Selection tool.**

3. **Choose Type ➪ Create Outlines, or press Ctrl+Shift+O (⌘+Shift+O).** At this point, most of the serifs on the letters overlap.

4. **Select all the letters, and choose Add to Shape Area from the Pathfinder palette.** This command gets rid of any unsightly seams between the letters. If

desired, create a rectangle and place it behind the letters. This makes the letters of the word stand out.

5. **Using the Pencil tool, draw a horizontal line from left to right across the rectangle.** Alt (Option)-copy several of this pencil-drawn path from the original down to the bottom of the rectangle. The example required the creation of five more paths.

6. **With the Direct Selection tool, randomly move around individual anchor points and direction points on each path, but try to avoid overlapping paths.**

7. **Color the stroke of each path differently, going from dark to light to dark.** In my example, I went from dark to light to dark to light and back to dark again.

8. **Blend the stroked paths together.**

9. **Open the Transparency palette, and choose Make Opacity Mask from the pop-up menu to mask the blend with the type outlines.** The mask you are creating is an opacity rather than a clipping mask. Your results should look similar to Figure 12-16.

Figure 12-16: This shows a reflective surface type blend created by blending and masking.

In the preceding steps, you press Alt (Option) to copy the path not only because it makes things easier, but also to ensure that the end paths in the blends have the same points in the same locations. This technique is much more effective than adding or deleting points from a path.

Tip

With slight transformations, you can use the same reflection blend for other objects in the same illustration and no one will be the wiser. A method that I often use is to reflect the original, scale it to 200 percent, and then use only a portion of the blend in the next mask.

Figure 12-17 shows how to use shape blends to create the glowing surface of a lit object, in this case a light bulb. The key to achieving this effect successfully is to draw the shape first and then use a copy of exactly the same path for the highlights. The relative locations of anchor points stay the same, and the number of anchor points never changes.

1. **Draw the shape you want to light.** Take your time to get it exactly the way you want it, because this path is the basis for everything else in this example. The example of the light bulb uses a fill of 30 percent Magenta, 80 percent Yellow, and a stroke of None.

2. **Copy the object and scale it down just a little bit, setting the origin on the base of the bulb.** Make two more copies of the object, each a little smaller than the previous copy.

3. **Change the color of each copy slightly.** In the example, the color of the light bulb's paths from inside to outside is as follows: Color the first (inside) path as 5 percent Magenta, 10 percent Yellow; the next path as 10 percent Magenta, 30 percent Yellow; and the last path as 15 percent Magenta, 40 percent Yellow. The outermost path should still be 30 percent Magenta, 80 percent Yellow.

4. **The paths should be in the correct top-to-bottom order, but if they are not, fix them.** To see if they are in the correct order, go to Preview mode. If the smaller paths are not visible, then send the outer paths to the back.

5. **Blend the paths together by selecting similar anchor point locations on each step.** Figure 12-17 shows the result. You can, of course, make additional modifications for an even more realistic appearance should you desire.

Figure 12-17: A light bulb created with blends almost seems to glow.

Blending symbols

The Blend tool can also blend symbols. Use the Symbol Sprayer tool to spray one symbol or drag the symbol from the palette. Select the symbols and blend them together. Not only can you blend like symbols, but different ones as well. Figure 12-18 shows a basic blend from a large flower symbol to a small flower symbol, and the spine was edited to an arch shape.

Cross-Reference   Chapter 5 covers the Symbol Sprayer.

Figure 12-18: Here is a flower symbol sized large and small and blended.

In blending different symbols, the blend may be a bit distorted. Even expanding the symbol won't change the blend outcome. Figure 12-19 shows several sets of blends between different symbols.

Blending envelopes

Not only can you blend symbols, but you also can take a blend and stuff it in an envelope-like shape with Warp effects. Simply select the blend and choose Effect ➪ Warp ➪ Arc, and then either press OK or choose another preset or create your own warp. Figure 12-20 shows two blends with two different Warp effects applied.

Cross-Reference   Chapter 11 covers Warp effects.

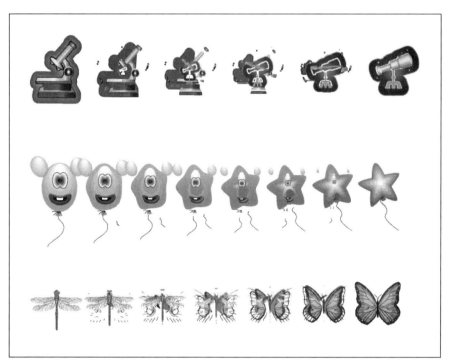

Figure 12-19: A blend between different symbols can produce some very interesting results.

Figure 12-20: You can create unusual effects by warping a blend's envelope.

Blending 3D objects

Another great use of blending is to blend 3D objects. You create a 3D object and then either create another one or duplicate and alter the original by pressing Ctrl+Alt+B (⌘+Option+B) to blend the two together. To change anything, select one of the objects in the blend, and use the Appearance palette make your edits. Figure 12-21 shows a 3D star blended with another 3D star on a curved spine.

Cross-Reference   For more on the Appearance palette, see Chapter 15. For more on 3D, see Chapter 16.

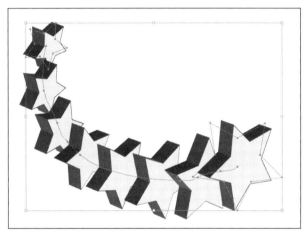

Figure 12-21: These 3D stars are blended together and still fully editable.

Tip   A really cool thing to do with the 3D stars is to select all objects and the blend, and then open the Layers palette. Choose Release to Layers (Sequence) from the palette menu. After you have done this, choose File ➪ Export and select Macromedia Flash (swf) in the Save as type list box (Format pop-up menu). Choose AI Layers to SWF Frames as the export type to create a File that you can open in your browser that becomes animated. It creates three files: an HTML file, a JPG file, and an SWF file. When you open the HTML file in your browser, it plays the SWF file using the JPG file.

Airbrushing shadows

To create a realistic shadow effect, the edges of an object must be a little fuzzy. The amount of fuzziness on the edges of the path is relative to the distance of the object from its shadow and the strength of the light source. These two areas also affect how dark the shadow is.

Airbrushing and the Magic of Stroke Blends

Blending can create effects that are usually reserved for bitmap graphics software, such as Adobe Photoshop CS2, but without the limitation of pixels. Blending identical overlapping paths together and varying their stroke weights and colors creates most of the effects described in this section. This technique can provide some of the best effects that Illustrator has to offer.

An important key to getting shape blends to look really good is to blend from the background color of the shape to the first blend, or to make that first blend the background color. This flows the blend smoothly into the background, so you can't tell exactly where the blend starts and stops.

Usually, the bottommost stroke has a heavier weight than the topmost stroke, and as the color changes from bottom stroke to top stroke, the colors appear to blend in from the outside.

To make really cool shadows, you can use either the soft mix effect, which can be used to darken areas, or the color adjust filter, which can be used to change the types of color in a selected area. The drop shadow filter creates hard-edged shadows, which are usually good only for creating text shadows quickly.

A second way to create cool shadows is to use stroke blends. Stroke blends can allow the shadows to fade smoothly into the background with a Gaussian Blur-like effect. You can combine stroke blends with the soft mix effect for even better effects. Follow these steps:

1. **Create a path (or copy it from an original object) for which you want to create a shadow (for example, create some text).** At this point, you may want to hide the object from which you are creating the shadow so that it doesn't get in your way, especially if this object is right above where you want to place the shadow.

2. **Fill the shadowed path with the color you want the shadow to be, and then make the stroke the same color, with a 0.5-point stroke weight.** In this case, if your text is black, you might want to use gray.

3. **Copy the shadow, and then choose Edit ➪ Paste in Back or press Ctrl+B (⌘+B).** Then change the stroke color to whatever the background color is (usually white, unless something else is under the shadow). Make the stroke weight twice the distance to which you want the shadow to fade out. In my example, I made the stroke 12 points.

4. **Now blend these two paths.** Blending is easy using the Object ➪ Blend ➪ Make command or by pressing Ctrl+Alt+B (⌘+Option+B). The shadow slowly fades in from the background color to the shadow color. Show the hidden objects (you may have to bring them to the front), and your shadow effect has been created, as shown in Figure 12-22.

Figure 12-22: Blends can produce an effect similar to airbrushed shadows, as shown here.

Creating glows

Glows are very similar to soft-edged shadows, but instead of a dark area fading into the background, a lighter area fades into the background. You can create a glow by using stroke blending.

Follow these steps to create a glow behind an object:

1. **Draw an object around which you want to create a glow.** In this example, I used the Ellipse tool to draw a circle with a red fill.

2. **Change the stroke to 6 percent Magenta, 60 percent Yellow, and 100 percent Black, and make the stroke about 40 points wide.** You can make the stroke wider if you want the glow to spread over a larger area.

3. **Select the object, and choose Edit ➪ Copy or press Ctrl+C (⌘+C) to copy it.**

4. **Choose Edit ➪ Paste in Front or press Ctrl+F (⌘+F) to paste a copy in front of the existing object.**

5. **Give the copied object a stroke of 6 percent Magenta and 62 percent Yellow, and a Weight of 1 point.**

6. **Select both objects by choosing Select ➪ All or by pressing Ctrl+A (⌘+A).**

7. **Blend the two edge paths together to create the glow behind the object.**

8. **Draw a Black rectangle around the outside edge of the object, and send it to the back by choosing Object ➪ Arrange ➪ Send to Back.** Figure 12-23 shows the result.

Note   When creating glows, make the initial glow area (around the edge of the object) lighter than the object edges if there are bright highlights in the object. Make the initial glow darker than the edges if the edges of the object are the brightest part of the object.

Figure 12-23: A "glow" added behind this object makes it look like a sun shining in the blackness of space.

Softening edges

You can soften edges of objects in a manner very similar to that of creating shadows. The reason you soften edges is to remove the hard, computer-like edges from objects in your illustration. You can soften edges to an extreme measure so that the object appears out of focus or just a tiny bit for an almost imperceptible change.

When determining how much of a distance you want to soften, look at the whole illustration, not just that one piece. Usually, the softening area is no more than one or two points (unless you are blurring the object).

To soften edges on an object, follow these general steps:

1. **Draw the object you want to soften.**

2. **Choose Edit ➪ Copy or press Ctrl+C (⌘+C) to copy the object.**

3. **Change the stroke to the color of the background and the weight to twice the width you want for the softening edge.** An amount of 3 or 4 points produces a good result in most cases.

4. **Choose Edit ➪ Paste in Front or press Ctrl+F (⌘+F).**

5. **Click the object to make sure the front object is selected.**

6. **Make the stroke on the object 0.25 point, the same color as the fill.**

7. **Choose Object ➪ Blend ➪ Make to blend the two objects.**

8. **Choose Edit ➪ Paste in Front or press Ctrl+F (⌘+F) to place a copy of the original object on top of the blended object.**

9. **Click outside of the objects to deselect them.** Figure 12-24 shows an example of how a softened edge looks when zoomed in to 800 percent.

Figure 12-24: Zooming in shows how the softened edge effect appears.

To blur an object, just make the bottom layer stroke extremely wide (12 to 20 points or more, depending on the size of the illustration) and blend as described in the preceding paragraphs.

Designing neon effects

To create neon effects with stroke blends, you need to create two distinct parts. Part one is the neon tubing, which by itself is nice, but it doesn't really have a neon effect. The second part is the tubing's reflection off the background, which usually appears as a glowing area. These two separate blends give the illusion of lit neon.

Note   Neon effects work much better when the background is very dark, though some interesting effects can be achieved with light backgrounds.

Basically, creating a neon effect simply requires that you make two copies of the blended object. The copy in front requires a blend where the top object has a smaller stroke weight and a brighter color to emulate the glow of a neon tube. The copy in the rear uses a wider stroke that blends to the darker color of the background. Figure 12-25 shows an example of the neon effect.

Figure 12-25: Neon candles are a good example of how you can use two blends to create an interesting effect.

Tip   Try crossing paths with neon, or for an even more realistic look, create "unlit" portions of neon by using darker shading with no reflective glow.

Another interesting effect that you can create that is similar to the neon effect is a backlighting effect. You can accomplish backlighting effects by creating a glow for an object and then placing that same object on top of the glow. By making the topmost object filled with black or another dark color, a backlit effect is produced.

Using Compound Paths

Compound paths are one of the least understood areas of Illustrator, but after you understand a few simple guidelines and rules, manipulating and using them correctly is simple.

Compound paths are paths made up of two or more open or closed paths. Where the paths cross with fills is a transparent hole. You can specify which paths create the holes by changing the direction of the paths via the reverse path direction option in the Attributes palette. The general rule is that paths traveling in the opposite direction of any adjoining paths form holes.

Creating compound paths

You can create compound paths of all sorts by following the steps described here. Make sure that none of the paths are currently compound paths or grouped paths before creating a new compound path, and then follow these steps:

1. **Create all the paths that you need for the compound path, including the outside path and the holes.**

2. **Select all the paths, and choose Object ➪ Compound Path ➪ Make or press Ctrl+8 (⌘+8).** Illustrator now treats the paths as one path. When you click one of the paths with the Selection tool, the other paths in the compound path are selected as well. Fill the object with any fill.

3. **Place the compound path over any other object.** (I used a placed EPS image for this example.) The inner paths act as holes that enable you to see the object underneath. Figure 12-26 shows a before and after example of creating a compound path.

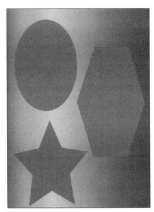

Figure 12-26: The left side shows the paths before being combined; the right side shows how the inner paths become holes in a compound path.

You can select individual paths by clicking them once with the Group Selection tool. As always, you can select points and segments within each path by using the Direct Selection tool. Clicking only once with the Group Selection tool on paths that you want to select is important. Clicking those paths more than once with the Group Selection tool selects all the other paths in the compound path. To click (for moving or copying purposes) the selected individual paths after the Group Selection tool has clicked them once, click them with the Direct Selection tool.

Note   Paths belonging to different groups cannot be made into a compound path unless all paths in all the groups are selected.

Here are some things you need to understand about compound paths:

✦ When you create a compound path, it takes on the Paint Style attributes of the bottommost path of all the paths that were selected and have become part of that compound path.

✦ You can create a compound path that is only one path, though there are few reasons to do so.

✦ If the singular compound path is selected as part of a larger compound path (with either the Direct Selection tool or Group Selection tool), the path directions may be altered.

✦ If you aren't sure whether an individual path is a compound path, check the Release option in the Object ➪ Compound Path submenu. If the Release option is available, then it is a compound path, if not, then it isn't a compound path.

Compound paths do not work in a hierarchical process as groups do. If a path is part of a compound path, it is part of that compound path only. If a compound path becomes part of another compound path, the paths in the original compound path are compounded only with the new compound path.

Releasing compound paths

When you want to release a compound path, select the path and choose Object ➪ Compound Path ➪ Release or press Shift+Ctrl+Alt+8 (Shift+⌘+Option+8). The path changes into regular paths.

If any of the paths appear as holes, they are instead filled with the fill of the rest of the compound path. The results may be a little confusing because these holes then seem to blend right in to the outer shape of the compound paths.

If the compound path that you are releasing contains other compound paths, they are released as well because Illustrator doesn't recognize compound paths that are within other compound paths.

Blending between Multiple-Path Compound Paths

You can blend between multiple-path compound paths.

1. Select the Blend tool, and click from one compound shape to the other shape.

2. While the initial blend between the two objects is still selected, double-click the Blend tool in the toolbox to open the Blend Options dialog box.

3. Select the Spacing drop-down list (pop-up menu), choose Specified Step, and enter a number. Remember that the larger the number you enter, the smoother the blend is.

4. Select Preview to see the results before you close the dialog box.

For really cool results, make sure the two objects are different colors. For smoothest blends, make sure that you don't have a stroke color applied to your shapes.

Understanding holes

Holes for donuts, Life Savers, and rings are quite simple to create. Just select two circles, one smaller than and totally within a larger circle, and choose Compound Path ➪ Make or press Ctrl+8 (⌘+8). The inside circle is then a hole.

A compound path considers every path within it to lie along the borders of the compound path. Path edges within an object appear to you to be on the inside of an object, but they appear to Illustrator to be just another edge of the path.

With this concept in mind, you can create a compound path that has several holes, such as a slice of Swiss cheese or a snowflake. Just create the outermost paths and the paths that you want to make holes, select all the paths, and then select Object ➪ Compound Path ➪ Make.

Tip You aren't limited to one set of holes. You can create a compound path with a hole that has an object inside it with a hole. In that hole can be an object with a hole, and so on.

Overlapping holes

Holes, if they really are paths that are supposed to be empty areas of an object, should not overlap. If anything, you can combine multiple holes that are overlapping into one larger hole, possibly by using Add to Shape Area in the Pathfinder palette.

If holes within a compound path do overlap, the result is a solid area with the same fill color as the rest of the object. If multiple holes overlap, the results can be quite unusual, as shown in Figure 12-27. (See "Reversing path directions," later in this chapter, to read more about multiple overlapping holes.)

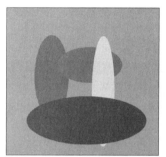 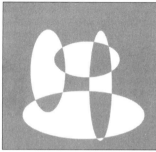

Figure 12-27: This figure shows overlapping holes before being made into compound paths (left) and after (right).

In most cases, you get the desired results with holes only if the outermost path contains all the holes. As a rule, Illustrator uses the topmost objects to "poke" holes out of the bottom-most objects. If you want holes to overlap, make sure that the holes are above the outside border.

Creating compound paths from separate sets of paths

Compound paths are very flexible. You can choose two sets of paths, each with an outline and a hole, and make them into one compound path. This technique is especially useful for making masks, but you also can use it to alleviate the repetition of creating several compound paths and selecting one of them at a time.

For example, if you have two shapes, a square and a circle, and want a round hole in each of them, you draw two smaller circles and put them into place. After you position the two shapes in the correct locations, you select them and the round paths inside each of them, and then you choose Object ➪ Compound Path ➪ Make or press Ctrl+8 (⌘+8). Each of the objects now has a hole, and they act as if they are grouped, as indicated in Figure 12-28. If you don't see a hole in each of the two objects, try again, but make certain that the small circles are above the other objects in the front-to-back order.

Figure 12-28: Compound paths can include separate shapes with holes.

To move separate objects that are part of the same compound path, select each object with the Group Selection tool, which selects an entire path at a time, and then move them. Remember that after they're selected, you should use the Direct Selection tool to move the selected portions of a compound path.

Working with type and compound paths

You have been using compound paths as long as you have been using computer PostScript typefaces. All PostScript typefaces are made of characters that are compound paths. Letters that have holes, such as uppercase B, D, and P and lowercase a, b, and d, benefit from being compound paths. When you place them in front of other objects, you can see through the empty areas to objects behind them that are visible in those holes.

Each character in a PostScript typeface is a compound path. When you convert characters to editable outlines in Illustrator, each character is still a compound path. If you release the compound paths, the characters with empty areas appear to fill with the same color as the rest of the character, as shown in Figure 12-29, because the holes are no longer knocked out of the letters.

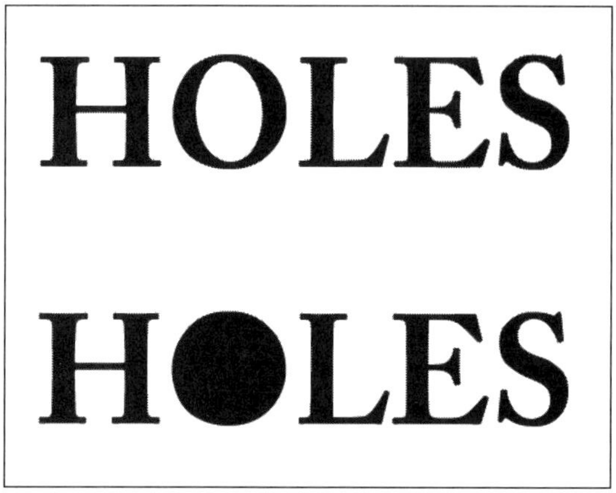

HOLES
H●LES

Figure 12-29: Type as it normally appears after you convert it to outlines (top) and after you release compound paths (bottom)

Note   Many times, type is used as a mask, but all the letters used in the mask need to be one compound path. Simply select all the letters, and choose Object ➪ Compound Path ➪ Make or press Ctrl+8 (⌘+8). This action creates a compound path in which all the letters form the compound path. Usually, all the holes stay the same as they were as separate compound paths (unless there is overlap between the objects).

Any letters that overlap in a word that you make into a compound path can change path directions and thus affect the "emptiness" of some paths. If letters have to overlap, use the Pathfinder Add feature on them first and then select all the letters and choose Object ➪ Compound Path ➪ Make or press Ctrl+8 (⌘+8).

Finding Path Directions

Each path in Illustrator has a direction. For paths that you draw with the Pen or Pencil tool, the direction of the path is the direction in which you draw the path. When Illustrator creates an ellipse or a rectangle, the direction of the path is clockwise.

If you're curious about which way a path travels, click any spot of the path with the Scissors tool and then choose Filter ➪ Stylize ➪ Add Arrowheads under the first sub-menu for Stylize. In the Add Arrowheads dialog box, make sure that the End button area only is selected and click OK. An arrowhead appears, going in the direction of the path. Figure 12-30 shows several paths and arrowheads appearing for each path.

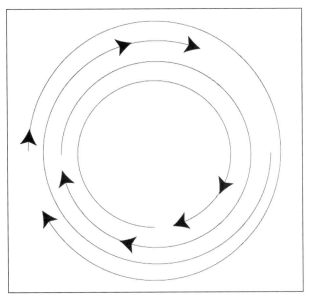

Figure 12-30: The arrows represent the direction of the paths.

Paths have directions for one purpose (one purpose that you need to know about, anyway), and that is to determine what the solid areas of a compound path and the empty areas become. The individual paths in a compound path that create holes from solid paths go in opposite directions.

If two smaller circles are inside a larger circle, they still punch holes in the larger circle because both of them are traveling in the same direction. But what happens when the two inside circles overlap? The area where they overlap is inside the empty area, but both holes go in the same direction. The intersection of the two holes is solid because of the winding path rule (see the next section for an explanation of winding).

Figuring out which way to go

Understanding the Winding Numbers Rule is helpful when you are dealing with compound paths. The Winding Numbers Rule counts surrounded areas, starting with 0 (outside the outermost edge) and working its way in. Any area with an odd number is filled, and any area with an even number (such as 0, the outside of the path) is empty, or a hole.

You can apply this rule to most compound paths — although taking the time to diagram the paths you've drawn and place little numbers in them to figure out what is going to be filled and what isn't is usually more time-consuming than doing it wrong, undoing it, and doing it right.

Reversing path directions

To change the direction of a path, select just the path using the Group Selection tool and choose Window ➪ Attributes. In the Attributes palette box, shown in Figure 12-31, click the other (not darkened) direction button.

Reverse Path Direction On   Use Non-Zero Winding Fill Rule

Reverse Path Direction Off   Use Even-Odd Fill Rule

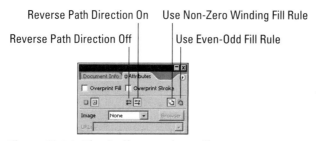

Figure 12-31: The Attributes palette allows you to control the path directions and fill rules.

When you change paths into compound paths, their direction may change. One element that is consistent when dealing with path directions is that holes must travel in the opposite direction from the outside path. As a result, if the Reverse Path Direction button is on for the holes, it is not on for the outside path. That scenario is the normal one when you create compound paths with holes. You can, if you so desire, check the Reverse Path Direction button for the outside path and uncheck it for the inside paths. The resulting image has the same holes as produced by the reversing of the path. Figure 12-32 shows a compound path and its path directions before and after some of the paths were reversed.

Caution

Never attempt to change path direction when all paths of a compound path are selected. Clicking once on either button makes all the paths in the compound path go in the same direction at this point, which means that no holes appear.

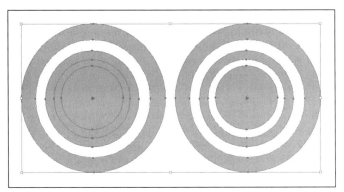

Figure 12-32: Reversing the direction of the paths in the illustration on the left fills those holes, as shown in the illustration on the right.

Faking a compound path

At times, using a compound path just doesn't work. You may need to cheat a little. Except in the most extreme circumstances, you can fake compound paths, but you need to make quite an effort.

If the background is part of a gradient, select the hole and the object that is painted with the gradient, apply the gradient, and use the Gradient tool to make the gradient spread across both objects in exactly the same way. This trick can fool even the experts.

Tip   One way to fake a compound path is by selecting the background, making a copy of it, making the hole a mask of the background area, and grouping the mask to the copy of the background.

Using Clipping Masks

In Illustrator, you use clipping masks to mask out parts of underlying objects that you don't want to see. The path that you draw in Illustrator defines the shape of the mask. Anything outside the mask is hidden from view in Preview mode and does not print.

Clipping Masks are objects that mask out everything but the paths made up by the mask, as shown in Figure 12-33. Clipping Masks can be open, closed, or compound paths. The masking object is the object whose paths make up the mask, and this object must be in front of all the objects that are being masked.

Figure 12-33: This shows an object, its mask, and the resulting masked object.

You can make clipping masks from any path, including compound paths and text. You can use masks to view portions of multiple objects, individual objects, and placed images.

Creating masks

To create a mask, the masking object (the path that is in the shape of the mask) has to be in front of the objects that you want it to mask. You select the masking object and the objects that you want to mask. Then you choose Object ➪ Clipping Mask ➪ Make or press Ctrl+7 (⌘+7). In Preview mode, any areas of the objects that were outside the mask vanish, but the parts of the objects that are inside the mask remain the same. Figure 12-34 shows an illustration with masks and without them.

Tip   Masks are much easier to use and understand in Preview mode than in Outline mode.

If you want to mask an object that is not currently being masked, you need to select the new object and all the objects in the mask, including the masking object. You then choose Object ➪ Clipping Mask ➪ Make or press Ctrl+7 (⌘+7). The mask then applies to the new object as well as to the objects that were previously masked. The new object, like all others being masked, must be behind the masking object.

Figure 12-34: The image on the left uses masks to hide portions of objects. The image on the right is the result of releasing those masks.

Like compound paths, masking does not work in hierarchical levels. Each time you add an object to a mask, the old mask that didn't have that object is released, and a new mask is made that contains all the original mask objects as well as the new object. Releasing a mask affects every object in the mask, as described in "Releasing masks," later in this chapter.

Tip   Grouping all the objects in a mask is usually a good idea, but group them only after you have created the mask. Having the objects grouped facilitates moving the mask and its objects and selecting them when you want to add other objects to the mask.

Masking raster images

There are two different ways to mask raster images. You accomplish the first method in Photoshop by creating a clipping path and saving it as an EPS image. For the second method, you use a clipping mask in Illustrator.

Each of the two methods has its strengths and weaknesses. The best solution is a combination of both methods. The main advantage to creating a clipping path in Photoshop is that you can adjust the path while viewing the image clearly at 16:1. (Viewing an image at 1600 percent in Illustrator displays chunky, unrecognizable blocks of color.) In this manner, you can precisely position the path over the correct pixels so that the right pixels are selected for masking. A disadvantage to using a clipping path is that compound paths in Photoshop adhere to one of two different fill rules, which control the way holes appear for differing path directions. Illustrator is much more flexible in this respect because you are able to change the path direction of each individual path with the Reverse Path Direction option in the Attributes palette.

Using a mask with other masks

You can mask objects that are masking other objects. Just make sure that you select all the objects in each mask and that, as with other objects, they are behind the path that you want to use for a masking object.

Note   You can apply a stroke or fill to a masking object. A fill and stroke of None replace any Paint Style attributes that you applied to the object prior to transforming it into a mask. But if you select the object after it is a mask, you can apply a stroke or fill to that mask. If you release the mask, the path that was the masking object continues to have a fill and stroke of None.

Releasing masks

To release a mask, first select the masking object (you may select other objects as well). Then choose Object ➪ Clipping Mask ➪ Release or press Ctrl+Alt+7 (⌘+Option+7), and the masking object no longer is a mask.

If you aren't sure which object is the masking object or if you are having trouble selecting the masking object, choose Select ➪ Select All or press Ctrl+A (⌘+A), and then choose Object ➪ Clipping Mask ➪ Release or press Ctrl+Alt+7 (⌘+Option+7). Of course, this action releases any other masks that are in the document — unless they were separate masks that were being masked by other masks.

To release all the masks in the document, even those masks that are being masked by other masks, choose Select All or press Ctrl+A (⌘+A) and choose Release Mask repeatedly. Usually repeating Release Masks three times gets everything, unless you went mask-happy in that particular document. You can also use the Select ➪ Clipping Masks option to check if any masks remain. If the Release menu option is enabled, then a mask still remains.

Masking and printing

As a rule, PostScript printers don't care too much for masks. They care even less for masks that mask other masks. And they really don't like masks that are compound paths.

Unfortunately, because of the way that Illustrator works, every part of every object in a mask is sent to the printer, even if you only use a tiny piece of an object. In addition, controlling where the masking object slices objects requires a great deal of computing power and memory. You can have a problem, for example, when you have more stuff to mask than the printer can handle.

More important than any other issue involved with masks and printing is the length and complexity of the masking path.

The more objects in a mask, the more complex it is. More anchor points and direction points coming off those anchor points add more complexity to the document. In other words, your printer enjoys a mask only if the masking object is a rectangle and you are not masking other objects.

Masking and compound paths

Creating masks from compound paths is especially useful when you are working with text and want several separate letters to mask a placed EPS image or a series of pictures that you created in Illustrator.

The reason that you need to transform separate objects into compound paths is that a masking object can be only one path. The topmost object of the selected objects becomes the masking object, and the others become objects within the mask. Creating a compound path from several paths makes the masking feature treat all the objects as one path and makes a masking object out of the entire compound path.

You can use compound paths for masking when you are working with objects that need to have holes as well as when you are working with text and other separate objects. Figure 12-35 was created by making one compound path from all the parts of the window frame and using that compound path as a mask.

Figure 12-35: Creating a compound path out of all the parts of the window frame made this window frame a clipping mask for the background.

Summary

Path blends, compound paths, and masks enable you to create some really fancy effects in your Illustrator documents. In this chapter, you learned the following important information about these topics:

✦ Using blends rather than gradients can produce some pretty cool realistic results.

✦ With Blend options, you can change the blend to steps, distance, or smooth color.

✦ You can blend from 3D objects to Symbols and use different objects.

✦ Compound paths are one or more paths that Illustrator treats as a single path.

✦ Compound paths give you the ability to put holes in your paths.

✦ Changing the direction of a path via the Attributes palette can change the holes in the compound path.

✦ Each character of type converted to outlines consists of a compound path.

✦ Masks are paths that overlay other Illustrator objects, showing the objects only through the masking path.

✦ When using text outlines as a mask, make sure that all the paths making up the text outlines are joined into a single compound path.

✦ ✦ ✦

Using Live Trace

In This Chapter

Understanding Live Trace

Learning Live Trace modes

Setting Live Trace options

Tracing with Live Trace

In this chapter, I introduce the new Live Trace tool that is included in Illustrator CS2. Live Trace takes the art of using bitmap images as the basis for Illustrator documents to a whole new and exciting level. You can use this tool to create vector-based graphics from raster images, but that description hardly even hints at the possibilities that Live Trace opens up for you.

Understanding Live Trace

As you are aware by now, Illustrator is primarily a vector-based graphics application. Quite simply put, Illustrator is able to handle vector images with far more adeptness than it can raster (or bitmap) images. To people, however, the format of an image is far less important than how that image appears. Sometimes, only a bitmap will do the job. For example, digital photos are always bitmap images — never vector images. If you need to use a digital photo in your Illustrator document, you have to import it as a bitmap.

Even though you have to import digital photos as bitmap images, you may not have to leave them in that format inside of Illustrator. There are many instances where a vector-based representation of the photo is just what you need. Consider the example shown in Figure 13-1. The image on the left is a digital photo and to the right is the result of using the Live Trace tool to convert the image into a drawing that looks like a hand-drawn sketch. If you're creating an image to use for a logo for a Web site advertising a pet-sitting business, the hand-drawn sketch appearance may well serve your needs better than the digital photo.

Figure 13-1: The left image is the raw imported bitmap, and the right image was traced using the Live Trace tool to produce a hand-drawn sketch appearance.

Previous editions of Illustrator have also been able to use imported bitmap images, and the Auto Trace tool did provide a method of converting those images into vector-based artwork. But the differences between the old Auto Trace tool and the new Live Trace tool are quite astounding. Simply put, just about the only thing the two share is the word "trace" in their names — Live Trace is that much better!

So just what does Live Trace do? Basically, Live Trace uses color or contrast information in an imported bitmap to create path and anchor points so that the bitmap image can be converted into a vector-based image. The tool uses the parameters that you set in the Tracing Options dialog box to determine how closely the vector image matches the bitmap image. Using various presets and options that are available in the dialog box, you can create a result that looks virtually identical to the bitmap, or you can go to the other extreme of having a result that contains only a few strokes that look like a very basic sketch with almost no detail. The important point to remember is that the Live Trace tool is extremely versatile, so you need to spend a little time trying out various options in order to achieve the final results you want.

Learning Live Trace Modes

Live Trace has three different tracing modes. These modes create very different end results, so a good place to start in understanding how Live Trace functions is to examine each of the three tracing modes.

You choose the tracing mode using the choices in the Vector drop-down list (pop-up menu) in the Tracing Options dialog box as shown in Figure 13-2. Use the Object ➪ Live Trace ➪ Tracing Options command to display the Tracing Options dialog box.

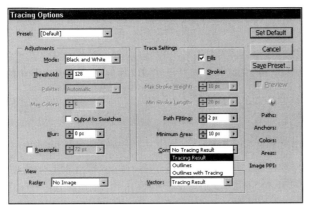

Figure 13-2: Choose the tracing mode from the Vector list in the Tracing Options dialog box.

Getting to know outline mode

In outline mode, the Live Trace tool creates strokes that outline any shapes in the bitmap image that seem to be a single fill area. Figure 13-3 shows an example of using the outline mode to trace a bitmap image.

Figure 13-3: This shows how the Live Trace tool traces an image in outline mode.

Tip Outline mode is also called fill mode because it outlines the fills in the image.

As Figure 13-3 shows, outline mode creates an image lacking any fills. You can, of course, add a fill yourself to any area later, but this mode is probably most appropriate for images where you want to produce a pen-and-ink style of drawing.

Using tracing result mode

In tracing result mode, the Live Trace tool creates stroked paths of variable widths as shown in Figure 13-4. In these examples, I selected the Color 6 preset to make it easier to see the differences between the tracing modes. The end result is an image that has fills without outlining strokes.

Figure 13-4: This shows how the Live Trace tool traces an image in tracing result mode.

Tip Tracing result mode is sometimes called stroke mode because it fills the strokes that are traced in the image.

The image in Figure 13-4 shows just one possible result you might see when using tracing result mode.

Combining outline and tracing result modes

If you choose the Outlines with Tracing option in the Vector drop-down list (pop-up menu), Illustrator combines outline mode and tracing result mode as shown in Figure 13-5.

Figure 13-5: This shows how the Live Trace tool traces an image combining outline mode and tracing result mode.

Tip   When a traced image is selected, you can use the Preview different views of the vector result button on the Control palette to see each of the different tracing modes. Likewise, you can use the Preview Different Views of the Raster Image button to see different views of the bitmap image under the tracing result.

Although you can do lots with just changing the tracing mode, that's only the tip of the iceberg. In the following sections, I cover how to use the other options in the Tracing Options dialog box to create exactly the effect you want.

Setting Live Trace Options

If you were to simply use the Object ➪ Live Trace ➪ Make command or click the Live Trace button on the Control palette without exploring the Live Trace options, you probably wouldn't gain much respect for the Live Trace tool. This tool is likely the most customizable tool contained in Illustrator. In fact, I can't even show you more than a very small sampling of the possibilities because it has so many options.

Understanding the Live Trace presets

Probably the best place to begin experimenting with the Live Trace options is by choosing one of the settings in the Preset drop-down list (pop-up menu) in the Tracing Options dialog box. After you have selected a preset that produces results close to your desired end result, you can play around with the remaining options in the dialog box to fine-tune the output.

Tip   Always make sure that you select the Preview check box in the Tracing Options dialog box. That way, you can see the effect of any selections you make immediately.

Figure 13-6 shows an example of the default preset option. In this case, the output is a black and white image with no shading.

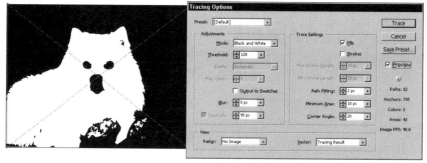

Figure 13-6: Using the default tracing preset produces a black and white image like this.

The next preset is the Color 6 preset shown in Figure 13-7. In this preset, the vector image has six colors.

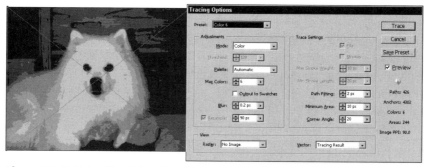

Figure 13-7: Using the Color 6 tracing preset produces a color image using six colors.

Figure 13-8 shows an example of the Color 16 preset. Although the appearance is similar to the Color 6 preset, Color 16 uses 16 shades for a more realistic appearance.

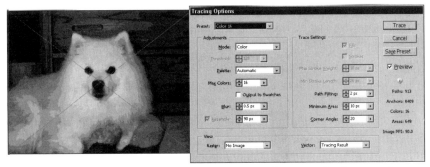

Figure 13-8: Using the Color 16 tracing preset produces a color image using 16 colors and more subtle shading.

Figure 13-9 shows an example of the Photo Low Fidelity preset. It can be a bit difficult to see the differences between Color 16 and Photo Low Fidelity, but Photo Low Fidelity tends to have fewer paths and anchor points than Color 16.

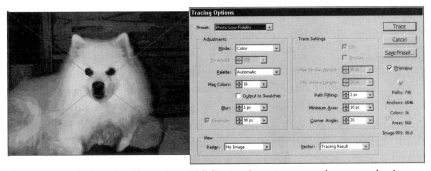

Figure 13-9: Using the Photo Low Fidelity tracing preset produces a color image using 16 colors but with a slightly different appearance than the Color 16 preset.

The Photo High Fidelity preset shown in Figure 13-10 produces a very realistic looking image. In this preset, 64 colors are used and the result looks very much like the original raster image.

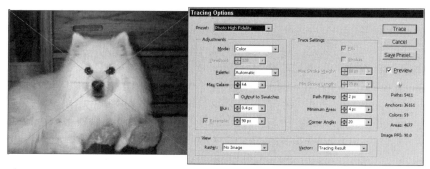

Figure 13-10: Using the Photo High Fidelity tracing preset produces a color image using 64 colors for an almost photographic appearance.

The Grayscale preset shown in Figure 13-11 produces a result similar to the Color 6 preset, but with all the colors replaced by shades of gray.

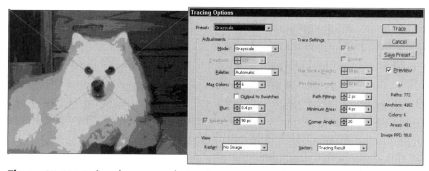

Figure 13-11: Using the Grayscale tracing preset produces a grayscale image using six shades of gray.

Believe it or not, the example shown in Figure 13-12 is the same image used in the previous examples. The only difference was the selection of the Hand Drawn Sketch preset. Obviously, this preset would work better with other raster images, but comparing the results for the same image throughout is interesting.

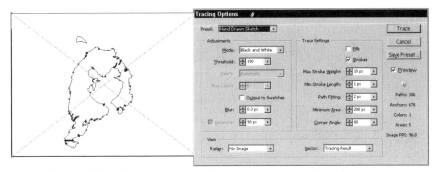

Figure 13-12: Using the Hand Drawn Sketch tracing preset produces a very different result with the sample image.

Figure 13-13 shows how the Detailed Illustration preset renders the image. In this case, the result is similar to the default preset.

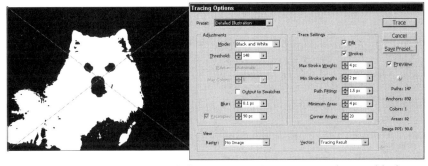

Figure 13-13: Using the Detailed Illustration tracing preset produces a black and white image.

Figure 13-14 shows an example of the Comic Art preset. Again, this preset is probably best suited to images other than the example we're using, such as ones with a lot of contrasting colors.

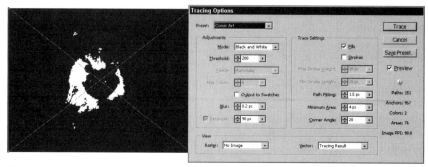

Figure 13-14: Using the Comic Art tracing preset produces a black and white image that can be very difficult to make out.

Figure 13-15 shows the image traced using the Technical Drawing preset. In this case, it's fairly easy to determine the image subject even if the results seem a little stark.

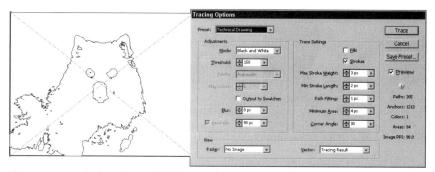

Figure 13-15: Using the Technical Drawing preset produces a black and white line drawing.

The Black and White Logo preset shown in Figure 13-16 is somewhat similar to the default and the Detailed Illustration presets, but for this image the results seem a bit more pleasing.

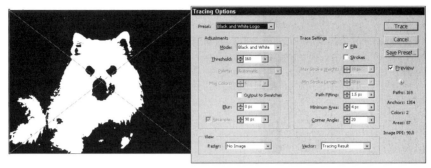

Figure 13-16: Using the Black and White Logo preset produces a black and white image that is fairly striking.

Figure 13-17 shows the Inked Drawing preset. Although the results are similar to the Black and White Logo preset results, this preset has a very different overall effect.

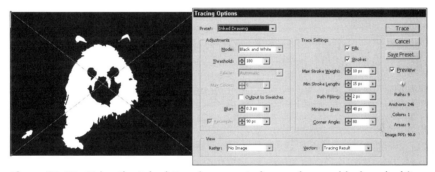

Figure 13-17: Using the Inked Drawing preset also produces a black and white image but with some interesting differences.

The final preset, Type, is shown in Figure 13-18. Again, the preset options produce a black and white image, but the end result shows more detail from the original raster image.

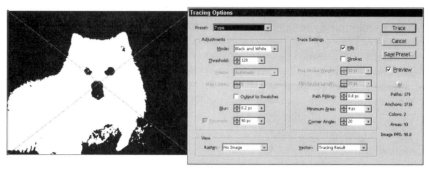

Figure 13-18: Using the Type preset also produces a black and white image, but with more detail than some of the other black and white presets.

Choosing custom Live Trace options

After you have selected a preset that gets you at least close to your desired result, you likely want to experiment with the other options in the Tracing Options dialog box. In doing so, you have the opportunity to fine-tune the appearance of the vector output.

These are the available options:

✦ **Mode:** This option enables you to choose Color, Grayscale, or Black and White for the format of the vector image.

✦ **Threshold:** This option allows you to choose the threshold between black and white (only for Black and White images).

✦ **Palette:** This option allows you to choose a custom library for color selection for Color and Grayscale images. The only choice here is Automatic unless you have loaded a custom library.

✦ **Max Colors:** Use this option to specify the number of colors to use (between 2 and 256) for Color and Grayscale images.

✦ **Output to Swatches:** Select this option to output the colors used to the Swatches palette.

✦ **Blur:** Use this to specify the size of the Blur filter to apply during raster image processing to remove small jagged edges.

✦ **Resample:** This option allows you to specify the sampling resolution to use on the raster image. You may want to choose a lower resolution to reduce the size of the document.

✦ **Tracing Fills/Strokes:** This option enables you to select the desired Trace mode.

✦ **Max Stroke Weight:** Use this to specify the maximum weight of a stroke that will convert into a stroked path.

✦ **Min Stroke Length:** Use this to specify the minimum length of a stroke that will convert into a stroked path.

✦ **Path Fitting:** Use this to control how closely paths should be traced.

✦ **Minimum Area:** This option enables you to specify the area (in pixels squared) that will be rejected during trace. Use this setting to reduce the complexity of the resulting vector image.

✦ **Corner Angle:** Use this to specify the sharpness of a turn in the raster image that will be turned into a corner in the vector image.

It's probably best to experiment with small changes in a single option at a time to narrow in on your desired results. As long as the Preview check box is selected, Illustrator redraws the vector image after each change you make. If you find that it takes too long to generate the previews, you can work with preview off, but doing so makes it more difficult to fine-tune the results.

Tracing Raster Images with Live Trace

Aside from choosing the set of options that will best suit your particular needs, actually using the Live Trace tool is quite simple. Follow these steps to trace a raster image using the Live Trace tool:

1. **Choose the File ➪ Place command to display the Place dialog box, as shown in Figure 13-19.**

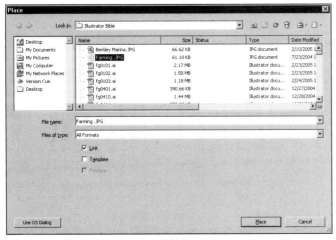

Figure 13-19: Open the Place dialog box to select a bitmap image to place into your document.

2. **Select the bitmap image that you want to trace.**

3. **Click the Place button to close the dialog box and return to your document.**

4. **Make sure that the newly placed image is selected.** If the image is not selected, click it with the Selection tool.

5. **Choose the Object ⇨ Live Trace ⇨ Tracing options command to display the Tracing Options dialog box.**

6. **Choose a preset from the Preset drop-down list (pop-up menu).**

7. **Click the Preview check box to preview the tracing.**

8. **Choose any options that you want in the Tracing Options dialog box.**

9. **Click the Trace button to close the Tracing Options dialog box and return to your document.**

You can also click the Tracing Presets and Options button on the Control palette and select a preset or the Tracing Options command from the drop-down list (pop-up menu). Then click the Live Trace button on the Control palette to trace the image.

Tip   Instead of using the spin controls to change the settings for one of the Live Trace options, click the existing value and enter the new value using your keyboard. This is especially important when the Preview option is selected or when you are entering values using the Control palette because Illustrator redraws the tracing whenever there is a value change.

After an image has been traced, you can modify the image in several ways. As explained in Chapter 14, you can use the Live Paint tool to change the colors in the image. Even if you traced the image in black and white, you can still colorize it. Another way to modify the traced image is to choose the Object ⇨ Expand command (or click the Expand button on the Control palette). If you expand the traced image, it becomes an ordinary Illustrator object and is no longer live. This means that you can't make any additional changes using the Live Trace tool, but you can use the other drawing tools to modify the image.

Summary

The Live Trace tool is one of the most important new features in Illustrator CS2. In this chapter, you learned how to use the Live Trace tool. Here are some important things you learned:

✦ The Live Trace tool replaces the Auto Trace tool that existed in previous versions of Illustrator.

✦ Live Trace has three modes for tracing raster images.

✦ Live Trace has a number of presets that you can use to quickly trace raster images.

✦ The Tracing Options dialog box offers an almost unlimited range of tracing options.

✦ You can use the Control palette to choose different views of both the original raster image and the traced vector image.

✦ Traced images can be converted into ordinary Illustrator objects using the Object ➪ Expand command.

✦   ✦   ✦

Using Live Paint

Adobe didn't stop with replacing the Auto Trace tool with the Live Trace tool. Illustrator CS2 also has a new "live" tool that you can use to fill paths — the Live Paint Bucket tool. This tool replaces the Paint Bucket tool of previous Illustrator versions with an improved tool that automatically detects regions of intersecting paths and fills them accordingly. This chapter introduces you to the new Live Paint Bucket tool.

Understanding Live Paint

Bitmap image-editing and creation programs have long had a fun yet often frustrating tool that is typically called a Paint Bucket tool. With just a click of the Paint Bucket tool, you can fill an enclosed area with a solid color. The Paint Bucket tool icon is always some variation on paint spilling out of a paint can, which seems like a very good icon for something that can be so hard to control. A single missing pixel around the perimeter of the area that you want to fill provides an escape route so that the fill spills out into areas you don't intend to paint. It's almost like trying to paint a room when a nosy cat is prowling around just waiting for a chance to cause some mischief.

When vector-based graphics applications like Illustrator took on the paint bucket metaphor, things were considerably different than they had been in the bitmap world. For one thing, in a vector-based application, objects are typically treated as a unit. If you want to change the fill color of an object, you typically don't have to worry about the dreaded missing pixel paint spill because each object is independent.

So, at this point you're probably wondering how the Live Paint Bucket tool improves on the Paint Bucket tool in previous versions of Illustrator. The new tool is better in a couple of subtle but very helpful ways. First, with the Live Paint Bucket tool, it's much easier to modify specific areas of an

In This Chapter

Understanding Live Paint

Setting the Live Paint options

Using Live Paint

object such as an image you traced with the Live Trace tool. That's because the Live Paint Bucket tool automatically detects the various independent regions as you move the tool over the object. As it detects each region, the Live Paint Bucket tool highlights the detected region, as shown in Figure 14-1. In this image I used the Live Trace tool to trace an old greeting card that I scanned. The highlighted areas are surrounded with a bright contrast to show the detected regions.

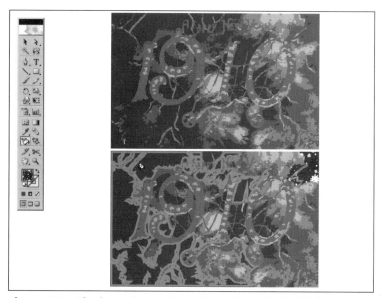

Figure 14-1: The lower image shows how Live Paint highlights a region as it is detected.

The Live Paint Bucket tool enables you to easily fill individual regions within an object rather than the object as a whole. Also, because the paint remains live, any changes you make to the regions are also reflected in the paint fill.

Note   Clicking a Live Trace object with the Live Paint Bucket tool converts the object into a Live Paint object. This precludes making additional changes to the object using Live Trace, so it's important to complete all your Live Trace adjustments before you use the Live Paint Bucket tool.

In addition to the Live Paint Bucket tool, Illustrator CS2 adds the Live Paint Selection tool. This tool allows you to select Live Paint regions without making any changes to those regions. In effect, the Live Paint Selection tool could be called the selection-only portion of the Live Paint Bucket tool. Using the Live Paint Selection tool, you can select more than one Live Paint region at a time, as shown in Figure 14-2 (the selected regions are filled with a dotted pattern to show that they are selected). The highlighted area under the mouse pointer indicates the current region that will be added to the selection.

Figure 14-2: The Live Paint Selection tool allows you to select regions without immediately modifying them.

Tip Clicking a Live Paint object with the Live Paint Selection tool makes it easier to preview the areas that the Live Paint Bucket tool will modify without actually making those changes.

Setting the Live Paint Options

You probably want to become familiar with the options that are available for controlling how the Live Paint Bucket tool works before you use the tool. It has only a few options, but they can have quite an effect on how well the tool meets your expectations.

The first set of Live Paint Bucket tool options are contained in the Live Paint Bucket Options dialog box shown in Figure 14-3. You display this dialog box by double-clicking the Live Paint Bucket tool in the toolbox.

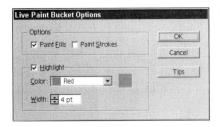

Figure 14-3: The Live Paint Bucket Options dialog box allows you to select basic settings for the Live Paint Bucket tool.

These settings are available:

✦ **Paint Fills:** When selected, this option enables the Live Paint Bucket tool to add the current fill color or pattern to the fill of a region you click.

✦ **Paint Strokes:** When selected, this option enables the Live Paint Bucket tool to add the current stroke color to the stroke of a region you click.

✦ **Highlight:** When selected, this option outlines the region that is automatically detected as you move the mouse pointer over a Live Paint object.

✦ **Color:** This option enables you to choose the color of the outline.

✦ **Width:** You use this option to set the width of the outline that the Live Paint Bucket tool draws around the region.

By default, the Paint Fills option is selected and the Paint Strokes option is deselected. Selecting both options and using a contrasting color for the stroke color can produce some interesting effects.

In addition to the options shown in the Live Paint Bucket Options dialog box, you can also control how the Live Paint Bucket tool responds to gaps. You set the gap options in the Gap Options dialog box shown in Figure 14-4. Choose the Object ⇨ Live Paint ⇨ Gap Options command to display this dialog box.

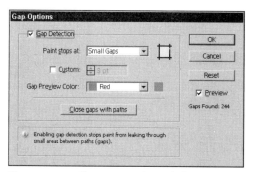

Figure 14-4: The Gap Options dialog box allows you to select settings for how the Live Paint Bucket tool deals with gaps in objects.

These gap options settings are available:

✦ **Gap Detection:** Select this check box to turn on gap detection. This option is off by default.

✦ **Paint stops at:** Choose Small Gaps, Medium Gaps, or Large Gaps from this list box. Illustrator finds fewer gaps when you choose a larger setting.

✦ **Custom:** Select this check box if you want to specify the size of the gap rather than using one of the preset options. If you select this option, use the text box to specify the size of gap you want to detect.

✦ **Gap Preview Color:** Choose a contrasting color to make the detected gaps stand out from your artwork.

✦ **Close gaps with paths:** Click this button to remove the gaps by inserting paths in place of the gaps.

Depending on the result that you are attempting to produce, you likely will find that using gap detection improves the smoothness of the Live Paint Bucket tool's results. With fewer gaps to contend with, the Live Paint Bucket tool generally finds simpler paths than it would in a drawing with many gaps.

Using Live Paint

You can use the Live Paint Bucket tool to fill objects that you have drawn, or you can use it to fill images that you created using the Live Trace tool. Either way, you begin by creating a Live Paint group so that Illustrator knows which objects you want to modify.

To create a Live Paint group, you use the Selection tool to select the object (or objects) that you want to include in the group. Then you click the selected object using the Live Paint Bucket tool. After an object is a part of a Live Paint group, Illustrator displays outlines around the detected regions as you move the Live Paint Bucket tool over the group. Figure 14-5 shows how the image appears as a region is highlighted.

Figure 14-5: The detected region under the Live Paint Bucket tool is highlighted to indicate the region that will be filled.

Figure 14-6 shows the result of clicking in the detected region with the Live Paint Bucket tool. In this example, I've moved the Live Paint Bucket tool out of the region and back into it to make the highlight reappear.

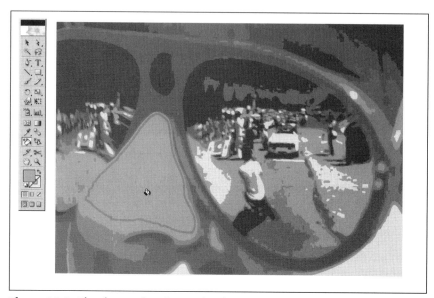

Figure 14-6: The detected region under the Live Paint Bucket tool is filled using the currently selected fill color.

If the Paint Strokes check box is selected in the Live Paint Bucket Options dialog box, the Live Paint Bucket tool's icon changes as shown in Figure 14-7 when the tool is over a stroke. Clicking the Live Paint Bucket tool over a stroke fills the stroke with the currently selected stroke color as shown in Figure 14-8.

You can also click a region in a Live Paint group using the Live Paint Selection tool to pick up the color from that region. You may, for example, decide that you want to pick up a color from one area to use to fill several other areas to reduce the clutter in a vector image traced by the Live Trace tool.

Figure 14-7: When the Paint Strokes option is selected, the Live Paint Bucket tool icon changes to indicate when the tool is over a stroke.

Figure 14-8: This shows the result of painting the stroke with the Live Paint Bucket tool.

Summary

The Live Paint Bucket tool provides you with a flexible vector-based paint tool that is considerably more powerful than the paint bucket tools you find in bitmap image editors. In this chapter, you learned the following:

✦ The Live Paint Bucket tool is the replacement for the Paint Bucket tool found in earlier versions of Illustrator.

✦ Live Paint groups remain live so that any changes you make to the paths are reflected in the fill you added using the Live Paint Bucket tool.

✦ Live Trace objects must be converted to Live Paint groups before you can use the Live Paint Bucket tool on them. This prevents you from making further modifications with the Live Trace tool.

✦ You can use the gap detection options to control how the Live Paint Bucket tool deals with gaps in the paths.

✦ You can choose to have the Live Paint Bucket tool paint fills, strokes, or both.

✦   ✦   ✦

Mastering Illustrator

P A R T

III

◆ ◆ ◆ ◆

In This Part

Chapter 15
Working with
Graphic Styles,
Filters, and Effects

Chapter 16
Creating 3D in
Illustrator

Chapter 17
Customizing and
Automating Illustrator

◆ ◆ ◆ ◆

Working with Graphic Styles, Filters, and Effects

◆ ◆ ◆ ◆

In This Chapter

Working with graphic styles

Using the Appearance palette

Using Photoshop filters

Working with effects

Experiencing the new Scribble effect

◆ ◆ ◆ ◆

Probably some of the most amazing illustrations you see in Illustrator come from using graphic styles, filters, and effects. Graphic styles can increase your productivity with any type of repeating symbol or set of attributes that you use daily. Set as a style, you can use it over and over again.

Filters and effects are similar when you look at their menus. Those of you looking to create special effects, look no further. In this chapter, you discover the difference between filters and effects as well as when to use them.

Along with filters and effects, you see a variety of artwork that uses filters, effects, and graphic styles all combined.

Understanding How Graphic Styles Work

Graphic styles have brought Illustrator to the front of the pack in illustration software. Graphic styles give you the ability to save all of an object's attributes in a palette. You can use the Graphic Styles palette to quickly add the attributes, such as transparency, effects, strokes, and fills to another object. Creating a Style is pretty darn easy. Simply create the look you want on an object, and then with your object selected, choose New Graphic Style from the Graphic Styles palette pop-up menu. That is it! Now you can use that style anytime you'd like. Seems like a breeze, but before diving headfirst into the Graphic Styles palette, first check out appearances.

The Appearance palette houses all the information about a selected object. The information includes the stroke information, fill information, any effects from the Effect menu, and transparency information. In this Appearance palette, you can continually edit, rearrange, and delete this style information.

You can't apply graphic styles to type unless you change the type to outlines.

Using the Appearance palette

The Appearance palette shows all strokes, fills, transparency, multiple fills, and any effects or transformations applied to that selected object. You open the Appearance palette by choosing Window ➭ Appearance. Figure 15-1 shows the Appearance palette.

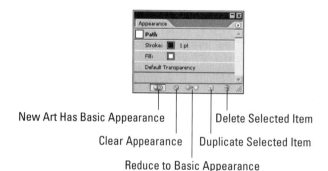

New Art Has Basic Appearance   Delete Selected Item

Clear Appearance   Duplicate Selected Item

Reduce to Basic Appearance

Figure 15-1: With an object selected, the Appearance palette displays the object's information.

The palette area shows the sequential order of the attributes that make up the object. Each time you add to the object, it gets listed above the previous entry. With this stacking order, you can drag other information, such as stroke weight, above or below the other entries, creating a different look to the object.

The Appearance palette's pop-up menu, shown in Figure 15-2, has a few options from which to choose. To access this menu, simply click the right-pointing arrow inside the circle located on the upper right of the palette. Under this menu, you can find the following: Add New Fill, Add New Stroke, Duplicate Item, Remove Item, Clear Appearance, Reduce to Basic Appearance, New Art Has Basic Appearance, Hide Thumbnail, and Redefine Graphic Style. Each of these items is discussed in detail later in this section.

Figure 15-2: The Appearance palette pop-up menu gives you additional options.

Editing and adding strokes and fills

Editing an item is as easy as double-clicking. Double-click the item you want to edit and make your changes, and the object immediately updates to your edits. When you double-click an effect in the Appearance palette, Illustrator displays the dialog box for that particular effect, as indicated in Figure 15-3.

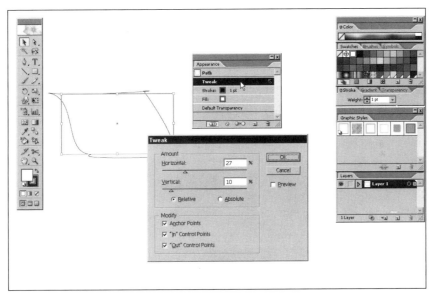

Figure 15-3: After you double-click an effect in the Appearance palette, Illustrator displays the dialog box for that effect.

The Appearance palette can also be used for editing. You can select a stroke or fill in the Appearance palette and do the edits in the Stroke or Fill palette. To edit a stroke or a fill, click one time in the Appearance palette to select the stroke or fill and then change the color of the stroke or fill and the stroke weight.

To edit the stroke weight and color by using the Appearance palette, follow these steps:

1. **Select the object with the Selection tool.** See Chapter 6 for more on the Selection tool.

2. **In the Appearance palette, select the stroke by clicking it one time.** You open the Appearance palette by choosing Window ➪ Appearance or by pressing Shift+F6.

3. **In the Color palette, choose a new color.** The color is automatically updated in the object.

4. **With the stroke still selected, change the stroke weight in the Stroke palette.** The weight of the stroke is instantly updated in the object.

Figure 15-4 shows an object in its original state and with the color and stroke weight changed. It is amazing to think that just a few minor changes can give a totally different look to the object.

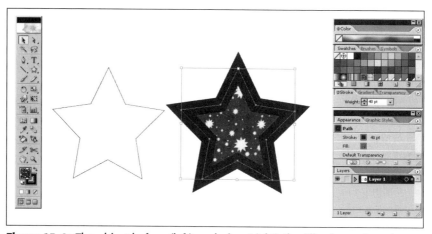

Figure 15-4: The object before (left) and after (right) the fill color and stroke weight were edited

Duplicating and removing items

Under the Appearance pop-up menu is a menu item you can use to remove an item — such as the stroke or fill — in the object's list. Click the item to select it, and then choose Remove Item from the pop-up menu (or click the Delete Selected Item icon at the bottom of the palette). The item is removed from the list and the object. Use this to edit a preset Style to customize it. Another way to remove an item is to select it and then click the trash icon at the bottom right of the Appearance palette.

You can also duplicate an object in the Appearance palette. Select the item you want to duplicate in the list in the Appearance palette, and then choose Duplicate Item from the pop-up menu. This comes in handy when you want to use some of the item's attributes, but not all. Duplicate the item, and then edit it as you want.

Clearing an appearance

Clearing an appearance removes the effects and changes the stroke and fill to None. If there are multiple fills or strokes, all are reduced to one stroke and one fill. You find the Clear Appearance option in the pop-up menu and in the icons at the bottom of the Appearance palette.

Reducing to basic appearance

Choosing Reduce to Basic Appearance from the Appearance palette pop-up menu (or clicking the icon at the bottom of the palette) removes all but one stroke and fill and all the effects. The remaining stroke and fill are assigned the default attributes (typically the bottommost stroke and fill color and the stroke weight of the bottommost stroke). If you didn't use a stroke, Illustrator reduces the object to the original fill color only. Similarly, if you didn't use a fill, Illustrator reduces the object to the original stroke color and weight. Figure 15-5 shows the object before and after applying Reduce to Basic Appearance. The end result looks a bit bland compared to the original.

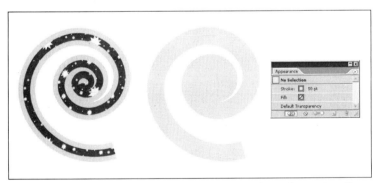

Figure 15-5: The object on the left has all its graphic styles and attributes. The object on the right has been reduced to a basic appearance.

Note   Reducing an object to the basic appearance is not the same as clearing the appearance. Clearing the appearance removes all the attributes while reducing to basic appearance only simplifies the object to a single stroke and fill.

Setting New Art preferences

If you select the New Art Has Basic Appearance option (either by clicking the button at the bottom of the Appearance palette or by choosing the option from the palette's pop-up menu), all art created afterward has a basic appearance of a white fill and a black stroke. If you do not select this option, as shown in Figure 15-6, all art created after using a style has the appearance of the last used style.

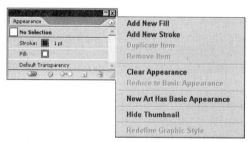

Figure 15-6: If the New Art Has Basic Appearance is not selected, all new art has the same attributes of the last style used.

Viewing thumbnails

In the Appearance palette, you have the option to view a small thumbnail of the selected object's style. The Thumbnail appears in the upper left of the Appearance palette. If you don't want to see this little thumbnail, choose Hide Thumbnail from the Appearance palette's pop-up menu. To see the thumbnail again, choose Show Thumbnail from the menu. I can think of no good reason to hide the thumbnail, but the option is available if you want to use it.

Redefining graphic styles

The Redefine Graphic Style option is available only when you apply one of the preset styles from the Graphic Styles palette. When you use the Redefine Graphic Style option, your new changes overwrite the original, and any objects that use that style immediately update to your new changes.

In order to redefine a graphic style, you must first select the style you want to redefine in the Graphic Styles palette. Then select an object that has the characteristics that you want to apply to the style. Finally, choose Redefine Graphic Style from the pop-up menu of the Appearance palette.

Caution Redefining a style completely replaces that style with the new style. The existing name is retained, but all other attributes are replaced. Unless you're absolutely sure that you want to replace all the style's attributes, it is probably safer to simply create a new graphic style using the Graphic Styles palette as discussed in the next section.

Working with the Graphic Styles palette

Now that you understand the Appearance palette, it is time to dive headfirst into the Graphic Styles palette. This magnificent little palette contains lots of creativity and amazing preset effects. The Graphic Styles palette shown in Figure 15-7 has few icons. The icons are Break Link to Graphic Style, New Graphic Style, and Delete Graphic Style. You find the guts of the palette in the pop-up menu, which you access by clicking the right-pointing arrow within the circle on the upper right of the palette. The following sections explain all the options found in the Graphic Styles palette's pop-up menu.

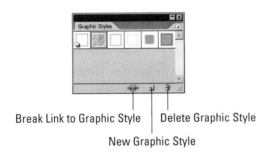

Figure 15-7: The Graphic Styles palette enables you to create and use graphic styles.

Break Link to Graphic Style | Delete Graphic Style
New Graphic Style

Creating a New Graphic Style

You use the New Graphic Style icon to make your selected object's attributes into a new style in the Graphic Styles palette. You can also create a new style by choosing New Graphic Style from the pop-up menu in the Graphic Styles palette. To create a new style, follow these steps:

1. **Create an object.** See Chapter 5 for more on creating objects.

2. **Add color to the fill and/or stroke, a stroke weight, and dash pattern if desired.**

3. **Add effects from the Effects menu.** You can include transformations, twists, distortions, or anything you like. For more on effects, see the section "Using Effects" later in this chapter.

4. **After the object looks just right, select the whole object.**

5. **Choose New Graphic Style from the pop-up menu in the Graphic Styles palette.** This displays the Graphic Style Options dialog box, shown in Figure 15-8, so that you can name the new style. Clicking the New Graphic Style button bypasses the Graphic Style Options dialog box (unless you Alt (Option) click the button) and simply gives the new style a default name of Graphic Style *x* where *x* is a number starting with 1.

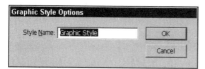

Figure 15-8: The Graphic Style Options dialog box allows you to name the new style.

6. **Enter a name for the New Graphic Style, and click OK.** This adds the new style to the Graphic Styles palette. The new graphic style now appears in the Graphic Styles palette.

7. **You can apply that new graphic style to any object you create.**

Tip

Another way to create a new graphic style is to drag the object thumbnail from the Appearance palette into the Graphic Styles palette. This automatically creates a new graphic style. If you want to name it, you can either double-click it in the Graphic Styles palette, or select it and choose Graphic Style Options from the pop-up menu.

Duplicating and merging graphic styles

Using the Graphic Styles palette menu, you can duplicate a style. Select a style in the palette, and choose Duplicate Graphic Style from the pop-up menu in the palette. This creates a duplicate swatch at the end of the list of graphic style swatches. Use this to alter and create your own custom style. You use Duplicate Graphic Style to duplicate a default swatch so that you don't overwrite the original swatch.

You can also take two different styles and combine them as one. Use the Merge Graphic Styles command found in the Graphic Styles palette menu. To combine two or more graphic styles, follow these steps:

1. **Press and hold the Shift key.**

2. **Click the graphic styles that you want to combine in the Graphic Styles palette.** To select non-contiguous graphic styles, press the Ctrl (⌘) key instead of the Shift key.

3. **Choose Merge Graphic Styles from the pop-up menu in the Graphic Styles palette.** The new combined graphic style is added to the end of the swatches in the Graphic Styles palette.

Deleting a graphic style

To delete a graphic style, select the graphic style in the Graphic Styles palette and choose Delete Graphic Style from the pop-up menu. Alternatively, you can click the trash icon at the bottom of the palette. A warning message appears asking, "Delete the Style Selection?" You can click either Yes to delete the style or No to cancel the action.

Breaking the link to a graphic style

You use the Break Link to Graphic Style option to break the graphic style from the object. The object still retains the appearance of the graphic style, but changes to the graphic style's definition no longer alter the object's appearance. A good use of this option is to find a graphic style that you like, but want to change. Fill an object with that graphic style, choose the Break Link to Graphic Style icon, and then alter the object as you want. When you have it as you like it, make it into a new style. Another good use for this option is when you want several objects to have the same basic style, but you want to make some subtle changes to some of them. If you break the link to the style for the objects that you don't want to change, you can quickly modify the remaining objects simply by modifying the style.

Understanding the other Graphic Styles palette options

Choosing Select All Unused selects all graphic styles that aren't used in the document. You can then choose to delete the unused graphic styles from the Graphic Styles palette.

Sort by Name sorts the Graphic Style swatches alphabetically. You probably won't find this very useful unless you choose one of the list views.

In the Graphic Styles palette, you can choose how you view the graphic style swatches. Choosing Thumbnail shows you a swatch of the graphic style. Choosing Small List View displays a small swatch next to the name of the graphic style. The Large List View displays a larger swatch next to the name of the graphic style.

The Override Character Color menu item overrides the object's original color with the graphic style. If you want to retain the original color qualities, uncheck the Override Character Color option in the Graphic Style palette's menu.

The Graphic Style Options lets you name or rename a graphic style swatch. You may not want to rename the standard swatches because doing so makes it harder to remember if you have a particular swatch open when you're looking at the names in a library.

Opening and saving Graphic Style Libraries

After you create a bunch of cool styles, you'll want to save them as a Library for future use. To save a Graphic Style Library, follow these steps:

1. **Choose Save Graphic Style Library from the Graphic Styles pop-up menu.**
   This opens the Save Palette as Graphics Style Library dialog box, shown in Figure 15-9. (Your dialog box may look a little different if you choose to display the standard dialog box instead of the Adobe dialog box.)

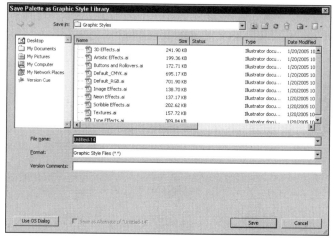

Figure 15-9: Use the Save Palette as Graphics Style Library dialog box to save your graphic styles in your own library.

2. **Enter a name for the library in the File name text box.**

3. **Click the Save button to save the file.**

To open a saved Library, follow these steps:

1. **Choose Other Library from the Open Graphic Style Library under the Graphic Style palette pop-up menu.** This launches the Open dialog box.

2. **Choose the saved file.**

3. **Click Open to open the library file.**

Using Filters in Illustrator

If you look at the Filter menu you see that filters are available for both Photoshop and Illustrator. The filters in Illustrator must be different from the filters in Photoshop because Illustrator deals with vector-based images and Photoshop works with bitmapped graphics. Many electronic artists use Photoshop as a staple of their graphics work. For them, the word "filter" conjures up thoughts of blurring and sharpening, as well as some of the fantastic effects that they can achieve by using filters from third parties, such as Alien Skin's Eye Candy.

The very term *filters* is based in photography terminology for special lenses that are attached to cameras to achieve special effects. Photoshop's filters are based on this concept, and they take it quite a bit further, creating controls for variety and exactness that a camera lens could never match.

Instead of just changing the appearance of objects or images, most of the filters in Illustrator perform tasks that took hours to do manually in previous versions of Illustrator. In a way, most of these filters work as intelligent macros, and they enable you to produce a variety of cool effects.

Some filters, such as the Zig Zag filter, seem to perform quite simple tasks. In reality, however, these filters are complex math-based programs that accomplish certain tasks faster than the fastest illustrator could dream of performing without them.

So why are all these functions in the Filter menu, shown in Figure 15-10, and not just functions within the software? Because none of them is really integrated into Illustrator; instead, each filter is an individual file called a plug-in, which resides in the Plug-Ins folder. For a filter to be available, the plug-in must be in the Plug-ins folder.

Figure 15-10: The Filter menu offers many possibilities for modifying objects in your Illustrator documents.

Finding the Plug-Ins folder

All the filters in Illustrator are in the Filter menu because a file with the same name as the filter is in the Plug-Ins folder. If the filter's file is not in the Plug-Ins folder, the filter does not appear in the Filter menu.

 Note The location of the Plug-Ins folder is dependent on the operating system. Generally, though, the Plug-Ins folder is a subfolder of the Illustrator program folder.

To see the list of all Illustrator's plug-ins, choose Help ⇨ About Plug-Ins (Illustrator ⇨ About Plug-Ins). In the About Plug-Ins dialog box, shown in Figure 15-11, choose the filter that you want to know about by clicking one time on it and then clicking the About button or by simply double-clicking the filter.

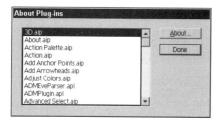

Figure 15-11: The About Plug-Ins dialog box shows all the filters that you have installed.

Understanding the color filters

The color filters in the Colors submenu of the Filter menu, shown in Figure 15-12, really take Illustrator's color capabilities to the next level in many ways. Unfortunately, they fall far short of Photoshop's color capabilities, but they're making good headway.

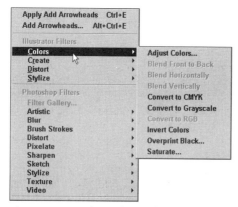

Figure 15-12: The Colors submenu provides access to all the color filters.

You can make some amazing changes using the color filters. Figure 15-13 shows an original illustration and the same illustration with a variety of color filters applied.

Figure 15-13: The top illustration is the original. The bottom illustration had various color filters applied.

Adjust Colors

The Adjust Colors feature increases and decreases process color fills in each color component. The percentages entered in Adjust Colors dialog box are absolute changes, meaning that a 10 percent decrease of Cyan when Cyan is 100 percent results in 90 percent, and a 10 percent decrease of Cyan when Cyan is 50 percent results in 40 percent, not 45 percent. If the increase makes the tint of a color greater than 100 percent, it stays at 100 percent, but other colors may still increase if they are not yet at 100 percent. If the decrease makes the tint of a color less than 0 percent, that color remains at 0 percent, but other colors may still decrease, as long as they are not yet at 0 percent. For example, a 25 percent increase to both Yellow and Magenta to a path with 80 percent Yellow and 50 percent Magenta results in the colors being 100 percent Yellow and 75 percent Magenta. Reapplying this filter results in 100 percent Yellow and 100 percent Magenta. Reapplying this filter at this point results in no change at all.

The Adjust Colors dialog box is shown in Figure 15-14.

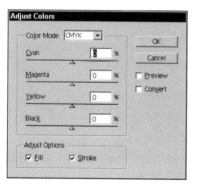

Figure 15-14: The Adjust Colors dialog box allows you to fine-tune the level of each color in a selection.

The Adjust Colors dialog box has several options. The Preview check box lets you see the changes that have been applied so far. The Convert check box automatically converts custom colors to process equivalents. The Fill and Stroke check boxes control whether the adjustments are applied to the fill, the stroke, or to both.

Tip   You can adjust colors using any color mode, even if your selected paths are different models. Click the Convert check box, and choose a different model.

Cross-Reference   For more on color modes, see Chapter 3.

Using the Color Blend filters

The Blend Front to Back, Blend Horizontally, and Blend Vertically filters blend the colors of at least three objects whose ending objects are either both process tints or both black tints. The Blend filters do not work with custom colors, patterns, or gradients. Using the Blend filters is very similar to using the Blend tool, but instead of making different shape and color blends, the Blend filters create new colors between objects automatically. If the ending paths' colors are different color types, the Blend filters may produce undesirable results.

The main differences between these filters are how each determines what the end paths are and in what direction the blend flows.

Understanding the Convert to filters

The three Convert to filters — Convert to CMYK, Convert to Grayscale, and Convert to RGB — enable you to change the color model of selected paths with a simple menu selection. In addition to switching between Grayscale, CMYK, and RGB, the Convert to filters change custom colors to those color models as well.

Using the Invert Colors filter

The Invert Colors filter works in what may seem like strange and mysterious ways on selected paths. Whatever the color of the path, Invert Colors takes the first three colors in the Paint palette (Cyan, Magenta, and Yellow) and subtracts them from 100. If the original color was a shade of Red (for example, where Cyan = 0%, Magenta = 100%, and Yellow = 100%), then Invert Colors makes the new color Cyan = 100%, Magenta = 0%, and Yellow = 0%.

For CMYK colors, the percentage of black is not affected by Invert Colors. If you are working with the RGB or Grayscale images, however, the Invert Color Filter produces a photographic negative effect.

Using the Overprint Black filter

Overprinting enables you to set black to print over the top of any color underneath. Overprinting prevents white gaps from showing up between colors and black areas. Choosing Filter ⇨ Color ⇨ Overprint Black displays the Overprint Black dialog box, shown in Figure 15-15, which enables you to apply overprinting of black to selected paths. You can select a number of options, including whether to add or remove overprinting from the selected objects. Another option lets you specify the minimal amount of black (as a percentage) that the printer uses to overprint.

Caution   Overprint Black affects only the object(s) selected when the filter is applied.

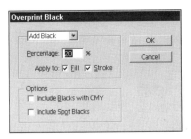

Figure 15-15: The Overprint Black dialog box allows you to control the overprinting options.

You can specify whether the overprint affects fills or strokes or both. The other options in the Overprint Black dialog box determine whether black overprints when combined with cyan, magenta, and yellow, or when part of a spot color.

The Overprint Black filter adds overprinting only to selected objects that are not currently overprinted when you select the Add Black choice from the drop-down list (pop-up menu) in the Overprint Black dialog box, and it removes overprinting from objects that currently have overprinting when you select the Remove Black choice.

Note   In the Attributes palette, the appropriate check boxes are selected when you use the filter on selected objects.

Understanding the Saturate filter

The Saturate filter adds or subtracts equal amounts of color to or from the selected objects. This filter does not correspond in any way to saturation changes made by Photoshop; instead, the color added is proportional to each color in a path.

The Saturate dialog box, shown in Figure 15-16, enables you to saturate or desaturate, depending on the direction you drag the slider. Dragging the slider to the left desaturates the selected object, reducing the intensity of the color fill. Dragging the slider to the right saturates the selected object, increasing the intensity of the color fill. The Preview check box in this dialog box is quite helpful, letting you see what is happening to the paths in real time. If the fill is set to none, attempting to change the intensity displays an error message.

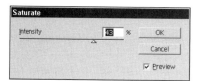

Figure 15-16: The Saturate dialog box enables you to change the color intensity of the selected objects.

Manipulating colors with the color filters

The color filters provide automated ways of changing colors on a variety of objects. Most of the filters work on paths that are filled with black or a process color, and some of them work on the strokes of the paths as well. The following sections describe various uses for the color filters.

Techniques for creating shadows and highlights

You can easily use color filters to create shadows and highlights for black and process-color paths. You create most shadows by simply creating a copy of the object and placing it under, and slightly offset from, the original. You can darken the copy in a number of ways, but the easiest way is to use the Adjust Colors filter. Figure 15-17 shows the result of the steps that you follow to create shadows and highlights.

You create highlights in the same way that you create shadows, but instead of darkening the copy, you lighten it.

Follow these steps to create shadows and highlights:

1. **Create an object that has several colors in it.** Although it may seem a little unusual, this object becomes the shadow. By creating the shadow first, you actually save several steps in the process. You may want to make this copy of the object a little darker so that it works well as a shadow. If you use text you'll need to convert the text to outlines.

2. **Group the individual elements in the object by selecting the elements and choosing Object ⇨ Group.**

3. **Copy the object by selecting it, holding down the Alt (Option) key, and dragging slightly up and to the left.** This copy is the main object.

4. **Choose Filter ⇨ Colors ⇨ Adjust Colors to open the Adjust Colors dialog box.** To lighten the copy evenly, I subtracted 20 percent from Cyan, Magenta, and Yellow, and 40 percent from Black.

5. **Again copy the object by selecting it, holding down the Alt (Option) key, and dragging slightly up and to the left.** This copy is the highlight.

6. **Use the Adjust Colors dialog box to decrease all four process colors by 40 percent if the background is dark or 20 percent if the background is light.** My background is dark, so I reduced the color in the highlight by 40 percent of each color.

Figure 15-17: The final results of the shadows and highlights applied to an object

Creating negatives with the color filters

You can produce negative images in Illustrator almost automatically by using the Invert Colors filter. For a process color, the Invert Colors filter subtracts the tints of cyan, magenta, and yellow from 100 percent and leaves black as is. On an object that is filled or stroked with black only, the filter subtracts the tint of black from 100 percent. RGB and Grayscale give photographic negatives where the black is treated as any other color.

To use this filter to create negatives, follow these steps:

1. **Select all the objects that you want to reverse.**

2. **Next choose Filter ➪ Colors ➪ Invert Colors.**

3. **Select each path, and check whether the paths have a process color fill that contains black.** If you find any fills that contain black, manually change black to the correct value.

Tip

After you check a path to see whether it is a process color that contains black, hide that path. Using this method can help you be sure that you have checked every path, and you do not have to worry about wasting time by rechecking paths.

Understanding the create filters options

Older versions of Illustrator included many create filters. Now the category is all but extinct, with only Crop Marks and Object Mosaic being the stragglers. As with most filters, you can manually perform the functions that the two create filters do, but using the filters is much easier. You find these two remaining options in the Filter menu's Create submenu.

Adding crop marks

Use the Crop Marks filter to add lines to the edges of your object, showing you how much to trim the object when printed. Figure 15-18 shows an example of the result of using this filter.

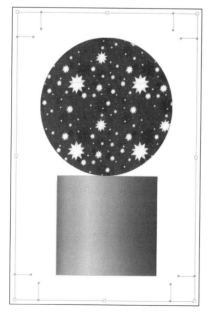

Figure 15-18: The Crop Marks filter adds crop marks to your document as shown here.

Cross-Reference   Crop marks are fully covered in Chapter 8.

Creating object mosaics

The Object Mosaic filter creates a series of tiles out of a placed bitmap image, as shown in Figure 15-19. Any size or color image may be used. When an image is converted through the Object Mosaic filter, it becomes a series of rectangles, each filled with a different color that most closely represents the underlying image.

Figure 15-19: This shows an image before (left) and after (right) applying the Object Mosaic filter.

Note   You cannot apply the Object Mosaic filter to a linked image — only an embedded one. Click the Embed button on the Control palette to change a placed image from linked to embedded.

In the Object Mosaic dialog box, shown in Figure 15-20, you can specify the number of tiles that the image is made up of and the space between the tiles. You also can specify a different size for the entire object mosaic.

The more rectangles, the more detail is in the mosaic. Bitmapped images are mosaics of a sort, with each pixel equal to one square.

Tip   If you need to apply the Object Mosaic filter to an illustration that you created in Illustrator, you can rasterize it by using the Object ⇨ Rasterize command. Do this at a low resolution (72 dpi works great for me), and then apply the Object Mosaic filter to the rasterized image.

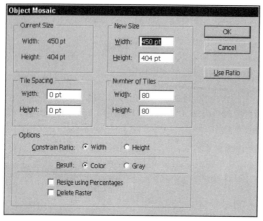

Figure 15-20: Use the Object Mosaic dialog box to specify the parameters for the object mosaic.

Use the following steps to create a fairly simple and basic mosaic in Illustrator:

1. **Create a bitmap file, and place it in Illustrator with the File ➪ Place command.** You do not need to use a high-resolution bitmap image. The Illustrator object mosaic looks just as good when you convert a 72-dpi image as when you convert a 300-dpi image.

2. **Click the Embed button on the Control palette to change the image from a linked one to an embedded one.**

3. **Choose Filter ➪ Create ➪ Object Mosaic to display the Object Mosaic dialog box, as shown in Figure 15-20.**

4. **In the Object Mosaic dialog box, enter the size that you want the mosaic to be and also the number of tiles across and down.**

   - **Current Size:** Current Size lists the size of the selected image.

   - **New Size:** Enter the size in width and height that you want the object mosaic to be. You can keep it the same size or enter a different size in width and height.

   - **Tile Spacing:** In the Tile Spacing area, enter the space between the tiles in width and height. To create an effect that is more like ceramic tiles, enter a number larger than the default of 0.

   - **Number of Tiles:** Enter the number of tiles you want to use to create the object mosaic. Keep in mind that using fewer tiles creates a less-detailed object mosaic. The greater the number of tiles, the better the detail is, but the longer it takes to create.

- **Options:** Under the Options area, choose from Constrain Ratio by width or height, the result to be in color or gray, whether to resize the image with percentages, and to delete the raster image. If you do not choose to delete the raster image, Illustrator leaves it in place underneath the resulting mosaic image.

5. **Click the Use Ratio button.** This keeps the same proportions as in the original image and may change the number of width or height tiles depending on whether you chose to constrain the ratio using width or height.

6. **Click OK when you are satisfied with the information that you have entered in the Object Mosaic dialog box.** Figure 15-21 shows the results that are produced by entering two different tile widths and heights into the Number of Tiles boxes.

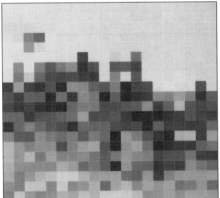 

Figure 15-21: The object mosaic on the left is 20 by 20 tiles while the object mosaic on the right is 80 by 80 tiles.

Combining the Object Mosaic and Round Corners filters

You can create some very exciting effects with the Object Mosaic filter when you use it in conjunction with other filters. The best ones to use with it are Round Corners, all the Distort filters, and most of the color filters, as well as the Transform Each function. In the following example, I combined the Object Mosaic filter with the Round Corners filter and the Transform Each function.

1. **Create an object mosaic with an average number of square tiles.** Use between 1,600 and 10,000 tiles, which would be from 40×40 to 100×100.

2. **Select all the mosaic tiles, and choose Filter ⇨ Stylize ⇨ Round Corners.**

3. **In the Round Corners dialog box, enter a large number.** I usually enter at least 10 points. As long as the tiles are not larger than 20 points wide, the Round Corners filter turns all the tiles into circles.

4. **Ungroup the tiles by choosing Object ⇨ Ungroup.**

5. **Choose Object ⇨ Transform ⇨ Transform Each to display the Transform Each dialog box.**

6. **In the Move section of the dialog box, enter a number in both text fields and check the Random check box and click OK.** I entered the number 5. See Figure 15-22 for the final results.

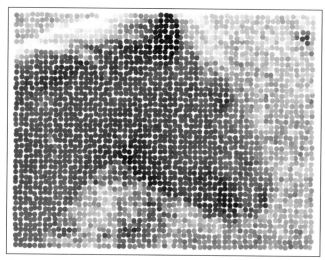

Figure 15-22: This shows an example of creating a Georges Seurat-like effect with the Object Mosaic filter.

Because of the way these tiles overlap, you can create a tiled or shingled roof quite easily, providing the original image is upside down. The next section describes this process in detail.

Creating an object mosaic with no white-space overlap

The following steps describe how to make the tiles in a mosaic overlap with no white space between them. This technique can easily create a background image or a funky illustration:

1. **Create an object mosaic from a raster image.**

2. **Ungroup the object mosaic by choosing Object ⇨ Ungroup.**

3. **Choose Object ⇨ Transform ⇨ Transform Each to display the Transform Each dialog box.**

4. **Make certain that the Preview check box is selected so that you can see the results as you make changes in the Transform Each dialog box.**

5. **Check the Random check box.**

6. **Enter the amount of movement for the tiles in the Move section.** In this example, I entered 10 points for both horizontal and vertical.

7. **Enter the percentage that the tile must be scaled up to eliminate the white space in the Scale area.** In this example, I entered 200%.

8. **Click OK to apply the transformations, and close the dialog box.** Figure 15-23 shows the results.

Figure 15-23: This shows the original image (left) and the result of creating overlapping random tiles with no white spacing between tiles (right).

Tip   To see the edges of the tiles more easily, place a 0.25-point 100% black stroke on them.

Understanding the Distort filters

The Distort filters create twists, bends, and alterations ranging from small to huge changes in the object's path. The filters under Distort are Free Distort, Pucker and Bloat, Roughen, Tweak, Twist, and Zig Zag.

Cross-Reference   For full coverage of the Distort filters, see Chapter 11.

Using the Stylize filters

The Stylize filters are used for a variety of functions — kind of a catchall for filters that really couldn't go anywhere else. With the Add Arrowheads filter, you can place arrowheads (all sorts!) on the ends of open paths. With the Drop Shadow filter, you can add a darkened shadow to a selected path. The Round Corners filter seems better suited to the Distort submenu, but Adobe has chosen to put it here. The Round Corners filter removes Corner Points and replaces them with Smooth Points.

Understanding the Add Arrowheads filter

The Add Arrowheads filter is exactly the same as the Add Arrowheads effect, but when used as a filter, you can't edit the arrowheads later. Using the Effects' Add Arrowheads enables you to go back in and edit later.

 Cross-Reference   For more on Add Arrowheads, see the Effects section later in this chapter.

Using the Drop Shadow filter

The Drop Shadow filter makes creating drop shadows for most paths a relatively simple task.

Unlike most other filters, selecting Drop Shadow affects both stroke and fill. In the Drop Shadow dialog box, shown in Figure 15-24, you may specify the offset of the drop shadow by entering values for how far across the drop shadow should move (X) and how far up or down it should move (Y). Positive numbers move the shadow to the right and down; negative numbers move the shadow to the left and up.

You have these options in the Drop Shadow dialog box (among others):

✦ **Mode:** Use this to choose the blending mode to apply.

✦ **Opacity:** This lets you set how much you can see through the shadow.

✦ **X and Y Offset:** The general rule in drop-shadowing is that the more the drop shadow is offset, the more elevated the original object looks. To make an object look as if it is floating far above the page, enter high offset values.

✦ **Blur:** This lets you enter how far the blur will go outward in pixels.

✦ **Color:** You choose this to set the shadow color to something other than black.

✦ **Darkness:** The percentage entered in Darkness is how much black is added to the fill and stroke colors. Darkness does not affect any of the other custom or process colors.

✦ **Create Separate Shadows:** Choose this to make the shadow separate from the object (ungrouped).

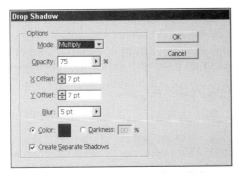

Figure 15-24: The Drop Shadow dialog box enables you to quickly produce drop shadow effects.

To create a drop shadow, do the following:

1. **Create and select the artwork that you want to give a drop shadow.**

2. **Choose Filter ➪ Stylize ➪ Drop Shadow to display the Drop Shadow dialog box, as shown in Figure 15-24.**

3. **Enter the amount that you want the drop shadow to be offset.**

4. **Enter the Opacity value.** This determines how see-through Illustrator makes the shadow.

5. **You can also set the mode for the shadow.** I chose Multiply. You can read move about the various modes in Chapter 7.

6. **Enter a value for Darkness.** The value that you enter in the Darkness field determines how much black Illustrator adds to the shadow to make it appear darker. Alternatively, you can choose a color for the shadow.

7. **If desired, check the Create Separate Shadows option (this is the default).** If you check the Create Separate Shadows box, the shadow is grouped to the original object.

8. **Click OK.** If the shadow isn't what you want, use the Undo command by pressing Ctrl+Z (⌘+Z), and then choose Filter ➪ Stylize ➪ Drop Shadow and create a new drop shadow. Figure 15-25 shows an example of text with a drop shadow.

Figure 15-25: This figure shows text with a drop shadow created using the Drop Shadow filter.

Using the Round Corners filter

You can use the Round Corners filter to create round corners just like (snap your fingers) that. This filter works on any path that has corner points, but the best results seem to be on polygons and stars or on type with very sharp corners.

Note   Round Corners replaces most corner points with two Smooth Points.

Selecting Round Corners changes all types of corner points to Smooth Points. In the Round Corners dialog box, shown in Figure 15-26, you specify what the radius of the Round Corners should be. The larger the number you enter for the radius, the bigger the curve is.

Note   Don't apply the Round Corners filter to a rounded rectangle to make the corners more rounded. Instead of making the corners rounder, the flat sides of the rounded rectangle curve slightly.

Figure 15-26: Use the Round Corners dialog box to specify the amount of rounding to apply.

To use the Round Corners filter, do the following:

1. **Select the artwork that you want to convert to rounded corners.** I used type converted to outlines in the example in Figure 15-27.

Figure 15-27: The original type (top), and after converting to outlines and applying Round Corners (bottom)

2. **Choose Filter ⇨ Stylize ⇨ Round Corners to display the Round Corners dialog box (refer to Figure 15-26).**

3. **Enter the amount that you want the corners to be rounded.** Entering a large number usually ensures that all points become as curved as possible.

4. **Click OK.**

You can use the Round Corners filter to smooth out overly bumpy edges. Using the Round Corners filter with Roughen can produce very smooth, flowing areas.

Reapplying the last filter used

Whenever you start Illustrator, the top menu item in the Filter menu reads "Apply Last Filter," but it is grayed out. This causes some confusion initially. After you use a filter, that filter's name appears where the menu once listed "Apply Last Filter." Thereafter, the name of the last filter that you used appears at the top of the menu. The key command for reapplying the last filter is Ctrl+E (⌘+E).

Tip   To return to the last filter's dialog box, choose Filter ⇨ (Name of Last Filter), located right below the Apply Last Filter option or press Ctrl+Alt+E (⌘+Option+E).

Using Photoshop-Compatible Filters in Illustrator

By themselves, these Photoshop filters are really neat. However, because many Illustrator users also have Photoshop, are they necessary?

For starters, these filters make things a bit easier than before Illustrator could use Photoshop filters, especially for creating features such as drop shadows and other special effects. Instead of having to allocate memory to Photoshop, you can do filter operations right in Illustrator.

Working with rasterized Illustrator artwork

Photoshop filters work only on pixel-based images. If you want to apply a Photoshop filter to your Illustrator artwork, you have to first rasterize it to turn it into a pixel-based image.

You have several ways to turn Illustrator art into pixels, but the best way is to use the Object ➪ Rasterize command, which transforms any selected artwork into pixel-based artwork, at the resolution you specify. Follow these steps to do this:

1. **Create your artwork in Illustrator.**

2. **Select the artwork by dragging the mouse over the top of it.** You can also choose the Select ➪ All menu command.

3. **Choose Object ➪ Rasterize to display the Rasterize dialog box, as shown in Figure 15-28.**

4. **Specify the resolution that you want to use.** Your final output determines the resolution. I chose 300 ppi so the printed piece looks nice. Choose Screen (72 ppi) if your final result will be on the Web or only viewed on a computer screen.

5. **Choose the background.** The background choices are white or transparent.

6. **Add any options you wish to use.** The options you can choose are Anti-aliasing options (Art Optimized, Type Optimized, or None), Create Clipping Mask, and Add space around object in points.

7. **Click OK to rasterize your artwork.**

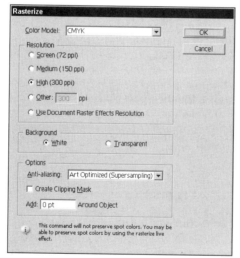

Figure 15-28: The Rasterize dialog box enables you to specify the parameters for converting vector art into a bitmap.

The rasterized art won't look different other than the path edges are gone and there is a box around the art. But now you can apply any of the Photoshop filters to this rasterized image.

Note   When Illustrator rasterizes artwork, the selected objects are joined together into a single object. Any hidden paths are eliminated in the process, and the resulting object can be edited only as a whole.

As an Illustrator user, you may not be familiar with having to decide resolution as you do in Photoshop. The quick rule is that the resolution of pixel-based images should be ½ to 2 times the line screen at which the piece will be printed. So if you'll be using a line screen of 133, your ppi should be between 199 and 266. It doesn't hurt to go higher than two times the line screen, but it is unnecessary. Because the math is easier, use double the line screen for the resolution.

Using Illustrator's Photoshop plug-ins

The Photoshop plug-ins are separated from the vector filters and appear below the vector filters (the logic being that you won't be using them as much as Illustrator filters, so why let them get in the way). The plug-ins are primarily special-effect plug-ins.

Photoshop filters work only on pixel-based and RGB images. Before starting this exercise, be sure that your document is in RGB color mode by choosing File ➪ Document Color Mode ➪ RGB. The following steps describe how to apply a Photoshop filter to an image, and Figure 15-29 illustrates the final result of these steps:

1. **Select the pixel-based image in Illustrator to which you want to apply the Photoshop filter.** For more on selecting images, see Chapter 6.

2. **Choose Filter ➪ Name of Photoshop filter submenu ➪ Name of filter.** For example, this could be Filter ➪ Texture ➪ Craquelure.

3. **In the filter's dialog box, adjust the settings and values.**

4. **Click OK in the Filter dialog box to produce the effect.**

One big limitation of using Photoshop filters in Illustrator is that you can't make any selections within the pixel-based image. A way around this is to create a copy of the image, apply the filter, and then mask the area to which you want to apply that effect.

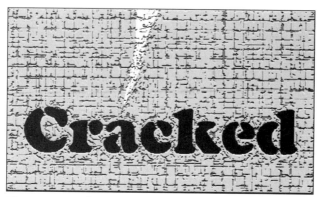

Figure 15-29: This is an example of a rasterized image with a Craquelure texture filter applied to it.

Using Effects

Effects are an intense set of commands. They apply their magic to any of the appearance attributes. Effects seem to have some of the same functions of filters. The one huge difference is that an effect is fully editable at any time. A Filter is permanent. After you apply the filter (short of undoing), it is not editable later. However, any effect you apply shows up in the Appearance palette. The Appearance palette is where you edit any of the applied effects.

To apply the last used effect quickly to another object, choose Effect ⇨ Apply Last Effect or press Ctrl+Shift+E (⌘+Shift+E). If you like the effect, but want to change some of the parameters, choose Effect ⇨ Last Effect or press Ctrl+Shift+Alt+E (⌘+Shift+Option+E).

Effects aren't limited to vector based objects. You can apply effects to raster images as well.

Understanding 3D effects

One of the biggest new features of Illustrator CS was the inclusion of three-dimensional abilities. There are few, if any, changes to the 3D features in Illustrator CS2, but because this is such a cool and intense feature, it's being covered in its own chapter.

Cross-Reference　For more on 3D, see Chapter 16.

Converting to Shape effects

The Convert to Shape effects take any selected object and fit it into a Rectangle, Rounded Rectangle, or Ellipse. The Convert to Shape effect puts a frame around your selected object. The frame is in one of the shapes that you choose (rectangle, rounded rectangle, or ellipse). Convert to Shape creates a new shape based on the original object's dimensions. Setting a negative value in the relative area decreases the size of the frame, and a positive number increases the size of the frame relative to the original size. To set the new size of the shape, enter the height and width values.

Figure 15-30 shows the Shape Options dialog box that appears when you choose any of the Convert to Shape effects. In this dialog box, you can choose the type of shape that you want to create from the Shape drop-down list (pop-up menu). You can also choose to create a shape that is set to a specific size by choosing the Absolute option or a shape that is resized by choosing the Relative option. The Corner Radius text box is used to specify the amount of corner rounding for rounded rectangles.

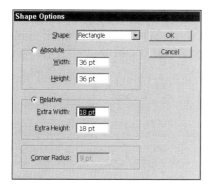

Figure 15-30: Use the Shape Options dialog box to specify how the Convert to Shape effects function.

Figure 15-31 shows an example of applying the Effect ⇨ Convert to Shape ⇨ Ellipse command to a star-shaped object. In this example, the Relative option was used and 18 extra points were added to both the width and height.

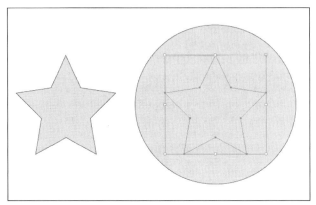

Figure 15-31: The original shape (left) and the shape that results from applying the Convert to Shape effect (right)

Distorting and transforming effects

The Distort & Transform effects include Free Distort, Pucker & Bloat, Roughen, Transform, Tweak, Twist, and Zig Zag. You may wonder why Transform effects appear in the Effect menu when you can do transformations in the Object menu. The big reason to apply a transformation under the Effect menu is that you can go back and edit that particular transformation at any time.

Cross-Reference   For in depth coverage of the Distort & Transform effects, see Chapter 11.

Creating Path effects

The Path effects that you can apply are Offset Path, Outline Object, and Outline Stroke. As with the Transform options, the Path options are the same as under the Object menu. The Path effects under the Effect menu are exactly the same as under the Object menu, except that the effects are live and editable at any time. This means that you can go back at any time and change any of the Path effects that you have applied.

Cross-Reference   For in depth coverage of the Path functions, see Chapter 6.

Understanding the Rasterize effect

The Rasterize effect has the same effect as the Object ➪ Rasterize menu command, but when applied as an effect, you can easily remove it at a later time by using the Appearance palette.

The Photoshop effects are on the bottom half of the Effect menu. These effects can be applied only to a rasterized image. To use these effects, first choose Effect ➪ Rasterize to display the Rasterize dialog box, shown in Figure 15-32.

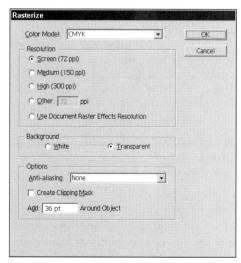

Figure 15-32: The Rasterize dialog box enables you to convert objects to raster objects using an effect that can be edited later.

In the Rasterize dialog box, you can set the resolution (from low to high or set your own). Choose from white or transparent background and the type of anti-aliasing. Other options are clipping mask or adding space around the object.

Cross-Reference See "Working with rasterized Illustrator artwork" earlier in this chapter for more information on rasterizing objects.

Stylizing effects

Under the Stylize effects are options that you can use to embellish paths and add effects to objects. The Stylize options are Add Arrowheads, Drop Shadow, Feather, Inner Glow, Outer Glow, Round Corners, and Scribble.

Using the Add Arrowheads effect

The Add Arrowheads effect is a boon to technical artists, sign makers, and anyone in need of a quick arrow. The number one complaint about the Add Arrowheads effect is that Illustrator offers too many arrowheads from which to choose. Some complaint!

Choosing Effect ⇨ Stylize ⇨ Add Arrowheads adds an arrowhead (or two) to any selected open path. If more than one path is selected, arrowheads are added to each open path. To use Add Arrowheads, select an open path and choose Effect ⇨ Stylize ⇨ Add Arrowheads to display the Add Arrowheads dialog box, as shown in Figure 15-33. In this box, you can pick which of the 27 different arrowheads you want to stick on the end of your path. Scale refers to the size of the arrowhead relative to the stroke weight of the path; you may enter any number between 1% and 1000% in this box. Choosing Start places the arrowhead at the beginning of the path (where you first clicked to draw it); choosing End places the arrowhead on the ending of the path (where you last clicked to draw it); and choosing Start and End places the same arrowhead on both the beginning and ending of the path. Reapplying this filter to the same paths continues to put arrowheads on top of arrowheads.

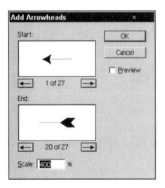

Figure 15-33: Use the Add Arrowheads dialog box to add markers to one or both ends of a path.

Figure 15-34 shows customized arrowheads created in Illustrator.

Note   Add Arrowheads does *not* work on closed paths.

Arrowheads are grouped to the paths that were selected when they were created; it is sometimes necessary to rotate the arrowhead by either ungrouping it or choosing it with the Direct Selection tool.

The size of the arrowheads is based on the width of the stroke, but you can alter each arrowhead's dimensions in the Scale text field in the Add Arrowheads dialog box.

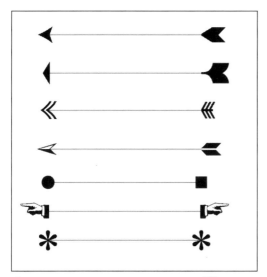

Figure 15-34: You can create many different types of customized arrowheads.

Using the Drop Shadow effect

The Drop Shadow effect is almost the same as the Drop Shadow filter, except that you can go back and edit the Drop Shadow effect at any time. For more details on Drop Shadow, see "Using the Drop Shadow filter" earlier in this chapter.

Understanding the Feather effect

The Feather effect adds a fade out to the selected object. Feather fades the object to transparent over a specified number in points. To add a Feather effect to an object, follow these steps:

1. **Select the object to which you want to apply the Feather effect.**

2. **Choose Effect ➪ Stylize ➪ Feather to open the Feather dialog box, shown in Figure 15-35.**

Figure 15-35: Use the Feather dialog box to set the distance over which objects fade out.

3. Enter the Feather Radius in points that you want in the Feather dialog box.

4. Click OK to see the Feather effect, as shown in Figure 15-36.

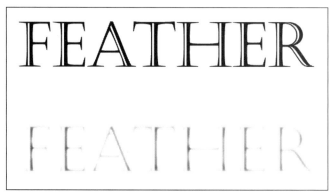

Figure 15-36: This shows the original (top) and faded out text (bottom) created using the Feather effect.

Using the Inner and Outer Glow effects

The Inner and Outer Glow effects create a softened glow on the inside or outside edge of the object. Choose Effect ➪ Stylize ➪ Inner Glow or Effect ➪ Stylize ➪ Outer Glow. In the dialog box, choose the blending mode for the glow as well as the Opacity, Blur distance, and whether the glow goes from the center or the edge. The Center option starts the glow from the center of the object; the Edge option starts the glow from the edge of the object. Figure 15-37 shows the Inner Glow dialog box.

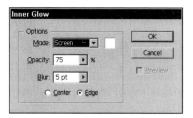

Figure 15-37: The Inner Glow dialog box enables you to create glowing effects in objects.

Round Corners

The Round Corners effect does the same thing as the Round Corners filter, except that you can go back and edit it at any time.

Cross-Reference

For more detail on the Round Corners function, see the section "Using the Round Corners filter" earlier in this chapter.

Understanding Scribble

The Scribble effect was new to Illustrator CS. It takes an illustration and adds a sketchy quality to it. You can choose from a variety of presets or create your own. The scribble effect can create a mass produced, mechanical look or a loose, flowing, childlike scrawl. The breakdown of what Scribble does is that it converts an object's stroke and fill to lines divided by transparency. The Scribble dialog box options let you alter the line style, density, looseness of the lines, and stroke width.

You find the Scribble effect under the Stylize submenu of the Effect menu. Figure 15-38 shows a portrait with two different Scribble effects applied. Within the Scribble dialog box are options that you can choose to change or customize your Scribbled art or to choose from preset Scribble effects.

Figure 15-38: Two different Scribble effects result in two very different looking portraits.

Using the Scribble presets

In the Scribble Options dialog box, you find a variety of preset options. Figure 15-39 shows the Scribble Options dialog box. These are the Scribble presets:

✦ **Custom:** Remembers the last settings you entered.

✦ **Default:** Applies 30° angled lines with varying thickness to the fill and stroke.

✦ **Childlike:** Applies 10° loopy angled lines that look very loose and as if a child had sketched them.

✦ **Dense:** Applies very tight 45° angled line with little space between lines.

✦ **Loose:** Applies very loose loopy –20° angled lines with lots of spacing between lines.

✦ **Moiré:** Applies tight –45° lines so close they actually create a moiré pattern with the fill.

✦ **Sharp:** Applies –30° angled lines tightly with little space between lines. Similar to Dense.

✦ **Sketch:** Applies –30° angled lines with a thicker stroke for the lines, but with little space between lines.

✦ **Snarl:** Applies 60° angled lines tightly together with loopy lines and a thin stroke weight.

✦ **Swash:** Applies a Figure-8 loop to the object with a thinner stroke weight and a symmetrical look to the lines.

✦ **Tight:** Applies a 30° angled line with tight lines and a thin stroke weight for an even line filled area.

✦ **Zig-Zag:** Applies a –20° angled line, a thin stroke weight for an even symmetrical look to the lines in the filled area.

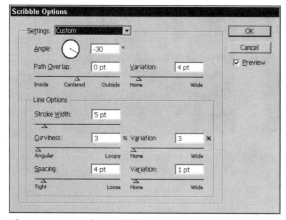

Figure 15-39: The Scribble Options dialog box provides enough options to create hundreds of very different scribble effects.

Working with the Scribble options

In the Scribble Options dialog box, you can find a variety of additional options to set, from Angle and Path Overlap to a Variation setting for Path Overlap. Line options are Stroke Width, Curviness, and Spacing, the latter two of which can have a Variation applied. You can choose from a preset value, or check the preview box and enter your own values to see immediate results.

You can set the following options for the Scribble effect:

✦ **Path Overlap:** This sets the amount the scribble lines stay inside or go beyond the object's edge.

✦ **Variation:** This sets how the scribble line lengths differ (loopy or angled) and how close together they are set.

✦ **Stroke Width:** This sets the width of the Scribble lines.

✦ **Curviness:** This sets how far the different Scribble lines curve from each other.

✦ **Variation:** This sets a range for how much the curviness may vary from line to line.

✦ **Spacing:** This sets the spacing amount between scribble lines.

✦ **Variation:** This establishes the range in which spacing magnitudes will fall.

✦ **Preview:** Check this to see the effect before applying it.

Using SVG Filters effects

You find SVG Filters under the Effects menu. Seems odd, Filters being under Effects instead of Filters. Well, that is because these pretty cool filters are XML-based and resolution independent. A perfect fit for vectors.

Cross-Reference For more on XML and SVG, see Chapter 19.

To access the SVG Filters, choose Effect ➪ SVG Filters. You have many different SVG filters from which to choose:

✦ **Alpha:** Creates transparent fluctuations

✦ **Bevel Shadow:** Creates a beveled shadow that is softened

✦ **Cool Breeze:** Creates fluctuations on the top edge of the object

✦ **Dilate:** Takes the fill outward to the edge of the object

✦ **Erode:** Takes away the fill from the edge of the object

✦ **Gaussian Blur:** Adds a soft shadow by blurring the object's edge

✦ **Pixel Play:** Uses light effects on the object

✦ **Shadow:** Creates a harsh shadow on the object

✦ **Static:** Uses a static fill in place of the original fill color

✦ **Turbulence:** Creates transparent fluctuations to the object

✦ **Woodgrain:** Creates a woodgrain effect to the object

Warp effects

The Warp effects are also part of the Effect menu. Chapter 11 covers these effects extensively.

Creating Photoshop filter effects

You can apply tons of Photoshop filter effects to any rasterized image. Turn your vector art into raster art, and apply effects from artistic to texturizing. The Photoshop filters found under the Filter menu are identical to the ones found under the Effect menu. The only difference is that when you use the Effect menu, you can go back and edit the Photoshop effect on the rasterized image. The main filters are Artistic, Blur, Brush Strokes, Distort, Pixelate, Sharpen, Sketch, Stylize, Texture, and Video.

These filters are the same as the ones you find in Photoshop, but you don't have to go back and forth between the applications to access them. Use them to create more exciting rasterized artwork.

Caution Be sure that you change the document colors space to RGB, or you'll find the Photoshop filter effects grayed out.

Summary

Graphic styles, filters, and effects provide some very powerful tools for manipulating objects in your Illustrator documents. In this chapter, you learned about these tools and the following related topics:

✦ Graphic Styles are where you can access saved Appearance settings.

✦ Choose from a wide range of graphic styles in the Graphic Style Libraries.

✦ Use the Appearance palette to edit an object's attributes.

✦ Filters add extra functionality to Illustrator through commands in the Filter menu.

✦ To use a filter, select the artwork that you want to "filterize" and select the filter from the Filter menu.

✦ The hardest aspect about filters is knowing what they do, and when and how to use them; the filters themselves are pretty simple.

✦ You can reapply the last filter quickly by pressing Ctrl+E (⌘+E).

✦ Access the last filter's dialog box by pressing Ctrl+Alt+E (⌘+Option+E).

✦ Adjust Colors adds and subtracts various amounts of process colors to and from multiple colored objects.

✦ The color blend filters look at two opposite paths and blend between the two colors.

✦ Saturate increases or decreases the amount of color in selected paths.

✦ The Object Mosaic filter takes rasterized files and converts them into Illustrator paths.

✦ Add Arrowheads creates arrowheads at the ends of open paths.

✦ Drop Shadow creates instant drop shadows.

✦ Round Corners changes Straight Corner Points into Smooth Points.

✦ Photoshop filters appear in the Filter menu under the Illustrator filters.

✦ Effects let you go back and edit at any time.

✦ Scribble effects can add a softer, sketchy look to your illustration.

✦ Reapply the last effect quickly by pressing Ctrl+Shift+E (⌘+Shift+E).

✦ Access the last effect's dialog box by pressing Ctrl+Shift+Alt+E (⌘+Shift+Option+E).

✦ Many Effects are similar to Filters, except that the Effects are fully editable and the Filters are more permanent.

✦   ✦   ✦

Creating 3D in Illustrator

✦   ✦   ✦   ✦

In This Chapter

Understanding 3D inside Illustrator

Extruding flat objects

Revolving paths around an axis

Adding highlights

Mapping 2D onto 3D objects

Other ways to add 3D to an illustration

✦   ✦   ✦   ✦

Creating depth and adding perspective has been the desire of many illustrators. This chapter shows how you can create three-dimensional images in Illustrator. Adding 3D to your package design, logo, or any illustration is a breeze. Take any path, type, or object, and model it into a 3D form, adding lighting and rotating it in three dimensions. Use 3D to take your artwork to the next level. Imagine a logo in three dimensions on a Web site rotating 360 degrees. The possibilities are endless.

Using 3D Inside Illustrator

One of the really cool features in Illustrator is the ability to create 3D inside the application. You use the Extrude command to pop a two-dimensional item into a three-dimensional world. You can revolve a path into a three-dimensional object with highlights and even map artwork onto an image in 3D. Not only can you revolve and extrude, but you can rotate the object as well. Because your 3D object is an effect, you can edit it at any time.

Take any flat shape and add depth with 3D, and you still retain all the editing abilities of the flat shape. Illustrator takes any changes you make later and incorporates them in the 3D form. Using the preview option, you can see what the object will look like. The extrude, revolve, rotate, and map artwork functions all appear in one clean, neat dialog box.

In the past, Adobe offered Adobe Dimensions, which was a three-dimensional creation program. With Dimensions, you could extrude and revolve two-dimensional paths to create three-dimensional art. You could also add depth and lighting effects to make the object appear realistic. Most of

Dimensions's capabilities are now inside Illustrator. The main difference in Illustrator is that you can't position multiple objects in 3D space. You can only position one object at a time. And Illustrator creates the 3D effect live rather than having to render, as Dimensions did.

Many 3D packages are on the market, ranging from high-end software, such as Caligari trueSpace, 3ds max, and Maya, to low-end programs. They all handle transforming high-end 3D into video, creating special effects, and making movies. And video artists use them in upscale game designs and animation. The low-end 3D programs include Swift 3D, Poser, and Strata. Poser allows you to create 3D models (people and animals), down to the facial hair and realistic skin. Strata can create a model, render the 3D, and animate the 3D objects. Illustrator's 3D abilities don't quite go that far, but it has come a long way for an illustrating program. Adobe took the three-dimensional qualities of Adobe Dimensions, created a cleaner, user-friendlier interface, and put it inside Illustrator.

Understanding the Three-Dimensional World

The concept of three dimensions should be more intuitive and easy for us to understand, because we are three-dimensional creatures who live in a three-dimensional world. But because most of our media are two-dimensional (reading, watching TV, working on a computer), adjusting to a three-dimensional digital world can be confusing and frustrating.

Changing from two dimensions to three dimensions

Television is a two-dimensional medium. The picture tube has height and width. Computer screens are two-dimensional. The pages of books are two-dimensional. Maps are two dimensional, even though the world is round. Most people think in two dimensions.

Most of the two-dimensional objects that we deal with may very well be replaced with three-dimensional objects. Three-dimensional life will become a reality as soon as technology makes it so. Holograms have been around for a while, and technology is making them more accurate and lifelike. Video games and virtual-reality glasses already simulate three dimensions through the use of holograms and computer-generated imagery; even the Viewmasters we grew up with give the three-dimensional effect.

Three-dimensional positioning

When you are trying to understand the concept of three dimensions on a computer screen, the most difficult aspect to grasp is depth. Left, right, up, and down are all simple concepts, but what about things that are closer or farther away? Maybe sometime in the future we will have to look up and down when we are driving.

Note   You are already thinking in three dimensions if you are familiar with Illustrator's Send to Back and Bring to Front commands. If you feel comfortable with stacking order and layers, then you are one step closer to working with three-dimensional positioning.

For more on arranging with Send to Back and Bring to Front, see Chapter 8.

Specify rotatic

You use three different indicators to position objects in the 3D Extrude & Bevel Options dialog box:

✦ **X is the object's horizontal location.** A value greater than 0 means that the object is positioned to the right of center (0). A value less than 0 (any negative number) represents an object to the left of center.

✦ **Y defines the object's vertical position.** A value that is greater than 0 means that the object is above center. A value that is less than 0 means that the object is below center.

✦ **Z represents the object's depth.** This variable indicates how far forward or backward the object is from the center. A value less than 0 means that the object is behind 0, or farther away. A value greater than 0 means that the object is in front of 0, or closer to you.

Figure 16-1 shows the X, Y, and Z values as you would see them initially in the 3D Extrude & Bevel Options dialog box (use Effect ⇨ 3D to open). In the dialog box, relative X (horizontal), Y (vertical), and Z (Depth) positions of selected objects can be rotated around those axes. In a direct, straight-from-the-front view, you cannot determine an object's Z position. From the default position, which is a view of the object from above and to the right of the front, you can determine all three positions visually.

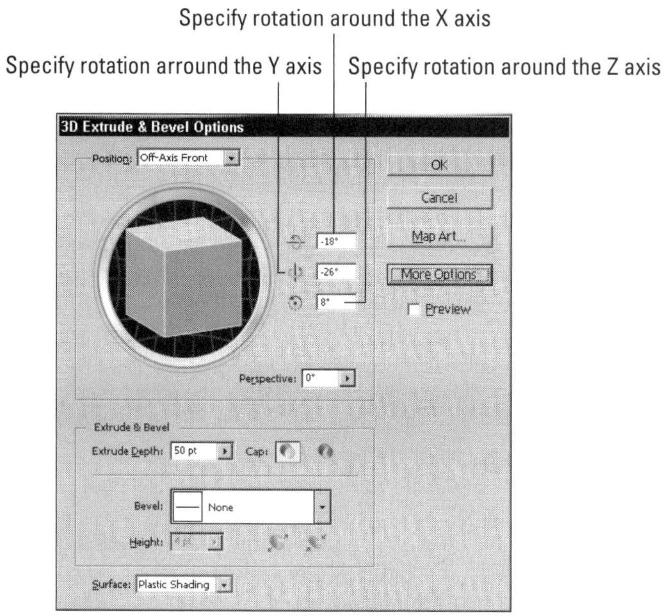

Specify rotation around the X axis

Specify rotation arround the Y axis | Specify rotation around the Z axis

Figure 16-1: The rotational values in the 3D Extrude & Bevel Options dialog box enable you to view an object in three dimensions.

Extruding and Revolving 2D Objects

Illustrator's 3D Extrude command adds sides, a top, and a back to an object. When extruding an object, you can fill the object or leave a hole in the middle (extruding the path but not the fill). Another option is to bevel the edges, which creates an amazing look for 3D text.

The Revolve command turns a path around a center axis, creating a 3D effect in a circular fashion. This is a great way to create a bottle, a chess piece, or any other revolved shape. Not only can you apply light and shading to the revolved object, but you can map artwork directly onto the face of the object.

Extruding flat art

Extruding is the process of giving two-dimensional art depth that is equal on every part of the artwork. Figure 16-2 shows the flat art and the same art extruded. When extruding art, you can retain the default depth (50 pt) or set the Extrude Depth slider to anywhere from 0 to 2000 points.

Figure 16-2: The original flat art (left) and the extruded art (right)

To create a basic extrusion on an object:

1. **Create an object to extrude.**

2. **Select the object.** See Chapter 6 for more on selecting objects.

3. **Choose Effect ⇨ 3D ⇨ Extrude & Bevel to display the 3D Extrude & Bevel Options dialog box.**

4. **Click the preview box.** This let you see the default settings on your selected object.

5. **Click OK.** Illustrator applies the 3D extrusion to your object using the default settings (unless you made any changes in the dialog box).

You can choose these options in the 3D Extrude & Bevel Options dialog box:

✦ **Extrude Depth:** This option lets you control how far in points the object's path is extruded. Drag the slider with the Preview button on to see a live preview of the depth.

✦ **Cap:** Choose whether to have the cap turned on for a more solid look or off for a hollow look.

✦ **Rotate:** Use the Rotate option to rotate your object around an X, Y, and Z axis.

✦ **Views:** The view option lets you change the view around the X, Y, and Z axis.

✦ **Position:** The position pop-up menu lets you choose from a variety of positions for your selected object. Choose a view from the Front, Back, Left, Right, Top, Bottom, Off-axis back, Off-axis left, Off-axis right, Off-axis top, Off-axis bottom, Isometric Left, Isometric Right, Isometric Top, and Isometric Bottom. You can also drag the box around to create a custom rotation.

That was just a basic extrusion. There is so much more you can do. To begin with, you can cap or uncap an object. Uncapping takes away the front and back panes making the object hollow. Capping puts a front and back pane on the object, making the object solid.

In the Position area in the top of the 3D Extrude & Bevel Options dialog box, you can rotate the object, move the view around the X, Y, and Z axis, and add perspective to the object. The default position is Off-axis front. Figure 16-3 shows guitars with extrusion, lighting, and altered views applied in 3D.

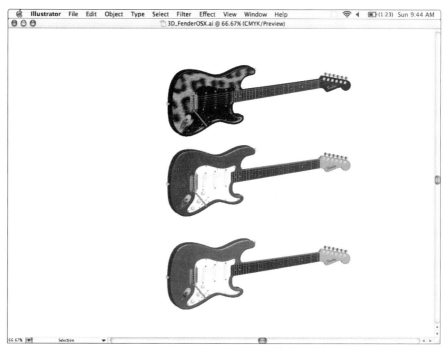

Figure 16-3: Guitars that were extruded, with lighting applied, and a rotated view

Cross-Reference   For more on lighting effects, see "Changing the Appearance of Three-Dimensional Objects" later in this chapter.

Extruding a stroke

One visually appealing effect that you can achieve is to take a dashed stroked line and use Extrude to make it 3D. This technique creates a bamboo look or individual bars.

Note   3D objects are inherently an extremely visual subject and most of the changes you make to them are quickly visible in the preview. Rather than giving you exact settings to reproduce the objects shown in the illustrations, I suggest you experiment to achieve results that please you. Your final results probably won't look just like the illustrations, but you'll have fun and learn more about how the settings interact that way.

Follow these steps to extrude a dashed line:

1. **Create an object with a dashed line stroke and no fill.** I used outlined text with a dashed stroke, but no fill.

2. **Choose Effect ⇨ 3D ⇨ Extrude & Bevel.** The Extrude & Bevel Options dialog box opens.

3. **Set the Extrude depth in points.** Alternatively, you can drag the slider, change the views by picking an option from the Position pop-up, or drag the box to a different view.

4. **Click OK to see the extruded dashed lines.** Figure 16-4 shows the resulting effect.

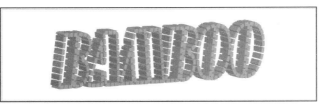

Figure 16-4: The extruded dashed stroke has a bamboo-type appearance.

Tip

Try using any of the Graphic Styles on your object before taking it into the 3D dialog boxes. You can come up with some pretty cool results.

Understanding bevels

The use of bevels can make or break your artwork. Bevels carve out an edge to your 3D object. You can use Illustrator's preset bevels, or, if you are feeling ambitious, you can create your own bevel.

Follow these steps to add a bevel to an object:

1. **Create an object to which you want to add 3D.**

2. **Choose Effect ⇨ 3D ⇨ Extrude & Bevel.** The Extrude & Bevel Options dialog box opens. (You can also apply an extrusion and change the position.)

3. **Choose a bevel from the drop-down menu.**

4. **Choose the height of the bevel and whether it bevels out or in.** The height option is how large or small you want the bevel to be. You set this option by dragging the Height slider to a bevel in points. The other option is whether you want to add the bevel to the outside of the object or subtract it from the

inside of the object. This make this determination, you click either the Bevel In or Bevel Out button.

5. **Check the preview box to see the bevel.** Leave the Preview box unchecked until you are done with your settings; otherwise it may take a while to preview your object.

6. **Click OK to see the final results.** Figure 16-5 shows the resulting bevel along the edge of the extruded path.

Figure 16-5: Adding a bevel to the artwork results in a very realistic-looking 3D effect.

Although the preset bevels are nice to use, you can also create your own custom bevel.

Follow these steps to add your own bevel to the Bevel menu:

1. **Open the Bevels.ai file found in the Adobe Illustrator Plug-ins folder.**

2. **Create the path you want to be your bevel in the Bevels.ai document.**

3. **Turn that path into a symbol.** You do this by choosing Window ➪ Symbols. Either drag the path to the Symbols palette, or select the path and click the New Symbol button in the Symbols palette. Or with the path selected, choose New Symbol from the Symbol palette drop-down menu.

Cross-Reference

For information on symbols, see Chapter 5.

4. **Rename the symbol.** To rename the symbol, double-click the symbol in the Symbols palette. Enter a name in the Symbol Options dialog box, and click OK.

5. **Choose File ➪ Save.** Doing this saves the new path symbol in the Bevels.ai file.

6. **Quit Illustrator, and start Illustrator again.** Now when you look at the Bevel menu in the 3D Extrude & Bevel Options dialog box, your new bevel is listed there. Now you can apply the custom bevel as you would any other bevel.

Revolving objects

Revolving, also called *lathing,* is the process of spinning a 2D object around an axis a specified number of degrees in order to create a 3D object. You can create things by revolving different objects around different axes. You can create a lamp, a chess piece, a wedge of cheese, and more.

Follow these steps to revolve a path:

1. **Draw a path first using any of the path tools (Pen, Pencil, or Line).** Figure 16-6 shows a simple path. For more on the different path tools, see Chapter 4.

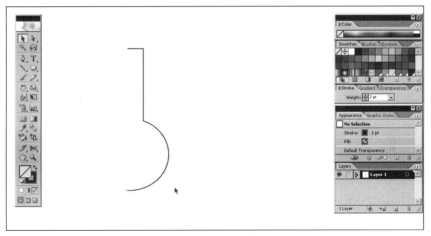

Figure 16-6: First draw the path to be revolved.

2. **Select the path, and choose Effect ➪ 3D ➪ Revolve to display the 3D Revolve Options dialog box, shown in Figure 16-7.**

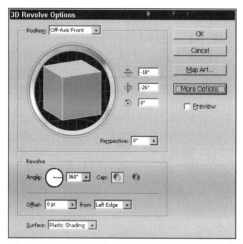

Figure 16-7: Use the 3D Revolve Options dialog box to create 3D objects by revolving a path.

3. **Click the Preview button to see the revolved object.**

4. **Click OK to finish the revolving.** Figure 16-8 shows the result of revolving the path we created. In this case the object is tilted a little to better show off the effect.

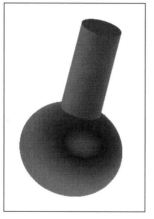

Figure 16-8: The revolved path looks like a 3D object.

The default option is to revolve the path 360 degrees. You can change that to any number between 1 and 360. A number less than 360 creates an open section like a wedge taken out of a round of cheese.

Rotating Objects

You can use the Rotate function found under the 3D effect submenu to rotate 2D and 3D objects. This rotation happens in 3D space. This is a great way to apply a sheared effect or perspective to an object that is 2D.

3D rotation is done in its own dialog box. Choose Effect ➪ 3D ➪ Rotate to open the 3D Rotate Options dialog box, as shown in Figure 16-9. In this dialog box, you can enter values in the text fields or you can click and drag the position square to the rotation you want. Make sure that you click the Preview button so you can see the rotation happen live.

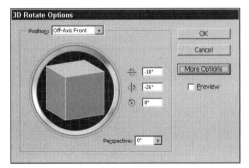

Figure 16-9: The 3D Rotate Options dialog box allows you to rotate an existing object.

Note   In most cases, you want to edit the existing effect by double-clicking it in the Appearance palette rather than using the Effect ➪ 3D ➪ Rotate menu command to rotate the existing object. Adding the Rotate effect to existing 3D objects can produce some very confusing results.

Changing the Appearance of Three-Dimensional Objects

Objects created in the 3D Extrude & Bevel Options dialog box are not only colored but also lit. With lighting comes additional specifications — shading and reflectivity. You control the light by its surface characteristics. If you don't see any lighting options, click the More Options button on the right side of the 3D Extrude & Bevel Options dialog box. This opens up the shading and light areas, as shown in Figure 16-10.

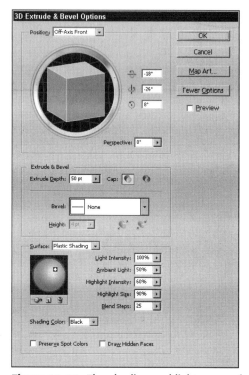

Figure 16-10: The shading and light areas of the 3D Extrude & Bevel Options dialog box enable you to exercise control over the lighting effects.

The Surface characteristics

The Surface properties control the look of the outside surface of the 3D object. You can create 3D objects that are just outlined, have no shading, have soft shading, or have intense, glossy shading. Your options are Wireframe, No Shading, Diffused Shading, and Plastic Shading. Figure 16-11 shows one object with each of the surface characteristics applied to them.

✦ **Wireframe** traces the curves of the object's geometric shape and fills the shape with transparent fill (there are no lighting options with this surface characteristic).

✦ **No Shading** fills the object with the same color as the original 2D object (there are no lighting options with this surface characteristic).

✦ **Diffuse Shading** adds a soft diffused light source on the object's surface.

✦ **Plastic Shading** adds a bright shiny light as if the object were made of plastic.

Figure 16-11: An object with all four surfaces applied from left to right (wireframe, no shading, diffuse shading, and plastic shading)

Understanding lighting

Lighting can be a little confusing in a 3D program. Because lights in 3D are positioned an infinite distance from objects, shading for different objects is the same, no matter what the position of the objects. For example, if the lights are in the upper left, objects on the far left have the same lighting as objects on the far right. If the lights were positioned closer, the shading would appear differently.

A good way to think of the lights that you create is that they resemble sunlight to us earthbound creatures. Light from the sun shines on an object in New York City almost exactly the same way it shines on an object in Boston. Because the sun is so far away, the difference in the position of the sun relative to the two cities is minute. If the sun were an infinite distance away and the earth were flat, the two cities would have exactly the same sunlight.

Because there are no shadows in Illustrator's 3D Extrude & Bevel Options dialog box, objects that are between the light source and another object let light pass through them so that the light can reach the "hidden" object.

Lighting options

In the lighting sphere in the 3D Extrude & Bevel Options dialog box, you can set a variety of lighting choices on your object. These buttons appear below the lighting preview sphere from left to right: Move selected light to back of object, New Light, and Delete Light.

You have these lighting options for Diffuse or Plastic Shading:

✦ **Light Intensity** controls how intense the light is. The values are from 0 to 100.

✦ **Ambient Light** changes the brightness of all the surfaces of the object. The values are from 0 to 100.

✦ **Blend Steps** adjusts how smooth the shading flows across the object. A lower number creates a more matte look. A higher number creates a glossy, shiny look.

If you are just using Plastic Shading, you can use these additional options:

✦ **Highlight Intensity** controls the reflecting light. A low number creates a matte look. A high number creates a glossy look.

✦ **Highlight Size** controls the size of the highlight on the object from 0 (none) to 100 (all).

Along with the lighting is the shading color. The default is black, but you can choose Custom, click the swatch that appears, and access the color picker. From the color palette, you can choose any color you wish.

Cross-Reference   For more on Color, see Chapter 7.

The lighting sphere shows the light on a surface. You can move the light around by dragging it to a new location. By clicking the New Light icon, you can add additional lights to the surface. The active light has a box around it. Each light can have different settings applied to it.

Note   The default setting is that all 3D objects must have one light. You can add as many as you like in addition to the default.

The Trash icon lets you delete lights. Select a light, and click the Trash icon to delete the light. The first icon is Move selected light to back of object. It sends that light behind the object for backlighting. Figure 16-12 shows an object with different lighting features applied to it.

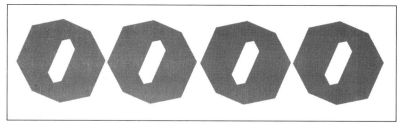

Figure 16-12: This figure shows an object with different lighting effects applied by using the lighting options in the 3D Extrude & Bevel Options dialog box.

Spot colors are automatically changed to process colors unless you check the Preserve Spot Colors box. When you check the Draw Hidden surfaces box, you can view the back faces through transparent surfaces.

Tip   If you hold down the Shift key while adjusting lighting in the 3D dialog box, you see the changes update in real time.

Using the Appearance palette with 3D

The amazing Appearance palette works wonders with 3D objects. If you have an object with multiple strokes and fills, and 3D, try moving the 3D to different areas of the Appearance palette. Move it above a fill or under a stroke, and see how different the object can look. Figure 16-13 shows an object with multiple attributes. I moved the 3D section to different areas to create different looks.

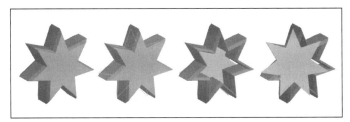

Figure 16-13: An original object (left) and the object after different attributes were moved in the Appearance palette (right)

Mapping 2D art to 3D surfaces

One of the most powerful features of 3D is the ability to wrap 2D objects around 3D surfaces. This feature alone makes upgrading or buying Illustrator worth the money. The Mapping feature is a great way to add a label to a bottle or any type of package design. Now your clients can see how their product will look before printing and packaging.

The most important concept to understand when you are mapping artwork is that each 3D object usually has several different surfaces, and each of those surfaces can have separate mapped artwork. The key to mapping 2D to 3D is to make a map out of the 2D object that you want to use and then turn it into a symbol. Any of Illustrator's symbols can be mapped onto 3D objects.

Follow these steps to create a 3D map out of a 2D object:

1. **Create the text (or other object) that you want to map onto the 3D art.**

2. **Drag the created text into the Symbols palette.** Doing this makes the text a new symbol.

3. **Create the path that you want to turn into 3D.** I chose a path to indicate a sign.

4. **Choose Effect ⇨ 3D ⇨ Extrude & Bevel to display the 3D Extrude & Bevel Options dialog box, shown in Figure 16-14.**

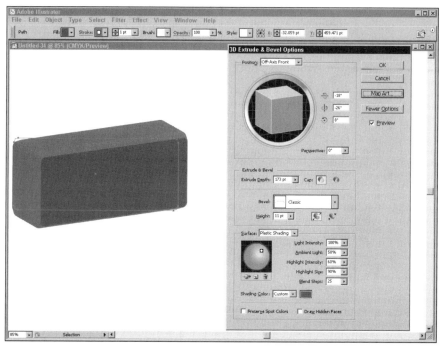

Figure 16-14: This figure shows the 3D Extrude & Bevel Options dialog box along with the path for a sign.

5. **Click the Map Art button to display the Map Art dialog box, shown in Figure 16-15.** In this dialog box, you can see the number of surfaces on the object, starting with surface 1.

6. **Choose the surface that you want to map.**

Note

As you choose a surface, the original highlights in red wireframe the surface you are selecting to make it easier for you to see where the mapping will occur.

7. **When you have the surface that you want to map, choose a symbol from the Symbol list box on the left.** The symbol you created is listed there, as shown in Figure 16-16.

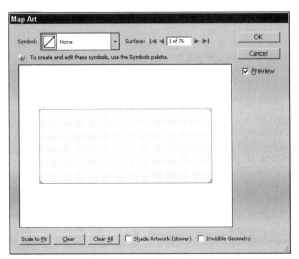

Figure 16-15: The Map Art dialog box enables you to place art on the surface of a 3D object.

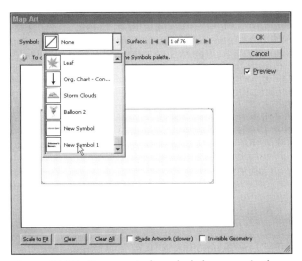

Figure 16-16: Your created symbol shows up in the Symbol list box.

8. **After you have chosen the art for all the surfaces, click OK to exit the Map Art dialog box.**

9. **Change the rotation or axis view if you want.**

10. **Click OK.** The final results are shown in Figure 16-17.

Figure 16-17: The final artwork is mapped onto the extruded object.

When you choose a symbol in the Map Art dialog box to map, the symbol appears in the center of the screen with a bounding box around it. This box gives you the ability to stretch, rotate, or move the object to fit the area you want.

The Map Art dialog box also has a preview button, which allows you to see the object mapped onto the shape. A cool thing to do is to use a cube and map artwork on all surfaces of the cube to make custom dice. Use the dice later in an animation for a Web page.

Cross-Reference   For more on Web stuff, see Chapter 19.

The Map Art dialog box has several other useful features:

✦ **Symbol:** Choose the 2D object to map onto your shape.

✦ **Surface:** All the object's surfaces are listed here. Apply mapped art to one surface or as many as you like.

✦ **Scale to Fit:** Choose this option to scale the mapped artwork to fit the whole surface.

✦ **Clear:** Use this to remove mapped artwork from the selected surface.

✦ **Clear All:** Use this to remove all mapped artwork from all surfaces.

✦ **Shade Artwork (slower):** This option shows the mapped artwork along with the shade and lighting applied. A preview takes longer with this option selected.

✦ **Invisible Geometry:** Choosing this option previews just the mapped art on the object with the object showing in wireframe.

Using Other 3D Techniques

Using Adobe Illustrator's 3D Effect isn't the only way to create depth in illustrations. You can do many things in Illustrator to create the illusion of depth. Drop shadows and blended shadows help define depth, but the most useful thing that you can do is to think about how a light source would hit an object and reflect back to the viewer.

Using gradients to make bumps and dents

When you place gradients on themselves and one gradient has a different direction than another, 3D effects appear. If you remember that highlights reflect off surfaces that bounce light to your eye, that principle should help you determine the direction of the gradients.

Of course, whether an object is coming at you or going away from you should be obvious, shouldn't it? Figure 16-18 shows ten different buttons. See whether you can determine which buttons are "innies" and which buttons are "outies." To assist you further, each button is on a standard background and has a button ring. The ring makes the direction of several of the buttons quite obvious.

Perspective drawing

Another newer aspect to Illustrator is the addition of perspective. The perspective option is found in the 3D Extrude & Bevel Options dialog box. This option gives your 3D object a perspective look. The perspective slider ranges from 0 to 160 degrees. The perspective is a simulated distance from the object in the actual file, as shown in Figure 16-19.

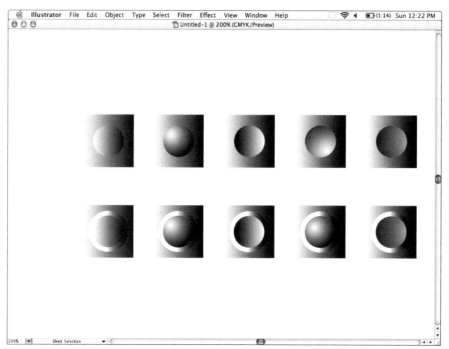

Figure 16-18: Innie and outie buttons show another 3D technique.

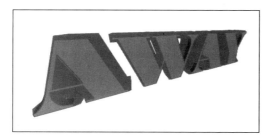

Figure 16-19: A 3D object with perspective applied

Guest Artist How-To: Using Illustrator to Create 3D Texture Maps (by Joe Jones)

I would never claim to be one of the best texture mappers, 3D modelers, or science-fiction illustrators around, although I certainly aspire to be, but the techniques I show here have worked pretty well for me so far.

Very early on when I was experimenting in a 3D environment, I quickly realized that the key to creating 3D images was to create texture maps with as much detail as possible. Creating a wireframe for every little intricate component that I wanted to show in my architecture would create incredibly huge files and probably take a couple of weeks to render. Not the thing to do! For me, it was logistically impossible to model everything, so I had to quickly come up with a system to create the necessary level of detail in my illustrations. I am currently still refining my process of creating 3D illustrations, which has already taken several years of development. Incredibly difficult, but very fun stuff!

Being able to have full control of each step and to see it all come together in 3D is nothing less than incredible to me. I've worked on every type of graphic and illustration projects you can imagine for more than 20 years now, but nothing comes close to the intimacy that I feel when working on 3D texture images. Although I'm sure a psychiatrist would claim that this is a form of escapism, I say, hey, an artist has to dream!

Well, without further ado, the following sections provide a brief description of each of the steps involved.

Conceptualization

I first created a slew of small conceptual thumbnails, sketches, and studies. Figure 16-20 shows the original conceptual sketch that I worked from for this piece titled "Port Merillia."

Figure 16-20: A sketch of the original concept

In the business of illustration, we have a saying: "Practice safe design and still use the concept!" In the end, concept is everything. Although in 3D illustration, true craftsmanship is in the model making and texture mapping, the concept still has to pull it all together for the illustration to work. I first developed a large series of conceptual sketches, one of which is shown in Figure 16-21, and then I defined the look of my architecture. I designed and built all the outline parts for the shape of each building as paths in Illustrator, which were later used in the modeling process in Ray Dream Studio. The actual texture mapping for each building is a process that starts in Illustrator, which I discuss soon.

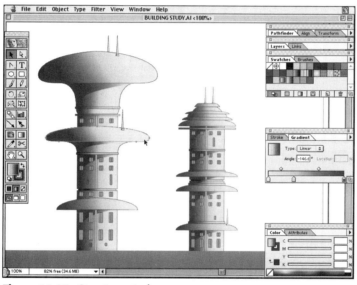

Figure 16-21: Structure study

Modeling

Yes, yes, I know that this is surely the poor boy's approach to 3D illustration. What can I say? It works, and I'm still not quite ready to drop several thousand dollars on applications such as Maya or 3ds max. Soon, maybe. Figure 16-22 is a conceptual vector study created in Illustrator. Here, I work on refining the scale, depth, color, and balance that I want from this piece.

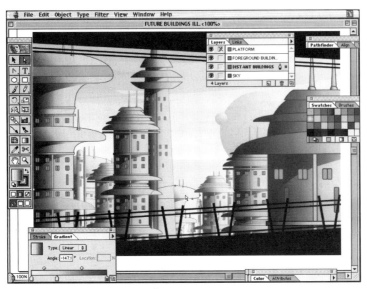

Figure 16-22: Structure study

Figure 16-23 shows the actual wireframe model of the dome element of just one structure after construction. It is now ready to be assembled with other modeled elements and have the texture map applied. To turn a basic shape into a 3D model, you must generate at least two separate paths — one is the shape of how it would look from the side, and the other is from the top. These paths are called *Cross Sections* and *Envelope Lines* and are essential in extruding or lathing a shape into a 3D model.

As you look at these illustrations, remember that for every single shape in each building, I had to produce at least two precise paths in Illustrator. I created all line work for the models, as well as the artwork for the texture mapping, at the same time to ensure that everything would fit and map correctly in the final steps. That's very important!

Texture mapping

Figure 16-24 shows the wireframe model of the dome element, with the texture map quickly applied for a better idea of its look, smoothness, and form.

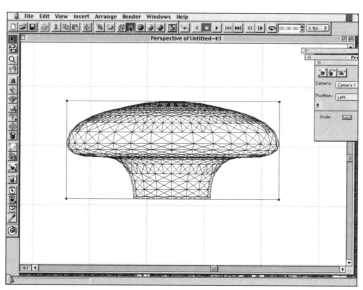

Figure 16-23: Dome wireframe

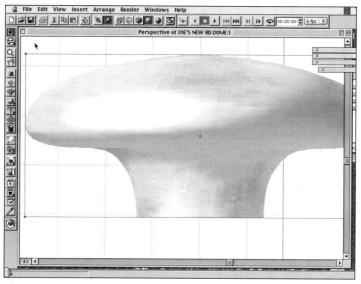

Figure 16-24: The dome with a texture map applied

All the custom mapping I created was based on my original sketches and more refined drawings, which had to be first carefully laid out in Illustrator, as shown in Figure 16-25. Starting with the circular base shape for the dome on the first layer, I created various panels, lights, and windows on separate layers for full control of these elements in Photoshop.

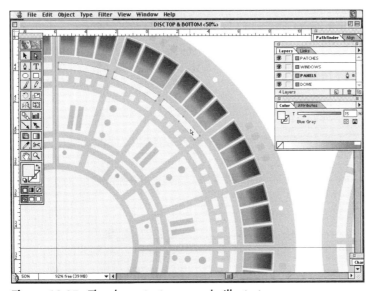

Figure 16-25: The dome texture map in Illustrator

I carefully constructed each map to proportionately match the building models that were built. To maintain their layers, I then exported these Illustrator files into Photoshop, where I added additional weathering and edge effect treatments.

Just like the dome map, the building map, shown in Figure 16-26, was created in a similar manner. Each element of the panels, patches, windows, and lights was set up on separate layers to be exported into Photoshop with the layers intact, to complete the final rendered map.

Figure 16-27 is the dome map file being brought into Photoshop. I started with some color correction and created the custom brushes that were needed for painting the weathered appearance.

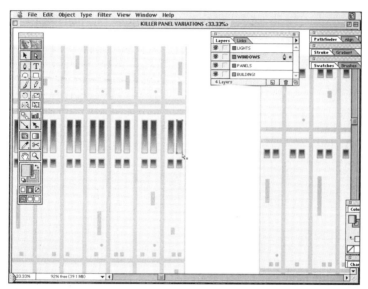

Figure 16-26: Building the texture map in Illustrator

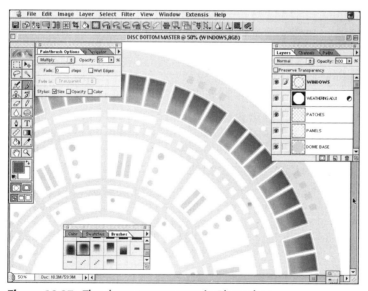

Figure 16-27: The dome texture map in Photoshop

As any experienced texture map artist will tell you, the appearance of weathering and signs of aging are critical to creating an illusion of reality. Figure 16-28 shows the final dome texture map with all its edge effects and hand-painted weathering. I worked both in Layers and Adjustment Layers in Photoshop to create this effect. When this map is applied to its model, it looks very convincing. Though the shapes in these maps are basic, this gives you some idea of the level of detail that can be created with a good texture map.

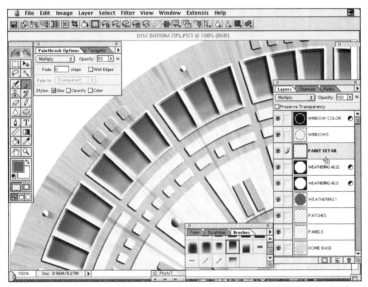

Figure 16-28: The weathered dome texture map in Photoshop

Figure 16-29 shows one of the many final building texture maps that I created. Again, I created its edge effects and hand-painted weathering in Layers and Adjustment Layers working in Photoshop.

To create certain effects, and especially the illusion of transparency and ambiance for the window and the lights, I first had to create this window mask for the dome in Illustrator, as shown in Figure 16-30. I then rasterized it as a grayscale file to be mapped in later. If done right, this creates a convincing effect without the pains of extensive modeling.

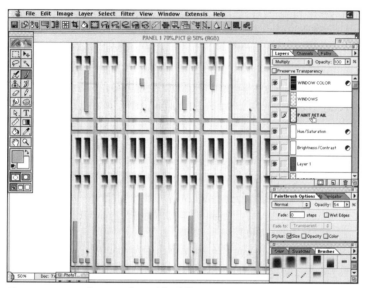

Figure 16-29: The weathered building texture map in Photoshop

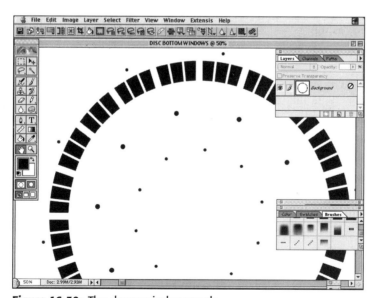

Figure 16-30: The dome window mask

Figure 16-31 shows four different texture maps applied to just one structure model. Add some light and atmosphere, and we're well on our way. What'd I tell you? Pretty convincing, huh!

Figure 16-31: The final dome texture maps

The final completed wireframe model partially rendered is shown in Figure 16-32. Of course, after all the texture mapping is applied to all the various models, this scene based on the original sketch needs to be built, lit, and then rendered. From there, the file is brought into Photoshop, where color correction and a ton of touch-up work is done. For example, the clothing for the figures is hand-painted using a digital tablet. We're not in Kansas anymore!

Cross-Reference See the color insert for more projects by Joe Jones and other leading Illustrator artists.

Figure 16-32: A sample of the final model

Summary

Creating 3D objects from 2D ones really brings your Illustrator documents alive. In this chapter, you learned about Illustrator's 3D effects, including these:

✦ You can extrude or revolve 2D objects to create 3D objects.

✦ You can add multiple lights and change the color of the shading on a 3D object.

✦ You can change the surface characteristics to be wireframe, no shading, diffuse shading, or plastic shading.

✦ You can map 2D artwork onto 3D objects.

✦ Layering gradients creates a 3D look.

✦   ✦   ✦

Customizing and Automating Illustrator

✦ ✦ ✦ ✦

In This Chapter

Customizing
Illustrator

Altering preferences

Changing the Startup
file

Creating actions

Customizing actions

✦ ✦ ✦ ✦

Y ou know that you can use Illustrator to do all types of incredible artwork, but you should also see the practical, real-world side of Illustrator where deadlines must be met and there's little or no time for play. This chapter focuses on real-world applications of Illustrator and how to get the most out of the software.

Who's Responsible for Illustrator?

Under the Help menu (Illustrator menu on a Macintosh), you'll find some useful information about the creators of Illustrator and its plug-ins.

About Illustrator displays a dialog box, shown in Figure 17-1, with the user information and credits for the Illustrator team (click the Credits button to see the list). The credits box lists everyone who ever helped with getting Illustrator updated and created and makes you aware of the large number of people who are involved in creating the software.

About Plug-Ins displays a dialog box, shown in Figure 17-2, that lists all the installed plug-ins. Selecting one of the items in the list and clicking About displays who made the plug-in and, occasionally, some useful or interesting information about that plug-in.

Figure 17-1: The Adobe Illustrator dialog box tells you information about your copy of Illustrator.

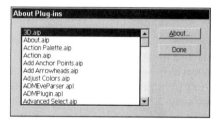

Figure 17-2: The About Plug-Ins dialog box shows which plug-ins you have installed.

Customization Options

No two illustrators work the same. To accommodate the vast differences among styles, techniques, and habits, Illustrator provides many settings that each user can change to personalize the software.

Illustrator provides five major ways to change preferences:

✦ The most dramatic and difficult changes are to a small file called Adobe Illustrator Startup. The startup file changes how new documents appear and which custom colors, patterns, and gradients are available.

✦ You can also control how Illustrator works by accessing the Preferences submenu, which you do by choosing Edit ➪ Preferences (Illustrator ➪ Preferences) or by pressing Ctrl+K (⌘+K). Within the Preferences dialog box, a number of different preference panels can be selected from the drop-down list (pop-up menu) at the top of the dialog box. You can go through each of the preference panels one by one by clicking the Next and Previous buttons or simply by choosing a preference panel from the Preferences submenu. The preference panels are General, Type, Units & Display Performance, Guides & Grid, Smart Guides & Slices, Hyphenation, Plug-Ins & Scratch Disks, File Handling & Clipboard, and Appearance of Black.

✦ A third way to make changes is by changing preferences relative to each document. You usually make these changes in the Document Setup dialog box, but a few other options are available. You can find more information on document-specific preferences later in this chapter.

✦ The fourth way to customize preferences happens pretty much automatically. When you quit Illustrator, it remembers many of the current settings for the next time you run it. These settings include palette placements and values in toolbox settings.

✦ The fifth way is to use the Window ⇨ Workspace commands to save your favorite workspace configuration or to reset the workspace to the default when you've really messed things up.

Illustrator has a few settings that you cannot customize. These features can really get under your skin because most of them seem like things that you should be able to customize. See the "Knowing What You Can't Customize" section later in this chapter for a list of these settings.

Modifying the Startup File

When you first run Illustrator, the program looks to the Illustrator startup file to check a number of preferences. Those preferences include window size and placement, as well as custom colors, gradients, patterns, zoom levels, tiling options, and graph designs.

Illustrator has two startup files — one for each color mode (RBG and CMYK). When launching Illustrator and starting a new document, you choose which color mode you want to work in.

New documents have all the attributes of the startup file for the selected color mode. Opened documents have all the gradients, custom colors, patterns, and graph designs of the startup file. Follow these steps to modify the startup file:

1. **Make a copy of the existing startup file.** Making a backup copy is very important, so you can revert to the original settings in case you make a mistake.

2. **Open the startup file.** The startup file is called either Adobe Illustrator Startup_CMYK.ai or Adobe Illustrator Startup_RGB.ai and is located in the

Plug-Ins folder in the Adobe Illustrator program folder. The file is an Adobe Illustrator document, so double-clicking the file opens Illustrator as well. Figure 17-3 shows the Adobe Illustrator Startup_CMYK file.

3. **To add something to the startup file, add the color, pattern, or gradient to the Swatches palette.** To add a graph design, create the graph design and apply it to a graph. Then place the graph in the startup file.

4. **To change the window size, just save the startup file with the window size that you want new documents to have.**

5. **To change the color swatches on the Swatches palette, add, replace, or delete color swatches while the startup file is open and then save the startup file.**

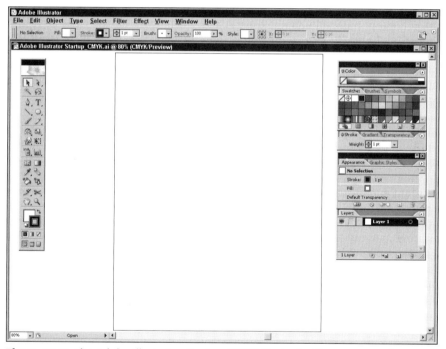

Figure 17-3: The Adobe Illustrator Startup_CMYK file looks like an empty document but is actually very important as the basis for new documents.

Caution

If you delete the Adobe Illustrator Startup file, most patterns, gradients, and custom colors are not available until you create a new startup file or place the original startup file from the CD-ROM in the Plug-Ins folder.

To check whether changes that you made in the startup file work, quit Illustrator and launch the program again. You cannot tell whether the changes are in place until you quit and reopen Illustrator. If there is a problem, replace the startup file with the backup copy you made in order to restore the original settings.

You can change both the window size of new documents and the viewing percentage. Most people seem to like documents to fit in the window when it is created.

Changing Preferences

The General portion of the Preferences dialog box, accessed by choosing Edit ➪ General ➪ Preferences (Illustrator ➪ Preferences ➪ General) or pressing Ctrl+K (⌘+K), contains most of the personalized customizing options for Illustrator. The options in this box affect keyboard increments, measuring units, and the way that objects are drawn. These options are considered personalized options because they are specific to the way that each person uses the program. Few people have the same preference settings as others have (unless they never change the defaults). The General portion of the Preferences dialog box is shown in Figure 17-4.

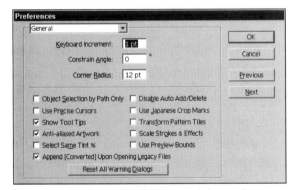

Figure 17-4: The General portion of the Preferences dialog box enables you to customize Illustrator.

Altering the Keyboard Increment option

The cursor key increment that you specify in this option controls how far an object moves when you select it and press the keyboard arrows.

The default for this setting is 1 point, which many people feel is small enough. I make my increment smaller when I am working in 800% or 1600% views.

Tip   While the arrow keys move selected objects the distance that is set in the keyboard increment option, Alt (Option) + the arrow key makes a copy of the object in that direction.

Using the Constrain Angle option

The Constrain Angle option controls the angle at which all objects are aligned. By default, rectangles are always drawn "flat," aligning themselves to the bottom, top, and sides of the document window. When you press the Shift key, lines that you draw with the Pen tool and objects that you move align to the Constrain Angle, or 45°, 90°, 135°, or 180°, plus or minus the constraining angle.

The Constrain Angle also affects how the four transformation tools transform objects. The Scale tool can be very hard to use when the Constrain Angle is not 0°, and the Shear tool becomes even more difficult to use than normal at different Constrain Angles. Pressing Shift when you are using the Rotate tool constrains the rotational angle to 45° increments added to the Constrain Angle.

Cross-Reference   For more on the Rotate tool and other transformational tools, see Chapter 11.

In Illustrator, 0° is a horizontal line and 90° is a vertical line. Figure 17-5 shows Illustrator angles.

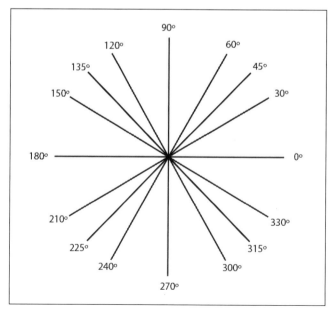

Figure 17-5: Angles in Illustrator are measured in a counterclockwise direction.

If you set the Constrain Angle at 20°, objects are constrained to movements of 20°, 65°, 110°, 155°, and 200°. Constrain Angles of 90°, 180°, and –90° (270°) affect only type, patterns, gradients, and graphs; everything else works normally.

When copying objects using the Alt (Option) shortcut, you can use the Shift key in conjunction with a Constrain Angle to duplicate objects at a specific angle. To copy with the Alt (Option) shortcut, press the Alt (Option) key while dragging an object and then release the mouse button before releasing the Alt (Option) key to produce a duplicate of the object at the new location.

Changing the Corner Radius option

The Corner Radius option affects the size of the curved corners on a rounded rectangle.

Cross-Reference   For a complete explanation of the corner radius and rounded rectangles, see Chapter 5.

The corner radius value changes each time you enter a new value in the Rounded Rectangle dialog box. This dialog box appears when you click the Rounded Rectangle tool without dragging in a document. If, for example, you create one rounded rectangle with a rounded-corner radius of 24 points, all rounded rectangles that you create from that point forward have a radius of 24 points. You can change the corner radius in only two ways: click the Rounded Rectangle tool without dragging in a document and then enter a new value in the Rounded Rectangle dialog box, or enter a new value in the Corner Radius text field in the Preferences dialog box.

The real advantage to changing the corner radius in the Preferences dialog box is that the corner radius affects manually created (dragged with the Rounded Rectangle tool) rounded rectangles immediately. Changing the corner radius in the Rectangle dialog box requires that you know the exact dimensions of the rectangle or that you draw a rectangle by entering information in the Rounded Rectangle dialog box (clicking with the Rounded Rectangle tool without dragging) and specify the corner radius. You must then delete the original rectangle in order to draw a rounded rectangle with the correct corner radius manually.

Caution   Because you can change the Corner Radius setting easily, be sure to check it before you draw a series of rounded rectangles manually. You cannot easily or automatically change the corner radius on existing rounded rectangles.

If you use 0 points as the Corner Radius setting, the corners are not rounded at all.

Adjusting the General options

The 11 check boxes in the General Options section of Preferences are Illustrator's version of the Battlestar Galactica ragtag fleet of unwieldy spacefaring craft. Some are quite powerful, and others seem like they aren't capable of transferring millions of people across the galaxy, much less defending themselves against the evil menace of the Cylon Empire. Okay, that wasn't the best analogy. The fact is, you won't find another place in Illustrator where so many totally unrelated options share the same dialog box, and I had to come up with a snazzy introduction.

Object Selection by Path Only

With Object Selection by Path Only checked, you have to select the object's path with a Selection tool to select the object, rather than click on the fill. If you uncheck this option, you can click on the fill with the Selection tool to select it.

The Use Precise Cursors option

Precise cursors are cursors that appear as a variation of a cross hair instead of in the shape of a tool. Figure 17-6 shows cursors that are different when the Use Precise Cursors option is on.

Tip   The Caps Lock key toggles between standard cursors and precise cursors. When the Use Precise Cursors option is checked, the Caps Lock key makes the cursors standard. When the Use Precise Cursors option is not checked, the Caps Lock key activates the precise cursors.

I usually keep this option on and rarely engage the Caps Lock key to change the cursors back to normal. In particular, I've found the precise cursor for the Brush tool to be quite useful, because the standard Brush cursor is one giant amorphous blob.

The Show Tool Tips option

This option displays little pop-up names for each of the tools if you rest your cursor above them for one second. It's a great idea to keep this option on, because not only do you see the name of the tool, but also the key to press to access that tool.

Tip   Illustrator lets you see the name of each swatch as you pass your cursor over it if you have Tool Tips active.

The Anti-aliased Artwork option

The Anti-aliased Artwork option turns on anti-aliasing for onscreen representation of vector objects. Curved and diagonal edges appear smooth instead of jagged (or "stair-stepped"). The resulting effect is for onscreen viewing only, and it won't affect output or rasterization of your artwork.

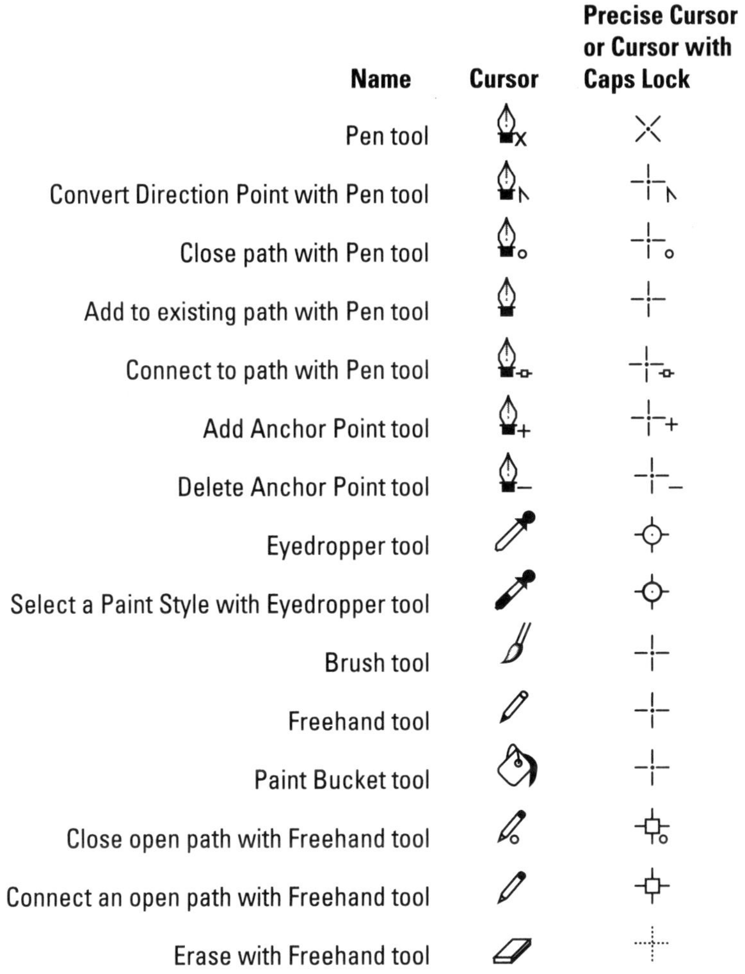

Name	Cursor	Precise Cursor or Cursor with Caps Lock
Pen tool		
Convert Direction Point with Pen tool		
Close path with Pen tool		
Add to existing path with Pen tool		
Connect to path with Pen tool		
Add Anchor Point tool		
Delete Anchor Point tool		
Eyedropper tool		
Select a Paint Style with Eyedropper tool		
Brush tool		
Freehand tool		
Paint Bucket tool		
Close open path with Freehand tool		
Connect an open path with Freehand tool		
Erase with Freehand tool		

Figure 17-6: This shows the regular cursors on the left and the precise cursors on the right.

Select Same Tint % option

This option specifies that the objects must have the same tint percentage when selecting objects with the same color. If this option isn't checked and you select a color, all tints of that color are selected.

Append [Converted] Upon Opening Legacy Files option

When you open an older version of an Illustrator file (prior to Illustrator CS), you get a dialog box telling you "This file contains text that was created in a previous version of Illustrator. This legacy text must be updated before you edit it." Because the text engine was revamped in Illustrator CS, all old type needs to be updated. By default, this option is checked so that all files with legacy type or other functions such as older files before gradients and transparency are updated when opening the file.

Disable Auto Add/Delete option

This option refers to the Pen tool's automatic add/delete feature. The default is unchecked. When the box is not checked, you can add or delete points while drawing with the Pen tool. As you are drawing a path with the Pen tool, you can click on the path to add more anchor points. You can also click an anchor point to delete it and continue to draw your path without having to switch tools. When you check this option, this feature is turned off.

The Use Japanese Crop Marks option

When checked, the Use Japanese Crop Marks option changes the standard crop marks, usually created with Filter ⇨ Create ⇨ Crop Marks, to Japanese Crop Marks, as shown in Figure 17-7.

The Transform Pattern Tiles option

Check the Transform Pattern Tiles option if you want patterns in paths to be moved, scaled, rotated, sheared, and reflected when you use the transformation tools. When this option is checked, opening a transformation dialog box (Move, Rotate, Scale, Reflect, or Shear) automatically checks the Pattern check box. When the option is not checked, the Pattern check box is not checked in the transformation dialog box. This option controls whether selected patterns are transformed when the transform palette is used.

I usually check the Transform Pattern Tiles box, which sets all patterns to automatically transform and move with the objects that are being transformed and moved. This feature is especially useful when you want to create perspective in objects because the transformations of patterns can enhance the intended perspective.

Figure 17-7: Standard crop marks (top) and Japanese crop marks (bottom)

The Scale Strokes & Effects option

When the Scale Strokes & Effects feature is on, it automatically increases and reduces line weights and applied effects relative to an object when you uniformly scale that object manually. For example, if a path has a stroke weight of 1 point and you reduce the path uniformly by 50 percent, the stroke weight changes to 0.5 point.

Note Scaling objects non-uniformly (without the Shift key pressed) does not change the stroke weight on an object, regardless of whether the Scale Strokes & Effects feature is on or off.

The Use Preview Bounds option

When you check the Use Preview Bounds option, it affects how the Info palette measures the dimension of the selected object. With the Use Preview Bounds checked, Illustrator's Info palette includes the size of the stroke width and other elements like feathered shadows in the dimensions.

Reset All Warning Boxes option

The Reset All Warning Boxes option puts back all of Illustrator's lovely warnings. For example, you get a warning when you try to delete a point and don't click on the point. You can turn this off by clicking the Don't show this again box. When you choose to reset all warning boxes, it is turned on again.

Changing Preferences for Type

The Type preferences enable you to customize your type options. You have nine type options to choose from. Figure 17-8 shows the Type section of the Preferences dialog box.

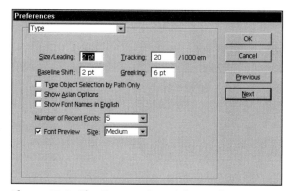

Figure 17-8: The Type section of the Preferences dialog box enables you to select the options for type used in your documents.

You can set these nine type preference options: Size/Leading, Baseline Shift, Tracking, Greeking, Type Object Selection by Path Only, Show Asian Options, Show Font Names in English, Number of Recent Fonts, and Font Preview. (When you select Font Preview, you have an additional option of Size.)

The Size/Leading option

You can use the keyboard to increase and decrease type size by pressing Ctrl+Shift+> (⌘+Shift+>) and Ctrl+Shift+< (⌘+Shift+<), respectively. You can increase and decrease leading by pressing Alt+↑ (Option+↑) and Alt+↓ (Option+↓), respectively. In the Size/Leading text box, you specify the increment by which the size and leading change.

You can increase or decrease the type size and leading only until you reach the upper and lower limits of each. The upper limit for type size and leading is 1296 points, and the lower limit for each is 0.1 point.

Tip

I keep my settings fairly high, at 10 points, because I have found that I require large point changes, usually quite a bit more than 10 points. If I need to do fine-tuning, I either type the exact size that I want or use the Scale tool.

The Baseline Shift option

The Baseline Shift feature moves selected type up and down on the baseline, independent of the leading. The increment specified in this box is how much the type is moved when you press the arrow keyboard commands. To move type up one Increment, press Alt+Shift+↑ (Option+Shift+↑). To move type down one increment, press Alt+Shift+↓ (Option+Shift+↓).

I keep the Baseline shift increment at 1 point so that I can adjust path type better; specifically, I like to be able to adjust the baseline shift of type on a circle.

The Tracking option

Tracking changes the amount of space between selected characters, and the setting in this text field represents the amount of space (measured in thousandths of an em space) that the keyboard command adds or removes. To increase tracking, you press Ctrl+→ (⌘+→); to decrease it, you press Ctrl+← (⌘+←).

To increase the tracking by five times the increment in the Type & Auto Tracing portion of the Preferences dialog box, press Shift+Alt+Ctrl+\ (Shift+Option+⌘+\). To decrease the tracking by five times the increment, press Shift+Alt+Ctrl+backspace (Shift+Option+⌘+backspace).

The value in the Tracking text field also affects incremental changes in kerning. Kerning is the addition or removal of space between one pair of letters only. Kerning is done instead of tracking when a blinking insertion point is between two letters, as opposed to at least one selected character for tracking.

The Greeking option

The number that you enter in this field defines the point at which Illustrator begins to greek text. Illustrator greeks text — turns the letters into gray bars — when the text is so small that reading it on the screen would be difficult or impossible. This change reduces screen redraw time dramatically, especially when the document contains a great deal of text.

The size in this text field is relative to the viewing magnification of the document. At a limit of 6 points, 6-point type at 100%, 66%, 50%, 25%, or smaller is greeked; but 6-point type at 150%, 200%, or larger will be readable. With the same limitations, 12-point type is greeked at 50% and smaller, but it is readable at 51% and larger.

The Type Object Selection by Path Only option

Checking this option makes it possible to select text by clicking on the text path itself. The default is turned off, allowing you to click anywhere on the type with the Selection tool to select the type.

The Show Asian Options option

Check the Show Asian Options option to be able to view and set the options for Asian fonts. The Asian fonts include Chinese, Japanese, and Korean.

The Show Font Names in English option

If you have a font from another language installed on your system (like Kanji, a Japanese character set), this option allows you to see these typefaces in the font/type menus as English words.

Setting the Number of Recent Fonts option

You use the Number of Recent Fonts option to specify how many font names are displayed in the Type ⇨ Recent Fonts submenu. You can choose a value between 1 and 15 from the drop-down list box. This option is especially useful if you have a large number of fonts installed on your system and you reuse several of the same fonts often. Choose a value that represents the largest number of fonts that you typically use in a single document.

Choosing a font preview size

When the Font Preview check box is selected, Illustrator displays fonts in the Type ⇨ Font menu using characters from the font. You can choose small, medium, or large size characters for the font preview from the Size drop-down list (pop-up menu). A smaller size allows more fonts to appear in the list without scrolling, while larger sizes make the subtle differences between certain fonts easier to see.

Using Units & Display Performance

The Units & Display Performance preferences enable you to select the measurement system you want to use and set the performance of the Hand tool. Figure 17-9 shows the Units & Display Performance section of the Preferences dialog box.

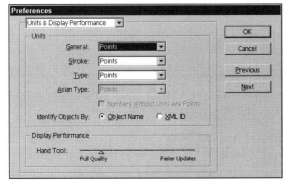

Figure 17-9: The Units & Display Performance section of the Preferences dialog box allows you to choose the units.

Changing Units settings

The General pop-up menu in the Units section changes the measurement system for the current document and all future new documents. The areas for which the measurement can be specified are General (which includes the Rulers), Stroke, Type, and Asian Type. Illustrator contains five different measurement units: inches, picas, points, millimeters, and centimeters.

✦ **General:** Applies to the measure tool and the Rulers

✦ **Stroke:** Applies to the weight of the path's stroke

✦ **Type:** Sets the type measurement increments

✦ **Asian Type:** Sets the type measurement increments for Asian type

Caution

Changing the General units in the Units & Display Performance Preferences dialog box changes the Ruler units in the Document Setup dialog box. Access this dialog box by choosing File ⇨ Document Setup or pressing Ctrl+Alt+P (⌘+Option+P).

The other areas under Units that can be changed are the Numbers Without Units Are Points check box and Identify Objects By (Object Name or XML ID).

✦ **Numbers Without Units Are Points:** When you enter a number with no measurement indicator (I for inches, p for points, and so on), the default is points.

✦ **Identify Objects By:** In this area, choose a radio button to identify objects by name or XML ID. If you save your document in SVG format for use with other Adobe products, choose XML ID to ensure that object names conform to XML naming conventions.

Being aware of which measurement system you are working in is important. When you enter a measurement in a dialog box, any numbers that are not measurement-system-specific are applied to the current unit of measurement. For example, if you want to move something 1 inch and you open the Move dialog box by choosing Object ➪ Transform ➪ Move or double-clicking the Selection tool, you need to add either the inch symbol (") or the abbreviation after you type 1 in the dialog box if the measurement system is not inches. If the measurement system is points or picas, entering 1 moves the object 1 point (or 1 pica), not 1 inch. If the measurement system is inches already, entering just the number 1 is fine.

Usually a corresponding letter or letters indicates the measurement system: in for inch, pt for points, and cm for centimeters.

Caution   The default measurement is points, so if you ever toss your preferences file or reinstall Illustrator, be aware that you may have to change the measurement system.

Changing Display Performance

The Hand tool's viewing performance is what you are adjusting under the Display Performance area. Drag the slider to the left so you see more quality when moving around your screen. Drag the slider to the right to get a quicker update with less quality viewing. A quicker update shows a rough preview as you are dragging rather than an exact preview of your illustration as you move around.

Changing Guides and Grid Preferences

The Guides & Grid section of Preferences lets you control the color and style of your guides and grids, and the spacing of your grid. Figure 17-10 shows the Guides & Grid section of the Preferences dialog box. Chapter 5 has the lowdown on using these options and grids and guides.

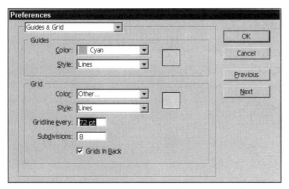

Figure 17-10: The Guides & Grid section of the Preferences dialog box enables you to fine-tune the guides and grid settings.

Tip   You can place grids in back of or in front of your image by checking or not check-ing the Grids In Back option in the Guides & Grid Preferences dialog box.

Adjusting Smart Guides & Slices

Smart Guides are helpers that show you the angle of the line and list the line as a path. You can check or uncheck four Display Options as well as adjust the angles and snapping tolerance. The Smart Guides snap to other objects aiding you in align-ing, editing, and transforming. Figure 17-11 shows the Smart Guides & Slices section of the Preferences dialog box. Slices are subdivisions of a Web-based graphic and used for Web pages. For more information on Slices and the Web, see Chapter 19.

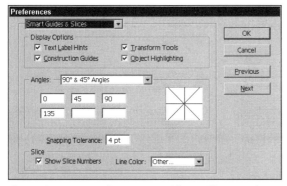

Figure 17-11: Use the Smart Guides & Slices section of the Preferences dialog box to set up the Smart Guides.

Changing Display options

These are the four Display Options:

✦ **Text Label Hints:** These hints pop up when you drag your mouse cursor over your object. They tell you what each area is. For example, if you drag your mouse cursor over a line, the hint pops up with the word "path." If you drag your mouse cursor over an anchor point, the hint says "anchor point."

✦ **Transform Tools:** When you are rotating, scaling, or shearing an object with this option checked, Smart Guides shows up to help you out.

✦ **Construction Guides:** This lets you view guidelines when using Smart Guides.

✦ **Object Highlighting:** This option highlights the object to which you are pointing.

Altering Angles

The Angles that you can choose in the Smart Guides & Slices dialog box let you pick what angles display guides when you drag an object. You can choose from seven presets or create Custom Angles. The lines indicate the standard guide angles. When you add your own angled lines, a line shows up representing the particular angle you entered.

Changing Snapping Tolerance

The Snapping Tolerance enables you to choose how close one object must be to another object before the first object automatically "snaps" to the second object. You set the Snapping Tolerance in points, and the lower the number, the closer you must move the objects to each other. The snapping tolerance default is 4 points. That means when you are within 4 points to another object, your selected object snaps to the second object. I tend to stick with the default.

Adjusting Slices

The options for Slices are the Show Slice Numbers check box and Line Color. The Show Slice Numbers shows the numbers for each slice, if checked. The Line Color option lets you change the slice lines to a color of your choice. The default is to use a contrasting color.

Cross-Reference   Slicing is covered in Chapter 19.

Changing Hyphenation

The Hyphenation section of the Preferences dialog box contains options for customizing the way Illustrator hyphenates words. At the top of the dialog box is a drop-down list (pop-up menu) that lists various languages. Select the default language. Typically, if you use Illustrator in English, you don't have to change anything. If you use a different language, you need to have that language installed on your computer. Then you can choose the language you want to use as a default. At the bottom of the dialog box is an area where you can add to the list of hyphenation exceptions. These exceptions are words that you don't want Illustrator to hyphenate under any circumstances. Figure 17-12 illustrates the Hyphenation section of the Preferences dialog box.

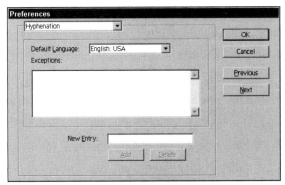

Figure 17-12: The Hyphenation section of the Preferences dialog box enables you to control how special words are hyphenated.

Adjusting the Plug-ins and Scratch Disks

The next preference item in the Preference drop-down list (pop-up menu) is a two-trick pony, the Plug-ins & Scratch Disks section of the Preferences dialog box, as shown in Figure 17-13. The first section in this dialog box enables you to specify a folder for plug-ins. The default is the Plug-ins folder in the Adobe Illustrator folder.

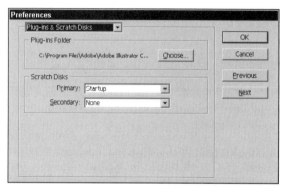

Figure 17-13: Use the Plug-ins & Scratch Disks section of the Preferences dialog box to specify file locations.

The second section in the Plug-in & Scratch Disks section of the Preferences dialog box lets you define what drives to use as scratch disks (places where Illustrator stores information when it runs out of RAM). Typically, you should assign the fastest, largest drive to be your primary scratch disk. The settings you choose don't take effect until you restart Illustrator.

Customizing the File Handling and Clipboard

The File Handling and Clipboard preferences let you change how the files are saved with extensions and links and how to handle the clipboard files. You set these preferences in the File Handling & Clipboard section of the Preferences dialog box, shown in Figure 17-14.

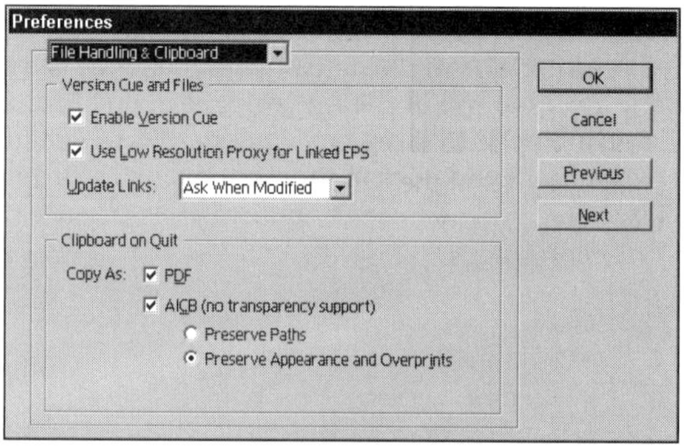

Figure 17-14: The File Handling & Clipboard section of the Preferences dialog box enables you to specify file sharing and the Clipboard options.

The File Handling preferences are used when saving and updating files. You can choose from these preferences:

✦ **Enable Version Cue:** Allows you to control file sharing using Adobe's Version Cue software (if you have the Creative Suite and Version Cue installed).

✦ **Use Low Resolution Proxy for Linked EPS:** Displays a low-resolution image for a Linked EPS to save in file space.

The Clipboard is another area that can be altered in preferences. When you copy and paste, the clipboard holds that information. Objects copied to the clipboard are PDF files by default. You can change that to AICB (Adobe Illustrator Clip Board), and you won't have any transparency support. Under the AICB, you can choose to Preserve Paths or Preserve Appearance and Overprints. All the AICB options enable you to do more with editing, but also take up more file space.

Setting the Appearance of Black Options

In the Appearance of Black section of the Preferences dialog box you have two options for controlling how Illustrator displays and prints black. In each case, you can choose to accurately depict black or make black into a deeper, richer appearing color. Figure 17-15 shows the Appearance of Black section of the Preferences dialog box.

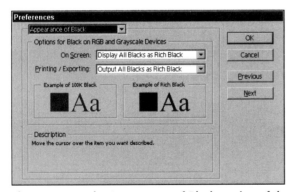

Figure 17-15: The Appearance of Black section of the Preferences dialog box enables you to control how Illustrator treats black sections of your documents.

Altering Placement and Toolbox Value Preferences

Most Illustrator users take many preferences for granted. But if Illustrator didn't remember certain preferences, most Illustrator users would be quite annoyed.

Palettes (including the toolbox) remain where they were when you last used Illustrator. Illustrator remembers their size and whether they were open. Values in the toolbox are still whatever you set them to last. For example, the options in the Paintbrush/Eyedropper dialog box remain the same between Illustrator sessions.

Adding Keyboard Customization

Those long-time users of Illustrator have noticed keyboard shortcut changes. Although they may be frustrating, there is a method to Adobe's madness. They want to make working between programs (Illustrator and Photoshop, for instance) seamless, and that means making keyboard shortcuts the same throughout their programs. If you liked a certain keyboard command, you can always customize the keyboard to what you like. Figure 17-16 shows the Keyboard Shortcuts dialog box. Choose Edit ➪ Keyboard Shortcuts to access this dialog box. In this dialog box, you can change and save your own settings. After you start to edit the Keyboard Shortcuts, the Illustrator Defaults changes to Custom and you can save your Custom settings. Next time you start Illustrator, your custom settings are available under the Illustrator Defaults pop-up.

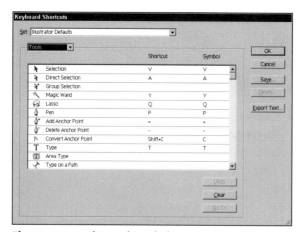

Figure 17-16: The Keyboard Shortcuts dialog box allows you to set up your own set of shortcuts.

Note You can't use the Ctrl (Command), Alt (Option), or function keys with other keys for tool shortcuts.

Knowing What You Can't Customize

Several things cannot be customized in Illustrator, and they can be annoying:

✦ Type information always defaults to 12-point Myriad, Auto Leading, 100% Horizontal Scale, 0 Tracking, Flush Left, Hyphenation Off. There is no easy way around this set of defaults.

✦ Every new document begins with only one layer. It's called Layer 1 and is colored light blue.

✦ When you create new objects, they are always 0% black fill and a 1-point stroke.

✦ The Selection tool is always the active tool.

Using Actions

Adobe has brought the same technology from Photoshop into Illustrator to ease mundane repetitive tasks. The Actions palette, shown in Figure 17-17, is opened by choosing Window ⇨ Actions. The tasks of applying color, object transformations, and text functions are easily automated using the Actions palette. Illustrator comes with some prerecorded actions, and you can create your own.

In the Actions palette, the box on the far left side toggles an item off or on. The next box toggles the dialog box off or on. The icons below enable you to record your own actions.

Using a Default Action

Accessing Default Actions requires little effort. To activate a Default Action, click the action to highlight it and then press the Play button.

Toggle item on or off

Toggle dialog box on or off

Collapse item

Expand item

Stop Playing/Recording   Delete Selection

Begin Recording   Create New Action

Play Current Selection   Create New Set

Figure 17-17: The Actions palette helps you automate Illustrator.

Creating a new action

If the numerous default actions aren't enough, you can create your own actions. To start recording a new action, you need to create a new action. Click the Create New Action icon at the bottom of the Actions palette or choose New Action from the Actions palette pop-up menu to open the New Action dialog box so that you can name the action. After entering a name (I prefer to give it a descriptive name so I know what action it does), you press the Record button and start doing your action. After you are finished, you can move the order or delete parts of your action.

Caution   Not everything can be recorded. If an action can't be recorded, Illustrator displays a warning dialog box.

Creating a new set

When you create a new action, it gets put in a folder with a set of actions. You can have multiple actions in a folder, or just one. A new action needs to be a part of a set (or in a folder). It can be an existing set or a new set. Think of actions as packages. To create a new set, click the New Set icon at the bottom of the palette or select New Set from the Actions palette pop-up menu.

What is recordable?

In Illustrator, not everything is recordable. As with anything, there are limits. The following actions are recordable in the Actions palette:

- ✦ **File:** New, Open, Close, Save, Save as, Save a Copy, Revert, Place, and Export
- ✦ **Edit:** Cut, Copy, Paste, Paste in Front, Paste in Back, Clear, Select All, Deselect All, and Select filters
- ✦ **Object:** Transform Again, Move, Scale, Rotate, Shear, Reflect, Transform Each, Arrange, Group, Ungroup, Lock, Unlock All, Hide Selection, Show All, Expand, Rasterize, Blends, Mask, Compound Path, and Cropmarks
- ✦ **Type:** Block, Wrap, Fit Headline, Create Outlines, Find/Change, Find Font, Change Case, Rows & Columns, Type Orientation, and Glyph Options
- ✦ **Filters:** Colors, Create, Distort, Stylize, and the Photoshop filters
- ✦ **View:** Guides-related only
- ✦ **Palettes:** Color, Gradient, Stroke, Character, MM Design, Paragraph, Tab Ruler, Transform, Pathfinder, Align, Swatch, Brush, Layer, and Attribute
- ✦ **Toolbox tools:** Ellipse, Rectangle, Polygon, Star, Spiral, Move (Selection tool), Rotate, Scale, Shear, and Reflect
- ✦ **Special:** Bounding-box Transform, Insert Select Path, Insert Stop, and Select Objects

Duplicating and deleting an action

You can duplicate an action when you want to modify an existing action but don't want to re-record the whole darn thing. To duplicate an action, first select an action in the Actions palette and then choose Duplicate from the Actions palette pop-up menu. This makes a copy of the action. To change the name of the action, double-click the action to open the Action Options dialog box, shown in Figure 17-18. You can change the name of an action this way, but not the name of the action set. You can also see which set the selected action is a part of. Assign a Function key here in the Options, especially if it is an action that you use repeatedly. You can also change the color of the action icon listed in the Actions palette. Deleting an action is pretty easy. Select the action that you want to delete and drag it onto the trash icon at the bottom of the palette or use the Actions palette pop-up menu item.

Figure 17-18: The Action Options dialog box enables you to rename or assign a shortcut key to an action.

Starting and stopping recording

To start recording, do one of the following:

+ Create a new action set and action.

+ Select an existing action, and click the Begin Recording icon at the bottom of the palette.

+ Activate an action, and select Start Recording in the Actions palette pop-up menu.

To stop recording, do one of the following:

+ Click the Stop Playing/Recording icon button.

+ Select Stop Recording in the Actions palette pop-up menu.

Inserting a menu item

If you have either duplicated an action or want to add to an action, you may want to insert an item into the action. To insert a menu item, activate an action, start recording, and select Insert Menu Item from the Actions palette pop-up menu. This allows you to record most menu items: File, Edit, Object, Type, Filter, and guide-related Views. You don't have to use this to record a menu item.

Inserting a stop

Insert Stop enables you to stop the playback of an action at a point where you may want to make the action stop so you can add something to a certain area each time you replay it. During your recording, select Insert Stop in the Actions palette pop-up menu. You can have some fun with this one. You are creating your own dialog box when you insert a stop, as shown in Figure 17-19. Put a message in this dialog box just for fun. Always allow the user to continue If he wants. That way, you continue with the rest of the action after the stop. This is great for using Actions to partially do the creation, but pauses so you can enter specifics in a dialog box.

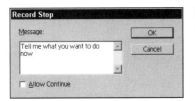

Figure 17-19: The Insert Stop command lets you create your own dialog boxes.

Action options

The Action options are where you can name or rename the action, move it to a set, assign a Function Key, or assign a Color to the Action. The Function key is a cool feature that lets you assign an "F" key number to an action so you can just press the F+number and your action starts.

Playback options

The Playback Options dialog box, which you access by choosing Playback Options from the pop-up Actions palette menu, lets you customize your actions even further. This dialog box is shown in Figure 17-20. You can accelerate, step through, or pause your Actions, as follows:

+ **Accelerated:** Plays the action all at once, quickly. This is great for monotonous, repetitive actions such as renaming figures or adding a tag line.

+ **Step By Step:** Plays the action one step at a time. This lets you decide whether you want to perform a step or add in-between steps.

+ **Pause For:** Stops at each step for the specified time. This is a good choice if you want to see closely how something was recorded and want to stop the recording at a certain spot.

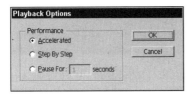

Figure 17-20: Use the playback options to control how fast your recorded action plays.

Inserting a selected path

You cannot record the Pen tool or the Pencil tool, but you can record a path. Follow these steps:

1. **Draw the path.**

2. **While the path is selected, start recording.**

3. **Choose Insert Select Path from the Actions palette pop-up menu.**

4. **Stop recording.**

You have just placed a path in your action.

Selecting an object

If you want to select an object to use later in your recording, you need to name and select an object or path first. Follow these steps:

1. **Select the object or path.**

2. **Choose Show Note from the Attributes palette pop-up menu.**

3. **Enter the name you want to give the object in the bottom field, and click the Actions palette to record the new setting.**

4. **When you need to select the object or path, choose Select Object in the pop-up menu, shown in Figure 17-21, type the name you gave it in the Attributes palette, and click OK.** The object or path is now selected.

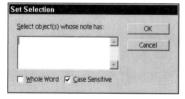

Figure 17-21: You can use the Set Selection dialog box to select objects by name.

Clearing, resetting, loading, replacing, and saving actions

Whew, even after creating a bunch of cool actions, you want more options. You can clear, reset, load, replace, and save actions. Now you can create, delete, load sets, and save to your heart's content. The following describes what each option does:

✦ **Clear Actions:** Deletes all the action sets in the Actions palette.

✦ **Reset Actions:** Resets the palette to the Default Actions.

✦ **Load Actions** *or* **Replace Actions:** Lets you navigate to a folder where the action sets are and lets you select one. You can find a ton of prerecorded actions and action sets on the application CD.

✦ **Save Actions:** Lets you save actions after you have recorded them. You must save your new action just like a file if you want to use it the next time you launch Illustrator. Select Save Action in the pop-up menu, and navigate to where you want to save your action set (maybe the Action Sets folder within the application folder).

Summary

You can customize and automate Illustrator to make the program work the way you like. In this chapter, you learned about the following topics:

✦ The different preference areas can be changed in Illustrator: Preferences, Keyboard shortcuts, and the Startup file.

✦ By changing the Adobe Illustrator Startup file, you can change the default colors, patterns, gradients, and zoom level of each new document created in Illustrator.

✦ Many preferences in Illustrator can be changed in the General panel of the Preferences dialog box.

✦ The Constrain Angle option controls the angle at which objects are drawn and moved when the Shift key is pressed.

✦ The General Units option controls how all measurements are controlled in Illustrator.

✦ Use the Actions palette to streamline repetitive tasks in Illustrator.

✦   ✦   ✦

Getting Art Out of Illustrator

✦   ✦   ✦   ✦

In This Part

Chapter 18
Understanding
PostScript and
Printing

Chapter 19
Creating Web
Graphics

✦   ✦   ✦   ✦

Understanding PostScript and Printing

CHAPTER

18

In This Chapter

Understanding
PostScript

Understanding the
difference between
composites and
separations

Determining when to
use process color
instead of spot color
separations

Printing separations
out of Illustrator

Understanding line
screens

Printing separations
from other programs

Understanding
trapping

Using Pathfinder Trap

Trapping after you
create an image in
Illustrator

Until the mid-1980s, computer graphics were, well, crusty. Blocky. Jagged. Rough. If we saw graphics that were done on computers in 1981 and printed to a black-and-white printer, we'd laugh so hard we couldn't breathe, stopping the laughter only when we realized that we actually could not breathe. Of course, in 1981, the world was gaga over the capabilities of computers and computer graphics. Those same pictures were admired, and the average person was generally amazed. The average designer, on the other hand, shuddered and prayed that this whole computer thing wouldn't catch on.

Desktop publishing was pushed to a level of professionalism in 1985 by a cute little software package called PageMaker. With PageMaker, you could do typesetting and layout on the computer screen, seeing everything on the screen just as it would eventually be printed. Well, almost. Aldus was the company that created PageMaker. In 1994, Adobe swallowed Aldus.

Problems aside, PageMaker would not have been a success if the laser printer hadn't handily arrived on the scene. Even so, there were problems inherent with laser printers, too: at 300 dpi (dots per inch), there were 90,000 dots in every square inch. A typical 8½ x 11-inch page of type had 8.5 million dots to put down. Computers were finally powerful enough to handle this huge number of dots, but the time it took to print made computers pretty much useless for any real work.

Several systems were developed to improve the printing process, and the one standout was PostScript from Adobe Systems. Apple licensed PostScript from Adobe for use on its first LaserWriter, and a star was born. Installed on every laser printer from Apple were two things from Adobe: the PostScript page description language, and the Adobe base fonts, which included Times, Helvetica, Courier, and Symbol.

PostScript became fundamental to Apple Macintosh computers and laser printers and became the standard. To use PostScript, Apple had to pay licensing fees to Adobe for every laser printer it sold. Fonts were PostScript, and if there ever was a standard in graphics, the closest thing to it was PostScript (commonly called EPS, for Encapsulated PostScript).

Today, the majority of fonts for both Macintosh and Windows systems are TrueType or OpenType fonts. However, many of the typefaces used in professional work are still PostScript, and almost all graphics and desktop-publishing software can read PostScript in some form. However, there are actually a greater number of TrueType fonts available.

You can print Illustrator documents in two ways: as a composite, which is a single printout that contains all the colors and tints used; or as a series of color separations, a printout for each color. Color separations are necessary for illustrations that will be printed on a printing press.

Understanding the Benefits of PostScript

A typical graphic object in painting software is based on a certain number of pixels that are a certain color. If you make that graphic larger, the pixels get larger, giving a rough, jagged effect to the art. To prevent these jaggies, two things can be done: Make sure that enough dots-per-inch are in the image so that when the image is enlarged, the dots are too small to appear jagged. Or define graphics by mathematical equations instead of by dots.

PostScript is a mathematical solution to high-resolution imaging. Areas, or shapes, are defined, and then these shapes are either filled or stroked with a percentage of color. The shapes are made up of paths, and the paths are defined by a number of points along the path (anchor points) and controls off those points (control handles, sometimes called curve handles or direction points) that control the shape of the curve.

Because the anchor points and control handles have real locations on a page, mathematical processes can be used to create the shapes based on these points. The mathematical equation for Bézier curves is quite detailed (at least for someone who, like me, fears math).

PostScript is not just math, though. It is actually a programming language and, more specifically, a page description language. Like BASIC, Pascal, Forth, SmallTalk, and C, PostScript is made of lines of code that are used to describe artwork.

Fortunately, the average user never has to deal directly with PostScript code; instead, the average user uses a simplified interface, such as Illustrator. Software that has the capability to save files in PostScript or to print to a PostScript printer writes this PostScript code for you. Printers that are equipped with PostScript then take that PostScript code and convert it to dots on a printed page.

Using PostScript

That most applications can handle EPS files and that most printers can print PostScript are of great benefit to users, but the strength of PostScript is not really in its widespread use.

If you create a 1-inch closed path in pixel-based drawing software and then enlarge that same path in any application, the path begins to lose detail. A 300-dpi path at twice its original size becomes 150 dpi. Those jagged edges become more apparent than ever.

If you create a 1-inch circle in Illustrator, you can enlarge it to any size possible without losing one iota of resolution. The Illustrator circle stays perfectly smooth, even enlarged to 200 percent because the circle's resolution depends on the laser printer or imagesetter that prints it. Therefore, a perfect 1-inch circle has the potential to be a perfect 2-foot circle (providing you can find a printer or imagesetter that can print a 2-foot diameter circle).

But scaling objects is only the beginning. You can distort, stretch, rotate, skew, and flip objects created in Illustrator to your heart's content, and still the object prints to the resolution of the output device.

Here's an example: A company wants its tiny logo on a 3-foot wide poster. If you use raster methods, the edges become fuzzy and gross-looking, pretty much unacceptable to your client. Your other conventional option is to redraw the logo at a larger size or to trace the blown-up version — a time-consuming proposition either way.

Illustrator's solution is to scan the logo, trace it either in another software tracing program or with the Live Trace tool, touch it up, and build your design around it. Afterward, output the illustration on a printer that can handle that size poster. There is no loss of quality; instead, the enlarged version from Illustrator often looks better than the scanned original.

Knowing What to Do Prior to Printing

Before you start the printing process, you may need to change or adjust a few items. For example, you may need to change the page size and orientation, or set how certain colors will separate. This section deals with the issues you should be aware of before you press Ctrl+P (⌘+P) to send your file to the printer.

Understanding document setup

Choosing File ➪ Document Setup, or pressing Ctrl+Alt+P (⌘+Option+P), enables you to set the initial page size of an illustration via the Artboard. Opening the Document Setup dialog box, shown in Figure 18-1, displays a wealth of options that assist in printing. If the Artboard is smaller than the printable page, then anything entirely outside the edges of the Artboard is cropped off when you print the illustration through Illustrator. Any objects that are partially on the Artboard print. Anything outside the Artboard print when you print the illustration through another application.

Cross-Reference   For more on document setup, see Chapter 3.

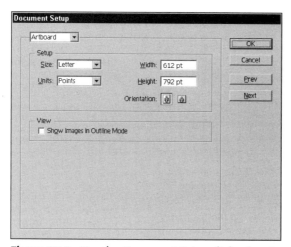

Figure 18-1: Use the Document Setup dialog box to specify the size of your Illustrator document.

Another area you can change in the Document Setup dialog box is the Show Images in Outline option, which enables you to choose whether placed images preview. Checking this box lets you see the placed image rather than a box with an X through it.

Printing composites

A composite printout looks very much like the image that appears on the screen. If you have a color printer, the image appears in color; otherwise, the colors are replaced by gray tints (see the next section, "Working with gray colors").

Note   Objects that are hidden or that exist on layers that are currently hidden do not print. Objects that exist on layers that have the printing option unchecked in the Layers Option dialog box also do not print.

When you are ready to print your document, choose File ➪ Print, or to press Ctrl+P (⌘+P). This action opens the Print dialog box, shown in Figure 18-2, where you may choose which pages to print, how many of each to print, and several other options. If you click the Cancel button, or press Esc, the dialog box disappears and no pages are printed. To print, click the Print button or press Enter (Return).

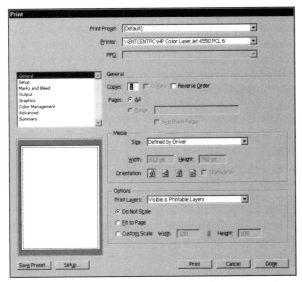

Figure 18-2: The Print dialog box provides many options for controlling how your Illustrator documents print.

The Print dialog box has a number of areas. You display each area by choosing an item from the list that appears along the left side of the dialog box.

The General area of the Print dialog box contains these options:

✦ **Copies:** The number that you enter here determines how many copies of each page will print.

✦ **Pages:** If you check the All radio button, all the pages that have art on them will print. If you select the Range radio button and enter numbers in the text field, only the pages that those numbers refer to will print

✦ **Media:** This handles the Size, Width, Height, and Orientation of the document.

✦ **Options:** This option determines how to print the layers and scaling options. In the Print Layers pop-up, choose from Visible & Printable Layers, Visible Layers, and All Layers. The Scaling Options are Do Not Scale, Fit to Page, and Custom Scale (enter a width and height in percentages).

The Setup option handles the following:

✦ **Crop Artwork to:** Choose from Artboard, Artwork Bounding Box, or Crop Area.

✦ **Placement:** Choose where you want the printing origin to start from relative to the edge of the paper.

✦ **Tiling:** This relates to paging. You can print Single Full Page, Tile Full Pages, or Tile Imageable Areas.

The Marks & Bleed option covers these items:

✦ **Marks:** This lets you check or uncheck the following options: All Printer's Marks, Trim Marks, Registration Marks, Color Bars, and Page Information. As for Printer's Mark Type, choose from Roman or Japanese. You can also set the Trim Mark Weight and offset from the art.

✦ **Bleeds:** This relates to how the art bleeds or extends off the page. This is used to make sure the art prints to the edge. Choose the top, bottom, left, and right. There is a Link button that is on by default, so if you change one, the rest change in synchrony.

The Output option covers these items:

✦ **Mode:** This controls whether the print will be a Composite (all colors together) or Separation (each color plate printed on its own page). Depending on your printer configuration, you may have an In-Rip Separation option. This option is for raster image processors that can perform the separation.

✦ **Emulsion:** This controls the positioning of the emulsion layer. Up (Right Reading) means that the layer is facing you, and you can read the text. Down (Right Reading) means that the layer is facing away from you, and the type is readable when facing away.

✦ **Image:** This controls whether the print will be a Negative or a Positive.

✦ **Printer Resolution:** This lets you change the printer's resolution (lines per inch/dots per inch). You can go only as high in resolution as your printer will allow. You can always go lower in resolution.

✦ **Check boxes:** These check boxes control whether all Spot Colors print as Process, or Black will Overprint.

✦ **Document Ink Options:** This controls how the ink is printed or converts a spot to a process color.

The options in the Graphics area are as follows:

✦ **Paths:** The Flatness setting adjusts the lines. Curved lines are defined by lots of tiny straight lines. The more accurate to the curved path, the better the quality and the slower it is to print. The lower accuracy to the path, the faster it prints, but the quality may not be as high as you might want.

✦ **Fonts:** This controls how PostScript fonts are downloaded to the printer. Some fonts are stored in the printer, but others that aren't standard on your printer can either be held on the printer or your computer.

✦ **Options:** The other options under Graphics are setting the PostScript language and Data format for type. You can check the Compatible Gradient and Gradient Mesh printing by converting the gradient or gradient mesh to a JPEG format. This area also is where you are informed of your Document Raster Effects Resolution (choose Effect ➪ Document Raster Effects Settings).

The options in the Color Management area are as follows:

✦ **Print Method:** The Print Method lists the Color Handling (whether the printer or Illustrator handles the colors), Printer Profile (the color management profile that you want to use), and Rendering Intent (the rendering intent to use when converting colors to a profile space).

The Advanced options are as follows:

✦ **Print as Bitmap:** Check this box to have your file print as a bitmapped image. This is useful to see a quick printout without the quality.

✦ **Overprint and Transparency Flattener Options:** In this area, you select whether you want to Simulate, Preserve, or Discard Overprints. You also choose the resolution from three presets or specify a custom resolution.

The Summary area lists the summary of the whole file. All the printing options you have chosen are listed here, and any warnings are listed at the bottom.

Tip   Choosing Level I PostScript options reduces errors when printing to an older printer.

Tip   When an illustration doesn't print, always choose Print Detailed Report. That way, you can read exactly what the error was.

Tip   Always save your file before printing.

Working with gray colors

When you are printing a full-color illustration to a black-and-white printer, Illustrator substitutes gray values for the process colors. In this way, the program creates the illusion that each color has a separate, distinct gray value. Of course, each color can't have its own unique gray value, so the colors have to overlap at some point.

Magenta is the darkest process color, ranging from 0% to 73% gray. Therefore, the darkest magenta will print is 73% gray. Cyan is second darkest, ranging from 0% to 57% gray. Yellow is extremely light, ranging from 0% to only 11% gray. Figure 18-3 shows a comparison of the four process colors at various settings and their printed results. The four bars show different values, indicated above the bars, for each process color. Within each bar is the percent of black that prints when you are printing that color at that percentage to a black-and-white printer.

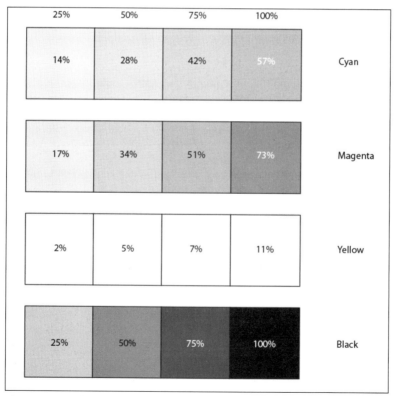

Figure 18-3: This shows how colors appear when printed on a black and white laser printer.

Different printers may produce different tints of gray. Lower-resolution printers, such as 300-dpi laser printers, do not create an accurate gray tint, because they use dots that are too large to create accurate tint patterns.

Using the Separation Setup

After you choose File ➪ Print and click the Output option on the left, the Print dialog box with the Output option appears, as shown in Figure 18-4. The left side shows how the illustration is aligned on the page and which elements will print with the illustration. The right side contains all the options for how the illustration is to print on the page.

The picture on the left side initially shows the illustration on a portrait-oriented page, even if landscape is selected in Illustrator.

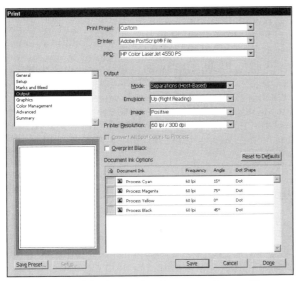

Figure 18-4: This shows the Output options with a separation setup selected.

Understanding the printer's marks and bleeds

The various marks shown on the page are the printer's marks defaults. The *trim marks* are used for cutting the image after it is printed. The *registration marks* are used when printing separations, and you can line up the registration marks to ensure that the print didn't get shifted and all looks as you planned.

The *bleeds* define how much of the illustration can be outside of the bounding box and still print. The default for bleed is 18 points, regardless of the size of the bounding box. To change the bleed, enter a distance in points in the Bleed text field. As you type the numbers, the bleed changes dynamically.

Bleeds are useful when you want an illustration to go right up to the edge of the page. You need to account for bleed when you create an illustration in Illustrator so that the illustration is the correct size with X amount of bleed.

Changing printer information

Illustrator uses a *PostScript Printer Description* (PPD) file to customize the output for your specific printer. To change the PPD, click the arrow at the right edge of the PPD list box in the Output area of the Print dialog box. Select the PPD file that is compatible with your printer.

Note   PPDs were created with specific printers in mind. Unpredictable and undesirable results can occur when you use a PPD for a different printer than the one for which it is intended. If you don't have a PPD for your printer and must use a substitute, always test the substitute PPD before relying on it to perform correctly.

If your printer's PPD is not included with Illustrator, you may be able to get it from the printer manufacturer directly by visiting the manufacturer's Web site.

When you choose a different PPD file, the information in the main panel changes to reflect the new selection. Certain default settings in the list boxes are activated at this time. You can change the settings at any time, but most of them will revert to the defaults if you choose a new PPD.

Changing page size

In the General area of the Print dialog box, the Media section has a drop-down list box (pop-up menu) that shows the available page sizes for the printer whose PPD is selected. For laser printers, few page and envelope sizes are supported. For imagesetters, many sizes are supported, and an Other option enables you to specify the size of the page on which you want to print.

Imagesetters print on rolls of paper or film. Depending on the width of the roll, you may want to print the image sideways. For example, on a Linotronic 180 or 230 imagesetter, paper and film rolls are commonly 12 inches wide. For letter-size pages, you should check the Transverse option to print the letter-size page with the short end along the length of the roll. For a tabloid page (11 x 17 inches), do not check the Transverse option because you want the long edge (17 inches) of the page to be printed along the length of the roll. If you check Transverse for a tabloid-size document, 5 of the 17 inches are cropped off because the roll is not wide enough. As always, when trying something new with printing, run a test or two before sending a large job.

Note The page size that you select in the Size drop-down list box (pop-up menu) determines the size of the page on the left side of the main panel. The measurements next to the name of the page size are not the page measurements; instead, they are the measurements of the imageable area for that page size. The imageable-area dimensions are always less than the dimensions of the page so that the margin marks can fit on the page with the illustration.

Changing the orientation

The Orientation setting controls how the illustration is placed on the page. You have four choices: portrait, landscape, portrait reversed, and landscape reversed.

Selecting Portrait causes the illustration to print with the sides of the illustration along the longest sides of the page. Selecting Landscape causes the illustration to print with the top and bottom of the illustration along the longest sides of the page.

Usually, the orientation reflects the general shape of the illustration. If the illustration is taller than it is wide, you usually choose Portrait orientation. If the illustration is wider than it is tall, you usually choose Landscape orientation.

Note It doesn't matter to Illustrator whether the illustration fits on the page in one or both of these orientations. If you can't see all four edges of the bounding box, chances are good that the illustration will be cropped. Orientation is quite different from Transverse. Orientation changes the orientation of the illustration on the page, but Transverse changes the way the page is put on the paper. It's a seemingly small difference, but an important one to understand.

Figure 18-5 shows an illustration that is placed on a page in both portrait and landscape orientations, with and without the Transverse option selected.

Understanding emulsion

Hang out around strippers (at a commercial printing company . . . get your mind out of the gutter), and you will hear them constantly talk about "emulsion up" and "emulsion down." In printing, emulsion is a photo-sensitive coating that is applied, dried, exposed, and then washed off leaving the areas to be printed open for ink to pass through. The non-printing areas retain the emulsion to prevent the ink from passing through. If you have a piece of film from a printer lying around, look at it near a light. One side is shinier than the other side. That side is the side without emulsion. When you are burning plates for presses, the emulsion side (dull side) should always be toward the plate.

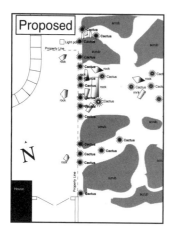

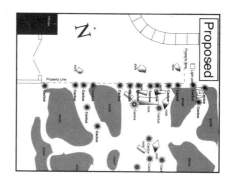

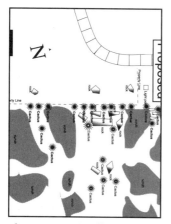

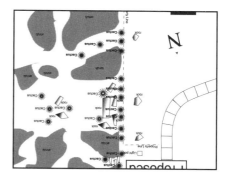

Figure 18-5: An illustration placed on a page in portrait orientation (upper left), landscape orientation (lower left), portrait with transverse checked (upper right), and landscape with transverse checked (lower right)

In the Output area of the Print dialog box, you use the Emulsion option to control which side the emulsion goes on. If you are printing negatives on film, choose Down (right reading) from the Emulsion pop-up menu. For printing on paper, just to see what the separations look like, choose Up (right reading). Always consult with your printer for the correct way to output film.

Tip Although "wrong reading" isn't an option in the Separation Setup dialog box, you can reverse an illustration by choosing the opposite emulsion setting. In other words, Down (right reading) is also Up (wrong reading), and Up (right reading) is also Down (wrong reading).

Thinking of the emulsion as the toner in a laser printer may help you understand this concept better. If the toner is on the top of the paper, you can read it fine, as always (Up emulsion, right reading). If the toner is on the bottom of the paper and you can read the illustration only when you place the paper in front of a light, the emulsion is Down, right reading. Thinking along these lines helped me back when I was new to the printing industry, and it should help you as well.

Changing from positive to negative to positive

You use the Image drop-down list box (pop-up menu) to switch between printing positive and negative images. Usually, you use a negative image for printing film negatives and a positive image for printing on paper. The default for this setting, regardless of the printer chosen or PPD selected, is Positive.

Working with different colors

At the lower right of the Output area of the Print dialog box, Document Ink Options list displays where you can select different colors and set them to print or not print, and set Custom Colors to process separately.

The list of colors contains only the colors that are used in that particular illustration. At the top of the list of separation colors are the four process colors in italic, if they, or spot colors that contain those process colors, are used in the illustration. Below the process colors is a list of all the spot colors in the document.

Tip If the illustration has any guides in it, their colors are reflected in the Document Ink Options list. From looking at the preview of the illustration in the Output options in the Print dialog box, you can't easily determine that these blank separations will print. The best thing to do is release all guides and delete them.

By default, all process colors are set to print, and all spot colors are set to convert to process colors. Clicking the Convert All Spot Colors To Process check box toggles between converting everything (checked) and spot colors (unchecked).

Each color in the list has its own frequency and angle. Don't change the angle or frequency for process colors because the separator has automatically created the best values for the process colors at the halftone screen you've specified. Instead, make sure that any spot colors that may be printing have different angles from each other so that no moiré patterns develop from them.

As soon as you type new values or check different options using the color list, the changes are applied.

Outputting a Color-Separated File

Color separations are necessary to print a color version of an illustration on most printing presses. Each separation creates a plate that is affixed to a round drum on a printing press. Ink that is the same color as that separation is applied to the plate, which is pressed against a sheet of paper. Because the ink adheres only to the printing areas of the plate, an image is produced on paper. Some printing presses have many different drums and can print a four-color job in one run. Other printing presses have only one or two drums, so the paper has to pass through the press four or two times, respectively, to print a four-color job.

The two types of color separations are process color separations and spot color separations. Each type has its own advantages and drawbacks, and you can use either type or a combination of both types for any print job. Process color separations typically use four colors (cyan, magenta, yellow, and black) to reproduce the entire range of colors. Spot color separations use a custom mixed ink to precisely render a specific color.

Tip   You should always determine which type of separation you want *before* you begin to create a job electronically.

Using spot color separations

Jobs that are printed with spot colors are often referred to as two-color or three-color jobs when two or three colors are used. Although you can use any number of colors, most spot color jobs contain only a few colors.

Spot color printing is most useful when you are using two or three distinct colors in a job. For example, if I needed only black and green to create a certain illustration, I would use only black and a green custom color for all the objects in the illustration.

There are three main reasons for using spot color separations rather than process color separations:

✦ It's cheaper. Spot color printing requires a smaller press with fewer drums. For process color separations, you usually need to use a press with four drums or run the job through a smaller press a number of times.

✦ Spot colors are cleaner, brighter, and smoother than the same colors that you create as process colors. To get a green process color, for example, you need to mix both cyan and yellow on paper. Using one spot color results in a perfectly solid area of color.

✦ You cannot duplicate certain spot colors, especially fluorescent and metallic colors, with process colors.

Learning Printing from the Experts

If you have never visited a printing company, make a point to visit one and take a tour. Most printing companies have staff members who are more than willing to explain their equipment and various printing processes. In a 30-minute tour with a knowledgeable guide, you can learn enough to save yourself hours of work, money, and misunderstandings.

When you are talking to a printing rep, find out what type of media they want your work on. Printing companies commonly use imagesetters that can output the job for you, and some companies even perform this service at no charge or for a significant discount if you have the job printed there.

Imagesetters are similar to laser printers, except that they produce images with a very high dpi, from 1273 to 3600, and sometimes higher. Imagesetters can print directly to RC (resin-coated) paper or to film negatives (or positives). The paper or film runs through the imagesetter and then must run through a developing process for the images and text to appear.

Most printing company salespeople can tell you when to give them negs (film negatives) and paper, and which service bureau to use if they don't have an imagesetter in-house. Many can tell you which software their clients prefer and which software packages create problems, and they can give you tips that can help you get your project through the process without problems.

A service bureau is a company that has on its premises an imagesetter and whose function is to provide the general community of desktop publishers with imagesetter output at a cost between $7 and $40 per page. Service bureaus often have color output capabilities and offer disk-conversion and other services that are sometimes needed by desktop publishers.

Better yet, do what I did: Work at a printing company for a short period of time. The first job I had out of college, working in the prepress department of a four-color commercial printer, taught me more than I learned in four years of school. The experience instilled in me some of the most important basic skills for graphics design that I still use and need every day. Ever wonder why your printer gets so grumpy when you say your negs won't be available until two days past the promised date? Working at a printing company can give you an understanding of job scheduling, an art of prophecy and voodoo that gives ulcers to printing company managers and supervisors.

The more you know about printing and your printer, the better your print job will turn out, and the fewer hassles you will have to deal with.

Illustrator creates spot colors whenever you specify a spot color in a swatch. If you use six different spot colors and black, you could print seven different spot color separations.

Spot colors do have their limitations and disadvantages. The primary limitation of using only spot colors is that the number of colors is restricted to the number of color separations that you want to produce. Remember that the cost of a print job is directly related to the number of different colored inks in the job.

The cutoff point for using spot colors is usually three colors. When you use four spot colors, you limit yourself to four distinct colors and use as many colors as a process color job that can have an almost infinite number of colors. Spot color jobs of six colors are not unusual, however. Sometimes people use more than three spot colors to keep colors distinct and clear. Each of the six colors will be bright, vibrant, and distinct from its neighbors, whereas different process colors seem to fade into one another.

Note   Spot colors are often incorrectly referred to as Pantone colors. Pantone is a brand name for a color-matching system. You can select Pantone colors as custom colors and use them in Illustrator, and you can print them as either spot colors or as process colors.

Printing process color separation

Process color separation, also known as four-color separation, creates almost any color by combining cyan, magenta, yellow, and black inks. By using various combinations of different tints of each of these colors, you can reproduce many of the colors (more than 16 million of them) that the human eye can see.

Process printing uses a subtractive process. You start with bright white paper and darken the paper with various inks. Cyan, magenta, and yellow are the subtractive primaries, and black is added to create true black printing, a color that the primaries together don't do very well.

The use of process color separation is advisable in two situations:

✦ When the illustration includes color photographs

✦ When the illustration contains more than three different colors

Choosing numerous colors

Everyone always says that you can create as many colors as you could ever want when you are using process colors. Maybe.

In Illustrator, you can specify colors up to $\frac{1}{100}$ percent accuracy. As a result, 10,000 different shades are available for each of the four process colors. So, theoretically, $10,000^4$, or 10,000,000,000,000,000, different colors should be available, which is 10 quadrillion or 10 million billion. Any way you look at it, you have a heck of a lot of color possibilities.

Unfortunately, most imagesetters and laser printers can produce only 256 different shades for each color. This limitation of the equipment (not PostScript) drops the number of available colors to 256^4, or 4,294,967,296, which is about 4.3 billion colors — only 1 billionth of the colors that Illustrator can specify.

This limitation is fortunate for us humans, however, because the estimate is that we can detect a maximum of 100 different levels of gray, probably less. As a result, we can view only 100^4, or 100,000,000, different colors.

We can run into a problem when we preview illustrations, however. An RGB monitor (which is the color format used on computers) can display up to 16.7 million colors, theoretically, if each Red, Green, and Blue pixel can be varied by 256 different intensities.

Another problem is that about 30 percent of the colors that you can view on an RGB monitor can't be reproduced by using cyan, magenta, yellow, and black inks on white paper. You can't create these unprintable colors in Illustrator, but you can create them in most other drawing and graphics software packages. These colors are for onscreen viewing pleasure only.

The secret to process color separation is that the four colors that make up all the different colors are themselves not visible. Each color is printed as a pattern of tiny dots, angled differently from the dots of the other three colors. The angles of each color are very important. If the angles are off even slightly, a noticeable pattern commonly known as a moiré emerges.

The colors are printed in a specific order — usually cyan, magenta, yellow, and then black. Although the debate continues about the best order in which to print the four colors, black is always printed last.

To see the dots for each color, use a magnifying device to look closely at something that is preprinted and in full color. Even easier, look at the Sunday comics, which have bigger dots than most other printed pieces. The different color dots in the Sunday comics are quite visible, and the only colors used are magenta, cyan, yellow, and black.

The size of the dots that produce each of these separations is also important. The smaller the dots, the smoother the colors appear. Large dots (such as those in the Sunday comics) can actually take away from the illusion of a certain unified color because the different color dots are visible.

Figure 18-6 shows how process colors are combined to create new colors. In the figure, the first four rows show very large dots. The top three rows are cyan, magenta, and yellow. The fourth row is all four process colors combined, and the bottom row shows how the illustration looks when you print it.

Process color printing is best for photographs because photographs originate from a continuous tone that is made on photographic paper from film, instead of dots on a printing press.

Figure 18-6: The top three rows display cyan, magenta, and yellow. The fourth row displays their combination. The fifth row displays the colors as they will print.

In Illustrator, you can convert custom colors to process colors either before or during printing. To convert custom colors to process colors before printing, select any objects that have a specific custom color and tint and click the process color icon. The color is converted to its process color counterpart, and all selected objects are filled with the new process color combination.

After you click the Process Color icon, if the selected objects become filled with white and the triangles for each process color are at 0%, you have selected objects that contain different colors or tints. Undo the change immediately.

To make sure that you select only objects that have the same color, select one of the objects and choose Select ➪ Same ➪ Stroke Color. Objects that have different strokes or objects with different tints of the same color are not selected.

You can convert custom colors to process colors in the Output options in the Print dialog box and in many page-layout programs.

Combining spot and process color separations

You can couple spot colors with process colors in Illustrator simply by creating both process and named spot colors in a document.

Usually, you add spot colors to process colors for these reasons:

✦ You are using a company logo that has a specific color. By printing that color as a spot color, you make it stand out from the other coloring. In addition, color is more accurate when it comes from a specific ink rather than from a process color combination. Often, the logo is a Pantone color that doesn't reproduce true to form when you use process color separation.

✦ You need a color that you can't create by using process colors. Such colors are most often metallic or fluorescent, but they can be any number of Pantone colors or other colors that you can't match with process colors.

✦ You need a varnish for certain areas of an illustration. A varnish is a glazed type of ink that results in a shiny area wherever you use the varnish. You commonly use varnishes on titles and logos and over photographs.

✦ You need a light color over a large area. The dots that make up process colors are most noticeable in light colors, but by using a spot color to cover the area with a solid sheet of ink that has no dots, you can make the area smoother and enhance it visually.

In some circumstances, you need to use a spot color as a spot color and also use it as a process color. Normally, you can't do both, but the following steps describe one way to get around this problem:

1. **If the color doesn't exist as a swatch, create a swatch for the color.**

2. **In the Swatch Options (double-click on the swatch), choose Spot Color in the pop-up menu and click OK.**

3. **Duplicate the swatch by dragging it on top of the New Swatch icon (the little piece of paper).**

4. **In the Swatch Options for the duplicated swatch, choose Process Color in the pop-up menu and click OK.**

Note   You can tell which swatch is which by looking at the lower-right corner of the swatches; the spot color swatch has a white triangle with a "spot" in it, and the process swatch is solid.

Using Other Applications to Print

Many other software programs, particularly page-layout software programs, incorporate color-separation capabilities. These programs usually enable you to import Illustrator files that have been saved as Illustrator EPS files.

When you produce color separations from other software, make sure that any custom colors in the Illustrator illustration are present and accessible in the document that the illustration is placed within. Usually, you can set the custom colors to process separately or to spot separately.

Note   You cannot change the colors of an imported Illustrator EPS document in a page-layout program, so be sure that the colors are correct for the illustration while it is in Illustrator.

Understanding Trapping

Trapping is one of the most important but least understood issues in all of printing. Trapping is the process of overprinting different colored areas so there won't be any gaps between them.

Traps solve alignment problems when color separations are produced. The most common problem that occurs from misalignment is the appearance of white space between different colors.

Note   Although Illustrator does incorporate a trapping filter, it is not a trap-happy piece of software. For detailed illustrations, it usually isn't worth your time to set the trapping inside Illustrator; instead, you want to have your printer do the work for you.

Note   The thought of trapping scares many graphic designers, not just because they don't know how to do it, but also because they aren't sure what trapping is and what purpose it serves. Understanding the concept of trapping is the hard part; trapping objects is easy (though somewhat tedious in Illustrator).

Figure 18-7 shows a spot color illustration with four colors. The top row shows each of the individual colors. The first illustration in the second row shows how the illustration prints if all the separations are aligned perfectly. The second illustration in the second row shows what happens when the colors are misaligned. The third illustration in the second row shows how the illustration looks when trapped, with black indicating where two colors overprint each other.

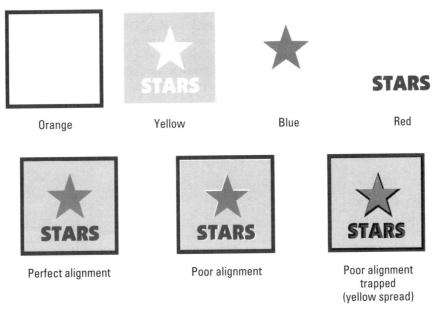

Figure 18-7: This spot color illustration shows individual colors (top) and aligned, misaligned, and trapped composites.

This example shows extreme misalignment and excessive trapping; I designed it just as a black-and-white illustration for this book. Ordinarily, the overprinting colors may appear a tiny bit darker, but they do not show as black. I used black so that you can see what parts of the illustration overlap when trapping is used. The trapping in this case is more than sufficient to cover any of the white gaps in the second illustration.

Trapping is created by spreading or choking certain colors that touch each other in an illustration. To spread a color, enlarge an object's color so that it takes up more space around the edges of the background area. To choke a color, expand the color of the background until it overlaps the edges of an object.

The major difference between a spread and a choke has to do with which object is considered the background and which object is the foreground. The foreground object is the object that traps. If the foreground object is spread, the color of the foreground object is spread until it overlaps the background by a certain amount. If the foreground object is choked, the color of the background around the foreground object is expanded until it overlaps the foreground object by a certain amount.

Tip   To determine whether to use a choke or a spread on an object, compare the lightness and darkness of the foreground and background objects. The general rule is that lighter colors expand or contract into darker colors.

Figure 18-8 shows the original misaligned illustration and two ways of fixing it with trapping. The second star has been spread by 1 point, and the third star has been choked by 1 point.

Original

Blue (star shape)
1-pt spread

Blue (star shape)
1-pt choke

Figure 18-8: The original illustration (left), fixing the star by spreading it 1 point (middle), and fixing the star by choking it 1 point (right)

Understanding misaligned color separations

Three common reasons why color separations don't align properly are that the negatives are not the same size, the plates on the press are not aligned perfectly when printing, or the gods have decided that a piece is too perfect and needs gaps between abutting colors. Trapping is required because it is a solution for covering gaps that occur when color separations do not properly align.

Negatives can be different sizes for a number of reasons. When the film was output to an imagesetter, the film may have been too near the beginning or the end of a roll, or separations in the same job may have been printed from different rolls. The pull on the rollers, while fairly precise on all but top-of-the-line imagesetters, where it should be perfect, can pull more film through when there is less resistance (at the end of a roll of film), or less film when there is more resistance (at the beginning of a roll of film). The temperature of the film may be different if a new roll is put on in the middle of a job, causing the film to shrink (if it is cold) or expand (if it is warm).

The temperature of the processor may have risen or fallen a degree or two while the film was being processed. Again, cooler temperatures in the chemical bays and in the air dryer as the film exits the process have an impact on the size of the film.

Film negatives usually don't change drastically in size, but they can vary up to a few points on an 11-inch page. That distance is huge when a page has several abutting colors throughout. The change in a roll of film is almost always along the length of the roll, not along the width. The quality of the film is another factor that determines how much the film will stretch or shrink.

Most strippers are quite aware of how temperature affects the size of negatives. A common stripper trick is to walk outside with a freshly processed negative during the colder months to shrink a negative that may have enlarged slightly during processing.

Check with your service bureau staff to see how long they warm up the processor before sending jobs through it. If the answer is less than an hour, the chemicals will not be at a consistent temperature, and negatives that are sent through too early will certainly change in size throughout the length of the job. Another question to ask is how often they change their chemicals and check the density from their imagesetter. Once a week is acceptable for a good-quality service bureau, but the best ones will change chemicals and check density once a day.

The plates on a press can be misaligned by either an inexperienced press operator or a faulty press. An experienced press operator knows the press and what to do to get color plates to align properly. A faulty press is one where plates move during printing or are not positioned correctly. An experienced press operator can determine how to compensate for a faulty press.

No press is perfect, but some of the high-end presses are pretty darn close. Even on those presses, the likelihood that a job with colors that abut one another can print perfectly is not very great.

If a job doesn't have some sort of trapping in it, it probably will not print perfectly, no matter how good the negatives, press, and press operator are.

Knowing how much you need to trap

The amount of trap that you need in an illustration depends on many things, but the deciding factor is what your commercial printer tells you is the right amount.

The most important thing to consider is the quality of the press that the printer will use. Of course, only the printer knows which press your job will run on, so talking to the printer about trapping is imperative.

Other factors to consider include the colors of ink and types of stock used in the job. Certain inks soak into different stocks differently.

Traps range from ¹⁄₁,₀₀₀ of an inch to ⁵⁄₁,₀₀₀ of an inch. Most traditional printers refer to traps in thousandths of inches, but Illustrator likes values in points for this sort of thing. Figure 18-9 is a chart with traps in increments of ¹⁄₁,₀₀₀, from 11,000 of an inch to ¹⁰⁄₁,₀₀₀ of an inch, and gives their point measurements. The trapped area is represented by black to be more visible in this example.

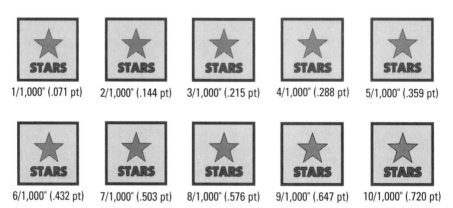

1/1,000" (.071 pt)   2/1,000" (.144 pt)   3/1,000" (.215 pt)   4/1,000" (.288 pt)   5/1,000" (.359 pt)

6/1,000" (.432 pt)   7/1,000" (.503 pt)   8/1,000" (.576 pt)   9/1,000" (.647 pt)   10/1,000" (.720 pt)

Figure 18-9: Different trap amounts

Remember that the greater the trap, the less chance there is that any white gaps will appear, but the trap may actually be visible. Visible traps of certain color pairs can look almost as bad as white space.

Trapping Illustrator files

In Illustrator, you accomplish manual (non-filter) trapping by selecting a path's stroke or fill and setting it to overprint another path's stroke or fill. The degree to which the two paths' fills or strokes overlap and overprint is the amount of trap that is used.

The most basic way to create a trap on an object is by giving it a stroke that is either the fill color of the object (to create a spread) or the fill color of the background (to create a choke).

Tip   Be sure to make the width of any stroke that you use for trapping twice as wide as the intended trap, because only half of the stroke (one side of the path) actually overprints a different color. In some circumstances, fixing a stroke that is not wide enough initially can be difficult.

Another way to create a trap is to use the Pathfinder palette. Follow these steps:

1. **Select all pieces of art that are overlapping or abutting.**

2. **Choose Trap from the Pathfinder palette.** You will find the Trap button when you choose Options from the Pathfinder pop-up menu.

3. **Enter the width into the Height/Width text field.**

4. **Click OK to apply the trap.**

Using complex trapping techniques in Illustrator

The preceding trap explanations are extremely simplified examples of trapping methods in Illustrator. In reality, objects never seem to be a solid color, and if they are, they are never on a solid background. In addition, most illustrations contain multiple overlapping objects that have their own special trapping needs.

I consider trapping to be complex when I can't just go around selecting paths and applying trap quickly. Complex trapping involves several different techniques:

✦ Create a separate layer for trapping objects. By keeping trapping on its own layer, you make myriad options available that are not available if the trapping is intermixed with the rest of the artwork. Place the new layer above the other layers. Lock all the layers but the trapping layer so that the original artwork is not modified. You can turn trapping on and off by hiding the entire layer or turning off the Print option in the Layers Options dialog box.

✦ Use the round joins and ends options in the Stroke portion of the Stroke palette for all trapping strokes. Round joins and ends are much less conspicuous than the harsh corners and 90-degree angles of other joins and ends, and they blend smoothly into other objects.

✦ Trap gradations by stroking them with paths that are filled with overprinting gradients. You cannot fill strokes with gradients, but you can fill paths with gradients. You can make any stroke into a path by selecting it and choosing Outline from the Pathfinder palette. After you have transformed the stroke into a path, fill it with the gradient and check the Overprint Fill box (in the Attributes palette) for that path.

Note   Whenever I start a heavy-duty trapping project, I always work on a copy of the original illustration. Wrecking the original artwork is just too easy when you add trapping.

When Trapping Yourself Isn't Worth It

Before you spend the long amounts of time that complex trapping entails and modify your illustration beyond recognition (at least in Artwork mode), you may want to reconsider whether you should do the trapping yourself.

If you estimate that trapping your job will require several hours of work, the chances of doing it correctly dwindle significantly. If the illustration includes many crisscrossing blends and gradations or multiple placed images, you may not have the patience to get through the entire process with your sanity intact.

If you determine that you cannot do the trapping yourself, you can have it done after the fact with Luminous TrapWise or Island Trapper, or you can have a service bureau with special output devices create trapping automatically. These services will undoubtedly cost more than doing the trapping yourself, but it will get done right, which is the important thing.

Summary

Printing Illustrator documents can often be quite a bit more complex than simply choosing File ➪ Print. In this chapter, you learned about a number of issues that directly affect the quality of the final printed output, including these:

✦ Illustrator can be interpreted as a good front-end for the PostScript page description language.

✦ Print separations from within Illustrator.

✦ Choose whether to print a composite or separations from the Print dialog box.

✦ Determine separation information in the Output section of the Print dialog box.

✦ Prevent potential white strips that can appear when a printer isn't perfectly aligned with trapping.

✦ Output options in the Print dialog box let you specify which colors print and at what angle and frequency they print.

✦   ✦   ✦

Creating Web Graphics

In This Chapter

Using Pixel Preview view

Learning Web-safe colors

Using the Save for Web interface

Understanding the Web formats and vector graphics for the Web

Applying SVG filters

Image slicing

Using CSS Layers

Creating interactive Web images

Using data-driven graphics variables

In concept, designing for the Web and designing for print are very similar, but in practice they both offer special tests to the patience of an Illustrator user. In this chapter, I discuss challenges that the designer faces when attempting to present ideas graphically that appeal to the eye and get the right point across. Web design encompasses more than just converting your picas to pixels.

Designing for the Web versus Designing for Print

A Web designer faces specific issues that a print designer never even thinks about. Consider these:

+ **A print designer chooses the specific color inks and paper with which to print, giving the designer complete control over how a reader sees it.** A Web designer has no way of knowing what kind of monitor a reader is using to view his Web site—a nice yellow color on one screen may end up looking orange or green on another monitor. Monitors also display at different resolutions (older machines may be set to 640×480 or 800×600, while newer ones may be 1024×768 or higher), meaning Web designers must make their Web sites work for all of them.

+ **A Web designer is always at the mercy of the Web browser.** In our ever-changing world, you can't know what a reader will use to view your Web site. When the Web first became popular, Netscape Navigator was the browser of choice. Microsoft's Internet Explorer is by far the most prevalent browser out there now. In the past few years, Apple introduced a browser called Safari to run specifically on the Mac platform. Now a browser called Firefox is rapidly becoming very popular. Because each browser displays type, uses styles, handles animation, shows frames, and even formats links differently, a Web site in Explorer can look very different from the same Web site in Navigator or Safari.

✦ **A Web designer must be conscious of how long it takes an average reader to download a page or graphic.** Although high-speed broadband connections are more popular, this is still an issue and limits Web designers from using large full color images or graphics. You still need to consider how many colors to use, what file types to use, and even what fonts to use.

✦ **The most alluring aspect of the Web is interactivity.** Web designers can take advantage of technologies that print designers can only dream of. Examples include having graphics change when a user moves his mouse (rollovers), making images come alive with animation. Other advantages are utilizing advanced programming techniques (called scripting) to deliver customized graphics tailored specifically to the reader or displaying a greeting based on the time of day.

Tip

Sometimes, a Web designer actually does know what monitor or system his viewers are using. When creating Web sites for use on intranets, which are employee-accessible internal company or organization networks, a designer can take advantage of that knowledge and use it to his benefit. For example, if a designer knows that everyone has a Windows computer running Internet Explorer, he can design just for that browser and not worry or care what the site may look like in Netscape, Safari, or Firefox.

Illustrator and the Web — the Basics

Illustrator is a great tool for creating Web graphics because it possesses all the necessary production tools, supports all the standard file types, and offers superb integration with other Web applications, such as Adobe Photoshop, Adobe ImageReady, Adobe GoLive, and Macromedia Flash. Even more important, because Illustrator is a vector-based application, you can easily repurpose graphics for both print and the Web, which means that you don't have to recreate your artwork for one or the other.

Although in theory you could create an entire HTML Web page using only Illustrator, no one would mistake Illustrator as the only tool you need for Web design. Illustrator's strength is creating graphics for a Web page or designing Web pages for assembly in an HTML editor, such as Adobe GoLive, Microsoft FrontPage, or Macromedia Dreamweaver. Brave designers may also utilize text-based HTML editors such as BBEdit. Illustrator is also perfect for creating vector-based graphics that you import into Macromedia Flash for creating truly interactive content.

Illustrator is well equipped to handle Web graphics, and before you actually run off and start creating them, I want to discuss some of the fundamental tools and functions that you need to understand. The first idea to remember is that all Web graphics are in RGB mode, so when you create a new document, make sure that you choose RGB. If you forget, you can always choose File ➪ Document Color Mode ➪ RGB to change to RGB color mode, as indicated in Figure 19-1.

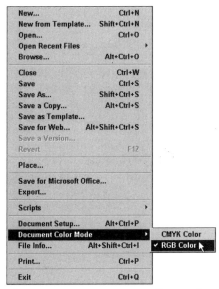

Figure 19-1: Be sure to specify RGB for the document's color mode for Web documents.

Understanding pixel preview

Sometimes, you just have to face the facts: Web graphics are always displayed in pixels. Even "vector-based" Web formats like Flash and SVG end up displaying on a computer screen, which means that they are viewed in pixel form. Although some monitors display at 96 or 105 ppi (pixels per inch), most still display graphics at 72 ppi. In either case, the resolution is *much* less than the 3450 dpi (dots per inch) that you see from your high-end imagesetter or even the 600 dpi that you see on printouts from your laser printer.

At such a low resolution, curved lines and text appear jaggy and can make your graphics look like they came from the early 1980s (Space Invaders and Asteroids come to mind). To compensate for low resolution on monitors, software programs usually employ a technique called *anti-aliasing*. By applying a gentle blur to the edge of your text or graphics, you eliminate the jaggedness of your image, replacing it with a smooth transition and a clean look, as shown in Figure 19-2. Illustrator uses anti-aliasing to allow you to preview your graphics and text onscreen beautifully. Don't worry; your printed output remains unaffected and your text looks crisp and sharp when you print from your laser printer or imagesetter.

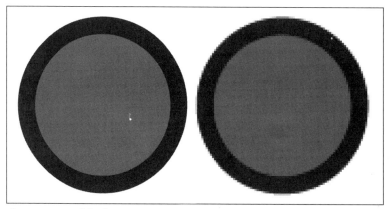

Figure 19-2: This demonstrates how art appears on a monitor with (left) and without (right) anti-aliasing.

Because the delivery medium for Web graphics is a computer screen, a Web designer cares very much about anti-aliasing. For one reason, although soft edges on your graphic may make large text and graphics pretty onscreen, they can also make small text fuzzy and unreadable, as shown in Figure 19-3.

> Small size text can be hard to read

Figure 19-3: Small anti-aliased text can be very hard to read.

Illustrator has a special preview mode called Pixel Preview (choose View ➪ Pixel Preview) that displays the graphics onscreen as actual rasters — the exact way they would display in a Web browser. Using Pixel Preview mode lets you know exactly how anti-aliasing affects your graphics. Because anti-aliasing is based on your monitor's pixel grid (see the "Thin Black Lines versus Fat Gray Lines" sidebar), moving your art around can affect its overall appearance. The first step in creating Web graphics from Illustrator is to turn on Pixel Preview. You can tell when you're in Pixel Preview mode by looking at the title bar of your document, as indicated in Figure 19-4.

Figure 19-4: The title bar indicates what view mode you are in.

Cross-Reference

For more on the various View modes in Illustrator, see Chapter 2.

Tip

You can turn off anti-aliasing to see how it affects your display by going into the General Preferences dialog box (Edit (Illustrator) ⇨ Preferences ⇨ General) and deselecting the check box for Anti-aliased Artwork. All artwork also appears anti-aliased when you're in pixel preview mode. Disabling anti-aliasing doesn't make your graphics look pretty onscreen, but it does slightly enhance the performance of Illustrator.

Using Web-safe colors

In this section, we look at a topic that many Web developers consider ancient history. Although the idea of *Web-safe colors* was quite important in the dark ages of Web development 10 years or so ago, very few people still surf the Web using the antique computers whose extreme limitations caused the need for limiting to a select few the number of colors used. Sure, Illustrator CS2 still offers support for Web-safe colors, but you can probably ignore the whole issue safely and not lose any sleep over the possibility that someone visiting a Web site you designed can't see exactly the color you intended.

As we mentioned earlier, one of the problems that a Web designer faced in the past was choosing a color that looked consistent, no matter what computer you viewed the Web site on. First, I want to explore the way monitors displayed colors. The average monitor could display at least 256 different colors onscreen at any one time. So what if one of the colors that you picked wasn't one of those 256 colors? In such cases, the monitor used a process called *dithering* to simulate that color onscreen.

Dithering is a process in which different colored pixels are placed in a pattern to match the desired color. This process is similar to four-color process printing, where dots of cyan, magenta, yellow, and black are used to simulate other colors. However, dithering can sometimes result in noticeable and ugly patterns, much like a moiré. Besides not displaying the exact color you wanted, dithering could make text or parts of your Web site unreadable (and you thought Web design was easy, right?).

Thin Black Lines versus Fat Gray Lines

Sometimes, the process of anti-aliasing produces results that are less appealing to the eye. Good examples of this are thin lines and small text. Anti-aliasing can make a thin black line look like a fat gray line, or it can make small crisp text an unreadable mush of pixels. Fortunately, Illustrator provides you with the tools to avoid these issues.

First, you should understand why these things happen. A pixel can either be on or off — you can't have a pixel that's only half-colored. By default, Illustrator always draws objects that "snap" to an invisible pixel grid. (You can turn off this feature by deselecting View ⇨ Snap to Pixel when you're in Pixel Preview mode). Illustrator also paints strokes on the center of a path. This means that if you select a 1-pixel stroke, Illustrator centers it on the path, effectively placing half a pixel on either side of the stroke. However, because you can't fill only half a pixel with color, Illustrator uses anti-aliasing to turn that 1-pixel black line into a 2-pixel gray line. If you turn off the Snap to Pixel option, and then move the line half a pixel in either direction (via the Move dialog), you see the 2-pixel gray line turn into a 1-pixel black line, as shown in Figure A.

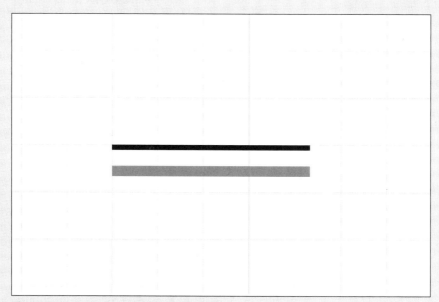

Figure A: A 1-pixel black line snapped to the pixel grid appears as a 2-pixel gray line when anti-aliased.

Small text actually reads better without anti-aliasing at all. Here, you can use Illustrator's Effects to your advantage:

1. Type some small text.

2. Choose Effect ⇨ Rasterize. This opens the Rasterize dialog box shown in Figure B.

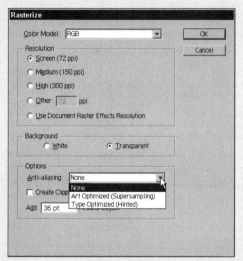

Figure B: The Rasterize dialog box

3. For the anti-aliasing option, choose None. This is shown in Figure B.

4. Click OK. Figure C shows text with and without anti-aliasing.

Web design

Web design

Figure C: Text with (top) and without (bottom) anti-aliasing applied

Because applying Rasterize in this way is a Live Effect, you can still make edits to your text with the Text tool as normal, yet the text can never be anti-aliased, as evidenced by Figure C. You can also use this technique for thin rules and lines.

To deal with this issue, developers came up with *Web-safe colors,* which is basically color that you know display correctly without dithering on any computer. Is it magic? Believe it or not, it's actually math. Windows and Mac computers both had 256 standard system colors. But they didn't use the same 256 colors for their system palettes. When you actually matched the two standard system palettes, only 216 colors were identical; the other 40 were different. This means that you could safely specify 216 colors that were guaranteed to display without dithering on any computer.

Illustrator has long had a Web-safe color palette. You access this palette by going to the Swatches palette menu, choosing Open Swatch Library, and selecting Web. All colors listed in this palette are Web-safe colors. You can also pick Web-safe colors directly from the Color palette. To do so, choose Web Safe RGB from the palette menu shown in Figure 19-5. When you drag the color sliders, Illustrator "snaps to" Web-safe colors. Clicking the color bar in the Color palette allows you choose a color that's outside of the Web-safe color gamut, and if you do so, Illustrator displays an "out-of-gamut" icon that looks like a 3D cube, as shown in Figure 19-6. Clicking that cube "snaps" your color to the nearest Web-safe color.

Figure 19-5: Choosing the Web-safe RGB option in the Color palette's menu

Figure 19-6: The "out-of-gamut" Web-safe color warning informs you that your current color selection is not a Web-safe color.

Understanding hexadecimal colors

Hexa-*what?* No, we're not trying to put a spell on you. In HTML-speak, colors are usually defined by hexadecimal code, which is based on a base-16 number system, where each digit is a number from 0 to F (15). Although you may not find it very intuitive to call a color "FFFF00" (red 255, green 255, blue 0), instead of yellow, Hex values allow designers to use specific colors (after all, "yellow" comes in plenty of shades). When you have the Color palette set to Web Safe RGB mode, you can enter Hexadecimal values for a specific color. If you open the Web-safe color palette, Illustrator also displays hexadecimal codes if you mouse over the swatches, as shown in Figure 19-7. You can also enter Hex values directly into the Find field to jump directly to a color.

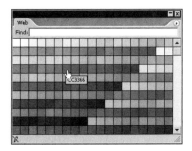

Figure 19-7: Hexadecimal values display in the Web-safe color palette when you point to a color swatch.

Optimizing and Saving Web Graphics

So you've created your lovely graphic and now it's time to save it in a format that a Web browser can understand and display. Back in the old days, Web designers were forced to export graphics with all these different settings and then open those graphics in a Web browser to see how they looked. More often than not, they ended up repeating this process until the graphics looked just right.

The exporting process is difficult because there's an important balance between file size and file appearance. In general, the more colorful and complex a graphic is, the larger its file size. But the larger the file size, the longer it takes to download the image. The average Web surfer isn't very patient, and if it takes too long to load a page, they move on to another one. So designers are forced to find that happy medium — an image that looks good enough, but that also downloads fast enough.

Note Two kinds of compression are available to you to help make files smaller. One is called *lossless*, which compresses the file without losing any data. The other is *lossy*, which throws out data that is deemed not important (by the mercy of the compression gods). With lossy compression, you usually have control over how much information gets tossed — the more data you choose to "lose," the higher the compression rate and the smaller the file.

Introducing the Save for Web dialog box

Several years ago, Adobe released a product called ImageReady, which gives designers a way to preview how Web graphics look with different file types, compression settings, and more, and to obtain real-time feedback on file size. This product was so monumental that Adobe built the basic ImageReady functionality, called *Save for Web*, into Photoshop, Illustrator, and GoLive.

Note   Today, Photoshop actually includes ImageReady as a separate companion application (most Photoshop users aren't even aware of this).

To use the Save for Web interface, choose File ➪ Save for Web and you're presented with a dialog box that takes up nearly the entire screen. There's good reason for this, because Save for Web has many different settings and options, as shown in Figure 19-8. The next section discusses what all these options are about. Get comfy; this is where things get busy.

Previewing Web graphics

The most notable and most important part of the Save for Web dialog box is the Preview pane. You can choose to either view your art in Original mode, Optimized, 2 Up, or 4 Up (the latter of which I find the most useful), where you can view your image in up to 4 different ways at once, allowing you to easily choose the best one. Here's how Save for Web works: You click one preview, choose settings, click another, choose different settings, and so on, and then you compare the different versions. You can then pick the one you think is best (all without leaving the dialog box).

Tip   The Save for Web dialog box honors Illustrator's Crop Marks for clip sizes. So if you want to easily export images for the Web in a particular size — even if you have other art on the page — you can draw a rectangle around the portion you want to export. You can then convert the rectangle to crops by choosing Object ➪ Crop Area ➪ Make, and then choose File ➪ Save for Web.

Along the left side of the dialog box are the four tools you use in Save for Web:

✦ **Hand Grabber tool:** Lets you move artwork around in the preview window.

✦ **Slice Select tool:** Allows you to choose with which slice you want to work.

Cross-Reference   For more about slices, see the section "Understanding Web Slicing" later in this chapter.

✦ **Zoom tool:** Lets you increase or decrease the magnification of your image.

✦ **Eyedropper tool:** Allows you to sample or select colors from your image (some functions in the Color Table require you to choose a color).

Toggle Slices Visibility

Eyedropper Color

Eyedropper Tool

Zoom Tool

Slice Select Tool

Hand Tool

Optimization Settings

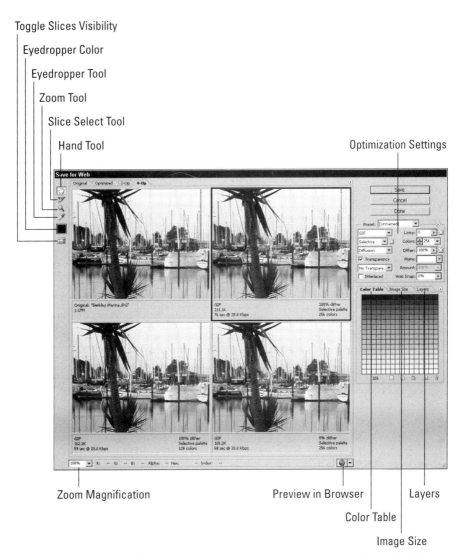

Zoom Magnification

Preview in Browser

Layers

Color Table

Image Size

Figure 19-8: The Save for Web dialog box gives you many options for optimizing your documents for the Web.

You also find two additional buttons here:

✦ **Eyedropper color:** This indicates the color chosen with the Eyedropper tool, or you can click on it, which brings up the Color Picker, allowing you to key in a specific color.

✦ **Slice Visibility:** Clicking this button either shows or hides the slices in your preview pane (not the art that's in them, just the slice boundaries and numbers themselves).

Located on the upper-right side of preview pane is a pop-up menu, shown in Figure 19-9, where you can choose a connection speed. Save for Web uses this setting to approximate how long it will take your graphic to load. Figure 19-10 shows that each preview pane lists a setting along with the estimated download time in the lower left of the preview pane.

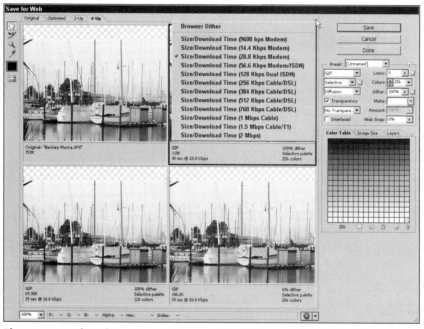

Figure 19-9: Choosing a connection speed enables you to optimize the document for different types of connections.

Approximate download times

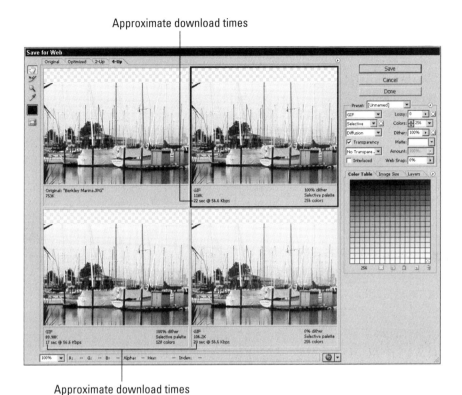

Approximate download times

Figure 19-10: Each preview lists a file-optimization setting and approximate download time in the lower-left corner of its box.

At the bottom of the palette, you have a zoom pop-up as well as feedback on colors and one of the handiest features — a button to preview your art in an actual Web browser of choice. Choosing this option launches a Web browser and not only displays the art but also all the information about the file, as well as the HTML source code to display it, as indicated in Figure 19-11.

Along the right side of the Save for Web dialog are all the settings you'd ever need (and some you'd probably never need) to customize your Web graphics to perfection. At the top are the Save, Cancel, and Done buttons (you'd use Done if you just wanted to specify Web settings but didn't want to export anything at that time). Pressing Alt (Option) turns Cancel and Done into Reset and Remember.

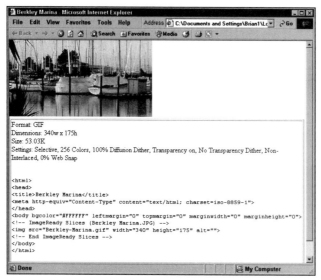

Figure 19-11: Along with a preview of your graphic, the browser displays all the file's settings.

Directly below is where you set the file format options, such as choosing among GIF, JPEG, PNG-8, PNG-24, SWF, SVG, or WBMP and all the specific settings that go with them. Figure 19-12 shows the drop-down list (on a Windows machine) where you choose the file format. You also have a Color Table palette that lets you control specific colors in your image, an Image Size palette, and a Layers palette where you can specify the output of CSS (Cascading Style Sheet) Layers (any top-level layer can be specified as a CSS layer here).

Figure 19-12: Choose a file format for the document from the drop-down list (pop-up menu).

Tip

Cascading Style Sheets are part of what DHTML (or Dynamic HTML, which is now part of the HTML 4.0 specification) is all about. CSS Layers give Web developers the ability to overlap images and slices, and to interactively show and hide each layer. You learn more about CSS layers later in the chapter.

Learning the Web-graphic formats

As stated in the previous section, you have many options for formats in the Save for Web dialog box shown in Figure 19-12. Which one should you use? Each of these format types has advantages and disadvantages, and understanding the difference between them will help immensely as you design and build Web pages. This section thoroughly discusses each format and walks you through the various options associated with each one.

Note   You should realize that no one setting is best suited for all Web graphics. Some settings are better suited for certain types of graphics. With experience, you'll come to understand and choose Web formats and settings with ease.

Understanding the GIF format

One of the most popular file formats for Web graphics, there's a never-ending controversy over how to pronounce GIF. Some say it with a soft G (as in Giraffe) while others pronounce with a hard G (as in Gift). Either way you say it, a GIF can contain a maximum of 256 colors, but more important, you can specify your image to have fewer colors to control file size. GIF uses a lossless compression algorithm and basically looks for large areas of pixels that are the same color to save file size. Lossless compression makes this format perfect for most flat color images, such as logos and text headlines.

The GIF format also has specific settings that can control how the GIF displays in a Web browser. Because GIF supports a maximum of 256 colors, you have to choose a color-reduction algorithm, which is basically how Illustrator forces all the colors to fit within a specific table of colors. You can go a step further by specifying exactly how many colors your GIF should contain as well, which can have a large impact on file size. If your image is just some black text, you can reduce your GIF to 4 or 16 colors with the same visual result — but get a huge file size saving.

You can choose different dither methods as well (to get colors that aren't in the color table to appear in your GIF). Here's where the different preview panes can really help you choose the best setting for your graphic; GIF also supports transparency, so that you can choose one color as a "none" color, allowing your image to have a transparent background (necessary for placing images on colored backgrounds). The Matte setting works in tandem with this. Anti-aliasing allows colors to blend into each other to create smoother transitions of color, but if you start off with art on a white background, you may see white pixels if you place that graphic on a non-white background. If you know the color on which you intend to display your graphic (that is, a background color), specifying that color as a Matte ensures that the graphic blends perfectly into the background.

You can also interlace a GIF, which means that the image quickly appears in a browser at a low resolution, and then improves in resolution and quality as it continues to load. This allows readers to start seeing graphics onscreen even while the page is still downloading. It's more of a psychological thing than anything else.

Using the JPEG format

If the GIF format is perfect for flat color images, the JPEG format (pronounced JAY-PEG) is the perfect format for photos and continuous tone graphics. JPEG was created originally to allow photographers to easily transmit photos electronically. Utilizing a lossy compression algorithm, JPEG can achieve some astonishing file savings by allowing you to compress a 10MB file to about 1MB in most cases.

Illustrator lets you set different levels of JPEG compression either by choosing options from a pop-up menu (Low, Medium, High, Very High, or Maximum) or by moving the Quality slider between 0 and 100. In the Save for Web dialog box, these settings refer to quality, not compression, so a setting of Maximum means maximum quality (and less compression), not maximum compression and lower quality. Because JPEG compression can result in files that have visible artifacts or look "chunky" (what you end up seeing are blocks of color rather than detail) you also have the option to apply a blur to minimize such artifacts. You can specify a blur setting of up to 2 pixels using the Blur slider (located under the Quality slider).

You can also set JPEG images to "progressive," which means that they load incrementally in a browser (similar to GIF's interlacing). You can also specify a Matte color for JPEG images (just as with GIFs).

Understanding the PNG format

When the GIF format became popular, an issue arose with regard to the patent holder who created the compression algorithm (Unisys). To get around possible legal issues, the PNG (Portable Network Graphics) format was born. Pronounced *ping,* the format offers lossless compression similar to GIF, but can support up to 32-bit color images and 256-level alpha channels for transparency (far more than the 256-color limit and 1-color alpha of GIF). An alpha channel is another term for the part of a file that's transparent. Save for Web allows users to save PNG images in PNG-8 and PNG-24 format, which offers support for more colors.

Because PNG can support continuous tone color, the format is great for both flat and photographic images. The additional settings you can apply to PNG images are similar to those that you can apply with GIF images.

Using the WBMP format

You use the Wireless Bitmap format specifically for graphics that you want to display on cell phones and PDA devices. The WBMP format is 1 bit, which means that pixels can be either black or white, so you're limited in choosing between different dithering methods (Diffusion, Pattern, and Noise) and a dithering amount.

You may remember that dithering is a process in which different colored pixels are placed in a pattern to match the desired color. For more on this subject, see the section "Using Web-safe colors," earlier in this chapter.

The SWF and SVG options are covered later in this chapter in the section "Creating Vector Graphics for the Web."

Choosing output options

When you've chosen how to optimize your graphics, you can click the Save button. Doing this opens the Save Optimized As dialog box, where you can choose to save your graphics in one of three different formats. These options are available in the Save as type list box:

✦ **Images only:** Saves just the images themselves

✦ **HTML and Images:** Saves the images and an HTML page that contains them

✦ **HTML only:** Saves just the HTML code without the images at all

Not all Web designers work alone. In many cases, a Web designer works hand-in-hand with a Web developer or someone who either writes code or defines how it's written. Because there are so many different ways of authoring HTML, many developers are very sensitive to how they write or how they build Web pages. Adobe certainly is aware of this because at the bottom of the Save Optimized As dialog is a pop-up menu called Settings. If you choose Other from the list, as shown in Figure 19-13, you'll be rewarded with the Output Settings dialog box, which is a dream come true for even the pickiest developer.

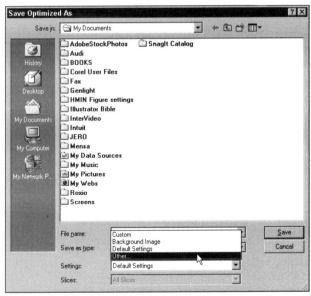

Figure 19-13: Choosing Other from the Save Optimized As dialog box gives you additional options.

The Output Settings dialog box has four separate panes, each of which offers a wealth of options:

✦ **HTML:** Shown in Figure 19-14, this pane allows you to specify exactly how the HTML code is formatted, along with options that you can include for better integration with other Adobe products such as ImageReady and GoLive. The Always Add Alt Attribute setting includes Alt attributes in all img tags, even where you don't specify them, which is a Section-508 (Government Accessibility) requirement (as well as a requirement to pass an HTML 4 or XHTML validation check).

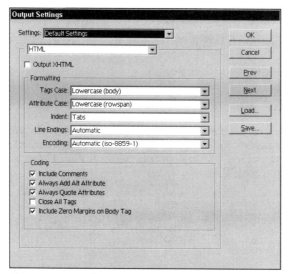

Figure 19-14: The HTML pane in the Output Settings dialog box

✦ **Slices:** Shown in Figure 19-15, this pane gives you control over how tables are coded in HTML and whether CSS layers are generated. You can also choose exactly how each slice is named. Slicing is covered in the sections "Understanding Web Slicing," and "Object-based Web Slicing" later in this chapter.

✦ **Background:** HTML allows you to specify a background color or a background image for the entire page (images *tile* or repeat to fill the entire page). In this tab, shown in Figure 19-16, you can specify what color or image you want for the background of your HTML page.

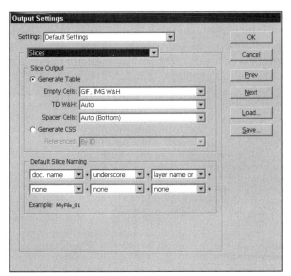

Figure 19-15: The Slices panel in the Output Settings dialog box

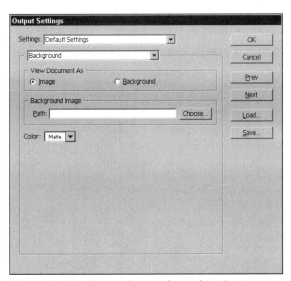

Figure 19-16: The Background panel in the Output Settings dialog box

✦ **Saving Files:** Shown in Figure 19-17, this pane lets you specify exactly how to name your files, as well as where you want to save them. The Include XMP option allows you to save metadata along with the files. XMP metadata comes from the File Info dialog box found under the File menu in Illustrator.

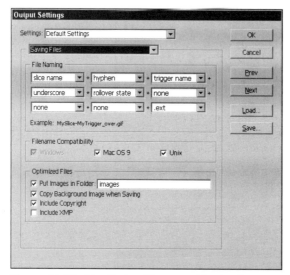

Figure 19-17: The Saving Files panel in the Output Settings dialog box

Creating Vector Graphics for the Web

Sure, the Web is a place where pixels abound, but that doesn't mean there's no room for vectors to play as well. In fact, vector-based Web graphics have become quite popular. They add the benefit of enlarging Web graphics without getting "the jaggies" and allow you to print better Web graphics from a browser. There are other benefits as well that we talk about as we discuss the two most popular vector Web formats — Flash and SVG.

Using Flash graphics

Once upon a time, a company called FutureWave developed a program called FutureSplash Animator that created vectors that you could display in a Web browser. The program let you animate vector shapes and place some cool animation in a Web page. The downside was that very few people knew about it, and to play the animations in a Web browser, you had to install a special plug-in.

One day, a company called Macromedia bought FutureWave and renamed FutureSplash to Flash. They also provided a browser plug-in for Flash to go along with their already popular Shockwave plug-in, calling it Shockwave Flash (SWF). The rest is modern-day Internet history. The Flash plug-in is now installed by default in every mainstream Web browser, and it has become the standard for creating interactive and engaging Web sites. Flash support is now even built into Apple's QuickTime video player, some cell phones, and some PDAs, and it continues to expand.

Note   Although Flash and Illustrator do share the similarity of being vector-based programs, Illustrator isn't a competing product to Flash. Adobe did try to unseat Macromedia's hold on the Web market with LiveMotion, but by the time LiveMotion reached version 2.0, Adobe cancelled it.

Although Illustrator can't do anywhere *near* the kinds of things that Macromedia Flash can do, it *can* export graphics in the SWF format. In fact, many designers who use Flash also use Illustrator to create their graphics and then import them into Flash to make them interactive.

To export graphics in the SWF format, choose File ➪ Export, select Macromedia Flash (SWF) from the Save as type drop-down list (Format pop-up), and click Export to display the Macromedia® Flash™ (SWF) Format Options dialog box, shown in Figure 19-18. For export options, you can choose from three different settings:

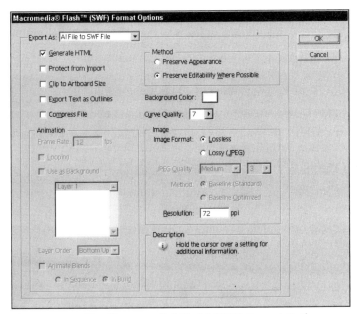

Figure 19-18: The Macromedia® Flash™ (SWF) Format Options dialog box enables you to save Illustrator documents in SWF format.

✦ **AI File to SWF File:** This option creates a single static SWF file from whatever is in your Illustrator file. This is perfect for when you want to display a static SWF image in your Web page.

✦ **AI Layers to SWF Frames:** This option creates a single animated SWF file from the layers in your Illustrator file. Each Illustrator layer becomes its own frame, allowing you to export animations right out of Illustrator. When you select this option, you can choose a frame rate as well as whether you want the animation to loop (see the next bulleted list for more on these options).

✦ **AI Layers to SWF Files:** This final option creates separate SWF files, each containing the contents of one layer in your Illustrator file. This is useful for designers who want to import individual art pieces into a Flash project.

Flash understands and takes advantage of Symbols, so if you define and use Symbols in your Illustrator file, they appear as Symbols when you open the SWF file in Flash. You also benefit from smaller file sizes when using Symbols in your SWF files. See Chapter 5 for more information on using Symbols in Illustrator.

You may also encounter these functions in the Macromedia Flash (SWF) Format Options dialog box:

✦ **Frame Rate:** This value is how many frames of the animation play each second.

✦ **Looping:** Selecting this option makes the animation continuously play over and over again.

✦ **Generate HTML:** One of the coolest options in this dialog box, this option not only creates the SWF file, but also creates the necessary HTML code to correctly display the graphic in a Web browser. It certainly takes the guesswork and gruntwork out of the equation and allows even novice Web designers to easily incorporate cool Flash graphics on their Web pages.

✦ **Protect from Import:** This assures you that others can't open the SWF to edit it.

✦ **Clip to Artboard Size:** This option sets the Flash movie boundary to the same size as your Illustrator artboard.

✦ **Export Text as Outlines:** This option exports text as outlines rather than as text.

✦ **Compress File:** Choosing this option results in a smaller size for the resulting SWF file.

✦ **Curve Quality:** This option lets you choose how precisely vector paths are calculated.

✦ **Preserve Appearance/Preserve Editability Where Possible:** You can either choose to Preserve Appearance or Preserve Editability. The latter option affects how SWF files display certain effects or appearances that Illustrator can apply to objects but that are not supported in Flash. In cases where Flash does not support the effect or appearance, the Preserve Appearance option rasterizes the object so that it looks correct. However, rasterizing the object may result in a file that isn't as editable when you open it in Flash.

✦ **Layer Order:** This allows you to export bottom or top layers first. Because the Flash Player loads the layers as they're encountered in the SWF file, this can affect how quickly your Flash movie begins playing.

✦ **Image Options:** These options come into play only if you have placed images or rasterized areas in your file. If you choose Lossless, your image is saved in GIF format, or you can choose Lossy and export your images as JPEG files, where you can choose quality and resolution (similar to those options we defined for JPEG earlier).

You can also save SWF files directly from the Save for Web dialog box, the benefit being that you can preview your art before you save.

For more on the Save for Web dialog box, see the section "Previewing Web graphics," earlier in this chapter.

Although the Save for Web dialog box can't preview SWF animations, you can use the Preview in Browser feature to see what your animation looks like before actually saving the file.

Illustrator uses Apple's QuickTime plug-in to preview SWF files in Save for Web. If you can't see a preview of your image when you choose SWF in Save for Web, make sure that you have QuickTime installed.

Creating SVG files

SVG stands for "Scalable Vector Graphics" and is an open standard format based on XML. To view SVG files in a Web browser, a plug-in is required, although future versions of Web browsers (Explorer, Navigator, Safari, and so on) most likely will provide built-in SVG support, because the format is becoming increasingly popular. One cool aspect of SVG is that you can edit it in any text editor and change values easily, thus changing the look of your graphic.

Other benefits of SVG are covered in the section "Using Data-Driven Graphics to Streamline Design Work" later in this chapter, where the XML text-based format is used to include variable content in a file.

Illustrator is actually one of the most robust tools available for creating SVG graphics. Illustrator not only can save files in the SVG format, but it can also open SVG files — even if they weren't created in Illustrator.

You can save SVG files directly out of Illustrator by choosing File ➪ Save and picking SVG from the Save as type list (Format pop-up menu), shown in Figure 19-19. You can also choose to save SVG files via Save for Web, as mentioned earlier in the chapter. Of course, the advantage to saving them from the Save for Web dialog box is that you can preview the results before you save them.

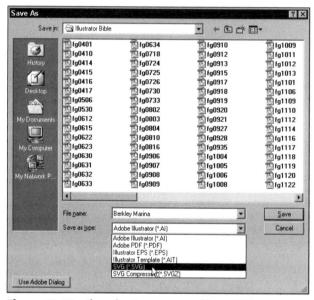

Figure 19-19: Choosing to save your file as SVG

When you save an SVG file, you can choose to embed fonts (where the font license agreement allows) and you can also choose whether to include linked images as separate links or to embed them and include them inside the SVG file. You'll also notice an option in the SVG Options dialog box, shown in Figure 19-20, to Preserve Illustrator Editing Capabilities. Turning this option on enables you to convert the file back into Illustrator without losing any native information. Because the option adds data into the file that only Illustrator can use, it increases the file size, so turn off this option if you don't need to edit the file later. Of course, saving a copy of the file as a regular file is always a good idea so that you don't lose any work.

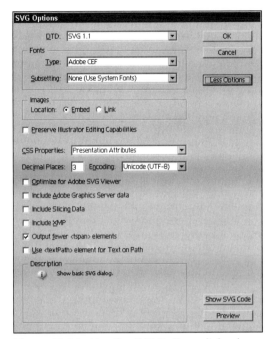

Figure 19-20: Use the SVG Options dialog box to specify settings for SVG files.

In the SVG Options dialog box, you also find a More/Less Options button where you can specify even more details about your SVG files. You can specify CSS Properties settings, choose how precisely vectors are calculated (decimal places), and choose text encoding formats. Optimize for Adobe SVG Viewer, which installs along with Illustrator, allows you to take advantage of certain features that only the Adobe SVG Viewer plug-in can offer. (This is currently the standard, so using it is a safe choice.) Include Slicing Data does exactly what it says: It includes Web-slice data in the file. (I cover Web slicing later in the chapter.)

Applying SVG filters

SVG filters are cool because they are attributes you can apply to your art in real time as they display in a Web browser. If you apply a drop shadow to text as an SVG filter, that text is still live and editable in your Web browser (you can select, copy, and paste it, and a search engine can "see" the text), yet it has a drop shadow applied to it when it displays on the Web page. Because you can zoom in on vector graphics in a Web browser, you can enlarge the SVG text as much as you want, and the drop shadow renders each time, ensuring a nice smooth drop shadow. (You won't get "the jaggies.")

Applying an SVG Effect is similar to applying any other effect. Figure 19-21 shows the SVG Filters submenu. Make your selection, and then choose Effect ➪ SVG Filters and choose one. You can't preview some of these filters in the Illustrator window, so previewing the file in your browser is a good idea. After you apply a filter, you can see it listed in the Appearance palette, shown in Figure 19-22, for that object or selection. Therefore, to edit or remove the effect, you use the Appearance palette.

Cross-Reference   Effects are covered in more detail in Chapter 15.

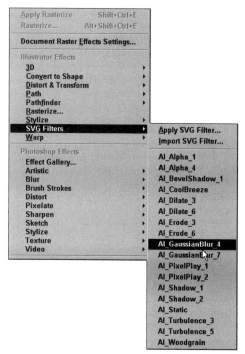

Figure 19-21: Use the Effect ➪ SVG Filters submenu to apply an SVG Filter effect to an object.

Illustrator comes with several SVG Filters. However, if you know SVG, you can also create your own effects by choosing Effect ➪ SVG Filters ➪ Apply SVG Filter and clicking the New SVG Filter icon button. Figure 19-23 shows an existing filter being modified. You can also import SVG filters from other Illustrator files by choosing Effect ➪ SVG Filters ➪ Import SVG Filter.

Figure 19-22: This shows the SVG Filter effect as it appears in the Appearance palette after it's applied.

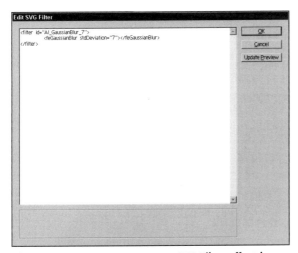

Figure 19-23: Create your own SVG Filter effect by modifying an existing SVG filter.

The SVG Interactivity palette

In reality, SVG is JavaScript-driven XML code. Illustrator allows you to add interactive options to graphics that you can save as SVG via the SVG Interactivity palette. Doing so requires the knowledge of JavaScript because you must select an object, choose an event from the pop-up shown in Figure 19-24, and write or reference a JavaScript to perform a specific function (change color, animate, resize, and so on).

Figure 19-24: Applying a JavaScript event via the SVG Interactivity palette

Note   The SVG format supports many levels of interactivity and animation. Although Illustrator cannot create or preview these effects directly, you can use a text editor to add these functions after you create the graphics. For more information on using SVG, check out the SVG Zone on the Web at www.adobe.com/svg.

Understanding Web Slicing

Throughout this chapter, the term slicing comes up. It refers to the process of cutting up Web graphics into smaller pieces to achieve several goals:

✦ Rather than waiting for one large graphic to load in a Web page, loading several different smaller pieces makes the graphic load faster.

✦ You don't have to force a graphic with several different parts or styles to use just one file format or compression setting. For example, if you have a graphic that has some text or a logo on one side and a photo or gradation of color on another side, rather than force the entire graphic to a larger size to make sure the gradient looks good, you can split the image into pieces and optimize the text and gradient differently, saving file size overall.

✦ You can assign links to a slice. By creating different slices, you can allow users to click different parts of a graphic, which link to different locations or pages on the Internet.

✦ You can assign rollovers to a slice. Rollovers are actually created outside of Illustrator (in ImageReady, for example), but you can still assign the slices right in Illustrator to save time in the workflow process. A rollover swaps one graphic for another when a user performs an action, such as moving the mouse over the slice. For example, you can make a graphic of a button look lit up when the user rolls the mouse over the button.

What the slicing process really does is divide your image into different pieces, which are described in HTML as a table. Figure 19-25 shows an example of such a table. Each cell of the table contains a different image, optimized as you specify with or without a link. Because a cell must be rectangular, you must make all slices rectangular as well. When the table is rendered in a Web browser, the image looks like a complete graphic.

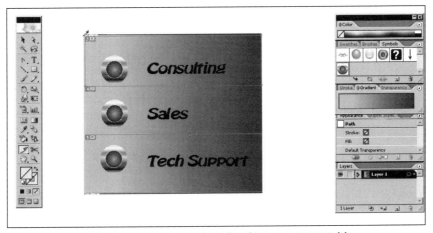

Figure 19-25: This shows a Web graphic sliced into an HTML table.

Object-based Web Slicing

Illustrator has two ways of applying slices. The traditional way is to choose the Slice tool from the toolbox and draw slices over your graphics. Figure 19-26 shows what a graphic might look like sliced. Numbered slices appear on your screen as you create the slices, and auto slices are created as well. (*User slices* are those that you create; *auto slices* are those that are automatically created to fill the rest of the table.) Slices don't print—they just indicate how the slice table is going to be created.

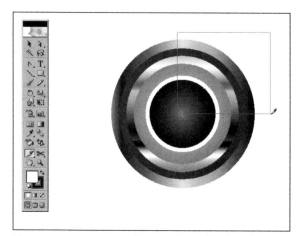

Figure 19-26: You can draw a slice with the Slice tool as shown here.

The downside of using this method is that if you ever want to edit your art, you may also need to update or redraw the slices. Illustrator includes a second way to create slices called *object-based slicing*. By applying slices as an attribute to an object rather than just drawing a separate shape, Illustrator creates a dynamic slice that moves and resizes itself based on the shape or selection to which it is assigned. You do this by first making a selection and then choosing Object ➪ Slice ➪ Make. Figure 19-27 shows the Slice submenu. A slice appears, but now when you edit that object, the slice grows or shrinks to fit the updated object.

Working with slices

Object-based slices don't need modifying — they are basically maintenance-free slices. But if you draw slices with the Slice tool, you can edit those slices using the Slice Selection tool, which allows you to move the slices as well as to resize them. The Slice Selection tool also allows you to select slices so that you can apply settings to them. You find the Slice Selection tool behind the Slice tool. Selecting a slice and choosing Object ➪ Slice ➪ Slice Options opens the Slice Options dialog box, shown in Figure 19-28, where you can specify the slice name, a URL link, Alt text (for Alternative text display in Web browsers), and more. The drop-down list (pop-up menu) at the bottom of the dialog box allows you to specify a background for that slice — each slice can have its own background color or image — and there's a Slice Type drop-down list (pop-up menu) that lets you specify the slice in one of three "states":

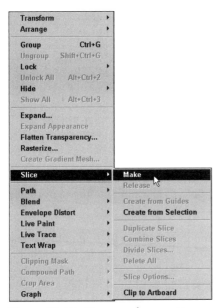

Figure 19-27: You can also create a dynamic object-based slice using the Object ⇨ Slice ⇨ Make command.

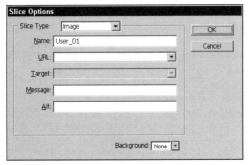

Figure 19-28: The Slice Options dialog box enables you to set parameters for a selected slice.

✦ **Image:** The contents of the slice, or table cell, are an image—GIF, JPEG, and so on—that you specify.

✦ **No Image:** The contents of the table cell are an HTML statement, which you can specify directly in the dialog box. This is useful if the graphic you have is just a placeholder for something else, such as QuickTime video clip or a script that loads a graphic.

✦ **HTML Text:** If the contents of the slice are displayed as text, this option becomes available, and Illustrator basically codes the HTML to display text rather than an image in the table cell.

Tip   Specifying slice options in Illustrator can save you time down the road if you're also using Photoshop, ImageReady, or GoLive. The options that you specify in Illustrator are stored and recognized in these programs.

Other functions from the Object ⇨ Slice submenu let you release an object-based slice, divide a single slice into multiple slices of equal size, create slices from either guides or selections (these won't be object-based slices), and combine multiple slices into a single slice. There's also an option called Clip to Artboard, which uses the artboard size as the table boundaries rather than the size of the art on your artboard. This is a great feature if you need to create a table of a specific size. By setting the document artboard size to the correct dimensions, you have one less thing to worry about.

After you've created all your slices, you can open the Save for Web dialog box and then use the Slice Select tool to choose individual optimization settings. You can press Shift and click to select multiple slices. If you're exporting HTML directly from Illustrator, click Save. However, if you plan to save your graphics as SVG to bring into GoLive, or if you intend to take your art into ImageReady, you can click the Done button to return to Illustrator.

Understanding CSS Layers

In HTML, you can describe only one "layer," which means that text and images can't overlap each other. You can't overlap images either. When CSS Layers were added to the HTML spec, Web designers finally had the ability to specify layers of information in a single HTML page. CSS, which stands for *Cascading Style Sheets,* gives designers and developers the ability to lay out elements of a page with pixel-by-pixel accuracy. It allows images and text to overlap each other.

The catch is that Web browsers don't always support CSS Layers in the same way, so use this feature with caution and lots of testing. Basically, Illustrator allows all top-level layers to be described as CSS Layers. You can turn this option on in the Layers palette of the Save for Web dialog box, shown in Figure 19-29. You can then choose what state you want each layer to assume (Visible, Hidden, and so on).

Figure 19-29: Choosing to export CSS Layers from the Save for Web dialog box

Getting Interactive

As mentioned earlier in this chapter, adding interactivity to a Web site is a great way for designers to add interest to sites as well as to add a functional element. Be it a cool animation or a navigation bar, Illustrator can help turn a static Web site into something that adds flair and value. Although Illustrator isn't Flash, LiveMotion, or even ImageReady, it can still hold its own when creating these kinds of elements.

Specifying an image map

Some Web sites feature a graphic that links to different pages or places depending on what part of the graphic you click. An *image map* is basically a set of coordinates (sometimes called *hotspots*) that you can apply to a Web graphic — with each coordinate taking the user to a link of your choice. Setting up an image map is really easy in Illustrator if you follow these steps:

1. **Select an object, and open the Attributes palette.** See Chapter 6 for more on selecting an object. To open the Attribute palette, choose Window ➪ Attributes.

2. **From the Image drop-down list (pop-up menu), choose Rectangle or Polygon.** You want to choose the latter for non-uniform shapes.

3. **Type the full link in the URL field as shown in Figure 19-30.** Illustrator stores each URL you use in a single file, so you don't have to repeatedly type the URL if you are using it again.

4. **Click the Browser button.** The Browser button that appears in the Attributes palette lets you quickly test your URL to make sure that it works.

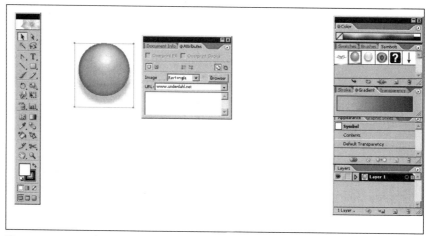

Figure 19-30: Selecting an image map, and specifying a URL

Note   Image maps are used less these days because slicing can achieve the same functionality and also add fancy effects like rollovers. However, there are still times when image maps are useful, such as when creating non-rectangular links. (Remember that slices are always rectangular.)

Image maps are written in several different ways, and you should speak to a Web developer or a technical contact at your Web-hosting company to find out which image map is best to use for your particular need and configuration. *Client-side* image maps reside inside the HTML code itself; *server-side* maps reside in a separate file that links to the HTML file.

Creating animations

Creating animations for the Web in Illustrator can be fun and is actually easy as well! Creating *animations* basically involves creating multiple images and playing them consecutively to give the appearance of motion. Each image in an animation is called a *frame*. In Illustrator, you animate using each layer in your file as a frame. You can then export your file as an SWF file and choose the AI Layers to SWF Frames option at export time to create your animation.

You can create unique and interesting animations when you combine Blends along with effects like 3-D and Scribble. Animating blends is easy because Illustrator has a feature called Release to Layers that automatically places each step of a blend onto its own layer — ready for exporting as an animated SWF.

The Release to Layers commands are found in the Layers palette menu, and you can choose between sequence and build. A sequence is much like traditional animation in that each frame contains a single image that moves from frame to frame. A build allows you to keep art in multiple frames and is useful for animating text, where you want letters to stay on the screen while others appear. For example, the animated word "hello" would contain "H" in the first frame, "HE" in the second frame, "HEL" in the third, and so on.

When you blend effects, Illustrator actually calculates each step of the blend individually, allowing you to create some spectacular effects, such as this one with the Scribble effect:

1. **Type the letter *A*.** Scale it so that it's nice and big (there's no need for you to squint at the screen).

2. **Choose Type ➪ Create Outlines to convert the text to a path.**

3. **Choose Effect ➪ Stylize ➪ Scribble.**

4. **Choose Sketch from the Settings drop-down list (pop-up menu).**

5. **Click OK to apply the effect shown in Figure 19-31.**

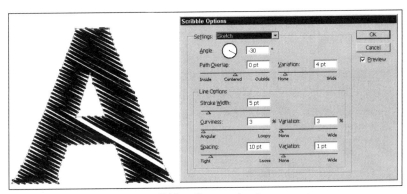

Figure 19-31: Applying a Scribble effect to the *A*

6. **Choose a color for the letter *A*.**

7. **Copy it by pressing Ctrl+C (⌘+C).**

8. **Paste in Front by pressing Ctrl+F (⌘+F).** Doing this makes a copy of the *A* right on top of the original one.

9. **With the new *A* still selected, give it a different fill color.**

10. **Use the Selection tool to select both letters.**

11. **Choose Object ➪ Blend ➪ Make.**

12. With the blended object still selected, choose Object ⇨ Blend ⇨ Blend Options to display the Blend Options dialog box.

13. Change the selection in the Spacing drop-down list to Specified Steps and choose 10 for the number of steps, as shown in Figure 19-32.

Figure 19-32: Specifying the number of blend steps

14. Now that you've created your blend, head over to the Layers palette and click on the little triangle to expose the contents of Layer 1.

15. Select the Blend layer, and choose Release to Layers (Sequence) from the Layers palette menu, as shown in Figure 19-33. Notice that the Layers palette now lists many more layers — and each layer now contains one step of the blend that you created in Step 13, as shown in Figure 19-34.

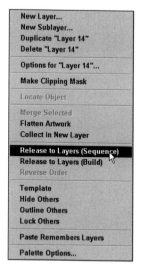

Figure 19-33: Choosing the Release to Layers (Sequence) option

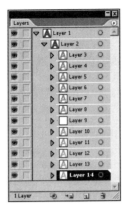

Figure 19-34: The Layers palette with all the new layers displayed

16. **Choose File ⇨ Save for Web, and select SWF for the image format.** You should now see only the first frame of the animation in your preview pane.

17. **Select Layers to SWF Frames in the Type of export drop-down list box.**

18. **To see what the animation looks like, click the Preview in Browser button.** If you're happy with the results as shown in Figure 19-35, go back to Save for Web and click the Save button.

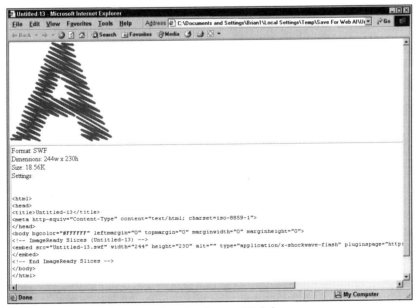

Figure 19-35: Viewing the animation in your Web browser

Adding rollovers with Adobe ImageReady

As mentioned earlier, Illustrator can't assign rollovers, but you can create your graphics, bring those graphics into ImageReady, and assign your rollovers there. This capability allows you to create your graphics with your familiar tools in Illustrator, take advantage of vector drawing tools and powerful text features, and even apply slice settings. You can quickly customize them in ImageReady.

Start out by planning your layers carefully and laying out your slices so that you can easily set up where your rollovers will go. The way you specify a rollover is to specify certain *states* for each slice. One state is for normal, one state is for mouseover, one state is for click, and so on. For example, if you want a button to change color or glow for a rollover, create the normal state on one layer; then create a separate layer for the mouseover state, and so on. When you bring the file into ImageReady, all you have to do is toggle which layer you want visible. Figure 19-36 shows the Layers palette listing the layers for a rollover.

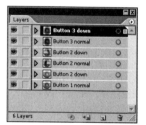

Figure 19-36: Layers set up for easy creation of rollovers in ImageReady

When you're finished, choose File ➪ Export and choose Photoshop (.PSD) from the Format pop-up. Most people don't know that you can export PSD files directly from Illustrator. You can then choose specific options, such as preserving layer information — even live text and slices. Figure 19-37 shows the Photoshop Export Options dialog box. Make sure that you check all these and then click Export. When you open that file in ImageReady, it's ready with text, layers, and slices all intact; you can assign your rollovers and export it to HTML (or to import into GoLive as a Smart Object).

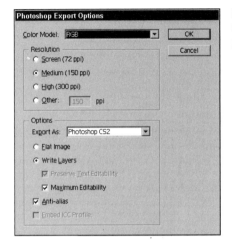

Figure 19-37: The Photoshop Export Options dialog box enables you to export PSD files from Illustrator.

Using Data-Driven Graphics to Streamline Design Work

Designing a business card can be fun. It's challenging to come up with a cool and clean design that gets the message across in a readable and usable format. What isn't fun is copying that card over and over, and typing different information for each employee in the company. Wouldn't it be great if you could do all the fun stuff yourself and then let the computer too all the tedious boring stuff?

That's where data-driven graphics comes into play. Sure, it's a mouthful to say, but it can save lots of time. You start off by creating a regular Illustrator file, which you use as a base file, or template. Figure 19-38 shows a business card template. This template contains your design, but you tag the content as *variables*. You then have a *script* fetch data from an external file, such as a text file or any ODBC-compliant database, and the script automatically generates customized files for you, while you go search for a nice beverage to enjoy. Now that you know the basic steps for creating data-driven graphics, the rest of the sections in this chapter walk you through how to go about performing those steps.

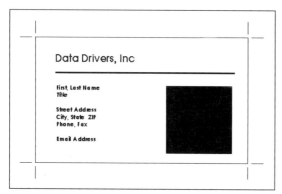

Figure 19-38: A sample data-driven graphics template will add data from another file.

Tip The data-driven graphics feature was originally created for Web graphics because that medium demands instant updates and graphics that are generated on-the-fly. However, it can prove very beneficial to print workflows as well.

Understanding variables

A variable is something that changes. In Illustrator, defining something as a variable means that "this will change." For example, when you type the name "Joe Smith" on a business card and then define it as a variable called "name," running the appropriate script replaces the words "Joe Smith" with whatever you have in the Name field of your database.

You can set four different kinds of variables in Illustrator:

✦ **Text:** A text variable is simply a string of text, either point text or area text, that gets replaced with new text. The font and style applied to that text remains. Only the characters themselves change — as in the example of the names on business cards.

✦ **Visibility:** You can apply visibility to any kind of object in Illustrator and control whether that object is shown or hidden. For example, you can show a starburst graphic in certain cases, but not others.

✦ **Linked image:** This kind of variable is specific to replacing linked images (any format). For example, if your business card design contains a picture of the employee, setting the image as a variable allows you to create business cards with each employee's photo on his or her card by replacing the value of the variable with the correct link.

✦ **Graph data:** Creating a graph in Illustrator is easy enough (sec Chapter 5), and by defining a graph as a variable, you can replace the data of that graph to generate customized graphs automatically. For example, you can automatically generate a weather chart by retrieving the latest weather forecasts from the Internet.

Using the Variables palette

You define Variables in Illustrator via the Variables palette, shown in Figure 19-39. The palette enables you to keep tabs of all your variables in a single location and allows you to define *data sets* as well. A data set is very much like a record in a database and stores information for a specific range of variables.

Cross-Reference See the section "Setting up a data-driven graphics template," later in this chapter, to see exactly how this works.

Figure 19-39: The Variables palette, with all four kinds of variables defined

You define a visibility variable by making a selection and clicking the Make Visibility Dynamic icon. Likewise, you define other variables by making a selection and clicking the "Make Dynamic" icon. These are context sensitive, so if you select text, the button is labeled "Make Text Dynamic," and if you select a graph, the button is labeled "Make Graph Dynamic."

Clicking the little camera icon in the upper left of the palette allows you to capture a data set. Data sets are stored in Illustrator as XML data, and you can both import and export variables and data sets from the Variables palette menu. Because XML is a standard format, Illustrator can very easily integrate into complex workflows and back-end systems.

Understanding scripting

A script is a list of commands that are contained in a single file. When you "run" a script, your computer follows the commands that are contained within the script. In reality, a script is much like computer programming code, except that it's what's called a "High Level" language in that it controls existing programs, rather than actually being a program itself. A script "tells" applications what to do. In fact, most scripting languages read almost like English — making them easier to learn and use.

Illustrator supports three different scripting languages:

✦ **AppleScript:** Created by the folks at Apple, this language works only on the Macintosh platform.

✦ **Visual Basic:** Created by Microsoft, this language works on the Windows platform.

✦ **JavaScript:** Originally developed by Netscape, this language is cross-platform.

Scripting versus Actions

If you've been paying attention, you remember a discussion about something called Actions back in Chapter 17. Because you're a smart person, you're probably wondering why you need scripting if you already have actions.

There are several big differences between actions and scripts.

✦ An action is simply a recorded sequence of events that you can play over and over, each time performing exactly the same way. A script can contain logic and therefore perform different steps depending on the situation.

✦ An action is a task that can be performed completely only within Illustrator. A script can involve multiple applications, not just Illustrator.

✦ An action is easy to create right in Illustrator. A script requires the knowledge of at least one of the scripting languages (AppleScript, VB Script or JavaScript). So although scripts are far more powerful, they are also far more difficult to create.

For example, you can write a script to automatically create a forecast graphic by going to a weather site on the Internet, retrieving temperature information for a particular city, and drawing a graphic. You can code the graphic so that temperatures below 32 degrees are colored blue, temperatures over 90 degrees are colored red, and temperatures between 75 and 85 have a smiley face with sunglasses. The script brings that info into Illustrator from another application (your Web browser) and then makes decisions based on that data within Illustrator. Actions are cool, but nowhere near as cool as scripts.

It takes much more work to write a script than it does to record an action, but a script can do much more and is more powerful than an action is.

Note   Not everything in Illustrator is Actionable, and not everything in Illustrator is Scriptable either. There are even some things that you can do with AppleScript or VB Script that you can't do with JavaScript. With each new version of Illustrator, you can record more and more features and commands of the application as Actions or Scripts.

Don't let all this talk about scripting scare you. Just because a script is a necessary step in the data-driven graphics process, it doesn't mean that you (the designer) have to do it. Some companies have developers on staff who know how to script, and you can have them write the required scripts for you. You can also hire a developer or consultant on a freelance basis to write your scripts. Because of the potential time-savings you gain when you utilize a script, this method can also prove very economical.

Setting up a data-driven graphics template

It's beyond the scope of this book to learn how to write a script to automatically fill a template, but it's easy to set up a template and create some sample data sets, which allow you to preview what your files will look like when they are filled with data.

1. **Using the text tool, click an empty part of the artboard to create some point text.** The example uses the words "Good Morning." Be creative and choose a nice font and even a drop shadow if you'd like.

2. **Switch to the Select tool, and select the type you just created.** For more on the Select tool, see Chapter 6.

3. **Choose Window ⇨ Variables to open the Variables palette.**

4. **Click the "Make Text Dynamic" button at the bottom of the palette as shown in Figure 19-40.** Alternatively, you can choose the "Make Text Dynamic" option from the Variables palette menu. Notice that a variable of type "Text" called Variable1 is created.

Figure 19-40: You define a Text variable using the Variables palette.

5. **Double-click the Variable1 item in the Variables palette to open the Variable Options dialog box.**

6. **Type a name for the variable.** Change the name of the variable so that you (or a script) can readily identify it. In the example, the name is changed to "greeting" as shown in Figure 19-41.

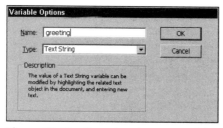

Figure 19-41: Changing the name of the variable to something more descriptive makes it easier to remember.

7. **Click OK.** You can also press Enter (Return).

8. **Click the little camera icon (this is the Capture Data Set button in the upper left of the Variables palette) to create Data Set 1.**

9. **Using the text tool, edit the text on your artboard to have it read something else.** The example now reads "Good Afternoon" instead of "Good Morning."

10. **Click the Capture Data Set button.** This creates Data Set 2.

11. **Edit the text on your artboard to change it again.** The example was changed from "Good Afternoon" to "Good Evening."

12. **Click the Capture Data Set button again, as indicated in Figure 19-42.** You now have three different data sets in your Illustrator file.

Figure 19-42: Capturing a third data set

13. **Using the left and right arrows in the Variables palette, click to step through all three of the data sets.** Note that as you switch among data sets, the text on your screen changes. This is extremely helpful when you create templates because it allows you, as a designer, to create a design that works well with different data. For example, a long word or name takes up more space than a short word does. Setting up several different data sets in your file allows you to preview how your design looks with different sets of data.

Taking advantage of data-driven graphics with Adobe GoLive

Beginning with version 6, GoLive added support for working with dynamically generated content. You can also use the variable feature in Illustrator to create those graphics in GoLive yourself, and it's really easy!

1. **Start by creating a template in Illustrator.** Design your art and then assign some variables.

2. **Choose File ➪ Save As.** Doing this opens the Save As dialog box.

3. **Choose SVG for the format, as indicated in Figure 19-43.** The SVG Options dialog box appears. The reason for choosing this format is that SVG is an open standards format based on XML and can contain variable content.

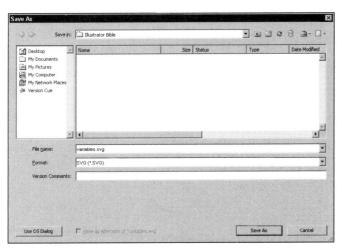

Figure 19-43: Save the file as SVG for use in GoLive.

4. **Click the Save As button to display the SVG Options dialog box.**

5. **Click the Preserve Illustrator Editing Capabilities check box.** Doing this allows you to reopen the SVG file in Illustrator later.

6. **Click the More Options button to display the advanced options section of the dialog box.**

7. **Make sure that the Include Adobe Graphics Server data check box is checked, as shown in Figure 19-44.**

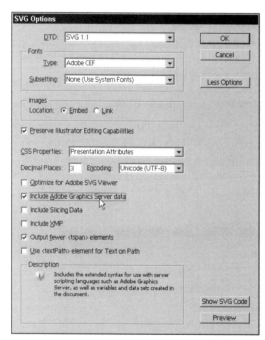

Figure 19-44: Checking the Include Adobe Graphics Server data option in the SVG Advanced Options dialog box includes the variables and data sets.

8. **Click OK.**

9. **In GoLive, open or create an HTML file.**

10. **From the Object palette in GoLive, drag an Illustrator Smart Object onto your page.**

11. **Using the point-and-shoot icon, load the SVG graphic that you created in Illustrator.** Because GoLive sees the variable content in the Illustrator SVG file, GoLive prompts you with a dialog box listing all the variables. Here, you can choose to replace text or change attributes of your variables.

You can change these variables at any time in GoLive by clicking the Variables button in the Inspector palette. It's a powerful way to quickly update your graphics without even launching Illustrator!

Summary

In this chapter, you found out the following:

✦ Pixel Preview mode displays graphics as they would appear in a Web browser.

✦ Save for Web lets you optimize graphics in one easy step.

✦ You can both open and save SVG files in Illustrator.

✦ Illustrator can export animated SWF files.

✦ You can easily bring sliced and optimized Illustrator files into Photoshop or ImageReady.

✦ Data-driven graphics can streamline repetitive tasks and help save time.

✦ Illustrator can define four kinds of variables in the Variables palette.

✦ Many variables are stored in XML.

✦ Illustrator supports AppleScript (Mac), VB Script (Windows), and JavaScript.

✦ Scripting is far more powerful than Actions.

✦   ✦   ✦

Shortcuts in Illustrator CS2

Illustrator has more keyboard commands, functions, and shortcuts than ever before. The tables in this appendix give you a quick reference to the commands, functions, and shortcuts for both Windows and Macintosh.

Caution Macintosh users should check to make sure that their function keys aren't assigned to complete any system tasks. In Macintosh's Keyboard & Mouse Control pane's Keyboard Shortcuts tab, you can assign or reassign keyboard shortcuts that are in conflict. This isn't the default value.

In This Appendix

Learning commands for every little thing

Using functions

Saving time with shortcuts

Menu Commands

Table A-1 The File Menu	
Command	**Shortcut**
New	Ctrl (⌘)+N
New from Template	Ctrl (⌘)+Shift+N
Open	Ctrl (⌘)+O
Browse	Ctrl (⌘)+Alt (Option)+O
Close	Ctrl (⌘)+W
Save	Ctrl (⌘)+S
Save As	Ctrl (⌘)+Shift+S
Save a Copy	Ctrl (⌘)+Alt (Option)+S
Save for Web	Ctrl (⌘)+Shift+Alt (Option)+S
Revert	F12[*]
Document Setup	Ctrl (⌘)+Alt (Option)+P
File Info	Ctrl (⌘)+Shift+Alt (Option)+I
Print	Ctrl (⌘)+P
Exit (Quit)	Ctrl (⌘)+Q (under the Illustrator menu for Mac OS X)

[*] In MacOS X 10.4 (Tiger), reassign in the Exposé & Dashboard System Preference pane.

Table A-2 The Edit Menu	
Command	**Shortcut**
Undo	Ctrl (⌘)+Z
Redo	Ctrl (⌘)+Shift+Z
Cut	Ctrl (⌘)+X
Copy	Ctrl (⌘)+C
Paste	Ctrl (⌘)+V

Command	Shortcut
Paste in Front	Ctrl (⌘)+F
Paste in Back	Ctrl (⌘)+B
Check Spelling	Ctrl (⌘)+I
Color Settings	Ctrl (⌘)+Shift+K
Keyboard Shortcuts	Ctrl (⌘)+Shift+Alt (Option)+K
General Preferences	Ctrl (⌘)+K (under the Illustrator menu for Mac OS X)

Table A-3
The Object Menu

Command	Shortcut
Transform ➪ Transform Again	Ctrl (⌘)+D
Transform ➪ Move	Ctrl (⌘)+Shift+M
Transform ➪ Transform Each	Ctrl (⌘)+Shift+Alt (Option)+D
Arrange ➪ Bring to Front	Ctrl (⌘)+Shift+]
Arrange ➪ Bring Forward	Ctrl (⌘)+]
Arrange ➪ Send Backward	Ctrl (⌘)+[
Arrange ➪ Send to Back	Ctrl (⌘)+Shift+[
Group	Ctrl (⌘)+G
Ungroup	Ctrl (⌘)+Shift+G
Lock ➪ Selection	Ctrl (⌘)+2
Unlock All	Ctrl (⌘)+Alt (Option)+2
Hide ➪ Selection	Ctrl (⌘)+3
Show All	Ctrl (⌘)+Alt (Option)+3
Path ➪ Join	Ctrl (⌘)+J
Path ➪ Average	Ctrl (⌘)+Alt (Option)+J
Blend ➪ Make	Ctrl (⌘)+Alt (Option)+B
Blend ➪ Release	Ctrl (⌘)+Alt (Option)+Shift+B

Continued

Table A-3 *(continued)*

Command	Shortcut
Envelope Distort ⇨ Make with Warp	Ctrl (⌘)+Alt (Option)+Shift+W
Envelope Distort ⇨ Make with Mesh	Ctrl (⌘)+Alt (Option)+M
Envelope Distort ⇨ Make with Top Object	Ctrl (⌘)+Alt (Option)+C
Envelope Distort ⇨ Edit Contents	Ctrl (⌘)+Shift+V
Live Paint ⇨ Make	Ctrl (⌘)+Alt (Option)+X
Clipping Mask ⇨ Make	Ctrl (⌘)+7
Clipping Mask ⇨ Release	Ctrl (⌘)+Alt (Option)+7
Compound Path ⇨ Make	Ctrl (⌘)+8
Compound Path ⇨ Release	Ctrl (⌘)+Alt (Option)+8

Table A-4
The Type Menu

Command	Shortcut
Create Outlines	Ctrl (⌘)+Shift+O
Show Hidden Characters	Ctrl (⌘)+Alt (Option)+I

Table A-5
The Select Menu

Command	Shortcut
Select All	Ctrl (⌘)+A
Deselect All	Ctrl (⌘)+Shift+A
Reselect	Ctrl (⌘)+6
Next Object Above	Ctrl (⌘)+Alt (Option)+]
Next Object Below	Ctrl (⌘)+Alt (Option)+[

Table A-6
The Filter Menu

Command	Shortcut
Apply Last Filter	Ctrl (⌘)+E
Last Filter	Ctrl (⌘)+Alt (Option)+E

Table A-7
The Effect Menu

Command	Shortcut
Apply Last Filter	Ctrl (⌘)+Shift+E
Last Filter dialog box	Ctrl (⌘)+Shift+Alt (Option)+E

Table A-8
The View Menu

Command	Shortcut
Outline/Preview	Ctrl (⌘)+Y (toggle)
Overprint Preview	Ctrl (⌘)+Shift+Alt (Option)+Y
Pixel Preview	Ctrl (⌘)+Alt (Option)+Y
Zoom In	Ctrl (⌘)++ (plus sign)
Zoom Out	Ctrl (⌘)+− (minus sign)
Fit in Window	Ctrl (⌘)+0 (zero)
	Double-click Hand tool
Actual Size (100%)	Ctrl (⌘)+1
	Double-click Zoom tool
Hide Edges	Ctrl (⌘)+H (toggle)
Hide Template	Ctrl (⌘)+Shift+W (toggle)

Continued

Table A-8 *(continued)*

Command	Shortcut
Show/Hide Rulers	Ctrl (⌘)+R (toggle)
Show/Hide Bounding Box	Ctrl (⌘)+Shift+B (toggle)
Show/Hide Transparency Grid	Ctrl (⌘)+Shift+D (toggle)
Show/Hide Text Threads	Ctrl (⌘)+Shift+Y (toggle)
Guides ⇨ Show/Hide Guides	Ctrl (⌘)+; (toggle)
Guides ⇨ Lock Guides	Ctrl (⌘)+Alt (Option)+;
Guides ⇨ Make Guides	Ctrl (⌘)+5
Guides ⇨ Release Guides	Ctrl (⌘)+Alt (Option)+5
Smart Guides	Ctrl (⌘)+U
Show/Hide Grid	Ctrl (⌘)+"(toggle)
Snap to Grid (Pixel)	Ctrl (⌘)+Shift+"
Snap to Point	Ctrl (⌘)+Alt (Option)+"

Table A-9
The Window Menu

Command	Shortcut
Align	Shift+F7 (toggle)
Appearance	Shift+F6 (toggle)
Attributes	Ctrl (⌘)+F11 (toggle)
Brushes	F5 (toggle)
Color	F6 (toggle)
Gradient	Ctrl (⌘)+F9 (toggle)
Styles	Shift+F5 (toggle)
Info	F8 (toggle)
Layers	F7 (toggle)

Pathfinder	Ctrl (⌘)+Shift+F9 (toggle)
Stroke	Ctrl (⌘)+F10 (toggle)

Command	Shortcut
Symbols	Ctrl (⌘)+Shift+F11 (toggle)
Transform	Shift+F8 (toggle)
Transparency	Ctrl (⌘)+Shift+F10 (toggle)
Type ➪ Character	Ctrl (⌘)+T (toggle)
Type ➪ OpenType	Ctrl (⌘)+Shift+Alt (Option)+T
Type ➪ Paragraph	Ctrl (⌘)+Alt (Option)+T
Type ➪ Tabs	Ctrl (⌘)+Shift+T

Table A-10
The Help Menu

Command	Shortcut
Illustrator Help	F1 (Windows only)
	Help key or Cmd+? (Mac only)

Toolbox Commands

Table A-11
Tool Selection

Function	Shortcut
Select the next pop-up tool	Drag to the right and release on desired tool
	Alt (Option)+click on a tool
Open tool dialog box	Double-click on the tool
Hide toolbox and palettes	Tab
Hide palettes	Shift+Tab

Table A-12
Selection Tools

Tool	Shortcut
Selection tool	V Ctrl+Tab with Direct Selection tool, and then hold Ctrl (⌘) Ctrl (⌘) with all other tools if Selection tool was the last tool used
Direct Selection tool	A (Mac and Windows) Ctrl+Tab with Selection tool, and then hold Ctrl (⌘)+Alt (Option) with Group Selection tool Ctrl (⌘) with all other tools if Direct Selection tool was the last tool used
Group Selection tool	Alt (Option) with Direct Selection tool Ctrl (⌘)+Alt (Option) with all other tools if Direct Selection tool was the last tool used
Magic Wand tool	Y
Direct Select Lasso tool	Q

Function	Procedure
Select one point	Click with Direct Selection tool
Select one segment	Click with Direct Selection tool
Select one path	Click with Group Selection tool
Select next group up	Click selected path again with Group Selection tool
Select top-level group	Click with Selection tool
Select additional	Shift+click
Select specific points	Drag with Direct Selection tool
Select specific paths	Drag with Selection tool
Deselect selected	Shift+click selected
Move selection	Drag
Duplicate selection	Alt (Option)+drag
Constrain to 45-degree movement	Shift+drag
Duplicate and constrain	Alt (Option)+Shift+drag
Proportionately resize object	Shift+drag Bounding Box handle

Function	Procedure
Resize from center	Alt (Option)+drag Bounding Box handle
Resize proportionately from center	Alt (Option)+Shift+drag Bounding Box handle
Select all	Ctrl (⌘)+A
Deselect all	Ctrl (⌘)+Shift+A
Select all objects with similar Fill, Stroke, Opacity, and/or Blending Mode	Click with Magic Wand tool
Add similar colored and stroked objects to current selection	Shift+Magic Wand tool
Subtract similar colored and stroked objects from the current selection	Alt (Option)+Magic Wand tool
Set Magic Wand options	Double-click on Magic Wand tool to open the Magic Wand palette

Table A-13
Path Tools

Tool	Shortcut
Pen tool	P
Add Anchor Point tool	= Alt (Option)+Delete Anchor Point tool Alt (Option)+Scissors tool
Delete Anchor Point tool	– Alt (Option)+Add Anchor Point tool
Convert Anchor Point tool	Shift+C Alt (Option)+Pen tool
Pencil tool	N
Smooth tool	Alt (Option)+Pencil tool Alt (Option)+Erase tool Alt (Option)+Paintbrush tool
Paintbrush tool	B
Scissors tool	C

Continued

Table A-13 *(continued)*

Function	Procedure
Create a straight corner point	Click with Pen tool
Create a smooth point	Drag with Pen tool
Continue existing open path	Click+drag with Pen tool on end point of existing path
Close open path	While drawing, click+drag with Pen tool on the initial end point Click+drag with Pen tool on each end point in succession Select path and join (Ctrl (⌘)+ J)
Constrain new point to 45 degrees from last point	Shift+drag with Pen tool
Constrain control handles to 45 degrees	Shift while dragging handle with Pen tool
Create a path	Click+drag a succession of points with Pen tool
Add anchor points to existing path	Click with the Pen tool on path
Delete anchor points from existing path	Shift+click with Pen tool on an anchor point
Convert anchor point to smooth point	Drag with Convert Direction Point tool on existing point
Convert smooth point to corner point	Click with Convert Direction Point tool on smooth point
Convert smooth corner to combination corner	Drag one handle with Direct Selection tool back into the anchor point
Convert smooth corner to curved corner	Drag one handle with Convert Direction Point tool
Draw freestyle paths	Drag with Pencil tool
View Paintbrush options	Double-click Paintbrush tool in toolbox
Reshape a path	Select points with Direct Selection, and then drag with Reshape tool
Split path	Click with Scissors tool
Slice multiple paths	Drag with Knife tool
Constrain Knife slice to straight lines	Option (Alt)+drag with Knife tool
Constrain Knife slice to 45 degrees	Shift+Option (Alt)+drag with Knife tool

Table A-14
Type Tools

Tool	Shortcut
Type tool	T Shift+Vertical Type tool
Area Type tool	Alt (Option)+Path Type tool Shift+Vertical Area Type tool Alt (Option)+Shift Vertical Path Type tool
Path Type tool	Alt (Option)+Area Type tool Shift+Vertical Path Type tool Alt (Option)+Shift+Vertical Area Type tool
Vertical Type tool	Shift+Type tool
Vertical Area Type tool	Alt (Option)+Vertical Path Type tool Shift+Area Type tool Alt (Option)+Shift+Area Type tool
Vertical Path Type tool	Alt (Option)+Vertical Area Type tool Shift+Path Type tool Alt (Option)+Shift +Area Type tool

Function	Procedure
Create individual type	Click with Type tool
Create type container	Drag with Type tool
Place path type on a closed path	Click path with Path Type tool Alt (Option)+click path with Type tool Alt (Option)+click path with Area Type tool
Place path type on an open path	Click path with Path Type tool Click path with Type tool Alt (Option)+click path with Area Type tool
Place area type on a closed path	Click path with Area Type tool Click path with Type tool Option (Alt)+click path with Path Type tool
Place area type on an open path	Click path with Area Type tool Alt (Option)+click path with Type tool Alt (Option)+click path with Path Type tool
Change vertical type to horizontal type	Choose Type ➪ Type Orientation ➪ Horizontal
Change horizontal type to vertical type	Choose Type ➪ Type Orientation ➪ Vertical

Continued

Table A-14 *(continued)*

Function	Procedure
Select entire text block	Click text block with Selection tool
Select one character	Drag across character with any Type tool
Select one word	Double-click word with any Type tool
Select one paragraph	Triple-click paragraph with any Type tool
Select all text in text block	Click in text block with any Type tool, and then press Ctrl (⌘)+A
Flip type on a path	Double-click the I-bar with any selection tool or just drag it to the opposite side

Table A-15
Line Tools

Tool	Shortcut
Line Segment tool	\

Function	Procedure
Create line segments using numbers	Click with the Line Segment tool
Draw a line segment	Drag with Line Segment tool
Constrain line segments to 45 degrees	Shift+drag with Line Segment tool
Create line segment from midpoint using numbers	Alt (Option)+click with Line Segment tool
Draw line segment from midpoint	Alt (Option)+drag with Line Segment tool
Move line segment while drawing	Spacebar+drag with Line Segment tool
Create multiple line segments	~+drag with Line Segment tool
Create arc segments using numbers	Click with the Arc tool
Draw an arc segment	Drag with Arc tool
Constrain arc segments to circular sections	Shift+drag with Arc tool
Create arc segment from the center	Alt (Option)+click with Arc tool
Draw arc segment from the center	Alt (Option)+drag with Arc tool

Function	Procedure
Move arc segment while drawing	Spacebar+drag with Arc tool
Create multiple arc segments	~+drag with Arc tool
Toggle arc between concave and convex	X+drag with Arc tool
Toggle between open and closed arcs	C+drag with Arc tool
Flip the arc	F+drag with Arc tool
Increase arc slope	↑+drag with Arc tool
Decrease arc slope	↓+drag with Arc tool
Create spiral using numbers	Click with Spiral tool
Draw spiral	Drag with Spiral tool
Constrain spiral angle	Shift+drag with Spiral tool
Move spiral while drawing	Spacebar+drag with Spiral tool
Create multiple spirals	~+drag with Spiral tool
Decrease spiral decay	Ctrl (⌘)+drag with Spiral tool
Increase spiral length and size	Alt (Option)+drag with Spiral tool (toggle)
Increase spiral length	↑+drag with Spiral tool
Decrease spiral length	↓+drag with Spiral tool
Create a rectangular grid using numbers	Click with the Rectangular Grid tool
Draw an rectangular grid	Drag with Rectangular Grid tool
Constrain rectangular grid to a square	Shift+drag with Rectangular Grid tool
Create a square rectangular grid	Alt (Option)+click with Rectangular Grid tool
Draw rectangular grid from the center	Alt (Option)+drag with Rectangular Grid tool
Move rectangular grid while drawing	Spacebar+drag with Rectangular Grid tool
Create multiple rectangular grid	~+drag with Rectangular Grid tool
Skew horizontal dividers to the left	X+drag with Rectangular Grid tool
Skew horizontal dividers to the right	C+drag with Rectangular Grid tool
Skew vertical dividers to the top of the rectangular grid	F+drag with Rectangular Grid tool
Skew vertical dividers to the bottom of the rectangular grid	V+drag with Rectangular Grid tool

Continued

Table A-15 (continued)

Function	Procedure
Increase vertical dividers	↑+drag with Rectangular Grid tool
Decrease vertical dividers	↓+drag with Rectangular Grid tool
Increase horizontal dividers	→+drag with Rectangular Grid tool
Decrease horizontal dividers	←+drag with Rectangular Grid tool
Create a polar grid using numbers	Click with the Polar Grid tool
Draw an polar grid	Drag with Polar Grid tool
Constrain polar grid to a circle	Shift+drag with Polar Grid tool
Create a circular polar grid	Alt (Option)+click with Polar Grid tool
Draw polar grid from the center	Alt (Option)+drag with Polar Grid tool
Move polar grid while drawing	Spacebar+drag with Polar Grid tool
Create multiple polar grid	~+drag with Polar Grid tool
Skew concentric dividers inward	X+drag with Polar Grid tool
Skew concentric dividers outward	C+drag with Polar Grid tool
Skew radial dividers counterclockwise	F+drag with Polar Grid tool
Skew radial dividers clockwise	V+drag with Polar Grid tool
Increase concentric dividers	↑+drag with Polar Grid tool
Decrease concentric dividers	↓+drag with Polar Grid tool
Increase radial dividers	→+drag with Polar Grid tool
Decrease radial dividers	←+drag with Polar Grid tool

Table A-16
Shape Tools

Tool	Shortcut
Rectangle tool	M
Ellipse tool	L

Function	Procedure
Create rectangle using numbers	Click with Rectangle tool or Rounded Rectangle tool
Draw rectangle	Drag with Rectangle tool
Draw square	Shift+drag with Rectangle tool
Create centered rectangle using numbers	Alt (Option)+click with Rectangle tool
Draw centered rectangle	Alt (Option)+drag with Rectangle tool
Draw square from center	Alt (Option)+Shift+drag with Rectangle tool
Move rectangle while drawing	Spacebar+drag with Rectangle tool
Create multiple rectangles	~+drag with Rectangle tool
Create rounded rectangle using numbers	Click with Rounded Rectangle tool
Draw rounded rectangle	Drag with Rounded Rectangle tool
Draw square with rounded corners	Shift+drag with Rounded Rectangle tool
Create centered rounded rectangle	Alt (Option)+click with Rounded Rectangle tool
Draw centered rounded rectangle	Alt (Option)+drag with Rounded Rectangle tool
Draw square from center with rounded corners	Alt (Option)+Shift+drag with Rounded Rectangle tool
Move rounded rectangle while drawing	Spacebar+drag with Rounded Rectangle tool
Create multiple rounded rectangles	~+drag with Rounded Rectangle tool
Create ellipse using numbers	Click with Ellipse tool
Draw ellipse	Drag with Ellipse tool
Draw circle	Shift+drag with Ellipse tool
Create centered ellipse using numbers	Alt (Option)+click with Ellipse tool
Draw centered ellipse	Alt (Option)+drag with Ellipse tool
Move ellipse while drawing	Spacebar+drag with Ellipse tool
Create multiple ellipses	~+drag with Ellipse tool
Create polygon using numbers	Click with Polygon tool
Draw polygon	Drag with Polygon tool
Constrain polygon angle	Shift+drag with Polygon tool

Continued

Table A-16 *(continued)*

Function	Procedure
Create centered polygon using numbers	Alt (Option)+click with Polygon tool
Draw centered polygon	Alt (Option)+drag with Polygon tool
Increase polygon sides	↑+drag with Polygon tool
Decrease polygon sides	↓+drag with Polygon tool
Move polygon while drawing	Spacebar+drag with Polygon tool
Create multiple polygons	~+drag with Polygon tool
Create star using numbers	Click with Star tool
Draw star	Drag with Star tool
Constrain star angle	Shift+drag with Star tool
Draw even-shouldered star	Alt (Option)+drag with Star tool
Move outer points only	Ctrl (⌘)+drag with Star tool
Increase star points	↑+drag with Star tool
Decrease star points	↓+drag with Star tool
Move star while drawing	Spacebar+drag with Star tool
Create multiple stars	~+drag with Star tool

Table A-17
Transformation Tools

Tool	Shortcut
Rotate tool	R
Reflect tool	O
Scale tool	S
Free Transform tool	E

Function	Procedure
Moving objects	Drag with the Selection or Free Transform tool
Constrain movements along 45-degree axis	Shift+drag with the Selection or Free Transform tool
Rotate using numbers	Alt (Option)+click with Rotate tool

Function	Procedure
Rotate from center of selection with numbers	Double-click with Rotate tool
Free Rotate (live)	Click with Rotate to set Origin, and then drag with Rotate tool
Free Rotate around selection center	Drag with Rotate tool
Constrain rotation to 45 degrees	Shift+drag with Rotate tool
Rotate a copy	Alt (Option)+drag with Rotate tool
Rotate pattern only	~+drag with Rotate tool
Scale using numbers	Alt (Option)+click with Scale tool
Scale from center of selection with numbers	Double-click with Scale tool
Free Scale (live)	Click with Scale to set Origin, and then drag with Scale tool
Free Scale around selection center	Drag with Scale tool
Constrain scaling to 45 degrees	Shift+drag with Scale tool
Scale a copy	Alt (Option)+drag with Scale tool
Scale pattern only	~+drag with Scale tool
Reflect using numbers	Alt (Option)+click with Reflect tool
Reflect from center of selection with numbers	Double-click with Reflect tool
Free Reflect (live)	Click with Reflect to set Origin, and then drag with Reflect tool
Free Reflect around selection center	Drag with Reflect tool
Constrain reflecting angle to 45 degrees	Shift+drag with Reflect tool
Reflect a Copy	Alt (Option)+drag with Reflect tool
Reflect Pattern only	~+drag with Reflect tool
Shear using numbers	Alt (Option)+click with Shear tool
Shear from Center of Selection with numbers	Double-click with Shear tool
Free Shear (live) with Shear	Click with Shear to set Origin, and then drag
Free Shear around selection center	Drag with Shear
Constrain shearing to 45 degrees	Shift+drag with Shear tool
Shear a copy	Alt (Option)+drag with Shear tool
Shear pattern only	~+drag with Shear tool

Table A-18
Distortion Tools

Tool	Shortcut
Warp tool	Shift+R

Function	Procedure
Twirl using numbers	Alt (Option)+click with Rotate tool
Free Twirl (live)	Drag with Twirl tool
Reshape distortion brush	Alt (Option)+drag with Warp, Twirl, Pucker, Bloat, Scallop, Crystallize, or Wrinkle tool
Constrain brush to horizontal or vertical movement	Shift+drag with Warp, Twirl, Pucker, Bloat, Scallop, Crystallize, or Wrinkle tool
Set distortion options	Double-click on the selected distortion tool

Table A-19
Symbol Tools

Tool	Shortcut
Symbol Sprayer tool	Shift+S

Function	Procedure
Add a single symbol	Click+Symbol Sprayer tool
Add multiple symbols	Drag+Symbol Sprayer tool
Remove symbols from set	Alt (Option)+Symbol Sprayer tool
Move the symbols in a set	Drag with the Symbol Shifter tool
Change the stacking order of the symbols	Alt (Option)+Symbol Shifter tool
Scrunch the symbols closer together	Drag with the Symbol Scruncher tool
Move the symbols farther apart	Alt (Option)+Symbol Scruncher tool
Increase the symbol size	Drag with the Symbol Sizer tool
Decrease the symbol size	Alt (Option)+Symbol Sizer tool
Rotate the symbols	Drag with the Symbol Spinner tool

Function	Procedure
Increase the symbol's transparency	Drag with the Symbol Screener tool
Decrease the symbol's transparency	Alt (Option)+Symbol Screener tool
Change the symbol's color	Drag with the Symbol Stainer tool
Restore the symbol's original color	Alt (Option)+Symbol Stainer tool
Apply a style to the symbol	Drag with the Symbol Styler tool
Remove the style from a symbol	Alt (Option)+Symbol Styler tool

Table A-20
Graph Tools

Tool	Shortcut
Column Graph tool	J

Function	Procedure
Create a Graph sized by numbers	Click with any Graph tool
Create a Graph sized by dragging	Drag with any Graph tool
Create a square or circular graph	Shift+drag with any Graph tool
Create a Graph from the center	Alt (Option)+drag with any Graph tool

Table A-21
Paint Tools

Tool	Shortcut
Gradient tool	G
Gradient Mesh tool	U
Live Paint Bucket tool	K Option (Alt)+Eyedropper tool
Eyedropper tool	I Alt (Option)+Paint Bucket tool

Continued

Table A-21 *(continued)*

Function	Procedure
Change Linear Gradient direction and/or length	Drag with Gradient tool
Constrain Gradient Direction to 45-degree angles	Shift+drag with Gradient tool
Change Radial Gradient size and/or location	Drag with Gradient tool
Change Radial Gradient origin point	Click with Gradient tool
Sample color to Color palette	Click with Eyedropper tool
Sample Screen color to Color palette	Shift+click with Eyedropper tool
Change Paint Style of selected objects	Double-click with Eyedropper tool on an object with the desired style
Measure a distance	Click the start and end location with the Measure tool
Measure a distance by 45-degree angles	Shift+click the start and end location with the Measure tool

Table A-22
Blend, Auto Trace, and Slice Tools

Tool	Shortcut
Blend tool	W
Slice tool	Shift+K

Function	Procedure
Blend between two paths	Click corresponding selected points on each path with Blend tool
Set Blend options	Double-click on the Blend tool
Auto Trace Images	Click area to be traced with Auto Trace tool
Divide artwork into slices	Drag+Slice tool
Constrain slice to a square	Alt (Option)+drag with the Slice tool
Slice selected objects	Drag+Slice Selected tool

Table A-23 Viewing Tools	
Tool	**Shortcut**
Hand tool	H Spacebar (when not entering text)
Zoom tool	Z Ctrl (⌘)+spacebar
Zoom Out tool	Ctrl (⌘)+Option (Alt)+spacebar Alt (Option)+Zoom tool
Function	**Procedure**
Reposition the page	Drag with the Hand tool
Fit the page within the document window	Double-click on the Hand tool
Moving page boundaries	Drag with the Page tool
Reset page boundaries	Double-click on the Page tool
Zoom in	Click with the Zoom tool Ctrl (⌘)++ (plus sign)
Zoom out	Alt (Option)+click with the Zoom tool Ctrl (⌘)+- (hyphen)
Zoom in to a specific area	Drag with the Zoom tool
Move the Zoom Marquee while drawing	Spacebar while dragging with the Zoom tool
Draw the Zoom Marquee from its center	Ctrl+drag with the Zoom tool

Type Commands

Table A-24 Type Shortcuts	
Action	**Shortcut**
Copy type on a path	Alt (Option)+drag the I-bar using any selection tool
Flip type on a path	Double-click the I-bar with any selection tool, or just drag it to the opposite side of the path
Move insertion point to next character	→ (right arrow)

Continued

Table A-24 *(continued)*

Action	Shortcut
Move insertion point to previous character	← (left arrow)
Move insertion point to next line	↓ (down arrow)
Move insertion point to previous line	↑ (up arrow)
Move insertion point to next word	Ctrl (⌘)+→
Move insertion point to previous word	Ctrl (⌘)+←
Move insertion point to next paragraph	Ctrl (⌘)+↓
Move insertion point to previous paragraph	Ctrl (⌘)+↑
Select (by highlighting) all type in story	Ctrl (⌘)+A when the insertion point is in the story
Select all type in document	Ctrl (⌘)+A when any tool but the Type tools are selected
Select next character	Shift+→
Select previous character	Shift+←
Select next line	Shift+↓
Select previous line	Shift+↑
Select next word	Ctrl (⌘)+Shift+→
Select previous word	Ctrl (⌘)+Shift+←
Select next paragraph	Ctrl (⌘)+Shift+↓
Select previous paragraph	Ctrl (⌘)+Shift+↑
Select word	Double-click word
Select paragraph	Triple-click paragraph
Deselect all type	Ctrl (⌘)+Shift+A
Duplicate column outline and flow text	Alt (Option)+drag column outline with Direct Selection tool
Insert discretionary hyphen	Ctrl (⌘)+Shift+- (hyphen)
Insert line break	Press Enter (Return) (on keypad)

Table A-25
Paragraph Formatting

Action	Shortcut
Display Paragraph palette	Ctrl (⌘)+Shift+M
Align paragraph flush left	Ctrl (⌘)+Shift+L
Align paragraph flush right	Ctrl (⌘)+Shift+R
Align paragraph flush center	Ctrl (⌘)+Shift+C
Align paragraph justified	Ctrl (⌘)+Shift+J
Align paragraph force justified	Ctrl (⌘)+Shift+F
Display Tab Ruler palette	Ctrl (⌘)+Shift+T
Align Tab palette to selected paragraph	Click Tab palette size box
Cycle through tab stops	Alt (Option)+click tab stop
Move multiple tab stops	Shift+drag tab stops
Cycle tab measurements	Click

Table A-26
Character Formatting

Action	Shortcut
Display Character palette	Ctrl (⌘)+T
Highlight font	⌘ (Ctrl)+Alt (Option)+Shift+M
Increase type size	Ctrl (⌘)+Shift+>
Decrease type size	Ctrl (⌘)+Shift+<
Increase type to next size on menu	Ctrl (⌘)+Alt (Option)+>
Decrease type to next size on menu	Ctrl (⌘)+Alt (Option)+<
Set leading to Solid (same as pt. size)	Double-click Leading symbol in Character palette
Increase Baseline Shift (Raise)*	Alt (Option)+Shift+↑
Decrease Baseline Shift (Lower)*	Alt (Option)+Shift+↓
Increase Baseline Shift (Raise) ×5*	Ctrl (⌘)+Alt (Option)+Shift+↑
Decrease Baseline Shift (Lower) ×5*	Ctrl (⌘)+Alt (Option)+Shift+↓

Continued

Table A-26 *(continued)*

Action	Shortcut
Kern/Track closer*	Alt (Option)+←
Kern/Track apart*	Alt (Option)+→
Kern/Track closer ×5*	Ctrl (⌘)+Alt (Option)+←
Kern/Track apart ×5*	Ctrl (⌘)+Alt (Option)+→
Reset Kerning/Tracking to 0	Ctrl (⌘)+Shift+Q
Highlight Kerning/Tracking	Ctrl (⌘)+Alt (Option)+K
Reset Horizontal Scale to 100%	Ctrl (⌘)+Shift+X

* Value/amount set in Preferences

Color Commands

Table A-27
Color Palette

Action	Shortcut
Show/Hide Color palette	F6 (toggle) Ctrl (⌘)+I (toggle)
Revert to default colors	D (White Fill, Black Stroke; Mac and Windows)
Toggle focus between Fill and Stroke	X
Choose current color in Color palette	, (comma)
Change paint to None	/
Apply to inactive Fill/Stroke (Fill when Stroke is active, Stroke when Fill is active)	Alt (Option)+click in color ramp on Color palette
Apply color to unselected object	Drag color swatch from Color palette to object
Apply color to selected object	Click swatch in Color palette
Copy Paint Style to unselected objects	Click unselected objects with Paint Bucket
Copy Paint Style from any (source) object to all selected objects	Click source object with Eyedropper
Tint process color	Shift+drag any Color palette slider
Cycle through Color modes	Shift+click Color Ramp (Grayscale, CMYK, RGB; Mac and Windows)

Table A-28
Swatches Palette

Action	Shortcut
Show/Hide Swatches palette	None
Toggle focus between Fill and Stroke	X
Add swatch	Click the New Swatch icon Drag from Color or Gradient palette into swatches
Replace swatch	Alt (Option)+drag from Color or Gradient palette into swatches
Duplicate swatch	Alt (Option)+drag swatch onto New Swatch icon in Swatches palette
Delete swatch	Drag to Trash icon in Swatches palette Click Trash icon with swatches selected
Select contiguous swatches	Shift+click first and last swatches
Select noncontiguous swatches	Ctrl (⌘)+click each swatch
Switch keyboard focus to Swatches palette (for selecting swatches by name as they are typed)	Ctrl (⌘)+Alt (Option)+click in Swatches palette
Apply color to unselected object	Drag color swatch from Swatches palette to object
Apply color to selected object	Click swatch in Swatches palette

Table A-29
Gradient Palette

Action	Shortcut
Choose current gradient in Gradient palette	. (period)
Show/Hide Gradient palette	Ctrl (⌘)+F9 (toggle)
Apply swatch to selected color stop on gradient palette	Alt (Option)+click swatch
Add new color stop	Click below gradient ramp
Duplicate color stop	Alt (Option)+drag color stop

Continued

Table A-29 *(continued)*

Action	Shortcut
Swap color stops	Option (Alt)+drag color stop on top of another
"Suck" color for color stop with Eyedropper	Shift+click with Eyedropper
Reset Gradient to default Black, White	Ctrl (⌘)+click in Gradient swatch
Apply color to unselected object	Drag color swatch from Gradient palette to object
Apply color to selected object	Click swatch in Gradient palette

Table A-30
Stroke Palette

Action	Shortcut
Show/Hide Stroke palette	Ctrl (⌘)+F10 (toggle)
Increase/decrease Stroke weight	Highlight Stroke field, use up or down arrows, press Enter (Return) when finished
Increase/decrease Miter amount	Highlight Miter field, use up or down arrows, press Enter (Return) when finished

Other Palettes

Table A-31
Miscellaneous Palette Commands

Action	Shortcut
Collapse/display Palette	Click box in upper-right corner
Cycle through Palette views	Double-click palette tab
Apply settings	Enter (Return)
Apply settings while keeping last text field highlighted	Shift+ Enter (Return)

Action	Shortcut
Highlight next text field	Tab
Highlight Previous text field	Shift+Tab
Highlight any text field	Click label or double-click current value
Increase value by base increment	Highlight field, ↑
Decrease value by base increment	Highlight field, ↓
Increase value by large increment	Highlight field, Shift+↑
Decrease value by large increment	Highlight field, Shift+↓
Combine palettes	Drag palette tab within other palette
Dock palette	Drag palette tab to bottom of other palette
Separate palette	Drag palette tab from current palette

Table A-32
Transform Palette

Action	Shortcut
Show/Hide Transform palette	Shift+F8
Copy object while transforming	Alt (Option)+Enter (Return)
Scale proportionately	Ctrl (⌘)+Enter (Return)
Copy object while scaling proportionately	Ctrl (⌘)+Alt (Option)+Enter (Return)

Table A-33
Layers Palette

Action	Shortcut
Show/Hide Layers palette	F7
New layer	Click New Layer icon
New layer with Options dialog box	Alt (Option)+click New Layer icon
New layer above active layer	Ctrl (⌘)+Alt (Option)+click New Layer icon

Continued

Table A-33 *(continued)*

Action	*Shortcut*
New layer below active layer	Ctrl (⌘)+click New Layer icon
Duplicate layer(s)	Drag layer(s) to New Layer icon
Change layer order	Drag layers up or down within Layer list
Select all objects on a layer	Alt (Option)+click that layer
Select all objects on several layers	Shift+Alt (Option)+click each layer
Select contiguous layers	Shift+click layers
Select noncontiguous layers	Ctrl (⌘)+click layers
Move objects to a different layer	Drag colored square to a different layer
Copy objects to a different layer	Alt (Option)+drag color square to a different layer
Hide/Show layer	Click Eyeball icon
View layer while hiding others	Alt (Option)+click Eyeball icon
View layer in Artwork mode	Ctrl (⌘)+click Eyeball icon
View layer in Preview while others are artwork	Ctrl (⌘)+Alt (Option)+click Eyeball icon
Lock/Unlock layer	Click Pencil icon
Unlock layer while locking others	Alt (Option)+click Pencil icon
Delete layer	Drag layer to Trash icon Select layer and click Trash icon
Delete layer without warning	Alt (Option)+drag layer to Trash icon Select layer and Alt (Option)+click trash icon

Miscellaneous Commands

<table>
<tr><td colspan="2" align="center">Table A-34
Viewing Shortcuts</td></tr>
</table>

Action	*Shortcut*
Zoom in	Ctrl (⌘)++ (plus sign) Click with Zoom tool
Zoom out	Ctrl (⌘)+- (hyphen) Alt (Option)+click with Zoom tool
Fit document in Window	Ctrl (⌘)+0 Double-click Hand tool
View at actual size (100%)	Ctrl (⌘)+1 Double-click Zoom tool
Artwork/Preview mode	Ctrl (⌘)+Y (toggle)
Show/Hide edges	Ctrl (⌘)+H (toggle)
Show/Hide guides	Ctrl (⌘)+;
Show/Hide grid	Ctrl (⌘)+"
Show/Hide rulers	Ctrl (⌘)+R
Hide selected objects	Ctrl (⌘)+3
Show all hidden objects	Ctrl (⌘)+Alt (Option)+3
Window mode (normal)	F (when in Full Screen mode in Mac or Windows)
Full Screen mode with menu	F (when in Window mode in Mac or Windows)
Full Screen mode (no menus)	F (when in Full Screen mode with menu in Mac or Windows)

Table A-35
Miscellaneous Commands

Action	Shortcut
Nudge selection*	Arrow keys
See special Status Line categories	Click status bar (lower-left corner)
Display context-sensitive menus	Ctrl+click (right-click)
Highlight last active text field	Ctrl (⌘)+~ (tilde)

* Value/amount set in Preferences

Generic Dialog Box Commands

Table A-36
Generic Dialog Box Commands

Action	Shortcut
Cancel	Esc
OK (or dark bordered button)	Enter (Return)
Highlight next text field	Tab
Highlight previous text field	Shift+Tab
Highlight any text field	Click label or double-click current value

✦   ✦   ✦

✦ ✦ ✦ ✦

In This Appendix

Meeting Illustrator
people

Finding Illustrator
resources

✦ ✦ ✦ ✦

People and Resources

T his appendix contains resources for related products, services, and other information that Illustrator users may find useful. All contact information is subject to change, of course.

Getting to Know the People Who Use Illustrator

You've seen their work — here's some background information on the Illustrator users who have contributed to the *Illustrator CS2 Bible.*

Joe Jones

E-mail: DujaVe@aol.com

A Denver native, Joe Jones has been a professional illustrator and graphic artist since 1983. In 1995, he started his own successful design firm, Art Works Studio. While working with diverse clients such as Adobe Systems, Sun America Trust, and Adidas, and performers such as Carlos Santana, Joe's passion for aviation, science fiction, and fantasy art has remained a focus in his life. Jones was named Special Guest Artist at the 21st, 22nd, and 23rd International Conferences on the Fantastic in the Arts. Joe's digital aviation design and illustration have landed him clients such as Rolls Royce, Frontier Airlines, and World Of Wings.

Joe's first work at the Smithsonian's National Air and Space Museum was put on permanent display in the summer of 2004. This work represents the first all-digital aviation illustration to be put on display at the museum. Joe's digital handiwork has been showcased in almost 20 books on Adobe Photoshop and Illustrator, including *The Illustrator 9 WOW! Book, Photoshop 6 Studio Secrets,* and the *Macworld Illustrator Bible* series. Visit him on the Web at www.artworksstudio.com.

Cory Gray

E-mail: corart@earthlink.net

Cory Gray is a commercial artist with a flair for cartoon art and a background in traditional illustration. Cory received associate of art degrees from the Colorado Institute of Art and Platte College for Digital Graphics. Since then, he has created numerous pieces for print production with expertise in high-end spot separation. His artwork has been featured on the cover of *Printwear* magazine. His accomplishments span a range of creative venues, including full wall murals, silkscreen designs, character concepts, and Cory's favorite, development and illustration for children's publications. Cory currently contributes graphic and illustrative techniques for silkscreen printing at Image West Apparel, Inc. Visit him on the Web at www.thegraydomain.com.

Brian Warchesik

E-mail: brianjudywar@earthlink.net

Brian Warchesik is a graphic designer in Denver. He also pursues his career as an illustrator from his home in Littleton, Colorado, where he lives with his wife, Judy. Brian's work has been featured in publications such as *Photoshop and Illustrator Synergy Studio Secrets* as well as Delta's in-flight magazine, *Sky Magazine,* and has recently done some work for the Business and Marketing Association of Colorado. His paintings have been featured in gallery showings, and he continues to love working. Reach him at 720-981-7722.

Todd Macadangdang

E-mail: toddm@adobe.com

An award-winning artist, instructor, and Adobe Illustrator guru, Todd closed his design firm in 1991 to focus on a career as a freelance illustrator. Since then, Todd has offered his services as illustrator, project manager, and creative director for numerous print, Web, and multimedia projects. Past clients include Paramount Publishing, Simon and Schuster, Viacom, AOL, The Learning Company, Worldcom, Adobe Systems, Siemens, Disney Online, and Nickelodeon. He is the current director of Illustratorworld.com and a member of the Illustrator development team at Adobe Systems in San Jose, California.

Jason McQuitty

E-mail: jasonmcquitty@adelphia.net

Born in Colorado Springs, Jason graduated from Rocky Mountain College of Art and Design with a bachelor of fine arts in illustration. Jason loves to work in Adobe Photoshop, Painter, and especially Adobe Illustrator. He specializes in comic book art, car illustration, and athlete illustration. You can contact Jason at 719-964-7540.

Martin Mendelsberg

E-mail: mendelsberg@msn.com

A graphic designer and educator, Martin Mendelsberg earned his master of fine arts degree from the University of Denver and his bachelor of fine arts from Minneapolis College of Art and Design. His foreign studies included Atelier 63 in the Netherlands. He has exhibited internationally in New Zealand, Australia, China, and the United States. His work is represented in permanent collections at Yale University, The New Zealand National Gallery, and Victoria University School of Architecture. His Hebrew "Torah" digital typeface is marketed in Tel Aviv, Israel, by Masterfont Ltd. Martin currently teaches design and typography at Rocky Mountain College of Art and Design in Denver.

Joe Barsin

E-mail: joebarsin@jebdesign.com

Joe Barsin has been a professional illustrator and graphic designer for more than 12 years. He and his wife, Eva, founded JEB Design, Inc., in 1998 and have lived in Annapolis, Maryland, ever since. To view Joe's work, visit www.jebdesign.com.

Chris Spollen

E-mail: cjspollen@aol.com

Chris Spollen received his art training at Parsons School of Design. He works in advertising, publishing, and editorial illustration. Among his recent clients are AT&T, Bell Labs, *Boys' Life, Byte Magazine,* Citibank, *Consumer Reports, Macworld,* Novell, *PC Magazine, Reader's Digest, Tandem,* VarBusiness, and *Woman's Day.*

Chris has developed a design-oriented architectural approach to illustration in which forms are fitted into the overall scheme, like pieces of a puzzle. He has been interviewed by *Byte, HOW, Macworld, Print,* and *Step-By-Step,* and has been a guest lecturer at the Art Director's Club of Long Island, the Graphic Artist Guild, and The Rochester Art Director's Club. He is listed in the *Contemporary Graphic Artists Who's Who* and the *Illustrator WOW! Book.* Visit him at www.spollen.com.

Brian Underdahl

E-mail: Consult@underdahl.net

Brian Underdahl is the author or coauthor of more than 70 books. He was the winner of the 2003 *Referenceware Excellence Award* for the Graphic Design and Multimedia category, awarded at the Waterside Publishing Conference. Brian writes on many different topics and does consulting work for small businesses on a contract basis. He has appeared on numerous TV shows such as *Computer Chronicles* and has been a featured guest on several radio shows as well. You can find the most recent listing of Brian's books and information about some current projects on the Web at www.underdahl.net.

Using Illustrator Resources

When you need support for a software product, the first place to look for help is, obviously, the company that produces the software. Here's the 411 on how to contact Illustrator's maker.

Adobe Systems, Inc.

Publisher of Adobe Illustrator, Adobe Photoshop, Adobe PageMaker, Adobe Streamline, Adobe Premiere, Adobe Dimensions, and several other products.

1585 Charleston Road
PO Box 7900
Mountain View, CA 94039-7900
www.adobe.com
Customer service: 800-833-6687
Technical support (available only to registered users with a valid serial number): 206-628-3953
BBS (First Class software): 206-623-6984

Of course, there's more to illustration creation than just product support. You need to learn the ins and outs of the software, you need to see examples of the works of others, and you want to talk to fellow users. The following sections point you in the right directions.

Using online design magazines

In addition to the main Adobe site, you'll want to peruse studio.adobe.com, which offers everything from tutorials to forums.

For you Mac users, www.macdesignonline.com/illustrator.html is an online magazine dedicated to Illustrator.

Find the Adobe Magazine archives online at `www.adobe.com/products/adobemag/archive/qaillu.html`.

For you Web designers, check out `www.digital-web.com/articles/adobe_illustrator_9`.

Finding Illustrator courses online

You can find a plethora of educational resources for Illustrator online, ranging from cheap to expensive, but everyone should find something available in his or her budget. The resources listed here are representative of what's available; these are not necessarily recommendations.

LVS Online

`http://northlite.50megs.com/illus/`

This site offers four Adobe Illustrator classes. According to the site, "classes begin at various times of the year, and run for 6 weeks. There are 5 sessions per year. Prices are $25 for new students and $20 for returning students."

Sessions.edu Online School of Design

`http://www.sessions.edu/syllabus/IllustratorAdv.html`

This site's advanced Illustrator course promises to help you "expand your Illustrator skills through challenging digital design projects."

The site calls this a "hands-on course," where "you'll create photo-realistic illustrations, complex patterns, rich designs, and learn how to speed your efforts with helpful workflow features. You'll build on your existing Illustrator skills to tackle high-end projects with depth, dimension, and wow-power."

Insight Software Training

`http://www.insight-software-training.co.uk/illustrator.htm`

This site offers training in your office; for a fee, they'll come directly to you and spend time helping you learn the software.

According to the site, "Insight Software Training Ltd supplies training courses in Adobe InDesign, Adobe Illustrator, Adobe Photoshop, Adobe PageMaker, QuarkXPress and CorelDraw. Our Adobe InDesign Training course is for Adobe InDesign CS, but we can supply training for Adobe InDesign version 1.5 and 2, although we strongly recommend you upgrade to the most recent version, Adobe InDesign CS."

Finding Illustrator courses at traditional schools

If you just want to learn to use the Illustrator software, you probably can find some type of Illustrator course at your local college or university. Many campuses offer workshops to students, staff, faculty, and the community at large.

For more serious study, consider the following design schools:

- ✦ **Art Institutes**

    www.artinstitutes.com

- ✦ **Minneapolis College of Art and Design**

    www.mcad.edu/

- ✦ **Rocky Mountain College of Art and Design**

    www.rmcad.edu/

- ✦ **Parsons School of Design**

    www.parsons.edu

Using Illustrator forums and archives

Other Illustrator users often have the solution you're seeking. Try exploring these forums and archives for many useful resources and tips.

Adobe Illustrator User Resources

http://graphicssoft.about.com/od/illustrator/

This archive offers Illustrator resources including tutorials, plug-ins, actions, brushes, templates, training and support resources, patches, updates, FAQs, and tips.

Seneca Design & Training

www.senecadesign.com/designgeek/illustrator.html

Visit this site to find an edited collection of Illustrator tips and resources for users at all levels.

Adobe Illustrator Tips and Techniques

Go to http://desktoppublishing.com/tipsillustr.html

Links for desktop publishing, fonts, and Web authoring are available at this site.

IllustratorWorld

http://www.illustratorworld.com/index.shtml

IllustratorWorld provides a forum where Illustrator artists can display their work. Users can share tips, ideas, and methods.

DigitalMediaDesigner

http://www.digitalmediadesigner.com/

Tips for Illustrator and other digital design media are available through this Web community.

Finding Illustrator products and services

Many plug-ins and other Illustrator-related products are available on the Web. The following listings are just a sampling.

Rick Johnson/Graffix

http://rj-graffix.com/

This supplier offers a variety of plug-ins for Illustrator.

Adobe Illustrator Business Card Design Tutorial and Templates

http://www.greatfxbusinesscards.com/illustrator.htm

Consider using Illustrator to create business cards. This vendor provides templates and an Illustrator tutorial.

Map Resources

http://www.mapresources.com/

Find maps for your graphic design projects in Illustrator and Photoshop formats.

Telegraphics

http://www.telegraphics.com.au/sw/

Telegraphics offers filters and other plug-ins for Illustrator and Photoshop.

✦   ✦   ✦

Index

Symbols and Numerics

, (commas), 141
/ (forward slash), 141
- (hyphen), 329
" (quotation marks), 144
~ (tilde), 131
3D effects
    discussed, 500
    texture mapping, 535–538
3D Extrude & Bevel Options dialog box, 515–516
3D objects
    blends, 425
    lighting, 525
    modeling, 534–535
    perspective drawing, 531
    surface characteristics, 524
    transparency, 229
3D Revolve Options dialog box, 521–522
3D Rotate Options dialog box, 523
100 percent view, zooming techniques, 32

A

About Plug-Ins dialog box, 544
Accelerated option, Playback Options dialog box, 569
actions
    clearing, 570
    creating new, 566–567
    default, 565
    deleting, 567–568
    duplicating, 567
    loading, 571
    menu items, inserting, 568
    naming, 569
    playback, stopping, 568–569
    recordable, 567
    replacing, 571
    resetting, 570
    saving, 571
    scripting versus, 642
    starting/stopping recording, 568
Actions palette, 24
active documents, 45
Actual Size command (View menu), 19
Add Anchor Point tool, 174, 176–177
Add Arrowheads filter, 494, 503–504

Add to shape area, Pathfinder palette, 195–196
Adobe Systems, Inc., as resource, 682
advanced options, printing, 581
ai (Illustrator Legacy) format, 64
airbrush effects, 425–426
Align palette
    description of, 24
    how to use, 265
    objects, 264
Align to Page option, Blend Options dialog box, 407
Align to Path option, Blend Options dialog box, 407
alignment
    center, 316
    left, 316
    objects, 264
    paths, 302
    right, 316
    strokes, 139
    type, 316
alpha effects, 509
ambient lighting, 525
anchor points
    Add Anchor Points tool, 176–177
    adding to paths, 175–176
    control handles, 74, 76–78
    converting, 190
    corner points, 75
    defined, 73
    deleting, 82, 177–179
    selecting all, 82
    smooth points, 75
    as transitional points, 97
Angle option, Calligraphic Brush Options dialog box, 105
Angle Threshold option, Simplify dialog box, 179
angles
    Constrain Angle value, 120, 548–549
    Corner Angle option, Tracing Options dialog box, 457
    custom, 278
    drawing shapes at, 120
    as guides, 278
animations, 634–637
Anti-aliased Artwork option, General preferences, 550
anti-aliasing, 604

Appearance of Black preferences, 563
Appearance palette
    Clear Appearance option, 475
    Delete Selected Item option, 474
    description of, 24
    editing options, 473–474
    menu access, 472
    Redefine Graphic Style option, 476
    Reduce to Basic Appearance option, 475
    Remove Item option, 474
    thumbnail views, 476
Arc Segment tool, 98–99
arcs, warp effects, 398
area graphs, 149
area type
    Area Type Options dialog box, 295–296
    discussed, 290
    good shapes for, 296
    list of, 294
    outlining areas of, 297
    placing in rectangles, 293
    selecting with, 297
arranging icons, 18
arrowhead effects, 494, 503–504
art
    copyrights, 247
    flat art, extruding, 516–518
    Photoshop program, placing into Illustrator
        program, 68–69
Art Brush Options dialog box, 108–109
Art Institutes Web site, 684
Artboard feature
    crop marks, 48
    hiding, 19
    measurement units, 49
    orientation options, 18, 50
    overview, 16
    separations, 48
    showing, 19
    size of, adjusting, 18, 49
    units for, adjusting, 18
Asian Type option, Units & Display Performance
    preferences, 557
Attributes command (Window menu), 247
Attributes palette, 24, 247
Auto Hyphenate function, vertical type, 304
Auto leading option, Justification dialog box, 318
auto slices, 629
Auto Trace tool, 4–5
averaging points, 186–188

B

backgrounds
    patterns, 355
    transparency options, 51–52
banding, blends, 405, 417
Barsin, Joe, contact information and contributions
        made by, 681
Base along option, Arc Segment tool preferences, 99
Baseline Shift function
    Type preferences, 555
    vertical type, 304
Bend option, Warp Options dialog box, 398
bevel effects, 519–521
bevel shadow effect, 509
Bezier curves, 79
bitmap fonts, 283
bitmap-image editing, Live Paint tool, 461
black and white images
    blends, 404
    fills, 136
Black and White Logo preset, Live Trace tool, 454
bleeds and marks
    PDF files, 61
    printing, 583–584
Blend Mode command, path selection, 169
blending modes
    adding to objects, 222
    list of, 221
    Magic Wand tool, 165
blends
    airbrush, 425–426
    banding, 405, 417
    black to white images, 404
    Blend Options dialog box, 406–407
    complex-shape, 419–420
    envelopes, 423
    expanding, 408
    filters, 484
    gradients versus, 401–402
    linear, 404–406, 413–414
    Live Blend feature, 407–408
    morphing, 402
    multiple objects, 407
    neon effects, 429–430
    nonlinear, 412
    path, 403–404
    radial, 415–416
    releasing, 408
    Replace Spine feature, 409
    Reverse Front to Back feature, 410

Reverse Spine feature, 410
softened edges, 428–429
specified steps, calculating, 414–415
symbols, 423
3D objects, 425
bloat effects, 386, 389–390
Blur option
Drop Shadow dialog box, 494
Tracing Options dialog box, 456
boundaries, patterns, 355
Bridge program, 8–9
Bring Forward command, object stacking order, 249
Bring to Front command, object stacking order, 249
browsing tools, 22
brush stroke type, transparency, 230
Brush Strokes command, path selection, 172
brushes
Art Brush Options dialog box, 108–109
Brush Library feature, 112–113
Calligraphic, 105–106
colorization tips, 112
custom, creating, 110
Document Info palette, 70
Pattern, 109–110
Scatter, 106–107
selecting new, 104
Brushes palette, 24
bubble effects, 234–235
bulge, warp effects, 398
bumps
bump and dent effects, 531
curves, 92

C

Calligraphic Brush Options dialog box, 105–106
Cap style, stroke attributes, 139
caps, new document setup, 51
Cascading Style Sheets (CSS), 632
cascading windows, 18
case, lowercase/uppercase, 328
center alignment, type, 316
Center function, vertical type, 304
Center option, Flare tool, 134
center point, drawing shapes from, 118
center-justified tabbing, 322
centimeters, measurement units, 267
Change All button, Find Font dialog box, 326
Change button, Find Font dialog box, 326

characters
attributes, 307
distortion, 334
fonts, 308
formatting, keyboard shortcuts, 671–672
hidden, 331
horizontal scale, 313
language options, 313
multinational options, 314
paragraph options, 315
rotation, 313
styles, 308
tabbing through, 308
vertical scale, 313
charts
organizational, 150–151
strokes, 341
Check Hidden Layers option, Find and Replace dialog box, 325
Check Locked Layers option, Find and Replace dialog box, 325
checking spelling, 327–328
childlike scribble effects, 508
circles
diameter and radius, 125
drawing, 118
Clean Up dialog box, 183–184
Clear All option, Map Art dialog box, 531
Clear Appearance option, Appearance palette, 475
Clear command (Edit menu), 41
Clear option, Map Art dialog box, 531
clearing actions, 570
clicking, mouse functions, 28
client-side image maps, 634
Clip Complex Regions option, Flatten Transparency dialog box, 227
clipping masks
compound paths and, 443
creating, 440–441
discussed, 439
in layers, 260
path selection, 172
raster images, 441
releasing, 442
Close command (File menu), 52
Close gaps with paths option, Gap Options dialog box, 465
closed paths, 74, 86–87

closing
    curved paths, 94–95
    documents, 52–53
    files, 52–53
    Illustrator program, 15
    palettes, 23
    paths, 92
    toolbox, 20
    windows, 17
CMYK (cyan, magenta, yellow, and black) color
        option, 213
Color blending mode, 221
Color Burn blending mode, 221
Color command (Window menu), 212
Color Dodge blending mode, 221
Color option
    Drop Shadow dialog box, 494
    Live Paint Bucket Options dialog box, 464
Color palette, 24
Color 6 preset, Live Trace tool, 450
Color 16 preset, Live Trace tool, 450
Colorization option
    Art Brush Options dialog box, 109
    Pattern Brush Options dialog box, 110
    Scatter Brush Options dialog box, 107
colors
    adding to text, 216
    Adjust Color filter, 483–484
    CMYK (cyan, magenta, yellow, and black), 213
    color commands, keyboard shortcuts, 672–674
    color management, printing options, 581
    color mode
        new document setup, 47
        swatches, 207
    Color Ramp feature, 214
    color space options, 211–213
    color swatches, 206–208
    colorization tips, brushes, 112
    fills, 137
    filters, 482–483
    gamut, 215
    grayscale, 212
    grids, 273
    guides, 276
    hexadecimal, 608–609
    HSB (Hue, Saturation, and Brightness) option, 212
    Invert Colors filter, 485
    layers, 255
    negatives, 487–488
    Overprint Black filter, 485
    process colors, 206

    RGB (red, green, blue), 212
    Saturate filter, 486
    slider values, 213–214
    spot colors, 11, 206, 209, 215–216
    strokes, 137
    transferring from object to object, 216–218
    Web safe, 213, 605–608
Columns option, Area Type Options dialog box, 296
combination corner points, 75, 95, 192
Comic Art preset, Live Trace tool, 453
commands
    Edit menu
        Check Spelling, 327
        Clear, 41
        Copy, 42, 348
        Cut, 42
        Export, 331
        Find and Replace, 325
        keyboard shortcuts, 650–651
        Paste, 42
        Paste in Back, 198, 250
        Paste in Front, 250
        Preferences, 22, 123
        Redo, 43
        Undo, 43
    Effect menu, keyboard shortcuts, 653
    File menu
        Close, 52
        Document Setup, 47
        Exit, 15, 52
        File Info, 71
        keyboard shortcuts, 650
        New, 45
        Open, 52
        Place, 457
        Print, 19, 237
        Revert, 55
        Save, 53
        Save a Copy, 55
        Save As, 54
        Save for Web, 56
    Filter menu, 653
    keyboard, 27
    Object menu
        Expand, 154
        keyboard shortcuts, 651–652
        Ungroup, 154
    Select menu, 652
    selecting, 26
    Start menu, 14
    Type menu, 652

View menu
  Actual Size, 19
  Fit in Window, 19
  Hide Artboard, 19
  keyboard shortcuts, 653–654
  New View, 40
  Preview, 38
  Show Artboard, 19
  Show Transparency, 225
  Show/Hide Rulers, 270
  Grid, 225
  Smart Guides, 277
Window menu
  Attributes, 247
  Brush Library, 113
  Color, 212
  Document Info, 69
  keyboard shortcuts, 654–655
  New Window, 36
  Symbol, 151
commas (,), 141
compatibility
  compatibility options, saving documents, 57–58
  compatibility problems, fonts, 335–336
composites, printing, 579–581
composition methods, type, 319
compound paths
  clipping masks and, 443
  creating, 431–432
  defined, 74
  discussed, 430
  holes, 433–434
  releasing, 432–433
  type and, 435–436
compression, 61
Concentric Dividers option, Polar Grid Tool Options
      dialog box, 102
conceptual sketching, 533–534
Connect Data Points option, Graph Type dialog box, 148
Constrain Angle value
  discussed, 120
  preferences, changing, 548–549
context-sensitive menus, 27
control handles
  defined, 74
  independent, 95
Control palette, 7, 15
Convert All Strokes to Outlines option, Flatten
      Transparency dialog box, 227
Convert All Text to Outlines option, Flatten
      Transparency dialog box, 227

Convert Anchor Point tool, 190
Convert Direction Point tool, 174
Convert to filters feature, 484
Convert to Shape effects, 501
converting
  anchor points, 190
  combination corner points, 192
  curved corner points, 193
  smooth points, 190–191
  straight corner points, 191
cool breeze effect, 509
copies, printing, 579
Copy command (Edit menu), 42, 348
Copy function, graphs, 143
copyrights, artwork, 247
Corner Angle option, Tracing Options dialog box, 457
corner points
  combination, 95, 192
  curved, 95
  description of, 75
Corner Points option, Roughen dialog box, 392
Corner Radius value
  preferences, changing, 549
  rounded rectangles, 123–124
corners, rounding backward, 126
Create Compound Path From Ellipses option, Polar
      Grid Tool Options dialog box, 102
Create New Layer icon, Layers palette, 258
Create New Sublayer icon, Layers palette, 258
Create Outlines function, vertical type, 304
Create Separate Shadows option, Drop Shadow dialog
      box, 494
Crop button, Pathfinder palette, 200
crop marks
  creating, 280
  discussed, 48
  filters, 488
  Japanese, 280, 552
cropping paths, 200
cross sections, 535
crystallize effects, 386
CSS (Cascading Style Sheets), 632
Current Size option, Object Mosaic dialog box, 490
Curve Precision option, Simplify dialog box, 179
curves
  Bezier, 79
  bumps, 92
  curved corner points, 95
  paths, 94–95
  Pen tool drawing, 92–94
  PostScript, 79
  S shapes, 93–94

Curviness option, Scribble Options dialog box, 509
custom angles, 278
custom brushes, creating, 110
Custom option, Gap Options dialog box, 464
custom patterns, 354
custom views, 40
customizing graphs, 145–146
Cut command (Edit menu), 42
Cut function, graphs, 143
cyan, magenta, yellow, and black (CMYK) color
    option, 213

D

Darken blending mode, 221
Darkness option, Drop Shadow dialog box, 494
dash patterns, strokes, 139
data points, graphs, 148
data sets, variables and, 641
date and time information, status bar, 28
decimal-justified tabbing, 322
default actions, 565
default preset, Live Trace tool, 450
Default Size option
    Polar Grid Tool Options dialog box, 102
    Rectangular Grid Tool Options dialog box, 101
Delete Anchor Point tool, 174
Delete Selected Item option, Appearance palette, 474
Delete Selection icon, Layers palette, 258
deleting
    actions, 567–568
    anchor points, 82, 177–179
    graphic styles, 479
    guides, 276
    layers, 260
    paths, 167
    shapes, 117
    swatches, 206, 208
dense scribble effects, 508
dent effects, 531
design magazines, as resource, 682–683
Detail option, Roughen dialog box, 392
Detailed Illustration preset, Live Trace tool, 453
diagonal-line patterns, 358–359
diagrams, organizational, 150–151
dialog boxes
    About Plug-Ins, 544
    Area Type Options, 295–296
    Art Brush Options, 108–109
    Blend Options, 406–407
    Check Spelling, 327

Clean Up, 183–184
Document Setup, 47–48, 50–51, 225
Drop Shadow, 494–495
Expand, 154, 237
File Info, 71
Find and Replace, 324–325
Find Font, 326
Flatten Transparency, 226–227
Gap Options, 464–465
Illustrator Legacy Options, 58
Import Options, Photoshop program, 9–10
Justification, 317–318
Keyboard Shortcuts, 22, 564
Live Paint Bucket Options, 463–464
Map Art, 528–531
Move, 372
New Document, 46
New Swatch, 207
Object Mosaic, 490
Offset Path, 271
Pattern Brush Options, 109–110
Place, 65–67, 457
Playback Options, 569
Polar Grid Tool Options, 102–103
Polygon, 128
Preferences, 22
Print, 19
Rasterize, 607
Rectangle, 122
Rectangular Grid Tool Options, 101–102
Roughen, 132, 391–392
Save for Web, 610
Save Palette as Graphics Style Library, 480
Save Selection, 173
Save Workspace, 10
Scatter Brush Options, 106–107
Scribble Options, 507–509
Set Selection, 570
Shape Options, 501
Simplify, 179
Slice Options, 630–632
Smart Punctuation, 328–329
Symbolism Tools Options, 153
3D Extrude & Bevel Options, 515–516
3D Revolve Options, 521–522
3D Rotate Options, 523
Tracing Options, 456–457
Transform Each, 376–377
Warp Options, 397–398
Warp Tool Options, 383

diameter, of circles, 125
Diameter option
  Calligraphic Brush Options dialog box, 106
  Symbolism Tools Options dialog box, 153
Difference blending mode, 221
diffuse shading, 524
DigitalMediaDesigner Web site, 685
dilate effect, 509
Direct Selection tool, 158, 163
Direction Handles command, path selection, 172
Direction option, Art Brush Options dialog box, 109
directions, paths, 436–438
disabling Tool Tips feature, 22
distortion
  characters, 334
  filters, 493
  free, 389
  tools, keyboard shortcuts, 666
Distortion Horizontal option, Warp Options dialog
      box, 398
Distortion Vertical option, Warp Options dialog box, 398
dithering, 605
diving paths, 198
docking palettes, 23–24
document color profile, status bar, 28
Document Info command (Window menu), 69
Document Info palette
  components, 70
  description of, 25
  Save option, 70
Document Setup dialog box, 47–48, 50–51, 225
Document Type Definition (DTD), 63
document window
  components of, 16–17
  overview, 15
  tiling, 18
documents
  active, 45
  closing, 52–53
  document setup, printing, 578
  exporting, 63–64
  general information, viewing, 69–71
  naming, 46
  new document setup, 45–47
  opening, 52
  saving
    compatibility options, 57–58
    as EPS file, 58–60
    file types and options, 57
    format options, 53–54
    last saved version, reverting to, 55

  as PDF file, 60–62
  Save a Copy command, 55
  Save As command, 54
  Save for Web command, 56
  Save option (Document Info palette), 70
  as SVG files, 62–63
  when to save, 55
  where to save, 54
dotted line display, rulers, 270
double quotes, new document setup, 50
double-clicking, mouse functions, 28
dragging, mouse functions, 28
Draw Filled Lines option, Graph Type dialog box, 148
drawing
  curves
    curved corner points, 95
    with Pen tool, 92–94
    S shapes, 93–94
  lines, straight, 90–92
  paths
    closed paths, 86–87
    discussed, 82
    open paths, 86–87
    using Pencil tool, 83–86
  shapes
    at angles, 120
    basic shapes, 116–117
    from center point, 118
    circles, 118
    drop shadows, 119
    ellipses, 127
    overview, 115
    polygons, 128–129
    rectangles, 120–121
    rectangles, rounded, 122–124
    squares, 118
    squares, rounded, 126
    stars, 130–133
    symmetric shapes, 118
    units of measure, 117
drop shadows
  Drop Shadow dialog box, 494–495
  filters, 494–495
  for shapes, 119
DTD (Document Type Definition), 63
duplicating
  actions, 567–568
  graphic styles, 478
  layers, 260
  swatches, 207–208

E

edge-to-edge lines, graphs, 148
Edit menu commands
    Check Spelling, 327
    Clear, 41
    Copy, 42, 348
    Cut, 42
    Find and Replace, 325
    keyboard shortcuts, 650–651
    Paste, 42
    Paste in Back, 198, 250
    Paste in Front, 250
    Preferences, 22, 123
    Redo, 43
    Undo, 43
editing
    path-editing tools, 174–175
    symbols, 154
    type, 306
educational resources, 683–684
Effect menu command, keyboard shortcuts, 653
effects
    airbrush, 425–426
    alpha, 509
    arcs, 398
    arrowhead, 494, 503–504
    bevel shadow, 509
    bevels, 519–521
    bloat, 386, 389–390
    blur, 456, 494
    bubbles, 234–235
    bulge, 398
    childlike scribble, 508
    Convert to Shape, 501
    cool breeze, 509
    crystallize, 386
    dilate, 509
    distortion
        characters, 334
        filters, 493
        free, 389
        tools, keyboard shortcuts, 666
    drop shadows
        Drop Shadow dialog box, 494–495
        filters, 494–495
        for shapes, 119
    embossed images, 236
    erode, 510
    Feather, 505–506
    fish, 399
    flag, 399
    ghosting, 235–236
    glow, 427, 506
    gravity, 301

    highlights, 486–487
    inflate, 399
    Inner Glow, 506
    mosaics, 489–493
    neon, 429–430
    Outer Glow, 506
    paper doll, 393
    Path, 502
    plug-ins
        About Plug-Ins dialog box, 544
        special effects, 499
    pucker, 385, 389–390
    rainbow, 301
    Rasterize, 502–503
    revolving objects, 521–522
    ribbon, 301
    rise, 399
    roughen, 391–392
    Round Corners, 496–497, 506
    scallop, 386
    Scribble, 507–509
    shadows, 378, 486–487, 510
    shells
        Spiral tool, 99
        warp effects, 398–399
    skew, 301
    softened edge, 428–429
    squeeze, 399
    stair step, 301
    static, 510
    3D
        discussed, 500
        texture mapping, 535–538
    transformations
        Free Transform tool, 373–374
        manual, 364–365
        moving objects, 372–373
        objects, 393
        paper doll effects, 393
        patterns, 360, 382–383
        portion-of-path, 381–382
        reflection, 367–368, 380–381
        reshaping, 370–371
        rotation, 366–367
        scaling options, 368–369
        shadows, 378
        shearing, 369–370
        tool options, keyboard shortcuts, 664–665
        Transform Each dialog box, 376–377
        Transform palette, 374–375
    turbulence, 510
    tweaking, 394–395
    twirl, 384
    twist, 395–396, 399

type, 301–302
warp, 384, 397–399
woodgrain, 510
wrinkle, 387–388
zig zag, 396–397, 508
elevator box, scroll bars, 34
ellipsis, 26, 127
embedded images, Document Info palette, 70
embossed images, 236
emf (Enhanced Metafile) format, 64
Empty Text Paths option, Clean Up dialog box, 184
Enable Version Cue option, File Handling and
        Clipboard preferences, 563
envelopes
    blending, 423
    envelope lines, 535
EPS (Encapsulated PostScript), 58–60
Erase tool, 88
erode effect, 510
every-line composition method, 319
Exclude overlapping shape area, Pathfinder palette, 197
Exclusion blending mode, 221
Exit command (File menu), 15, 52
Expand button, Pathfinder palette, 198
Expand dialog box, 154, 237
expanding
    blends, 408
    gradients, 237
Export command (Edit menu), 331
exporting
    documents, 63–64
    text, 331–332
extrusion
    flat art, 516–518
    strokes, 518–519
Eyedropper tool, 218, 610

F
Feather effect, 505–506
fidelity values, Pencil tool preferences, 84
fight-clicking, mouse functions, 28
file formats, 63–64
File Handling and Clipboard preferences, 562–563
File Info dialog box, 71
File menu commands
    Close, 52
    Document Setup, 47
    Exit, 15, 52
    Export, 331
    File Info, 71
    keyboard shortcuts, 650
    New, 45
    Open, 52
    Place, 457

Print, 19, 237
Revert, 55
Save, 53
Save a Copy, 55
Save As, 54
Save for Web, 56
files
    closing, 52–53
    opening, 52
    tab-delimited, 143
Fill Arc option, Arc Segment tool preferences, 99
Fill Color command, path selection, 170
Fill Color option, Magic Wand tool, 165
Fill Grid option
    Polar Grid Tool Options dialog box, 102
    Rectangular Grid Tool Options dialog box, 101
Fill & Stroke command, path selection, 170
filled lines, graphs, 148
fills
    applying, 140–141
    black and white, 136
    color options, 137
    combining with strokes, 139–140
    defined, 78
    in focus, 141
    gradient meshes, 137
    gradients, 137
    how to use, 136
    object stacking order, 250
    open paths, 79
    patterns, 137
    process colors, 137
    spot colors, 137
    text, 136
film strip example, strokes, 347
Filter menu commands, keyboard shortcuts, 653
filters
    Add Arrowheads, 494, 503–504
    Adjust Color filter, 483–484
    blends, 484
    color, 482–483
    Convert to, 484
    Crop Marks, 488
    Drop Shadow, 494–495
    Invert Colors, 485
    last used, reapplying, 497
    Overprint Black, 485
    Round Corners, 496–497
    Saturate, 486
    Stylize, 494–497
    SVG, 509–510
    uses for, 481
Find and Replace dialog box, 324–325
Find Font dialog box, 326

Find Whole Word option, Find and Replace dialog
        box, 325
finding
    finding and replacing text, 324–325
    fonts, 326
First Line Indent function, vertical type, 304
fish, warp effects, 399
Fit in Window command (View menu), 19
Fit option, Pattern Brush Options dialog box, 110
flags, warp effects, 399
Flare tool
    editing options, 135
    highlighting options, 135
    uses for, 134
Flash program, Web graphics, 620–621, 623–624
flat art, extruding, 516–518
Flatten Transparency dialog box, 226–227
Flattener Preview palette, 25
Flip option
    Art Brush Options dialog box, 109
    Pattern Brush Options dialog box, 110
flipping type, 302
Flush Left function, vertical type, 304
Flush Right function, vertical type, 304
flyouts, 21
Font function, vertical type, 304
Font Preview option, Type preferences, 556
fonts
    bitmap, 283
    compatibility problems, 335–336
    Document Info palette, 70
    EPS files, 59
    finding, 326
    Font submenu, 286
    glyphs, 288
    hinting method, 336
    Multiple Master, 285
    OpenType, 284–285, 320–321
    PostScript, 284
    Recent Fonts submenu, 287
    size of, 288
    TrueType, 284
formats
    GIF, 615
    JPEG, 616
    PNG, 616
    types of, 63–64
    WBMP, 616–617
forward slash (/), 141
free distortion effects, 389
Free Transform tool, 373–374

free-form selections, Lasso tool, 166
Full Screen Mode, 40
full-color illustrations, printing, 582–583
functions
    Auto Hyphenate, 304
    Baseline Shift, 304, 555
    Center, 304
    Copy, 143
    Create Outlines, 304
    Cut, 143
    First Line Indent, 304
    Flush Left, 304
    Flush Right, 304
    Font, 304
    Hang Punctuation, 304
    Justify All Lines, 304
    Justify Full Lines, 304
    Leading, 304
    Left Indent, 304
    mouse, 28
    Paste, 143
    Right Indent, 304
    Size, 304
    Tab Rule, 304
    Trap, 201–202

G

gamut color option, 215
gap detection feature, Live Paint tool, 7
Gap Options dialog box, 464–465
gaussian blur effect, 510
General option, Units & Display Performance
        preferences, 557
General preferences
    Anti-aliased Artwork option, 550
    Japanese Crop Marks option, 552
    Object Selection by Path Only option, 550
    Reset All Warning Boxes option, 554
    Scale Strokes & Effects option, 553
    Select Same Tint % option, 552
    Show Tool Tips option, 550
    Transform Pattern Tiles option, 552
    Use Precise Cursors option, 550
    Use Preview Bounds option, 554
general printing, 579–580
ghosting effects, 235–236
GIF formats, Web graphics, 615
global swatches, 207
glow effects, 427, 506
Glyph scaling option, Justification dialog box, 318
Gradient and Mesh Resolution option, Flatten
        Transparency dialog box, 227

Gradient palette, 25
gradients
    blends versus, 401–402
    bubbles, creating, 234–235
    bumps and dents, 531
    expanding, 237
    fills, 137
    ghosting effects, 235–236
    Gradient palette, 231–232
    linear, 232
    preset, 231
    printing, 237
    radial, 232–233
    swatches, 206
Graphic Styles palette
    description of, 25
    New Graphic Style option, 477–478
graphics
    styles
        breaking links to, 479
        deleting, 479
        Document Info palette, 70
        duplicating, 478
        libraries, 480
        merging, 478
        overriding, 479
    SVG (Scalable Vector Graphics)
        filters, 509–510
        Interactivity palette, 25
        saving documents as, 62–63
        support for, 11
        Web graphics, 623–627
    Web
        animations, 634–637
        CSS (Cascading Style Sheets), 632
        data-driven graphics, 639
        Flash graphics, 620–621, 623–624
        GIF formats, 615
        hexadecimal colors, 608–609
        image maps, 633–634
        interactivity, 633–637
        JPEG formats, 616
        output options, 617–620
        PNG format, 616
        previewing, 610–614
        rollovers, 638
        scripting, 641–643
        slicing, 628–632
        SVG files, 623–627
        WBMP format, 616–617
        Web-safe colors, 605–608

graphs
    area, 149
    basic, 144–145
    Copy function, 143
    customizing, 145–146
    Cut function, 143
    data points, 148
    data variables, 641
    edge-to-edge lines, 148
    filled lines, 148
    grouped-column, 147
    labels, 144
    legends, 144
    line, 148
    Paste function, 143
    pie, 149
    printing options, 581
    radar, 150
    scatter, 150
    spreadsheet example, 142–143
    stacked-column, 147–148
    tab-delimited files, 143
    tick marks, 146
gravity effects, 301
gray area, scroll bars, 34
gray colors, printing full-color illustrations, 582–583
Gray, Cory, contact information and contributions
        made by, 680
grayscale color option, 212
Grayscale preset, Live Trace tool, 452
Greeking option, Type preferences, 556
Grid Colors option, Document Setup dialog box, 225
Grid Size option, Document Setup dialog box, 225
Grid tool
    how to use, 100–101
    Polar Grid Tool Options dialog box, 102–103
    Rectangular Grid Tool Options dialog box, 101–102
grids
    colors, 273
    discussed, 271
    grid patterns, 357
    gridlines, 272–273
    Snap to Grid feature, 272
    Snap to Point feature, 272
    spinning, 274
    styles, 273
    subdivisions, 273–274
    turning off, 272
Group Selection tool
    how to use, 163–164
    uses for, 158

grouped path selection, 160–161
grouped-column graphs, 147
grouping objects, 251–252
guides
    angles as, 278
    colors, 276
    creating, 275
    deleting, 276
    discussed, 274
    locking, 275
    moving, 275
    preferences, changing, 276
    pulling from rulers, 275
    releasing, 275–276
    Smart Guides feature, 277
    styles, 276
    unlocking, 275
Guides & Grid preferences, 558–559

H

H option, Transform palette, 269, 375
Halo option, Flare tool, 134
Hand Drawn Sketch preset, Live Trace tool, 452–453
Hand Grabber tool, 610
Hand tool
    location of, 20
    scrolling with, 35
Hang Punctuation function, vertical type, 304
hanging indents, 317
Hard Light blending mode, 221
headlines, 324
height
    new document setup, 47
    rectangle drawings, 122
Height option, Area Type Options dialog box, 296
hexadecimal colors, 608–609
hidden characters, 331
hiding
    Artboard feature, 19
    objects, 247
    palettes, 21
    rulers, 270
    toolbox, 20–21
highlight effects, 486–487
highlight options
    Flare tool, 135
    Live Paint Bucket Options dialog box, 464
    Mesh tool, 239–241
    new document setup, 50
highway example, strokes, 351–352

hinting method, fonts, 336
holes, compound paths, 433–434
Horizontal Dividers option, Rectangular Grid Tool
    Options dialog box, 101
Horizontal option, Warp Options dialog box, 398
horizontal scale, type, 304, 313
hotspots, 633
HSB (Hue, Saturation, and Brightness) color option, 212
Hue blending mode, 221
hyphen (-), 329
hyphenation
    preferences, 561
    text, 318–319

I

icons, arranging, 18
Illustrator Legacy (ai) format, 64
Illustrator Legacy Options dialog box, 58
Illustrator program
    closing, 15
    exiting, 52
    opening, 14
    and Photoshop program, moving between, 67–68
IllustratorWorld Web site, 685
image maps, 633–634
images
    bitmap-image editing, Live Paint tool, 461
    black and white
        blends, 404
        fills, 136
    raster
        clipping masks, 441
        Live Trace tool, 457–458
Import Options dialog box, Photoshop program, 9–10
inches, measurement units, 267
indention
    hanging, 317
    paragraphs, 316–317
independent control handles, 95
individual type, 290
inflate, warp effects, 399
Info palette, 25
Inked Drawing preset, Live Trace tool, 455
Inner Glow effect, 506
Insight Software Training Web site, 683
Intensity option, Symbolism Tools Options dialog box,
    153
interactivity, Web graphics, 633–637
Intersect shape area, Pathfinder palette, 197
intrapath selecting, 159

Inverse command, path selection, 169
Invert Colors filter, 485
Invisible Geometry option, Map Art dialog box, 531
Isolate Blending option, Transparency palette, 222

J

Japanese crop marks, 280, 552
join style, strokes, 139
joining points, 188–189
Jones, Joe, contact information and contributions
        made by, 679–680
JPEG formats, Web graphics, 616
Justification dialog box, 317–318
Justify All Lines function, vertical type, 304
Justify Full Lines function, vertical type, 304

K

kerning, 311–313
keyboard commands, 27
keyboard shortcuts
    character formatting, 671–672
    color commands, 672–674
    dialog boxes, 678
    distortion tools, 666
    Edit menu commands, 650–651
    Effect menu commands, 653
    File menu commands, 650
    Filter menu commands, 653
    graph tools, 667
    line tools, 660–662
    Object menu commands, 651–652
    paint tools, 667–668
    paragraph formatting, 671
    path tools, 657–658
    Select menu, 652
    selection tools, 656–657
    shape tools, 662–664
    symbol tools, 666–667
    tool selection, 655
    transformation tools, 664–665
    Type menu commands, 652
    type tools, 659–660
    View menu commands, 653–654
    viewing tools, 669
    Window menu commands, 654–655
Keyboard Shortcuts dialog box, 22, 564
Knife tool
    path-editing, 174
    sectioning paths, 181
Knockout Group option, Transparency palette, 223

L

labels, graphs, 144
landscape view
    Artboard feature, 50
    new document setup, 47
    printing options, 585
language options
    characters, 313
    new document setup, 50
Lasso tool
    object selections, 166
    uses for, 158
last saved version, reverting to, 55
layer comps, 9
layers
    Check Hidden Layers option, Find and Replace
        dialog box, 325
    Check Locked Layers option, Find and Replace
        dialog box, 325
    clipping masks in, 260
    colors, 255
    creating new, 255, 260
    deleting, 260
    duplicating, 260
    Layers palette, 256–258
    locking, 255, 257
    merging, 261
    naming, 255, 257
    object location, 260
    objects in
        moving, 259
        printing, 256
    previewing, 255
    reverse stacking order, 261
    showing, 255
    sublayers, 260
    templates, 262
    uses for, 253
Layers palette, 25
Leading function, vertical type, 304
leading increments, 310–311
left alignment, type, 316
Left Indent function, vertical type, 304
left-justified tabbing, 322
legacy text, 331
legal option, new document setup, 46
legends, graphs, 144
Length X-Axis option, Arc Segment tool preferences, 99
Length Y-Axis option, Arc Segment tool preferences, 99
letter option, new document setup, 46

Letter spacing option, Justification dialog box, 318
libraries, graphic styles, 480
Lighten blending mode, 221
lighting effects, 525
Line Art and Text Resolution option, Flatten
        Transparency dialog box, 226
line graphs, 148
Line Segment tool, 97–98
linear blends, 404–406, 413–414
linear gradients, 232
lines
    line patterns, 356
    line tools, keyboard shortcuts, 660–662
    as measurement unit, 270
    straight, 90–92
Link Block Series command, path selection, 171
Link option (Place dialog box), 66
linked image variables, 640
linked images, Document Info palette, 70
linking palettes, 23–24
Links palette, 25
Live Blend feature, 407–408
Live Paint Bucket Options dialog box, 463–464
Live Paint tool
    bitmap image-editing, 461
    gap detection feature, 7
    Gap Options dialog box, 464–465
    how to use, 465–466
    image examples, 6
    Live Paint Bucket Options dialog box, 463–464
    overview, 5
    uses for, 218
Live Trace tool
    Auto Trace tool comparisons, 4–5
    Black and White Logo preset, 454
    Color 6 preset, 450
    Color 16 preset, 450
    Comic Art preset, 453
    default preset, 450
    Detailed Illustration preset, 453
    Grayscale preset, 452
    Hand Drawn Sketch preset, 452–453
    Inked Drawing preset, 455
    outline mode, 447–448
    overview, 3
    Photo High Fidelity preset, 451
    Photo Low Fidelity preset, 451
    Preset drop-down list, 449
    raster images, 457–458
    result mode, 448
    Technical Drawing preset, 454
    Tracing Options dialog box, 456–457
    Type preset, 455
    uses for, 445
loading actions, 571
locking
    guides, 275
    layers, 255, 257
    objects, 246
loose scribble effects, 508
lower and upper stroke limits, 138
lowercase, 328
Luminosity blending mode, 221

M

Macadangdang, Todd, contact information and
        contributions made by, 680
magazines, as resource, 682–683
Magic Wand tool
    object selections, 165
    uses for, 158
magnification levels, Zoom tool, 29
Make/Release Clipping Mask icon, Layers palette, 257
manual reflections, 368
manual transformations, 364–365
Map Art dialog box, 528–531
map elements, strokes, 346–350
Map Resources Web site, 685
Mark Data Points option, Graph Type dialog box, 148
marks and bleeds
    PDF files, 61
    printing, 583–584
masks, clipping
    compound paths and, 443
    creating, 440–441
    discussed, 439
    in layers, 260
    path selection, 172
    raster images, 441
    releasing, 442
Match Case option, Find and Replace dialog box, 325
Max Colors option, Tracing Options dialog box, 456
Max Stroke Weight option, Tracing Options dialog
        box, 456
maximizing windows, 17
McQuitty, Jason, contact information and
        contributions made by, 681
Measure tool, 267–268
measurement units
    Artboard feature, 49
    centimeters, 267
    equally spaced apart, 271

inches, 267
Measure tool, 267–268
methods of, 265
millimeters, 267
with objects, 270
picas, 267
pixels, 267
points, 267
ruler options, 270
type, 308–309
unit of measurement changes, 266
media, printing options, 580
memory, RAM, 254
Mendelsberg, Martin, contact information and
    contributions made by, 681
menus
commands, selecting, 26
context-sensitive, 27
opening, 26
overview, 15
selecting, 26
submenus, 26
Merge button, Pathfinder palette, 199
merging
graphic styles, 478
layers, 261
paths, 199
swatches, 208
Mesh tool
highlights, 239–241
how to use, 238
shading, 239–240
Metadata pane, Bridge program, 9
Method option, Symbolism Tools Options dialog
    box, 153
millimeters, measurement units, 267
Min Stroke Length option, Tracing Options dialog
    box, 457
minimizing
palettes, 23
windows, 17
Minimum option, Tracing Options dialog box, 457
Minneapolis College of Art and Design Web site, 684
Minus Back button, Pathfinder palette, 201
misspelled words, spell checking options, 327
Miter Limit option, stroke attributes, 139
Mode option
Drop Shadow dialog box, 494
Tracing Options dialog box, 456
modeling, 3D objects, 534–535

modes, blending
adding to objects, 222
list of, 221
Magic Wand tool, 165
morphing, blends, 402
mosaic effects, 489–493
mouse functions, 28
Move option, Transform Each dialog box, 377
moving
guides, 275
layer objects, 259
objects, 249, 372–373
paths, 167
patterns, 360
between Photoshop and Illustrator programs,
    67–68
symbols, 156
multinational options, character selection, 314
Multiple Master fonts, 285
multiple objects, blends, 407
Multiply blending mode, 221

N
Name option
Art Brush Options dialog box, 109
Calligraphic Brush Options dialog box, 105
Pattern Brush Options dialog box, 110
Scatter Brush Options dialog box, 107
naming
actions, 569
documents, 46
layers, 255, 257
swatches, 207
Navigator palette
description of, 25
scrolling with, 36
zooming with, 33–35
negative images, 487–488, 587
neon effects, 429–430
New command (File menu), 45
New Document dialog box, 46
New Graphic Style option, Graphic Styles dialog box,
    477–478
New Size option, Object Mosaic dialog box, 490
New Swatch dialog box, 207
New View command (View menu), 40
New Window command (Window menu), 36
nonlinear blends, 412
Normal blending mode, 221
Number of Tiles option, Object Mosaic dialog box, 490

O

Object menu commands
    Expand, 154
    keyboard shortcuts, 651–652
    Ungroup, 154
Object Mosaic dialog box, 490
Object Selection by Path Only option, General
        preferences, 550
Object status, Layers palette, 257
object-based slices, 630
objects
    alignment, 264
    attributes, selecting, 247
    crop marks, 280
    Document Info palette, 70
    grouping, 251–252
    hiding, 247
    locking, 246
    measuring, 265–266
    moving, 249, 372–373
    pasting, 250–251
    revolving, 521–522
    rotating, 523
    sizing, 269
    stacking order, 248–251
    3D
        blends, 425
        lighting, 525
        modeling, 534–535
        perspective drawing, 531
        surface characteristics, 524
        transparency, 229
    tiling, 279
    transformations, 393
    ungrouping, 252
Offset option, Area Type Options dialog box, 296
Offset Path dialog box, 271
offset paths, strokes, 11
100 percent view, zooming techniques, 32
online courses, resources, 683–684
Opacity command, path selection, 171
opacity masks, Transparency palette, 223–224
Opacity option
    Drop Shadow dialog box, 494
    Magic Wand tool, 165
Opacity slider, Transparency palette, 219–220
Open command (File menu), 52
open paths
    defined, 74
    drawing, 86–87
    filled, 79

opening
    Document Setup dialog box, 18
    documents, 52
    files, 52
    Illustrator program, 14
    menus, 26
    Page tool, 19–20
    Pathfinder palette, 193
    Preferences dialog box, 22
    Smooth tool, 88
    toolbox, 20
    windows, 36
OpenType fonts, 284–285, 320–321
Optical Margin Alignment punctuation, 320
Options value, Graph Type dialog box, 146
organizational charts, 150–151
orientation
    Artboard feature, 50
    new document setup, 47
    printing options, 585
    type, 331
Outer Glow effect, 506
Outline button, Pathfinder palette, 200–201
outline mode, Live Trace tool, 447–448
outlines, creating, 332–334
outlining paths, 185–186, 200–201
output options
    printing, 580–581
    Web graphics, 617–620
Output to Swatches option, Tracing Options dialog
        box, 456
overlapping holes, 433–434
Overlay blending mode, 221
Overprint Black filter, 485
Overprint Fill option, Attribute palette, 247
Overprint Preview mode, 39
Overprint Stroke option, Attribute palette, 247

P

Page tool, 19–20
page-layout software programs, printing options, 594
pages, Align to Page option, Blend Options dialog box,
    407
Paint Fills option, Live Paint Bucket Options dialog
        box, 464
Paint stops at option, Gap Options dialog box, 464
Paint Strokes option, Live Paint Bucket Options dialog
        box, 464
paint tools, keyboard shortcuts, 667–668
Paintbrush tool, 103

painting
  brushes
    Art Brush Options dialog box, 108–109
    Brush Library feature, 112–113
    Calligraphic, 105–106
    colorization tips, 112
    custom, creating, 110
    Document Info palette, 70
    Pattern, 109–110
    Scatter, 106–107
    selecting new, 104
  Live Paint tool
    bitmap image-editing, 461
    gap detection feature, 7
    Gap Options dialog box, 464–465
    how to use, 465–466
    image examples, 6
    Live Paint Bucket Options dialog box, 463–464
    overview, 5
    uses for, 218
Palette option, Tracing Options dialog box, 456
palettes
  Actions, 24
  Align, 264–265
  Appearance
    Clear Appearance option, 475
    Delete Selected Item option, 474
    description of, 24
    editing options, 473–474
    menu access, 472
    Redefine Graphic Style option, 476
    Reduce to Basic Appearance option, 475
    Remove Item option, 474
    thumbnail views, 476
  Attributes, 24, 247
  Brushes, 24
  closing, 23
  Color, 24
  Control, 7, 15
  docking, 23–24
  Document Info
    components, 70
    description of, 25
    Save option, 70
  Gradient, 231–232
  Graphic Styles, 477–478
  hiding, 21
  Layers, 256–258
  linking together, 23–24
  list of, 24–25
  minimizing, 23

Navigator
  description of, 25
  scrolling with, 36
  zooming with, 33–35
  overview, 15, 22
Pathfinder
  Add to shape area, 196
  Crop button, 200
  Divide and Outline Will Remove Unpainted
    Artwork option, 195
  Divide button, 198
  Exclude overlapping shape area, 197
  Expand button, 198
  Intersect shape area, 197
  Merge button, 199
  Minus Back button, 201
  opening, 193
  Outline button, 200–201
  overview, 193
  Precision option, 195
  Remove Redundant Points option, 195
  Subtract from shape area, 196
  Trap function, 201–202
  Trim button, 199
  resizing, 23
  separating from other, 24
  showing, 21
  size of, adjusting, 23
  Swatch Library, 210–211
  tabbing, 23–24
  tearing apart, 23–24
  toggling display of, 21
  Transform, 269, 374–375
  Transparency
    blending modes, 220–221
    features, 218–219
    Isolate Blending option, 222
    Knockout Group option, 223
    opacity masks, 223–224
    Opacity slider, 219–220
  Variables, 641
  zooming, 23
paper doll effects, transformations, 393
paragraphs
  formatting, keyboard shortcuts, 671
  indention, 316–317
  spacing before and after, 317
  tabbing options, 315
parallel strokes, 344–346
Parsons School of Design Web site, 684
Paste command (Edit menu), 42

Paste function, graphs, 143
Paste in Back command (Edit menu), 198, 250
Paste in Front command (Edit menu), 250
pasting objects, 250–251
Path effects, 502
Path Fitting option, Tracing Options dialog box, 457
Path Overlap option, Scribble Options dialog box, 509
Path tool, 290
Pathfinder palette
    Add to shape area, 195–196
    Crop button, 200
    description of, 25
    Divide and Outline Will Remove Unpainted Artwork
        option, 195
    Divide button, 198
    Exclude overlapping shape area, 197
    Expand button, 198
    Intersect shape area, 197
    Merge button, 199
    Minus Back button, 201
    opening, 193
    Outline button, 200–201
    overview, 193
    Precision option, 195
    Remove Redundant Points option, 195
    Subtract from shape area, 196
    Trap function, 201–202
    Trim button, 199
paths
    alignment, 302
    anchor points
        Add Anchor Points tool, 176–177
        adding, 175–176
        control handles, 74, 76–78
        converting, 190
        corner points, 75
        defined, 73
        deleting, 177–179
        smooth points, 75
    averaging points, 186–188
    cleaning up, 183–184
    closed, 74, 86–87
    closing, with Pen tool, 92
    compound
        clipping masks and, 443
        creating, 431–432
        defined, 74
        discussed, 430
        holes, 433–434
        releasing, 432–433
        type and, 435–436

cropping, 200
cross sections, 535
curved, closing, 94–95
defined, 73
deleting, 167
directions, 436–438
dividing, 198
drawing
    closed paths, 86–87
    discussed, 82
    open paths, 86–87
    using Pencil tool, 83–86
fills, 78
joining points, 188–189
merging, 199
moving, 167
offsetting, 184–185
open
    defined, 74
    drawing, 86–87
    filled, 79
outlining, 185–186, 200–201
path blends, 403–404
path tools, keyboard shortcuts, 657–658
path-editing tools, 174–175
resectioning, 181–182
reshaping, 182
sectioning, 181–182
selecting
    Blend Mode command, 169
    Brush Strokes command, 172
    clipping masks, 172
    custom paint style selections, 173–174
    Direct Selection tool, 158
    Direction Handles command, 172
    Fill Color command, 170
    Fill & Stroke command, 170
    free-form selection, 166
    Group Selection tool, 158, 163–164
    grouped paths, 160–161
    intrapath selecting, 159
    Inverse command, 169
    Lasso tool, 158
    Link Block Series command, 171
    Magic Wand tool, 158, 165
    methods, 157–158
    Opacity command, 171
    redoing, 168
    saving selections, 173
    Select menu commands, 167–169
    selecting all, 161–162

Selection tool, 158, 162
stray points, 172
Stroke Color command, 171
Stroke Weight command, 171
Style command, 171
Symbol Instance command, 171
text objects, 172
whole paths, 159
single points, 82
spacing, 302
splitting, 180–181
strokes, 78, 81
traps, 201–202
trimming, 199
type on, 300–302
Pattern Brush Options dialog box, 109–110
pattern objects, Document Info palette, 70
pattern swatches, 206
patterns
backgrounds, 355
boundaries, 355
custom, 354
default, 353–354
diagonal-line, 358–359
fills, 137
grid, 357–359
line, 356
moving, 360
pattern tiles, 352–353
seamless, 355
symmetrical, 356
transforming, 360, 382–383
transparent, 359–360
Pause For option, Playback Options dialog box, 569
PDF (Portable Document Format), 60–62
Pen tool
curved paths, closing, 94–95
curves, drawing, 92–94
drawing rules, 96–97
how to use, 89–90
paths, closing, 92
straight lines, drawing, 90–92
tracing templates, 262
Pencil tool
ease of use, 83
how to use, 84–85
preferences, setting, 84–85
tracing templates, 262
perspective drawing, 3D objects, 531
Photo High Fidelity preset, Live Trace tool, 451
Photo Low Fidelity preset, Live Trace tool, 451

Photoshop program
art, placing into Illustrator program, 68
and Illustrator program, moving between, 67–68
Import Options dialog box, 9–10
Photoshop (psd) format, 64
picas, measurement units, 267
pie graphs, 149
Pixar (pxr) format, 64
Pixel Preview mode, 39
pixels
measurement units, 267
pixel play effect, 510
preview, 603–604
Place dialog box, 65–67, 457
placing text, 331–332
plastic shading, 524
Playback Options dialog box, 569
plug-ins
About Plug-Ins dialog box, 544
special effects, 499
Plug-ins and Scratch Disks preferences, 561–562
PNG (png) format, 64
pointing, mouse functions, 28
points
anchor points
Add Anchor Points tool, 176–177
adding to paths, 175–176
control handles, 74, 76–78
converting, 190
corner points, 75
defined, 73
deleting, 82, 177–179
selecting all, 82
smooth points, 75
as transitional points, 97
corner points
combination, 95, 192
curved, 95
description of, 75
measurement units, 267
smooth points
converting, 190–191
description of, 75
Polar Grid Tool Options dialog box, 102–103
polygons, drawing, 128–129
pop-up tools, selecting, 21
Portable Document Format (PDF), 60–62
portrait view
Artboard feature, 50
new document creation, 47
printing options, 585

positive images, printing options, 587
PostScript Printer Description (PPD), 584
PostScript system
    benefits of, 576–577
    curves, 79
    PostScript fonts, 284
PPD (PostScript Printer Description), 584
Precision option, Pathfinder palette, 195
preferences
    Appearance of Black, 563
    Constrain Angle option, 548–549
    Corner Radius value, 549
    File Handling and Clipboard, 562–563
    General preferences
        Anti-aliased Artwork option, 550
        Japanese Crop Marks option, 552
        Object Selection by Path Only option, 550
        Reset All Warning Boxes option, 554
        Scale Strokes & Effects option, 553
        Select Same Tint % option, 552
        Show Tool Tips option, 550
        Transform Pattern Tiles option, 552
        Use Precise Cursors option, 550
        Use Preview Bounds option, 554
    Guides & Grid, 558–559
    Hyphenation, 561
    Plug-ins and Scratch Disks, 561–562
    Type
        Baseline Shift option, 555
        Font Preview option, 556
        Greeking option, 556
        preference options, 554
        Setting the Number of Recent Fonts option, 556
        Show Asian Options option, 556
        Show Font Names in English option, 556
        Size/Leading option, 555
        Tracking option, 555
        Type Object Selection by Path Only option, 556
    Units & Display Performance, 557–558
Preferences command (Edit menu), 22, 123
Preferences dialog box, 22
Preserve Alpha Transparency option, Flatten
        Transparency dialog box, 227
Preserve Overprints and Spot Colors option, Flatten
        Transparency dialog box, 227
Preset option, Flatten Transparency dialog box, 226
presets
    gradients, 231
    Live Trace tool
        Black and White Logo, 454
        Color 6, 450

        Color 16, 450
        Comic Art, 453
        default, 450
        Detailed Illustration, 453
        Grayscale, 452
        Hand Drawn Sketch, 452–453
        Inked Drawing, 455
        Photo High Fidelity, 451
        Photo Low Fidelity, 451
        Technical Drawing, 454
        Type, 455
Pressure Pen option, Symbolism Tools Options dialog
        box, 153
pressure-sensitive tablets, 106
Preview command (View menu), 38
Preview option, Scribble Options dialog box, 509
previewing
    layers, 255
    type, 302
    Web graphics, 610–614
Print command (File menu), 19, 237
Print dialog box, 19
printing
    advanced options, 581
    color management options, 581
    composites, 579–581
    document setup, 578
    full-color illustrations, 582–583
    general, 579–580
    gradients, 237
    graphics options, 581
    landscape view, 585
    layer objects, 256
    marks and bleeds, 583–584
    orientation options, 585
    output options, 580–581
    page size, changing, 584–585
    page-layout software programs, 594
    portrait view, 585
    positive and negative images, 587
    PPD (PostScript Printer Description) files, 584
    process color separation, 588
    setup options, 580
    spot color separations, 588
    trapping process, 594–596
process colors
    fills, 137
    printing, 588
    swatches, 206
products and services, as resource, 685
Programs command (Start menu), 14

psd (Photoshop) format, 64
pucker effects, 385, 389–390
punctuation
    Optical Margin Alignment, 320
    Roman Hanging, 319
    Smart Punctuation dialog box, 328–329
pxr (Pixar) format, 64

Q

quotation marks ("), 144
quotes, new document setup, 50–51

R

radar graphs, 150
radial blends, 415–416
radial gradients, 232–233
radius, of circles, 125
Radius option, Polygon dialog box, 128
rainbow effects, 301
RAM (Random Access Memory), 254
raster images
    clipping masks, 441
    Live Trace tool, 457–458
Rasterize dialog box, 607
Rasterize effect, 502–503
Raster/Vector Balance option, Flatten Transparency
        dialog box, 226
Rays option, Flare tool, 134
recordable actions, 567
Rectangle tool, 120–121
rectangles
    area type in, 293
    drawing, 120–124
    as measurement unit, 270
    Rectangle dialog box, 122
Rectangular Grid Tool Options dialog box, 101–102
red, green, blue (RGB) color option, 212
Redefine Graphic Style option, Appearance palette, 476
Redo command (Edit menu), 43
redoing path selection, 168
Reduce to Basic Appearance option, Appearance
        palette, 475
reflection, transformations, 367–368, 380–381
registration marks, 583
releasing
    blends, 408
    clipping masks, 442
    compound paths, 432–433
    guides, 275–276
Remove Item option, Appearance palette, 474

Remove Redundant Points option, Pathfinder
        palette, 195
Replace option (Place dialog box), 67
Replace Spine feature, blends, 409
replacing
    actions, 571
    text, 324–325
Resample option, Tracing Options dialog box, 456
resectioning paths, 181–182
Reset All Warning Boxes option, General
        preferences, 554
resetting actions, 570
Reshape tool, 370–371
reshaping paths, 182
resizing palettes, 23
resources
    Adobe Systems, Inc., 682–683
    design magazines, 682–683
    educational, 683–684
result mode, Live Trace tool, 448
Reverse Front to Back feature, blends, 410
Reverse Path Direction buttons, Attribute palette, 247
Reverse Spine feature, blends, 410
reverse stacking order, layers, 261
Revert command (File menu), 55
revolving objects, 521–522
RGB (red, green, blue) color option, 212
ribbon effects, 301
Rick Johnson/Graffix Web site, 685
right alignment, type, 316
Right Indent function, vertical type, 304
right-justified tabbing, 322
Rings option, Flare tool, 135
rise, warp effects, 399
Rocky Mountain College of Art and Design Web site, 684
rollovers, 638
Roman Hanging punctuation, 319
Rotate option
    Transform Each dialog box, 377
    Transform palette, 269, 375
rotation
    characters, 313
    objects, 523
    path of objects, 379–380
    transformations, 366–367
    transforming patterns, 360
Rotation option, Scatter Brush Options dialog box, 107
Rotation relative to option, Scatter Brush Options
        dialog box, 107
Roughen dialog box, 132, 391–392

Round Corners effect, 496–497, 506
rounded rectangles, drawing, 122–124
rounded squares, drawing, 126
Roundness option, Calligraphic Brush Options dialog
    box, 106
Rows option, Area Type Options dialog box, 296
rulers
    dotted line display, 270
    pulling guides from, 275
    showing/hiding, 270

S

S shapes, drawing, 93–94
Saturate filter, 486
Saturation blending mode, 221
Save a Copy command (File menu), 55
Save As command (File menu), 54
Save command (File menu), 53
Save for Web command (File menu), 56
Save for Web dialog box, 610
Save Palette as Graphics Style Library dialog box, 480
Save Selection dialog box, 173
Save Workspace dialog box, 10
saving
    actions, 571
    documents
        compatibility options, 57–58
        as EPS file, 58–60
        file types and options, 57
        format options, 53–54
        last saved version, reverting to, 55
        as PDF file, 60–62
        Save a Copy command, 55
        Save As command, 54
        Save for Web command, 56
        Save option (Document Info palette), 70
        as SVG file, 62–63
        when to save, 55
        where to save, 54
    path selections, 173
Scalable Vector Graphics. *See* SVG
Scale option, Transform Each dialog box, 377
Scale Strokes & Effects option, General preferences, 553
Scale to Fit option, Map Art dialog box, 530
Scale tool, 368–369
scallop effects, 386
Scatter Brush Options dialog box, 106–107
scatter graphs, 150
Scissors tool
    path-editing, 174
    splitting paths, 180–181
Screen blending mode, 221

screen modes, 40
screening symbols, 153
Scribble effect, 507–509
Scribble Options dialog box, 507–509
scripting, Web graphics, 641–643
scrolling
    with Hand tool, 35
    with Navigator palette, 36
    scroll bars, 34
scrunching symbols, 153
seamless patterns, 355
Search Backwards option, Find and Replace dialog
    box, 325
sectioning paths, 181–182
Select menu commands, keyboard shortcuts, 652
Select Same Tint % option, General preferences, 552
selecting
    paths
        Blend Mode command, 169
        Brush Strokes command, 172
        clipping masks, 172
        custom paint style selections, 173–174
        Direct Selection tool, 158, 163
        Direction Handles command, 172
        Fill Color command, 170
        Fill & Stroke command, 170
        free-form selection, 166
        Group Selection tool, 158, 163–164
        grouped paths, 160–161
        intrapath selecting, 159
        Inverse command, 169
        Lasso tool, 158
        Link Block Series command, 171
        Magic Wand tool, 158, 165
        methods, 157–158
        Opacity command, 171
        redoing, 168
        saving selections, 173
        Select Inverse command, 169
        Select menu commands, 167–169
        selecting all, 161–162
        Selection tool, 158, 162
        stray points, 172
        Stroke Color command, 171
        Stroke Weight command, 171
        Style command, 171
        Symbol Instance command, 171
        text objects, 172
        whole paths, 159
    pop-up tools, 21
    swatches, 207, 209
    type, 305–306

Selection tool
  activating, 158
  how to use, 162
Send Backward command, object stacking order, 249
Send to Back command, object stacking order, 249
Send to Current Layer command, object stacking order, 249
Seneca Design & Training Web site, 684
sentence case, 328
server-side image maps, 634
services and products, as resource, 685
Set Selection dialog box, 570
Setting the Number of Recent Fonts option, Type preferences, 556
setup options, printing, 580
Shade Artwork option, Map Art dialog box, 531
shading
  diffuse, 524
  Mesh tool, 239–240
  plastic, 524
shadow effects, 378, 486–487, 510
Shape Options dialog box, 501
shapes
  for area type, 296
  blending, 419–420
  deleting, 117
  drawing
    at angles, 120
    basic shapes, 116–117
    from center point, 118
    circles, 118
    drop shadows, 119
    ellipses, 127
    overview, 115
    polygons, 128–129
    rectangles, 120–121
    rectangles, rounded, 122–124
    squares, 118
    squares, rounded, 126
    symmetric shapes, 118
    units of measure, 117
  shape tools, keyboard shortcuts, 662–664
sharp scribble effects, 508
Shear option, Transform palette, 269, 375
Shear tool, 369–370
shells
  Spiral tool, 99
  warp effects, 398–399
Shockwave Flash (SWF), 621
shortcuts. See keyboard shortcuts
Show Artboard command (View menu), 19
Show Asian Options option, Type preferences, 556

Show Font Names in English option, Type preferences, 556
Show Images in Outline Mode option (Document Setup dialog box), 50
Show Original option, Simplify dialog box, 179
Show Tool Tips option, General preferences, 550
Show Transparency Grid command (View menu), 225
Show/Hide column, Layers palette, 256–257
Show/Hide Rulers command (View menu), 270
showing
  Artboard feature, 19
  palettes, 21
Sides option, Polygon dialog box, 128
Simplify dialog box, 179
Simulate Colored Paper option, Document Setup dialog box, 225
single points, paths and, 82
single quotes, new document setup, 50
Single word justification, Justification dialog box, 318
single-line composition method, 319
site maps, organizational, 150–151
size
  of Artboard feature, adjusting, 18, 49
  of fonts, 288
  of palettes, adjusting, 23
  of symbols, 153, 156
  of type, 309
Size function, vertical type, 304
Size option
  Art Brush Options dialog box, 109
  Pattern Brush Options dialog box, 110
  Roughen dialog box, 392
  Scatter Brush Options dialog box, 107
Size/Leading option, Type preferences, 556
sizing objects, 269
sketch scribble effects, 508
skew effects, 301
Skip button, Find Font dialog box, 326
Slice Select tool, 610
Slice tool, 182
slices
  auto, 629
  object-based, 630
  Slice Options dialog box, 630–632
  user, 629
slider values, color options, 213–214
Slope option, Arc Segment tool preferences, 99
small caps, new document setup, 51
Smart Guides feature, 277
Smart Punctuation dialog box, 328–329
Smooth Color option, Blend Options dialog box, 407
Smooth option, Roughen dialog box, 392

smooth points
    converting, 190–191
    description of, 75
Smooth tool, 88
smoothness values, Pencil tool preferences, 85
snails, Spiral tool, 99
Snap to Grid feature, 272
Snap to Point feature, grids, 272
Snapping Tolerance option, guides, 278
snarl scribble effects, 508
Soft Light blending mode, 221
softened edge effects, 428–429
sorting swatches, 208–209
spacing before and after paragraphs, 304, 317
Spacing option
    Scatter Brush Options dialog box, 107
    Scribble Options dialog box, 509
spacing paths, 302
special effects. See effects
Specified Distance option, Blend Options dialog
        box, 407
Specified Steps option, Blend Options dialog box, 407
spell checking, 327–328
spinning grids, 274
Spiral tool, 99
splitting paths, 180–181
Spollen, Chris, contact information and contributions
        made by, 681
spot colors
    creating, 215–216
    defined, 11
    Document Info palette, 70
    fills, 137
    spot color separations, printing options, 588
    swatches, 206, 209
spreadsheets, graphing example, 142–143
squares
    drawing
        basic squares, 118
        rounded squares, 126
    as measurement unit, 270
squeeze, warp effects, 399
stacked-column graphs, 147–148
stacking order, objects, 248–251
staining symbols, 153, 156
stair step effects, 301
Standard Screen Mode, 40
stars, drawing
    basic stars, 130–131
    dynamic starbursts, 131–133
Start menu commands, Programs, 14

startup file, 545–547
static effect, 510
status bar
    current tool information, 28
    date and time information, 28
    document color profile, 28
    overview, 16, 27
    version cue status, 28
Step By Step option, Playback Options dialog box, 569
straight corner points, 75, 191
straight lines
    drawing, 90–92
    Simplify dialog box, 179
Stray Points option, Clean Up dialog box, 183
stray points, path selection, 172
strikethrough text, 12, 308
Stroke Color command, path selection, 171
Stroke Color option, Magic Wand tool, 165
Stroke option, Units & Display Performance
        preferences, 557
Stroke palette, 25
Stroke Weight command, path selection, 171
Stroke Weight option, Magic Wand tool, 165
Stroke Width option, Scribble Options dialog box, 509
strokes
    alignment, 139
    applying, 140–141
    attributes, changing, 138–139
    charts, 341
    colors, setting, 137
    combining with fills, 139–140
    creative solutions, 339–340
    dash patterns, 139
    defined, 78
    extruding, 518–519
    film strip example, 347
    highway example, 351–352
    map elements, 346–350
    object stacking order, 250
    offset paths, 11
    parallel, 344–346
    Pencil tool preferences, 85
    ten-point paths, 343
    three-point paths, 342
    upper and lower limits, 138
    usage rules, 340
    weight, changing, 137
Style command, path selection, 171
Style option
    Graph Type dialog box, 146
    Warp Options dialog box, 398

style sheets, 632
styles
    characters, 308
    graphics
        breaking links to, 479
        deleting, 479
        Document Info palette, 70
        duplicating, 478
        libraries, 480
        merging, 478
        overriding, 479
    graphs, 145
    guides, 276
    symbols, 153, 156
Stylize filters, 494–497
subdivisions, grids, 273–274
sublayers, creating, 260
subscripts, new document setup, 51
Subtract to shape area, Pathfinder palette, 196
superscripts, new document set, 51
surface characteristics, 3D objects, 524
Surface option, Map Art dialog box, 530
SVG (Scalable Vector Graphics)
    filters, 509–510
    Interactivity palette, 25
    saving documents as, 62–63
    support for, 11
    Web graphics, 623–627
swatches
    adding to Swatches palette, 211
    color, 206–208
    creating new, 206, 208
    deleting, 206, 208
    deselecting, 207
    duplicating, 207–208
    global, 207
    gradient, 206
    merging, 208
    naming, 207
    New Swatch dialog box, 207
    pattern, 206
    selecting, 207, 209
    showing all, 206
    sorting, 208–209
    spot colors, 209
    Swatch Library palette, 210–211
    thumbnail views, 211
    viewing, 209
Swatches palette, 25, 205
SWF (Shockwave Flash), 621

switching between tools, 22
Symbol Instance command, path selection, 171
Symbol option, Map Art dialog box, 530
symbols
    blending, 423
    creating new, 154–155
    editing, 154
    location of, changing, 156
    moving, 156
    screening, 153
    scrunching, 153
    sending backward, 156
    sizing, 153, 156
    staining, 153, 156
    styles, 153, 156
    Symbol Screener tool, 156
    Symbol Scruncher tool, 156
    Symbol Shifter tool, 156
    Symbol Sizer tool, 156
    Symbol Spinner tool, 156
    Symbol Sprayer tool, 151–152
    Symbol Stainer tool, 156
    Symbol Styler tool, 156
    Symbolism Tools Options dialog box, 153
    tools, keyboard shortcuts, 666–667
    transparency, 156, 229
Symbols palette, 25
symmetric shapes, drawing, 118
symmetrical patterns, 356

T

Tab Rule function, vertical type, 304
tabbing
    center-justified, 322
    decimal-justified, 322
    left-justified, 322
    overview, 308
    palettes, 23–24
    paragraphs, 315
    right-justified, 322
tab-delimited files, graphs, 143
Targa (tga) format, 64
Target icon, Layers palette, 257
Technical Drawing preset, Live Trace tool, 454
Telegraphics Web site, 685
Template option (Place dialog box), 67
templates
    discussed, 261
    layers, 262
    tracing, 262

ten-point stroke paths, 343
text. *See also* type
    colors, adding, 216
    exporting, 331–332
    fills, 136
    finding and replacing, 324–325
    hyphenation, 318–319
    kerning, 311
    legacy, 331
    object stacking order, 250
    placing, 331–332
    spell checking, 327–328
    strikethrough, 12, 308
    threaded, 286, 322–323
    underlined, 12, 308
Text Flow option, Area Type Options dialog box, 296
Text Format (txt) format, 64
text objects, path selection, 172
text variables, 640
texture mapping, 535–538
tga (Targa) format, 64
threaded text, 286, 322–323
3D effects
    discussed, 500
    texture mapping, 535–538
3D Extrude & Bevel Options dialog box, 515–516
3D objects
    blends, 425
    lighting, 525
    modeling, 534–535
    perspective drawing, 531
    surface characteristics, 524
    transparency, 229
3D Revolve Options dialog box, 521–522
3D Rotate Options dialog box, 523
three-point stroke paths, 342
Threshold option, Tracing Options dialog box, 456
thumbnail views
    Appearance palette, 476
    swatches, 211
tick marks, graphs, 146
tight scribble effects, 508
tilde (~), 131
Tile buttons, Pattern Brush Options dialog box, 110
Tile Spacing option, Object Mosaic dialog box, 490
tiling
    objects, 279
    windows, 18
title case, 328
toggling palettes, 21
Tolerance option, Magic Wand tool, 165
Tool Tips feature, 22

toolbox
    closing, 20
    hiding, 20–21
    opening, 20
    overview, 15
    tool selection, 21
tools
    Add Anchor Point, 174, 176–177
    Arc Segment, 98–99
    Auto Trace, 4–5
    browsing, 22
    Convert Anchor Point, 190
    Convert Direction Point, 174
    Delete Anchor Point, 174
    Direct Selection, 158, 163
    Erase, 88
    Eyedropper, 218, 610
    Flare
        editing options, 135
        highlighting options, 135
        uses for, 134
    flyouts, 21
    Free Transform, 373–374
    Grid
        how to use, 100–101
        Polar Grid Tool Options dialog box, 102–103
        Rectangular Grid Tool Options dialog box, 101–102
    Group Selection
        how to use, 163–164
        uses for, 158
    Hand
        location of, 20
        scrolling with, 35
    Hand Grabber, 610
    keyboard shortcuts, 655
    Knife
        path-editing, 174
        sectioning paths, 181
    Lasso
        object selections, 166
        uses for, 158
    Line Segment, 97–98
    Live Paint
        bitmap-image editing, 461
        gap detection feature, 7
        Gap Options dialog box, 464–465
        how to use, 465–466
        image examples, 6
        Live Paint Bucket Options dialog box, 463–464
        overview, 5
        uses for, 218

Live Trace
    Auto Trace tool comparisons, 4–5
    Black and White Logo preset, 454
    Color 6 preset, 450
    Color 16 preset, 450
    Comic Art preset, 453
    default preset, 450
    Detailed Illustration preset, 453
    Grayscale preset, 452
    Hand Drawn Sketch preset, 452–453
    Inked Drawing preset, 455
    outline mode, 447–448
    overview, 3
    Photo High Fidelity preset, 451
    Photo Low Fidelity preset, 451
    Preset drop-down list, 449
    raster images, 457–458
    result mode, 448
    Technical Drawing preset, 454
    Tracing Options dialog box, 456–457
    Type preset, 455
    uses for, 445
Magic Wand
    object selections, 165
    uses for, 158
Measure, 267–268
Mesh
    highlights, 239–241
    how to use, 238
    shading, 239–240
Page, 19–20
Paintbrush, 103
Path, 290
Pen
    curved paths, closing, 94–95
    curves, drawing, 92–94
    drawing rules, 96–97
    how to use, 89–90
    paths, closing, 92
    straight lines, drawing, 90–92
    tracing templates, 262
Pencil
    ease of use, 83
    how to use, 84–85
    preferences, setting, 84–85
    tracing templates, 262
pop-ups, 21
Rectangle, 120–121
Reshape, 182, 370–371
Scale, 368–369

Scissors
    path-editing, 174
    splitting paths, 180–181
selecting from toolbox, 21
Selection
    activating, 158
    how to use, 162
Shear, 369–370
shortcuts, customizing, 22
Slice, 182
Slice Select, 610
Smooth, 88
Spiral, 99
switching between, 22
Symbol Screener, 156
Symbol Scruncher, 156
Symbol Shifter, 156
Symbol Sizer, 156
Symbol Spinner, 156
Symbol Sprayer, 151–152
Symbol Stainer, 156
Symbol Styler, 156
Vertical Type, 292
Zoom, 29–30, 610
Zoom Out, 30
Tools palette, 25
tracing
    Live Trace tool
        Auto Trace tool comparisons, 4–5
        Black and White Logo preset, 454
        Color 6 preset, 450
        Color 16 preset, 450
        Comic Art preset, 453
        default preset, 450
        Detailed Illustration preset, 453
        Grayscale preset, 452
        Hand Drawn Sketch preset, 452–453
        Inked Drawing preset, 455
        outline mode, 447–448
        overview, 3
        Photo High Fidelity preset, 451
        Photo Low Fidelity preset, 451
        Preset drop-down list, 449
        raster images, 457–458
        result mode, 448
        Technical Drawing preset, 454
        Tracing Options dialog box, 456–457
        Type preset, 455
        uses for, 445
    templates, 262
Tracing Fills/Stroke option, Tracing Options dialog
    box, 456

Tracing Options dialog box, 456–457
tracking and kerning, 311–313
Tracking option, Type preferences, 556
Transform palette, 25, 269
Transform Pattern Tile option, General
         preferences, 552
transformations
    Free Transform tool, 373–374
    manual, 364–365
    moving objects, 372–373
    objects, 393
    paper doll effects, 393
    patterns, 360, 382–383
    portion-of-path, 381–382
    reflection, 367–368, 380–381
    reshaping, 370–371
    rotation, 366–367
    scaling options, 368–369
    shadows, 378
    shearing, 369–370
    tool options, keyboard shortcuts, 664–665
    Transform Each dialog box, 376–377
    Transform palette, 374–375
transitional points, anchor points as, 97
transparency
    applying, 220
    brush stroke type, 230
    EPS files, 59
    flattening process, 226, 228
    new document set, 51–52
    symbols, 156, 229
    3D objects, 229
    Transparency Grid feature, 225
    transparent patterns, 359–360
Transparency palette, 25
    blending modes, 220–221
    features, 218–219
    Isolate Blending option, 222
    Knockout Group option, 223
    opacity masks, 223–224
    Opacity slider, 219–220
Trap function, Pathfinder palette, 201–202
trapping process, printing issues, 594–596
Trim button, Pathfinder palette, 199
trim marks, 583
trimming paths, 199
TrueType fonts, 284
turbulence effect, 510
turning off grids, 272
tweaking effects, 394–395
twirl effects, 384
twist effects, 395–396, 399
txt (Text Format) format, 64

type. *See also* text
    alignment, 316
    area type
        Area Type Options dialog box, 295–296
        discussed, 290
        good shapes for, 296
        list of, 294
        outlining areas of, 297
        placing in rectangles, 293
        selecting with, 297
    composition methods, 319
    compound paths and, 435–436
    editing, 306
    effects, 301–302
    flipping, 302
    headlines, 324
    horizontal scale, 313
    individual, 290
    leading increments, 310–311
    measuring, 308–309
    orientation, 331
    outlines, 332–334
    Path tool, 290
    on paths, 300–302
    previewing, 302
    punctuation, 319–320
    selecting, 289, 305–306
    size of, changing, 309
    threaded text, 322–323
    type tools, keyboard shortcuts, 659–660
    vertical, 302–304
    Vertical Type tool, 292
Type menu commands, keyboard shortcuts, 652
Type Object Selection by Path Only option, Type
         preferences, 556
Type option
    Arc Segment tool preferences, 99
    Document Setup dialog box, 50–51
    Graph Type dialog box, 146
    Units & Display Performance preferences, 557
Type palette, 25
Type preferences
    Baseline Shift option, 555
    Font Preview option, 556
    Greeking option, 556
    preference options, 554
    Setting the Number of Recent Fonts option, 556
    Show Asian Options option, 556
    Show Font Names in English option, 556
    Size/Leading option, 555
    Tracking option, 555
    Type Object Selection by Path Only option, 556
Type preset, Live Trace tool, 455
typographer's quotes, new document setup, 51

U

underlined text, 12, 308
Undo command (Edit menu), 43
Ungroup command (Object menu), 154
ungrouping objects, 252
units
  measurement
    Artboard feature, 49
    centimeters, 267
    equally spaced apart, 271
    inches, 267
    Measure tool, 267–268
    methods of, 265
    millimeters, 267
    with objects, 270
    picas, 267
    pixels, 267
    points, 267
    ruler options, 270
    type, 308–309
    unit of measurement changes, 266
  new document setup, 47
Units & Display Performance preferences, 557–558
unlocking guides, 275
Unpainted Objects option, Clean Up dialog box, 184
up and down arrows, scroll bars, 34
upper and lower stroke limits, 138
uppercase, 328
Use Low Resolution Proxy for Linked EPS option, File Handling and Clipboard preferences, 563
Use Outside Rectangle As A Frame option, Rectangular Grid Tool Options dialog box, 101
Use Precise Cursors option, General preferences, 550
Use Preview Bounds option, General preferences, 554
user slices, 629

V

Value Axis option, Graph Type dialog box, 146
variables
  data sets, 641
  graph data, 641
  linked image, 640
  text, 640
  Variables palette, 641
  visibility, 640
Variables palette, 25
Variation option
  Calligraphic Brush Options dialog box, 106
  Scribble Options dialog box, 509
version cue status, status bar, 28
Vertical option, Warp Options dialog box, 398
vertical scale, type, 304, 313
vertical type, 302–304
Vertical Type tool, 292

View menu commands
  Actual Size, 19
  Fit in Window, 19
  Hide Artboard, 19
  keyboard shortcuts, 653–654
  New View, 40
  Preview, 38
  Show Artboard, 19
  Show Transparency Grid, 225
  Show/Hide Rulers, 270
  Smart Guides, 277
viewing
  documents, general information in, 69–71
  swatches, 209
  viewing tools, keyboard shortcuts, 669
views
  creating new, 40
  custom, 40
  Outline mode, 36–38
  Overprint Preview mode, 39
  Pixel Preview mode, 39
  Preview mode, 36–38
  screen modes, 40
visibility variables, 640

W

W option, Transform palette, 269, 375
Warchesik, Brian, contact information and contributions made by, 680
warp effects, 384, 397–399
Warp Options dialog box, 397–398
Warp Tool Options dialog box, 383
waves, warp effects, 399
WBMP format, Web graphics, 616–617
Web graphics
  animations, 634–637
  CSS (Cascading Style Sheets), 632
  data-driven graphics, 639
  Flash graphics, 620–621, 623–624
  GIF formats, 615
  hexadecimal colors, 608–609
  image maps, 633–634
  interactivity, 633–637
  JPEG formats, 616
  output options, 617–620
  PNG format, 616
  previewing, 610–614
  rollovers, 638
  scripting, 641–643
  slicing, 628–632
  SVG files, 623–627
  WBMP format, 616–617
  Web-safe colors, 605–608
Web safe colors, 213, 605–608

Web sites
    archives and forums, 684–685
    online courses, 683–684
    online design magazines, 682–683
    products and services, 685
weight, of strokes, 137
whirlpools, Spiral tool, 99
width
    new document setup, 47
    rectangle drawings, 122
Width option
    Area Type Options dialog box, 296
    Live Paint Bucket Options dialog box, 464
Window menu commands
    Attributes, 247
    Brush Library, 113
    Color, 212
    Document Info, 69
    keyboard shortcuts, 654–655
    New Window, 36
    Symbol, 151
Window Metafile (wmf) format, 64
windows
    cascading, 18
    closing, 17
    maximizing, 17
    minimizing, 17
    opening new, 36
    tiling, 18
wmf (Window Metafile) format, 64

woodgrain effect, 510
Word spacing option, Justification dialog box, 317
workspace, managing, 10
wrinkle effects, 387–388

X

X option
    Drop Shadow dialog box, 494
    Transform palette, 269, 375
X values, 3D Extrude & Bevel Options dialog box, 515

Y

Y option
    Drop Shadow dialog box, 494
    Transform palette, 269, 375
Y value, 3D Extrude & Bevel Options dialog box, 515

Z

Z value, 3D Extrude & Bevel Options dialog box, 515
zig zag effects, 396–397, 508
zooming
    default levels, 31–32
    to fit in window size, 32
    with Navigator palette, 33–35
    100 percent view, 32
    palettes, 23
    specific magnifications, 33
    zoom control, 16
    Zoom Out tool, 30
    Zoom tool, 29–30, 610